Clerical Office Procedures

Fifth Edition

James R. Meehan
*Professor of Business Education and
Dean of Administration, Emeritus
Hunter College
of the City University of New York*

William R. Pasewark
*Professor
Texas Tech University*

Mary Ellen Oliverio
*Professor of Education
Teachers College
Columbia University*

Published by

K37 **SOUTH-WESTERN PUBLISHING CO.**

CINCINNATI   WEST CHICAGO, ILL.   DALLAS   PELHAM MANOR, N.Y.
BURLINGAME, CALIF.   BRIGHTON, ENGLAND

ISBN: 0-538-11370-7

Library of Congress Catalog Card Number: 70-186699

1 2 3 4 5 6 7 K 9 8 7 6 5 4 3

Printed in the United States of America

PREFACE

The office is the center of many innovations that are making it a more efficient place and at the same time a more pleasant, rewarding place for all employees. Clerical tasks to be done by human beings are still necessary; their nature, though, is changing constantly. These changes underscore the need for competent workers — workers who understand procedures and processes.

Learning to complete clerical tasks with skill and understanding is an exciting venture. *Clerical Office Procedures* has as its general purpose the introduction of the student to the challenge and dignity of working with attention and intelligence. A job well done — a job thoroughly understood — is likely to gain appreciation from an employer. However, more importantly, a job well done results in personal satisfaction that is sustaining and confidence-building. It is this self-confidence that students will develop as they read about and learn the skills described in *Clerical Office Procedures*.

Few jobs in modern business are devoid of *clerical tasks*; to learn how to handle them is to have some of the most valuable work abilities any student can develop. A primary goal of *Clerical Office Procedures* is to give students an understanding of important clerical functions performed in offices and at the same time to develop in students a comprehension of the application of these functions to related office procedures. The student will be prepared to undertake any one of several office jobs when he has completed the study of this text. At the same time he will have a comprehension of the business office and its major functions so that he will continue to develop in his first job and be eligible for additional responsibility and promotion.

Clerical Office Procedures is organized to assist the student in meeting these goals:

1. Mastery of office tasks that are central to the smooth functioning of departments that handle mail, central files, copying and duplicating, financial records, purchasing and selling, inventories, and typewriting

2. Understanding of the purposes of the tasks that are handled by the several departments in a typical organization

3. Awareness of the kind of personal and business behavior that is most conducive to pleasant, rewarding relationships with fellow associates

4. Comprehension of the total process of information circulating through an organization

iii

A thorough revision of this text was undertaken so that the material presented would reflect the most up-to-date practices and policies of business and governmental operations. Emerging innovations were reviewed, considered, and written into the text so that the most recent information on each topic is presented.

End-of-chapter materials have been completely rewritten. These materials include

Reviewing What You Have Read — questions that reinforce the key points of the text presented in each part

Making Decisions — problems that require thought-provoking, realistic solutions

Working with Others — case studies that require a reasonable approach to solving everyday problems of human relationships in the office

Using Language — exercises that review areas of general weakness in language usage

Using Arithmetic — exercises that review basic arithmetic applications for developing accuracy and understanding

Performing Office Tasks — assignments that simulate the work performed in offices to assist the student in gaining practical experience

Although not necessary for the completion of the various exercises at the end of each part, stationery and business forms that provide realistic practice are available in a correlated workbook.

To assist the student in that most critical of all areas for beginning office employees — spelling and vocabulary — the authors have attempted to enlarge and strengthen the student's knowledge of the English language by inserting in the margin definitions of all terms that may be new or may cause confusion in mastering this course. The definitions are limited only to their application in the text. A good dictionary will provide more comprehensive usage for the terms chosen for emphasis in this course.

A modern textbook requires the cooperation of many people. Business firms and government agencies have generously provided information about current and developing office procedures, as well as forms, photographs, and other illustrations. Experienced office employees, supervisors, and executives have been enlightening and informative. Countless numbers of teachers have cooperated by providing their students' reactions to suggested materials and exercises. To all these generous, thoughtful people, we acknowledge gratefully our indebtedness.

James R. Meehan
William R. Pasewark
Mary Ellen Oliverio

CONTENTS

UNIT 1

A CAREER IN THE MODERN OFFICE

GENERAL OFFICE CLERK

ccurate and dependable typi
ng manual typewriter to typ
tations, payroll reports, in
, billing, purchase order
neral. Hours 8 to 4:3
s area. Send resum
Enquirer.

Part 1   Career Opportunities

Part 2   Preparing for Your Career

PART 1 CAREER OPPORTUNITIES

Sheila Farnsworth works in the home office of a large insurance company in Hartford, Connecticut. She holds the position of file clerk in the central records department. This department receives thousands of requests each working day for information about insurance policies from agents and policyholders. The clerks must be able to locate the needed records in seconds. Sheila does a variety of jobs, including typing labels for new file folders, locating records, and putting new items in proper files. She likes the variety in her work. She also believes that maintaining accuracy in all tasks is a continuing challenge to her and her fellow workers.

Tom Hammer is a messenger in an advertising firm in San Francisco. He has had this job for six months and is learning the operations of every department in the firm. His messenger duties take him all over San Francisco. He also works in the mail room where he helps to open and distribute mail. He aids the manager of the duplicating department and at times assists the display manager in setting up exhibits for clients. Tom enjoyed his art classes in high school; and, when he studied clerical office procedures, he began to see a way of combining these two interests.

Nancy Diaz is the receptionist in an office of the United States Department of Agriculture in Washington, D.C. Nancy grew up on a farm in western Texas and finds her farm background helpful as she talks with visitors who call at the office. Nancy maintains the collection of bulletins that are available to callers. She also does typing tasks when she is not talking with visitors or directing them to the various offices. At her desk she maintains a calendar of all appointments for the six officials whose offices are in her suite. She also makes appointments by telephone and handles requests for appointments that come in the mail.

Sheila, Tom and Nancy are providing services that make it possible for the work of these organizations to continue smoothly, accurately, and promptly. They are employed in a general class of occupations which the federal government calls *clerical workers*.

ROLE OF THE MODERN OFFICE

As you learn more about the modern office, you will see that it is an important part of every organization. It serves as the memory of the organization through the records it keeps. It is the communications center. The flow of information to and from an organization is an important function of the office. This means that telephone calls must be handled quickly and efficiently, that mail must be opened and distributed promptly, and that information for the general public must be presented accurately and attractively.

DUTIES OF OFFICE EMPLOYEES

Among the major tasks of office workers which you will learn how to perform during your study of clerical office procedures are the following.

Producing Mailable Letters

Beginning office workers with such job titles as general clerk, clerk-typist, typist-stenographer, and transcribing machine operator spend much of their time in the important task of producing letters. These workers must know how to set up letters attractively, how to spell and punctuate correctly, and how to type with speed and accuracy.

Illus. 1-1
A transcribing machine operator spends much time producing attractive letters.

IBM Corporation

Processing Data

Many clerical workers aid in **processing data** in the office. Processing data refers to a wide range of office activities. It includes such tasks as tallying checks received in payment for goods sold, determining the total hours worked by each employee, and calculating the total of all bills received during a day. Clerical workers who process data often work with highly efficient equipment, which they have learned to operate. Key punch operators, computer operators, and calculating machine operators are some of the basic positions for carrying out this important function. These employees understand the special language of numbers and symbols used for processing data. They record information in readily usable form for the machines, determine totals on calculating machines, and prepare reports for those who need them for their work.

Illus. 1-2
Young man operating the
console of a computer

Federal Life Insurance Company
(Mutual)

Processing Mail

Almost 100 billion pieces of mail are delivered in the United States each year. Much of this mail **originates** in business, government, or service organizations and is delivered to other organizations. To keep the mail moving, clerks use procedures that you will learn, for they are useful whether you are employed in a small office or in a large office.

Maintaining Records

Maintaining accurate records and files is one of the most important tasks in the modern office. The records are the memory of the organization. Not only do they provide a history of the company, but they also contain current information which provides the basis for future decisions.

The files in an office may be as simple as an alphabetic card file of names or as complex as a computer. No matter which filing system is used, every office worker is involved in maintaining records. When you type a carbon copy of a letter, you are preparing material for the files. When you calculate a payroll, you are preparing information for the files. Filing and records management are so important that no business could exist without them.

Greeting People

Many office workers spend much of their time assisting customers and callers. Some office workers who spend most of their time performing this task are called receptionists. Successful receptionists are cheerful, cooperative, interested in helping others, and sensitive to the needs of people. You will learn how to be courteous and efficient in assisting callers. You will learn how your own behavior in dealing with your co-workers will make your office a more pleasant place in which to work.

Illus. 1-3
Receptionist uses inter-com to notify an executive of a caller arriving for an appointment.

Philips Business Systems, Inc.

Using the Telephone

The telephone is an important source of communication both within an organization and in its transactions with other businesses. To complete telephone calls quickly and efficiently, proven methods of using the telephone have been established. You will learn much about the correct use of the telephone and about the variety of equipment and services provided by the telephone company.

Photocopying and Duplicating Business Papers

Multiple copies of many business papers — letters, memorandums, reports — are needed if all persons who must see them are to be kept up to date. As an office worker, you will use photocopying equipment and, very likely, will prepare materials for duplication on different kinds of machines. There are office workers in duplicating departments who devote much of their time to performing duplicating services for the entire organization. You will learn much about these services and how to prepare masters and stencils skillfully.

Preparing Business Reports

In every office many hours are spent in planning and preparing business reports. Reports are needed to keep customers informed of new developments and products; reports are needed to keep the owners informed of the condition of the business; reports are needed to keep management informed of production and sales figures. As an office worker, you will undoubtedly have tasks related to the preparation of reports. During your study of clerical office procedures, you will learn how to perform these tasks.

Illus. 1-4
Compiling information for reports is a never-ending task. Telephone, intercom, files, and written records assist in this clerical function.

Philips Business Systems, Inc.

Purchasing, Selling, and Controlling Inventories

Regardless of the nature of the organization, the office will have the responsibility for purchasing, selling, and maintaining inventories. After manufacturing firms purchase raw materials, inventories must be kept of the raw materials, goods partially completed, and finished products. They, of course, sell the finished products. Service organizations, such as insurance companies, utility companies, and publishing companies, buy a wide variety of supplies and equipment to **facilitate** their work. They record and maintain inventories of these purchases. They sell policies, units of electricity or telephone service, or subscriptions to magazines or newspapers.

facilitate: to make easier

You will understand an organization better if you have a knowledge of these important functions. You will also learn the technical language associated with these activities.

Performing Financial Duties

While accounting clerks and bookkeeping machine operators spend all their time in performing financial duties, many other office workers are at times also involved. You will, therefore, want to know the proper procedures for handling financial duties.

Illus. 1-5
Financial record keeping is necessary in purchasing, selling, and controlling inventories.

Victor Comptometer Corporation

KINDS OF OFFICE POSITIONS

There are many kinds of office positions. Each has its own qualifications, and persons with special interests and talents will find some more appealing than others. Within some office positions, there are often different grades. For example, there are clerical positions classified as Clerk I, Clerk II, Clerk III, and Clerk IV. The general nature of the work done by all these clerks is similar; however, Clerk II has a job requiring more responsibility than Clerk I; Clerk IV has a more responsible job than Clerk III. Persons who do satisfactory work at a lower level are frequently promoted to the next grade. The work at a lower level is usually considered a training opportunity for the next higher position.

In this book you will become acquainted with the tasks of a variety of typical office positions. However, secretarial and stenographic work will not be covered, since these positions require a knowledge of stenography. Nevertheless, if you know stenography and then study clerical office procedures, you will be able to combine your skills and knowledges to qualify for many more office positions.

Several beginning clerical positions, along with their requirements, for the state of Missouri are described on page 9. Notice the basic requirements for the two levels shown.

OFFICE WORKERS IN THE AMERICAN LABOR FORCE

specialization:
doing just one job
or one part of one
job
systematic:
arranged in order;
organized; planned

When office workers were first employed in American businesses more than a hundred years ago, they were considered general office workers. Each was expected to do all the tasks of the office. There was little **specialization**. However, as American businesses grew larger and developed **systematic** procedures, the office worker became a specialist. Today we have some general clerks, but there are far more specialized clerical workers. Through developing skills to a high level, the office worker in the modern office becomes a more valuable worker.

What Business Expects of Office Workers

Executives and supervisors responsible for office workers often ask the question: How productive are these workers? By this question they mean: How much should every office worker complete in an hour? a day? a week? In a central typing department, for example, the supervisor determines how many letters a typist should complete each day. The supervisor sets standards for the typists and expects them to produce at least the minimum number of letters that is considered satisfactory for a day's work.

CLERICAL POSITIONS
Missouri Personnel Division
Jefferson City, MO

POSITION	REQUIRED KNOWLEDGES, SKILLS, AND ABILITIES
Clerk I	Knowledge of modern office practices, procedures, and equipment Knowledge of business English, spelling, and arithmetic Ability to understand and follow simple oral and written directions Ability to make simple arithmetical computations and tabulations
Clerk II	Same Requirements as for Clerk I, plus Ability to maintain moderately complex clerical records and to prepare reports from such records Ability to make relatively complex arithmetical computations and tabulations accurately and with reasonable speed Ability to assign, supervise, and review the work of several clerical subordinates
Clerk-Typist I	Same Requirements as for Clerk I, plus Ability to type accurately from plain copy at the rate of 30 words a minute as evidenced by a passing grade in a typing performance test
Clerk-Typist II	Same Requirements as for Clerk I and Clerk II, plus Ability to type accurately from plain copy at the rate of 40 words a minute as evidenced by a passing grade in a typing performance test
Account Clerk I	Working knowledge of office methods and procedures and familiarity with the uses of standard office equipment Knowledge of bookkeeping principles and practices Ability to make arithmetical calculations with speed and accuracy
Account Clerk II	Same Requirements as for Account Clerk I, plus Working knowledge of appropriation and budget account procedures Ability to direct the flow of a considerable volume of detailed work and to plan, lay out, and review the work of clerical employees engaged in routine tasks

POSITION	REQUIRED KNOWLEDGES, SKILLS, AND ABILITIES
Duplicating Equipment Operator I	Considerable knowledge of the operation, adjustment, and maintenance of a multilith press and duplicating equipment such as mimeograph and ditto Considerable knowledge of the various kinds of papers, inks, and chemicals used in duplicating work Ability to operate multilith and other machines used in duplicating work Ability to instruct new employees in the operation and maintenance of duplicating equipment Ability to keep simple clerical records
Duplicating Equipment Operator II	Same Requirements as for Duplicating Equipment Operator I, plus Some knowledge of modern office procedures, methods, and equipment Ability to maintain duplicating equipment in good working order and to make routine repairs and adjustments
Key Punch Operator I	Knowledge of general office practices and procedures Knowledge of the methods and equipment used in punching and verifying tabulating cards in connection with mechanical recording of statistical and accounting data Ability to acquire skill in the operation of key punch machines
Key Punch Operator II	Same Requirements as for Key Punch Operator I, plus Skill in the operation of key punch machines and key punch verifying machines Ability to read small printed words and numbers accurately and rapidly

Source: Missouri Personnel Division
117 East Dunklin Street
Jefferson City, MO 65101

Illus. 1-6
State of Missouri
Clerical position requirements

Supervisors realize that the production of office employees is a result of their being on time every day, their willingness to cooperate with each other, and their ability to follow instructions carefully.

How the Office Worker Views Productivity

productivity: yielding or furnishing results, benefits or profits

As a future office worker, you will want to understand the need for paying attention to your **productivity**. How efficiently are you doing each job? How carefully are you listening to and following instructions? How rapidly are you completing your tasks? To ask yourself such questions and then consider your answers will lead you to improve your way of working and, therefore, what you are able to accomplish in a day. An office worker who earns his salary is the most promising candidate for a promotion to a better position.

REWARDS OF CLERICAL POSITIONS

There are many rewards for working in a business office. However, to enjoy the benefits of a business career, you must first prepare yourself to qualify for employment and then continue your education and apply your skills so that you will always be ready for every promotional opportunity that presents itself. The following are some of the advantages of working in a business office.

Working Conditions

Most offices are attractively furnished and tastefully decorated. Most clerical workers enjoy the surroundings in which they work. Today many offices are air-conditioned. Some of them are carpeted and scientifically lighted so that fatigue, noise, and eyestrain are greatly reduced.

Most office employees work from 35 to 40 hours a week, five days a week. Almost all organizations pay clerical workers for any overtime they are asked to work. Organizations realize that clerical workers work more efficiently and more accurately with modern office equipment; therefore, you will find many laborsaving machines and other office aids are available for your use.

Salaries

Salaries vary in different parts of the country and at different times, depending upon many factors including prevailing business conditions, the cost of living, and the available supply of competent office workers. Beginning office workers can expect to earn from $75 to $110 a week, with fringe benefits adding another $10 to $20 to their weekly salaries. Clerical workers with several years of experience earn $135 a week or more.

Fringe Benefits

Besides their regular salaries, clerical workers receive an additional 15 to 25 percent of their salaries in what are known as fringe benefits. These benefits usually include pay for sick days, holidays, and vacations; health insurance and group life insurance; and often major medical and dental care. Sometimes educational benefits are included. These benefits are provided to make the office employees' lives more pleasant and more secure than they would otherwise be.

Opportunities for Employment

Clerical workers are needed everywhere — in insurance, banking, industry, service organizations, television and radio, medicine, museums, libraries, schools, government offices — and the needs continue to mount as our society demands better goods and services to improve our standard of living. It is difficult to find a service or good that can be provided without the aid of at least one clerical worker. People want the goods they ordered delivered quickly. They want telephone service to be prompt and courteous. They want to receive their paychecks on time. They want to have their appointments scheduled correctly. They want their insurance premiums calculated accurately. Can you imagine the many kinds of clerical work that must be done if all these wants and many others are to be satisfied?

As you explore the qualifications office workers must have and become skilled in office procedures, you will find many ways to use your talents so that you gain satisfaction from your work and make your own personal contribution to our society.

REVIEWING
WHAT YOU
HAVE READ

1. Why is the office considered an important place in the modern organization?
2. What are the titles of some of the workers who produce letters as one of their tasks?
3. What is the meaning of *processing data*?
4. What is the major responsibility of a receptionist?
5. Why are reports prepared?
6. How does a Clerk II position differ from a Clerk I position?
7. What is meant by *job specialization*?
8. What does the businessman expect of his clerical workers?
9. How can an office worker improve productivity?
10. What are two advantages of a clerical position?

1. One of your friends says to you, "I like working with numbers, knowing what things cost, and how much was spent. Is there any place in office work for me?" What would you say to your friend?
2. What difference should the study of clerical office procedures make in the way you work on your first office job?

Carole is a file clerk in a large company. There are twelve file clerks in the filing department in addition to a supervisor. Carole thinks the work she is doing is mere routine and quite dull. She does the same thing day after day and is able to do it without thinking, she believes. She doesn't associate with the other file clerks. One day the supervisor asks Carole this question: "Carole, did you have all the correspondence from the Research and Development office to file yesterday?" Carole's response was, "You don't expect me to pay attention to the source of the copies I file, do you? I really don't remember what I did yesterday!"

What do you think of Carole's attitude in general and of her response to her supervisor?

A noun is a name of a person............ Sheila, Nancy, Tom, employer, businessman, messenger

name of a place.............. Hartford, Dallas, mail room

name of a thing.............. duplicator, folder, calendar, telephone

name of a condition
or relation............... pleasure, satisfaction, efficiency, responsibility

Copy the sentences below on a separate sheet of paper and underline all nouns.

Example: You will learn how to prepare masters and stencils.

1. The receptionist answers the telephone all day.
2. Records are maintained in many forms.
3. The typist produces mailable letters quickly.
4. Promotions are given to good employees.
5. Fringe benefits are considered a part of the rewards for working.
6. The productivity of office workers is increased when machines are available.
7. Office workers are needed in organizations from Maine to California and from Florida to Washington.
8. Ruth and Victor both enjoy the responsibilities they have in their jobs in the mail room of a large insurance company.
9. Multiple copies of many papers are required in modern businesses.
10. Manufacturing organizations purchase raw materials, maintain inventories of materials, goods in process, and finished goods.

Below are some numbers with the operation you are to perform indicated in each instance. Write the problems on a separate sheet of paper and complete them.

$3 + 4 = ?$	$4 + 12 = ?$	$342 + 321 = ?$	$\$21.95 + \$195.45 = ?$
$9 - 2 = ?$	$13 - 5 = ?$	$20 - 14 = ?$	$\$14.95 - .29 = ?$
$9 \times 3 = ?$	$12 \times 2 = ?$	$142 \times 105 = ?$	$\$25.50 \times 25 = ?$
$12 \div 2 = ?$	$28 \div 7 = ?$	$196 \div 14 = ?$	$\$450.00 \div 25 = ?$

PERFORMING OFFICE TASKS

1. You have learned about ten tasks that are regularly performed by office workers. During this course you will have many experiences to help you become skilled in completing these tasks. Prepare an outline with the major headings of these key tasks and under each heading indicate the specific skills and abilities you hope to develop.

   Example: WHAT I EXPECT TO LEARN THIS YEAR

   A. To produce mailable letters

      (a) I must improve my knowledge of letter styles.
      (b) I must improve my skill in placing copy attractively on the page.
      (c) I must improve my basic speed and accuracy in typewriting.

2. Below are four questions relating to clerical positions. Choose two of these and write one short paragraph about each.

   A. Why are answering the telephone and placing calls important tasks?

   B. What kinds of fringe benefits are provided for office workers?

   C. Why should clerks in mail rooms use standard procedures?

   D. When is an office worker given a promotion?

PART **2**

PREPARING FOR YOUR CAREER

Laurie Heinman began working as a clerk-typist in the personnel office of a broadcasting company in New York City when she graduated from high school. She had been in her job for about six months when she was asked, "What do you like about this, your first full-time job?" Laurie answered, "I like many things about this job. The people here are very nice, and they have taught me so much about this company. The procedures here are well organized so that if you follow instructions you will do your work in the right way. I like the sense of order, of neatness, of efficiency in this office. I am really continuing the way of working that I was taught in my high school classes, and also I am gaining valuable experience in an important department of a large organization. You know, if the department that hires new employees doesn't do its job carefully, the whole company suffers. I like being in this department."

INTERESTS AND ABILITIES IMPORTANT FOR OFFICE WORK

Every major occupational field has basic skill requirements. Persons who work in forests or on the sea have interests and talents that are apt to differ from those of singers or actors. While there are some general interests and talents, there are also some that are **unique** to particular occupations. Successful office workers tend to have certain interests and abilities in common.

unique:
single;
alone

An Interest in the Organization and How It Functions

Many people must cooperate if the office work of an organization is to be completed efficiently. Therefore, you must be interested in learning how all the operations of a company blend together in order to understand the usefulness of what you do as it relates to the total function of the organization. Each person has a relationship to the purposes of the company. It is not certain that you will do your best work unless you understand this relationship. Fundamental to understanding this relationship is your interest in the organization.

Illus. 1-7
The work of each person is related
to the total function of the company.

Western Electric Co., Inc.

Mr. Stonington, the supervisor of a large office, was commenting about a young employee whose ability impressed him when he said, "Allen is deeply involved in his work. He wasn't satisfied until he fully understood our complete operation. He is a valuable young worker, and we appreciate what he does."

An Interest in Working with Others

If you enjoy doing things with others you will find an office a pleasant place in which to work. An office is not a place for the person who wishes to work alone. The completion of almost all office tasks requires the cooperation of others. If tasks are to be finished satisfactorily, office workers must understand what is going on and make their contribution to the total production. To work with others means that the **coordination** of the efforts of many different people is necessary.

coordination:
a common
action, movement,
or condition

It was 2:30 when Dorothy's employer approved the final draft of a 12-page report that she had typed for him. He then asked if it would be possible to have it duplicated and distributed that afternoon. When she went to the duplicating department Dorothy learned that the work was scheduled tightly for the entire afternoon, but the supervisor looked over the jobs and found one that could be postponed. He had one of the operators run off Dorothy's stencils at once. Dorothy stayed to help collate the report. When the job was finished, she commented, "Thank you for your cooperation. You really saved the day for Mr. Adams and me." The supervisor replied, "Ordinarily we do work in the order in which it comes in; but, of course, emergencies do come up now and then, and we try to do our best to help."

Illus. 1-8
Cooperating with others
in revising schedules is
often necessary to
accomplish the job.

Vincent Nanfra

An Ability to Be Accurate

Office workers who rarely make errors are extremely valuable. Accuracy is a basic ability that can be developed if you are willing to give careful attention to details. Accuracy reflects your care in checking your own work. An accurate worker is aware of the quality of every task performed.

Joan is a typist in a statistical typing department where she types tables of numbers many hours each day. Her supervisor appreciates the quality of her work. "Joan," said the supervisor, "is our best typist. I can depend upon her to produce a perfect table every time. She never overlooks an error in her copy. Furthermore, she types with attention to what she is typing; often she finds errors that were overlooked in the department that prepared the rough draft. Joan is a valuable employee."

"The job that Bill Meredith does requires accuracy," said his supervisor. "If payments are recorded to the wrong account, you can imagine how disturbed our customers become. Bill is careful to check account numbers as a means of making sure of the account to be credited." Bill works in a large department store office and handles customers' charge accounts.

Illus. 1-9
Verifying work results
in unquestioned accuracy
and happy customers.

Wilson Jones Company,
Division of Swingline, Inc.

An Ability to Work Fast

Speed is one of the abilities of the competent office worker. A typist who is unable to maintain an acceptable rate of accuracy and speed cannot be kept on the payroll. A clerk who appears upset and frantic as she attempts to complete a job does not possess the basic skill required for her job.

Amy lost her job as a general office worker because she was unable to turn out enough work to justify her salary. To her credit she tried hard; however, she accomplished very little, and she failed to realize that she was not producing at the level that was expected of her. Every errand that she went on took at least an hour; other clerks completed errands in ten to fifteen minutes. If she was asked to get something from the files, it always took her at least half an hour. She wasted endless time trying to figure out where the requested filed material was. She never seemed to understand the filing system, but eventually she would locate what was wanted. She did not grasp things quickly; she never seemed to be able to get to the point of what she was really supposed to do. Amy did not have the ability to work with reasonable speed in an office position.

An Ability to Use Standard Procedures

The methods used to perform the work of the modern office are constantly changing and improving. Many of these changes are the result of suggestions made by alert office employees. However, most offices have standard procedures that are followed in doing a great many tasks.

For example, in one large firm the mail is received at 9:30 in the morning. It is opened and separated by departments. It is then delivered to the various departments according to a regular schedule.

Statements to customers of a department store with last names *A* through *G* are mailed on the afternoon of the 16th of each month. If the 16th falls on a nonworking day, then the statements must be mailed on the afternoon nearest the 16th. These are just two illustrations of standard procedures.

Consider another example. Let's say that you are a file clerk in the central filing department of a large corporation and that all the file clerks follow the same procedure when answering the telephone.

1. You are at the desk when the telephone rings, and you answer it immediately.
2. Before lifting the telephone, you pick up a pencil from your desk and place a message pad in position for taking notes.
3. You answer the telephone by saying, "Central Files, . . . (mention your full name) speaking."
4. Generally the calls are from other departments in the company that are requesting files. Record the name of the file requested the first time it is stated by the calling party. If there is any doubt about the name, request the spelling. Begin writing as soon as the name is spelled.
5. If you are busy with another task, drop this latest request into the proper tray for immediate pickup by the first clerk free for another assignment.

Standard procedures provide a means of working in the same way time after time so that errors are unlikely to occur.

Systems specialists are employed by many organizations to determine the most efficient procedures to use. Office workers must be willing to follow the instructions that apply to the tasks they perform.

BASIC SKILLS THAT HAVE MANY APPLICATIONS IN THE OFFICE

As you already know, the basic skills of reading, writing, and arithmetic are constantly used in your personal life. These skills will be of primary value in an office. This is the way the insurance business stresses the importance of basic skills to young people:

"Whatever job you get, you will need the three basic skills: reading, writing, and arithmetic. Many life and health companies have training manuals to tell you about your job and what you have to know to do it well. Being able to read those manuals and other written materials is **essential**.

"Equally essential is writing legibly. One life insurance personnel executive tells of an enormous problem that grew out of an employee not writing clearly. His company has two million customers called policy holders. One day, one of them wrote in and gave a change of address. The clerk who got the letter put the change of address down on a card but wrote the street number **illegibly**. The card went to another clerk to type the change for the computer that contains all the addresses of policyholders. That person, because of the illegible writing, copied the address incorrectly. The error went into the computer and for months the policyholder's premium notices and other communications from the company went to the wrong address. No great damage was done but the policyholder

essential:
of the nature of something; of great importance

illegibly:
not readable

Illus. 1-10
An error entering a computer can cause much inconvenience for a customer, and correction can be costly for a company.

Donald Greenhaus

was, quite understandably, irritated with the company and put to a great deal of trouble to get the error corrected. The company spent time and money in finding and correcting the error — all because of illegible writing and careless work.

"Much of the business of life and health insurance companies involves numbers and entails correspondence with customers. This is true of many businesses. The basic skills of working carefully with numbers and being able to express yourself clearly and gracefully are important in nearly any job.

"If you are not proficient in reading, writing, and arithmetic, you will be handicapped in your career, no matter what field you enter. Now is the time to improve these basic skills."[1]

What the Institute of Life Insurance is saying about basic skills is exactly what all types of organizations say when they think of fully competent workers. Fortunately, it is never too late to make up for weaknesses you may have in these basic skills. In fact, during your study of clerical office procedures, you will have many opportunities to develop your skills and to apply them to office work.

APPEARANCE AND BEHAVIOR IN THE OFFICE

Business executives want their organizations to be orderly and attractive. They try to employ office workers who are neat and who behave properly. If you are to become a satisfactory office worker, you should be aware of improvements you might make in your appearance and in your conduct.

Health

Good appearance and an alive, alert manner begin with good health. A person who fails to get sufficient sleep, to eat proper foods, and get a reasonable amount of exercise is unlikely to enjoy good health. Lack of **stamina**, intense feelings of fatigue, and inability to work consistently may result from failure to take care of one's health.

stamina: staying power; endurance

Rest. Do you get enough rest every night? Are your hours for going to sleep and for getting up approximately the same day after day? Lou was one young man who could not answer yes to these two questions.

---

[1]Institute of Life Insurance, Educational Division, *It's Up to You — A Guide to a Career in Life and Health Insurance* (New York City, 277 Park Avenue, 1971), pp. 8–10.

"No," said Lou, when asked about his sleeping habits, "I never get much sleep at night. I often stay up until 2 or 3 in the morning talking with my friends. I enjoy that. But when the alarm goes off at 7 the next morning, I find it hard to get up. Sometimes I just turn off the alarm and go back to sleep. Then when I get up I realize that I have overslept. I just loaf most of the day and stay up late again the next night. Even if I do get up when the alarm goes off, I am so tired all day that I don't get much done. In fact, I often feel ill and go around half asleep."

Is Lou behaving as he should? Is he developing good habits for maintaining good health and vitality?

Illus. 1-11
Health, energy, and strength are the rewards for this young data processing trainee who has respect for his physical and mental well-being.

Product Innovations, Inc.

Food. Proper foods are needed to maintain a fully functioning body with all the energy that you need for the activities in which you participate. Nutrition experts say that a good breakfast is important if you are to have sufficient energy and a feeling of well-being. Do you begin the day with a good breakfast which you eat in an unhurried fashion? Properly selected foods for lunch and dinner help assure a balanced diet.

Exercise. To function well you need exercise every day. In your leisure hours you should plan activities that you like and that will give you a chance to use muscles not used in your regular work.

Tammy is a pretty young typist in a local public utilities company. She is lively, yet relaxed. When she was asked about her health habits she said, "I am careful to eat three meals a day, and I don't just eat favorite foods that I know have little nutritional value. I am one of those persons who must have eight hours of sleep every night if I am to feel fit the next day. The world seems fuzzy to me, and I have little patience if I have had only a few hours of sleep. To keep my weight at the right point on the scale, I get regular exercise. I'm not the world's best tennis player, but I do play three or four times a week, and I enjoy it very much. I am also a hiker."

Posture

How would you describe your posture? Do you sit and stand with your head up and back straight? Or do you sit with your shoulders slumped and your legs coiled around the chair legs? Do you walk with a quick, lively step; or do you drag your feet when you walk? Good posture, more so than expensive clothes, can make you an attractive and handsome person.

Personal Grooming

There are basic rules for personal care that all office workers are expected to follow. You are already acquainted with these, but you must remember them when you enter the business world.

1. Take a bath or shower at least once each day.
2. Use an antiperspirant or deodorant daily.
3. Brush your teeth at least twice each day.
4. Wash your face thoroughly twice each day.
5. Keep your fingernails clean and trimmed.
6. Wash your hair regularly.

Attire

There is no standard dress code for all offices. We live in a society that allows considerable freedom in the selection of clothing. Most companies respect this freedom, but assume that employees will use good judgment in determining their office clothing. In general, organizations tend to prefer that their employees dress in clothing that is acceptable workday attire in the community. Casual clothing, as well as formal attire, is considered out of place for the office.

From your own experience in offices and other businesses in your community, you are aware of acceptable attire for work. You will want to choose clothing that does not attract special attention to you and clothing that is comfortable to wear and easy to maintain.

Businessmen expect employees to treat each other with respect and pleasantness. Considerate and cheerful social behavior towards your co-workers makes the office a better place in which to work. Your employer will expect you to be cordial and courteous to customers, clients, and other visitors.

While personalities vary, yours should show your concern for others and your interest in their welfare. Some important rules to remember are:

1. Speak softly to others so as not to disturb persons who are working within hearing range.

   Lillie was a good worker, but she was called the "loud one" behind her back because, when she entered a room, everyone knew she had arrived. She talked loudly to everyone she met. When the supervisor learned of Lillie's nickname, she knew that she must talk with her. Lillie was surprised; she had not realized that her conduct was disturbing to others. Lillie took her supervisor's advice, and before long the nickname was forgotten.

2. Listen carefully and patiently when you are asked a question or spoken to by a fellow worker or a visitor.

   Jeanne is a very popular receptionist in a large publishing company in Denver. Much of her popularity is created by the pleasant manner in which she talks to everyone who approaches her desk. Visitors often comment about "how patient that young lady is — and how helpful." She always seems to have time to help a caller.

3. Greet your fellow workers in the morning and say good-night at the end of the day.

   Iris lost her job for a number of reasons. Among her failures were her sullen attitude and her refusal to respond to others. She came in every morning and, even though others said good-morning to her, she never responded. She would never look up when someone came to her desk requesting information from her. Her supervisor talked with her, but he was unable to change her attitude or her behavior.

4. Introduce a stranger to a person with whom you may be talking or working.

   Ben was proofreading a report with Tom when Sally came to the desk. Ben looked up and said, "Hi, Sally. What can I do for you?" "Ben, I need three copies of the Lamont report, and I understand you have extra copies here." "Yes we do. Sally, this is Tom Barry; Tom, this is Sally Rolson, Mr. Tuttle's secretary. Sally, Tom is our new assistant." "I am happy to meet you, Tom. I hope you'll like working here. We do, don't we, Ben?"

5. Give others a chance to go through a door, onto a bus, into an elevator.

Larry never goes through the entrance on the floor where he works without looking back. If someone is behind him he holds the door for the other person to pass through, too. He also allows persons who are waiting for an elevator to step onto the elevator first. Larry is considered a thoughtful, courteous young man.

WHAT BUSINESSMEN EXPECT

The business world is an important part of our society. Businessmen are very much aware of their standing in the community, and what they expect of new employees is not likely to surprise you. Employers want to encourage the finest kind of behavior in their organizations. They want young workers who have gained a sense of what is important from their educational experiences as well as from their general living experiences. They need young people who have skills that are reasonably well developed; they want these new workers to become productive within a short period of time. Furthermore, they want young workers who have respect for others and who will work with them in a cheerful and courteous manner.

REVIEWING
WHAT YOU
HAVE READ

1. Why should an office worker have an interest in how his organization functions?
2. Why should an office worker want to work with others?
3. What is the attitude of an office worker who is accurate?
4. Is someone who is rushing through a job doing it speedily? Explain.
5. In what way is a standard procedure useful in an office?
6. In what ways do poor health habits interfere with a person's work?
7. What kind of clothing is appropriate for the office?
8. What are the personal grooming habits that office workers should follow regularly?
9. Describe social behavior as it relates to office work.
10. A businessman cares only for the skills of the office worker; nothing else is of interest to him. React to this comment.

1. Three young women are living in an apartment in a large city about 100 miles from their home town. They like their office jobs very much; they also like living in a large city. When they leave their offices in the evening, they generally meet for a quick snack and then go shopping or see a movie. Often they are not home until after midnight, when they eat something more since they seldom have dinner. Usually when the alarm goes off at seven, they find it difficult to get up and get ready for work; so they often go back to sleep and then jump up and dash out at the last minute to get to their offices on time, but without breakfast.

What do you think of this pattern of living?

2. Mr. Phillips explained to Bradford Stiles, the new mail clerk, the procedure for opening the mail and organizing it for distribution to the various departments. Bradford listened attentively, for he wanted to do his first task properly. He is one of several mail clerks who handle the same tasks.

What is the value of the procedure that Mr. Phillips explained?

Deborah, a young office worker, makes this comment to you:

"You know you can't let others take advantage of you. I know what my job is, and I do it. When I have finished my job, I read a magazine or just look out the window. I don't go looking for other work. When someone asks me to help him, I say I have my own work to do. I'm not going to get involved in doing other people's work. Each person has his job, and he should expect to do it."

In what ways do you think Deborah misunderstands the work of an office?

On a separate sheet of paper write the past tense for each of these words.

pay	think
say	study
keep	begin
record	understand
verify	leave
break	count
sleep	force
go	swim
inform	argue
drive	include

How much do you recall? Below are some questions that require basic arithmetic. Show your calculations on a separate sheet of paper.

1. Miss Sayles purchased the following items at a local stationery store: a felt pen at 69 cents, a roll of masking tape at $1.19, a tube of glue at 79 cents, and three rolls of transparent tape at 39 cents each. What is the total cost of her purchases?
2. If pencils are 6 cents each, how much will a gross (144) of pencils cost?
3. If the interest on a savings account is 5 percent a year, how much interest is earned in one year on an account of $500?
4. If an order for six yards of plastic wrap costs $6.36, what is the price for each yard?
5. Ruth Schultz has four boxes of envelopes and each box contains 500 envelopes. How many envelopes does she have?

6. The price of the adding machine is $169.95, less a discount of 10 percent. How much should the check be to pay for the adding machine if the cash discount is taken?

7. A quire of stencils (24 = 1 quire) is priced at $2.64. What is the price of one stencil?

8. Grade A paper costs $2.45 a ream, while Grade B paper costs $1.95 a ream. What is the difference in price of these two grades of paper?

9. You find a plastic tape that is priced at 59 cents a roll. You need 12 rolls. What will the cost be?

10. You need 24 feet of masking tape, which is sold by the yard. How many yards do you need? What is the cost if masking tape is priced at 3 cents a yard?

PERFORMING OFFICE TASKS

1. Your teacher will probably want to have information about you just as an employer would want information about an applicant. Write a short report about your background, including part-time and full-time employment, if any, and the schools you have attended. Also, list the business courses you have taken in this and other schools.

2. You have just studied the interests and abilities that are considered necessary for good office workers. Write a short report on the interests and abilities that you consider important to develop during this year. You may, if you wish, include skills that you have learned in other business courses or through actual work experience.

UNIT 2

BASIC SKILLS FOR OFFICE JOBS

OFFICE CLERKS

Variety of interesting dutie
ight typing. Neat handwritin
ust like to work with figure
be accurate. High scho
ate. Off-street parking pr

CITY CARPET C
ST. 822-714

Part 1   Reading and Listening
Part 2   Handwriting
Part 3   Computing

PART 1 READING AND LISTENING

When Elaine Sawyer applied for a position as a general clerical worker with the Ishler Systems Company, she took a clerical aptitude test that included checking the correctness of names, computing answers to business problems, and interpreting instructions. She completed each part of the test ahead of time and used the extra minutes to read over what she had done. As she handed her test to the personnel clerk in charge she was glad that she had been fully prepared for this test. She had studied carefully in her office procedures courses in her school, and she felt confident that she could meet the demands of an employer. She commented after she was hired by Ishler Systems, "You don't learn how to read and write and work with numbers just to pass tests in school. These skills are used daily in all kinds of work. I see the value of these skills more and more each day."

READING

Your employer will expect you to be skillful in several kinds of reading. You must be able to read a wide variety of written communications and understand what you have read. You must be able to read instructions, explanations, summaries, and other types of communications quickly and accurately so that you will know what you are to do. You will also be expected to know how to read information in dictionaries, atlases, and schedules.

Reading for Understanding

You will learn a great deal about your job through reading. You must be able to comprehend what you read — that is, read with understanding — so that you will be able to make what you read a part of your knowledge. When Barbara was employed as an office worker in a large insurance company, she was given a brochure that described her work and responsibilities. Here is part of the bulletin:

domain:
place under control
of one person

Your Desk Is Your **Domain.** The desk to which you have been assigned is yours to maintain in an orderly manner so that you can work efficiently. Please remember that papers are to be on your desk temporarily — they are to be taken care of by you quickly and accurately and then forwarded to the proper office.

The drawers of your desk are sufficient for the stock of supplies that you should have available for your work. Do not use the top of your desk as a storage area. Materials that belong in the files should be in the files. Papers temporarily taken from files should be kept in a tray or drawer, where they can be located easily when needed. Your desk surface and drawers should be neatly arranged to provide immediate **access** to pens, pencils, and other supplies.

access: condition of being easy to reach

How should such a passage be read so that you understand it well? Here are some suggestions:

1. *Determine the general topic of the text.* Ask yourself questions such as these before you begin to read:
   (a) Since the heading is, "Your Desk Is Your Domain," then what is likely to be discussed?
   (b) Why is it important that this message be understood?

2. *Read through the text quickly to get an overview.* Your understanding will be greater if you first skim the text to get a *general* idea of what you are going to read.

3. *Read through the text a second time.* During this reading give attention to the details so that you have a thorough understanding of the ideas presented. If you read "Your Desk Is Your Domain" carefully, the ideas listed here should now be part of your knowledge.

   (a) You alone will be using your desk.
   (b) To work well, you must keep your desk orderly.
   (c) The desk surface is your work area, and it should not be cluttered with papers and supplies.
   (d) The papers that come to your desk are to be handled quickly and accurately and then sent to the next location.
   (e) Papers that cannot be handled immediately should be filed or kept in a drawer or tray.
   (f) The drawers of the desk have enough space for all the supplies that you should keep at your desk.

4. *After you have completed reading the message, ask yourself questions to see if you really understand what you have read.*

    (a) What are the main points of the message?

    (b) What do you understand now about your responsibilities for keeping an orderly desk that you did not understand before you read the passage?

Reading for Specific Information

Frequently you must get information from references in the office. Spelling of words must be checked in a dictionary; the price of a product must be obtained; the time for an afternoon flight must be found.

Specific details are often provided in charts or tables with the use of symbols and abbreviations that are explained either at the beginning of the reference or as footnotes. You must understand the symbols and abbreviations to get the complete information sought.

Many tasks that you will be asked to complete will require your reading the instructions so that the task is done exactly as requested. To follow instructions correctly requires careful, thoughtful reading.

Reading a Dictionary. When you want to check the spelling of a word or its meaning, the dictionary is a helpful reference. Peggy, a typist, thought the word *accompanyed* looked incorrect so she looked up the base word *accompany* in a dictionary. This is what she found:

ac com pa ny . . . *v.* - nied, nying . . . .

How did she read the past tense? Peggy noted that the dictionary indicated the final syllable of the past tense. Therefore, the spelling is *accompanied*. (The *ny* of *accompany* is changed to *nied*.)

In addition to checking the spelling, you will find that the dictionary is a source for the following information:

1. Pronunciation of a word
2. Form of word, such as noun, adverb, adjective
3. Spelling of plural, past tense, gerund forms of the word, if **irregular** in form
4. Words that are **synonymous** with the given word
5. Meaning of the word

irregular: not following the customary rules
synonymous: alike or nearly alike in meaning

Reading Instructions. There are many ways of completing tasks, and the careful office worker checks the instructions before beginning a new task. Here is an example of instructions that were given to typists in a billing department of a small appliance center.

Illus. 2-1
You will learn a great deal about your job by carefully reading everything connected with it.

Smith-Corona

INSTRUCTIONS: This form is to be prepared in triplicate. The final copy is for your files. Be sure to list unit price as well as **extension**. Indicate handling and shipping charges for out-of-city orders.

extension:
total price after the unit price is multiplied by the number of units ordered

The typist knew that she had to make three copies; however, only the original and one carbon copy would be forwarded. She would keep the final carbon copy in her files. She also knew that she had to indicate the price of each unit: that is, if the customer purchased two table lamps at $19.95 each, then she had to indicate that each lamp was $19.95 and the two were $39.90. Furthermore, since this purchase was for delivery within the metropolitan area there were no handling and shipping charges.

Another typist was asked to prepare a bibliography with these instructions:

Please type, using double space throughout, a rough draft of the attached card bibliography. Entries are to be listed alphabetically by author, and then by title. Make two copies.

The typist immediately realized that the cards were not necessarily in correct alphabetic order. She first put them in order, noting that if one author had two or more references, the titles were put in place in alphabetic order. She knew she would need the original plus one carbon copy.

Getting Specific Information. Office workers must check many different sources to get the specific information they need.

Debbie was asked to check the schedules of two airlines to determine if there was a flight to Boston on Thursday around four. This is what Debbie found:

TO: **BOSTON** (EST)						
12:30p L	1:14p	82	NON-STOP	☕	727	Ex Sa
1:30p L	2:18p	314	NON-STOP	☕	727	Daily
2:30p L	3:18p	94	NON-STOP	☕	727	Daily
3:30p L	4:18p	690	NON-STOP	☕	727	Ex Sa
4:00p J	5:02p	164	NON-STOP	☕	707	Daily
4:30p L	5:20p	578	NON-STOP	☕	727	Ex Sa
5:30p L	6:20p	366	NON-STOP	☕	727	Daily
6:30p L	7:21p	228	NON-STOP	☕	727	Ex Sa
7:30p L	8:18p	296	NON-STOP	☕	727	Daily
11:50p L	12:33a	502	NON-STOP	☕	727	Ex Sa

TO BOSTON, MASS.

K	9 20A	10 10A	484	ExSu	S	o
K	12 40P	1 30P	62			o
K	2 40P	3 30P	20			o
K	3 30P	4 20P	4			o
N	8 35P	9 30P	416			o

Illus. 2-2 Airlines schedules

There are several flights that might be convenient. One airline has a flight at 3:30, another at 4, and one at 4:30; the other airline has a 3:30 flight.

Ronald got from the stockroom one pair of salt and pepper shakers in the Fruits and Flowers pattern. He had to record the price of this item. He checked the price list and recorded the price, which was $16.00 a pair.

Illus. 2-3
Portion of a page from a dinner ware catalog

PATTERN:				
Chinese Bouquet	AOG	Group I	Green Bouquet	AV	Group I
Coronation	BAT	Group II	Market Garden	FR	Group III
Fruits and Flowers	BFR	Group IV	Queen Victoria	VBO	Group III
			Rothchild Bird	RO	Group II

STOCK No.	DINNER WARE	I AOG AV	II BAT RO	III FR VBO	IV BFR
734	Teacup and saucer	14.00	18.00	20.00	21.00
1515	Bread and butter plate	6.75	9.00	10.00	10.50
1518	Salad plate	7.75	10.75	11.00	11.50
1524	Dinner plate	13.00	15.25	18.50	19.00
	Place setting – 5 piece	41.50	53.00	59.50	62.00
42	Covered vegetable – medium	68.00	73.50	76.00	79.00
43	Covered vegetable – small	56.50	62.00	65.00	67.50
75	Covered muffin	28.00	34.00	34.00	34.00
86	Covered vegetable dish	68.00	79.00	79.00	85.00
229	Sauce boat – ½ pint	17.00	22.50	22.50	25.50
234	Sauce boat – ¾ pint (fast stand)	39.50	45.00	45.00	56.50
249	Ladle – 5¼" long	4.00	5.50	5.50	6.50
250/260	Salt and pepper – 2¼" tall	12.50pr	15.00pr	15.00pr	16.00pr
251	Twin Salt	9.00	10.25	10.25	11.25
259	Sugar Shaker – 5"	12.00	14.50	14.50	15.25
262	Eggcup (single)	6.25	7.50	7.50	8.00
263	Eggcup (double)	9.00	12.50	12.50	14.00
311	Compote	56.50	62.00	62.00	62.00
329	Fruit saucer	6.25	9.00	9.50	10.50
330	Oatmeal bowl	8.50	12.00	12.50	14.00
372	Jam jar – 4½" tall	20.00	22.50	22.50	25.00
420	Tray – 11¼"	31.00	36.50	36.50	39.50
436	Sandwich dish – 14½"	28.50	34.00	34.00	34.00
439	Round tray – 14"	51.00	56.50	56.50	62.00
443	Three section hors d'oeuvre	28.50	34.00	34.00	34.00
505	Hot water plate	34.00	40.00	40.00	42.00
530	Crescent salad	12.50	15.25	17.00	17.50

Paprikas Weiss Importers

LISTENING

Many businesses depend on frequent oral communications. The large stock exchanges, for example, handle buy and sell orders by oral agreements. Department stores do much selling and reordering of goods by telephone. Supervisors give instructions to employees; employees seek assistance from co-workers; telephone callers ask for information and leave messages. The listener has been *attentive* if he hears accurately what the speaker says.

How well do you listen? If you always listen when someone is talking to you and know what has been said to you, you are a good listener. Also, if you don't have to ask the speaker to repeat what he said, you are listening. But, if a member of your family or a very close friend has said to you, "You aren't listening to a *word* I am saying." or "Did you *really* hear what I said?" or "Will you please *listen* to me for a few minutes?" you probably weren't listening carefully. Your failure to listen in a work situation is shown by your not following procedures properly or by your need to ask additional questions.

To be a good listener you will want to keep the following in mind.

Listen Carefully

Give your full attention to the person who is talking to you. What does *give your full attention* mean? It means that your mind is following

Illus. 2-4
Give your full attention to the person who is talking to you.

Girl Scouts of the United States of America

the speaker. Your mind is not on something else. You are not thinking of what you want to say next instead of listening. You are not guilty of thinking about what you are going to do when you leave the office at five while the supervisor is explaining the details of a job.

Listen for Thoughts

The message the speaker is trying to communicate to you is more than a collection of words; the message requires an understanding of facts in relation to a particular situation.

Paul's supervisor came to his desk with a handwritten report and said, "I've just completed a first draft of a report that must be mailed by the end of the week. I would like to see what it looks like in type, and then I can make changes and additions. Please type this as a rough draft, using triple spacing. Could I have it shortly?"

What thoughts did Paul's supervisor convey to him if he was listening? Among them were these:

1. This is the first draft of a report.
2. A speedy job of typewriting is desired.
3. The copy is to be triple-spaced. It is not necessary that this be an attractive job.

If Paul had *not* been listening for thoughts, he may not have realized that this was a rough draft. He may have taken time to correct errors in the copy and typed the report as a final copy.

Summarize as You Listen

This is actually done along with the preceding step of listening for thoughts. As you listen for key thoughts, you will want to organize them so that at the end of the conversation you have a clear knowledge of what was said.

Review What You Heard

Since it is possible to hear something at the moment it is told to you and then quickly forget it, you may want to think through what you have just heard and, if you have pencil and pad at hand, make notes which assure you of the correct information. Recalling will reinforce the message in your memory.

REVIEWING WHAT YOU HAVE READ

1. What kinds of reading does the businessman expect of his office workers?
2. Why is reading for understanding important?
3. Of what value is skimming?

4. How does the second reading of a passage differ from skimming?
5. What is the value of asking yourself questions when you have finished reading something?
6. Describe what is meant by *giving full attention to what you are hearing.*
7. List three examples that show the necessity of listening carefully in a business office.
8. If you are a good listener, how do you listen?
9. List four steps that are necessary if you are to be a good listener.
10. In what way can you improve your ability to remember what you have heard?

MAKING DECISIONS

1. Kay was asked to locate a hotel in San Francisco that had facilities for business meetings. She used the *Hotel and Motel Red Book* as a reference to find this information. Below is part of a page from this book. Is there a hotel listed that has the facilities she needs?

Illus. 2-5

Hotel and Motel Red Book

2. A new photocopying machine was purchased for the office where Brenda works. A representative of the company came to the office and demonstrated the use of the machine. Brenda was thinking of an unfinished job on her desk and didn't listen attentively to the demonstrator. The next day when she had to use the machine she realized that she didn't know how to use it. What should Brenda do?

Jack is an accounting clerk in a large office where it is necessary to work co-operatively. His fellow workers know that he seldom listens to instructions and is constantly doing jobs incorrectly. This means that the work of others is disrupted while corrections are made. Jack seems to "tune the speaker out" and then doesn't know what must be done when he begins his work. He then guesses what he has to do. What should his supervisor say to him about this problem?

**USING
LANGUAGE**

Pronouns are words that serve as substitutes for nouns. They must agree with their antecedents (nouns for which they stand) in person, number, and gender.

Examples: Ruth does all *her* work on an electric typewriter. *Ruth* (third person, singular number, feminine gender) is the antecedent of *her*, which is the same person, number, and gender.
The supervisor referred to the new file clerk *who* is doing a very good job. *Clerk* is the antecedent of *who*, which is the relative pronoun used to refer to a person.

On a separate sheet of paper write the following sentences, indicating correct pronouns.

1. Chester and David will get (his, their) new typewriters within a week.
2. The supervisor, as well as the file clerks, begins (his, their) work day promptly at 8:45.
3. Valerie did not know what (she, her) assignment was for the afternoon.
4. The committee passed (its, their) resolution after several hours of discussion.
5. The employer is not sure if Sally is the one (which, who) is contributing most to getting the job done on time.
6. When will the report be ready for (I, me)?
7. If I were (he, him), I don't believe I would undertake that job at this time.
8. To (who, whom) should this memorandum be forwarded?
9. All the members of the group expressed (his, their) opinions in writing.
10. The decision will have to be made between John and (I, me).

**USING
ARITHMETIC**

On a separate sheet of paper find the answers to the following problems.

1.	143 +231	2.	356 +490	3.	289 +899	4.	934 +785	5.	532 +389
6.	9786 −145	7.	5632 −1245	8.	7498 −670	9.	3562 −1989	10.	5740 −5391
11.	127 ×61	12.	143 ×13	13.	543 ×28	14.	678 ×36	15.	351 ×29

**PERFORMING
OFFICE
TASKS**

1. Type each of the names and addresses at the top of page 37 on a 5″ x 3″ card (or on a piece of paper cut to this size). Use single spacing. Type the name on the first line in this order: Last name, first name, middle name or initial. Use ZIP abbreviations instead of full state name.

Frank W. White
568 Dogwood Drive
Little Rock, Arkansas 72201

Leland T. Thompson
570 Midwood Road
Muncie, Indiana 47301

Ralph N. Rothenberg
1454 - 54th Street
Chicago, Illinois 60604

Antonio W. Tesori
7581 Spring Avenue
Bridgeport, Connecticut 06601

Thomas O. Tobias
690 Beulah Road
Wilmington, Delaware 19809

Charles M. Ross
5702 Carleton Drive
Fresno, California 93705

ABBREVIATIONS	
Standard	ZIP
Ala.	AL
Alaska	AK
Ariz.	AZ
Ark.	AR
Calif.	CA
Colo.	CO
Conn.	CT
D.C.	DC
Del.	DE
Fla.	FL
Ga.	GA
Hawaii	HI
Idaho	ID
Ill.	IL
Ind.	IN
Iowa	IA

2. The recommendations below for typing names and addresses on envelopes have been issued by the United States Postal Service.

(a) Addresses are single-spaced.
(b) The bottom line of the address must contain the names of the city and state and the ZIP Code. The ZIP Code is usually typed two spaces after the state.
(c) The state name should be typed in full or abbreviated according to the two-letter ZIP Code abbreviation (see Appendix D, page 617).
(d) The next to the last line of the address (including the apartment number) should be reserved for the street address or the Post Office box number.
(e) A building name (including suite number), if used, should appear on the line above the street address.

Type each of the following names and addresses on an envelope (or pieces of paper cut to the size of a small envelope, 6½″ x 3⅝″). Follow the recommendations in the arrangement of the name and address.

Mrs. F. T. Neville
157 Watts Boulevard
Greenwood Terrace Apartments
San Diego, California 92108

Mr. Daniel McDow
174 - 14th Street
Louisville
Kentucky 40207

Mr. Theodore Murray
472 Wayne Avenue
Walnut Grove
Mississippi 39189

Mrs. Ivan F. Oshinsky
Oak Towers
511 Waverly Place
New York City 10004

PART 2 HANDWRITING

Antonio Diaz is an order clerk in a large appliance store where many customers order replacement parts for appliances. Antonio knows the importance of a clear handwriting, for if he records one number that is not legible, the wrong part will be ordered. This means that a customer who expected to get his order in two weeks will be delayed while the misordered part is returned and the proper part ordered. Antonio writes each number and letter clearly so that the order clerk in the central office will have no problems following up on customer orders.

Handwriting continues to be used in the business office even though typewriters, card punch machines, and calculating machines record millions of letters and numbers. Illegible penmanship costs United States businessmen large sums in scrambled orders, lost time, missent shipments, and other forms of inefficiency. The Handwriting Foundation estimates that poor penmanship costs business about $100 million a year.[1]

Many business forms are still completed by hand. It is important that your handwriting be easily read, which means that it must be legible. Forms that you prepare in longhand must be read by others. If others are to read them quickly and accurately, there must be no question about the numbers and letters. Good handwriting requires your continuous attention. You probably had some practice in penmanship, but you may have become somewhat careless since then and you may have lost some of your good writing skill. You will now have a chance to develop this useful business skill for office use.

ACCEPTABLE STYLES OF HANDWRITING

Your handwriting is acceptable if it can be read by anyone who knows the English language and understands Arabic numerals. Various styles of handwriting are considered adequate. Look at these two samples of penmanship at the top of page 39. One is a vertical style. The other is slanted. Both are acceptable.

---

[1]Costello, John, "Executive Trends," *Nation's Business*, Washington: Chamber of Commerce of the United States (July, 1970), p. 11.

Good writing comes by practice.

Good writing comes by practice

Note that these handwriting samples meet these requirements:

1. Letters are all slanted in the same direction.
2. The spacing between letters is approximately equal.
3. Words are separated from each other by approximately the same amount of space.
4. Capital letters are about twice as large as small letters, and letters are in proper proportion.
5. Letters that cause **confusion** if written improperly, such as *a*'s, *e*'s, *c*'s and *o*'s, are clearly different.
6. All *t*'s are crossed, and all *i*'s are dotted.
7. Rounded and pointed parts of *m*'s, *n*'s, *u*'s, and *v*'s are clear.

confusion: uncertainty; difficulty

HOW TO IMPROVE YOUR HANDWRITING

How would you rate your own handwriting? Is it acceptable when evaluated by the standards listed? On a piece of lined paper write the following two paragraphs in your natural handwriting.

It is possible to improve the quality of your handwriting. To do so will require some attention to good writing techniques.
Office workers are characterized by their ability to make good judgments, follow proper techniques, and use extra effort to improve skills.

Now, look at the specimen of your handwriting that you have just completed and notice if it meets the requirements listed on page 39.

If you are satisfied that your writing is legible and attractive, you may want to see if you can improve your rate of writing without causing your writing to become illegible.

If your writing is not as good as it should be, review your manner of writing. Check the following points about your writing techniques:

1. Do you give yourself enough space in which to write easily? You should have sufficient desk space so that your arms can rest comfortably on the desk. There should be enough room so that your arms are free to move away from the body slightly. Your desk should be sufficiently clear of books and papers to allow you to arrange your writing paper conveniently for writing.

2. Do you use a hand position that makes it easy to produce clear, complete letters?

    (a) Do you hold your pen comfortably and in a manner that gives you full control over the letters that you are making? (A standard procedure for holding the pen or pencil is to hold it about an inch above the point, between the thumb and the side of the middle finger, near the base of the fingernail.)

    (b) Are you writing in a manner that prevents your becoming tired?

3. Do you give attention to completing each letter before you move on to the next letter?

PRINTING

There are times when office workers need to use printing because it is normally easier to read than writing. Business firms frequently specify that certain information requested on their business forms, usually names and addresses, be printed or typed to insure **legibility**.

legibility:
readability

You can learn to print neatly and attractively if you follow these simple rules:

1. Use a vertical position for the main part of each letter.

Illus. 2-8

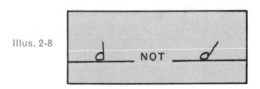

2. Maintain a uniform size for all alphabetic forms.

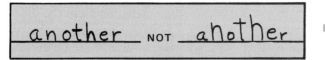

Illus. 2-9

3. Use a **consistent** style for printing; that is, do not mix capital letters with lower case letters.

consistent:
the same way
every time

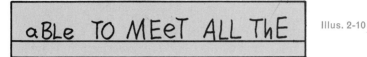

Illus. 2-10

WRITING NUMBERS

Numbers are an important part of daily business life. They must show exact amounts of money, correct telephone numbers, quantities desired. Numbers must be written clearly so that they can be read quickly and accurately. These numbers are legible:

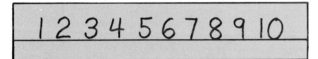

Illus. 2-11

1. Notice that all the numbers are of the same height.
2. Notice that the 6, 8, 9, and 0 are *closed*.
3. Notice that only 4 and 5 require more than a single stroke.

NUMBERS IN COLUMNS

Often numbers are recorded in columns and must be written to fit into prelined spaces. The numbers you write in columns must be written within the space allowed for each digit, or the values of the numbers may be confused by the reader. Notice the difference in the two illustrations:

Correctly aligned   Incorrectly aligned

Correctly aligned	Incorrectly aligned
4980	4980
59821	59821
39856	39856
1291	1291
4678	4678

Illus. 2-12

READING HANDWRITING

deciphered:
make out the mean-
ing of something
that is puzzling

Office workers spend much time reading the handwriting of others. Instructions are often handwritten, copy to be typewritten is sometimes handwritten, and signatures often must be **deciphered** so that the response can be written to the proper person. Here are some aids to help you read writing that is not legible.

1. Note carefully how the same number or letter is written in places where you are certain of the number or letter. For example, how are letters written in simple words, such as *the, and, but, sales*, etc.? How are the numbers written in the date or in an amount that you already know, such as the amount of the invoice that was sent to the person whose handwriting you are now trying to decipher?

2. Print those parts of a word that you are certain of; it may give you a clue as to the rest of the word.

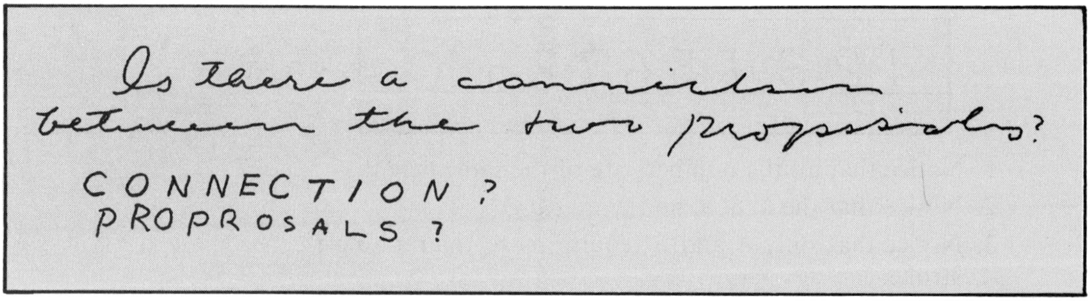

Illus. 2-13

3. Record the numbers that are clear and then attempt to determine what the remaining numbers must be. For example, if a dress manufacturer is identifying one of your products, knowing the nature of the writer's business may indicate which product he wants.

Illus. 2-14

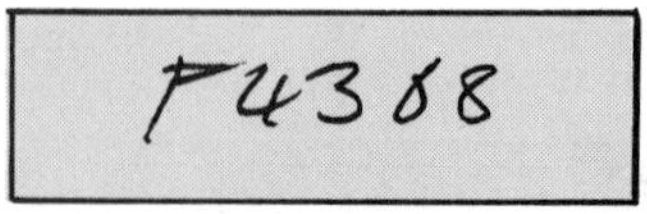

Is this F4308 or F4368 or P4368? Since this is a dress manufacturer, he is not likely to be specifying F4308, which is a heavy zipper for mattress covers, or P4368, which is a snap for children's pants. The item must be F4368, which is a lightweight zipper for jersey fabrics.

Learning to read the handwriting of others is a type of detective work and will require your following through a wide variety of clues.

You will be satisfied, though, when you realize that you have successfully identified the name, the word, or the amount that was causing hesitancy.

1. What is legible handwriting?
2. What are some uses for handwriting in the office?
3. If your *a*'s and *o*'s look very much alike, what should you do to improve legibility?
4. How much desk space do you need to write easily?
5. When is printing used in the office?
6. Why should printed letters be of uniform size?
7. What is meant by a *consistent style* in making letters?
8. Which numbers must be *closed* if they are to be legible?
9. How should numbers be written in columns?
10. How can you determine what an illegibly written word might be?

MAKING
DECISIONS

1. Betsy is the receptionist in a chemical manufacturing company. She takes many messages each day. She leaves the messages on the desks for the executives. One day she realized that the secretaries to the executives were asking her again and again to read the telephone numbers she had recorded. What would you suggest to Betsy to reduce the number of questions she receives from the readers of her messages?
2. Neil copied a paragraph from a magazine article on photocopiers and then attempted to determine how satisfactory his handwriting was. Here is a sample of his writing. How would you evaluate it?

Illus. 2-15

Here is a way to arrive at your true copy cost. For simplicity we will use a Brown and White 1000 machine, total volume being 20,000 usable letter-size copies monthly

WORKING
WITH
OTHERS

Sharon was talking with a friend one afternoon about her handwriting. Among her comments was this: "I think you are born with a good handwriting. There is no way to improve your writing; so I don't see why I should bother with mine, which is obviously poor." What would you say to Sharon if you were her friend?

Verbs are words that express action or a state of being. They are closely related to subjects and must agree with their subjects in person and in number.

Examples: The file *clerks go* to lunch at one o'clock.

The *supervisor goes* to a department meeting weekly.

On a separate sheet of paper copy the following sentences, using the correct verb in each case.

1. The three mail clerks (is, are) planning a weekend trip to the mountains.
2. The typist (want, wants) to complete the report by noon.
3. Each inventory clerk (plan, plans) his own work in the morning.
4. The outline for the report was (organize, organized) early last month.
5. When all parts of this exhibit are received tomorrow, the shipping clerk (wraps, will wrap) it for shipment.
6. Jerry and Philip (go, goes) to lunch at one o'clock each day.
7. The mail was (distribute, distributed) by noon yesterday.
8. The receptionist (receives, received) three long-distance calls last Friday.
9. The general clerk (files, filed) the correspondence each Monday.
10. Will the messenger (take, takes) this package to midtown tomorrow morning?

1. Each day Tricia gets requests for bulletins; checks for the bulletins are enclosed with the requests. As she opens each letter, she records the amount of the check on a sheet. At the end of the day on November 11, she had the following listing:

$1.50
.75
2.25
2.50
.50
3.25
.75
1.25
3.75
2.25

Record these amounts on a separate sheet of paper and find the total.

2. Wanda maintained a record of the supplies she got from the Central Supply Department. At the end of the month she worked out the total cost of the supplies she had used during the past month. Below is her record for October.

Supplies, October, 197–

1 box (500) of envelopes at	$3.25 a box
1 box (500) of envelopes (Kraft) at	4.05 a box
4 reams of letterhead paper at	2.30 a ream
1 gallon of Ditto fluid at	2.50 a gallon
6 dozen pencils at	.60 a dozen
2 rolls of Scotch tape at	.94 a roll
2 boxes of stencils at	3.90 a box
1 can of ink liquid at	2.84 a can
1 box (100 sheets) of carbon paper at	4.40 a box
2 typewriter ribbons at	1.96 each
1 box (500) of envelopes (Kraft) at	4.05 a box

Record these amounts on a separate sheet of paper and find the total.

PERFORMING OFFICE TASKS

Edith works in a small stationery store where customers are able to order all styles of stationery with their names and addresses on it. For each order that Edith accepts, she must fill in a form indicating clearly what is to be printed on the stationery. Below are listed the names and addresses of three customers who have ordered stationery. On plain sheets of paper, draw the lines as shown in the form and then print the names and addresses shown below.

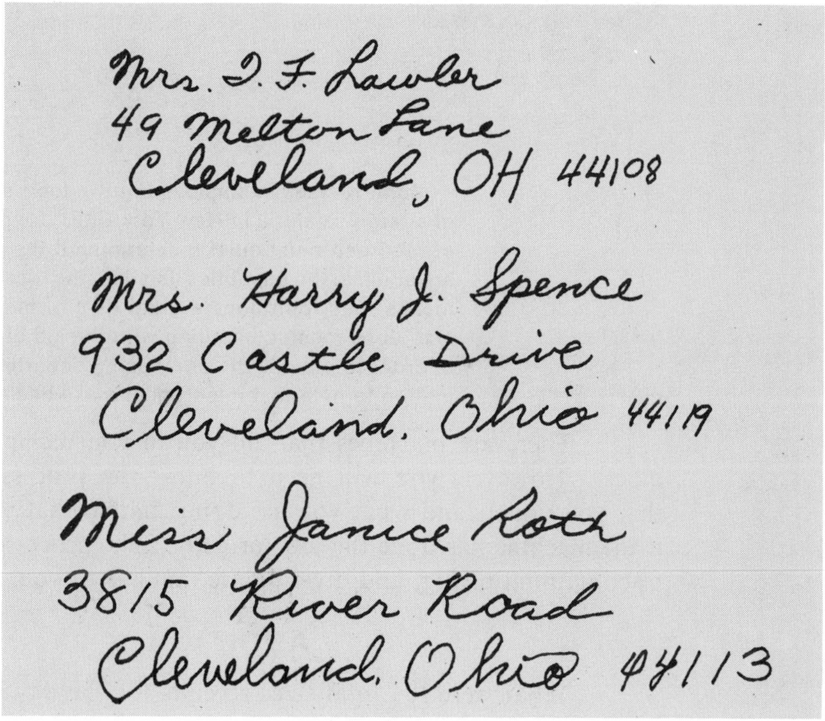
Mrs. I. F. Lawler
49 Melton Lane
Cleveland, OH 44108

Mrs. Harry J. Spence
932 Castle Drive
Cleveland, Ohio 44119

Miss Janice Roth
3815 River Road
Cleveland, Ohio 44113

Coles Stationery Shop
39 Park Avenue
Cleveland Ohio 44103

NAME ON STATIONERY : (Please print)

____

ADDRESS ON ENVELOPE (Please print)

____

____

Illus. 2-16

John Kierzek is employed in the food services department of a large cafeteria in New York City. John receives all orders of food and must quickly determine if the quantities delivered are equal to the quantities listed on the receiving slip. This task means that John does a great deal of mental arithmetic. He also does much computing with the aid of an adding machine in order to provide the purchasing department with cost information to help that department make decisions wisely.

computing: finding answers by arithmetical work

There are machines that aid you in your **computing** tasks in the office. However, you will need to know the processes thoroughly so that you understand what you are doing and so that you can determine if the machine has done the job correctly. The processes of adding, subtracting, multiplying, and dividing are familiar to you.

ADDITION

What were the total sales receipts for the day? How much was spent out of the petty cash fund this week? How many calls were received in the office this past week? All these questions require a *total* — the sum you get when you *add* numbers together.

The checks received in one office in the morning's mail were for the following amounts: $13.50, $2.75, $150.00, $75.35, and $1.75. To find the sum, recall these helpful rules.

1. Items should be written carefully so that each digit is legible.
2. Items should be recorded so that the decimal points are aligned.

$$\begin{array}{r} \$\ 13.50 \\ 2.75 \\ 150.00 \\ 75.35 \\ 1.75 \\ \hline \end{array}$$

3. Add digits in groups of two or more.

$$
\begin{array}{rrrrr}
\$ & 1^1 & 3^2 & 5^1 & 0 \\
 & & 2. & 7 & 5 \\
1^1 & 5 & 0. & 0 & 0 \\
 & 7 & 5. & 3 & 5 \\
 & & 1. & 7 & 5 \\
\hline
\$2 & 4 & 3. & 3 & 5 \\
\end{array}
$$

4. Double-check the total by adding in the opposite direction. If you added from top to bottom the first time, double-check by adding from bottom to top.

Addition is a commonly used skill in a business office. Here are two examples:

At the end of each week, the general office clerk in a small insurance office checked the petty cash fund. During the week receipts showing the payments from petty cash were placed in an envelope. On Friday afternoon the receipts were totaled. Below are the receipts for the week of September 20.

Date September 20, 197–	No. 149	No. 150	No. 151	No. 152	No. 153	No. 154
	Amount	Amount	Amount	Amount	Amount	Amount
Paid to Clinton Supply Co.	$ 1 25	$ 1 10	$ 3 90	$ 2 15	$ 1 98	$ 2 47
For Masking tape						
Charge to: Supplies						
Payment received: L.T. Jeffrey — Approved by	LTC	LTC	LTC	LTC	LTC	LTC

Illus. 2-17
Petty cash receipts

A receptionist in a large company was asked to keep a record of the number of incoming calls she received each day. She was to keep this record for a week. To make this task easy she used a tally sheet as shown in Illus. 2-18 at the top of page 48. Each time she picked up the receiver she made a tally mark on her sheet. Notice how quickly she was able to determine the number of calls, since she recorded her tallies in groups of five.

SUBTRACTION

As you recall from your study of arithmetic, subtracting is a process of "taking away." To subtract is to deduct one number from

Telephone Calls			
Day	Morning	Afternoon	Total
Monday	𝍱𝍱 𝍱𝍱 //	𝍱𝍱 𝍱𝍱 𝍱𝍱 /	28
Tuesday	𝍱𝍱 𝍱𝍱 𝍱𝍱	𝍱𝍱 𝍱𝍱 ////	29
Wednesday	𝍱𝍱 𝍱𝍱 𝍱𝍱 ///	𝍱𝍱 𝍱𝍱 𝍱𝍱 /	34
Thursday	𝍱𝍱 ////	𝍱𝍱 𝍱𝍱 ///	22
Friday	𝍱𝍱 𝍱𝍱 𝍱𝍱 𝍱𝍱 /	𝍱𝍱 𝍱𝍱 ///	34
	75	72	147

Illus. 2-18
Tally sheet of
incoming telephone
calls

another number. The *minuend* is the number from which the *subtrahend* is subtracted to find the *difference*.

At the end of the week, the total payments from petty cash were $12.85. The petty cash fund was $25.00. How much was left in the petty cash fund?

$25.00 Minuend
−12.85 Subtrahend
—————
$12.15 Difference

A receptionist for the personnel interviewers kept a record of the number of interviews held each day. One interviewer asked how many interviews were yet to be held on a particular afternoon. The receptionist had scheduled 28 interviews and checked each as it was completed by one of the interviewers. She noted that 17 were completed. She was able to quickly tell the interviewer how many were still to be completed by subtracting 17 from 28.

28
−17
———
11 Interviews yet to be completed

To check the accuracy of a subtraction problem, add the subtrahend to the difference and the total should equal the minuend.

$12.15   11
+12.85   +17
————   ———
$25.00   28

MULTIPLICATION

Multiplication is the process you use to simplify the adding of numbers. It is really repeated addition. What is the sum of 5+5+5+5? As you know, you can add these and get the total, 20. Or you may get the answer by *multiplying* 5 × 4 = 20.

5 Multiplicand

×4 Multiplier

20 Product

Many office tasks will require that you multiply. If a typist has a mailing to prepare, she must first check to see how many envelopes she will need before getting more from the central supplies department. If she finds that she has 3 boxes, each of which contains 500 envelopes, she will multiply 500 by 3 to learn that she has 1,500. These will be enough for a job that requires about 900 envelopes.

Decimal Point Placement

To determine where the decimal point is placed in the product, you must count the numbers to the right of the decimal point in both the multiplicand and the multiplier. These two figures are *added* to determine how many places to the left of the product the decimal point is placed.

$ 15.67 Multiplicand	2 places to the right	
×14 Multiplier	0 places to the right	
6268		
1567		
$ 219.38 Product	Decimal 2 places to the left	

$ 195.00 Multiplicand	2 places to the right	
×.0125 Multiplier	4 places to the right	
97500		
39000		
19500		
$2.437500 Product	Decimal 6 places to the left	

Rounding Numbers

In the preceding example, the product is $2.437500. Amounts of money are generally rounded to the nearest cent. In this instance .4375 is nearest to .44; therefore, the product would be considered $2.44.

A simple rule to follow is this: If the first digit to the right of the cents position is 5 or more, add 1 to the cents digit; if it is less than 5, **disregard** it. Therefore:

$15.353 becomes $15.35
1.456 becomes   1.46
10.455 becomes   10.46

Estimating the Product

A good office worker is always aware of the importance of numbers, and the process of **estimating** is a measure of this awareness. To estimate the product, you should look at the multiplicand and round it to the nearest simple number and then do the same with the multiplier. Estimating gives you an idea of *about* what the product should be.

As an example, if you had to order 11 reams of paper at $1.98 each, what would be the approximate cost? To estimate, consider the $1.98 as $2.00 and the 11 as 10. The exact answer should be *near* $20.00. The exact answer *is* $21.78. If you had estimated the answer, you would not have accepted an exact answer of $2.17 or $217.80.

Multiplying by 10, 100, 1,000 . . . .

To multiply by 10, 100, 1,000 or of higher powers of 10, you merely add as many zeros to the multiplicand as there are zeros in the multiplier to get the product.

$$167 \times 10 = 1,670$$
$$186 \times 100 = 18,600$$
$$146 \times 1,000 = 146,000$$

If there is a decimal point in the multiplicand, then you must move the decimal point in the product to the right for as many digits as there are zeros in the multiplier.

$$45.85 \times 100 = 4585.00 \text{ or } 4,585$$
$$.125 \times 1,000 = 125.000 \text{ or } 125$$

DIVISION

Division is a process of separating into parts. For example, a typist has 85 copies of a bulletin and wants to determine how many packets of 5 bulletins she will have. To find the number of packets she will have, she must divide 85 by 5.

$$\begin{array}{r} 17 \\ 5)\overline{85} \\ 5 \\ \hline 35 \\ 35 \\ \hline \end{array}$$

Divisor 5)85 Dividend
   17 Quotient

$85 \div 5 = 17$

The number divided is called the *dividend*.

The number by which the dividend is divided is called the *divisor*.

The result of this process is called the *quotient*.

To check the accuracy of the computation, multiply the quotient by the divisor — $17 \times 5 = 85$. The product of this check is the same as the dividend in the original problem.

Decimal Point Placement

In those cases where there is a decimal point in the dividend and the divisor is a whole number, the decimal point in the quotient is aligned with the decimal in the dividend.

$$\begin{array}{r} 1.3 \\ 15)\overline{19.5} \\ 15 \\ \hline 45 \\ 45 \\ \hline \end{array}$$

Since division can be done with only a whole number divisor, move the decimal point in the divisor to the end. Then move the decimal in the dividend the same number of places to the right, and place the quotient decimal point directly above this. It may be necessary to add zeros to the dividend to have enough places.

$$\begin{array}{r} 12. \\ 15.135\,)\overline{181.620} \\ 151\ 35 \\ \hline 30\ 270 \\ 30\ 270 \\ \hline \end{array}$$

Dividing by 10, 100, 1,000 . . . .

To divide by 10 or 100 or 1,000 or a higher power of 10, you move the decimal point to the left in the dividend for as many places as there are zeros in the divisor. The dividend then becomes the quotient. This is a very useful division shortcut.

$$156 \div 10 \quad = 15.6$$
$$4567 \div 100 \quad = 45.67$$
$$15.3 \div 1000 = \quad .0153$$

Remember that when you have a whole number, the decimal point follows the last digit:

156 is the same as 156.

FRACTIONS AND DECIMALS

If your office career involves computing, you will work not only with whole numbers (60, 45, 21) but also with parts of whole numbers, which are expressed either as fractions or decimals.

A *fraction* is a representation of one number divided by another—¾, ½. The number above the line is called the *numerator*; the number below is called the *denominator*.

¾ is three fourths

or

3 divided by 4

or

3 over 4

All fractions can be expressed as decimal parts. To change the fraction ¾ to a decimal, you must divide the numerator by the denominator—in this example $3 \div 4$:

```
        .75
   4) 3.00
      2 8
      ____
       20
       20
      ____
```

equivalent:
equal in amount or
value

The decimal **equivalent** of ¾ is, therefore, .75.

Office employees who work with numbers usually know from memory the decimal equivalents of the common fractions. Below is a list of frequently used fractions and decimals.

Fraction	Decimal	Fraction	Decimal
1/2	.5	4/5	.8
1/3	.3333	1/6	.16667
2/3	.6667	5/6	.83333
1/4	.25	1/8	.125
3/4	.75	3/8	.375
1/5	.2	5/8	.625
2/5	.4	7/8	.875
3/5	.6		

Unit 2 / Basic Skills for Office Jobs

PERCENTAGES

A *percentage* is a *part of a hundred.* Any whole number is 100 percent of itself; that is, 68 is 100 percent of 68. If someone asks you what is 50 percent of a group of 68, he is asking what **proportion** of 68 represents 50 percent of that group. Since 50 percent is the same as ½ or .5, you can determine the answer to the question by multiplying 68 by ½ or by .5. The answer is 34. Remember that a percent(age) is a proportion of the number.

proportion: the relation of one part to the whole

Twenty-five percent of the staff of a local insurance company is composed of clerical workers. There are 452 members on the staff. How many are clerical workers?

100 percent of the workers = 452

25 percent of the workers = x

You can find out how many of the staff are clerical workers by multiplying 452 by .25 which equals 113. There are 113 clerical workers on the staff of 452. To check your computation, divide 113 by 452.

```
    452                .25 or 25 percent
   ×.25          452) 113.00
   ----              90 4
   2260              ------
   904               22 60
   ------            22 60
  113.00             ------
```

Illus. 2-19
Most computing is done by calculator.

Marchant

Part 3 / Computing

53

A *discount* is a reduction of a debt usually allowed for a cash or prompt payment. A discount is stated as a percentage. For example, a large manufacturer allows customers a 2 percent discount if payment of an invoice is made within 10 days of receipt of the invoice. An invoice of $1,500 less a discount of 2 percent (if paid within 10 days) would result in payment of $1,470 by the customer.

$1,500
× .02
———
$30.00 Amount of discount

$1,500
− 30
———
$1,470 Amount of payment

REVIEWING WHAT YOU HAVE READ

1. What does *computing* mean?
2. In order to get a sum, which operation must be performed?
3. Why is it a good idea to record tallies in groups of five?
4. What is the answer of a subtraction problem called?
5. What is the relationship of addition to multiplication?
6. What is a *product* in multiplication?
7. How do you multiply a number by 10 or 100 mentally?
8. What is the *quotient* in a division problem?
9. What process is required to change a fraction into a decimal?
10. What is the decimal equivalent of ¼?

MAKING DECISIONS

1. In order to determine how busy each file clerk is, the supervisor has asked each clerk to keep a record of how many files she pulls from the file drawers each hour. Elizabeth feels she has a good memory and will keep track of how many she pulls by merely counting them mentally as she pulls them.
   What do you think of this procedure? Would you recommend some other way?
2. Barbara checks the supply cabinet to determine which additional supplies she needs. This is what she finds:
   ¼ box of envelopes (each box holds 500)
   4 packages of large envelopes (each package has 25)
   ¼ ream of letterhead (a ream has 500 sheets)
   2 packages of carbon paper (each package has 100 sheets)
   ½ ream of second sheets (a ream has 500 sheets)
   What is the quantity of each item that is available?

WORKING WITH OTHERS

Dolores is a typist in the purchasing department. She has made up a purchase order (see page 55) for some supplies. She asks you to check her arithmetic to be sure that she has no errors. How would you check it? On a separate sheet of paper describe the checking procedure that you would use. Then check this form and write out what you would tell Dolores about any errors that you found.

Unit 2 / Basic Skills for Office Jobs

Coles Stationery Shop

39 Park Avenue, Cleveland, Ohio 44103 Area Code 216 391-4040

PURCHASE ORDER

TO:

Gibson Supply Company
4408 Euclid Avenue
Cleveland, OH 44103

DATE June 27, 197-   TERMS   2/10 net 30

ORDER
NO. 21503   SHIP VIA   UPS

QUANTITY	CAT. NO.	DESCRIPTION	PRICE	TOTAL
12 bottles	RC-4	Rubber Cement--4 oz.	.29	3.48
12 bottles	M-7	Mucilage--1.5 oz.	.19	2.18
6 bottles	PL-6	Paste--Liquid--6 oz.	.69	4.24
12 rolls	ST-1296	Scotch Tape--1/2" x 1296"	.56	6.72
12 rolls	ST-300	Scotch Tape--3/4" x 300"		
		(Dispense Pack)	.29	3.48
36 rolls	MT-232	Masking Tape--3/4" x 2160"	.89	32.04
36 rolls	MT-236	Masking Tape--1" x 2160"	1.19	42.84
12 rolls	DP-123	Dymo Tape--Plastic 1/2"		
		(Black)	1.10	13.20
12 rolls	DP-124	Dymo Tape--Plastic 1/2"		
		(Blue)	1.10	13.20
				121.38

Illus. 2-20

USING
LANGUAGE

Below are pairs of words that cause confusion in both oral and written communications:

good — desirable, right, proper

well — success in doing something; state of health

effect — the result of

affect — to influence the result

except — to leave out

accept — to receive

learn — to acquire some new knowledge or skill

teach — to aid another in acquiring a new skill or knowledge

farther — indicates distance

further — additional; more; to a greater degree or extent

On a separate sheet of paper write each of the following sentences choosing the word which correctly completes the sentence:

1. Jane told Ruth that she would (learn, teach) her to use the new correction paper.
2. Tom said that he would give (farther, further) attention to the report today.
3. The job was done (good, well) by the three typists.
4. What is the (affect, effect) of a coffee break on our productivity?
5. Who is the person in this office who can (accept, except) the ballots?
6. The supervisor praised the (good, well) job that Betsy did yesterday.
7. How much (farther, further) must we travel to get to the convention site?
8. Vicki told me that she will (learn, teach) this new job to anyone who comes to her.
9. Everyone is in favor of the change in layout (except, accept) Paul.
10. Did the memorandum we received yesterday (affect, effect) your holiday plans?

Copy the following problems on a sheet of paper and perform the operations indicated.

1.	$13.45	2.	$2,194.50	3.	$3,945.00
	12.95		180.95		4.50
	4.65		1,463.75		123.91
	+ 98.40		+ 981.50		+ .87

4.	4,390.00	5.	298.75	6.	398.19
	− 981.51		− 24.88		−129.98

7. $489 × 15% =

8. $385 × 25% =

9. $195.50 × 12% =

10. $9,361.46 ÷ 46 =

11. $4,248 ÷ 18 =

12. $3,968.44 ÷ 14 =

13. ½ = ?%

14. ¾ = ?%

15. ⅓ = ?%

Complete the computations required for each of these problems on a separate sheet of paper.

1. A receptionist in a national rental car office at a busy airport fills in the forms when customers return their rented cars. Among the computations that the receptionist must perform is the determination of the mileage cost. Here are the figures on four of the forms from one morning's work. The cost is 15 cents a mile. What is the mileage charge for each?

345 miles
189 miles
489 miles
102 miles

2. An inventory clerk checked the lamps in stock. He found the following:

Stock No.	Units	Selling price
L 12	4	$32.95
L 36	11	24.95
L 32	8	29.98
L 56	14	21.50
L 71	3	59.95

What is the total selling price of this stock?

UNIT 3

PRODUCING MAILABLE LETTERS

DICTAPHONE TYPIST

roduction office of large dow
vn dress manufacturer ha
active position for exper
d dictaphone typist. Cor
ffers good salary with e
inge benefits. Pleasa
nditions in a mode
ley Brothers, 2

PART 1 LETTER FORMATS

Lucille Mason works for the McGuire Sewing Machine Company, which employs three salesmen. Each of the salesmen wants his letters typed in a different style. Mr. Pierce told Lucille, "I like my letters to be typed in block style. It's easy for you to type, and I think it looks great." Mr. Raven said, "Lucille, please type all my correspondence in modified block style. That's the style most people prefer." Mr. Gatis, the youngest salesman said, "Lucille, I'd like you to type my letters in the simplified style. I think it is more modern." Lucille carefully made a note of which style each salesman preferred.

COST OF A LETTER

The Dartnell Corporation recently reported that the average cost of a business letter is $3.31. This includes the cost of the time spent to dictate and type the letter, the cost of the paper, envelopes, and other supplies. It also includes office **overhead**, such as space, equipment, and lighting. Since letters do cost money, it will be to your advantage to know very thoroughly the different letter styles so that you can type them accurately and quickly.

overhead: expense

THE FIRST IMPRESSION

The recipient or addressee of a letter (the person who receives the letter) sees the total letter on the sheet of paper and forms an impression before he begins to read the message. A well-placed letter with clean, even type will make a very good first impression. Such a letter will encourage the recipient to read the letter with the care that your employer would like his letter to receive. A poorly typewritten, carelessly placed letter may fail to get the attention it deserves. It will be your responsibility to judge each letter you typewrite in a critical fashion and with this question in mind: How will this letter look to the receiver?

A letter gives a good first impression if

1. Margins, indentations, and spacing are pleasing to the eye.

2. Parts of the letter are correctly placed according to the style selected.
3. There are no obvious erasures and no strikeovers.
4. It is clean — has no smudges or fingermarks.
5. Type is even and clear.

LETTER STYLES

Letter style refers to the placement of the parts of the letter (see Part 2 of this unit, pages 69 and 75). The most popular letter styles are the modified block, block, and simplified. Many companies use the same style in all their offices, while other companies permit each office or each person to decide which letter style to use. Your employer will tell you which letter style you should use.

Modified Block Style

The modified block style is the letter style used most often in the office. Instead of being typed at the left margin (when compared with the block style), the following parts are typed starting at the **horizontal** center of the page: date, complimentary close, typed name, and official title. For parts of the letter see Illus. 3-6, page 69.

horizontal: parallel to a base line; across

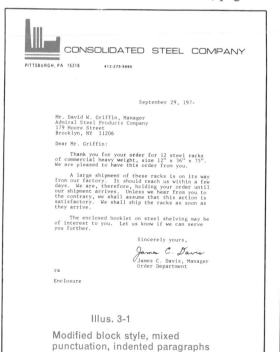

Illus. 3-1

Modified block style, mixed punctuation, indented paragraphs

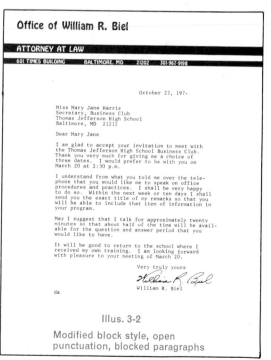

Illus. 3-2

Modified block style, open punctuation, blocked paragraphs

The first line of each paragraph in a modified block style may be indented (Illus. 3-1, page 59) or may be blocked (Illus. 3-2, page 59).

Block Style

In the block style, you begin typing all lines of the letter at the left margin. This style, of course, is one of the easiest to type because you don't use the tabulating key. It is a modern style (Illus. 3-3 below, left) and is gaining popularity in many offices.

Simplified Style

The simplified style was introduced by the Administrative Management Society and is sometimes called the AMS Style. It is the easiest letter style to type and the Administrative Management Society reports that the use of this style results in a cost savings of 10.7 percent.

omit:
to leave out

In the simplified style, type all lines at the left margin and **omit** the salutation and the complimentary close. Type a subject line in all capital letters a double space below the inside address. Begin the body of the letter a double space below the subject line. Type your employer's name and title in all capital letters on the fourth line below the last line of the letter (Illus. 3-4 below, right).

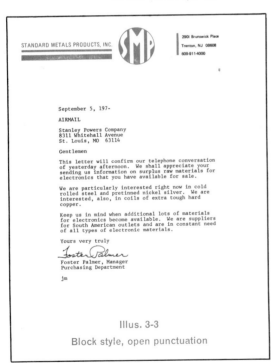

Illus. 3-3

Block style, open punctuation

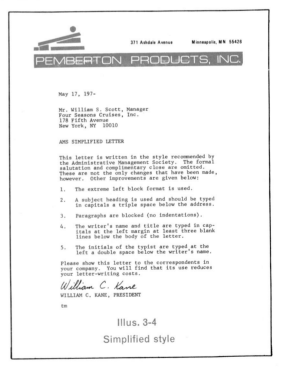

Illus. 3-4

Simplified style

LETTER PUNCTUATION

Letter punctuation refers to the use of punctuation marks after the salutation and complimentary close of a letter. The most **frequently** used styles of punctuation are open and mixed.

frequently:
often; repeatedly

Open Style

In the open style, you do not type any mark of punctuation after the salutation and complimentary close (see Illus. 3-2, page 59). This style is gaining in popularity because it takes less time to type.

Mixed Style

If your employer would like you to use the mixed style of punctuation, you would type a colon after the salutation and a comma after the complimentary close (see Illus. 3-1, page 59).

There are several ways of combining letter styles and of punctuating letters. For example, you could type a letter in modified block style with open punctuation, in modified block style with mixed punctuation, in block style with open punctuation, or in block style with mixed punctuation. The punctuation styles do not apply to simplified letters because you do not type a salutation or complimentary close.

SIMPLIFYING THE TYPEWRITING OF LETTERS

Many office managers attempt to reduce the cost of letters in one or more of these ways:

1. Using open punctuation. **Eliminating** marks of punctuation after the salutation and complimentary close is clearly a timesaving feature of open punctuation.

eliminating:
getting rid of;
setting aside

2. Omitting names that appear in the letterhead. For example, there is no need to typewrite the name of the company below the complimentary close if it appears in the letterhead. Also, the typewritten name and title of the dictator need not appear in the closing lines if they are in the letterhead.

3. Typewriting letters in block or simplified style. These letters can be typed faster than other letter styles because every line is started at the left margin and the tabulating key is not used. In addition, in the simplified letter the salutation and complimentary close are omitted.

4. Using a standard line length for all letters. When the length of letters varies, the typist can save time by

establishing a standard line length and varying the distance between the letterhead and the date and between the complimentary close and the reference initials. Some offices use a six-inch line for all letters, and a skillful typist can make each letter attractive with this standardization.

INTEROFFICE MEMORANDUMS

In the office in which you will be employed, you may type many short business notes or reports on forms called interoffice memorandums. These memorandums remain within the organization itself. They are brief and to the point because their only purpose is to communicate with other members of the organization quickly and clearly. The chief advantage of these forms is that they can be typed quickly. Titles (*Mr.*, *Mrs.*, *Dr.*, etc.), the salutation, the complimentary close, and the formal signature are usually omitted.

The forms, with the heading *Interoffice Memorandum*, may be printed on half sheets or whole sheets of paper, which generally is a less expensive paper than the company letterhead. The printed words *To*, *From*, *Date*, and *Subject*, with enough writing space after each of them, may be included in the heading of the form. Usually the company name also appears on the interoffice memorandum.

APEX CORPORATION   **INTEROFFICE MEMORANDUM**

To: Gary Keyton   **Date:**   October 21, 197–

From: Stan Pruitt   **Subject:** Interoffice Memos

Start the interoffice memo a double space below the typewritten heading material and block it at the left margin.

Since the writer's name is in the heading there is no need to type it at the end of the message. The typist's initials are placed a double space below the message. All end-of-letter notations such as the typist's initials and carbon copy information are typed as they are in letters.

cm

cc Jim Hereford

Illus. 3-5

You should double-space after the last line of the heading and the first line of the message. Short messages of not more than five lines may be typed double space; longer messages should be typed single space. Reference initials should be typed at the left margin a double space below the last line of the message. When enclosures are sent with a memorandum, the enclosure notation should be typed a double space below the reference initials.

An interoffice memorandum is often sent to a number of people within the organization. In such cases carbon copies may be used. The names of all who are to receive copies, however, should be listed on the original and on all carbon copies. Another practice is to type the original and one carbon file copy with the names of the recipients. The original, with any special enclosures, is sent to the first person on the list. When he is finished with it, he draws a line through his name and sends the memorandum along to the next person on the list. This is repeated until all the interested persons have seen it. This practice is most satisfactory when there is an enclosure or an attachment with the interoffice memorandum that is either too long or too difficult to reproduce.

REVIEWING WHAT YOU HAVE READ

1. What does letter style refer to?
2. Which are the most frequently used letter styles?
3. Which parts of a letter are changed in the modified block style when compared with the block style? Where do you type these parts in the modified block style?
4. Can you indent paragraphs in the modified block style?
5. Explain how you would type a block style letter.
6. How would you type a simplified style letter?
7. How would you type a letter with the open style punctuation?
8. How would you type a letter with the mixed style of punctuation?
9. What are four ways to simplify the typing of letters?
10. What is the major advantage of writing a short business note or report in the form of an interoffice memorandum?

MAKING DECISIONS

You work for Mr. Anderson and Mr. Todd. Mr. Anderson has requested that you type all his letters in block style with open punctuation. Mr. Todd has never mentioned a preference for one of the letter styles. You don't know for sure how to type Mr. Todd's letters. What should you do?

WORKING WITH OTHERS

Marsha Peterson works in the office of Hooser Machine Company. Anita, another office employee, has told Marsha that Mr. Hooser wants all his letters typed in the modified block style. Marsha had typed the block style letter in high school and felt it was much easier and faster to type. Should Marsha try to persuade Mr. Hooser to change to block style?

There are three degrees of adjective comparison: positive, comparative, and superlative. The comparison is used to indicate increasing and decreasing degrees.
(a) Most adjectives of one syllable are compared by adding er or est to the word.
(b) Most adjectives of more than one syllable are compared by using the words more, most, less, or least before the adjective.
(c) Other adjectives are compared irregularly.

Examples:

Positive	Comparative	Superlative
(a) light	lighter	lightest
(b) expensive	more expensive	most expensive
(c) good	better	best

On a separate sheet of paper type three columns with the headings, Positive, Comparative, and Superlative and write the forms of comparison for the following adjectives.

1. fine *finer- finest.*
2. fast
3. durable
4. little *littler less least*
5. old
6. far
7. beautiful
8. useful
9. blue
10. late
11. short
12. strong
13. hard
14. high
15. satisfactory

The Dartnell Corporation Institute of Business Research in a report dated 1973 states that the cost of an average letter is as follows:

Cost Factor	Average Costs
Dictator's Time	$ .72
Secretarial Time	.99
Nonproductive Labor	.26
Fixed Charges	.86
Materials Cost	.10
Mailing Cost	.21
Filing Cost	.17
	$3.31

1. What would the total cost of the letter be if costs could be decreased to the following: Dictator's Time, 64 cents; Secretarial Time, 90 cents; Nonproductive Labor, 20 cents; Fixed Charges, 86 cents; Materials Cost, 10 cents; Mailing Cost, 16 cents; Filing Cost, 15 cents?

2. If you can decrease costs as described in Item 1, in comparison with the $3.31 cost of the average letter determined by the Dartnell Corporation:
(a) How much money can your company save on each letter?
(b) What will be the percentage of savings?

1. Make a collection of five business letters. For each letter, describe briefly what might be done to make the letter more attractive.

2. Type the letter at the top of page 65 in modified block style with indented paragraphs. Use mixed punctuation. Type one carbon copy.

Mr. Earl Imhoff
Darby Employment Service
4020 Princeton Avenue
Tampa, FL 33606

Dear Mr. Imhoff

Thank you for taking the time to discuss employment opportunities at Darby Employment Service with me last Wednesday afternoon. I deeply appreciate your interest. The suggestions you made during the interview will help me qualify for the office position I really want.

I plan to take office education courses at Dutchess Community College next semester. They will be offered during evening hours in the Continuing Education Program. I have already found part-time employment as a clerk-typist in the Placement Office of the College. The day-to-day work in the Placement Office should give me valuable office experience.

After I have completed the courses in the program and have acquired the office experience you consider essential, I hope you will grant me another interview.

Sincerely yours

Dora Stewart

3. Compose a brief letter in which you describe the block form. Type the letter in block style with open punctuation. Address it to your teacher.

4. Type the following letter in simplified style. Type one carbon copy.

Mrs. Eleanor McBeth
4305 - 27th Street
Joliet, IL 60433

CREDIT CARD

Your excellent credit record enables you to receive our nationwide credit card for your personal use. Mrs. McBeth, the charge card that is enclosed will enable you to purchase almost any kind of merchandise you might want anywhere in the United States.

On the first of each month you will receive an itemized statement of all purchases for the preceding month. No interest charge is made if we receive your payment by the 10th of the month.

We know that you will enjoy using your new credit card and look forward to getting to know you better.

DOUGLAS KLINGMAN, CREDIT MANAGER

Enclosure

PART 2 PARTS OF A LETTER

Maxine Sutton worked as a typist for the Helton Finance Company. She often typed letters for the manager, Mr. Edward Haney. Mr. Haney said, "Maxine, this letter must go out today. Send it by airmail, and say we are sending the catalog under separate cover." Maxine remembered from her high school office procedures class that, when a letter indicates a separate cover notation, it should also indicate how the item was sent; so she asked, "How are we sending the catalog?" Mr. Haney replied, "We'll send it by parcel post." Maxine typed the letter and added the separate cover parcel post mailing notation.

STANDARD PARTS OF A LETTER

To understand the business letter, you should know the parts of a letter and why each part is needed. You will not use all parts of a letter on every letter you type. However, some parts, such as the date and signature, are always included in a letter. You will need to use your judgment and the preference of your employer to decide which parts should be included in each letter. The standard parts of a letter listed below are illustrated on page 69.

1. Letterhead
2. Date Line
3. Inside Address
4. Salutation
5. Body
6. Complimentary Close
7. Signature, Typed Name, and Title
8. Reference Initials
9. Enclosure Notation
10. Carbon Copy Notation

Letterhead

The letterhead (Item 1, page 69) on a firm's stationery is usually made up of the firm's name, address, and telephone number. The letterhead can be used to identify the nature of the firm's business by including a slogan, picture, or symbol of the firm.

Since the letterhead is the first part of a letter a recipient notices, it should be attractive, easy to read, and representative of the firm. You will want to take the letterhead into consideration when you type the letter so the letter looks attractive and balanced on the page.

Date Line

The date line (Item 2, page 69) on a letter is very important because it tells you and the recipient when the letter was typed. Also, if your employer has written to a person several times, he can use the date to refer to one of the earlier letters and the reader will know exactly which letter is meant.

The date line contains the name of the month written in full, the date of the month, and the year. A correct date line would be January 10, 197–. Abbreviated forms of the date, such as 1/10/7– or Jan. 10, 197– should not be used in a business letter.

Inside Address

The inside address (Item 3, page 69) is typed on the fourth line below the date at the left margin. You can use the inside address on a letter to guide you in filing the carbon copy in your office. For example, if you just typed a letter to Mr. Allen Gray, you would look at the inside address to determine where to file the carbon copy of the letter. Since the envelope is often thrown away when the letter is opened, the inside address also tells who should receive the letter when it arrives at its destination.

Name and Company Lines. The name of the person and the company should be typed to **conform** exactly with the style used by the person and the company receiving the letter. For example, if you were typing a letter to a man who writes his name *Edward R. Voiers*, you would not type his name *E. R. Voiers*.

conform: agree

Official Titles. When a person's official title is included in the address, it may be placed on either the first or second line. If the title is placed on the first line, it is separated from the person's name by a comma. Since either placement is correct, you should choose the one that will give better balance to the length of the lines in the address.

Street Address Line. When the name of the street is a number from one to ten inclusive, the street name is spelled out (367 Second Avenue or 381 Tenth Street); figures are used for street names that are numbers above ten. When a street is identified by figures, the house number is separated from the street number by a hyphen with a space on either side, 157 - 179th Street. If the street number is preceded by East, West,

North, or South, however, the hyphen is not necessary — for example, 589 South 117th Street.

City, State, and ZIP Code Line. The name of the city is separated from the name of the state by a comma.

The United States Postal Service has **designated** two-letter abbreviations for states to be used with the ZIP (Zone Improvement Plan) Code. A list of two-letter state abbreviations can be found on page 617 in Appendix D. These approved abbreviations are written in all capital letters and without periods. Use of the ZIP Code reduces mailing costs and speeds mail deliveries by allowing the use of automated equipment.

The ZIP Code number should be typed on the same line as the city and state with one or two spaces after the state and with no mark of punctuation between the state and ZIP Code number.
Forms for addresses are:

```
Mr. William F. Wells, Vice-President
The American Copying Company
3546 Broad Street
Philadelphia, PA  19140

Mr. James A. Satterfield
President, Consultants Limited
465 Avenue of the Americas
New York, NY  10011
```

You should avoid abbreviations except in those cases where an abbreviation will make a more balanced line. In general, abbreviations give a somewhat careless appearance to a letter and they can make a letter more difficult to read. When you type the inside address, try to make the lines as **uniform** in length as possible.

uniform:
the same

Salutation

The salutation (Item 4, page 69) is a greeting to the person to whom the letter is written. You type it a double space below the address. The salutation may be formal or informal depending upon the circumstances. For example, if your employer sends a letter to a senator, you use a more formal salutation than if he writes a letter to a good friend.

The salutations below are arranged from the most formal to the least formal. Notice the capitalization used in each.

For Men	*For Women*
Sir	Madam
Dear Sir	Dear Madam
Dear Mr. Simon	Dear Mrs. (Miss) Whitman
Dear John	Dear Jane

1 Printed Letterhead	1 ICBC INLAND

INLAND CORRUGATED BOX COMPANY   7660 CHESTER ROAD   COLUMBUS, OHIO 43206   614 872-4552

2 Date   2 May 19, 197-

                                                                    3 blank lines

3 Inside   3 Mr. James A. Gordon
Address   3421 North 58th Street
                Austin, TX 78212
                                                                    1 blank line

4 Salutation 4 Dear Mr. Gordon
                                                                    1 blank line

Thank you for your letter of May 14 in which you asked for the guidelines that we follow in preparing sales letters. In our firm we try to write attractive and convincing sales letters with a minimum amount of expense.

We use a letter that is generally accepted in business and yet requires the least time to type. Here are some suggestions to help you make your letters more effective.

5 Body   5   1. Use open punctuation.

   2. Use a modified block style. (You may prefer an extreme block style. This means that the date, complimentary close, signature, and title of the dictator start at the left margin.)

   3. When in doubt about the placement of the parts of a sales letter, use this letter as a model.

Carbon copies of sales letters prepared in both modified block and extreme block styles are enclosed for your inspection. After you have decided upon the letter style that you prefer, concentrate on the wording so that you may produce better sales letters.

                                                                    1 blank line

6 Complimentary
Close   6 Sincerely yours

7 { Signature
    Typed Name   7 { Kenneth H. Rhodes   3 blank lines
    Title   Kenneth H. Rhodes
                                         Sales Manager

8 Reference   8 ht   1 blank line
Initials

9 Enclosure   9 Enclosures   1 blank line
Notation

10 Carbon   10 cc Mr. Wayne B. Monroe   1 blank line
Copy
Notation

Illus. 3-6

Model letter, modified block style,
open punctuation, blocked paragraphs

For a Corporation	For a Firm of Women
Gentlemen	Ladies
For a Firm of Men	For a Firm of Men and Women
Gentlemen	Ladies and Gentlemen
	Dear Mrs. Smith and Mr. Jones

Body

You should always single-space the body (Item 5, page 69) of the letter except for very short messages. Double-space between paragraphs for a neat, attractive appearance. You may indent the paragraphs, or you may begin them even with the left margin depending upon the letter style.

Keep the right margin as even as possible and about as wide as the left margin. You can do this by setting the right margin stop from five to eight spaces beyond the point where you want the line to end, so that the bell will ring just before the space where the line ends. You will still have space to complete a short word or add a hyphen for a word that must be hyphenated before the carriage stops moving.

Complimentary Close

The complimentary close (Item 6, page 69) is the *good-bye* of the letter. You should type it a double space below the body of the letter. Only the first word of the complimentary close is capitalized. There are formal and informal complimentary closes, and you should use a complimentary close that fits the formality of the letter. If a letter contains the salutation *Gentlemen*, for example, you should use the *Yours very truly* or *Very truly yours* type of complimentary close. However, if the letter contains the salutation *Dear Mr.* or *Dear* (first name), a less formal complimentary close, such as *Sincerely* or *Sincerely yours*, is appropriate. The complimentary closes listed below are arranged from most formal to the least formal.

Yours respectfully	Very sincerely yours
Respectfully yours	Sincerely yours
Very truly yours	Yours sincerely
Yours very truly	Sincerely
Yours truly	Yours cordially
Yours very sincerely	Cordially yours

Signature, Typed Name, and Title

Your employer signs his name (Item 7, page 69) between the complimentary close and his typed name (Item 7, page 69). Type your employer's name on the fourth line below the complimentary close. His name is typed in the closing lines because sometimes it is hard to read a handwritten signature.

Sometimes the name of the company is typed as part of the signature. If this is the case, type the company's name in all capital letters on the second line below the complimentary close. You then type the name of your employer on the fourth line below the company name. Your employer's official title (Item 7, page 69) may be typed on the same line as his name or on the line below the typed name.

Sincerely yours

HAWTHORN HARDWARE COMPANY

Bryan M. Hawthorn

Bryan M. Hawthorn, President

If your employer is a man, do *not* use his personal title, such as *Mr.* or *Dr.*, before his name. If your employer is a woman, however, type *Miss* or *Mrs.* before her legal name (her legal name is her first name, middle initial, and married last name) so that if the person wants to reply to her letter, he will know the correct title for the inside address and salutation. The title *Miss* or *Mrs.* may be typed either with or without parentheses. Some examples of women's correct signature lines follow.

Signature of an Unmarried Woman	*Signature of a Married Woman or Widow*
Yours sincerely,	Very truly yours
Eva M. Kelly	*Alice B. Canter*
Miss Eva M. Kelly	Mrs. Alice B. Canter
or	or
(Miss) Eva M. Kelly	(Mrs.) Alice B. Canter

You must be sure that each letter is signed, either by your employer or yourself, before you fold it and insert it in an envelope for mailing. If you sign the letter with your employer's name, be sure to initial the signature as follows:

Sincerely yours,

Robert E. Maxwell

Robert E. Maxwell   *M. H.*

Reference Initials

To indicate who typed the letter, place your initials (Item 8, page 69) in lower case letters a double space below the official title even with the left margin. Sometimes you will see the initials of the dictator before the typist's initials; but this is unnecessary work, since everyone knows who dictated the letter from the typed name below the signature.

Enclosure Notation

An enclosure is anything placed in the envelope with the letter. You should indicate at the end of the letter that you are sending enclosures with the letter. This **notation** (Item 9, page 69) reminds you to include the items that should be sent with the letter. It also can be used by the person who receives the letter to check to see that all the enclosures are in the envelope.

Type the enclosure notation at the left margin two spaces below the reference initials. If you are enclosing only one item, you may merely type the word *Enclosure*. If you are including more than one item, you may type the word *Enclosures* and the number of items such as

```
rg

Enclosures 2
```

You may also list each enclosure. Be sure to type only one enclosure on each line and to indent the name of each enclosure five spaces from the left margin.

```
rg

Enclosures
      Price List
      Circular
      Sample X-14
```

Carbon Copy Notation

When your employer wants to send carbon copies of a letter to other people, you should indicate this on the letter by typing *cc* followed by the names of those who are to receive copies. The carbon copy notation (Item 10, page 69) is typed at the left margin two lines below the reference initials if there is no enclosure. If there is an enclosure notation, you type the carbon copy notation two lines below the enclosure notation.

```
Enclosures 2

cc Roy McWhorter
```

If carbon copies are sent to several people you list their names.

```
cc Vernon Lewis
   Fred Nix
   Gary Standefer
```

If your employer does not want the person to whom the letter is addressed to know that a carbon copy has been sent to someone else, you may type a *blind carbon copy* notation. You should type *bcc* or *bc* and the name of the person who is to receive the carbon copy on the carbon copy but *not* on the original letter. The notation on the *carbon copies* would appear as

```
bcc Miss Sharon Castillo
```

To type a blind carbon copy notation, you simply place a card or heavy piece of paper over the notation position on the original copy, type the notation, and remove the card. Another way to type a blind carbon copy notation is to release the paper release lever and remove only the original and first carbon sheet from your typewriter. Then turn the remaining sheets and carbon back to the normal position for a carbon copy notation and type the blind carbon copy notation even with the left margin. Using either of these methods, the blind carbon copy notation will be on the carbon copies but not on the original.

The carbon copies of a letter are sent to the individuals listed in the carbon copy notation; therefore, you must type an envelope for each recipient. You may have to get their addresses from a card file of frequently contacted individuals or from previous correspondence. Check each recipient's name with a check mark after you have typed the envelope for the individual recipient.

OTHER LETTER PARTS

There are several other letter parts which may be included in a letter. They are not used as often as the standard parts; but their use varies with the nature of the correspondence. For example, an insurance company may use a subject line on almost every letter, because it is an easy way of indicating a particular policy number or file number. The following **optional** letter parts are illustrated on page 75.

optional:
having a choice

1. Mailing Notation
2. Attention Line
3. Subject Line
4. Separate Cover Notation
5. Postscript

Mailing Notation

When your employer wants to use a special postal service to send a letter, such as registered mail, airmail, or special delivery, you should include a mailing notation (Item 1, page 75) on the letter. You type the mailing notation even with the left margin between the date line and the first line of the inside address with one blank line above and below the mailing notation. You should type the mailing notation in all capital letters.

Some companies type the mailing notation only on the carbon copy, but placing it on the original letter helps to remind you that it should go by airmail or special delivery, and it indicates to the recipient that the letter is important.

Attention Line

Sometimes your employer may want a letter to be addressed to a company but he wants a **specific** person in the company to read the letter. In this case you can type an attention line (Item 2, page 75) a double space below the inside address. Even though companies use attention lines, there is actually little need for them. If the letter is to be directed to an individual, his name should be placed on the first line of the inside address. You may also use an attention line when you are writing to a position within a company but do not know the name of the individual holding that position. In this case, the attention line would be *Attention Purchasing Agent.*

Illus. 3-7
Producing attractive mailable letters is very important in the modern business office.

INLAND CORRUGATED BOX COMPANY   7660 CHESTER ROAD   COLUMBUS, OHIO 43206   614 872-4552

April 14, 197-

1 MAILING NOTATION

1 AIRMAIL

Ferguson & Walters
634 Main Street
Harrisburg, PA   17101

2 ATTENTION LINE

2 Attention Mr. James C. Maxwell

Gentlemen

3 SUBJECT LINE

3 BOOKLET ON CORRUGATED FIBER BOXES

It required six months for us to gather and condense into
a 28-page booklet all the information the shipper needs for
the selection, packing, sealing, and shipping of corrugated
fiber shipping boxes.

Under separate cover we are sending you a copy of this useful booklet. Please accept it with our compliments.

We would also like to send you samples of a new composition
packaging material which we have developed. You will be
amazed when you test this lightweight, durable material.
If you would like to see samples of this new material, just
check and mail the enclosed card.

Yours very truly

William A. Johnson

William A. Johnson
Sales Manager

ve

Enclosure

4 SEPARATE COVER NOTATION

4 Separate Cover

5 POSTSCRIPT

5 We are working on a similar booklet about our wooden shipping
crates. This booklet should be available by the end of the
year.

Illus. 3-8
Letter illustrating optional parts

If you do use an attention line, you should make the salutation on the letter agree with the company name on the first line of the inside address rather than with the attention line.

```
Almond Construction Company
321 Forbes Boulevard
Pittsburgh, PA  15222

Attention Mr. Whitney T. Drews

Gentlemen:


Mr. Whitney T. Drews
Almond Construction Company
321 Forbes Boulevard
Pittsburgh, PA  15222

Dear Mr. Drews:
```

Notice that the salutation when the attention line is used is *Gentlemen*; it agrees with the first line of the inside address, *Almond Construction Company*. The salutation when the attention line is *not* used is *Dear Mr. Drews*; it also agrees with the first line of the inside address.

Subject Line

Your employer may want to use a subject line (Item 3, page 75) to emphasize the key topic of a letter. When you use a subject line, type it a double space below the salutation. You then double-space between the subject line and the first paragraph of the body of the letter. You may type the subject line even with the left margin or centered on the page. You may precede the topic by the word *Subject*, although this is not necessary.

Separate Cover Notation

When your employer sends an item to the person addressed in the letter but it is too large to go in the envelope with the letter, you should indicate this by a separate cover notation (Item 4, page 75). Type the separate cover notation at the left two lines below the last notation.

If you are sending only one item under separate cover, you may merely type the words *Separate Cover*. If you are sending two or more items, you may type the words *Separate Cover* followed by the number of items you are sending.

```
Separate Cover 2
```

Your employer may also want you to indicate the means of transportation used for sending the separate cover material.

    Separate Cover—Express

You may also list the items to be sent under separate cover.

    Separate Cover—Third-Class Mail
        Sample C-12
        Price List

Postscript

Sometimes your employer may want to add a postscript (Item 5, page 75) to a letter. A postscript is a short message that is typed on the second line below all other notations. The postscript is often used to emphasize a special point by setting it apart from the rest of the letter. You may use the abbreviation *PS* before the message, although it is not necessary.

Indent the first line of the postscript if you indented the paragraphs in the body of the letter; block the first line of the postscript if you blocked the paragraphs in the body of the paragraph.

**REVIEWING
WHAT YOU
HAVE READ**

1. Will you use all parts of a letter on every letter you type? How do you decide which parts should be included?
2. Why is the date line important?
3. How can you and the company who receives the letter use the inside address on a letter?
4. In what two ways can the official title of a person be typed in the inside address on a letter?
5. What is the rule of capitalization for the complimentary close?
6. Where do you type the reference initials? Should you include your employer's initials as well as your own?
7. How can you and the person who receives the letter use the enclosure notation?
8. When is a blind carbon copy notation used?
9. Where do you place the mailing notation on a letter?
10. When is a postscript used?

**MAKING
DECISIONS**

1. If your employer asks you to type an airmail letter to a customer and says, "It is very important that we get this information to him this week," do you think it would be a good idea to put a mailing notation on the letter? Why or why not?
2. Your employer is writing a letter to Mr. George Darrell, a business acquaintance and good friend in another city. What would be an appropriate salutation and complimentary close?

**WORKING
WITH
OTHERS**

Penny Mueller, an office worker at the Tipton Insurance Company, often signs letters for her employer, Mr. Sandman. She always signs Mr. Sandman's name and puts her initials below his name. Evelyn, another office worker, also frequently signs letters for her employer, Mr. Howerton, but she never puts her initials after the signature. Evelyn said to Penny, "Why should I put my initials on the letter? It just tells whoever receives the letter that I signed the letter. I want people to think that Mr. Howerton signs all his letters himself." Do you think that Evelyn's reason for not initialing the letters to which she signs her employer's name is correct? Can you give at least one good reason for adding your initials when you sign your employer's name? Do you think it is a good practice? Why or why not?

USING LANGUAGE

The following adverbs are often used incorrectly. After reading the definitions below, on a separate sheet of paper type each of the sentences and insert the adverb that will correctly complete each sentence.

too — an adverb, meaning also or more than enough.

to — a preposition, meaning toward or into a certain direction or condition

well — an adverb, except when you are speaking of health; when referring to health, well is an adjective.

good — an adjective in most cases; sometimes it is used as a noun.

very — an adverb expressing degree.

real — an adjective of quality.

1. She, (to, too) always included the ZIP Code on her letters.
2. Although he is a beginning typist, he types (well, good).
3. Although the inside address was (very, real) clearly written, Kimberly typed the wrong address.
4. She, (too, to), went to work for the Hardin Equipment Company.
5. Although Jack had a sprained ankle, he performed his job (very, real) well.
6. Are you feeling (well, good) today?
7. There was a (real, very) difference in the quality of the two letters.
8. She is a good worker; she read her letters (well, good).
9. She sent the (real, very) important letter by Special Delivery.
10. Do you think he did (well, good) on his typing exam?

USING ARITHMETIC

On a separate sheet of paper figure the Gross Pay of each employee by multiplying the Hourly Rate times the Hours Worked.

Employee	Hourly Rate	Hours Worked	Gross Pay
1	$1.60	40	64.00
2	2.45	40	108.00
3	2.30	35	80.50
4	1.60	32	51.20
5	1.85	40	74.00
6	1.98	40	79.20
7	2.15	38	81.70
8	1.90	35	66.50
9	1.64	36	59.04
10	1.78	40	71.20

PERFORMING OFFICE TASKS

1. In most offices, you will type the standard parts of a letter many times a day. So that you will become familiar with the standard parts of a letter, type the letter used in the illustration on page 69 exactly as illustrated; however, do not type the colored explanations in the margin. Notice where each part of the letter is placed on the page.

2. Type the appropriate salutations for each of the following letters addressed to
   (a) Mr. John McConnell, a good friend of your employer *Dear John*
   (b) Miss Laura Thames, a real estate broker from whom your employer is buying some property *Dear miss Th*
   (c) Melrose Cosmetics, a firm of women to whom you must write about an error in a monthly statement *Ladies & G*
   (d) Hillcrest Pipe Company, Inc., a corporation with which you frequently correspond *Gents*
   (e) Mrs. Thomas Taylor and Miss Jennifer Waiel, owners of a small business from which you purchase supplies *Dr mrs Taylor & miss waiel*

3. Sometimes you will be required to type a letter which has one or more of the optional parts of a letter. To familiarize yourself with the optional parts of a letter, type the letter (not the colored explanations in the margins) on page 75 exactly as it is illustrated. Note carefully how and where each of the optional parts of a letter is typed.

4. Your employer is writing to
   (a) Custom Brake Company, 1512 South Fourth Street, Wichita Falls, KS 67204. He wants the letter to go to Mr. Alvin Timms. Type an appropriate inside address, attention line, and salutation.
   (b) Mosler Industrial Fixtures Manufacturing Co., 4009 Frankford Avenue, Philadelphia, PA 19124. He wants this letter to go to Mr. Robert Sides. Type an appropriate inside address and salutation when you do *not* use an attention line.

5. You are typing a letter for your employer, Mr. Lee R. Cromer, President of Cromer Furniture Company, to a prospective customer and are enclosing ten colored pictures of some furniture. Type an appropriate complimentary close, typewritten company name, your employer's name and title, reference initials, and enclosure notation for the letter.

PART 3 TYPING THE LETTER

Annette Marshall had written personal letters for many years, but she didn't realize how important letters are in business until she began to work as a typist for Mr. Lovell at the Lovell Lumber Company. Mr. Lovell said, "Annette, the letters that we send from our office are very important to our success in business. The first thing our customers notice about a letter they receive is how it looks. That first impression is important because it may decide how they accept the message in the letter. Since most of our letters are sent to possible customers, we want all letters to be neat and attractive so that they will make a good first impression." Annette then knew Mr. Lovell expected a high quality of work on his letters. She now appreciates the time and effort she gives to producing well-placed, attractive letters with neat corrections.

ESTIMATING THE PLACEMENT OF A LETTER

Placing a letter attractively on a page is a skill that you will develop with experience. To place letters attractively on the page, you must be able to judge whether a letter is short, medium, or long.

Your letters will look well balanced on the page if the side margins are even and the bottom margin is slightly wider than the side margins. Until you have developed the skill to attractively place the letters on the page, you may use a Letter Placement Table (illustrated on page 81) to estimate the spacing for your letters. For example, if you are typing a short letter (that is, the letter contains 100 or fewer words), leave two-inch side margins and type the date on Line 20. If you are typing a letter with from 101 to 300 words in it, the side margins are 1½ inches but the line on which you type the date varies (see Column 4 on the Letter Placement Table). After you have typed several letters, you will be able to judge whether the letter is short, medium, or long and will no longer have to refer to the Letter Placement Table.

Your employer may prefer that you keep the typing line the same length for all letters you type regardless of their length. If this is the case, you can balance the letter on the page by varying the space between the

LETTER PLACEMENT TABLE

(1) Actual Words in Body of Letter*	(2) Letter Length	(3) Width of Side Margins	(4) Type Date on Line**
Up to 100	Short	2″	20
101–150	Medium { 1	1½″	18
151–200	2	1½″	16
201–250	3	1½″	14
251–300	4	1½″	12
301–350	Long	1″	12
More than 350	Two-Page	1″	12

*Actual Words in Body of Letter represents the complete words — not the average five-stroke words used to measure typing speed.
**Count lines from top edge of paper.

Illus. 3-9

letterhead and the date line. If the letter is long, you will leave less space between the letterhead and the date line; if the letter is short, you will leave more space between the letterhead and the date line.

TYPING THE SECOND PAGE

Some letters you will type may take more than one page. As you can see from the Letter Placement Table, you type the two-page letter with one-inch side margins. When you type the second page, you will keep the same one-inch margins.

When you are typing a two-page letter, you must type a heading on the second page. This heading will include

1. The name of the person to whom the letter is written, as it appears in the inside address
2. The page number
3. The date

Either the spread form or the block form is considered correct.

```
Mr. Norman Childs              2              April 20, 197-


     I plan to arrive in Chicago at 10:06 a.m. on TWA Flight 348.
     If possible, I would like to meet you to discuss the details
```

Illus. 3-10
Spread form of heading

```
Mr. Norman Childs
Page 2
April 20, 197-

        We are shipping to you under separate cover the three
No. 16550 chairs that you ordered on March 19, 197-.

        If you have any questions about the refund, please do
not hesitate to write us since our Credit Department is very
```

The block form is the easier to type since you do not have to center the page number or backspace for the date.

Leave at least an inch (6 line spaces) at the top of the page before you begin typing the heading and triple-space after the heading. You should try to finish a paragraph on the first page so that you can start a new paragraph on the second page. If you can't do this, you must leave at least two lines of the paragraph at the bottom of the first page and carry over at least two lines of the paragraph to the top of the second page.

Always use bond paper of the same quality as the letterhead for the second and **succeeding** pages of a letter. Do not use letterhead paper for any page but the first.

succeeding:
next in order

MAKING CARBON COPIES

When you are working in an office, you will almost always make a carbon copy of the correspondence you type; so you must learn how to make attractive, clean carbon copies.

Assembling Carbon Packs

assemble:
put together

A *carbon pack* is a collection of materials that includes a letterhead, carbon sheets, and copy paper. The quickest way to **assemble** a carbon pack is to arrange all the materials you will need in your desk drawer so that you can pick up the paper easily and quickly. If your desk drawer has sloping dividers for your stationery, arrange it in the order shown in the illustration. If you do not have a desk drawer with dividers, label file folders with the headings, *Letterhead, Carbon, Copy Paper*, and insert the correct paper in each folder. Arrange in the order shown in the illustration. Pull the paper in the folders forward so that you can easily pick up the paper from each folder.

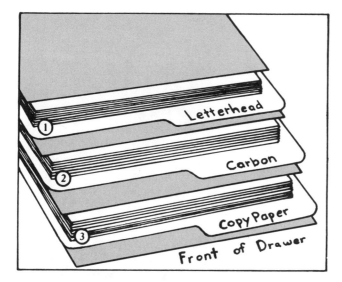

Illus. 3-12
Desk drawer
carbon pack
assembly

To assemble a carbon pack, take a sheet of letterhead paper and pull it toward the carbon paper in the next slot. Pick up a sheet of carbon paper and pull both sheets toward the copy paper slot and pick up a sheet of copy paper. Take out all three sheets and jog them on the desk to **align** them. If you need more than one carbon copy, go through the above procedure once and then continue picking up as many sheets of carbon and copy paper as you need but do not use more than one letterhead.

align:
make even

Some office workers like to assemble carbon packs in a different way:

1. Arrange the letterhead and second sheets and slip them behind the platen. Be sure they are firmly anchored.
2. Flip the pack forward over the front of the typewriter.
3. Turn the last sheet, which is the letterhead, back and insert a piece of carbon, shiny side facing you, repeating this until all carbons have been inserted.
4. Turn the platen knob, bringing the papers into typing position.

Inserting a Carbon Pack in the Typewriter

To insert the carbon pack in the typewriter, you should use the paper release lever, slip the pack into the machine with the shiny side of the carbon facing you, snap the paper release lever into position, and turn the platen rotating knob to bring the paper into writing position. If you must insert a thick carbon pack, place the flap of a long envelope or a folded sheet of paper over the top of the pack and remove the envelope or paper after the pack has been turned to the position for typing.

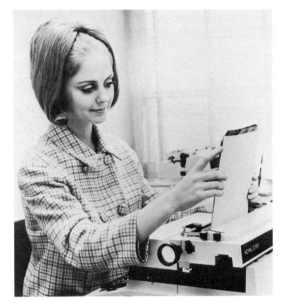

Illus. 3-13
Quickly assembling
and inserting a
carbon pack in your
typewriter will
improve your typing
production rate.

Administrative Management Society

Using Preassembled Carbon Packs

Some offices use preassembled carbon packs. These carbon packs have copy paper already assembled in the correct order with carbon sheets attached. They are easy to use and make good carbon copies. Fingerprints and smudges are eliminated because your fingers never touch the carbon.

Illus. 3-14
Preassembled carbon pack

The Carter's Ink Company

Handling Carbon Copies

The following steps will assure attractive, clean carbon copies:

1. Handle the carbon paper carefully so that the carbon is not transferred to your fingers where it can smudge the original and the carbon copies.
2. Never squeeze the assembled sheets together too hard. A thumb print or fingernail scratch on a sheet of carbon paper may spoil the appearance of the carbon copy.
3. If there are marks on the copy paper from the paper-bail rolls, use carbon paper with a hard finish or have the paper-bail rolls adjusted by a serviceman.
4. To make many carbon copies, use lightweight carbon paper and lightweight paper. When you are making only two or three carbon copies, you may use a medium-weight carbon paper.
5. Use a medium-finish carbon paper for regular work, and a soft-finish carbon paper when you are making eight or ten copies.
6. Never use a wrinkled sheet of carbon paper because it will cause a carbon smudge on the copy sheet.
7. Always keep carbon paper in a flat folder or box away from dust, moisture, and heat.
8. Always replace the carbon paper you are using before the copies become too light to read.

By using carbon paper which is one-half inch longer than your letterhead paper, you can easily remove carbon without smudging because you can take hold of the carbon that extends from the bottom of the pack.

MAKING CORRECTIONS

Making corrections that cannot be noticed is a skill which you will want to develop so that your typed letters will always be attractive and neat. Strikeovers give your work an untidy, careless appearance, and you should never give a letter with a strikeover in it to your employer for his signature. A good erasing procedure is to

1. Move the typewriter carriage to the right or left to prevent erasure **particles** from falling into the typewriter. You may also turn the cylinder knob either forward or backward to position the error in a convenient place to erase it.

   particles: pieces

2. Insert a plastic or metal erasure shield or a 5″ x 3″ card directly behind the original but *in front of* the first sheet of carbon paper.

3. Use an erasing shield with cutouts to protect the adjoining letters or lines while you are erasing.

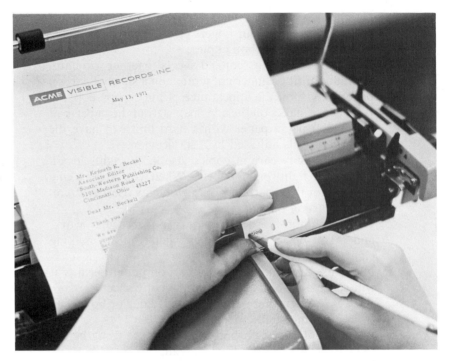

4. Erase the error using a circular movement for more than one letter and using an up and down motion for only one letter.
5. Remove the shield or 5″ x 3″ card and place it behind the first copy sheet but *in front of* the second sheet of carbon paper.
6. Continue erasing the carbon copies moving from the front to the back.
7. Check the alignment to be sure that you will be typing on the same line as before.
8. Strike the correct key or keys lightly, repeating the stroking until the desired shading is achieved.

By following this simple procedure, you will develop the ability to make corrections so that they are unnoticeable. You can use the shield or 5″ x 3″ card to separate the carbon paper from the copy paper so that you keep your hands clean.

There are times when the correction of an error requires that an extra letter or a word be inserted. A letter may be added if the letters are typed in such a way that each one occupies less space than it did before.

On some machines, this is done by striking the first letter, then holding the backspacer down slightly and striking the second letter, and continuing in this manner until the complete word has been typed. You may want to practice this skill, called *squeezing*, if you have not as yet perfected it.

At other times, the correction of an error requires that a letter be omitted. A letter may be omitted without spoiling the appearance of the page if the remaining letters are typed in such a way that each one occupies more space than it did before. This is done by striking the first letter, striking the space bar, then depressing the backspacer slightly and holding it in that position while striking the second letter, and continuing this operation until the complete word has been typed. This is called *spreading*.

If you are using an electric typewriter, you may have to use slightly different procedures for spreading and squeezing. On some electric typewriters, you will have to hold the carriage by hand while you type the letters in the correct places. On other electric machines, you will find a half-space key that will aid you in proper placement.

There are other ways to make corrections on typewritten work. You may use a white correction liquid to paint over the error. After it has dried you type in the correction. You may also use a correction tape which you insert directly over the error before retyping the incorrect letter. This covers the error with a white chalky film. You then backspace and type the correction. Correction fluids and tapes are considered superior to erasing since they avoid the rubbing away of the surface of the paper and the possibility of bits of the eraser falling into the typewriter.

TYPING AN ENVELOPE

After you have typed the letter, you should immediately type the envelope. Place the envelope face up with the flap over the top of the letter and enclosures, if any. This will prevent you from putting a letter in the wrong envelope.

You should address a large No. 10 envelope (9½" x 4⅛") if the letter is one or two pages and if you have enclosures. A small No. 6 envelope (6½" x 3⅝") is used with half-size letterheads, statements, and sometimes one-page letters.

Type the address on a small envelope 2 inches from the top and 2½ inches from the left edge of the envelope. When typing on a large envelope, leave a 2½-inch top margin and a 4-inch left margin.

The following items should be placed on the envelope as shown in Illus. 3-16, page 88.

1. Type *mailing notations*, such as REGISTERED MAIL, AIRMAIL, or SPECIAL DELIVERY, in capital letters under the stamp.

2. Type *special notations*, such as HOLD FOR ARRIVAL or PLEASE FORWARD, in all capital letters a triple space below the return address.
3. Type an *attention line*, immediately below the name of the company in the address.

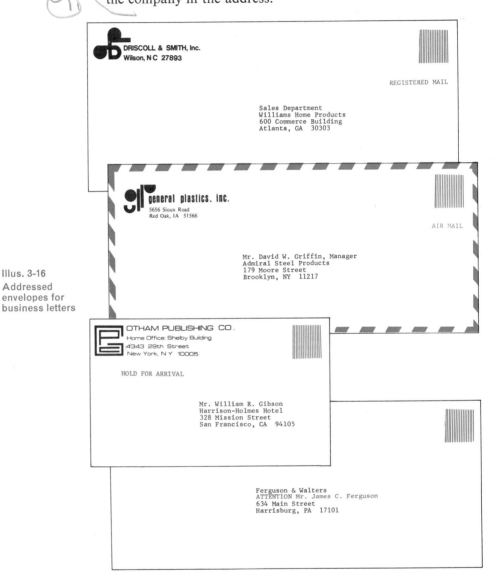

Illus. 3-16
Addressed envelopes for business letters

DRISCOLL & SMITH, Inc.
Wilson, N C 27893

REGISTERED MAIL

Sales Department
Williams Home Products
600 Commerce Building
Atlanta, GA 30303

general plastics. inc.
5656 Sioux Road
Red Oak, IA 51566

AIR MAIL

Mr. David W. Griffin, Manager
Admiral Steel Products
179 Moore Street
Brooklyn, NY 11217

OTHAM PUBLISHING CO.
Home Office: Shelby Building
4343 29th Street
New York, N Y 10005

HOLD FOR ARRIVAL

Mr. William R. Gibson
Harrison-Holmes Hotel
328 Mission Street
San Francisco, CA 94105

Ferguson & Walters
ATTENTION Mr. James C. Ferguson
634 Main Street
Harrisburg, PA 17101

USING WINDOW ENVELOPES

Window envelopes are used in business so that you don't have to address envelopes. The address on the letter, statement, or invoice shows through the window. Their use not only saves time but prevents letters being put into wrong envelopes.

The address must be written so that it can be seen through the window after the letter or bill is folded. Some businesses have a mark printed on their stationery to show the location for the address. The first few letters should be checked to see whether they are correctly folded to show through the window. The method of folding the letter or bill for the window envelope is different from the method of folding used for an ordinary envelope. Methods of folding letters are described in Unit 5, Part 2, under "Outgoing Mail."

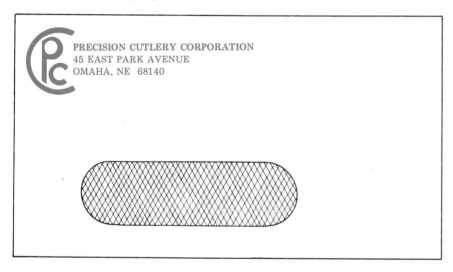

PRECISION CUTLERY CORPORATION
45 EAST PARK AVENUE
OMAHA, NE 68140

Illus. 3-17
Window envelope

USING BUSINESS REPLY ENVELOPES AND CARDS

Your company can get a business reply permit from the post office. This permits you to enclose a special business reply envelope or card that

FIRST CLASS
PERMIT NO. 436
DAYTON, OHIO

BUSINESS REPLY MAIL
NO POSTAGE STAMP NECESSARY IF MAILED IN THE UNITED STATES

POSTAGE WILL BE PAID BY

Newsweek
117 EAST THIRD STREET
DAYTON, OH 45402

Illus. 3-18
Business reply card

the addressee may return without paying postage. The post office collects postage from your company when it receives the returned envelopes and cards.

Such envelopes and cards are frequently used when a firm is sending out correspondence to which replies are invited such as sales literature inviting inquiries from prospective customers. The amount collected for a business reply envelope or card is two cents more than the ordinary postage. A business reply envelope that is enclosed in a No. 6¾ envelope should be of slightly smaller size, such as No. 6¼. Likewise, a No. 9 business reply envelope should be used for an enclosure in a No. 10 envelope.

REVIEWING WHAT YOU HAVE READ

1. Which two types of headings can you type on the second page of a two-page letter?
2. If you can't finish a paragraph on the first page of a letter, how many lines of the paragraph must you leave at the bottom of the first page, and how many lines must you carry to the top of the second page?
3. How many sheets of letterhead paper do you need if you are typing a letter with three carbon copies?
4. How do you insert a carbon pack in the typewriter?
5. If you have a thick carbon pack, what can you use to help you insert the pack in the typewriter?
6. Why do you move the typewriter carriage to the right or left when making an erasure?
7. What other ways are there to make corrections on typewritten work other than erasing?
8. After you have typed the envelope, how should you place it with the letter and enclosures to prevent you from inserting material in the wrong envelope?
9. Where do you type the attention line on an envelope?
10. What are two reasons for using window envelopes?

MAKING DECISIONS

Your employer has asked you to type a letter with six carbons. What type of carbon and copy paper would you use to get good carbon copies?

WORKING WITH OTHERS

Judy works as a typist in the office of the Knight Carpet Company. Jan, the other typist, has just recently graduated from high school and this is her first job. Judy works for Mr. Randolph and Jan works for Mr. Pryor. Mr. Pryor has recently asked that Jan type several letters over because the erasures were so poor. Jan was quite upset by this because she wanted to do a good job. She hesitated to ask Mr. Pryor about the erasures because she knew he was very busy. Judy has seen the letters that Jan was asked to type over and thought she could show Jan how to make acceptable, unnoticeable erasures. How can she tactfully help Jan without hurting her feelings?

On a separate sheet of paper complete the following sentences by choosing the correctly spelled word.

1. The (activities, activeties) of the club are very worthwhile.
2. Although Marvin needed a helper, he could not find an (assistance, assistant).
3. We have not found very many persons who have (sufficient, suficient) background for the job.
4. Although we won the game, we must (continue, cuntinue) to improve.
5. Each person's (training, traning) is very important to his success.
6. They installed shatter-proof glass in the windows to insure the (safty, safety) of the workers.
7. Mr. Henderson was (sincerely, sincerily) sorry to see George leave his job.
8. It is sometimes hard to (maintain, maintian) a *B* average.
9. (Generaly, Generally) we go to a movie on Saturday night.
10. The (immediate, immedeate) future is unknown.

Your employer has asked you to estimate how much stationery you use during a month. You know that you type about ten letters a day and that you make at least one carbon copy for each letter. Half of the letters require one extra carbon copy. Of course, you type an envelope for each letter. You estimate that you have to retype one letter and one envelope a day. You use about five sheets of carbon paper a week. Figure the total number of sheets of letterhead paper, copy paper, carbon paper, and envelopes you use in a month (4 weeks) working five days a week.

1. For the following different length letters, give the width of the side margins and the line on which you would type the date.
   (a) A letter with 110 words in the body of the letter
   (b) A letter with 224 words in the body of the letter
   (c) A two-page letter with 333 words in the body of the letter
   (d) A letter with 93 words in the body of the letter

2. Type the following letter in block style with open punctuation. Make one carbon copy. Carefully correct all errors using one of the methods described in the text. Type an appropriate sized envelope.
Mr. Ronald Ramsey, Principal
Jackson Elementary School
124 Temple Street
Tucson, Arizona 85713
Dear Mr. Ramsey:
As you know, KBTL Radio each year invites boys between the ages of 10 and 13 to a special camp for two weeks. Each elementary school in Tucson is allowed to send in the names of two applicants. We would appreciate your sending us the names of two boys who would benefit the most from this experience.
As always, KBTL Radio will pay all expenses for the boys; but they can take spending money if they wish. The camp will provide qualified supervisors to lead the boys in horseback riding, boating, swimming, tennis, and assorted crafts. Transportation will be provided to and from the camp.
May we receive the names of the two deserving boys from your school by June 4? We know they will have an exciting two weeks at the camp.
Sincerely yours
Jerry Winborn, Manager

3. Your employer, Mr. Hodges, is writing a letter to Mr. Stephen Schultz, 1113 East Newscombe Street, Adams City, Colorado 81424. Type both the block and spread forms of a second-page heading.

4. Type an envelope for the following letters. Be sure to type all special notations in the proper place on the envelopes.

   (a) An airmail letter addressed to Mr. James Daniel, 2403 Acuff Road, Boston, MA 02138

   (b) A letter to Mr. Garland Newsom, 1219 Avenue D, Wichita, KS 67217. Since Mr. Newsom has recently moved and you do not know his new address, type an appropriate forwarding notation on the envelope.

   (c) A one-page letter with two enclosures to Mr. William Kleine, 235 Indiana Street, San Jose, CA 95116

   (d) A two-page special delivery letter to Wolfe Body Shop, 2611 Avenue G, Houston, TX 77050. It is sent to the attention of Mr. Jack Rister, Credit Manager.

PART 4 USING DICTATING AND TRANSCRIBING MACHINES

Although Jessie Parks has been employed in the office of the McKee Corporation for almost a year, she had not used a transcribing machine in her work until just recently. Last week her employer, Mr. Roger Sanders, said, "Jessie, last night I recorded several letters on the transcribing machine because I will be out of the office most of the day. Could you transcribe them for me while I am away from my desk this morning? I'll be back this afternoon to sign them." Jessie realized that one of the advantages of a transcribing machine is that her employer can dictate letters whenever he has free time during and after office hours. She knew that this must be a great convenience to all business executives.

ADVANTAGES OF MACHINE DICTATION

Dictating and transcribing machines are used in most businesses today. More and more companies know the many advantages of using this equipment.

Dictating machines permit your employer to dictate whenever he wishes. Instead of waiting to dictate to a person who can take shorthand, your employer merely picks up the microphone and dictates. Instructions to the transcriber as well as correspondence can be dictated at the same time.

Using dictating and transcribing machines is less time-consuming than other methods of recording information. When dictation is given to a stenographer, the time of both the dictator and the stenographer is used to just record the information. An employer could write the message in longhand and then have it typed. A competent dictator, however, can dictate a message much faster than he can write it in longhand.

Your employer can take a portable machine with him on trips and send the recordings back to the office to be transcribed. When he returns to the office, the letters are ready for his signature.

KINDS OF DICTATION AND
TRANSCRIPTION MACHINES

Whether a portable unit, a standard unit, or a remote control network system is used in a particular business will depend upon the operations of the company.

Portable Units

These small transistorized units allow an executive to dictate while away from the office such as at home, in a car, or on a trip. In fact, several airlines provide portable machines for businessmen who want to dictate while on a flight. There is also a service that provides a dictating machine at the departure point of flight or at a hotel. The recording which the executive has dictated can be mailed back to his own office for transcription.

Illus. 3-19
Portable dictating equipment can be used anytime anywhere.

Philips Business Systems, Inc.

Standard Units

Separate machines for dictation and transcription are available. The executive has one machine on his desk for dictating, and the transcriber has a different machine on her desk for transcribing. Combination units are also available and are popular in offices where there is a limited amount of dictation. With a combination unit you can dictate and transcribe on the same machine. Because only one person can use such a unit at a time, the work must be carefully planned so that a transcriber is not using the machine to transcribe when the executive needs it to dictate.

Remote Control Systems

A remote control system means that the belt, disc, or tape (called a recording) on which the message is recorded is not located near the dictator. The dictator speaks into a special telephone handset, and the message is ready to be transcribed at the transcriber's desk. A light appears on the transcribing unit. The transcriber can begin transcribing even before the dictator completes dictating.

There are several types of systems. An executive can dial a special number on his desk telephone and is connected to a dictating machine that is ready to record what he says. An executive at a branch office can record

Illus. 3-20
An executive can use a regular outside telephone to call into the office where dictating machines are ready to record.

Dictaphone Corporation

on a dictating machine at the home office in another town. In another system an executive can use a regular outside telephone to call into the office where the dictating machines are available.

A network of dictating and transcribing equipment permits many executives throughout a company to use the same dictating machine. An executive dictates into a microphone or into his telephone which is connected to a centralized dictating machine in a *transcribing pool*. This is a group of typists who transcribe material from transcribing machines. A supervisor generally **coordinates** the work of the typists and helps them with any special problems they may have.

In a company where a network system has been installed, executives tend to use the service as a **supplement** to that provided by their secretaries. When their secretaries have unusually heavy workloads, the executives use the central service so that their secretaries need not transcribe the dictation. Typists in the central transcription pool prepare the transcription which is returned to the executives' offices for signature.

DICTATING

Most dictating machines are operated by controls on a hand microphone. Keys or buttons are used to (1) start and stop dictation; (2) backspace for repeating a few words of the dictation, (3) indicate corrections, and (4) show the length of each dictated letter. If corrections or special instructions must be made, they can be dictated along with the message. After the dictation is completed, the recording is removed from the machine and transcribed.

WORD PROCESSING

Because the amount of paper work in business continues to increase and the cost of this work continues to rise, more and more businessmen are seeking ways to improve the processing of paper work. They want

Illus. 3-21
This transcribing machine operator inserts a belt on a transcribing unit. Notice the indicator slip which shows corrections, length of letters, and other instructions.

Dictaphone Corporation

to increase efficiency by decreasing the amount of time, effort, and material it takes to process words. This will decrease expenses and increase profits, and a company cannot continue unless it makes a profit.

One of the expensive office activities is recording the executive's thoughts in typewritten form on a piece of paper such as a report or a letter. For example, The Dartnell Corporation reports the cost of an average business letter increased from $1.83 in 1960 to $3.31 in 1972. To **convert** those words that are in the mind of a dictator into typewritten words on paper is called *word processing*.

convert:
to change

The procedure for one type of word processing system is described below.

Dictation and Transcription

1. The executive dictates his thoughts into any kind of dictating machine.
2. The typist at a word processing station transcribes on a sheet of paper in the typewriter called a *hard copy*. At the same time the information is recorded on a magnetic card, sometimes called a *Mag Card* or on a reel of magnetic tape. The term *MT/ST* is often used when the recording is on magnetic tape and it means *Magnetic Tape/Selectric Typewriter*. The Mag Card or the tape is called the *magnetic copy*.

Illus. 3-22
Transcriber inserts magnetic card into console of Magnetic Card Selectric Typewriter

IBM Corporation

3. The hard copy is really a rough draft copy, and it tells the typist what is stored on the magnetic copy in the console unit. Since the hard copy is to be a rough draft, the typist can transcribe at a rate much faster than if she were transcribing final copy. If an error is made, the typist merely strikes over the mistake and the magnetic copy is automatically corrected.

Proofreading and Corrections

1. The dictator reads the rough draft hard copy and makes necessary corrections.
2. The typist places the rough draft in the typewriter and types corrections on the rough draft copy. The corrections are automatically made on the magnetic copy.

Playback

1. The rough draft copy is replaced in the typewriter with letterhead paper.
2. Several control knobs and keys are set on the console and a start button is pushed.
3. The typewriter, controlled by the magnetic tape or card, types out the final copy at about 175 words a minute without a single error.
4. Information on the magnetic copy can be stored indefinitely, and the same letter can be typed over and over if it is a form letter.

FORM LETTERS

In many offices some kinds of letters are written over and over again and it is, therefore, economical to compose letters that can be used in response to similar requests. Companies often build their own files of form letters and organize a coding system so that they can quickly locate an appropriate letter. Often form letters are written with different paragraphs so that the typist has a choice and can thus select the paragraph that is most appropriate for a particular recipient.

Letters acknowledging orders, sending out requested information, requesting references for prospective employees, and thanking companies or individuals for references are just a few of the instances where form letters are useful. Illustrations of form letter paragraph inserts follow.

Prospective Customer

1.   It was a pleasure to talk with you when you visited our booth at the recent _____ Convention. The material you requested is enclosed.

2. _____ who represents our company in your city will call you soon and arrange an appointment at your convenience, as you requested.

3. For further information about our products, please write to us; or you may call

_____, our representative in

your city. His telephone number is

_____.

Requesting Reference

_____ has applied for a position with our company and has given your name as a reference. We would appreciate your completing the attached form and returning it in the enclosed self-addressed stamped envelope. There is space for any additional comments you may wish to make.

Thank you for your courtesy in responding to this request.

TRANSCRIBING

Transcribing machines are equipped with ear pieces or headsets that either fit into the ears or rest gently against the ears. You insert the

Illus. 3-23
Transcribing equipment is timesaving. The operator can adjust speed control, volume control, and tone control to suit her needs.

IBM Corporation

dictated recording in the transcribing machine, then place the indicator slip (a strip of scaled paper which shows corrections, length of letters, and other instructions) in the slot provided for it. Adjust speed control, volume control, and tone control to suit your particular needs.

When you first learn to transcribe, listen for a few words, a phrase, or a sentence, stop the machine, typewrite the words, start the machine again, listen for a few more words, and repeat this until the dictation has been transcribed. As your ability increases, you should be able to stop and start the transcribing machine without pausing in your typing. You will also not have to backspace so often to relisten to the dictation.

Special instructions to the transcriber may be dictated along with the regular dictation. A system of marks is used on the indicator slip to show the beginning and ending of each letter and where special instructions are given on the recording. These marks aid you in judging the length of the letter and in planning its placement on the letterhead. You should listen to the corrections and special instructions before beginning to type from the recording.

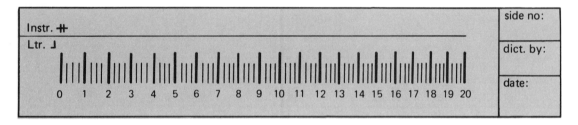

Illus. 3-24 Indicator slip

If you work for a large company you will probably have an office manual which will tell you the style of letter to use and the procedure for returning finished transcription to the person who dictated it. Transcribed materials are usually returned to the dictator in a folder with the most urgent messages on top ready for signing. An unused belt, disc, or tape, along with a new indicator slip, are placed in the folder with the completed dictation. Place the envelope for each letter face up with the flap over the top of the letter and any accompanying enclosures. If the folder is sent to the dictator by messenger or through the company mail system, it may be placed in a large envelope which is addressed to the recipient.

TRANSCRIBING SUGGESTIONS

Your transcription rate can be increased and the number of time-consuming errors can be reduced if you follow suggestions of experienced transcribers as listed on the next page.

1. Listen to the corrections and special instructions before transcribing any of the dictated material.
2. Use the indicator slip as a guide for the proper placement of material to be transcribed.
3. Be sure that you understand the meaning of the dictation before typing so that you will avoid

   (a) errors in grammar
   (b) errors in punctuation
   (c) errors in spelling
   (d) confusion of **homonyms**, such as *their* for *there*
4. Develop the ability to remember dictation in order to avoid the overuse of the repeat key.
5. Develop the skill of an expert — keep the typewriter moving as much as possible but stop the transcribing unit when necessary. Listen to one phrase ahead of your typewriting.
6. Use the parts of the typewriter to advantage, especially the tabulator and the variable line spacer.

homonyms: words pronounced alike but different in meaning

IMPROVING TRANSCRIPTION

Transcribing ability is improved through correct practice and knowing about transcribing problems you will encounter. Some of the common transcribing problems and solutions are discussed below.

Incorrect Information

Incorrect information such as a wrong price, date, or name may have been dictated. If the dictator did not know about the mistake, correct it if you are absolutely sure that there is an error. Always attach a note to the letter indicating what was changed and why.

If the dictator knows about the mistake, he will correct the error at the time by recording over it (this is possible only on magnetic tape dictating machines) so that you hear only the corrected version. On other machines he may mark the indicator slip where the error occurs and dictate the correction wherever space is available on the recording. Before you start transcribing listen to the recording at the point where the error was made and then to the correction and type only the corrected information.

Incomplete Information

Occasionally the dictator may not have information, such as a current address, readily available to him, and he may request that you find the information and insert it in the correct place in the transcription. In such a case, you may have to look in the files or in accompanying correspondence to find the information.

Grammatical Errors

If you are certain there is a grammatical error in the dictation, it is proper for you to correct it. But if you are not certain, or if your correction would change the message in any way, you should check with the dictator before making the revision. Most grammatical errors are easily corrected by changing, adding, or deleting a word or two.

Punctuation Errors

Dictators may make errors in punctuation, if they dictate punctuation. If you are not sure whether there is a punctuation error, check a reference manual. Most dictators do not give punctuation; therefore, it is the responsibility of the transcriber to supply correct punctuation marks.

Homonyms

Give special attention to homonyms such as *mail, male; knot, not;* and *peace, piece.* Normally you will know the correct word by the way it is used in the sentence. If this isn't possible, consult a dictionary, your supervisor, or the dictator.

You may not know either the spelling or the meaning of some unfamiliar words. Sometimes the words will be spelled for you on the recording. If they are not, first you should check the accompanying correspondence, the files, or a dictionary. If you can't find the words ask your supervisor or the dictator.

OTHER USES OF DICTATING EQUIPMENT

Dictation equipment can be used in many different ways to increase the efficiency of an executive by conserving his time and energy. For example, many companies have form letters which have been prepared to answer routine correspondence. The busy executive does not want to take time to dictate a complete letter when a form letter is available. He need only supply extra information required to complete the form letter. Therefore, he dictates the needed information and requests that the transcribing machine operator type the letter and include the extra facts in their correct places.

Many executives also use a portable dictating unit to record messages or reminders to themselves or to their staffs. The messages are later transcribed and distributed as directed.

Some executives want a transcript of speeches they make, and this can be done with dictating equipment. Meetings can be recorded, and minutes can be typed from the recording. A businessman can greatly increase his efficiency by using dictating equipment.

1. What are the major types of dictating and transcribing machines?
2. What is a transcribing pool?
3. What does the term *word processing* mean?
4. What is an indicator slip?
5. If a dictator made an error and he used an indicator slip to show where the error was located, what procedure would you follow to make sure that you typed the material correctly?
6. How is the transcribed material usually returned to the dictator?
7. Is it a good practice for you to correct errors in grammar or punctuation made by the dictator?
8. What should you do if you come across a word that is very unusual, and you don't know how to spell it or what it means?
9. How can dictating machines be used to prepare form letters for mailing?
10. What are some of the other uses of dictating equipment in business today?

MAKING DECISIONS

1. Why do you think it is a good idea to listen to corrections and special instructions before you begin to type from the tape?
2. What do you think is the main advantage of a portable dictating machine?
3. Whenever Mr. Harris dictates material on a dictating machine, he often fails to prepare an indicator slip. How would you ask him to remember to prepare one for you?

WORKING WITH OTHERS

Dianna Porter is a transcribing machine operator for Mr. James Murray. He dictates almost all his correspondence on a dictating machine, and Dianna transcribes it. Dianna has trouble understanding many of his sentences, because he dictates slowly in a very low voice and he mumbles. This has presented quite a problem for Dianna, because it takes her so long to transcribe the material. She has to listen to almost every sentence at least twice. Even then she is not always sure that she has transcribed the material correctly.

Should Dianna tell Mr. Murray about this problem? How can Dianna encourage Mr. Murray to speak plainly when dictating?

USING LANGUAGE

Words that are pronounced alike but are different in meaning are known as homonyms. They can be very confusing, especially when you are transcribing material from a dictating machine. On a separate sheet of paper type the word that correctly completes the following sentences:

1. As Janie became more experienced in her new job, she was (allowed, aloud) to take over many more responsibilities.
2. Terrie was enrolling in an office procedures (coarse, course) where she would learn how to operate a transcribing machine.
3. Jonathan did not like the (bare, bear) wall in the office; so he painted a landscape picture to put there.
4. Although she had (herd, heard) his voice many times, she did not recognize it on the dictation tape.
5. After Larry had worked in an office, he found it was better not to (meddle, medal) in other people's business.
6. Yolanda searched (threw, through) four files before she found the misplaced letter.

7. (There, Their) jobs were carefully analyzed to determine which tasks they performed.
8. There were (two, to, too) dictating units in the office — a standard unit and a combination unit.
9. In a letter she transcribed, Margaret misspelled Seattle, the (capital, capitol) of Washington.
10. You should use the indicator slip (to, too, two) guide you in properly placing a letter on the page.

USING ARITHMETIC

Your employer, an insurance adjuster, has a standard dictating and transcribing unit which he wants to trade in for a new model. He also wants to purchase a portable unit to take with him to record notes about the extent of damages when he is adjusting a claim. A local business machine dealer told your employer he would allow him $75.00 on the price of a new machine if he traded in his old machine. The new standard unit for the office costs $326.34 and the portable unit costs $185.56.

What is the total cost to your employer to trade in his old machine for a new standard unit and to purchase a portable unit?

PERFORMING OFFICE TASKS

1. Write letters to several dictating machine dealers and ask for information on their latest standard and portable dictating units. Prepare a bulletin board display with the information you receive.
2. If dictating and transcribing machines are available, dictate the following letter on a machine and then transcribe it. This letter contains several errors which you should correct as you dictate and transcribe.

If dictating and transcribing machines are not available, type the letter in rough draft form, make the corrections needed, and type the letter in block style with open punctuation.

Mr. Edward H. Richardson, Richardson Engineering Company, 1420 Hickory Drive, Richmond, Vir. 23222 Dear Mr. Richardson (¶1) We have just introduced our latest portable dictating machine, the EXECUTIVE. You will be satisfied with no other machine once you have tried the EXECUTIVE. (¶2) The portable dictating machine for the busy business man is not a new idea. Our EXECUTIVE with it's small overall dimensions and lightweight battery are new concepts. Our new battery will outlast any other battery on the market today. (¶3) We would like you to use the EXECUTIVE for two weeks on a trail basis. Take it with you where ever you go. We will even furnish you with two free cassettes for recording your important dictation. If at the end of the trial period you do not believe that the EXECUTIVE is the best portable recording machine made, simply return it to us. (¶4) If you would like to experiment with the EXECUTIVE, please call our office at 947-8340. We shall deliver your EXECUTIVE and cassettes immediately. Sincerly yours Michael J. Desmond Sales Manager

UNIT 4

PROCESSING DATA

DATA INPUT CLERK — To han
dle cash receipts and prepar
DP input documents for ac
unts receivable function. Ex
ience not required but mus
ble to handle considerabl
e of detailed informatio
ely and rapidly. Legibl
g is necessary; mini
required. Call 381

PART 1

THE OFFICE WORKER PROCESSES DATA

In his Clerical Office Procedures class, Paul Rizzuto visited Data Services, Incorporated, a data processing firm that provides such services as inventory control, sales analysis, and customer billing for business firms. Paul said to the manager, Frank Travis, "We have been studying about data processing in class. It seems that the term is used in many different ways. Can you give us a good definition?" Mr. Travis replied, "Many people do have mistaken ideas about data processing. Actually everyone processes data in some way every day. Of course, here at Data Services we are concerned mainly with electronic data processing since we do use a computer; but you also process data when you work with a pencil and paper. Most people, though, when they hear the term data processing, think of computers with lights flashing and buzzers sounding." As Paul continued the tour of the computer installation with his class, his understanding of the importance of data processing increased; and he knew that he wanted to learn more about the use of data processing in business today.

WHAT IS BUSINESS DATA PROCESSING?

Data simply means the words (such as *invoice*, *balances*), numbers (such as *382*, *4½*), and symbols (such as *#*, *%*) that businesses use in order to make decisions. *Processing* means arranging the data in a series of steps in an organized manner. When the words, numbers, and symbols are organized so that they have meaning, the result is called *information*. *Data processing*, therefore, is arranging words, numbers, and symbols to provide information. *Business data processing* means arranging words, numbers, and symbols about business **transactions** to provide useful information.

transactions: business dealings such as selling or purchasing goods

Whether you realize it or not, you are constantly processing data mentally. Suppose a friend asks you to go to a movie. In deciding if you should or should not go, you are processing data. Some of your data would be the cost of the movie and how much money you have, the length of the movie and how much time you have available, the distance from your home to the theater, the different means of transportation, and whether you believe you would enjoy the movie. In order to give your friend your answer, you must first process all your data. Although business decisions usually involve more important matters, the procedures used are similar.

Data by itself is often meaningless. For example, if twenty sales invoices arrived in your office, it would be impossible to know the total dollar amount of sales by simply looking at the twenty separate invoices. The data must be added together to arrive at a total. This adding of numbers is processing data. The report which results from the processing can be useful to your employer in making many very important decisions about the business.

Data about business transactions is collected, processed, and reported to provide people in the company with information. The data needed by a business will depend upon many factors, such as the size and type of business. The information needed by the owner of a small service station would not be the same as that needed by the executive of a large steel corporation. The more complex the operations of a firm the more different types of information it needs. The method for processing data will depend on such factors as the amount and kind of data and the time and money available for processing the data.

Some people think that data processing is a recent development. The term *data processing* is new, but the activity is not new. The processing of numbers, words, and symbols has progressed from manual methods through several stages to **sophisticated** electronic computers.

sophisticated: complicated or complex

THE NEED FOR PROCESSED DATA

Data is needed for two major reasons — internal use (within the company) and external use (outside the company).

Internal information is used to perform the daily activities of the business and to plan the future of the business.

External information is used to provide data to **stockholders,** government agencies, unions, customers, suppliers, and creditors.

stockholders: owners of the business

Some information serves several purposes. Payroll records, for example, give internal information for payment of salaries and also external information for financial reports to the government and to unions.

METHODS OF PROCESSING DATA

Data may be processed by manual, mechanical, unit record, or electronic means. There are similarities among these methods as well as differences.

Processing Data Manually

The human mind was the earliest means of processing data. When a person hears or sees data, this becomes information to be stored in the brain. The brain is the processor which performs the operations upon the data. The information that results can be in the form of the written or spoken word, or both.

Let's say you are asked to process an order. With the manual method of processing data, you write a sales slip giving data, such as date, customer's name, customer's address, terms, quantity, and other vital information. The other records such as the invoice, journal entry, ledger entry, and customer's statement are copied in handwriting.

It is easy to make errors in routine work, such as copying data from one form to another. The speed and accuracy of manual data processing are **comparatively** low; and, for large volumes of work, the cost to process each document is comparatively high.

comparatively:
estimated or judged
by comparison

New York Telephone
Company

Illus. 4-1 Manual means of processing data

Processing Data Mechanically

When the intelligence of the office worker is combined with the speed and accuracy of machines, an efficient system can be designed. Equipment such as typewriters, calculating machines, and bookkeeping machines (see Part 3 of this unit) are combined to perform several operations.

If you process a sale using the mechanical means of processing data, you will probably handwrite the sales slip but you will perform the calculations by using an electronic calculator. By using a bookkeeping machine, the journal and ledger entries can be posted and the customer's statement prepared. Thus, you combine your intelligence with the speed and accuracy of machines to form a mechanical data processing system.

Processing Data by Unit Record (Punched Card) System

The unit record method of processing data is also called the *punched card* system because information is recorded on a card in which holes have been punched. It is called a unit record system because only one type of information is recorded on a single card.

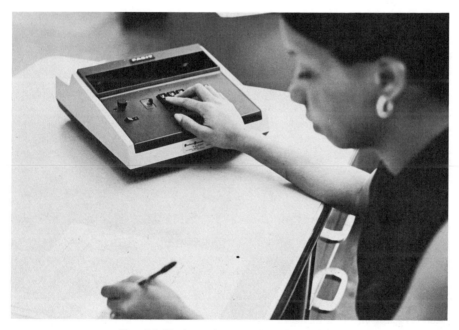

Illus. 4-2 Mechanical means of processing data

Printed numbers and letters at the top of the card show what each hole or holes below it represent. The card shown in Illus. 4-3 has 80 columns and, therefore, can contain 80 characters.

Compared with the manual and mechanical systems of data processing, unit record equipment handles larger volumes of data with greater speed and accuracy at a relatively lower cost. The punched card system consists of the *card punch, verifier, sorter, tabulator,* and *collator.* These machines are illustrated in Part 3.

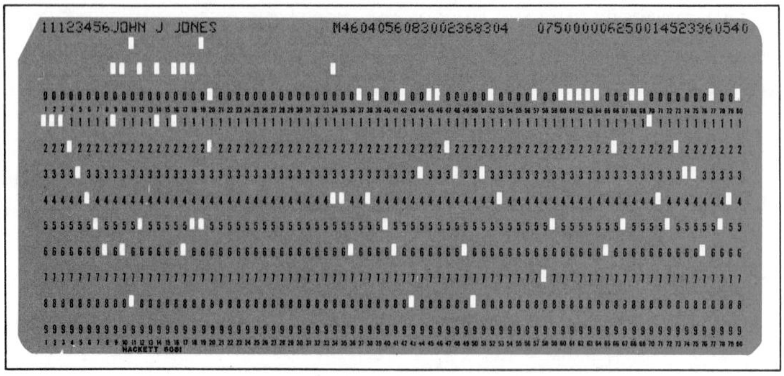

Illus. 4-3 Punch card

If you process a sale by the unit record method, you usually hand-write or typewrite the sales slip. It provides the information needed to process the data by the unit record method. The sales slip data is punched

IBM Corporation

Illus. 4-4 Unit record means of processing data

into a card designed for this purpose and verified. The holes punched into the card give the information in the form of a code that can be understood by the card punch machines. The punched cards are processed by machine to produce the journal entry, the ledger entry, and the statement.

Processing Data by an Electronic (Computer) System

     The electronic computer is the latest tool developed by man to aid him in processing data. For business or government agencies dealing with great numbers of records, none of the previously mentioned data processing methods is fast enough. It is almost impossible to describe a computer's many uses. The computer helped land men on the moon! It is used for arranging class schedules, sorting and routing mail, assisting doctors in **diagnosing** and controlling diseases, printing this book, navigating ships, verifying income tax returns, keeping airline reservations in order. Part 4 of this unit will take you through the basic steps of electronic computer processing.

diagnosing: identifying the cause of a condition or problem

     Let's say that you are asked to supply a sales slip for the processing of a sale using electronic data processing equipment. You may either

IBM Corporation

Illus. 4-5 Electronic means of processing data

handwrite or type this sales slip. Information from the sales slip is then punched into data cards to be processed by the computer. The processing, or arranging, of the data is performed by a list of instructions to the computer called a *program*. The computer consists of several units which will be discussed in Part 4 of this unit. The computer can prepare the invoice, journal entry, ledger entry, and statement for the customer. It can also store the information for future reference.

1. Define business data processing.
2. Is data processing a recent development?
3. What are the two major needs for data processing?
4. Identify four methods of processing data and briefly explain each.
5. What are two disadvantages of manual data processing?
6. Why is processing data mechanically a more efficient system than manual data processing?
7. Name five machines that make up the unit record system.
8. What is another name for the unit record system?
9. What is the latest method of processing data?
10. List five ways in which electronic data processing is used.

MAKING DECISIONS

You often hear the statement "Man is being replaced by the machine." Do you think electronic data processing will ever completely take the place of man in the business world? Explain why or why not.

WORKING WITH OTHERS

Mr. Daton started in the hardware business thirty years ago. At that time, his inventory was small, and he could handle every area of his business himself. As the years passed, his business grew and Mr. Daton prospered. He now has five full-time office employees to help him handle the increasing work load. Even so, Mr. Daton is faced with a growing problem in his office. Despite his efforts to keep pace with his growing business, his records get more and more out of date. They seem to be less accurate than they were. His employees are neglecting their other responsibilities in the office in an effort to handle the paper work which they perform manually.

What would you suggest Mr. Daton do to get his office operating efficiently again?

USING LANGUAGE

A conjunction is a word used to connect words, phrases, or clauses. Conjunctions can be *coordinate* or *subordinate*. A *coordinate* conjunction is independent; it connects equal elements in a sentence. The coordinate conjunctions are *and, but, for, neither,* and *nor*. A *subordinate* conjunction is dependent in that it connects unequal elements in a sentence. Examples of coordinate and subordinate conjunctions are:

You *and* I are elected (coordinate conjunction).
The man left hurriedly *lest* he be seen (subordinate conjunction).

On a separate sheet of paper type the coordinate or subordinate conjunctions in each of the following sentences.

1. The term *data processing* is new, but the activity is not new.
2. Since electronic data processing machines save some businesses many thousands of dollars, you should understand how they operate.
3. Accuracy is very important in all businesses because errors can be costly and time consuming.
4. Data is carefully checked by at least two different people, since it is important that the data put into an electronic system of processing data be accurate.
5. The mechanical method of processing data is faster than the manual method, provided that you can operate the machines efficiently.

6. Originally data was processed only by the manual method, but that process was very slow.
7. Many businesses are using electronic data processing systems because they are faster and more accurate than mechanical methods.
8. Human beings become tired doing routine work, but computers do not get tired.
9. He wrote the sales slip, but he performed the calculations on an electronic calculator.
10. They were short of help that afternoon, since several of the card punch machine operators had colds.

USING ARITHMETIC

You work for the Thompson Wholesale Beauty Supply House. The company does not have an electronic or mechanical data processing system. All data must be processed manually. It is your job to double-check all invoices prepared by co-workers to make sure they are correct.

Type the following partial invoices on a sheet of paper. Check the invoices for accuracy in arithmetic. Cross through any errors you find and supply the correct amounts.

Item	Price	Quantity	Amount
X271	$ 1.75 doz.	4 doz.	$ 7.00
V303	4.17 ea.	5	28.05
Z111	5.50 doz.	3 ½ doz.	19.25
A101	7.99 ea.	18	148.42
			$172.62

Item	Price	Quantity	Amount
F719	$ 3.24 doz.	8 ¼ doz.	$ 28.35
L101	4.50 ea.	29	130.05
K210	.12 ea.	65	7.80
H112	23.75 ea.	1	27.35
			$193.55

PERFORMING OFFICE TASKS

The following letter was received from a customer complaining about an error made on his monthly statement.

Gentlemen:

I am again returning this statement to you because it is incorrect. As I told you last month, I did not purchase the lawn chair charged to me on May 19; yet it has not been subtracted from my account.

Will you please straighten this out? I will pay the bill as soon as this correction is made.

Very truly yours,

Charles Townsend

As soon as you check the complaint you discover that an error was made when writing the account number so that the lawn chair was charged to the wrong account.

1. Write a letter explaining the situation to Mr. Townsend at 2304 Grove Street, N.E., Salem, OR 97303.
2. How does an error like this affect customer relations?
3. What can be done to prevent errors like this from happening again?

PART **2**   THE DATA PROCESSING CYCLE

Sprawls & Reed Oil Company employs over 2,000 workers and has several branch offices. Most of the paper work is processed by a computer located in the home office. Alvin Siever, a recent high school graduate, accepted a position at Sprawls & Reed Oil Company in the Data Processing Department. Alvin was anxious about the job at first, but his former bookkeeping teacher told him that data processing isn't complicated after the basics are mastered. Alvin studied a unit on data processing in his bookkeeping class in high school and remembered that the teacher used flow chart symbols to explain how the data was processed. When he was going through a training program at Sprawls & Reed Oil Company, many of these same symbols were used to explain the procedures to be followed in processing the data for each of the branch offices. Alvin found that no matter what data was processed, it always went through certain steps. These steps made up what his supervisor called the *data processing cycle*.

STEPS IN THE DATA PROCESSING CYCLE

Before a business report is prepared, the data to be used in the report must follow a series of steps called the data processing cycle. The steps in the data processing cycle are (1) origin, (2) input, (3) processing, and (4) output.

Step 1 — Origin of Data

Origin means the beginning or start of something. In business the information to be processed originates in a variety of business papers. The business papers used to record data for the first time are called **source documents**. For example, when you go to a store to buy a tape deck on a charge account, the sales clerk fills out a sales slip with your name and address, telephone number, description of the item you bought, and the price. Writing this information on the sales slip is the origin of data about your purchase of the tape deck. Other source documents may include invoices, time cards, or checks.

source:
point of origin

Step 2 — Input of Data

In Step 2 the data from the source document is recorded in such form that it can be easily manipulated, or processed. If the information is to be processed manually, this step may involve putting the information about your sale in a Sales Journal so that the store can get a total sales figure for the month. If the information is to be processed automatically by electronic equipment, this step may involve punching the data from the source document onto cards or tapes so that it can be processed on electronic equipment. The information is punched into a card or tape by using a card punch, illustrated on page 110.

Step 3 — Processing of Data

The next step is to actually process the data. This may involve classifying, **calculating**, and summarizing the data. When you purchased your tape deck, the information concerning the sale was written on a sales slip. The information on the sales slip is processed (added, subtracted, multiplied, divided, or summarized) to prepare a monthly bill for you and to provide reports, such as the Monthly Sales Report, needed to run the business efficiently. The different machines used to process the data will be discussed in Part 3 of this unit.

calculating: determining something mathematically

Illus. 4-6
Information on sales slips is processed to prepare monthly bills, sales records, and other reports for running a business efficiently.

National Cash Register Company

Step 4 — Output of Data

The final step in the data processing cycle is the output of data. In this step the information that has been processed is organized and arranged in a usable form. The output document may take a variety of forms. Quite often it is a statement, an invoice, or a report. The output from your purchase of a tape deck may include a monthly bill to you and a sales report for the store. When data is processed electronically, the output may be another punched card rather than a written report. The monthly utility bill you receive at your home is usually in the form of a punched card. This punched card can be processed automatically when it is returned to the company with payment.

FLOW CHART SYMBOLS

The steps in the data processing cycle can be shown using a *flow chart*, which is a diagram of how something moves or flows in a business. Flow charts are used in business because symbols make it possible to **visualize** the processes easier than words. Also, flow chart symbols can save time because fewer words have to be used.

visualize:
to see or form a
mental image

Some of the sybols and their meanings are shown below.

Illus. 4-7
Flow chart
symbols

Symbol	Meaning	Symbol	Meaning
	Document		Sort
	Keying operation		Input/Output
	Transmittal tape		Process
	Manual operation		Magnetic disk
	Punched card		Flow (movement)

Recording the sale of a tape deck using a combination of manual, mechanical, unit record, and electronic computer methods would be charted as shown below.

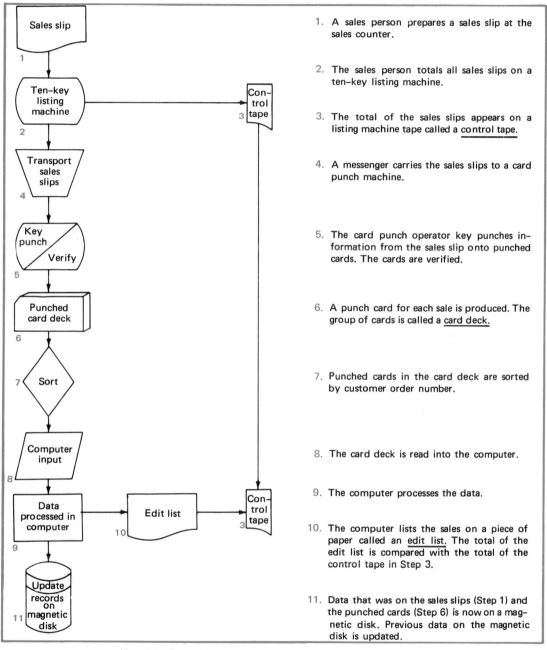

1. A sales person prepares a sales slip at the sales counter.

2. The sales person totals all sales slips on a ten-key listing machine.

3. The total of the sales slips appears on a listing machine tape called a control tape.

4. A messenger carries the sales slips to a card punch machine.

5. The card punch operator key punches information from the sales slip onto punched cards. The cards are verified.

6. A punch card for each sale is produced. The group of cards is called a card deck.

7. Punched cards in the card deck are sorted by customer order number.

8. The card deck is read into the computer.

9. The computer processes the data.

10. The computer lists the sales on a piece of paper called an edit list. The total of the edit list is compared with the total of the control tape in Step 3.

11. Data that was on the sales slips (Step 1) and the punched cards (Step 6) is now on a magnetic disk. Previous data on the magnetic disk is updated.

Illus. 4-8   Record of a sale through various data processing steps

COMMON MACHINE LANGUAGE

Data recorded by one machine can be transmitted and processed by other machines. This process that unites the work of data processing machines is sometimes called *integrated data processing* or *IDP*. The processing of data by machines with a minimum of human effort is called *automation*.

So that one machine can process data from another machine, data must be recorded in a form that can be understood by both machines, and it is called *common machine language*. Common machine language is either a hole punched in paper or magnetic impulses (invisible electrical signals) on plastic tape similar to the plastic tape on your tape deck at home. Each hole in the paper and each magnetic impulse on the plastic tape represent letters, numbers, or symbols that can be understood and therefore processed by machines.

MACHINES THAT CAN READ PRINT

Data represented by holes in punched cards and magnetic impulses on tape can be read by machines, but it cannot be read very well by people. Printed data can be read by people, but until recently it could not be read by machines. This meant that printed data on paper had to be converted to holes in paper or to electrical impulses on plastic tape before it could be understood by machines.

Machines now make it unnecessary to convert printed data on paper into another form for the machines to read.

Magnetic ink character recognition (*MICR*) and *optical scanning* machines will read printed characters (data). In the MICR method, characters are printed on documents with special magnetic ink that machines can read.

Illus. 4-9
Check with magnetic ink numbers

In the optical scanning method, numbers are printed with ordinary ink; but each character has a special shape which can be read by a light beam. The light beam is then converted into electrical impulses on magnetic tape or in printed form on other documents. Some optical scanning machines can even read handwritten numbers.

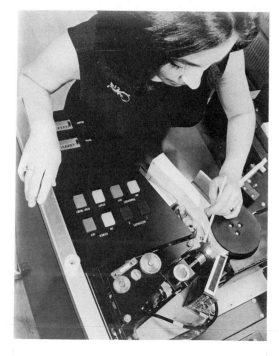

Illus. 4-10
Optical scanning machine

Honeywell

REVIEWING WHAT YOU HAVE READ

1. What are the four basic steps in the data processing cycle?
2. Explain briefly what takes place in each step of the data processing cycle.
3. What does *origin* mean?
4. Define a *source document.*
5. Give some examples of source documents.
6. Name four forms that an output document can take.
7. What is a flow chart?
8. Why use flow chart symbols in business?
9. What does each of these symbols represent in a flow chart?

 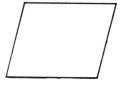 

10. In the flow chart on page 116 what step follows the punched cards being sorted by customer order number.

MAKING DECISIONS

In which businesses would you expect to find wide use of MICR and optical scanning equipment? Why?

You are a clerk in the Accounting Department of the Wade Moving Company. Because of increasing costs in the department, Mr. Gillespie, who is head of the department, has asked all employees to flow chart the procedures involved in their work. These charts will be used to study the department's work so that it can be improved.

Harold, a fellow employee, has had a great deal of experience in the department; and he tells you that he resents having to describe his work on flow charts.

What should you reply to Harold?

A preposition connects a noun or a pronoun with some other element of the sentence and shows the relationship between them. Some often misused prepositions are *in, into, between,* and *among.* Study how each of these words should be used and then type the correct preposition for each of the phrases below on a separate sheet of paper.

in — used after a verb expressing the idea of rest or, in some cases, motion within a certain place.

into — used after a verb that indicates the motion of a person or a thing from one place to another.

between — used only in reference to two persons or objects

among — used only in reference to three or more persons or objects

1. to distinguish _____ the two steps (between, among)
2. to enter _____ an agreement (in, into)
3. to divide the bonus _____ us three (between, among)
4. to dive _____ a pool (in, into)
5. to work _____ the data processing department (in, into)
6. disagreement _____ labor and management (between, among)
7. to go _____ the computer rental business (in, into)
8. a discussion _____ the supervisor and the employee (between, among)
9. to choose _____ the four of them (between, among)
10. to store material _____ a file (in, into)

Mr. Carter owns a furniture store. As an added incentive to customers, he offers a discount (a deduction from the original price) to customers who pay cash for their purchases. The amount of the discount varies.

The steps in determining the cost of a purchase can be expressed in a flow chart as follows:

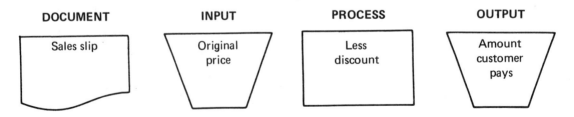

DOCUMENT	INPUT	PROCESS	OUTPUT
Sales slip	Original price	Less discount	Amount customer pays

What would the output be for the sales (shown at the top of page 121) made by Mr. Carter?

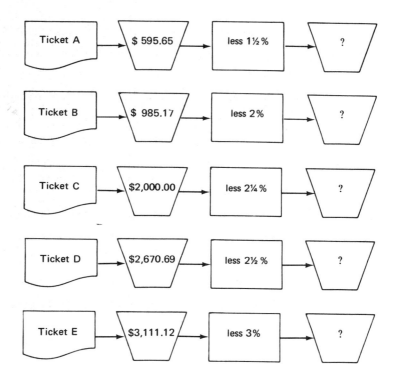

Ticket A	$ 595.65	less 1½ %	?
Ticket B	$ 985.17	less 2%	?
Ticket C	$2,000.00	less 2¼ %	?
Ticket D	$2,670.69	less 2½ %	?
Ticket E	$3,111.12	less 3%	?

PERFORMING OFFICE TASKS

As an office worker, you may be required to make a flow chart of office procedures. To develop your understanding of flow charts:

1. Make a flow chart showing the sale of a tape deck on credit. Use a combination of manual, mechanical, card punch, and computer methods. Lay the flow chart paper over the symbols. With a pencil, trace the symbols onto the flow chart paper in the order in which you want your flow chart to appear. If you have a workbook, use the flow chart paper and sheet of flow chart symbols provided. If you do not have a workbook, place a sheet of regular 8 ½" x 11" white paper over the proper symbols on page 116 of this textbook. Since your chart will be handdrawn, the symbols may not look as precise as those you traced.

2. Make a flow chart showing the cash sale of a record player. Show the following steps:

   (a) The sales person prepares a sales slip at the sales counter.
   (b) The sales person receives cash from the customer.
   (c) The sales person determines how much change to give to the customer.
   (d) The sales person gives the change and merchandise to the customer.
   (e) All sales slips for the day are added on a ten-key listing machine to get the total sales for the day.
   (f) The total of the sales slips appears on a listing machine tape called a control tape.

PART 3 | DATA PROCESSING MACHINES

At 4:30 one afternoon Ellen's boss, Mr. Powell, said, "Andy isn't here to total our sales for the day. Will you add up today's invoices?" Mr. Powell placed a stack of invoices on Ellen's desk and showed her how to list figures on a new electronic calculator. Because Ellen had learned about the ten-key listing machine in school, she was able to add the figures on the electronic calculator after a brief demonstration by Mr. Powell.

There are many different kinds of calculating machines, and each is designed to process data in a special way. Office workers should know what each machine can do, when it should be used, and how it is operated.

CALCULATING MACHINES

The amount of work you do on a calculator will depend on the business in which you are working. Some of the duties you may perform using a calculator are checking a report containing **computations**, figuring the payroll, and preparing budgets.

computations: amounts added, subtracted, multiplied, or divided

There are several kinds of calculating machines. Since there are many manufacturers of these machines, there are many different models of each type. Don't let this confuse you. Just know the features of each type. Then if you know how to operate one model of each type, with a little additional practice, you will be able to operate other models of the same type. As a comparison, if you know how to drive one model of automobile, with very little practice you can drive another model automobile.

Electronic Calculators

The electronic calculator is the most modern of all the calculators and is replacing many other types of calculating machines. Models are **available** that will perform every kind of computation that is needed in a business office.

available: present in such form as to be usable

They compute very rapidly because numbers are entered on a keyboard with a touch system, and calculations are made electronically. They multiply and divide automatically; and, because of their computing speed, they are very efficient for multiplication and division problems. Some models can store amounts in separate memory registers until needed later in the calculations.

There are two types of electronic calculators — printing and non-printing. Computations are done electronically on these calculators, but on most machines the printing is mechanical; that is, a wheel or bars strike the paper tape to print answers. Computations of electronic printing calculators are shown on a paper tape so that they can be checked for accuracy against the original document.

Illus. 4-11   Monroe electronic printing calculator

Illus. 4-12   Burroughs display calculator

Computations for nonprinting calculators (sometimes called electronic display calculators) are shown by lighted figures in a window directly above the keyboard. They are used when a printed record of the calculations on a tape is not needed. Display calculators have no moving parts and are completely silent. Portable, battery-operated models that can be held in one hand are available.

Singer
Business
Machines

Illus. 4-13   Portable electronic calculator

Ten-Key Listing Machines

As the name implies, a ten-key machine has only ten figure keys on the keyboard. Amounts are entered on the keyboard and printed on the paper tape in the order in which they are read. Each figure key, including the 0, or cipher key, is depressed separately. For example, to list $50.60 you would depress the 5, 0, 6, and 0 keys and then depress the motor bar.

Illus. 4-14
Ten-key listing
machine

Singer
Business
Machines

Because the machine has only ten figure keys, all within easy reach, you will be able to enter amounts on the keyboard without looking at the keys after a few hours of instruction. Touch operation will increase your production rate and greatly reduce your chances of omitting amounts or **transposing** figures in an amount.

transposing:
putting one in
place of the other

Ten-key listing machines are used for addition and subtraction.

Mechanical Printing Calculators

There are many mechanical printing calculators in offices, but in time they will be replaced with electronic printing calculators. Mechanical printing calculators have ten-figure keyboards and like the other ten-key machines can be operated by touch.

Illus. 4-15
Mechanical printing
calculator

Remington Rand

Calculations printed on the tapes can be checked against source documents from which the computations are made. They are all-purpose machines with automatic multiplication and division. Some models have memory storage.

Full-Keyboard Listing Machine

A full-keyboard listing machine (also known as a *full-bank adding machine*) has from five to twenty columns of keys ranging in **ascending** order from 1 to 9. There are no 0 keys on the keyboard; zeros are printed automatically. The full-keyboard listing machine is used primarily for addition and subtraction.

ascending:
rising upward

Illus. 4-16
Full-keyboard
listing machine

Remington Rand

Some listing machines have movable carriages which hold statements and ledger cards. If you work in a small company, you will be able to do your billing work on the listing machine itself.

Rotary Calculators

You use a rotary calculator for multiplying and dividing numbers with many **digits**. You can use decimal markers on the keyboard and in

digits:
the Arabic
numerals 1 to 9
and 0

Illus. 4-17
Rotary calculator

Monroe

the answer dials to guide you in recording amounts with decimals. Rotary calculators are used to solve all types of problems, but they are being replaced in offices by electronic calculators.

CASH REGISTERS

The cash register is widely used in business to process data. It can be used to record a transaction and also to give a receipt to the customer. Special cash registers are available that also show the correct change due a customer.

audit tape:
paper tape on which transactions are recorded

The cash register records all cash sales, charge sales, receipts on account, or paid-out items on an **audit tape**. At the end of each day, the audit tape is used to determine whether the amount of cash in the cash register drawer agrees with the cash amount on the tape.

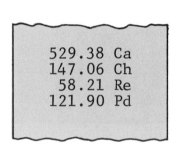

```
529.38 Ca
147.06 Ch
 58.21 Re
121.90 Pd
```

Illus. 4-18
Audit tape

Singer
Business
Machines

Illus. 4-19
A modern cash register

BOOKKEEPING MACHINES

Bookkeeping machines are also known as *billing* machines. The main advantages of bookkeeping machines are their ability to tabulate from one position to another and to print at high speeds. Such reports as statements, invoices, and checks can be prepared on a bookkeeping machine much more rapidly and accurately than they can be handwritten.

Bookkeeping machines can perform addition; subtraction; and, with a special attachment, multiplication and division.

Illus. 4-20
Bookkeeping
machine

National Cash
Register Company

Bookkeeping machines are particularly valuable in preparing **repetitious** data, such as customer billing.

repetitious:
occurs again and
again

ACCOUNTING MACHINES

These machines work faster and more automatically than book-keeping machines. They are not, however, as efficient as computers. This machine has a *central processing unit* (sometimes called a *CPU*) that programs the work for the machine to do. The program is stored on paper tape in cabinets beside the machine. The operator sends data into the system using a keyboard similar to a typewriter but with additional keys.

Illus. 4-21
Accounting
machine

Burroughs Corporation

UNIT RECORD SYSTEM

As was mentioned in Part 1 of this unit, the unit record method of processing data is also called the punched card system because data is recorded by punching holes in a card. The five machines used in the unit record system are illustrated here, and a brief description of how they are operated is given.

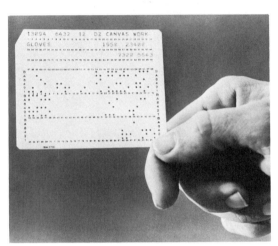

Illus. 4-22
Punched paper card containing 96 columns.

IBM Corporation

Card Punch Machine

The purpose of the card punch machine is to transfer data into a card by means of a punched code. The card punch operator reads the

Illus. 4-23
Card punch machine

IBM Corporation

source document and depresses keys that punch holes in the cards. The holes represent numbers, letters, and symbols. The machine automatically feeds, positions, and ejects each card. The operator must strike the proper keys in the correct sequence.

Verifier

Since accuracy is so essential, card verifying is necessary to check original card punching. A different operator usually verifies the original punching by striking the keys of a verifier while reading from the same source of information used to punch the cards. The verifying machine

Illus. 4-24
Card verifier

IBM Corporation

compares the key struck with the hole already punched in the column on the card. A difference causes the machine to stop, indicating a difference between the two operations.

Sorter

Imagine sorting from 800 to 1,000 cards a minute with complete accuracy! This is one of the outstanding advantages of the punched card system. After the punched cards have been verified, they are sorted into

Illus. 4-25
Sorter

IBM Corporation

numeric or alphabetic order according to the information that has been punched in them. Payroll cards, for example, may be sorted alphabetically according to the last and given names of the employees or numerically according to their time card numbers.

Tabulator

After the cards have been sorted, they are fed through a tabulator to transcribe and print automatically the information punched in the cards. The tabulator will print names and other descriptive information from a group of cards, add or subtract punched amounts, and print totals and

Illus. 4-26
Tabulator

IBM Corporation

grand totals only, without listing either the descriptive information or the separate amounts punched into the individual cards. Tabulating machines operate at speeds ranging from 100 to 150 cards a minute depending upon the type of machine used.

Collator

merged:
combined; united;
blended

Sometimes information is required from two or more card files. The cards from the files must be brought together and **merged** or matched before further processing is possible. A collator is used for this purpose.

Illus. 4-27
Collator

IBM Corporation

A collator can (1) merge two decks of punched cards in numeric sequence, (2) match the cards from two files having the same numeric data punched in them in a particular field, (3) select from a deck of cards only those cards having a certain number or a series of numbers in a specified field, or (4) check a file of cards to make sure that they are in **sequential** order.

sequential:
following in a series

REVIEWING WHAT YOU HAVE READ

1. Under what circumstances might you use calculating machines?
2. Name the two types of electronic calculators.
3. How is the paper tape of the electronic printing calculator used?
4. Where do the computations of a nonprinting calculator appear?
5. How would you enter the amount $25.70 on a ten-key listing machine?
6. Why use the touch method when entering amounts on the ten-key listing machine?
7. What is the primary use of the full-keyboard listing machine?
8. With what type computations would you use a rotary calculator?
9. How is an audit tape used?
10. What are the main advantages of bookkeeping machines?

MAKING DECISIONS

1. Janice must get the total for this column of numbers:

$$ 24.30
78.69
3.74
126.05
19.83
48.31$$

She should list the numbers and check her answers on a paper tape.
Close to her desk are a full-keyboard listing machine and a printing calculator. Which machine should she use? Why?

2. Why do you think many businesses use cash registers? Can you think of some specific examples of stores that use cash registers?

3. Why is it necessary for the punched cards in a unit record system to be verified?

WORKING WITH OTHERS

You work for the First State Bank as a bookkeeper. Mr. Lamont, your supervisor, has just introduced you to Karen, a new employee. Mr. Lamont wants you to help Karen learn how to operate a ten-key listing machine.

Which points about the ten-key listing machine would you tell Karen so that she could become a fast, efficient worker on the ten-key listing machine?

On a sheet of paper list the words in Column 1. Then write the number of the definition for each word from Column 2. Check a dictionary if you are not sure of the definition of any word.

Example:

(a) accumulate	(8) to collect or bring together

Column 1	Column 2
(a) accumulate	(1) one who has legal right of ownership
(b) invoice	(2) carry through with dispatch
(c) valid	(3) itemized list of merchandise sent to a purchaser
(d) acknowledgment	(4) capable of being supported or defended
(e) expenditure	(5) statement of estimated income and expenses
(f) automation	(6) act of recognizing a fact to give it validity
(g) proprietor	(7) an outlay of money; disbursement
(h) expedite	(8) to collect or bring together
(i) miscellaneous	(9) automatic equipment that replaces some hand operation
(j) budget	(10) consisting of diverse things

You work for the Adams Advertising Agency. Some of the customer accounts are shown below. The amounts on the left side of the accounts are debits (amounts customers owe us). The amounts on the right are credits (amounts customers paid us).

What is the balance (debits less credits) for each account?

Which calculating machine in the office would you use to get the answers? Explain your choice.

(a) **Carousel Dress Shop**

$375.75	$375.75
50.11	
80.32	

(d) **Jack's Cycle Shop**

$150.00	$ 75.00
30.00	
25.93	

(b) **Hamburger Heaven**

$ 28.11	$
75.25	

(e) **The Stereo Center**

$ 65.00	$
25.20	

(c) **Bookworm Shop**

$ 15.00	$ 50.00
15.00	
20.00	

(f) **Cindy's Candy Shop**

$ 10.95	$
5.75	

Visit one or more offices in your community to find out which calculating machines are being used. Also find out which particular kinds of jobs are being done on the various machines. If possible, request some of the business forms that are used in connection with these jobs. Prepare a typewritten report on your visit, attaching the forms collected. Be prepared to make an oral presentation to the class.

PART 4

ELECTRONIC COMPUTER DATA PROCESSING

When Tony Oliva graduated from high school he began working in the Data Processing Department of the Denco Electronic Supply Company. He performed a wide variety of tasks including delivering messages, loading cards into punched card equipment, typing, and getting records ready to be put into the computer. Mr. Elmer Nicholson, head of the Data Processing Department, just returned from a computer school in Baltimore, Maryland, and told Tony about his experiences at the school. This increased Tony's interest in data processing and particularly in becoming a programmer. As Tony became more experienced, Mr. Nicholson let Tony perform more and more jobs directly related to data processing. About a year later Mr. Nicholson called Tony into his office and said, "Tony, you have the ability to become a programmer; and, of course, I already know how interested you are in this kind of work. Our company sometimes sponsors outstanding employees in getting additional education so that they can be promoted. We have decided that you have the ability and the desire to make the most of this opportunity. We are enrolling you, at our expense, in the Programmer's Course at North Hampton College." Tony looked forward to going to school and knew that everything he learned at school and on the job would help him become a better employee with a bright future.

FEATURES OF ELECTRONIC COMPUTERS

The computer plays a vital role in the lives of most people today. The business world needs faster and more accurate information to serve customers better and for decision-making. The computer can supply this information because of three features — speed, accuracy, and storage.

Speed

If you were asked to multiply two 10-digit numbers, say 3,575,212,134 by 2,456,754,137, it would be a difficult task with a pencil and paper. This would be an impossible task if you tried to perform the calculations mentally and to remember the original numbers along with the answer for future reference. Most electronic computers, however, could do this calculation along with storing the results in a few *nanoseconds*. A nanosecond is one billionth of a second.

Accuracy

Accuracy is very important in all businesses. When large numbers of items are processed, it is easy to make errors. In using computers, however, errors can be reduced because the information is verified before it is put into the computer. The computer then follows the same instructions each time without getting tired or bored. Human beings become tired and bored when doing repetitive work and, as a result, make errors.

Storage

Many different kinds of data can be stored in a computer. Usually the data to be processed and the instructions for processing the data are stored in the computer by using magnetic drums, tapes, or disks. The computer is able to find this data very quickly when it is needed.

Illus. 4-28
Processing data by
an electronic
computer system

IBM Corporation

HOW A COMPUTER WORKS

flexible:
responding to new
or changing
situations

The human mind is a **flexible** but very unreliable processor of information. Human beings, however, are needed to handle situations where judgment is required. Electronic data processing combines the talents of people who are slow, inaccurate, and intelligent with computers which are fast, accurate, and not intelligent. Combining the advantages of the human mind and the electronic computer gives the businessman an efficient system of providing information for decision-making and service to customers.

Illus. 4-29
A small computer

IBM Corporation

Computers process data electronically. A typical electronic computer system uses three groups of linked machines or devices (input, processing, and output) to process data.

Input

Computers are fed data to be processed and instructions that tell the computer how to process the data. The instructions and data are recorded on different types of media which are sometimes called "software." The major types of media are punched paper tape, punched paper cards, magnetic plastic tape, and magnetic disks.

Punched Paper Tape. Holes in the paper tape represent letters, numbers, and symbols as shown on the right of Illus. 4-30.

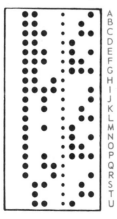

Illus. 4-30
Punched paper tape

Punched Paper Cards. Information can be put into a computer with the same punched cards used in unit record system described on page 109.

Magnetic Plastic Tape. Just as you cannot see your voice recorded on the plastic tape of your tape deck, you cannot see the magnetic impulses or spots on the plastic tape used for processing data. When you play back your tape recorder at home, music is produced. When you play back the data processing tape, information in the form of words, numbers, and symbols is printed on paper.

Magnetic Disks. A magnetic disk can be compared with a home phonograph record as magnetic tape is compared with a reel of tape on your tape deck. Magnetic disks have an advantage over magnetic tape because the computer can go directly to an item of information and retrieve it without examining all the data on the disk. To retrieve information that is stored on magnetic tape, you must start at the beginning and play the tape until you get to the desired information. This **technique** of locating information on magnetic disks is called *random access.*

technique: method or way of doing something

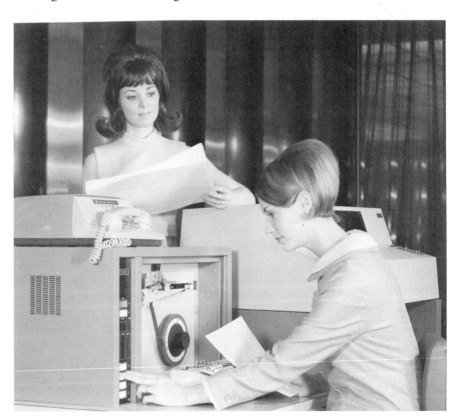

Illus. 4-31
Magnetic tape is one kind of input in electronic computer data processing.

Data on the software media is sent into the computer by input devices and machines that may be located in the same room as the computer. It is also possible to place data in the computer with machines that are far away from the computer but connected to the computer with electrical wires.

Business is constantly searching for ways to automatically collect accurate data at its source and record it in a common language that can be processed later. This makes it possible to process data accurately and rapidly with the least amount of human effort. For example, to decrease the number of times the same data about a sale must be rewritten, some modern cash registers send sales data such as customer name, date, articles purchased, and price directly to a computer to which they are connected.

Illus. 4-32
A large computer

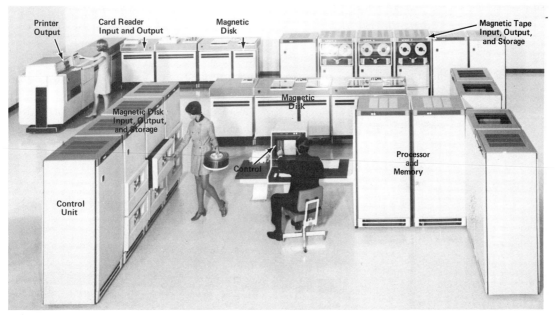

Printer Output
Card Reader Input and Output
Magnetic Disk
Magnetic Tape Input, Output, and Storage
Magnetic Disk Input, Output, and Storage
Magnetic Disk
Control
Processor and Memory
Control Unit

National Cash
Register Company

Processing

The central processing unit of the computer includes three sections:

1. The *storage section* temporarily stores data, instructions, final results, and any other information that can be **advantageously** stored within the computer.
2. The *process section* **manipulates** the data. Computing — addition, subtraction, multiplication, and division — is performed here.
3. The *control section* could be called the nerve center of the data processing system. It receives each instruction

advantageously: favorably

manipulates: arranges; processes

of the program and analyzes it to determine the operation to be performed. The movement of data into or out of storage is supervised by the control section. It controls the action execution of the operation. It **monitors** and supervises the flow of data within the system. It notifies the operator when attention is required.

Output

The output devices are used to take the results of the processing out of the system. Output information can be on a continuous form, called a print-out; on up-dated magnetic tapes or disks, punched paper tape or cards; or displayed on a television-like screen at a terminal unit.

Visual display units are connected directly with a computer close by or many miles away. For example, a branch office in Tucson may not keep a complete set of records on its customers. The salesman may want to know the type of merchandise that a specific customer ordered during the last three months, and this information is stored in the home office computer in Denver.

The operator types on the terminal unit requesting information from the computer. In a few seconds the computer will cause the information to appear on the screen of the terminal unit.

Illus. 4-33
Computer terminal
unit

IBM Corporation

By having a knowledge of the ways data can be processed, you are better prepared to perform your job in a modern office on computer software or on printed documents such as payrolls, ledgers, and statements.

REVIEWING WHAT YOU HAVE READ

1. List three features of an electronic computer system and comment briefly on each.
2. How does the electronic computer provide businessmen with a more efficient system?
3. What do the holes in paper tape represent?
4. What are the three linked units in a typical electronic data processing system?
5. Name four types of software used in processing data.
6. How does magnetic plastic tape used in data processing resemble your tape recorder at home?
7. What is the advantage of magnetic disks over magnetic tape?
8. Name the three sections of the processing unit in an electronic computer.
9. Describe the function of the control section.
10. Briefly describe how you would operate a visual display unit of a computer in order to obtain information.

MAKING DECISIONS

1. Why are business firms changing to electronic computer data processing systems?
2. What is the effect of electronic computer data processing on office employment?

WORKING WITH OTHERS

You work for the Omaha Insurance Company as a card punch operator in the Unit Record Department. Mr. Gillian, your supervisor, has just told you that you are being promoted to a programmer. He asks you to explain to Marilyn, your replacement, how to operate the card punch machine. Mr. Gillian also suggests that you begin your explanation by telling Marilyn how important her work will be to the rest of the department.

What would you say to Marilyn when explaining to her how important her work is to the department?

USING LANGUAGE

Numbers can be written as figures or as words. Two very frequent uses of numbers in business are amounts of money and dates. Amounts of money, except in legal documents, should be written in figures. Amounts less than one dollar are written in figures with the word *cents* following. In writing even sums of money, the decimal and ciphers are omitted.

Except in formal or legal writing, the day of the month and the year are usually written in figures. You use an *st, d*, or *th* only when the day is written before or is separated from the month. Some examples follow:

We enclose our check for $21.75
The meeting was held on the 5th and 6th of July.

On a separate sheet of paper rewrite any of the following sentences in which numbers are expressed incorrectly.

1. The purchase price of the electronic calculator was three hundred twenty dollars and fifty-eight cents.
2. A roll of paper tape for the ten-key listing machine costs $.89.

3. Mr. Loomey's full-keyboard listing machine had a trade-in value of about $60.00.
4. On April seven, 197–, Mr. Dodd purchased a printing calculator for the Accounting Department.
5. The Business Machines Conference will be held on the 10th and 11th of September.
6. The cash register showed the total of the purchase was $128.43.
7. Mr. Johnson had used his ten-key listing machine since the 12 of August, 196–.
8. Although Mrs. Harrison knew the rotary calculator was very good, she did not want to pay over $150 for a used machine.
9. The business machines dealer said the new calculators would be delivered on the 3 of January.
10. Mr. Finley estimated that the rotary calculator and the ten-key listing machine would cost about $350.00.

USING ARITHMETIC

Your company pays $1 for 1,000 punch cards. During the first week of January, you punched 7,400 cards. During the second week, you punched exactly half this amount. In the third week you punched 7,500 cards and then 7,000 cards in the fourth week.

1. How many cards did you punch during the four weeks of January?
2. What is the cost of one card?
3. What was the total cost of the cards you punched during that four-week period?

PERFORMING OFFICE TASKS

IBM TRAINEES

Rotate shifts. Opportunity to learn operation of console. Will train. Good starting salary and fringe benefits. High school graduate. Some clerical experience preferred, but not necessary.

An Equal Opportunity Employer

Write to Mr. Leonard Cornell, Liberty Life Insurance Company, 2314 Sixth Street, Lubbock, TX 79414, for an appointment.

You have had a year of experience in the Unit Record Department of a local manufacturing company when you see the above advertisement in your daily newspaper. Write a letter, block style, open punctuation, to Mr. Cornell telling why you are interested in pursuing a career in electronic computer data processing and what your qualifications are.

UNIT 5

MAILING AND SHIPPING SERVICES

MESSENGER
MAIL CLERK

Excellent opportunity for rece
gh school graduate with d
e to enter the banking fiel
rs 8:30 A.M.–5 P.M. Mond
gh Friday. No experien
ary.
Personnel Department
Friday 9 A.M.–4 P.M
NAL BANK

PART 1   INCOMING MAIL

Lorraine does general office work for a small company. One of her duties is to be responsible for incoming mail. This requires a good deal of care, since she must see that all the orders, correspondence, inquiries, and packages are delivered to the correct persons. Special delivery and registered mail and envelopes marked Personal or Confidential must receive extra care.

The people with whom Lorraine works know that when they receive their mail all the enclosures will be with the correspondence (or, if not, the letter will be so marked), it will be date and time stamped, and it will be delivered to their desks promptly.

HANDLING INCOMING MAIL

The United States Postal Service presently handles about 86 billion pieces of mail every year. One of your first duties in an office may be to assist in handling the ever-increasing volume of mail.

The system of handling the mail will depend upon the size and type of business in which you are employed. In a large office the incoming mail is opened, sorted, and distributed by the mail department. In a small office, you may be expected to open, read, sort, and route all the incoming mail.

Opening the Mail

When the volume of incoming mail is very large, the letters are opened in the mail department with an automatic mail opener. It trims a narrow strip off one edge of each envelope. The amount taken off is so small that there is little risk that the contents will be damaged. In order to reduce the chances of cutting the contents, the envelopes may be jogged on the table before they are placed in the opener so that the contents will fall away from the edge that is to be trimmed.

transparent: clear; can be seen through

If you work in a small office and are responsible for opening the mail, you may use a letter opener, a paper knife, or a hand-operated letter opener. If you should cut a letter or an enclosure as you are opening an envelope, use **transparent** mending tape to put it together again.

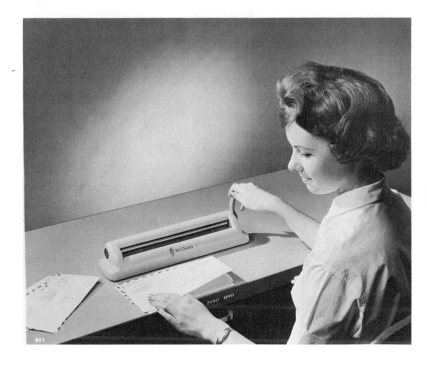

Illus. 5-1
Hand-operated
letter opener

Pitney Bowes

After you have opened the envelopes, remove the letters and other enclosures carefully. Look at each letter and its enclosures as soon as they are removed and attach the enclosures to the letter. If an enclosure is missing, you should note the omission in the margin of the letter. You may be expected to make up a special memorandum and keep it on file if the missing enclosure is a check, a money order, cash, or stamps.

Keep the envelopes until you have examined each letter for the signature and the address. If either is missing on the letter, attach the envelope to the letter. Sometimes a check is received with no other means of **identification** except the envelope in which it was mailed. If the date of the letter is different from the postmark, keep the envelope. Sometimes the envelope of an important **document** is stapled to the document because the date of mailing may prove to be of some importance. If, after you have thrown away the envelope, you notice that the return address is not printed or typed on a letter, you may be able to find the address in a telephone directory, a city directory, or in the correspondence files. Once in a while you may make an error by opening a personal or confidential letter. If this happens place the letter back in the envelope and write on the outside "Sorry — opened by mistake," and add your initials. Don't let this happen too frequently, however. Personal mail should remain personal and should be delivered to the addressee's desk unopened.

identification:
a means of telling
to whom something
belongs

document:
a written or printed
paper that furnishes
information, such
as a letter, a con-
tract, a deed, or an
invoice

Dating the Mail

After you have checked the incoming mail for enclosures, return addresses, and signatures, mark it with the date and time. You can do this with a pen or pencil, a rubber stamp, or a time stamp machine.

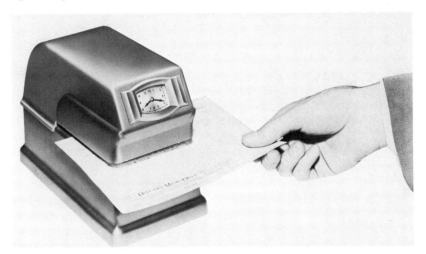

Illus. 5-2
Time stamp

This time stamp prints the year, month, date, hour, and minute of receipt of letters, telegrams, and other documents.

IBM Corporation

Sorting and Routing Mail

If you work in a small office, you may have many responsibilities related to the mail. After you have opened the mail, you check it carefully for addresses, signatures, and enclosures. Next, you will date and time stamp the mail. Then you will *route* the mail, which means sorting it according to addressee or department.

If you work in the mail room of a large company, the mail is sorted by departments. Sorting bins or trays, with a separate compartment for each department, are used for this purpose. After the mail has been sorted, it is delivered by a mail clerk or a messenger. Usually mail is delivered several times a day, the first mail of the day being the heaviest.

When sorting and routing the mail in a large company, usually all orders are directed to the order department. Correspondence regarding credit is sent to the credit department. Inquiries concerning products are sent to the sales department. Checks and correspondence related to the payment of bills are sent to the accounting department. Personal and confidential mail is delivered *unopened* to the addressee. Correspondence addressed to individuals in the company is routed directly to them.

Special delivery letters and registered mail are usually not delivered with the regular mail. They should be handled promptly upon receipt and brought to the addressee's attention quickly.

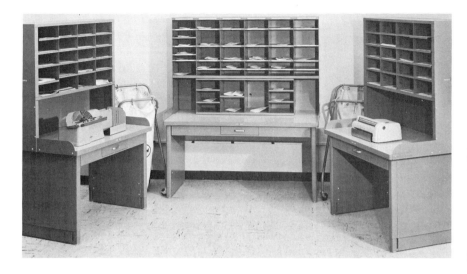

Illus. 5-3
Mail sorting bins and other mail equipment in a small company

Pitney Bowes

Some correspondence and often important articles in magazines or newspapers may be referred to more than one executive or department. Your incoming mail may contain material such as this that must be routed. Many firms use either a rubber stamp or a duplicated routing slip with the names of all the departments or executives to whom this material is sent. It is routed and delivered with regular mail.

```
Please read the attached material and pass
it on to the persons indicated.

                       Date        Date
Refer to:           Received    Passed on

W. N. Ames          _____    _____
M. P. Conrad        _____    _____
N. A. Davis         _____    _____
P. F. Evans         _____    _____
C. X. Hill          _____    _____
F. J. Klein         _____    _____
S. D. Larsen        _____    _____
P. J. Murtagh       _____    _____
N. W. Nelson        _____    _____
J. L. Peterson      _____    _____
J. W. Robinson      _____    _____
G. A. Simpson       _____    _____

Return to:
```

Illus. 5-4
Routing slip

One of these slips is attached to each piece of mail that should be distributed to others. The names of those who are not to receive it are crossed off.

KEEPING MAIL RECORDS

As you read certain letters, you will notice promises of materials that are being sent under separate cover. To be sure that you receive them, you should keep a record of mail expected in another package. Check at least twice a week to see which items have not been received so that you can remind your supervisor or the addressees of delayed mail. When the delayed mail is received, send it to the department or the person to whom the original letter was routed. One type of record for separate cover mail is illustrated below.

DATE OF ENTRY	ARTICLE	FROM WHOM	DATE SENT	DEPARTMENT	INDIVIDUAL	DATE RECEIVED
3-12	Catalog	A. H. Martin & Co	3-11	Purchasing		3-14
3-14	Book	F. Stevens	3-12	Advertising		3-18
3-18	Tickets	G. H. Simms	3-15		P. L. Martin	3-21
3-20	Folders	Kimball Bros	3-18	Filing		3-23
3-22	Catalog	Bryce & Maye	3-20	Purchasing		

Because of its special importance, you may find it necessary to keep a record of the receipt of mail that is insured, special delivery, or registered. Use a form similar to the one illustrated below.

RECEIVED		FROM WHOM		FOR	KIND OF MAIL RECEIVED
DATE	TIME	NAME	ADDRESS	DEPARTMENT OR INDIVIDUAL	
10-1	8:15 a.m.	R. J. Walker	New York City	Accounting	Registered
10-1	9:20 a.m.	Mrs. V. Jones	Denver, Colo.	O. Miller	Insured
10-2	2:15 P.M.	Art Shop, Inc.	Chicago, Ill.	Sales	Special - Delivery

PHOTOCOPYING MAIL

When reading the mail for sorting and routing, you may at times notice that the subject matter is of equal importance to two or more persons or departments. Suppose the letter contains an order and also an inquiry about a new product. In order to speed delivery to both the order department and the sales department you will photocopy the letter and make a notation on the original to the order department that you have sent a copy to the sales department.

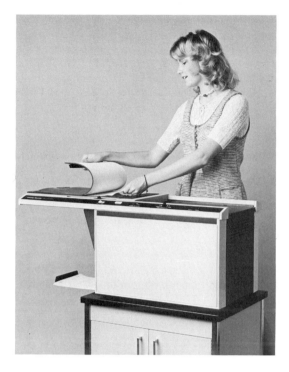

Illus. 5-7
It may be necessary to photocopy some correspondence for fast delivery to several departments.

Pitney Bowes

DISTRIBUTING THE MAIL

Depending on the size of the company you may or may not be responsible for distributing the mail. If you are, you will have the necessary supplies to carry out this task. Your equipment may be a cart, a lightweight mail basket, or it may be something as simple as an alphabetized expanding folder.

REVIEWING WHAT YOU HAVE READ

1. When you open incoming mail with an automatic letter opener, how do you avoid cutting the contents of the envelope?
2. Why should you inspect the enclosed contents of every letter as soon as they are removed from the envelope? For what particular enclosures should you look?
3. A letter is received but the enclosure is missing. What should you do?
4. Under what circumstances should you attach the envelope to the contents of a piece of mail?
5. A letter is received in which reference is made to a package coming under separate cover. How can you remind yourself to look for the package later?

MAKING DECISIONS

1. Under what circumstances is incoming mail likely to be opened by hand? by machine?
2. Do you believe it is important to time stamp all mail that is received? If so, why?

As assistant to Miss Larson, the secretary to the treasurer, you open and read the mail, time stamp it, and attach related files. One morning — because the mail is a half-hour late — you are rushing, since Miss Larson needs information that has just come in for a report that the treasurer must have ready in the next hour. You open and read a letter from the president of the company to the treasurer questioning the accuracy of some of Miss Larson's figures. You then notice that the envelope is marked **CONFIDENTIAL!** What should you do now?

**USING
LANGUAGE**

1. A period is used at the end of a declarative or imperative sentence.
   Example: In the mail room the mail is sorted by departments.
2. A period is used to mark an abbreviation. (Some approved exceptions are FBI, OK, SEC.)
   Example: a.m., p.m., pp. (pages), etc., Dr., i.e. (that is)
3. A period is used to express decimals and between dollars and cents when expressed in figures.
   Example: $3.75 $5.45

On a separate sheet of paper write the following sentences and insert periods where necessary.

1. Breakfast was served at 8 am; lunch was served at noon; dinner was served at 7 pm
2. The fund was set up by Harriman and Co
3. Mrs Jones and Miss Harding were present at the graduation
4. Pp 15 to 25 were missing from the report
5. T M Canter was supervisor of the Shipping Department
6. The president left for Maine at 2 pm — ie that was the time his plane departed
7. Dr Armstrong left for Washington, DC, at the same time
8. Thirty-seven percent when written as a decimal is 37
9. One half of $5 is $250
10. When Miss Anderson delivered the mail at 10 am, Mr Hardy asked her why she was late

**USING
ARITHMETIC** Below is a list of insurance fees (in addition to postage) which must be paid on items up to the value indicated.

FEES (IN ADDITION TO POSTAGE)

Amount of Insurance	Fee
$0.01 to $15	$0.20
15.01 to 50	.30
50.01 to 100	.40
100.01 to 150	.50
150.01 to 200	.60

You work for a jewelry store that often mails jewelry to other firms for repairs and to customers. On a separate sheet of paper show the insurance fee that would be charged for each of the pieces of jewelry listed at top of page 149.

Item	Value
Man's plain gold ring	$ 75
Lady's pearl necklace	25
Man's watch	175
Woman's lapel pin	17
Diamond earrings	200
Black onyx cuff links	85
Man's stretch watch band	20
Ruby tie tac	40
Two-piece fraternity pin with chain	60
Gold bracelet with three small emeralds	200

PERFORMING OFFICE TASKS

Compose and type an interoffice memorandum to one of your classmates instructing her how the company for which you both work wishes incoming mail handled. Her responsibility will be to date stamp the mail and route it. All orders will be directed to the order department. Correspondence regarding credit will be sent to the credit department. Personal and confidential mail will not be opened, but will be directed to the addressee. Inquiries concerning products will be sent to the sales department. Checks and correspondence related to payment of bills will be sent to the accounting department. Make your instructions clear regarding handling of enclosures. The only time she will write on any letter is in the event an enclosure is not with the mail or if she makes a photocopy. Correspondence addressed to individuals in the firm will be routed directly to them. Tell her under which circumstances an envelope will be attached to the correspondence when it is passed on to the department or individual addressee. Give her instructions as to what action she should take regarding special delivery mail.

PART 2 OUTGOING MAIL

"Penny, along with the regular mail today, there are a few special items. Send the letter to Mr. Dauten in Seattle airmail. The signed contracts on the Wirmel agreement should be sent registered mail with a return receipt requested. Also, send these samples back to the Research Department in Newark by parcel post and insure them for $50." Penny, who is a mail clerk in the office of a small company, knows how to prepare the outgoing mail, the different kinds of mail service that are available, and how to use them. Her supervisor knows that he can rely on Penny to send mail quickly and efficiently.

A complete listing of postal services with the details for their use can be found in the *Postal Service Manual* of the United States. Postal services and rates are changed from time to time; therefore, it is important for an office to have either an up-to-date copy of the *Postal Service Manual* or the *Mailer's Guide to Postal Service* which contains all the information about **domestic mail**. Either may be purchased from the Superintendent of Documents, United States Government Printing Office, Washington, D.C. 20402.

domestic mail: mail that stays within this country

You should be able to select the proper mailing service for all the different types of outgoing mail. For instance, a letter may be sent by special delivery to insure prompt delivery, by airmail if it is to go a great distance, or by certified or registered mail if it contains valuable papers. A fee for special delivery or for special handling may be added to fourth-class mail to insure the prompt delivery of parcel post packages. For a small fee, a return receipt, which is proof that an item has been received, may be requested when using insured, certified, or registered mail.

HANDLING OUTGOING MAIL

The system of handling outgoing mail, like the system of handling incoming mail, depends upon the size and the type of business in which you are employed. In a small office a mail clerk usually is responsible for all the details connected with outgoing mail. In a large office the mail is collected from each department several times throughout the day by a messenger or a mail clerk and taken to the mailing department where it is sealed and stacked near the *postage meter*, which is a machine that automatically prints the amount of postage, the postmark, and the mailing date on the envelope.

Folding and Inserting Letters

Folding a business letter properly is not a difficult process, but care should be taken that the creases are straight and that they are made without harming the neatness of the letter. Paper, 8½″ x 11″, to be inserted in an ordinary — No. 6 — envelope (6½″ x 3⅝″) is folded and inserted as follows:

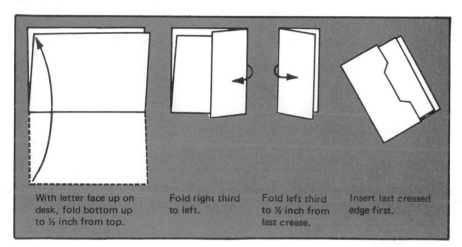

Illus. 5-8

| With letter face up on desk, fold bottom up to ½ inch from top. | Fold right third to left. | Fold left third to ½ inch from last crease. | Insert last creased edge first. |

Only two folds are necessary if the letter is to be placed in a large — No. 10 — envelope (9½″ x 4⅛″):

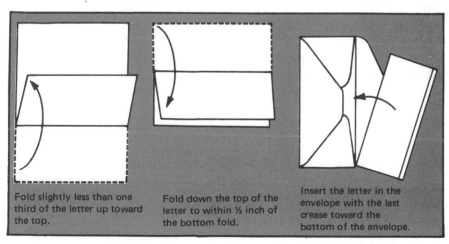

Illus. 5-9

| Fold slightly less than one third of the letter up toward the top. | Fold down the top of the letter to within ½ inch of the bottom fold. | Insert the letter in the envelope with the last crease toward the bottom of the envelope. |

A letter should be inserted in an envelope in such a way that it will be in a normal reading position when it is removed from the envelope and unfolded. The enclosures that accompany the letter should be folded with the letter or inserted so that they will come out of the envelope at the same time the letter is removed.

For a large No. 10 window envelope, 8½″ x 11″ letter sheets are folded as shown below:

Illus. 5-10

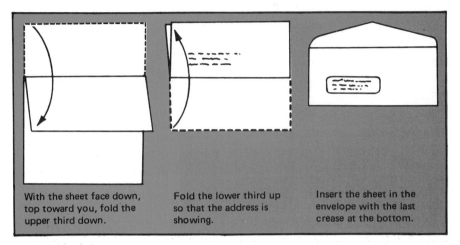

With the sheet face down, top toward you, fold the upper third down.

Fold the lower third up so that the address is showing.

Insert the sheet in the envelope with the last crease at the bottom.

Small No. 6 window envelopes are also available; they are used mostly for bills or statements that are designed to fit with only a single fold.

Sealing Envelopes

If you should have to seal a large number of envelopes without the use of a sealing machine, spread about ten envelopes on a table, address down, flap open, one on top of the other with the gummed edges showing. Brush over the gummed edges with a moist sponge or a moistener to soften the glue so that the flaps can be closed quickly and sealed. When sealing, start with the top envelope, the one nearest you, and work down to the first one placed on the table.

Stamps

You may also put postage stamps on rapidly by arranging six to eight envelopes on top of each other, showing just the upper right part of each one. Moisten the strip of stamps with a damp sponge and put on one stamp after the other. You can save time and increase your efficiency this way.

Postage stamps may be purchased in sheet, booklet, or coil form. The bound booklets of stamps are preferred for personal and home use;

business firms find it better to work with the 100-stamp sheets or the coiled stamps. Coiled stamps are often used in business because they can be quickly placed on envelopes and packages and because they are less likely to be lost or damaged than are individual stamps.

Precanceled Stamps and Envelopes

For an advertising campaign your employer may wish to use precanceled stamps or precanceled stamped envelopes. Their use reduces the time and cost of handling mail. Precanceled stamps and envelopes are purchased from the post office with the cancellation lines already stamped on them. When the sorted mail is returned to the post office, it is not necessary for the letters to go through the canceling machine again. Therefore, the mail is **dispatched** more quickly. Precanceled stamps and envelopes cannot be used for first-class mail.

dispatched:
sent

Stamped Envelopes and Cards

Another means of saving your time is through the use of stamped envelopes of different **denominations** which may be purchased in various sizes — singly or in quantity lots. The return address will be printed on them by the post office for a small fee if the envelopes are purchased in quantity lots.

denominations:
values, such as
8 cents or 10 cents

First-class postal cards may be purchased in single or double form. The double form is used when a reply is requested on the attached card. Airmail postal cards are also available, but only in the single form.

If you are left with spoiled stamped envelopes and cards (if uncanceled), you may exchange them for stamps, stamped envelopes, or postal cards. You may also obtain an exchange on stamps if you happen to buy the wrong denomination.

Metered Mail

The most efficient device you can use to put postage on any class of mail is the postage meter machine. This machine prints the postmark and the proper amount of postage on each piece of mail. The imprint of a fully automatic metering machine may also carry a slogan or a line or two of advertising, such as IT'S SMART TO BE THRIFTY, next to the postmark. Metered mail is neither canceled nor postmarked at the post office; therefore, it is processed and dispatched quickly.

The meter of the postage machine is set at the post office for the amount paid at the time. The meter registers the amount of postage used on each piece of mail, the amount of postage remaining in the meter, and the number of pieces that have passed through the machine. The meter locks when the amount paid for has been used; it is then necessary to take it to the post office again to pay for more postage. Additional postage should be bought before the meter locks. You will find the postage meter very easy to operate, and it will save you a great deal of time.

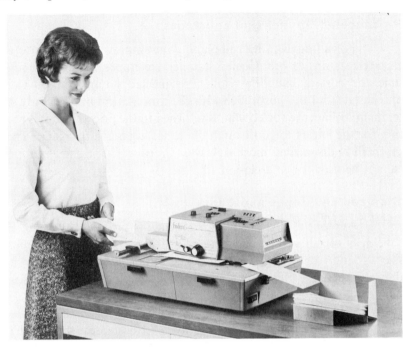

Illus. 5-11
In a small office a desk-top postage meter is used for stamping and stacking outgoing mail.

Singer Business Machines

ZIP Codes

To assure prompt delivery of your mail always use ZIP Codes. Their use increases the speed, accuracy, and quality of *all* mail service. The ZIP Code is a five-digit number that identifies the destination of a piece of mail. For instance:

9	45	77
Area	Sectional Center or Large City	Local Zone

The *9* identifies one of ten large areas made up of three or more states into which the entire country has been divided. The next two figures, *45*, represent the sectional center or large city within that area. And, finally, the *77* represents the local delivery zone within that city or sectional center.

The code should appear on the last line of *both* the envelope address and the return address following the city and state. Two spaces should be left between the last letter of the state and the first digit of the code. The address should be typed in block form:

Fisher Division
The Simmons Company
2350 Washington Avenue
San Leandro, CA 94577

All Zip Codes can be found in the *National Zip Code Directory*.

OPTICAL CHARACTER READER (OCR)

The post office is installing Optical Character Readers, electronic equipment which will speed up the mail. This equipment can read printed or typewritten addresses and sort letters with speed and accuracy.

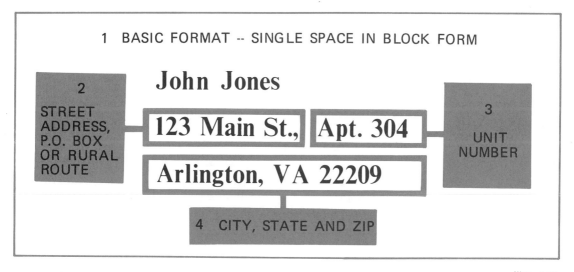

Illus. 5-12

Even if your post office does not have OCR equipment yet, the following rules will help to speed the processing of your outgoing mail.

1. *The Basic Format.* The address should be typed single space in block form.

2. *Street Address*, *P.O. Box*, or *Rural Route*. These should be shown on the line immediately above the City, State, and ZIP Code.

3. *Unit Number.* Mail addressed to occupants of a multi-unit building should include the number of the apartment, room, suite, or other unit. The unit number should appear immediately after the street address on the same line — never above, below, nor in front of the street address.

4. *City*, *State*, and *ZIP Code.* They should appear in that order on the bottom line of the address.

ITEMS TO CHECK BEFORE MAILING

Before mailing outgoing correspondence, check each envelope first to be sure that

1. The address on the envelope agrees with the inside address of the letter.
2. The ZIP Code is typed on the last line of *both* the envelope address and the return address.
3. Any special notations, such as Registered, Special Delivery, and Airmail, have been noted on the envelope.
4. The typed address on a label for a package to be sent separately agrees with the address on the envelope.

Finally, to skip one sorting operation at the post office, separate and identify the *Local* and the *Out-of-Town* mail. Free self-sticking, wrap-around labels are available at most post offices. The use of these wrap-around labels is another procedure that assures better service at the post office.

DOMESTIC MAIL SERVICE

Domestic mail is that sent within the United States, its territories and possessions, Army-Air Force (APO) and Navy (FPO) post offices, and also mail for delivery to the United Nations, New York City. You can speed the mail delivery and reduce the cost of mailing if you use the right mailing service at the right time. A United States Postal Service official states that millions of dollars are wasted each year because of the general lack of knowledge of postal services. He estimates that **extravagance** adds at least 10 percent to the annual cost of all domestic mailing. You can always get up-to-date postal information free of charge at the Information window of your local post office.

extravagance: spending much more than is necessary

CLASSES OF DOMESTIC MAIL

Your employer will expect you to know the different kinds of domestic mail most widely used by business firms. The six kinds of domestic mail listed below will be considered separately.

1. First-class mail — letters, postal cards, and postcards
2. Second-class mail — newspapers and magazines
3. Third-class mail — circulars and other miscellaneous printed matter
4. Fourth-class mail — parcel post
5. Airmail
6. Mixed classes of mail

First-Class Mail

First-class mail is usually sealed letters only; however, the following mail must also be sent first class:

1. All matter sealed against postal inspection
2. Postal cards (cards sold by the post office with stamps imprinted on them) and postcards (privately purchased mailing cards on which stamps are put)
3. Business reply cards and envelopes
4. Matter, partly in written form, such as statements of account, checks, punched cards, and filled-in forms
5. Other matter in written form, such as typewritten reports and documents

Second-Class Mail

In today's news-conscious world, certain newspapers and magazines are sent at second-class rates of postage which are lower than parcel post or third class. Authorization to publishers and news agents to mail at bulk second-class rates must be obtained from the Postal Service.

Third-Class Mail

What is third-class mail? Almost every day you receive in your own home circulars and advertisements that have been sent through the mails at third-class rates. This mail is used for materials that cannot be classified as first- or second-class mail and that weigh less than 16 ounces. The same material in parcels weighing 16 ounces and over is considered fourth-class mail. The following may be sent by third-class mail service:

1. Circulars, books, catalogs, and other printed matter
2. Merchandise samples

Envelopes may be sealed if marked *Third Class* anywhere on the envelope. In the absence of such a marking, sealed envelopes will be subject to first-class mail rates.

Fourth-Class Mail (Parcel Post)

Fourth-class mail is also known as parcel post. It includes merchandise, printed matter, and all other mailable matter not included in first-, second-, or third-class mail that weighs 16 ounces or more. Parcel post rates are determined according to (1) the weight of the parcel and (2) the distance the parcel is being sent. There are limitations on the weight and size of parcel post packages.

Parcel post packages may be sent sealed or unsealed. Unless it is clearly marked *First Class* a sealed package is usually treated as parcel post by the postal sorters regardless of the amount of postage paid.

Airmail

The swiftest means of sending mail a distance of 200 miles or more is by air. It need not be used for shorter distances because first-class mail is usually delivered within 200 miles as quickly as airmail. Airmail is carried by air and the fastest connecting ground carrier; therefore, the rate is higher than for other domestic mail. It is given the quickest handling in both dispatch and delivery, but it is not given special delivery unless a special delivery fee has been paid in addition to the airmail postage. Stamped airmail envelopes with a red, white, and blue border design may be purchased at any post office. Plain envelopes and regular stamps may also be used for airmail. Should you use an ordinary envelope for airmail, be sure to print or type in capital letters the word *AIRMAIL* below the postage and above the address on the right side of the envelope or paste Airmail labels on the front and back of the envelope. Any matter that is acceptable in domestic surface mail may be sent by airmail with the exception of items that might possibly be damaged by changes in temperature or atmospheric pressure.

Mixed Classes of Mail

affixed:
attached

Sometimes it is better to send two pieces of mail of different classes together as a single mailing to be sure that they both arrive at the same time. A first-class letter may be attached to the outside of a large envelope or parcel of a different class of mail, or it may be enclosed in a large envelope or parcel. When a first-class letter is *attached*, the postage is **affixed** to each part separately. When a first-class letter is enclosed, its postage is added to the parcel postage and affixed on the outside of the package. The words *First-Class Mail Enclosed* must be written, typed, or stamped below the postage and above the address. A piece of mixed mail is handled and transported by the post office as mail matter of the class in which the bulky portion falls — not as first-class mail.

MAILING SUGGESTIONS FOR FAST DELIVERY

There are many ways to help the United States Postal Service move your mail fast. Here are four suggestions for hastening the processing and delivery of your outgoing mail:

1. *Mail early and often.* Mail earlier in the day *and often*, regularly at 11 a.m. and 4 p.m., for example, to avoid

getting your mail caught in the five o'clock rush. Most post offices receive about three-quarters of the day's mail in the late afternoon or early evening.

2. *Check collection times.* If you ordinarily mail from a building lobby or street mail box, check the "Hours of Collection" listed on the box. Collections are made only once a day at some street mail boxes. If you should miss the last daily collection and want your mail to move fast, take it directly to the nearest post office.

3. *Keep Local Metered Mail separate from Out-of-Town Metered Mail.* If you are using metered mail, use separate labels for *Local Metered Mail* and *Out-of-Town Metered Mail* to make certain that your metered mail skips one sorting operation as well as canceling and postmarking at the post office.

4. *Use ZIP Codes in both the mailing address and in the return address.* To assure speedy delivery of your mail, *always use ZIP Codes.* Make sure your addressing is clear, complete, and correct. Check to be sure that you have written the *correct street number* in the mailing address. Remember that all envelopes should carry your return address with your ZIP Code so that undeliverable mail can be returned to you.

INTERNATIONAL MAIL

Mail is now sent to all parts of the world, either by air or surface transportation, in ever-increasing volume. International mail is divided into two general categories — postal union mail and parcel post. Postal union mail is further divided into two groups — *LC* mail and *AO* mail. LC mail (letters and cards) consists of letters, letter packages, and postal cards. AO mail (articles, other) includes printed matter, samples of merchandise, matter for the blind, and small packets.

The postage for letters and postal cards mailed to Canada and Mexico is the same as that for the United States. To all other countries the rates are higher and the weights are limited. Overseas parcel post packages must be packed even more carefully than those for delivery within the continental United States. A *customs declaration* form must be attached to each parcel with an accurate and complete description of its contents.

SPECIAL POSTAL SERVICES

The United States Postal Service also provides many special services, such as those listed on page 160:

1. Special Delivery
2. Special Handling
3. Registered Mail
4. Certified Mail
5. Insured Mail
6. COD Service
7. Tracing Mail
8. Recalling Mail

Special Delivery

Special delivery provides the fastest handling and delivery service for any kind of mail. Special delivery mail is handled at the post office of destination with the same promptness given to first-class mail and, in addition, is given immediate delivery (within prescribed hours and distances). The fees charged are in addition to the regular postage. They vary according to the weight of the letter or parcel. The mail must be stamped or marked *Special Delivery*.

Special Handling

On payment of a fee in addition to the regular postage, a parcel labeled *Special Handling* will be given the same prompt handling and delivery service as is given to first-class mail. Special handling parcels are delivered the same way that parcel post is ordinarily delivered — on regularly scheduled trips, not special delivery. The fees are lower than special delivery fees. Special handling services may be used only with parcels sent as third- or fourth-class mail.

Registered Mail

Mail is registered to give protection to valuable and important mail. Money, checks, jewelry, stock certificates, and bonds are included in the valuable items frequently sent by registered mail. Important items include contracts, bills of sale, leases, mortgages, deeds, wills, and vital business records. Registration provides insurance, a receipt for the sender, and proof of delivery. Mail may be registered for insurance up to $10,000 if no other insurance is carried. If other insurance is carried, postal insurance liability is limited to a maximum of $1,000. All classes of mail may be registered provided the first-class or airmail rate is paid.

Before your mail will be accepted for registration, the post office requires that you
1. Seal it. Masked tape or transparent tape cannot be used to seal registered mail.
2. Have the complete names and addresses of *both* the sender and the addressee on the mail.
3. Declare the *full* value of the mail to the postal clerk.

You will be given a receipt showing that the post office has accepted the registered mail for transmittal and delivery. For an additional fee you may obtain a *return receipt* to prove that the registered mail has been delivered.

Certified Mail

If your mail has no value of its own (such as a letter, a bill, or an important notice) and yet you want proof of mailing and delivery, you may find it less expensive to send it by *Certified Mail*. It provides a receipt for the sender and a record of delivery. No insurance coverage is provided for certified mail.

Insured Mail

Third- or fourth-class mail, or airmail containing third- or fourth-class matter, may be insured for up to $200 against loss or damage. A receipt is issued for insured mail. It should be kept on file until the insured mail has arrived in satisfactory condition. If an insured parcel is lost or damaged, the post office will **reimburse** you for the value of the merchandise or the amount for which it was insured, whichever is the smaller.

reimburse:
to pay back

COD Service

Merchandise may be sent to a purchaser COD, that is, *collect on delivery*, if the shipment is based on an order by the buyer or on an agreement between sender and addressee. The seller may obtain COD service by paying a fee in addition to the regular postage. The maximum amount collectible on one package is $200. The total fee varies with the amount to be collected, the weight of the package, and the distance it is to travel.

Tracing Mail

If mail has not been delivered within a reasonable time, you may make a written request to have it traced. The post office will supply you with a form for tracing a piece of mail. Although the post office will co-operate in every possible way, it is almost impossible to trace unregistered, uninsured, or uncertified mail, especially if it does not carry a return address. Consequently, all mail should carry a complete return address and valuable or important mail should be registered, certified, or insured.

Recalling Mail

Once in a great while it may be necessary to recall a piece of mail you have already mailed. This will require prompt action on your part.

Go to the post office in your mailing zone to recall a letter mailed to a local address or to the central post office to recall a letter mailed out of town. Fill in Form 1509 (*Sender's Application for Withdrawal of Mail*) and the post office will have the piece of mail returned to you.

Outgoing mail, as you can see, may mean first-class mail, fourth-class mail, and even mixed mail. It may mean domestic, foreign, and special service mail. Your knowledge and understanding of postal services and effective mail handling can save your employer time and money and can increase the efficiency of his business. Anytime you are faced with an unusual problem involving mailing, call the postmaster or the superintendent of mails at your local post office. He or one of his assistants will furnish the latest official information.

REVIEWING WHAT YOU HAVE READ

1. Why would you use precanceled stamps and envelopes with outgoing mail?
2. What are the advantages of using metered mail?
3. How is payment made for postage used in a postage meter machine?
4. Why are ZIP Codes now used with all classes of mail?
5. What kind of mail must be sent at the first-class rate?
6. What is included in second-class mail?
7. What is the weight limit of third-class mail?
8. What is the other name for fourth-class mail? How does it differ from other classes of mail?
9. What are the differences between *Special Delivery* and *Special Handling?*
10. What is the maximum amount collectible on a single COD package?

MAKING DECISIONS

1. If your employer asked you to mail the following items for him, what mailing service would you use for each and why?
   (a) A stock certificate for fifty shares of American Telephone and Telegraph Company stock
   (b) An important lightweight package containing copies of a speech your employer will deliver at a convention
   (c) A package to the research department of your company containing a sample portion of a product on which a complaint has been filed
   (d) A business letter to be mailed a distance of 1,500 miles
   (e) A business letter to be mailed a distance of 175 miles, but one that should be delivered as quickly as possible
2. In a business office in which you are working (a) several letters are returned because of incorrect and incomplete addresses, and (b) others are delivered with insufficient postage for which the recipients must pay. What would you suggest to correct such occurrences?

WORKING WITH OTHERS

Just before closing time Mr. Arnold asked Mary Reynolds, the mail clerk in a small office, to remove an important letter from the regular mail and send it airmail, special delivery. In the rush to get the mail out before five o'clock, Mary forgot about the letter. It was metered and mailed first class.

Five days later Mr. Arnold commented to Mary when she stopped by his office to pick up his mail that he could not understand why he had not received a reply to the letter, since the requested information was very important and he should have received it within three or four days.

Should Mary explain that the letter was accidentally mailed at the first-class rate, or should she offer no explanation and hope for a reply in the next day's mail?

USING LANGUAGE A few of the more important comma usages follow:

1. To set off a nonrestrictive phrase or subordinate clause. (A phrase or clause is nonrestrictive if the main clause in the sentence expresses a complete thought when the nonrestrictive phrase or clause is omitted.)
2. To set off phrases or expressions at the beginning of a sentence when they are loosely connected with the rest of the sentence.
3. To set off parenthetical words, clauses, or phrases.
4. To set off words and phrases used in apposition.
5. To separate two or more adjectives if they both precede or follow the noun they modify, provided each adjective modifies the noun alone.

On a separate sheet of paper type the following sentences and insert commas where needed.

1. Mr. Holbrook who is now in Europe will send you a cable soon.
2. Generally speaking a telegram will receive more attention than a letter.
3. An ancient developmental typewriter was the only machine available.
4. Miss Elder my secretary should be here presently.
5. You may therefore draw this conclusion.

USING ARITHMETIC

1. It costs 11 cents an ounce to send an airmail letter in the United States. When Jerry weighed a three-page letter, the letter and envelope weighed two ounces. How much postage did Jerry put on the envelope?
2. Jerry took an envelope containing contracts to the post office and requested the postal clerk to send them by registered mail with a return receipt requested. The contracts were sent first-class mail at 8 cents an ounce. They weighed three ounces. The registration fee was 80 cents. For a return receipt showing to whom and when the contracts were delivered, there was an additional fee of 25 cents. How much did it cost to mail the contracts?
3. Jerry also took the samples for the Research Department with him to the post office. Since he sealed the package, he marked it Fourth Class. The parcel weighed less than two pounds. His chart showed that the parcel post fee was 75 cents. The insurance fee for $50 is shown in Part 1, page 148. What was the total postage charge to send the samples?

PERFORMING OFFICE TASKS

1. Using an 8½" x 11" sheet of paper and an ordinary No. 6 envelope, fold the paper as you would a letter and insert it in the envelope.
2. Using three sheets of 8½" x 11" paper and a large No. 10 envelope, fold the three sheets together and insert them in the envelope.
3. Using an 8½" x 11" sheet of paper and a large No. 10 window envelope fold the sheet and insert it in the envelope. (If you do not have a window envelope, fold the sheet as though it would be inserted in a window envelope.)

4. Address envelopes of either 6½" x 3⅝" (No. 6) or 9½" x 4⅛" (No. 10) for the following names and addresses. If envelopes are not available, type the addresses on slips of paper of approximately one of these sizes. You may assume that these names and addresses were taken from the classified directory of New York, N.Y.

Acme File Company, 30 Warren Street, 10007

Airport Duplicating Service, 510 East End Avenue, 10028

American Stationery Company, 59 East 44th Street, 10017

Apollo Supply Company, 139 Varick Street, 10013

Buckeye Printing Company, 30 West 59th Street, 10019

Chase Office Supply Company, 10 West 35th Street, 10001

City Systems, 59 Ann Street, 10038

Columbia Stationers, 199 East 14th Street, 10003

Cosmopolitan Supply Company, 410 West 24th Street, 10011

Dale Ribbons, 92 Park Avenue, 10016

Diamond Equipment Company, 210 East 27th Street, 10016

Duplicating Service, Inc., 10 Park Row, 10038

Embassy Manufacturing Company, 400 West 59th Street, 10019

Empire Filing Equipment, 192 Seventh Avenue, 10011

Equity Equipment, 310 West 46th Street, 10036

General Equipment Company, 92 Fourth Avenue, 10003

Globe Service Corporation, 10 East 39th Street, 10016

Guide Systems, Inc., 179 West 37th Street, 10018

Howard Stationery Company, 92 John Street, 10038

Hygrade Desk Company, 129 Fifth Avenue, 10003

PART 3 VOLUME MAIL

A few weeks before Bill Ryan graduated from high school he saw this advertisement in the daily newspaper.

MAIL CLERK

Applicants should have a high school diploma and Pennsylvania driver's license. Duties to consist of delivering company mail, filling literature requests, handling volume mail, and operation of various mailing equipment.

SIEHL CATALOG SALES COMPANY

459 Township Avenue
Pittsburgh, Pennsylvania
An Equal Opportunity
Employer

Bill was looking for a job that would permit him to be outdoors at times. Since the position sounded interesting and challenging, he answered the advertisement. After an interview with the personnel director and the supervisor of the mail department, Bill was hired and started working a few days after graduation.

Bill's job is challenging. He is learning to operate many kinds of machines used for mailing. He is learning the different kinds of mail that a large company sends. He is learning that he can save the company large sums of money just by using the correct postal service.

AIDS FOR VOLUME MAILING

There are many mailing aids that business firms use in advertising campaigns and in making announcements of new products and services.

Mailing Lists

Many firms keep lists of their customers, **prospective** customers, subscribers, clients, or others to whom they address mail repeatedly. A firm may use a number of mailing lists for different purposes — for instance, to advertise a new product, to announce a new service, or to **institute** a new policy. Special mailing lists of all kinds of prospective

prospective:
expected in the future

institute:
to establish or start

buyers, both nationwide and regional, can be purchased. One of your duties may be developing the mailing list and keeping it up to date.

Mailing Lists on File Cards

The names and addresses of a mailing list are frequently kept on 5″ x 3″ cards that are filed in alphabetic order. These cards may be grouped under various classifications, such as doctors, druggists, jewelers, and stationers. The different groupings may be indicated by colored tabs, or the cards for each group may be filed in separate drawers or compartments in the card file.

The cards may also be filed by subject — the subject that the prospective customer has been interested in or may be interested in later.

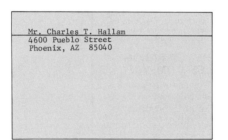

```
Mr. Charles T. Hallam
4600 Pueblo Street
Phoenix, AZ  85040
```

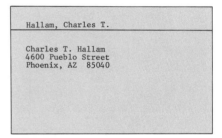

```
Hallam, Charles T.


Charles T. Hallam
4600 Pueblo Street
Phoenix, AZ  85040
```

Up-to-Date Mailing Lists

Unless mailing lists are kept up to date, they soon lose much of their usefulness. The names on all mailing lists are constantly changing as newcomers move into the sales area and others move out. Additions, deletions, and corrections of names and addresses should be made whenever the information is received. You learn of many of the necessary changes in addresses when mail is returned because of nondelivery.

The post office will assist you in maintaining an up-to-date mailing list. It will make corrections on a mailing list or correct individual addresses if requested to do so. For a small fee it will also supply the ZIP Codes for an entire mailing list.

Chain Feeding of Envelopes for a Mailing List

The names and addresses on a mailing list are usually typed on the envelopes if the list is used infrequently. A chain feeding method of inserting and addressing the envelopes will save a great deal of time in typing from the list. The four steps in the widely used front-feed method follow:

1. Stack the envelopes *face down*, with the flaps toward you, at the side of the typewriter.

2. Address the first envelope; then roll it back (toward you) until a half inch shows above the alignment scale.

3. Insert the next envelope from the front, placing it between the first envelope and the cylinder.

4. Turn the cylinder back to remove the first envelope and to position the second one. Continue the "chain" by feeding all envelopes from the front of the cylinder.

5. The envelopes will stack themselves in order at the back of the cylinder. Remove them after about every sixth envelope is typed.

Illus. 5-14
The front-feed method of chain feeding of envelopes

IBM Corporation

Addressing Machines and Addressing Services

You may use an addressing service or, if your office has it, an addressing machine in addressing a large number of envelopes. Because mailing lists are used over and over again, the names and addresses are often stenciled or embossed so that the envelopes can be automatically addressed on an addressing machine. Two widely used styles of addressing machines are the Addressograph, which prints from a metal plate; and the Elliott, which prints from a stencil plate. Also, some businesses are now using their computers for addressing large numbers of envelopes.

The Addressograph. The Addressograph is often used for addressing envelopes and cards for permanent mailing lists. It may also be used to print the inside addresses on letters or to print names, addresses, numbers, and other identifying information on bank statements, monthly bills, time cards, paychecks, dividend checks, and other business forms. The plates can be coded so that an automatic selecting device can be used as the letters are addressed. Classification tabs can be attached to the address plates of a particular mailing list, and the automatic selector will then select and print only these plates without changing the order of any of the plates in the file.

Elliott Addressing Machine. The stencil address plates used in the Elliott addressing machine can be prepared on a typewriter. When a small attachment is used, the small stencil plates are typed in much the same manner as ordinary stencils. The stencil addressing equipment is not often used to print inside addresses on letters or other material that should give the appearance of being completely typed. The plates are, however, often used for mailing lists with frequently changing addresses.

Illus. 5-15
The metal plate addresser-printer has many uses in volume mailing.

Pitney Bowes

Computer Addressing. Some large firms use their computers for addressing envelopes and cards. The computer can print the addresses directly on the cards and envelopes, or it can print address labels which have an adhesive backing. When adhesive-backed labels are printed, they are then attached to the front of the envelopes.

PRESORTING VOLUME MAIL

You will get faster delivery of a large volume of important mail if you presort and separate it by the five-digit ZIP Code areas. For ease in handling, mail should be presorted three times:

1. From 0 to 9 according to the first digit of the ZIP Code to route each piece of mail into one of the ten large geographic areas of the country
2. According to the second and third digits to route the mail into a large post office or designated sectional center within the geographic area
3. According to the fourth and fifth digits which represent the delivery area or the post office of delivery

For example, a letter with the ZIP Code 60635 following the mailing address would be routed into the Midwest by *6*, the first digit in the ZIP Code; into Chicago by *06*, the second and third digits; and into a local post office in Chicago for delivery by *35*, the fourth and fifth digits in the ZIP Code.

Mail separated by five-digit ZIP Code areas bypasses all state and sectional center sorting operations, and arrives at the delivery area or post office of delivery ready for sorting into the carriers' mail routes.

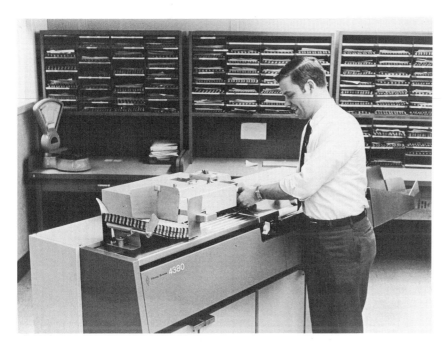

Illus. 5-16
Postage meter machine for heavy volume mail. This machine feeds, seals, meter stamps, counts, and stacks 200 envelopes a minute.

Pitney Bowes

TRAYING VOLUME MAIL

You can speed the processing of a large volume of first-class mail through the postal system by switching to trays, modern mail containers recommended by the Postal Service. The trays will be provided by the

Postal Service and picked up at your place of business at no additional cost. However, your mail must be placed in the trays with the addresses and postage faced in one direction. Traying saves valuable processing time and permits the Postal Service to dispatch your mail sooner.

For assistance with presorting or traying volume mail call your local post office and ask for either your postmaster or the customer service representative.

REVIEWING WHAT YOU HAVE READ

1. What is the purpose of keeping a mailing list?
2. What steps can you take to keep your mailing lists current and correct?
3. What is the major difference between the Addressograph and the Elliott addressing machine?
4. What are two advantages of presorting volume mail by five-digit ZIP Code areas?
5. What is meant by *traying volume mail*?

MAKING DECISIONS

1. Suppose that the firm for which you work is considering using a postage meter machine instead of ordinary postage stamps for its outgoing mail. What do you think are the advantages that might come from the use of such a machine? the disadvantages?
2. Postal authorities report that millions of letters and parcels become part of undeliverable *dead letter mail* every year. What can you suggest to avoid having some of your volume mail become dead letter mail?

WORKING WITH OTHERS

You are employed as a mail clerk for a nationwide mail order company and prepare many packages for mailing. Your supervisor has instructed you to address only one side of the package, since in the past few months many packages have been returned for lack of postage caused by postal clerks glancing hastily at the wrong side of the package and concluding that the package did not have postage. The secretary to the supervisor of the order department has on several occasions brought rush packages to you and asked you to weigh them and mail them. In doing so, you have noticed that she has placed address labels on both sides of the package. How would you solve this problem?

USING LANGUAGE

1. The following terms were taken from Unit 5, Parts 1, 2, and 3. Write the meaning of each term. Consult the text or a standard dictionary if you are not sure of the definition.

    (a) computer addressing
    (b) domestic mail
    (c) LC and AO international mail
    (d) mailing lists
    (e) mixed mail
    (f) postal cards
    (g) precanceled stamps
    (h) return receipt
    (i) tracing mail

2. Type the correct spelling of each of the following words used in mailing:

(a) accurate   or acurate
(b) applicable   or applicible
(c) bulky   or bulkey
(d) catagories   or categories
(e) cataloges   or catalogs
(f) certified   or certefied
(g) circulers   or circulars
(h) exceding   or exceeding
(i) mailible   or mailable
(j) prescribed   or perscribed
(k) receipt   or reciept
(l) transmited   or transmitted
(m) underlinning   or underlining

USING ARITHMETIC

1. You have received a statement from your local post office for $7.50 for placing ZIP Codes on a volume mailing list. If the post office charges $1.50 a thousand names for this service, how many thousand ZIP Codes were furnished?

2. You have just completed preparing 250,000 catalogs for mailing at the third-class rate of 1.6 cents for each catalog. How much postage is required for this mailing?

3. You have been assigned the preparation of 300,000 labels for a special sales promotion program. The machine you will use to prepare this mailing will print 1,000 labels a minute. How many hours will it take to complete this job?

PERFORMING OFFICE TASKS

1. Your employer, Mr. John Randolph, General Manager of Randolph Office Equipment and Supply Company, has instructed you to order the latest edition of the Postal Service Manual. Inasmuch as you do not have an order form for this purpose, you will write a letter. If necessary, check with the library or the post office to determine the amount of the remittance that should accompany the order.

Randolph Office Equipment and Supply Company letters are written in modified block form (no paragraph indentations) with mixed punctuation.

2. Fifty envelopes must be addressed for mailing of statements on the first of the month. On a separate sheet of paper describe how you would chain feed these envelopes into your typewriter in order to complete this job as quickly and accurately as possible.

4 AIR AND SURFACE SHIPPING

Jim O'Neill is employed in the order department of a nation-wide mail-order house. Since all the orders are received by mail or from the company's distribution outlets in large cities, Jim must have an above average knowledge of the various shipping methods. Although the actual packaging of the orders is done in the shipping department, Jim has schedules and rates for different ways of shipping at his fingertips. This is necessary for two reasons — first, the customer must pay shipping charges on all orders; therefore, the least expensive method is used. Secondly, if an order is to be rushed — as is often the case at Christmas time — packages must be shipped the fastest way possible, but with shipping cost kept in mind. Jim is not alone in being aware of shipping costs. Every business must be very aware of this factor, since, in most cases, shipping costs are included in the price of the product; and every company wants to keep its prices as low as possible to meet competition.

"What's the best way to send that package?" your employer may ask. It may be just a small parcel urgently needed by a customer, or it may be a large package of advertising materials. Your employer may consider the speed of delivery to be of much more importance than the cost. Whatever the case may be, if your job involves mailing and packaging, you must be familiar with the various ground and air shipping services.

Every business firm uses a number of different shipping services to deliver parcels and to distribute large commodities. As an alert and intelligent employee, you should be familiar with the advantages of each service. You may be required to decide how small parcels should be sent. You may be called upon to prepare the necessary forms for express and freight shipments for which trains, planes, trucks, and buses are used. Occasionally you may be asked to prepare the forms for tracing a shipment or for filing a claim for goods damaged in transit.

RECENT DEVELOPMENTS IN SHIPPING

With the great increase in volume, the shipping of goods in the United States and Canada has undergone many rapid changes in the past few years. Trucks have replaced trains for a great deal of shipping across the nation, and shipping by air is becoming widespread.

Recent developments in packaging have also aided the shipping process. Lightweight, theft-proof containers are being used in place of heavy wooden crates. In addition, shipping terminals and airports have been equipped with automatic equipment which uses high speed conveyer belts to handle packages of all sizes. Railroad terminal yards have been equipped with automatic switching equipment and closed-circuit TV to save time and shipping costs.

METHODS OF SHIPPING

Goods may be shipped to various points by railway, truck, bus, planes, or by a combination of two or more of these services. Each of these services has its own advantages: some offer faster delivery; some offer a higher degree of safety; some are less expensive; and some are much more convenient for the shipper, for the receiver, or for both. The values of each of these services should be known to the shipper so that he may select the best and the most suitable shipping service.

Shipping Guides

Where can you look for the information you and your employer need about shipping? Various guidebooks are printed to assist you in selecting the method of shipment that is best for each shipment. There are several guides which are widely used in business offices and which you will find very helpful.

The United States Postal Service Manual gives complete information about all classes of mail.

The Express and Parcel Post Comparative Rate Guide gives a complete list of all express stations and the comparative charges between express and parcel post shipments.

Leonard's Guide gives rates and routings for freight, express, and parcel post.

Parcel Post

Also called fourth-class mail, parcel post is a method of transporting goods that is used most often when small items are to be shipped to widely scattered places. Some details of parcel post service are discussed in connection with the classes of mail in Unit 5, Part 2. Parcel post shipments are handled by the United States Postal Service. The cost of sending a package parcel post depends on the weight of the package and the distance it is to travel.

Air Parcel Post

When speed is important in the delivery of a package, you will probably send the parcel by air. The delivery time can be greatly reduced by using air parcel post. The rates are higher than for ordinary parcel post. Increasingly, air parcel post is being used to carry merchandise to distant and isolated places. This is especially true for Hawaii and Alaska and other areas where surface travel is slow.

REA Express

A telephone call to the nearest REA Express office will bring an express truck to your door to pick up packages of all kinds and sizes. This is a very fast and convenient way to ship packages. Delivery is usually made directly to the home or office of the addressee. The cost of shipping depends upon the weight of the shipment and the distance it has to travel.

Illus. 5-17
Signing receipts for delivery of packages is usually a clerical responsibility.

REA Express

Air Express

You will find air express the swiftest method of commercial transportation. This service includes shipping by air to all parts of the United

States and to most foreign countries. Air express shipments receive special pick-up and delivery service. Almost all types of goods, including machine parts, **perishable** foods, printed materials, and flowers, are moved by air express. Small packages or shipments may be placed on regular passenger planes. Large or bulky shipments are usually sent by special air freight cargo planes.

perishable:
may become ruined
or destroyed

Bus Express

Most bus lines throughout the country offer package express service. This is a particularly useful service when **destination** points are located where there is no airport and when speed of delivery is important. Many points receive same day delivery — many within a few hours — which may be even faster than air service. Frequent and direct bus trips between the cities and the fact that terminals are usually located in business districts account for the speed of handling and delivery.

destination:
the place to which
something is sent

Illus. 5-18
Business depends upon the services of specialized carriers of small packages.

United Parcel Service

United Parcel Service

United Parcel Service is the nation's leading carrier of small packages weighing up to 50 pounds. It rates are **competitive** with parcel

competitive:
compare favorably
with

post. In addition, each package is insured for up to $100. The service is provided over most of the nation. It offers shippers other features, which are not available with parcel post, including pickup of packages at the shipper's place of business.

Truck Transportation

Another shipping service which your employer may use is truck transportation. The truck is the best type of local transportation available. Arrangements can easily be made with a trucking company to make regular calls at your place of business to pick up and deliver goods. Truck transportation is also available for long-distance hauls. Some long-distance truck firms offer overnight service to insure the prompt delivery of goods.

Railway Freight Service

For shipping bulky articles and goods for which the speed of delivery is not important, railway freight service is often used. The cost of shipping by rail is lower than the cost of shipping by truck or any other method.

Illus. 5-19
Railway freight is often used when speed of delivery is not important.

Union Pacific Railroad

MARKING GOODS FOR SHIPMENT

Whether goods are shipped by freight, express, parcel post, or some other way, it is important to the prompt movement and proper delivery of shipments that the goods be marked correctly. The rules of the carriers require that the shipper mark each package plainly, legibly, and durably. In marking shipments, the following rules should be observed in order to insure the proper delivery of packages:

1. The addressee's name and address must be shown.

2. The word *From* should **precede** the name and address of the shipper. This explanation is of great assistance to both the shipper and the carrier if the shipment gets lost, is unclaimed, or is refused by the addressee.

3. Packages containing articles easily broken should be marked *Fragile* or *Handle with Care*. Packages containing merchandise that is perishable, such as fruit, should be marked *Perishable*.

4. Marking should be done with a brush, stencil, crayon, or rubber stamp. If lettered by hand, a good clear style of lettering should be used. Labels should be prepared on a typewriter and fastened securely to the packages.

precede:
to go ahead or in front of

Illus. 5-20
Proper packaging is important if merchandise is to withstand rough handling in shipping and storage and reach its destination undamaged.

Administrative Management Society

PACKAGING

Goods for shipment must be packaged properly if they are to be delivered without damage. It is the responsibility of the shipper to properly package the item for shipment. The item to be shipped, the method of transportation to be used, and the distance to be traveled will be the determining factors in packaging. The decision on a damage claim is often decided on the basis of how well the goods have been packaged.

TRACING

modes:
styles, kinds, or
methods

It may be necessary to trace a shipment if the goods are not delivered within a reasonable time. All carriers in all **modes** of transportation provide tracing services. Information required to trace a shipment is:

1. Shipper's name and address
2. Name and address of the person to whom the goods were shipped
3. Shipping date
4. Quantity of packages involved
5. Shipping receipt
6. Routing used

CLAIM FOR LOSS

You submit a claim to the transportation company for a total or partial loss if the shipment is not delivered, if it is totally or partially destroyed, or if it is delivered in a damaged condition. Claims for loss are presented by either the shipper or the addressee, depending upon who owns the goods.

REVIEWING WHAT YOU HAVE READ

1. What are some of the more recent developments in shipping services?
2. What shipping guides are commonly used in business offices?
3. What are the advantages of air express?
4. What are some of the advantages of United Parcel Service?
5. What are some of the rules you should follow in marking goods for shipment?

MAKING DECISIONS

1. How will you ship a small parcel to a customer in a large city 1,500 miles away if the parcel is needed quickly?
2. How will you ship a small carton of merchandise to a customer in a suburb ten miles away if the merchandise is needed within the next few days?
3. How will you ship a package to a customer in a town along a major highway about 200 miles away if the town has no airfield and is 50 miles from the nearest railroad station?
4. When would you recommend that a shipment of merchandise be made by air rather than railroad?
5. When would you recommend that a parcel be shipped by air parcel post instead of by ordinary parcel post?

Mr. Howard C. Patton, an executive of a large brokerage firm in New York City, instructed Jeanette Wilson, a new clerical worker in the office, to photocopy the entire file folder of a client with a large account. The client had moved to Hawaii; so Jeanette was also told to wrap the photocopies and mail them by air parcel post to the manager of the firm's branch in Honolulu.

Two weeks later Mr. Patton received a telephone call from the manager of the Honolulu branch. He said that the records had not been received. However, much to his embarrassment, the client had already called but he could not suggest investments because he had no record of the customer's holdings.

Mr. Patton then learned that Jeanette had delayed mailing the photocopies because she said that she did not have the time to wrap them. Furthermore, she felt that it was not her job to wrap and mail packages. She believed this to be the function of the mail department. When she finally had them ready, she mailed them by ordinary parcel post.

What do you think of Jeanette's attitude with regard to wrapping and mailing of packages? What was wrong with shipping the records by ordinary parcel post? If you were in Mr. Patton's place, what would you do?

Adjectives are used to indicate an increasing or decreasing degree of quality· quantity, or manner. The three degrees of comparison are positive, comparative, and superlative.

Example: *Positive*	*Comparative*	*Superlative*
light	lighter	lightest
useful	more (less) useful	most (least) useful

On a separate sheet of paper list the adjectives in the sentences below and indicate which degree of comparison is used.

1. The clerk called the trucking firm and asked that a small pick-up truck stop at the office to pick up the package.
2. Of all the merchants on Fifth Avenue, Mr. Clay had the prettiest window display.
3. The dispatcher's list contained three bulky pickups which the small pick-up truck could not hold.
4. The package was wrapped less securely than it should have been.
5. The typewriter, the books, the calculator, the stove, and the produce had to be crated carefully before shipment to either a close or far destination.
6. A larger box could not be found.
7. The driver spoke most softly even though the anger showed on his face.
8. Of the two order clerks, she wrote the more legibly.
9. Companies demand prompt movement and proper delivery of their shipments.
10. The building contained much ventilation, more light, and the most space of any of the warehouses they examined.

1. A firm ships 250,000 packages a year as follows:
   25 percent are shipped by air express.
   30 percent are shipped by truck.
   30 percent are shipped by railway freight.
   The remainder are shipped by parcel post.

How many packages are shipped by each method? On a separate sheet of paper compute your answers.

2. You have the following packages to be sent parcel post:
Three 2-pound packages at 75 cents, 80 cents, and $1.05 each. (The cost differs because each is going to a different destination.)
Four 1-pound packages at 60 cents each
One 7-pound package at 75 cents
Three 10-pound packages at $1.20 each
What is the total postage charge for these packages?

PERFORMING OFFICE TASKS

1. Make a study of the following shipping services available in your community and be prepared to report your findings orally to the class and in writing to your teacher:
   (a) REA Express Service
   (b) Bus Express
   (c) United Parcel Service
   (d) Truck Service
   (e) Railway Freight Service

2. What transportation service would you suggest for shipping the following from your local community:
   (a) A standard manual typewriter to a college you are entering 100 miles away
   (b) The 24 volumes of the *Encyclopaedia Britannica* to a relative 500 miles away
   (c) An electronic desk calculator weighing 30 pounds to a branch office 50 miles away
   (d) An electric stove weighing 300 pounds to your employer's home 10 miles out of town
   (e) Twenty cases of produce to a market 70 miles away

UNIT 6

BUSINESS FILING

GENERAL OFFICE WORK

for small trucking firm. Typi
me bookkeeping. Able to s
and maintain filing syste
-day week. Good frir
its. Send resume to B
quirer.

PART 1 RECORDS CONTROL

"Carol, get me the files on the Jenkins contract. Mr. Jenkins is on the phone with a question." Mr. Ashburn knows that Carol will find the contract and bring it to him within minutes. In addition to her other fine qualities, Carol understands the importance of being able to file business papers properly and of *finding* them quickly when they are needed.

Compare Carol with the girl who thought to herself: Where is it? I know I put that letter away carefully so that I could find it quickly — but where? These were the thoughts that raced through the mind of a file clerk as she searched nervously for the letter for which her boss was impatiently waiting. *If only she had filed it correctly in the first place!* Don't let this happen to you!

Illus. 6-1
File it correctly so that it can be found quickly!

Remington Rand

In our high-speed "computer age" it might surprise you to learn that paper work must accompany every business action. Even a telephone call may require papers to place an order, report on a shipment, or make a payment. The information contained in these papers forms the basis for a variety of decisions and moves the business forward.

All the records which you will file will be important to the continued successful operation of your firm. The records become part of the *memory* of the organization. Not only do the records provide a history of the business, but they also provide a basis for future decisions. In today's business offices, important decisions are based upon available up-to-date information. The risks are too great for management's decisions to be based upon guesses or hunches.

The proper care of records is also important to every family. Everyone has records to keep — insurance policies, appliance guarantees, bills, receipts, apartment leases. Those who do not keep these personal records in order soon see their insurance policies **lapse** because the premiums have not been paid; service cannot be obtained when an appliance breaks down because the guarantee cannot be found; bills become overdue; or an item is charged for twice because the receipt from the first payment cannot be found.

lapse:
run out, expire, or end.

RECORDS CONTROL

Every important record, whether it belongs to the nation's largest business or to its smallest, must be stored where it can be found when needed. The regular way in which a business keeps track of its records and correspondence is called *records control*. Since business information is created and spread about in so many different ways, a records control program plays an important role in providing the "business intelligence" of any firm for which you may work.

Four main areas with which records control is concerned are:

1. *Files Management* — Developing effective information (or filing) systems, deciding upon the particular type of equipment and supplies needed for each of the systems, and controlling and improving the different systems.

2. *Information Retrieval* — Developing effective and rapid methods of retrieving, or finding, filed information.

3. *Records Protection* — Deciding what the vital records of a firm are and developing a program for protecting them. (*Vital* records are the important papers of a business that are needed to continue operating after a fire or some other disaster.)

4. *Records Retention and Disposition* — Determining which records should be kept, where they should be kept and for how long; deciding when and how outdated records should be destroyed.

FILES KEPT BY THE OFFICE WORKER

As an office worker, you may be responsible for keeping your employer's business records in an orderly fashion. You may be expected to decide which material should be filed, where it should be filed, and how it should be filed. A great deal of mail that is addressed to your employer (advertisements, announcements, and other third-class mail) need not be filed at all. When you are first employed, a brief discussion of the files with your employer should prove helpful in deciding which material should be thrown away and how the material to be filed should be classified. Most large firms have a records retention schedule which can help you classify materials as to their importance. In addition to the regular business files of your office, your employer may ask you to keep a separate file of his personal correspondence which may include records of his civic and professional activities.

CENTRAL FILES

economical: operating with little waste; saving

Many firms find it **economical** to maintain a central file of all materials that may be needed by different departments or by the entire organization. It is also possible that a large department within an organization, such as the purchasing department, may centralize its own files.

Because the file clerks in a central file department are well-trained specialists and are properly supervised, faster and better filing service is provided. A central file department eliminates the keeping of duplicate copies of material and makes for more efficient use of filing equipment and filing floor space. The central file department should always serve as an active information file — not just as a place for filing old and unneeded records. It is the file clerk's responsibility to know where and how to file records correctly and how to retrieve them instantly when requested.

FILING

What is filing? *Filing* is a system of arranging and storing business papers in a neat, orderly, and efficient manner so that they can be located easily and quickly when they are wanted.

neglected: given little attention; left undone

Filing is one of the *most important* — yet one of the most **neglected** — duties in many offices. Errors in filing may be funny in cartoons, but they are costly and embarrassing in a business office.

In order to *find* material efficiently, you must follow standard rules and procedures for filing. Not only must you know the rules of filing and apply them but you must also keep your files up to date by giving some part of every day to filing. Otherwise you may get so far behind that you will have to search through the files and then the unfiled material on your desk when you are asked to produce information.

SYSTEMS OF FILING

The most important reason for having a filing system is so that you can locate information quickly. Filing systems should be developed based upon the way records are called for, or the way they are used.

Alphabetic Name Files

Since most business records are referred to by the name of a firm, these names determine the type of filing system that will be used. This system of filing, known as an *alphabetic file*, is the most widely used in business. When you look for a firm name in a telephone directory, you are using this system.

Illus. 6-2
Alphabetic
name file

The Globe-Wernicke Systems Co.

Alphabetic Subject Files

Another filing system found in most business offices is an *alphabetic subject file*. The Yellow Pages of a telephone directory are arranged in alphabetic subject file order. Under the letter *E* in the Yellow Pages you will find such subject headings as Employment Agencies, Employment Contractors — Temporary Help, Employment Counselors, and Employment Service. Most offices have both an alphabetic company name file and also a subject file.

Geographic Files

To find the names of customers and prospective customers in the parts of the country in which they are located, some offices maintain geographic files. A geographic file may be set up according to the name of a state and then be further subdivided by the sales territories within the state, or by cities, towns, or counties. Sales offices and magazine publishers are two users of geographic filing systems.

Numeric Files

Since some business papers are identified by number rather than by name, numeric files are frequently used. Life insurance companies file their policies by the policy number. However, in addition to the main numeric file, an alphabetic file by the names of all policyholders (listing their policy numbers as well) is also kept on cards or on computer tape for fast retrieval.

Chronological Files

Another basic filing system is the chronological file, a file maintained in the order of time according to the year, month, and day. For example, an automobile insurance company would keep a chronological file showing the exact day of the year on which each automobile owner's insurance policy **expires**. This helps the company prepare and mail a new policy to each owner before his current automobile insurance expires.

expires:
comes to an end

A desk calendar is one form of chronological filing. Other chronological files of unfinished, pending, or follow-up work may be kept in a *tickler file*, a file arranged according to the days of the month. Since it is almost impossible to remember everything that must be done on a given business day, a chronological file should be developed and checked daily so that proper action may be taken at the right time.

THE CARE OF RECORDS

For business purposes, records are classified in four general groups: vital, important, useful, and nonessential. All records considered essential to the operation and growth of an organization, such as the financial statements, legal papers, and tax records, are classified as *vital records*. At least 43 percent of the business firms that lose their vital records in a fire, flood, or tornado are forced to go out of business. These records should be protected by microfilming them and storing the microfilm in a fireproof cabinet, or by photocopying them and filing the copies in another location.

Now let us consider the next two classifications: important and useful records. *Important records* are those which could be replaced, such as personnel records, but only at great expense. These records should also receive a degree of protection because of their confidential nature. *Useful records*, such as the records of accounts payable, are those which can be replaced — but with some delay and inconvenience. They should be kept in regular file cabinets.

Finally, we must be concerned with nonessential records. *Nonessential records*, such as press releases, are those which soon outlive their usefulness — perhaps some of them should never have been filed in the first place. They should be destroyed to save valuable file space and floor space. Records management experts estimate that over 40 percent of the material in active office files is nonessential and can be safely destroyed in short order — or immediately — without any embarrassment or inconvenience to anyone.

Illus. 6-3
The proper care of records is necessary. These records survived a scorching fire because of careful storage in fireproof files.

Shaw-Walker

RECORDS CONTROL IN THE OFFICE

Much of your time will be spent on records control. When you are typing a letter, you are preparing a record (the carbon copy) for the files. When you are reading and deciding what to do with incoming mail, you are preparing materials for filing. The result of almost *all* your office duties will be placed in the files.

To be valuable in any office you should thoroughly understand business filing and records control procedures. These procedures and the supplies and equipment with which you will be working are covered in the parts that follow.

REVIEWING WHAT YOU HAVE READ

1. Why do business firms keep records?
2. Name and describe four main areas of records control and management.
3. Define the term *filing*.
4. Name five systems of filing.
5. Give an example of a *vital* record. An *important* record. A *useful* record.

MAKING DECISIONS

1. What problems could a business have if it did not have an orderly way of storing and finding important business papers?
2. If you work in a business that has a central file department with filing specialists to take care of the records of the business, why will it still be necessary for you to have a knowledge of filing and records control?
3. What is the most important factor to consider in setting up a filing system?
4. How do you decide if a business paper is a useful or a nonessential record? How is each handled in filing?

WORKING WITH OTHERS

Sheila Baker, a recent high school graduate, accepted her first full-time position as a clerk-typist in the purchasing department of a very large company. During her first two weeks of work, the woman supervisor of the department acquainted her with the department's operations. The supervisor also explained the tasks and duties for which Sheila alone would be responsible.

After introducing Sheila to her co-workers and giving her an overview of the purchasing department and what it does, Mrs. Williams, the supervisor, explained to Sheila the filing system used in the department. Sheila was then given several correspondence files to read and prepare for filing. While having lunch with several of the girls in the department, Sheila commented that she didn't know if she would stay on this job or not. "After all," she said, "I accepted this position to be a clerk-typist, not a file clerk."

Is Sheila correct in having doubts about her new position? Could the supervisor have chosen another way of teaching Sheila the basics of her job? How can reading correspondence and preparing it for filing help a new employee?

USING
LANGUAGE On a sheet of paper list the words in Column 1. Then write the number of the definition for each word from Column 2.

Example:

| (a) retrieval | (3) act or process of recovering or finding |

Column 1

(a) retrieval
(b) manually
(c) retention
(d) disposition
(e) chronological
(f) essential
(g) inconvenient
(h) document
(i) capacity
(j) client
(k) embarrassment

Column 2

(1) not suitable, unfit
(2) confusion or distress of thought, speech, or action
(3) act or process of recovering or finding
(4) act of ordering or arranging in an orderly way
(5) relating to or involving the hands
(6) a maximum measure of content or output
(7) arranged by date or by order of occurrence
(8) official paper; writing conveying information
(9) a person who engages the professional services of another
(10) act of keeping in possession or use
(11) belonging to the nature of things

USING
ARITHMETIC

1. Betty's supervisor asked her what materials she had ready for the files. When Betty checked her desk, she found four stacks of various files. One contained 25 contracts; the second contained 10 letters; the third consisted of 4 case histories; and the fourth was a miscellaneous stack of 7 different items. How many files did Betty have to take care of before she would be ready for another assignment?

2. Five file clerks handle all the requests for file records in a large insurance company. Two of the clerks are new and are able to retrieve and file 15 percent of all requests (each girl handles 15 percent). One experienced file clerk is able to take care of 30 percent of the files. The remaining two file clerks each take care of 20 percent of the files. If 2,500 requests are received each day, how many files does each girl retrieve and file each day?

PERFORMING
OFFICE
TASKS

You have just accepted a position with the City Haul Trucking Company, Inc., 105 Grand Boulevard, South St. Louis, Missouri 63103, which just began operations a month ago. This company picks up local parcels — small and medium sized — for delivery to large interstate trucking companies. Since St. Louis is a connecting point between the eastern and western sections of the country, it will be necessary to have a filing system which incorporates many features. Files will have to be set up for accounts payable and accounts receivable, purchases, receipts, costs of truck maintenance, payroll, personnel, correspondence, records of daily pickups and daily deliveries, and claim files for lost or damaged parcels.

Consult the Yellow Pages of your local telephone directory under Filing Equipment, Systems & Supplies, and then compose and type letters to be sent to at least two companies explaining your problem, requesting information, literature, and the assistance of one of their representatives.

PART 2

ALPHABETIC FILING RULES FOR NAMES OF INDIVIDUALS

When Diane Grollman was hired as a file clerk in the office of Mr. Walter Stalder, the sales manager, she was surprised to be told that one error in filing could cost as much as $92. Diane quickly realized that if she was going to be valuable to Mr. Stalder she would have to recall and use all the filing rules that she had learned in school. Diane's care in filing and her knowledge of proper procedures have made it possible for her to work without having misfiled one item in over two years.

A filing system is costly to set up and maintain. Therefore, if the system you use is to be worth this high cost, the information in it must be available when it is needed. This means that business correspondence and other filed materials must be arranged in an exact and established order.

FILING RULES

Every filing method makes use of filing rules. Only if you know the standard rules for filing, and apply them the same way every time, can you find the filed materials quickly when they are needed.

The most widely used method of filing is based on the alphabet; however, because of difficulties involved in indexing some materials or because of the great volume of materials filed, other filing methods have been developed. These are numeric, geographic, and subject filing.

procedures:
particular ways of doing something

In certain cases, where more specialized filing **procedures** are used, you will need on-the-job training to fully understand these methods. By following one set of filing rules and recognizing the importance of records control, you will be of great assistance to your employer and play an important role in the successful operation of your office. Since every business, regardless of its size, uses one or more alphabetic filing method, it is important that you learn the rules for alphabetic filing.

ALPHABETIC INDEXING FOR INDIVIDUALS

One of the first steps in filing procedures is *indexing*. When you arrange names for filing purposes, you are indexing. The rules for alphabetic indexing begin at the top of page 191.

1. Personal Names

When you consider the name Walter B. Anderson, each word and each initial or abbreviation is a separate *indexing unit*. Thus, you have three indexing units. The units of an individual's name are considered in

```
┌──────────────────────────────────┐
│ Anderson, Walter B.     72        │
├──────────────────────────────────┤
│ Walter B. Anderson                │
│ 575 Crane Road                    │
│ Middletown, NY 10940              │
└──────────────────────────────────┘
```

this order: (a) last name, or surname; (b) first name, initial, or abbreviation; (c) middle name, initial, or abbreviation. Therefore *Anderson* is the first indexing unit, *Walter* is the second, and *B.* is the third. (In the examples, the names are in alphabetic order.)

INDEX ORDER OF UNITS

Names	Unit 1	Unit 2	Unit 3
Walter B. Anderson	Anderson	Walter	B.
Henry David Brown	Brown	Henry	David
Edward J. Cox	Cox	Edward	J.
A. B. Davis	Davis	A.	B.

2. Surnames (Last Names)

When the last names of individuals are different, the alphabetic order is determined by the last names alone. *The letter that determines the order of any two names is the first letter that is different in the two names.* In the following lists the underlined letter in each last name determines the alphabetic order of that name when compared with the preceding name. Note that when one last name is the same as the first part of a longer last name, the shorter name goes before the longer. This is often called the *nothing before something* rule of filing order.

Last Names	Last Names	Last Names
Hall	Hoffman	Johns
Hill	Hoffmann	Johnston
Hull	Hofmann	Johnstone

3. Last Names Containing Prefixes

A last name containing a prefix is considered as one indexing unit. The common prefixes include *D'*, *De*, *Del*, *du*, *Fitz*, *La*, *Mac*, *Mc*, *O'*, *Van*, *Von*, and *Von der*. Spacing between the prefix and the rest of the last name, or capitalization of the prefix makes no difference when indexing. Note that the prefixes *Mac* and *Mc* do not go before other names beginning with the letter *M* but are placed in strict alphabetic order.

INDEX ORDER OF UNITS

Names	Unit 1	Unit 2	Unit 3
Frances C. D'Arcy	D'Arcy	Frances	C.
Mario L. Del Favero	Del Favero	Mario	L.
Robert J. du Pont	du Pont	Robert	J.
Malcolm Paul MacDonald	MacDonald	Malcolm	Paul
James J. Manning	Manning	James	J.
Helen C. McConnell	McConnell	Helen	C.
Charles H. Mead	Mead	Charles	H.
Mary M. O'Shea	O'Shea	Mary	M.
Henry T. Van Allan	Van Allan	Henry	T.
Carol A. Van Derbeck	Van Derbeck	Carol	A.
Elsie D. von Koch	von Koch	Elsie	D.

4. Compound Last Names

A compound last name (*Fuller-Smith*, for example) is indexed as two separate units. The hyphen is ignored. In a last name such as *St. Claire*, *St.* is considered to be the first unit (in spelled-out form as *Saint*) and *Claire* the second unit. *St.* is not considered a prefix as in Rule 3 because it is an abbreviation for the word *Saint*. The prefixes in Rule 3 are not abbreviations.

INDEX ORDER OF UNITS

Names	Unit 1	Unit 2	Unit 3
Michael Ross-Harris	Ross(-)	Harris	Michael
Robert J. Ross	Ross	Robert	J.
Allen Ross-Sanders	Ross(-)	Sanders	Allen
George J. Rosse	Rosse	George	J.
Edwin St. Claire	Saint	Claire	Edwin
Gerald St. John	Saint	John	Gerald
Marie T. Satone	Satone	Marie	T.
Harold Twigg-Porter	Twigg(-)	Porter	Harold

5. Given Names (First Names)

When the last names are alike, you consider the first names in determining the alphabetic order. When the last names and the first names are both alike, the middle names determine the alphabetic order, as illustrated at the top of page 193.

INDEX ORDER OF UNITS

Names	Unit 1	Unit 2	Unit 3
William A. Smith	Smith	William	A.
Winifred C. Smith	Smith	Winifred	C.
Walter Clark Thompson	Thompson	Walter	Clark
Walter Crane Thompson	Thompson	Walter	Crane

6. Initials and Abbreviated First or Middle Names

A first initial is considered an indexing unit and goes before all names that begin with the same letter. An abbreviated first or middle name (*Wm.* for *William*, for example) is usually treated as if it were spelled in full. Originally a nickname — *Bob* for *Robert*, *Larry* for *Lawrence*, etc. — was always indexed as if written in full. Recently, however, many names **formerly** considered nicknames have become given names. Unless the first name is thought to be a nickname — *Tom* for *Thomas* — it should be indexed as written.

formerly:
in times past

INDEX ORDER OF UNITS

Names	Unit 1	Unit 2	Unit 3
R. Robert Brogan	Brogan	R.	Robert
Robt. R. Brogan	Brogan	Robert	R.
Robert Richard Brogan	Brogan	Robert	Richard
Sam F. Brogan	Brogan	Sam	F.
Sam'l George Brogan	Brogan	Samuel	George

7. Unusual Names

When you can't decide which part of a name (usually a foreign name) is the last name, the last part of the name as written should be considered the last name. This type of name is often cross-referenced as explained on page 210.

INDEX ORDER OF UNITS

Names	Unit 1	Unit 2	Unit 3
Juan Maria Mallendez	Mallendez	Juan	Maria
Boyd Nelson	Nelson	Boyd	
Arthur Patrick	Patrick	Arthur	
Lee Kuan Yew	Yew	Lee	Kuan
Geza Zsak	Zsak	Geza	

8. Identical Personal Names

When you have identical names in filing, they are indexed by the usual procedure; but the filing order is determined by the parts of the address as follows:

    (a) Town or City Name
    (b) State Name
    (c) Street Name
    (d) House Number (in numeric order)

	INDEX ORDER OF UNITS			IDENTIFYING ELEMENTS (another way to determine alphabetic order when the names are the same)			
Names	Unit 1	Unit 2	Unit 3	City	State	Street	House Number
Charles G. Grant 145 Beach Street Kingston, IL 60145	Grant	Charles	G.	Kingston	Illinois	Beach	145
Charles G. Grant 204 Pearl Street Kingston, NY 10124	Grant	Charles	G.	Kingston	New York	Pearl	204
Charles G. Grant 177 State Street Kingston, NY 10124	Grant	Charles	G.	Kingston	New York	State	177
Charles G. Grant 350 State Street Kingston, NY 10124	Grant	Charles	G.	Kingston	New York	State	350

9. Seniority in Identical Names

A term indicating seniority, such as *Senior* or *Junior*, or *II* (*Second*) or *III* (*Third*), is not considered an indexing unit. The term is used as an identifying element in determining the alphabetic order for filing purposes.

	INDEX ORDER OF UNITS		IDENTIFYING ELEMENTS
Names	Unit 1	Unit 2	Seniority Titles
John Young	Young	John	
John Young, IV	Young	John	(Fourth)
John Young, Jr.	Young	John	(Junior)
John Young, Sr.	Young	John	(Senior)
John Young, III	Young	John	(Third)

10. Titles

(a) A personal or professional title or degree is usually not considered in filing, but it is put in parentheses at the end of the name.

(b) When a religious or foreign title is followed by a first name only, it is indexed as written.

INDEX ORDER OF UNITS

Names	Unit 1	Unit 2	Unit 3
(a) Dr. Alfred G. Brown	Brown	Alfred	G. (Dr.)
Arthur E. Brown, M.D.	Brown	Arthur	E. (M.D.)
Raymond C. Ellis, Ph.D.	Ellis	Raymond	C. (Ph.D.)
Mme. Jeannine Patou	Patou	Jeannine (Mme.)	
Mayor John J. Ryan	Ryan	John	J. (Mayor)
Lieut. Earl T. Stewart	Stewart	Earl	T. (Lieutenant)
Senator Ralph Williams	Williams	Ralph (Senator)	
(b) Brother Andrew	Brother	Andrew	
Father Henry	Father	Henry	
King George	King	George	
Lady Anabel	Lady	Anabel	
Prince Philip	Prince	Philip	
Princess Margaret	Princess	Margaret	
Sister Mary Martha	Sister	Mary	Martha

11. Names of Married Women

If it is known, the legal name of a married woman should be used rather than her husband's name. When a woman marries, the only part of her husband's name that she legally **assumes** is his last name. Her legal name includes either (a) her first name, her maiden last name, and her husband's last name, or (b) her first name, her middle name, and her husband's last name. In other words, a married woman's legal name could be *Mrs. Jane Foster Burke* or *Mrs. Jane Melinda Burke* but not *Mrs. Marvin J. Burke.*

The title *Mrs.* is put in parentheses after the name but *it is not considered in filing.* Her husband's name is given in parentheses below her legal name.

assumes:
takes; receives;
takes upon oneself

INDEX ORDER OF UNITS

Names	Unit 1	Unit 2	Unit 3
Mrs. Thomas (Mary Parker) Smith (Mrs. Thomas Smith)	Smith,	Mary	Parker (Mrs.)
Mrs. Theodore Smith	Smith,	Theodore (Mrs.)	
Mrs. Frank (Evelyn Marie) Zeller (Mrs. Frank Zeller)	Zeller,	Evelyn	Marie (Mrs.)

REVIEWING WHAT YOU HAVE READ

1. How many indexing units are there in the name *Gerald V. Wilcox*?
2. What is meant by the *nothing before something* rule?
3. Is *Van Der Veer* considered one, two, or three filing units?
4. How is an abbreviated first name like *Benj.* treated?
5. If two people have last names that are alike, what will determine the order in which their names are indexed?
6. Is the city or state considered first when filing identical names?
7. Which is the correct order for indexing *Jr., Sr., III, IV*, or *Fourth, Junior, Senior, Third*?
8. What is done about the *Dr.* in *Dr. James B. Moulton*?
9. How are religious and foreign titles treated in indexing?
10. What is the legal name of a married woman?

MAKING DECISIONS

1. What confusion might be caused if last names containing a prefix were not treated as one unit?
2. Why are foreign names often difficult to index?

WORKING WITH OTHERS

Rita Dutton assists the vice-president and his secretary in the legal department of a large manufacturing company. Among other duties, she is responsible for all the legal files of the department. Most of these are maintained in separate confidential files in the vice-president's office. She is often interrupted by telephone calls. Executives of the company and other persons who must talk with her boss cause his office to be occupied the greater part of the day. Their days are so busy that Rita finds it difficult to properly file the records that must be kept in the vice-president's office. If you were Rita what would you do to keep control of the files for which you are responsible?

USING LANGUAGE

A good practice is not to use a capital unless a rule exists for its use. Four basic rules of capitalization are:

1. Capitalize the first word of a sentence.
   Example: He asked if we were ready to go.
2. Capitalize the first word of a direct quotation.
   Example: He asked, "Are you ready to go?"
3. Capitalize proper nouns and adjectives.
   Example: Beaumont High School   Mexican music
4. Capitalize the important words of titles
   Example: *A Short History of the English People*

Type the following sentences on a separate sheet of paper using capitalization wherever necessary.

1. a condensed version of his new novel will appear in the march issue of the reader's digest.
2. the new york firm had all its vital records on microfilm stored underground at a secret location in altoona, pennsylvania.
3. when he was in independence, missouri, he visited the truman library.
4. when she opened the drawer marked contracts and agreements, she was surprised at the number of files it contained.
5. dean lindsey told his secretary to file the volume entitled an inquiry into the nature of certain nineteenth century pamphlets in the school library.

USING ARITHMETIC

1. On a separate sheet of paper solve the following problems.

$$25.46 \times .1 \qquad 32.58 \times .01 \qquad 76.89 \times .001$$

2. On a separate sheet of paper solve the following problems.

$$.1)\overline{25.46} \qquad .01)\overline{32.58} \qquad .001)\overline{76.89}$$

PERFORMING OFFICE TASKS

In completing the following filing exercise, you will need one hundred 5″ x 3″ filing cards, or plain paper cut to about that size. (When the dimensions of a card are mentioned, the first number indicates the width of the bottom edge, and the second number indicates the depth. With a 5″ by 3″ card, the 5″ means that the bottom edge is 5 inches wide, and the 3″ means that the card is 3 inches in depth. Normally, however, these cards are referred to as 3″ by 5″ cards.)

(a) Type each of the following names in index form at the upper left-hand side of a card.
(b) Type the number of each name in the upper right corner of the card. (These numbers will aid in checking the answers.)
(c) After the names have been properly indexed and typed, together with their respective numbers, arrange the cards in alphabetic order.

1. Dr. Herman G. Hofmann
2. Salvatore L'Abbate
3. Joan Neuhaus
4. Shirley M. Schecter
5. Mrs. Adele C. Welsh
6. Mrs. Minnie B. Ballau
7. Ernest Sanford Black
8. Lloyd C. Carpenter
9. Thomas F. Corey
10. David E. Forbes-Watkins
11. Harry D. Van Tassell
12. Stanley Schechter
13. Arthur Neuhaus
14. Henry M. Kaufmann
15. George A. Heinemann
16. Vicki Forbes
17. Maryalice Corey
18. Mrs. Evelyn M. Cannon
19. Sidney J. Bernstein
20. Albert Theron Baldwin
21. Hartzell P. Angell
22. Mrs. Bessie Berkowitz
23. Joseph A. Colombo
24. Mrs. Agnes F. Burns
25. John A. Farrell
26. Arnold H. Hansen-Sturm
27. Arthur Jacobs
28. Robert L. Michalson
29. Viggo Rambusch
30. W. Anthony Ullman
31. E. Cooper Taylor
32. Nicholas Rambone
33. James D. McLean
34. C. Albert Jacob, Jr.

35. Rev. Herbert W. Hansen
36. John Farrell
37. Paul G. Clarke, Jr.
38. Gino Borsesi
39. Thomas L. D. Berg
40. Bette P. Albert, M.D.
41. Robert S. Hackett
42. Olaf Ellison
43. Mrs. Evelyn E. Clarke
44. Charles W. Borman
45. Thomas L. Beckett, Ph.D.
46. Norman J. Abrams, D.D.S.
47. Mrs. Sharon Ennis
48. Edwin C. McDonald, Jr.
49. Alfred H. Phillips
50. Anthony Y. Szu-Tu
51. Julia B. Fee
52. N. R. Heinneman
53. Julia Ann Kaufman
54. Kazan Michel
55. William St. John
56. Seymour C. Ullmann
57. Patrick Colombo
58. George L. Cady
59. Marvin T. Bernstein
60. Mrs. Lillian M. Backer
61. David B. Bandler, Jr.
62. Malcolm Carpenter, M.D.
63. Mrs. J. Black
64. D. Howard Daniels
65. Maxine Friedman
66. Richard D. Hoffman
67. Annette C. LaBelle
68. Arabelle J. O'Brien, M.D.
69. Madelyn Russell Segal
70. Harold A. Welch
71. Richard D. Zirker
72. Mrs. Gladys Smythe
73. James F. O'Neill
74. R. O. Ennis
75. James A. Gilmartin
76. Thomas M. Ellis
77. Samuel H. Clark
78. Robert D. Block
79. Edward J. Barrett
80. Albert V. Marcus
81. Joseph Lloyd Barnett
82. Samuel Clark
83. A. Marvin Gillman, M.D.
84. Leo J. Madden, D.D.S.
85. William M. Smith
86. Gloria Younger
87. Dr. William Bloch
88. A. V. Danielson
89. Harry A. Humphries
90. Carol Philipps
91. Barbara Ann Barken
92. Wilford R. Young
93. Joseph E. Black
94. Irving T. Siegel
95. James E. Clark, Jr.
96. William J. O'Neil
97. Malcolm MacDonald
98. Harry S. Humphreys
99. Louis M. Friedmann
100. Henry L. Daniels

PART 3

ALPHABETIC FILING RULES FOR BUSINESS FIRMS AND OTHER ORGANIZATIONS

Judy Melvin was the first assistant Mr. Howard Bivens hired when he started Ambex Paper Products six months ago. She is amazed at the number of different organizations — business firms, government agencies, religious bodies, schools, newspaper and magazine publishing companies — that call on Ambex for its products. Judy has spent a great deal of time establishing the filing system. Mr. Bivens depends completely on Judy to see that the files are up to date at all times. With the help of a records consultant, Judy has assumed complete supervision of the filing system and is gradually becoming expert in alphabetizing. The filing system Judy established is truly a pleasure with which to work.

ALPHABETIC INDEXING FOR BUSINESS FIRMS AND OTHER ORGANIZATIONS

The alphabetic indexing rules presented in Part 2 are also used in filing for business firms and other organizations. Businesses, however, can sometimes present special indexing problems. A mastery of the following rules should give you the confidence you need when you have to file materials for other than names of individuals.

12. Business or Firm Names

The following rules determine the indexing of a business or firm name:

(a) As a general rule, the units in a firm name are indexed in the order in which they are written. The word *and* is not considered an indexing unit.

(b) When a firm name includes the full name of a person, the person's last name is considered as the first indexing unit, his given name or first initial as the second unit, his middle name or initial as the third; and the rest of the firm name is then considered.

(c) Occasionally a business name contains the name of a person (for example, *Arthur Murray* or *Fanny Farmer*) who is so well known that it would confuse most people if the name were to be **transposed**. In such cases, the name is indexed as it is popularly known and cross-referenced. For example, *Fanny Farmer Candy Shops, Inc.*, would be cross-referenced as *Farmer, Fanny Candy Shops, Inc.*

(d) The name of a hotel or motel is usually indexed in the order in which it is written. However, if the word *Hotel* or *Motel* appears first, it is transposed to allow the most clearly identifying word to become the first indexing unit (for example, *Hotel McKitrick* is indexed as *McKitrick Hotel*).

INDEX ORDER OF UNITS

Names	Unit 1	Unit 2	Unit 3	Unit 4
Ames Art Shop	Ames	Art	Shop	
Hotel Ames	Ames	Hotel		
Brown and Son Realty Co.	Brown (and)	Son	Realty	Company
Campbell Soup Company, Inc.	Campbell	Soup	Company	Incorporated
Citizens National Bank	Citizens	National	Bank	
John Hancock Mutual Life Insurance Co.	John	Hancock	Mutual	Life
John H. Kramer Shoe Repair Shop	Kramer	John	H.	Shoe
Michigan Savings and Loan Co.	Michigan	Savings (and)	Loan	Company
Modern Tile Store	Modern	Tile	Store	
Montgomery Ward and Company	Montgomery	Ward (and)	Company	
Motel Morris Gift Shoppe	Morris	Motel	Gift	Shoppe
L. Morrison Moss Supply Co.	Moss	L.	Morrison	Supply
Singer Wallpaper and Paint Company	Singer	Wallpaper (and)	Paint	Company

13. Alphabetic Order of Business or Firm Names

The first units of firm names determine the alphabetic order when those units are different. The second units determine alphabetic order when the first units are alike. The third units determine alphabetic order when the first and second units are alike.

Names	Unit 1	Unit 2	Unit 3	Unit 4
Gunn Printing Company	Gunn	Printing	Company	
Gunn Radio Shop	Gunn	Radio	Shop	
Hess Beauty Shoppe	Hess	Beauty	Shoppe	
Mary Hess Beauty Salon	Hess	Mary	Beauty	Salon
Hess Specialty Shop	Hess	Specialty	Shop	
Irwin Shoe Distributors	Irwin	Shoe	Distributors	
Irwin Shoe Mart	Irwin	Shoe	Mart	

14. Articles, Prepositions, and Conjunctions

(a) The articles (*a, an, the*); prepositions (*of, on, for, by*, etc.); and conjunctions (*and, &, or*) are *not* considered as indexing units and should be put in parentheses.

(b) However, when a preposition is the first word in a business name (as in *At Home Bakery* or *In Town Motel*), the preposition is treated as the first indexing unit.

INDEX ORDER OF UNITS

Names	Unit 1	Unit 2	Unit 3	Unit 4
L. S. Andrews & Co.	Andrews	L.	S. (&)	Company
A Bit of Scotland	Bit (of)	Scotland (A)		
By the Sea Inn	By (the)	Sea	Inn	
First National Bank of Cincinnati	First	National	Bank (of)	Cincinnati
The House of Design	House (of)	Design (The)		
In Between Book Store	In	Between	Book	Store

Illus. 6-4

A good file clerk is able to retrieve records instantly when they are requested.

15. Abbreviations

An abbreviation in a firm name is indexed as if it were spelled in full. Single-letter abbreviations are also indexed as though spelled in full. If the meaning of the abbreviation is not *definitely* known, however, the name should be indexed as it is written.

INDEX ORDER OF UNITS

Names	Unit 1	Unit 2	Unit 3	Unit 4
Amer. Paper Co.	American	Paper	Company	
Ft. Lee Stores, Inc.	Fort	Lee	Stores	Incorporated
Penn Central R.R.	Penn	Central	Railroad	
St. Vincent's Hosp.	Saint	Vincent's	Hospital	
U.S. Rubber Co.	United	States	Rubber	Company
YWCA	Young	Women's	Christian	Association

16. Single Letters

When a firm's name is made up of single letters, each letter is considered as a separate indexing unit. The spacing between the single letters is not considered in indexing. Firm names made up of single letters are filed before words beginning with the same letter because of the *nothing before something* rule.

INDEX ORDER OF UNITS

Names	Unit 1	Unit 2	Unit 3	Unit 4
A & A Auto Parts	A (&)	A	Auto	Parts
ABC Printers	A	B	C	Printers
A C Cleaners	A	C	Cleaners	
A–Z Dry Cleaners	A (–)	Z	Dry	Cleaners
Acme Rug Co.	Acme	Rug	Company	
WNBC	W	N	B	C
X-Cel Advertising Service	X (-)	Cel	Advertising	Service

17. Hyphenated and Compound Names and Words

(a) Hyphenated firm names are indexed as if they were separate words; thus, they are separate indexing units (for example, *Allis-Chalmers*).

(b) Each part of a hyphenated "coined" word (such as *The Do-It-Ur-Self Shop*) is considered to be a separate indexing unit.

(c) A single word written with a hyphen (a word containing a prefix, such as *anti-, co-, inter-, mid-, pan-, trans-, tri-*) is filed as one indexing unit.

INDEX ORDER OF UNITS

Names	Unit 1	Unit 2	Unit 3	Unit 4
(a) McGraw-Edison Company	McGraw(-)	Edison	Company	
Shaw-Walker	Shaw(-)	Walker		
Stokens-Van Buren, Inc.	Stokens(-)	Van Buren	Incorporated	
(b) Bar-B-Q Drive-Inn	Bar(-)	B(-)	Q	Drive(-)
C-Thru Window Company	C(-)	Thru	Window	Company
Econ-O-Me Cleaners	Econ(-)	O(-)	Me	Cleaners
(c) Inter-State Truckers Assoc.	Inter-State	Truckers	Association	
Mid-City Garage	Mid-City	Garage		
Pan-American Insurance Co.	Pan-American	Insurance	Company	

18. Two Words Considered as One

If separate words in a firm's name are often considered or written as one word, these words as a group should be treated as one indexing unit. The use of a hyphen or spacing is of no indexing **significance**. This rule does away with the separating of similar names in the files. Examples of such words include *airport, carload, crossroads, downtown, eastside, goodwill, halfway, mainland, railroad, seaboard*, and points of the compass words, such as *northeast, northwest, southeast*, and *southeastern*.

significance: importance

INDEX ORDER OF UNITS

Names	Unit 1	Unit 2
Down Town Garage	Down Town	Garage
Good Will Agency	Good Will	Agency
The Half-Way Restaurant	Half-Way	Restaurant (The)
North Eastern Airlines	North Eastern	Airlines

19. Titles in Business Names

(a) A title *in a business name* is treated as a separate unit and is indexed in the order in which it is written.

(b) The titles *Mr.* and *Mrs.* are indexed as written *rather than* spelled in full.

Names	Unit 1	Unit 2	Unit 3	Unit 4
Dr. Posner Shoe Co., Inc.	Doctor	Posner	Shoe	Company
Madame Adrienne French Cleaners	Madame	Adrienne	French	Cleaners
Mr. Foster's Shops	Mr.	Foster's	Shops	
Sir Michael, Ltd.	Sir	Michael	Limited	

20. Compound Geographic Names

Compound geographic names containing two English words (such as *New York*) are treated as two separate indexing units, but compound names written as one word (such as *Lakewood*) are considered as one indexing unit.

Names	Unit 1	Unit 2	Unit 3	Unit 4
Ft. Wayne Finance Co.	Fort	Wayne	Finance	Company
New Jersey Thruway Res't	New	Jersey	Thruway	Restaurant
Newport Knitting Co.	Newport	Knitting	Company	
St. Louis Post Dispatch	Saint	Louis	Post	Dispatch

21. Numbers

indicate:
to show; to point out

A number in a business name is treated as though written in full and is considered one indexing unit (regardless of the length or number of digits). In order to use a smaller number of letters to **indicate** a number, four-digit numbers are written in hundreds and five-digit numbers are written in thousands. For example, the four-digit number *1,250* would be written *twelve hundred fifty* instead of *one thousand two hundred fifty*. The five-digit number *10,010* would be written *ten thousand ten*.

Names	Unit 1	Unit 2	Unit 3	Unit 4
A-1 Envelope Co.	A(-)	One	Envelope	Company
40 Winks Motel	Forty	Winks	Motel	
42nd Street Playhouse	Forty-second	Street	Playhouse	
40,000 Investment Association	Forty Thousand	Investment	Association	
The 400 Cake Shop	Four Hundred	Cake	Shop (The)	
4th Federal Loan Co.	Fourth	Federal	Loan	Company

22. Foreign Names

    (a) Each separately written word in a compound foreign name is considered as a separate indexing unit. The words *San* and *Santa* mean *Saint* and are, therefore, indexed separately.

    (b) A foreign prefix is combined with the word that follows it and is indexed as one filing unit (as explained in Rule 3, Part 2, page 191).

    (c) Unusual foreign names are indexed as written.

INDEX ORDER OF UNITS

Names	Unit 1	Unit 2	Unit 3	Unit 4
(a)				
Mesa Verde Distributors	Mesa	Verde	Distributors	
Puerto Rico Travel Bureau	Puerto	Rico	Travel	Bureau
San Francisco Chronicle	San	Francisco	Chronicle	
Terre Haute City Service	Terre	Haute	City	Service
(b)				
Du Bois Fence & Garden Co.	Du Bois	Fence (&)	Garden	Company
LaBelle Formal Wear Shops	LaBelle	Formal	Wear	Shops
Las Vegas Convention Bureau	Las Vegas	Convention	Bureau	
Los Angeles Wholesale Institute	Los Angeles	Wholesale	Institute	
(c)				
Ambulancias Hispano Mexicana	Ambulancias	Hispano	Mexicana	
Iino Kauin Kaisha Imports	Iino	Kauin	Kaisha	Imports
Mohamed Esber, Cia	Mohamed	Esber	Cia	

23. Possessives

    The *apostrophe s* (*'s*), the singular possessive, is *not* considered in filing. An *s apostrophe* (*s'*), the plural possessive, *is* considered as part of the word. Very simply, consider all letters to be in the indexing unit up to the apostrophe; drop those after it.

INDEX ORDER OF UNITS

Names	Unit 1	Unit 2	Unit 3	Unit 4
Brook's Jewelry Store	Brook('s)	Jewelry	Store	
Brooks' Brothers Clothing	Brooks'	Brothers	Clothing	
Paul's Limousine Service	Paul('s)	Limousine	Service	
Pauls' Real Estate Agency	Pauls'	Real	Estate	Agency

24. Identical Business Names

(a) Identical names of two or more businesses are arranged in alphabetical order according to the names of the cities in the addresses. The name of the state is disregarded unless the towns have the same name.

(b) If several branches of one business are located in the same city, the names of those branches are arranged alphabetically or numerically by streets. If more than one branch is located on the same street in the same city, the names are arranged according to the numeric order of the building numbers. Names of buildings are not considered unless street names are not given.

	INDEX ORDER OF UNITS			IDENTIFYING ELEMENTS			
Names	Unit 1	Unit 2	Unit 3	City	State	Street	House Number
(a) Office Supplies Company Akron, Ohio	Office	Supplies	Company	Akron	Ohio		
Office Supplies Company Canton, Ohio	Office	Supplies	Company	Canton	Ohio		
Office Supplies Company Lansing, Michigan	Office	Supplies	Company	Lansing	Michigan		

(b)
National Food Market
  225 Main Street
  Columbus, Ohio
	National	Food	Market	Columbus	Ohio	Main	225

National Food Market
  187 Prospect Street
  Columbus, Ohio
	National	Food	Market	Columbus	Ohio	Prospect	187

National Food Market
  United Building
  341 Stone Drive
  Columbus, Ohio
	National	Food	Market	Columbus	Ohio	Stone	341

National Food Market
  722 Stone Drive
  Columbus, Ohio
	National	Food	Market	Columbus	Ohio	Stone	722

National Food Market
  Young Building
  Columbus, Ohio
	National	Food	Market	Columbus	Ohio	Young	

25. Churches, Synagogues, and Other Organizations

(a) The name of a church or synagogue is indexed in the order in which it is written unless some other word in the name more clearly identifies the organization.

INDEX ORDER OF UNITS

Names	Unit 1	Unit 2	Unit 3
First Baptist Church	Baptist	Church	First
The Chapel at Brown & Vine	Chapel (at)	Brown (&)	Vine (The)
Congregation of Moses	Congregation (of)	Moses	
Trinity Lutheran Church	Lutheran	Church	Trinity
St. Paul's Church	Saint	Paul's	Church

(b) The name of a club or any other organization is indexed according to the most clearly identifying unit in its name. For example, the most clearly identifying unit in *The Ancient Order of Mariners* is *Mariners*.

INDEX ORDER OF UNITS

Names	Unit 1	Unit 2	Unit 3
Fraternal Order of Eagles	Eagles	Fraternal	Order (of)
Loyal Order of Moose	Moose	Loyal	Order (of)
Local 200, Retail Store Employees Union	Retail	Store	Employees
Rotary Club	Rotary	Club	

26. Schools

(a) The names of elementary and secondary schools are indexed first according to the name of the city in which the schools are located, and then by the most **distinctive** word in the name.

distinctive: easily identified

INDEX ORDER OF UNITS

Names	Unit 1	Unit 2	Unit 3	Unit 4
Indian Prairie School, Kalamazoo, Michigan	Kalamazoo	Indian	Prairie	School
Oakwood Elementary School, Kalamazoo, Michigan	Kalamazoo	Oakwood	Elementary	School
Oakwood Junior High, Kalamazoo, Michigan	Kalamazoo	Oakwood	Junior	High
Pershing School Portage, Michigan	Portage	Pershing	School	

(b) The names of colleges or universities are indexed according to the most clearly identifying word in the name.

INDEX ORDER OF UNITS

Names	Unit 1	Unit 2	Unit 3
Albany Business Col.	Albany	Business	College
Indiana Business School	Indiana	Business	School
Iowa State University	Iowa	State	University
University of Iowa	Iowa	University (of)	
Northwestern University	Northwestern	University	
Slippery Rock State College	Slippery	Rock	State

27. **Newspapers and Magazines**

(a) The name of a newspaper is indexed in the order in which it is written unless the city of publication does not appear in its name. In that case, the name of the city is inserted before the name of the newspaper.

INDEX ORDER OF UNITS

Names	Unit 1	Unit 2	Unit 3	Unit 4
The Canton Herald	Canton	Herald (The)		
The Journal Gazette Ft. Wayne, Indiana	Fort	Wayne	Journal	Gazette (The)
The New York Times	New	York	Times (The)	
The Wall Street Journal, New York, NY	New	York	Wall	Street

(b) The name of a magazine is indexed in the order in which the name is written. A cross-reference may be made listing the publisher, as described on page 210.

INDEX ORDER OF UNITS

Names	Unit 1	Unit 2	Unit 3
Administrative Management	Administrative	Management	
Harvard Business Review	Harvard	Business	Review
The Office	Office (The)		
Reader's Digest	Reader's	Digest	

28. **Federal Government Offices**

The names of all federal government agencies and offices are indexed under United States Government. They are indexed as shown at the top of page 209.

(a) United States Government
(b) Name of the department
(c) Name of the bureau
(d) Name of the division or sub-
    division
(e) Location of the office
(f) Title of official, if given

```
+-------------------------------------------+
| District Director                         |
| Internal Revenue Service                  |
| Indianapolis, Indiana  46204              |
+-------------------------------------------+
```

would be indexed

```
+-------------------------------------------+
| United States Government                  |
|     Treasury (Department of)              |
|     Internal Revenue Service              |
|     Indianapolis                          |
|     District Director                     |
+-------------------------------------------+
```

Names	INDEX ORDER OF UNITS

District Director
Agricultural Research Service
Federal Building
Tallahassee, Florida 33602
	United States Government
	   Agriculture (Department of)
	   Agricultural Research Service
	   Tallahassee
	   District Director

Bureau of International Commerce
U.S. Department of Commerce
Philadelphia, Pennsylvania 19108
	United States Government
	   Commerce (Department of)
	   International Commerce (Bureau of)
	   Philadelphia

Division of Employment Statistics
Bureau of Labor Statistics
U.S. Department of Labor
Cleveland, Ohio 44199
	United States Government
	   Labor (Department of)
	   Labor Statistics (Bureau of)
	   Employment Statistics (Division of)
	   Cleveland

Customs Service
U.S. Department of the Treasury
San Francisco, California 94102
	United States Government
	   Treasury (Department of the)
	   Customs Service
	   San Francisco

Data Processing Center
Veterans Administration
St. Paul, Minnesota 55511
	United States Government
	   Veterans Administration
	   Data Processing Center
	   St. Paul

(Note: Rule 28 also applies to foreign government names.)

29. Other Political Subdivisions

The names of other political subdivisions — state, county, city, or town government — are indexed according to

(a) Geographic name of the subdivision, such as *New Jersey, State* (*of*); *Westchester, County* (*of*); or *Philadelphia, City* (*of*)
(b) Name of department, board, or office
(c) Location of the office
(d) Title of the official, if it is given

Names	Unit 1	Unit 2	Unit 3	Unit 4
Police Department Alliance, Ohio	Alliance	City (of)	Police	Department
Clinton Co. Park Commission Dubuque, Iowa	Clinton	County (of)	Park	Commission
Municipal Public Works Div. Lancaster, Pa.	Lancaster	City (of)	Public	Works
State Health Department Columbus, Ohio	Ohio	State (of)	Health	Department

30. Subjects

Sometimes it is better to file materials according to subject rather than under the name of the person or business. The reason for this is that the subject may be more important than the name of the person or business. Applications for employment are examples of this type of indexing. The applications are of major importance; the names of the applicants are of secondary importance.

INDEX ORDER OF UNITS

Names	Unit 1	Unit 2	Unit 3	Unit 4
C. J. Browning (Advertiser)	Advertisers:	Browning	C.	J.
R. M. Smith (Advertiser)	Advertisers:	Smith	R.	M.
H. L. Kramer (Application)	Applications:	Kramer	H.	L.
Jack Myer (Application)	Applications:	Myer	Jack	
J. Frank Smith (Application)	Applications:	Smith	J.	Frank

CROSS-REFERENCING

consist:
made up of

What will you do when a letter or other material to be filed could be asked for by more than one name? Examples are firm names that **consist** of two or more surnames, the names of married women, and the names of magazines. You may look for the name according to an indexing order that is not shown on the piece of correspondence or on the file card. For example, you may remember only the name *Goodman* in the firm name *Bergdorf-Goodman*; you may not remember a married woman's legal name — you may remember only that her husband's name is *Thomas Devine*; or you may remember the name of a magazine, *Life*, but not the name of the publisher, *Time, Inc.*

In such instances, a cross-reference sheet should be filled out and filed under the other title. It should indicate where the material is actually

ER

William Carter Co.
815 Lakeland Dr. Kansas City, MO 64151 Area Code 816 891-1129

JUN 15 197 - 2-12 PM

June 14, 197-

Allis-Bowen Products, Inc.
9621 East Tracy Street
Los Angeles, CA 90028

Attention Mr. B. P. Warren

Gentlemen

Thank you for your letter of June 12 in which you inquired about the possibility of our printing for you
a booklet giving a short description of your company
and an illustrated description of the products that
you manufacture.

Before we are able to quote prices on a publication of
this kind we need the following information:

1. An estimate of the length of the booklet

2. The approximate number and dimensions of
   illustrations

3. The size of the page desired

4. The kind and quality of paper and cover
   stock.

We shall be glad to give you an exact quotation on cost
of the booklet as soon as we receive this information.

At the present time we are in a position to give you
prompt as well as efficient service. We can assure you
of an attractive booklet with suitable type, clear illustrations, and strong binding.

Very truly yours

Earl E. Whitmore
Earl E. Whitmore

ecb

Illus. 6-5
Coded letter

CROSS-REFERENCE SHEET

Name of Subject   Whitmore, Earl E.
                   Kansas City, MO 64151

Date of Item   June 14, 197-

Regarding   Request for further information as
                   basis for quotation on printing a
                   booklet

              SEE

Name of Subject   Carter, William, Company
                   815 Lakeland Drive
                   Kansas City, MO 64151

Illus. 6-6
Cross-reference sheet

The line drawn under the name *Carter Co.* in the letterhead above indicates the name under which the letter should be filed. The line drawn under the name *Whitmore*, which is extended into the margin and marked with an "x," indicates that the letter may be called for by Whitmore's name rather than by the name of the company. Consequently, the cross-reference sheet above was prepared and should be filed under the name *Whitmore*, *Earl E.* (The notation *ER* is a release mark, which indicates that the paper is ready to be filed. *June 15 . . . 2-12 PM* is a time stamp indicating when the letter was received.)

filed. If a photocopying machine is available, it is more efficient, more accurate, and faster to make a photocopy than to fill out a cross-reference sheet. The photocopy should then be filed under the other title.

Although cross-referencing is important for locating filed information quickly, care should be taken in deciding which records really need to be cross-referenced. Too much cross-referencing takes a lot of time and a lot of space. Too little cross-referencing will cause needless and costly delays in getting important information.

Cross-Reference for a Company Known by More than One Name

If the name of a firm is *Rogers-Turner Food Mart*, the original piece of correspondence should be indexed as it is written. You should, however, make a cross-reference card or sheet for the second name in the title. Consequently, if you remember only the second name, *Turner*, you will find on the cross-reference for *Turner* "See Rogers-Turner Food Mart."

Cross-Reference for the Name of a Married Woman

You will file the original piece of correspondence for a married woman under her legal name, that is, her given first name, her maiden last name, and her husband's last name. Her husband's given name might be cross-referenced to find the filed piece of correspondence faster. If the legal name of a married women is *Mrs. Dorothy Lee Hall*, this name should be indexed on the original piece of correspondence; and a cross-reference card or sheet based on her husband's name should be prepared.

Hall, Dorothy Lee (Mrs.)	Hall, Raymond C. (Mrs.)
Mrs. Raymond C. Hall 1230 Fifth Street Marion, IA. 52302	<u>See</u> Hall, Dorothy Lee (Mrs.)
Illus. 6-7	Illus. 6-8

1. In what order are the units of a business name considered for filing purposes?
2. What is done when units of an individual name are included in a firm name?
3. How are the words *and*, *of*, and *for* treated in indexing?
4. In a firm name what differences are made in indexing between two words combined with a hyphen and a single word containing a hyphen — for example, *Walker-Gordon Mills, Inc.,* and *Mid-Hudson Electric Co.*?

5. What are the rules for geographic names?
6. State simply the rule for indexing possessive words.
7. Give examples of subject titles that would be used in preference to the names of the persons or businesses that are concerned.
8. What is a cross-reference?
9. What is the advantage of using photocopies as cross-reference copies?
10. Give two examples of types of names that are frequently cross-referenced.

MAKING DECISIONS

1. Why is each word in a geographic name treated as a separate indexing unit?
2. For what purposes other than filing would a company make use of the rules for alphabetic indexing?

WORKING WITH OTHERS

Louise Allen has been with the Lily Soap Company since it was started over thirty years ago. She developed the filing system for the firm and is now supervisor of the central files. Her filing procedures are used in all the executive offices so that materials sent to the central files can be filed and found quickly.

She has her own fixed ideas about filing rules; for instance, the customers' names beginning with *Mac* and *Mc* are placed ahead of all the other names in the *M* section of the alphabetic files. This is but one of the variations in alphabetic filing at the Lily Soap Company.

New employees are confused because the system is so different from the rules of filing they have been taught. They waste much time and energy filing and finding correspondence. Louise is not willing to accept any suggestions for change, claiming that the system has been operating successfully for over thirty years.

If you were to be employed as a file clerk at the Lily Soap Company, how would you attempt to adjust to the differences between company practice and the filing rules you learned in school? How would you plan to get along with Louise?

USING LANGUAGE

On a separate sheet of paper write the plural of each of the following words. After you have written the plural forms, check your answers in a dictionary.

1. attorney	6. company	11. series
2. belief	7. delivery	12. statistic
3. business	8. prefix	13. studio
4. chief clerk	9. salesman	14. trade-in
5. city	10. secretary	15. youth

USING ARITHMETIC

1. Your employer has received the following discounts on the purchases indicated. On a separate sheet of paper show your computation of the discounts and the net amount of each purchase.

Article	Price	Discount
Table	$70.00	12½%
Golf cart	15.50	30%
Binoculars	69.50	20%
Shaver	21.90	16⅔%
Paintbrush	1.89	25%

2. The price of a desk lamp is reduced 40 percent from the original price of $5.95. How much will you pay for the desk lamp at the reduced price?

1. In each of the following names of individuals select the *first* indexing unit.

   (a) R. Harold Dana
   (b) Hubert Smith-Johnson, Jr.
   (c) Lois J. McDowell
   (d) Veronica Blake
   (e) Father Francis
   (f) Chairman Frank Simpson
   (g) Mrs. John Hanson
   (h) President Walter C. Schott
   (i) T. J. Fairleigh, News Commentator
   (j) Attorney Edward K. Wilcox

2. In each of the following business names select the *second* indexing unit.

   (a) The Holden Paper Company
   (b) Woodward & Lothrop
       Department Store
   (c) A to Z Cleaning Service
   (d) Trans-Canada Air Lines
   (e) North West Wholesale Furriers
   (f) Tommy Tucker's Toys
   (g) Johnson-Hardin
       Produce Company
   (h) San Bruno Public Warehouse
   (i) A-1 Window Washers
   (j) St. Louis Pharmaceuticals, Inc.

3. In each of the following names select the *first* indexing unit.

   (a) Provident Bank & Trust
       Company of Cleveland
   (b) Michigan State University
   (c) National Association of
       Life Underwriters
   (d) Exchange Club
   (e) St. Gertrude's Church
   (f) University of Cincinnati
   (g) Disabled American Veterans
   (h) Camden Savings and Loan
   (i) Yale Alumni Association
   (j) Miss Hall's Preparatory School
       for Girls

4. Is the order of the names in each of the following pairs correct? Type the pairs of names on a separate sheet of paper. Make any corrections in indexing order that are necessary.

   (a) H. M. Jones
       Henry M. Jonas
   (b) Carl O'Bannon
       J. B. Obannon
   (c) Mrs. Rena Lawson Carter
       Harold Lawson-Carter
   (d) Professor Walter Hampton
       Walter Charles Hampton
   (e) George Carpenter, II
       George Carpenter, III
   (f) Sister Julia
       Julia Sisson
   (g) Ernest V. Mellon, Sr.
       Ernest V. Mellon, Jr.
   (h) Dr. Frank Tarkington
       Frank D. Tarkington
   (i) Francine the Florist
       Francis J. Flanagan
   (j) Charlie's Place
       Charlie Porter, Plumbing

5. Indicate the order in which the parts of the following titles are considered in indexing.

   (a) Board of Education
       Hamilton County, Oregon
   (b) Pennsylvania State
       Department of Highways
   (c) Central Trust Company
       of Delaware
   (d) Department of Public Welfare
       City of Minneapolis, Minnesota
   (e) Phillips & Woods (Real Estate)
   (f) Division of Unemployment
       Compensation
       Ohio State Employment Service
   (g) Oakwood First National Bank
   (h) M. Meredith Weatherby
       (Application for Employment)
   (i) The Gerald Gerrard Gun Shop
   (j) The War College
       U.S. Department of Defense

6. Arrange the following names in correct alphabetic order in each group.

Group 1
(a) H. Duncan McCampbell
(b) Mack Campbell
(c) The Campbell Soup Company
(d) J. C. MacCampbell

Group 2
(a) Martin and Ulberg
(b) Martin C. Ulberg
(c) Martin-Ulberg, Inc.
(d) K. Martin Ulberg, M.D.

Group 3
(a) Rosewood Delicatessen
(b) Olde Rosewood Tea Shoppe
(c) Rose Wood (Mrs.)
(d) Roselawn Public Library

Group 4
(a) Five Corners Car Wash
(b) Five-Corners Creamery
(c) Five O'Clock Shop
(d) 15th Avenue Apartments

Group 5
(a) Williams Ave. Brake Service
(b) William's Coiffures
(c) Williams' Sons (Brokers)
(d) Williamson Heater Company

Group 6
(a) La Maisonette
(b) Lamson & Towers Advertising
(c) Lamps & Lighting, Inc.
(d) Laap Brothers Furniture

Group 7
(a) 2 in 1 Cleaning Service
(b) 22d Street Theater
(c) Twenty-One (Restaurant)
(d) Twosome Dance Club

Group 8
(a) Mrs. J. C. (Barbara) Sands
(b) Santa Barbara Police Dept.
(c) St. Barnaby's Episcopal Church
(d) Barbara St. John

Group 9
(a) Boy Scouts of America
(b) Boy's Scouting Club
(c) Boy and Bike Shop
(d) Boys' and Dads' Day Committee

Group 10
(a) J. & L. Fruit Market
(b) Jones & Laughlin Steel
(c) J. L. Jones Jr.
(d) J. L. Jones, Sr.

7. In completing this exercise you will need fifty 5″ x 3″ file cards or plain paper cut to about that size.

(a) Type each of the following names in index form at the top of a card. Type the number of each name in the upper right corner of the card. (These numbers will aid in checking the answers.) Type the name and address below the indexed name. (See illustration on page 191.)

(b) After the names, numbers, and addresses have been typed, arrange the cards alphabetically.

(c) Save these cards for use in assignments in Unit 7.
   (1) Janitrol Heating Service, 6602 No. Clark St., Chicago, IL 60626
   (2) Kitty's Korner Kitchen, Cooper Bldg., Marietta, OH 45750
   (3) Mlle Jeanette Cecil Sagan, 3 Rue de la Pais, Paris, France
   (4) Janitor Supplies & Equipment Co., 9 W. 7th St., Akron, OH 44314
   (5) Robert P. Van der Meer, 221 Watervliet St., Detroit, MI 48217
   (6) Jerome Labelson, Apt. 3B, 60 Sutton Place, South, New York, NY 10022
   (7) Williams & Williams, Tax Consultants, Suite 12, Statler Hotel, Cleveland, OH 44141
   (8) Jasper J. Seaman, Chalfonte Hall, Campus Station, Durham, NC 27707

(9) Meyer Lufkin & Son, Commercial Bldg., 9th & Walnut, Omaha, NE 68108

(10) Meyer, E. Jones & Millikin Co., 210 N. State St., Albany, NY 12210

(11) Youman & Garties Mfg. Company, 316 Spring St., N.W., Atlanta, GA 30308

(12) The World-Telegram News, Dallas, TX 78421

(13) Raymond J. Vandermeer, 3920 Alamo Drive, Houston, TX 77007

(14) Mid Way Service Station, Junction State Routes 7 & 9, Osburn, ID 83849

(15) Ringling Bros.-Barnum & Bailey Circus, Winter Headquarters, Sarasota, FL 33580

(16) Greenstone Zion Reform Temple, Cor. Reading & Vine Sts., Greenstone, PA 17227

(17) William's U-Fix-It Shop, 4920 Carthage Rd., Richmond, VA 23223

(18) Seamen's Rest, 60 Front St., New Orleans, LA 70130

(19) Wati Rajhma, Room 2100, United Nations Secretariat, New York, NY 10017

(20) Oberhelman Bros. Flooring, Inc., 420 Vine St., Seattle, WA 98121

(21) P. M. Diners' Clubhouse, 22 Regent St., Louisville, KY 40218

(22) Society for the Sightless, 1404 K St., N.W., Washington, D.C. 20005

(23) J. & K. Seaman Hauling Line, 160 N. First St., Ottumwa, IA 52501

(24) 29th Street Mission, 13 - 29th St., San Francisco, CA 94110

(25) La Belle Dresses, 18 Circle Drive, Rogers, CT 06263

(26) Rosenswig's Dept. Store, 6920 Appletree Rd., Wilmington, DE 19810

(27) R. & L. Benjamin & Company, 14 West Decatur St., Ft. Smith, AR 72901

(28) Mayor Michael O'Berne, City Hall, Baltimore, MD 21202

(29) Midway Seafood House, 3109 Collins Ave., Miami Beach, FL 33839

(30) Boy's Hobby Shop, 1010 Pacific Blvd., Portland, OR 97220

(31) Automatic Food Dispenser Co., 112 High St., Colorado Springs, CO 80904

(32) Automatic Food Dispenser Co., 19th & Ewald Sts., Camden, NJ 08105

(33) Automatic Food Dispenser Co., Camden, OH 45311

(34) Boys' Hobby Haven, 730 Pine St., St. Joseph, MO 64504

(35) Lufkin Central Savings Society, 9 So. Main St., Lufkin, TX 75901

(36) Rosen's Fresh Fruit Market, 1403 La Cienega St., Los Angeles, CA 90035

(37) Kitty-Kat Products, Ashport, TN 38003

(38) Long Island Railroad, 69–75 Rockefeller Plaza, New York, NY 10020

(39) Adolph G. Meier Lumber Co., First St. at B. & O. R.R., Columbus, OH 43201

(40) Dr. John W. Barnhart, 22 Medical Arts Bldg., Oak Park, IL 60403

(41) John Barnhart, 635 Capitol Ave., Springfield, IL 62701

(42) Drury Hill Farms, Inc., Box 10, Route 4, Drury, PA 18222

(43) Carthage Mills, Inc., Springvale, GA 31788

(44) Police Department, Drury, PA 18222

(45) P. M. Dinersman Company, 1614 Meridian St., Indianapolis, IN 42625

(46) Branford & Branford Co., Artesia, MS 39736

(47) Branford, Branford and Branford, Attorneys, Union Life Bldg., St. Louis, MO 63155

(48) Olde Seaport Inn, Front and Plum Sts., Alexandria, VA 22313

(49) John L. Barnhart, Sr., 2226 Washington Avenue, Fargo, ND 58102

(50) Ninety and Ninth Apartments, 90th St. at 9th Ave., New York, NY 10024

PART 4 FILING EQUIPMENT AND SUPPLIES FOR CORRESPONDENCE

The following conversation took place between James Dobson, a lawyer, and Lucille Ruebel, a clerk-typist in his office.

"Lucille, why are all of our contracts folded? I would like to be able to give our clients a copy that hasn't been creased."

"Mr. Dobson, there really isn't much choice with our filing equipment. The drawers aren't wide enough to take legal papers unless they are folded. Yet we have to put prepared contracts in the files in order to protect them until the client picks them up. If you would like, I'll be glad to see what filing equipment is available for the kinds of paper we must store."

Knowing the indexing rules for filing is absolutely necessary. But, unless you have the proper filing equipment and the correct supplies, you will not have an efficient filing system. Don't be like the young office worker who wanted to take an automobile trip. She planned her trip and studied the road maps carefully. When she got into her car, however, it wouldn't start. Her equipment was defective, and so she could not accomplish her purpose. Unless your filing equipment and supplies are correct, your filing system will "break down."

FILING EQUIPMENT

Good tools are necessary if you are to make your filing system work for you. In large offices filing equipment is usually ordered through the purchasing department, and filing supplies are available from the stockroom. However, in a small office you may make recommendations and assist your employer in purchasing equipment and supplies. This will require careful study to make correct decisions. Whether you work in a large office or a small office, you will be more efficient if you are familiar with the kinds of equipment and supplies that you will be using on your job.

Proper storage of records is necessary in all businesses. The *size* of the material to be filed is the first factor to be considered; the *number of items* to be filed each day is second.

Standard filing cabinets are available for storing the two most common sizes of business records: letter size (8½″ x 11″) and the legal size (8½″ x 13″ or 8½″ x 14″). Other cabinets are designed to house card files, visible records, punched cards, computer print-outs, blueprints, and other materials.

Vertical Files

The typical pull-out drawer file cabinet — the **vertical** file — is used in most business offices. Vertical file cabinets are manufactured in two-, three-, four-, and five-drawer units. Two-drawer vertical file cabinets are used beside the desk and contain only the most active records. Three-drawer vertical file cabinets are often referred to as counter-height cabinets. Five-drawer vertical file cabinets are replacing four-drawer units since they occupy the same amount of floor space, but contain an additional drawer.

Office space in the business districts of many large cities is very expensive and may rent for as high as $15 a square foot; so a saving in floor space for filing cabinets can greatly reduce the cost of housing records.

Every business office has correspondence files. Correspondence files consist of letters, telegrams, teletype messages, purchase orders, invoices, memorandums, reports, and interoffice messages. Reading the correspondence files of any company is the easiest way to learn the nature

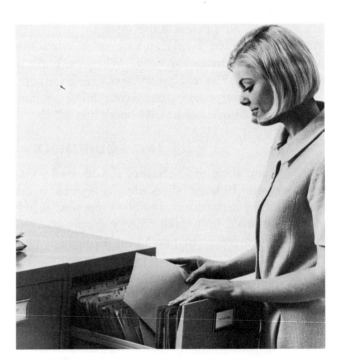

Illus. 6-9
Three-drawer vertical file cabinets are often referred to as counter-height cabinets.

Kelly Services

of its business and the history of its transactions. Active correspondence files are usually kept in desk-side two-drawer files; while files on completed transactions are kept in three-, four-, or five-drawer files in other areas of the office.

Lateral and Shelf Files

Because of the increasing number of records that must be kept in expensive office space, many organizations are now using **lateral** and shelf files. The lateral cabinets look a lot like a chest of drawers and are frequently used as area dividers or low partitions. Often a lateral cabinet is placed behind a desk to house records constantly referred to, such as current correspondence, sales reports, price lists, and production reports.

lateral: directed toward or coming from the side

In shelf filing, papers are held in folders placed on shelves in an upright position. Some shelf files are built with open shelves (like the shelving of library books); others are equipped with sliding doors to protect the records. Some are equipped with sliding shelves which draw out sidewise, similar in operation to the pull-out drawer in a typical file cabinet.

Units that are seven or eight shelves high provide the **maximum** amount of filing area for the floor space while keeping the records within reach. While much floor space can be saved by using shelf files, many records management consultants believe that individual records cannot be filed or found as quickly as in vertical files, particularly when sliding doors are used to protect the shelf files. They believe shelf filing is most effective for storing records that are not frequently requested.

In addition to the standard filing equipment mentioned here, there is a great deal of specialized filing equipment that is used in microfilming and in the data processing field which is described and illustrated in Part 4 of Unit 7.

Illus. 6-11
Shelf files provide a maximum amount of filing area.

FILING SUPPLIES

Since your filing duties will be concerned mostly with alphabetic name and subject files, which are often combined in one system, you should know how to use the tools within a file drawer to their greatest advantage.

Unit 6 / Business Filing

Each drawer in a correspondence file contains two different kinds of filing supplies — guides and file folders. The *guides* in an alphabetic correspondence file divide the drawer into alphabetic sections and serve as signposts for quick reference. They also provide support for the folders and their contents.

File folders hold the papers in an upright position in the file drawer. They are made of heavy paper stock and serve as a container to keep papers together.

Guides

Guides are heavy cardboard sheets which are the same size as the folders. Extending over the top of each guide is a tab upon which is marked or printed a notation or title called a *caption*. The caption indicates the alphabetic range of the material filed in folders behind the guide. For example, a guide may carry the caption *A* which tells you that only material starting with the letter *A* is to be found between that guide and the next guide. This tab may be part of the guide itself, or it may be an attached metal or plastic tab. Sets of guides may be purchased with printed letters or combinations of letters and numbers that may be used with any standard filing system. Other guide tabs are blank, and the specific captions are made in the user's office.

Guides may be obtained with a rod projection that extends below the body of the guide. The projection contains a metal eyelet through which a file drawer rod may be run, thus holding the guides in place and preventing the folders from slipping down in the drawer.

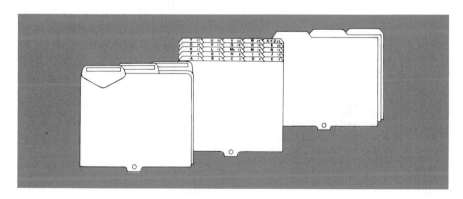

Illus. 6-12
File guides
with metal eyelets
for drawer rods

Kinds of Guides. Guides are classified as primary or secondary. The *primary guides* indicate the major divisions — alphabetic, numeric, subject, geographic, or chronological — into which the filing system is divided. *Secondary guides* (also called auxiliary or special name guides) are subdivisions of the primary guides and are used to highlight certain types of information, for example, to indicate the placement of special folders (such as those for *Advertising* or *Applications*). They are also used to indicate a section of the file in which many folders with the same first indexing unit are placed. For example, if a file contains many individual folders for the name *Brown* behind the primary guide with the caption *B*, a secondary guide with the caption *Brown* might be placed in the file drawer to aid in finding one of the *Brown* folders.

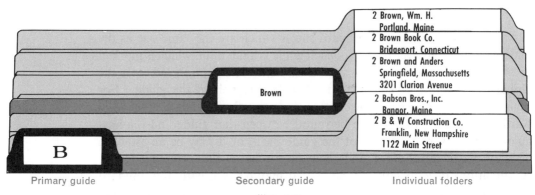

| Primary guide | Secondary guide | Individual folders |

2 Brown, Wm. H.
Portland, Maine

2 Brown Book Co.
Bridgeport, Connecticut

2 Brown and Anders
Springfield, Massachusetts
3201 Clarion Avenue

2 Babson Bros., Inc.
Bangor, Maine

2 B & W Construction Co.
Franklin, New Hampshire
1122 Main Street

Brown

B

Illus. 6-13

Number of Guides. If individual folders are to be located quickly, not more than ten should be filed behind any one guide. The number of guides, however, will depend on the actual use of the file and the amount of material in each folder. Anywhere from 15 to 25 guides in each file drawer will help in finding and filing in most filing systems.

CHART SHOWING PRIMARY GUIDE CAPTIONS FOR VARIOUS ALPHABETIC SUBDIVISIONS

Illus. 6-14

10 A-Z	25 A-Z	40 A-Z	60 A-Z	80 A-Z	120 A-Z	160 A-Z	Guide No.
A–B	A	A	A	A	A	A	1
C–D	B	B	Am	Ae	Al	Ai	2
E–G	C	Be	B	An	An	Am	3
H–J	D	Bo	Be	B	Ar	An	4
K–L	E	C	Bi	Bar	B	Ar	5
M	F	Ci	Br	Be	Bar	B	6
N–R	G	Cr	By	Bi	Be	Bam	7
S	H	D	C	Bo	Ben	Bas	8
T–V	I	Di	Ce	Br	Bi	Be	9
W–Z	J	E	Co	Bu	Bo	Ben	10

The Globe-Wernicke Systems Co.

Folders

A folder is made of a sheet of heavy paper that has been folded once so that the back is about one-half inch higher than the front. Folders are larger than the papers they contain so that they protect them. Two standard folder sizes are *letter size* for papers that are 8½″ x 11″ and *legal size* for papers that are 8½″ x 13″ or 8½″ x 14″.

Folders are cut across the top in two ways — so that the back is straight (straight cut) or so that the back has a tab that projects above the top of the folder. Such tabs bear captions that identify the contents of each folder. Tabs vary in width and position. The tabs of a set of folders that are one-half cut are half the width of the folder and have only two positions. *One-third cut* folders have three positions, each tab occupying a third of the width of the folder. Another standard tab is *one-fifth cut* which, as you can see, has five positions. Other folders "hang" from a metal frame placed inside the file drawer.

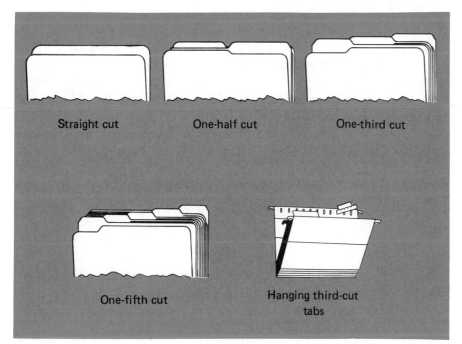

Straight cut   One-half cut   One-third cut

One-fifth cut   Hanging third-cut tabs

Illus. 6-15

Miscellaneous Folders. A miscellaneous folder is kept for every alphabetic primary guide. It is called a *miscellaneous* folder because it contains filed material from more than one person or firm. When there are fewer than six pieces of filed material to, from, or about the same person or firm, these documents are placed in a folder bearing the same caption as the primary guide it serves. For example, if the caption on the primary guide is *B*, the caption on the miscellaneous folders will also be *B*.

Individual Folders. When six pieces of filed material to, from, or about one person or subject have accumulated in the miscellaneous folder, an individual folder for this material is prepared. The caption on the tab of an individual folder identifies the correspondent. Obviously materials will be found faster if they are filed in an individual folder rather than in a miscellaneous folder.

Special Folders. When an organization files a large amount of material that relates to one subject (such as applications for employment) all this related material is placed in a special folder. The caption identifies the subject or the name of the material. A special folder may be prepared to file all identical last names, thus removing them from the miscellaneous folder. For example, all the *Smiths* may be removed from the miscellaneous folder and placed in a special folder, thus permitting material filed under *Smith* to be found faster.

Capacity of Folders. Folders should never become overcrowded. Each separate folder should contain not more than one inch of filed material. Most file folders have *score lines* at the bottom that are used to widen each folder and thereby increase its capacity. When the folder begins to fill up, the first score is creased; as more pieces of filed material are inserted, the remaining scores are creased.

When a folder can hold no more material it should be subdivided into two or more folders. Subdivisions may be made according to date or by subject:

Jones Company January–March	Jones Company Orders
Jones Company April–June	Jones Company Receipts

The subdivided folder should be properly identified. *Folder 1* or *Folder 2* does not indicate what is in the folder.

Miscellaneous folders should be examined often so that individual and special folders may be prepared to expand the filing system.

Labels

There are two principal kinds of labels for filing — folder labels and file drawer labels. Folder labels come in a variety of colors. Each company has its own system of identifying file folders by the use of color. You will find the use of color in filing a great help in locating particular files in a matter of seconds and thus acts as a money-saving device in keeping costs under control. Drawer labels are usually white.

Folder Labels. The captions on folder labels may be printed by hand or typewritten. It is better if they are typewritten because they can be read more easily. Labels are glued to the folder tabs.

Consistency in typing captions on labels is important. The captions should always be typed in exact indexing order (*Brown John A* — not *John A. Brown*). Punctuation other than a hyphen or dash is usually omitted. In order to insure uniformity in the files you should type the first letter in the caption at the same point on each label, usually two spaces from the left edge. Type the name on the label so that after the labels have been attached to the folders, the names will appear at the top edge of each tab. For ease in reading, upper and lower case letters should be used. In a subject file, however, the caption of the main subject is sometimes typed in all upper case letters to make it stand out. The subdivision file labels are then typed in upper and lower case.

consistency: agreement of parts to one another or a whole

Labels must be kept in good condition and must be replaced when torn or difficult to read. Hard-to-read or torn labels tend to delay the finding of filed materials.

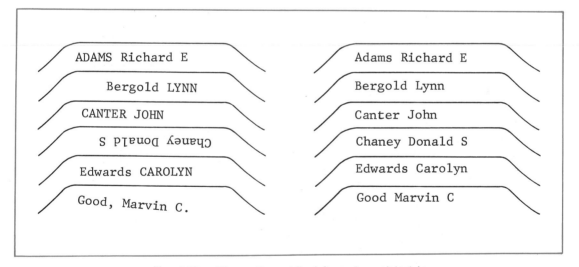

Illus. 6-16   The captions at the left are inconsistent in their punctuation, capitalization, and placement. Captions may be typed in all capital letters or as shown at the right.

Drawer Labels. Drawer labels are used to identify the contents of each file drawer. To locate filed material quickly, the labels must be specific, easily read, and up to date. The information should appear on the drawer front as illustrated at the top of page 226.

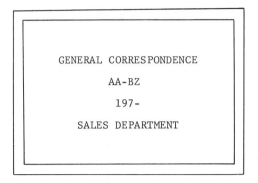

GENERAL CORRESPONDENCE

AA-BZ

197-

SALES DEPARTMENT

Line 1 — Description

2 — Index

3 — Year

4 — Unit or department

Illus. 6-17

When the contents of a cabinet are changed in any way, the drawer label must be corrected immediately.

POSITIONS OF GUIDES AND FOLDERS

Since the tabs on guides and folders take up only part of the space available, they may appear in several positions. In any filing system, the tabs in each position should be of the same width. Specific positions should be reserved for each type of guide and folder. When guide positions are made with regard to the position of the folders, the filing system becomes well organized. An example of this is an alphabetic system in which four filing positions are used.

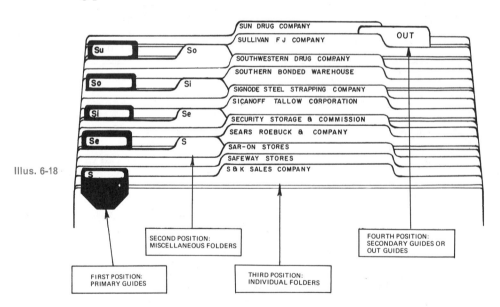

Illus. 6-18

1. First position: Reserved for primary guides indicating the major divisions of the system.

2. Second position: Reserved for miscellaneous folders. Miscellaneous folders carry the same caption as the primary guides and are placed at the end of each category, *immediately in front of the next primary guide.*

3. Third position: Reserved for individual folders filed directly behind the primary guides.

4. Fourth position: Reserved for secondary guides or out guides. (An out guide is put in the file to indicate that a folder has been borrowed.)

FILING ACCESSORIES

In addition to filing cabinets, guides, and folders, there are many **accessories** that will make your filing job easier. Some of these are a table or desk to be used when arranging material for the files, file boxes or baskets into which material is placed, and a sorter for arranging papers before they are filed.

accessories: things which aren't necessary but which add efficiency, effectiveness, or beauty

REVIEWING WHAT YOU HAVE READ

1. Why would a five-drawer vertical file be preferred to a four-drawer file?
2. What are the three different types of folders that will be found behind any particular guide in a file drawer?
3. What is a miscellaneous folder, and where is it placed in relation to the primary guide and the other folders?
4. What information should a drawer label contain?
5. What is the purpose of an out guide?

MAKING DECISIONS

Mrs. Peggy Cummings, who heads the United States operation for a French cosmetic company, has placed Marion Walters in charge of the filing department of the research division for developing new cosmetics. Cosmetic formulas are guarded very carefully. One of Marion's most important responsibilities is to personally maintain the highly confidential files of newly developed products. These files are locked when not in use.

This week at lunch a close friend and fellow employee asked Marion about the ingredients in a new face powder. The employee (and friend) said that her doctor was performing a series of allergy tests on her and she would like to cooperate by giving him this information in order to help him find the source of her difficulty as quickly as possible. What should Marion do?

WORKING WITH OTHERS

Jean Fowler is employed in the Central Records Department of the Adams Electric Company. When Bill Stone, one of the young men in the Accounting Department, phones for information about invoices and other records, he always identifies himself as J. B. Adams, President of the company. Jean has become well aware of the fact that he is joking and usually gives him a smart answer.

One day Jean received a telephone call from a man who identified himself as J. B. Adams. Thinking that the caller was the alleged humorist in the Accounting Department, Jean gave him a very smart answer. Her caller proved to be the real but somewhat astonished J. B. Adams, President of the company.

Jean recovered quickly and supplied Mr. Adams with the information he asked for. Later she began to worry about what had happened and about her general conduct in telephone conversations, particularly when dealing with the young man in the Accounting Department.

Should Jean call the President and try to explain her unusual behavior, or should she try to forget the incident and hope the President will forget it too? What recommendations would you make concerning Jean's behavior?

USING LANGUAGE

Of the following 20 words, at least ten have been misspelled. Type the entire list giving the correct spelling of each misspelled word.

1.	accessories	11.	miscellaneous
2.	chronalogical	12.	obviously
3.	consistency	13.	partition
4.	distroyed	14.	primery
5.	efficiency	15.	reciepts
6.	essential	16.	refered
7.	facilitate	17.	retrievel
8.	familar	18.	correspondence
9.	guarentees	19.	similar
10.	latteral	20.	verticle

USING ARITHMETIC

1. Along with your other duties, you maintain the stock of office supplies for the office. On Monday morning when you check the supplies you find the following have been used since last Monday morning:

80% of the letterheads
60% of the file folders
12.5% of the erasers
25% of the typewriter ribbons
20% of the plain white bond paper

List these items on a separate sheet of paper and convert the decimals to fractions.

2. If you earn $90 a week, how much will you be paid each month?
If you save $3 a week, how much will you save in a year before interest is added?
If your rent is $80 a month, how much will housing cost you for a year?
If your insurance policy premium is $40.36 annually, how much do you pay semi-annually?

On a separate sheet of paper show your answers as well as how you computed them.

PERFORMING OFFICE TASKS

List five or more places where your name is on file indicating in each instance just how it is filed. For example, list how your name is filed for Social Security purposes, for school records, for life insurance, for a charge account, for a driver's license, for a public library card, in a telephone directory.

UNIT 7

RECORDS MANAGEMENT

FILE CLERK

SALARY $90-95

Major midtown motion pictu
mpany seeks an alert f
rk experienced in subje
. Pleasant office, excelle
its plan. Call Sue Goldbe
ppointment.
7000 EXT. 264
rtunity Employ

PART 1 — BASIC FILING PROCEDURES

Audrey Frierson has worked in the office of Mr. Walter Carrelli since he started the Carrelli Air-Conditioning Company a year ago. Audrey, with the help of a filing consultant, set up the filing system in the beginning and has supervised its expansion. When new employees are hired, Audrey explains the filing procedures that they are to use. Among the many things Audrey stresses are the proper collection, inspection, and cross-referencing of materials to be filed.

Effective filing procedures begin long before any material is actually placed in the files. If they are properly applied, systematic filing procedures will in the long run save you time which you can use to perform other important office duties. But, of even greater importance, well-organized and carefully followed filing practices insure the prompt retrieval of filed records.

COLLECTING PAPERS FOR THE FILES

The basic reason for having a filing system is to be able to find information when it is needed. Unless materials are filed promptly and properly, this is not possible.

Correspondence and other business papers that are to be filed should be gathered in an orderly manner. Materials to be filed should be kept in a special basket or tray which is usually marked *File*.

INSPECTING

In large offices several times a day a messenger collects the papers to be filed in the central files. In a small office it may be your duty to collect the materials to be filed. After the files have been collected the next step in the filing process is to inspect each document to be filed.

During the inspection process you look for a *release mark*, which is your authority to file each letter. This mark indicates that action has been taken on the letter, and it is released for filing. The release mark is usually indicated by the initials of an authorized person in the upper left corner of the letter.

Since it is assumed that carbon copies are ready to file, they do not bear release marks. Many firms prepare carbon copies on paper with the words F I L E C O P Y printed in large outline letters across the face of the sheet. Frequently colored paper is used for the file copy.

In addition to checking for the release mark, you should examine records for completeness. All correspondence that is clipped together is examined and stapled (if it belongs together) in the upper left corner. The reply is stapled on top of the incoming letter. Paper clips, rubber bands, or straight pins are never placed in the file drawer. Torn papers should be mended at this time.

INDEXING

Although every step in the filing process is important, the indexing step is particularly significant. *Indexing* is the process of determining how a document is to be filed. An incorrect decision at this time may mean a lost letter. At the very least, it means lost time in locating the letter. It is necessary, therefore, to scan or read each letter carefully to determine the *key name* or title that best identifies the material.

The way materials are requested usually determines the way they should be indexed. An incoming letter could be filed under the name appearing on the letterhead, the name of the person signing the letter, the name of a person or business mentioned in the body of the letter, or the subject of the letter. For example, a letter announcing a new fire-resistant filing cabinet would probably be filed under the heading "Office Equipment" in a folder labeled "Filing Cabinets" rather than under the name of the distributor appearing on the letterhead.

Copies of outgoing letters could be filed under the name of the addressee, the name of a person or business mentioned in the letter, or the subject of the letter. If a letter is of a personal nature, it is filed under the name of the person to or by whom it is written, even though the letter may have been written on a company letterhead. If there is any doubt about how a document should be indexed, the person who has released the record for filing should be consulted.

CODING

After the exact indexing order has been chosen, the document is marked or coded. A document may be coded in several different ways. The indexing units may be underlined.

|Acme Dry Cleaning Corporation

R. Robert |Wagner

Or the units may be numbered.

1   2   3   4

Acme Dry Cleaning Corporation

2   3   1

R. Robert Wagner

If the name or subject does not appear in the letter, it must be written in, preferably in the upper right portion of the paper. All coding is done with a colored pencil. Coding aids in filing the record each time it is removed from the file as it does not need to be reread.

CROSS-REFERENCING

Although selecting the indexing caption is **relatively** simple in most cases, there are always some records that might be requested in different ways. For example, your firm might receive a letter from a good customer recommending an applicant for a position. Obviously this letter of recommendation should be filed with other records referring to the applicant and would be filed in the applicant's folder in the "Applications" section. It may be well, however, to keep a record of the letter in the customer's folder. The name of the applicant, therefore, is underlined on the letter as the primary indexing unit. The customer's name (of secondary importance in this instance) is also underlined and an *X* placed at the end of the line in the margin to show that a cross-reference should be made.

A cross-reference sheet (usually of a distinctive color) is prepared with the name and address of the customer, the date of the letter, a brief description of the letter, and where the letter is filed following the "SEE." This cross-reference is then placed in the customer's folder, in its proper

date **sequence** with the other papers, as a record of the letter.

Rather than prepare regular cross-reference sheets, many companies prefer using a photocopy of the original. This speeds retrieval since a complete copy of the record is available at each file point. Do not forget, however, to underline and place an *X* on each copy, so that you will know in which folder each is to be filed.

Many hard-to-index documents should be cross-referenced in several places, for this is your one opportunity to think of the number of ways by which material may be requested. Too much cross-referencing requires considerable time as well as filing space; however, too little cross-referencing may delay retrieval.

If a permanent cross-reference is desired, a cross-reference guide is prepared. This is a **manila** card the same size as a file folder, with a tab

CROSS-REFERENCE RECORD

FIRM NAME or SUBJECT *Dye* ① *(for Synthetic Fibers)* ②③   File No. O 47.2

Date 2/25/7- Remarks

SEE *Alco Clothing Co.*   File No. A 47.2

1421 Leeland Road

Bedford, Ma 01730

Date 2/28/7-   Signed *Mr. Betz*

FILE CROSS-REFERENCE RECORD UNDER NAME OR
SUBJECT LISTED AT TOP OF THIS SHEET, AND IN
PROPER DATE ORDER.
THE PAPER REFERRED TO SHOULD BE FILED
UNDER NAME OR SUBJECT LISTED UNDER "SEE"

Illus. 7-2. Cross-reference for letter

ALCO CLOTHING COMPANY
1421 LEELAND ROAD • BEDFORD, MA 01730
PHONE 617-421-3746

19- FEB 28 AM 9:44

February 25, 197-

R.L.D.

Mr. Robert L. Downs
Color-Lite Manufacturing Co.
1874 Rockney Road
Boise, ID 83705

Dear Mr. Downs

We are in the process of expanding our line
to include synthetic fibers. This makes it necessary for us to seek sources of supplies of dyes
that are compatible with synthetic fibers. Your
company has been suggested as a possible source
of supply.

Would you please send us your catalog of
dyes so that we may make our evaluation? If
there is additional information that you think
may be of assistance to us, we would appreciate
seeing it.

Sincerely yours

Albert Hayes
Albert Hayes
Purchasing Agent

el

Illus. 7-1 Letter properly released and coded

in the same position as those used for individual folders. A situation requiring a permanent cross-reference guide might be as follows: The name of a company with which you do a great deal of business is changed. Another folder is prepared for the new name and all the material is placed in this folder. The old folder is now replaced with a permanent cross-reference guide with the retrieval information typed on the label:

Adams and Smith Manufacturing Co.
See Adams and Jones Manufacturing Co.

If a special form is not available, use the back half of the folder as a cross-reference guide by cutting off the front flap of the folder at the score line. The cross-reference guide remains in the file as long as the name or subject is still active. (See page 259 for additional information on cross-referencing.)

SORTING

After the records have been coded and the necessary cross-reference sheets prepared, the material is ready to be sorted. *Sorting* is the process of arranging the records in indexing order before placing them in the folders.

Illus. 7-3
Daily filing time can be greatly reduced by using proper indexing and sorting equipment.

Yawman & Erbe

Sorting serves two important purposes. First, it saves actual filing time. Since the records are in exact indexing order, you are able to move

A. INSPECTING means seeing that the letter has been released for filing. GTF indicates that this letter has been released.

B. INDEXING means determining the key name under which the correspondence should be filed. This letter should be filed under Shipley-Langston Stores.

C. CODING means determining and marking the exact indexing order. The correct order is (1) Shipley (2) Langston (3) Stores.

D. CROSS-REFERENCING means trying to decide if the letter might be requested in some other way. This letter should be cross-referenced under (1) Langston (2) Shipley (3) Stores. The X indicates that it has been cross-referenced.

E. SORTING means arranging all the records in indexing order before placing them in the files. This letter would be sorted under S.

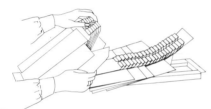

F. PLACING RECORDS IN THE FILES simply means storing the correspondence in the proper place until it is needed.

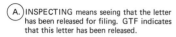

B. **C.**
1   2   3
X
SHIPLEY-LANGSTON STORES

D.

873 Mallard Drive
Costa Mesa, CA 92626
Telephone 714-633-0525

A. GTF

197- MAR 20 AM 10:45

March 18, 197-

Mrs. Grace T. Froman, President
Foremost Fashions, Inc.
2142 Granada Avenue
San Francisco, CA 94112

Dear Mrs. Froman

You were right! Your spring collection of dresses is the fastest moving line we have ever carried. After being on our racks for only two weeks, about 40 percent of our stock has been sold.

I wish you could be here to listen to our customers' compliments. Being wise shoppers, they realize the versatility, practicality, and economy of your dresses. We have never before witnessed such complete acceptance by the consumer.

We send our congratulations on your success. If the present sales pace continues, you should receive a substantial follow-up order within the next two weeks.

Sincerely yours

George B Verner

George B. Verner
Manager

sv

Illus. 7-4 Basic filing procedures

quickly from drawer to drawer, thus saving time and energy for other important tasks. Second, if documents are requested before they are filed, they can be found quickly.

If the volume of filing is high, special sorting trays or compartments should be used. Sorting trays are equipped with alphabetic, numeric, or geographic guides, depending upon the classification system you are using. When you sort materials alphabetically, for example, records beginning with the letter *A* are placed behind an *A* guide; those beginning with *B*, behind a *B* guide, and so on through the alphabet. After the materials have been rough sorted, they are removed from the sorting tray and placed in exact alphabetic order (fine sorting). If the volume of material is low, this same procedure may be followed on your desk top.

PLACING RECORDS IN THE FILE

After the records have been fine sorted they are placed in the files. A systematic routine should always be followed:

1. Locate the proper file drawer by examining drawer labels.
2. Scan the primary guides in the drawer to locate the major alphabetic section desired.
3. Check to see if an individual or special folder has been prepared for this material. If so, file the record here.

Illus. 7-5
Don't allow folders to bulge. Bulging folders encourage filing errors.

4. If no individual or special folder is available for this particular record, file the letter in the miscellaneous folder for the section.

ARRANGING MATERIALS IN FOLDERS

Letters should always be placed in folders with the front of the letter facing the front of the folder and the top of the letter at the left side.

In *individual* folders, letters are arranged according to date, with the *most recent* record in front. In *miscellaneous* folders, documents are arranged alphabetically by name; if there are two or more records for the same individual or company, they are arranged according to date, with the most recent record first. In a *special* folder, the records are arranged alphabetically by name and then by date in each group of names.

TWENTY FILING HINTS

Twenty filing hints recommended by experienced filing supervisors are given on the following pages.

1. Be a good housekeeper. Well-organized, carefully administered files encourage accurate filing and rapid retrieval. What is more, you will enjoy filing!

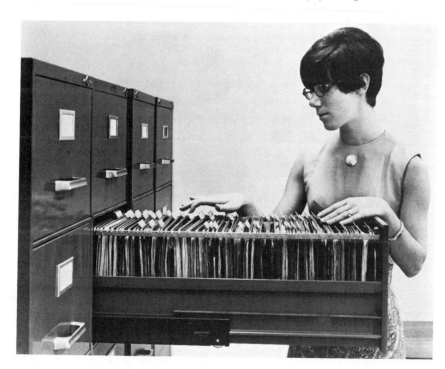

Illus. 7-6
Expand your system by preparing special and individual folders whenever possible.

Oxford Pendaflex Corporation

2. Don't foolishly economize on file supplies. Good quality supplies hold up through continued hard use; poor quality supplies soon wear out and hinder the efficiency of the system. Choose the right supplies for the right records with a particular system in mind.

3. Before refiling any folder that has been removed from the files, quickly examine its contents. You may find a lost document by performing this simple procedure. Always "jog" the contents of a folder before returning it to the file.

4. Set aside a definite time each day for filing. Remember: records belong in the file — not in or on desks.

5. Constantly analyze your filing system and recommend ways in which it can be improved. Your employer will appreciate any suggestion for an improved information system. Seek the advice of your office supplies dealer. Constantly review the various business publications. They'll keep you informed on the latest products and new developments in the field of records management.

6. Let color help. Use different color labels for different file years or periods. A well-planned color scheme will aid in prompt filing and retrieving.

7. Keep your system simple. If others must use your files, be certain they understand how the system works, but insist that you do all the filing and refiling. Provide a handy place for them to place the materials they have removed from the files. They will be glad to cooperate — and it will guarantee file accuracy.

8. File the most active records in the most easily reached parts of the file cabinets. Active records belong in the top drawers, less active documents in bottom drawers. This saves both time and energy.

9. Use your filing cabinets only for filing, not for storing office supplies and other items. File only vital records in the special fire-resistant equipment that has been purchased for their protection.

10. Don't allow folders to bulge. Bulging folders encourage filing errors. When necessary, subdivide individual folders into monthly folders. Expand your system by preparing special and individual folders.

11. Separate records that must be maintained in the files for long periods of time from those of temporary value.

12. If smaller than normal sized documents are placed in file folders, glue or tape them to standard size paper. They will be easier to find.

13. If a particular document was difficult to retrieve, cross-reference it when it is finally found. It will save time when it is requested again.

14. Protect the tabs on guides and folders. Always lift a folder or guide by the side — never by the tab. Replace folder labels as soon as they are difficult to read.

15. Don't fill a file drawer to capacity. Leave at least six inches of working space in each file drawer. It speeds up your work and prevents papers from being torn.

16. To avoid accidents, close a file drawer immediately after using it; and open only one drawer at a time.

17. Use the proper filing tools. A rubber finger helps separate documents; a file shelf makes you more efficient at the file; a file stool conserves your energy (yes, you can file sitting down).

18. Mend all torn documents before placing them in a file folder.

19. Follow a regular program of removing inactive records from the active files.

20. Be certain to follow, without **variation**, the office procedures that have been established to protect vital records.

variation:
change

REVIEWING WHAT YOU HAVE READ

1. How are letters and other papers gathered together for filing and by whom?
2. Do carbon copies of outgoing letters need release marks?
3. Is *indexing* something that is written?
4. What are the various captions under which incoming letters could be filed?
5. Under what captions may copies of outgoing letters be filed?
6. Under what caption is a personal letter filed?
7. What is coding and how is it done?
8. Explain the process of cross-referencing?
9. What is used to establish a permanent cross-reference?
10. How are letters arranged in *individual* folders? in *miscellaneous* folders? in *special* folders?

MAKING DECISIONS

1. Why are indexing and coding so important in filing?
2. It is said that cross-referencing can be overdone. Under what circumstances might this be true?
3. Why is the most recent letter placed in front in an *individual* folder?

In the office of the Walters Shoe Company, Mr. J. B. Wilkins has received a letter asking for an answer to an earlier letter written by the National Leather Company. The unanswered letter was found in the *special* folder of the National Leather Company. The letter bears the initials JBW as a release-for-filing mark, but Mr. Wilkins says he does not remember initialing the letter. The initials were actually placed there by mistake by Mr. Wilkins' secretary. What should the file clerk do in this situation?

All twenty key words listed below are used in filing. After you have studied the example, type the key word and the word or phrase you believe is *nearest in meaning* to the key word.

Example: facilitate — (a) appreciate (b) depreciate (c) *make easier* (d) negotiate

1. *adhere* — (a) to expect (b) to hold closely (c) to part (d) to loosen
2. *appropriate* — (a) approximate (b) apt (c) fitting (d) unsuitable
3. *caption* — (a) finishing stone (b) heading or title (c) rank of captain (d) seizure
4. *comprehensive* — (a) compelling (b) complex (c) extensive (d) limited
5. *consistent* — (a) consonant (b) incompatible (c) incongruous (d) tribunal
6. *conventional* — (a) contrary (b) customary (c) jovial (d) well informed
7. *distinctive* — (a) distasteful (b) sound harsh (c) intemperate (d) individual
8. *document* — (a) a particular principle (b) an established opinion (c) any written item (d) ownership of land
9. *effective* — (a) exhausted of vigor (b) flowing out (c) producing intended results (d) show enthusiasm
10. *identical* — (a) idealistic (b) matching (c) unlike (d) visionary
11. *initial* — (a) beginning (b) concluding (c) inheriting (d) suggesting
12. *legible* — (a) branch of military science (b) multitude (c) valid (d) capable of being read
13. *primary* — (a) humble (b) last (c) main (d) proud
14. *procedure* — (a) a disposition (b) course of action (c) to defer action (d) to progress
15. *propel* — (a) foretell (b) multiply (c) project (d) prove
16. *retention* — (a) silent (b) rejoinder (c) remedy (d) memory
17. *retrieval* — (a) recovery (b) retraction (c) retrenchment (d) retribution
18. *sequence* — (a) separation (b) series (c) seriousness (d) sermon
19. *variation* — (a) deviation (b) sameness (c) truthfulness (d) word for word
20. *vital* — (a) unimportant (b) expendable (c) resounding (d) essential

On a separate sheet of paper show your computations and the answers to the following problems.

1. In order to earn money for Christmas you sold boxes of Christmas cards on which you received a commission of 25 cents a box. You sold 84 boxes. How much Christmas money did you earn?
2.   1% of $60 is _____.
   10% of $94 is _____.
   100% of $28 is _____.
   1000% of $15 is _____.
3. Your starting salary of $94.50 a week is equal to how much a month?

1. The following letters pertaining to the application of John A. Dillon are filed in the "Applications" folder of the firm where you work. Indicate the order, from front to back, in which the letters should be placed in this folder.

4 (a) Henry & Currier Company's March 8 letter of recommendation

7 (b) John A. Dillon's March 12 letter stating that he will call on March 15

2 (c) Your firm's March 3 letter to Mr. Dillon asking him to come in for an interview

9 (d) John A. Dillon's March 18 letter accepting the position

3 (e) Your firm's March 5 letter to the Henry & Currier Company asking for information about Mr. John A. Dillon

6 (f) Your firm's March 11 letter to Mr. Dillon asking him to come in for a second interview

8 (g) Your firm's March 17 letter offering Mr. Dillon a position in the cost accounting department

1 (h) John A. Dillon's March 1 letter of application

5 (i) Your firm's March 9 letter to Henry & Currier Company thanking them for their cooperation

2. The following letters are filed in the Harvey O. Jackson individual folder. Indicate the order, from front to back, in which the letters should be placed in this folder.

1 (a) Harvey O. Jackson's order of April 1

3 (b) Your firm's letter of April 8 enclosing the April 6 invoice

5 (c) Harvey O. Jackson's letter of April 30 enclosing a check

4 (d) A cross-reference sheet dated April 10

6 (e) Your firm's letter of May 3 acknowledging the check of April 30

2 (f) Your firm's invoice of April 6 for the April 1 order

3. The letters listed below are filed in the "To-Tw" miscellaneous folder. Indicate the order, from front to back, in which the letters should be placed in this folder.

2 (a) Your firm's letter of September 30 to Arthur Towne, Jr.

1 (b) The receipted invoice sent to you on September 21 by Albert Town

3 (c) Towne and Lovitt's order of September 2

6 (d) Your firm's letter of September 28 to Richard G. Twitchell

4 (e) Your firm's invoice of September 6 covering the September 2 order from Towne and Lovitt

5 (f) An advertising circular and letter dated September 14 sent to your employer by H. J. Tweed

4. This is a continuation of the alphabetic indexing exercise begun in Unit 6, Part 3.

(a) Type the following names in index form on 25 file cards. Type the number in the upper right-hand corner and the name and address below the indexed name as you did in Unit 6, Part 3.

(b) Incorporate these 25 cards in proper filing order with the 50 cards prepared in Unit 6, Part 3.

(c) Save the cards for the assignment following Unit 7, Part 4.

(51) X-Cel Paints & Varnishes, 532 Mill St., Pittsburgh, PA 15221

(52) Theodore C. Haller, 59 E. 10th St., Charleston, WV 25303

(53) Henry R. Elston, II, 660 N. Michigan Ave., Chicago, IL 60611

(54) XYZ Electrical Repair Service, 2d and Main Sts., Lexington, KY 40507

(55) Countess Flora's Dance Academy, Chase Hotel, St. Louis, MO 63166

(56) Mrs. K. D. Ingles (Hazel Parks), 40 Sheridan Dr., Providence, RI 02909

(57) Quick Brothers Florists, 6720 Turkey Run Rd., Nashville, TN 37202

(58) Charles T. Hallam, 4600 Pueblo St., Phoenix, AZ 85041

(59) Hall-Kramer Printing Co., Inc., 7700 S. Wells St., Chicago, IL 60621

(60) R. Nelson Forrester, 377 Desert Drive, Reno, NV 89504

(61) Robert N. Forrest, 781 University Ave., Minneapolis, MN 55413

(62) Sister Julietta, Sacred Heart Academy, Racine, WI 53401

(63) William A. Graves, 239 N. Vineyard Drive, Kenosha, WI 53140

(64) Mrs. Arthur P. Matthews (Helen), 5229 Crest Drive, Cleveland, OH 44121

(65) Town & Country Furniture Co., Town & Country Shop-In, Centerville, IN 47330

(66) U.S. Electrotype Corp., 2101 - 19th St., Long Island City, NY 11105

(67) Prince George Hotel, St. Thomas, Virgin Islands 00801

(68) Les Trois Chats Inn, 48 Henri St., Quebec, Province of Quebec, Canada

(69) 29 Palms Motel, U.S. 60 at First St., Twenty-Nine Palms, CA 92277

(70) Venice Yacht Club, 29 Oceanside Drive, Venice, CA 90291

(71) Mr. Morris Book Store, 6th & Pike Sts., Mt. Morris, IL 61054

(72) State Auditor, Columbus, OH 43216

(73) Hire-the-Handicapped Committee, 30 Le Veque Tower, Denver, CO 80201

(74) Hamilton County SPCA, Colerain & Blue Rock Sts., Cincinnati, OH 45223

(75) Port-au-Prince Imports, Inc., 21 Main St., Gulfport, MS 39501

PART 2

CHARGE-OUT, FOLLOW-UP, TRANSFER, AND RETENTION

> After five years of operations, the Nickerson Printing Company has expanded to the point where it needs a central filing system. A new filing clerk has just been hired. Julia Coombs, Mr. Nickerson's office manager, has supervised the files since the company was founded. Until the central files are set up and are being maintained by the new clerk, Julia will continue to oversee the use of the files. Julia knows that it is necessary to maintain the system of charging out files, following up on correspondence, and transferring and storing records. Until the new file clerk learns the system, she will have to look to Julia for guidance.

Records are kept because they contain needed information; filing systems are developed in order to retrieve this information promptly and efficiently. Yet if records are often removed from the files without *charging* them to the borrower, the system will soon become useless. It will certainly not be worth the time, effort, and money that have gone into its development and maintenance.

Since the people who borrow records from the files are busy, they may neglect to return these documents to the files. Although every worker should feel responsible for maintaining an effective office information system, it is your responsibility to protect the records placed under your control. Therefore, a charge-out and follow-up system must be developed to insure the return of borrowed documents to the files.

CHARGE-OUT

There are times when executives or other employees will need materials that are stored in your files. When materials are borrowed from your files, you should prepare a form that identifies the records removed. This form (usually 5″ x 3″ or 6″ x 4″) is known as a *requisition* card and has spaces for a full description of the material borrowed, the name and department of the borrower, the date the material was removed from the file, and the date it is to be returned.

Charge-Out Forms

In addition to the requisition card, four kinds of forms are commonly used when material is taken from the files. They are *out guides*, *out folders*, *carrier folders*, and *substitution cards*.

Out Guides. An out guide is a pressboard guide with the word *OUT* printed on its tab. It is placed in the files when an entire folder is borrowed. There are two forms of out guides. One type is ruled on both sides, and the charge information is written directly on the guide. When the folder is returned, the out guide is removed and the charge information crossed out. The guide is then ready for further use.

analyze:
to study

The other kind of out guide has a pocket into which a requisition card is placed. This form is preferred since it is faster to use and the charge information is usually more legible. The requisition cards may later be used to **analyze** the activity of the files. A tabulation of the cards will determine how often the files are used and which records are most active.

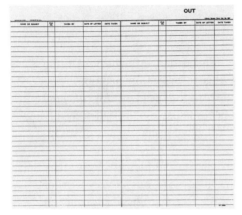

Remington Rand

Illus. 7-7 Ruled out guide

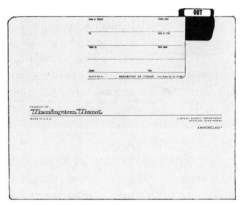

Remington Rand

Illus. 7-8 Out guide with pocket

Out Folders. Some firms prefer using out folders when an entire folder is requested from the files. If additional material reaches the files before the regular folder is returned, it is temporarily filed in the out folder. This material is then filed in the regular folder when it is returned.

Carrier Folder. A carrier folder is useful in reminding the borrower to return records to the files. It is of a different color from the regular folders with the words *RETURN TO FILES* printed on it. The requested material is removed from the regular folder and sent to the borrower in a carrier folder. An out card or guide is placed in the regular folder containing the charge-out information. The regular folder remains in the file to hold any material placed in the file before the carrier folder is returned. A carrier folder saves the regular folder from the wear and tear it would receive when removed from the files.

Substitution Cards. A substitution card is a tabbed card, usually salmon-colored, that is placed in a folder when single documents are borrowed. The word *OUT* is printed on the tab. The charge-out information may be recorded on the card itself or on a requisition form inserted in a pocket of the substitution card. A substitution card is basically the same as an out guide.

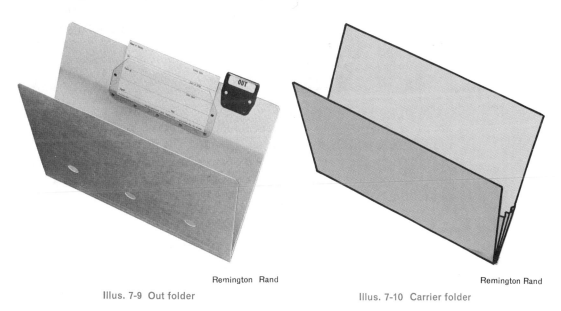

Remington Rand

Illus. 7-9 Out folder

Remington Rand

Illus. 7-10 Carrier folder

Photocopies

To avoid removing important papers from the files, many firms prepare photocopies of a requested record. When this method is used, the document is removed from the files and copied on a copying machine. The original document is then refiled and the photocopy sent to the borrower with instructions to destroy it after use. This method is generally used when single documents are requested rather than an entire folder.

Length of Charge Time

Borrowed materials are usually used by the borrower immediately and should be returned to the files as soon as possible. The longer records

are away from the files, the more difficult it is to get them back; furthermore, they are likely to be lost or discarded. Most firms charge out records for only one week (with weekly extensions, if found necessary). It is
best to have short charge-out periods and prompt follow-up of materials
not returned to the files.

FOLLOW-UP

If you work in a large office, you may be required to maintain
follow-up files for various persons, or you may require a follow-up file
for recovering files that have been held overtime. Two frequently used
follow-up files are the card tickler file and the dated follow-up folder file.

Card Tickler Files

A card tickler file consists of a set of 12 monthly primary guides
and 31 daily secondary guides. Important matters to be followed up are
recorded on cards and placed behind the appropriate month and day guides
in the file. A card tickler file may be used to follow up records that have
been borrowed from the files or to follow up other matters that require
attention.

Dated Follow-Up Folders

This file resembles the card tickler file except that a folder is available for each day of the month. Items that require follow-up are placed in

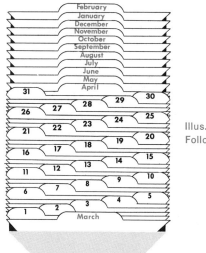

Illus. 7-12
Follow-up file

the correct day folder, and the folder is then placed behind the appropriate monthly guide. For example, a folder may contain a photocopy or an extra carbon of an outgoing letter that requests an answer by a certain day. On that particular day you should check to see if an answer to the letter has been received. If not, follow-up action is taken. By using photocopies and extra carbons for follow-up, the correspondence can be filed in its proper place and the official folder is always complete. This procedure saves a great deal of time.

TRANSFER

Office files should contain only those records that are needed to operate efficiently. If inactive or outdated records are never removed from the files, needed information becomes more and more difficult to **retain** and retrieve. Every organization should adopt a plan of removing inactive documents from the active files by *transferring* these records to a records center.

retain:
to keep

Removing inactive records from the office files serves three important purposes:

1. Active records can be filed and retrieved quickly.
2. Expensive office space and file equipment are kept at a minimum.
3. Costs are reduced since transferred records are housed in inexpensive file equipment, usually cardboard transfer cases.

It is important to remember that not every document received in an office should be filed; not every document retained in the active file should be transferred.

Transferring File Folders

Records that must be kept for long periods of time should be separated from those of temporary value when placing records in transfer cases. Miscellaneous, special, and individual folders are usually transferred from the active to the inactive files when they are no longer needed. Each transferred folder should be stamped *Transfer File* to prevent it being returned to the active files should it be requested from the records center. Many firms use different colored folder labels to identify their file periods.

The Records Center

A records center is an important part of any transfer program. This center houses documents no longer needed for daily reference. Records may be stored at the center indefinitely or for a temporary period only. Inactive records are inexpensively maintained in the center, since all the floor space can be **utilized** (floor to ceiling filing) and inexpensive equipment can be used to house the records.

Documents maintained in the center must be accurately indexed and controlled so that they will be available if requested. Without **adequate** indexing, protection, and control of these inactive records, all the time and effort spent in the transfer program have been wasted.

utilized:
made use of

adequate:
enough to get a
job done

RETENTION

Every organization is faced with the problem of how long to retain its records. Because of the growing volume of paper work, many firms have established *record retention schedules*. This schedule identifies the retention value of every record created or received by an organization and determines which records must be retained and for how long. Useless records occupy expensive floor space and costly equipment; they hinder the rapid retrieval of needed information.

While certain documents must be retained permanently, most records created and received in the average business organization have a limited period of usefulness. The National Records Management Council estimates that 95 percent of all corporate paper work over a year old is rarely, if ever, referred to again. Most record authorities estimate that 40 percent of all stored records can be legally destroyed.

Even though every organization must develop its own retention schedule, factors that affect the retention period of business records include

1. Legal requirements (federal, state, and local)
2. Office use (those records needed to operate on a daily basis)
3. Historical documents
4. Vital records

A retention schedule can be adopted only after a thorough study of the record requirements of a particular organization. Legal counsel should always be sought. Once a schedule is adopted, it must be continually revised to meet changing conditions and needs.

REVIEWING WHAT YOU HAVE READ

1. Why should all materials taken from files be *charged out* to the person taking them?
2. What is a requisition card?
3. What are the two types of out guides? Which is better?
4. What is the difference between an out guide and a substitution card?
5. How is the out folder used?
6. What are the advantages of releasing photocopies rather than original documents from the files?
7. Describe a card tickler file and tell of its use.
8. Why are inactive records removed from the office files?
9. Why should a transferred folder be stamped *Transfer File*?
10. List four factors that affect the retention schedule of business records.

MAKING DECISIONS

The filing department of a certain business is so small that no one person is responsible for the keeping of a record of material borrowed. Each person who needs correspondence from the files removes it from the folders, signs his name in a record book kept for this purpose, and takes the correspondence with him. Can you recommend any improvement in this system?

WORKING WITH OTHERS

Your company has a rule that all materials requisitioned from the files must be returned within 48 hours. One of the company executives has a habit of holding folders for a week or more frequently creating problems in the filing room.

What action could the records supervisor take to try to improve this situation?

USING LANGUAGE

Two uses of the comma are:

1. To separate long coordinate clauses that are joined by the conjunctions *and, but, for, neither, nor,* and *or.* The comma is placed before the conjunction.
2. To separate words, phrases, or clauses in a series. A comma follows each item in the series.

Type the following sentences on a separate sheet of paper and insert commas where necessary.

1. The supervisor said that out guides substitution cards and out folders are used frequently.

2. Carson's folder contained 20 pieces of correspondence but the Moore folder contained more than 30 pieces of correspondence.
3. Only one file clerk was in the records department for it was during the lunch hour when I requested the file.
4. Mr. Jones Mr. Wilson Mr. Gates and Mr. Hill requested files at the same time.
5. Neither Mr. Jones nor Mr. Gates had to wait long but Mr. Wilson's and Mr. Hill's files took a few minutes to find.

USING ARITHMETIC

On a separate sheet of paper solve the following problems.

1. If Mary could file 20 files in a half hour, how many could she file in two hours·
2. Twenty percent of a total of 342 pieces of correspondence remain to be filed· How many pieces of correspondence must yet be placed in the files?
3. If a file cabinet costs $145 and your employer will receive a 25 percent discount, how much will the file cabinet cost?

PERFORMING OFFICE TASKS

1. Type captions on folder labels for each of the following authors, who contributed articles to a recent issue of *The Office*, a magazine of management, equipment, and automation. (If folder labels are not available, type the names on blank sheets of paper approximately 3½″ x 1½″.)

George H. Harmon	Joe E. Torrence
Arthur L. Ratz	Charles A. Agemian
Jord H. Jordan, Jr.	Denis S. Greensmith
J. A. Mosher	Theodore K. Cobb
Wesley S. Bagby	T. M. Galloway
Thomas G. Morris	E. Philip Kron
Richard I. Tanaka	Patrick R. Gaffney
Frank Plasha	Carl W. Golgart
Bruce I. Blackstone	John H. Dunham
Bernard Goldstein	Robert E. Bennis
G. Peter Ignasiak	Ellsworth H. Morse, Jr.
Clarence E. Franke	K. R. Atkins, Jr.
James D. Parker, Jr.	Donald F. Evans
William W. Newell	Walter M. Carlson

Type the name without punctuation on the upper half of the folder label about two spaces from the left edge, as illustrated.

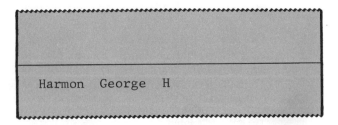

Harmon   George   H

2. After the names in Problem 1 are indexed in alphabetical order type the list on a single sheet of paper. Center the heading, AUTHORS OF THE JANUARY ISSUE, and type the list in two double spaced columns.

PART 3

NUMERIC, SUBJECT, AND
GEOGRAPHIC FILING

Allison Taylor was recently hired as a junior clerk-typist in the office of Mr. Harold Skeen, the General Sales Manager for Midwest Appliance Wholesalers, Inc. This company distributes household appliances to all parts of the United States. Allison was asked to work in the filing department for one week so that she could become accustomed to the filing systems used and so that she could get a quick picture of how the business operates. She quickly discovered that, in addition to an alphabetic filing system, Midwest Appliances used a numeric system for stock numbers and orders, a subject system for major appliances, and a geographic system for sales territories.

You will probably be more concerned with alphabetic correspondence filing methods than with numeric, subject, or geographic. To assist your supervisor properly, however, you may need to understand other filing systems and how they operate. You may be required to request records from a filing department that uses one of the other systems. You may also be required to code correspondence which will be filed in the central files.

Records must be filed in the manner by which they will be called for — by name, by number, by subject, or by geographic area. When you have correspondence with a customer, you know that it will be filed alphabetically by the company name. However, if your employer asks that copies of the sales reports be sent to the managers of each territory, you will make use of a geographic file. In a purchasing department, you will keep a numeric file by the purchase order number. All the **forecasts** of **anticipated** expenditures for your department for the coming year will be filed by the subject caption *Budgets* not under *Controller Jamison*.

forecasts: estimates of future events

anticipated: expected

NUMERIC FILING

With the widespread use of data processing systems for repetitive and statistical operations in many organizations, numbers have become important in identifying many records in today's businesses. In general, only large systems use numeric filing. Records that are frequently identified by number and filed in a numeric sequence are insurance policies, purchase orders, sales orders, contracts, licenses, customers' charge accounts, bank accounts, and credit card accounts. Many large government agencies, such as the Social Security Administration, the Veterans Administration, and state motor vehicle bureaus, file their records in numerical order.

Illus. 7-13
Many records are filed in numerical sequence, and many kinds of businesses and government agencies use numerical files.

Oxford Pendaflex Corporation

Since it would be impossible to remember the file number of every business paper, an alphabetic card index of the numerically filed material is maintained by name or by subject as a cross-reference. Numeric filing systems are *indirect* in finding and filing because, in most instances, reference must be made to the alphabetic card index before a document is found or coded.

A numeric file usually consists of three parts:

1. The file itself, in which the documents are filed by an assigned number and in which the guides and folders bear numeric captions.

2. An index card control file, in which names or subject titles are arranged alphabetically.

3. An *accession* book or *register*, in which a record of assigned numbers is kept.

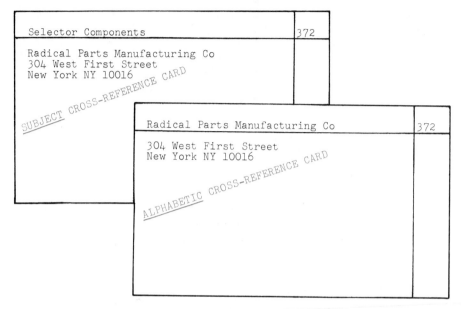

Selector Components   372

Radical Parts Manufacturing Co
304 West First Street
New York NY 10016

SUBJECT CROSS-REFERENCE CARD

Radical Parts Manufacturing Co   372

304 West First Street
New York NY 10016

ALPHABETIC CROSS-REFERENCE CARD

Illus. 7-14
Index control cards

NUMERIC ARRANGEMENTS

There are several arrangements of numbers that may be used in numeric filing:

1. The numbers may be in consecutive order (consecutive number filing).

2. Certain portions of a long number may be used as the first indexing unit (**terminal**-digit and/or middle-digit filing).

3. The number may be combined with letters of the alphabet (alpha-numeric filing).

terminal:
last or ending

Consecutive Number Filing

In this arrangement documents are filed in strict numeric sequence. The number is written in the upper right portion of the paper, and an alphabetic card is typed as a cross-reference to the assigned number. The papers are filed in numerical sequence in folders, and the card is filed alphabetically in the index. Additional papers related to the same subject are checked against the card index and coded with the same number.

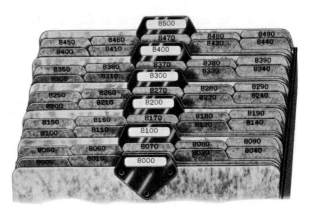

Illus. 7-15
Consecutive number file. Documents are filed by number and cross-referenced in alphabetic and subject card files.

Shaw-Walker

Legal Files. In legal firms a number (for example, 607) is assigned to a client and as additional matters are handled for the same client, they are given a secondary number (607-1 — Will) to separate the new material. An alphabetic cross-reference card is made for each client as well as for each item the legal firm is taking care of for the client. Individual folders are prepared for each and are filed numerically:

607   John W. Rodgers
607-1 Will
607-2 Real Estate Holdings
607-3 Income Tax Records
607-4 Insurance

Project and Job Files. Consecutive numeric filing is used for these two types of records primarily because there are related drawings, blueprints, and artwork connected with the correspondence and such material is controlled more easily through a numbering system. Almost always it is necessary to subdivide the correspondence by subject. Drawings will have secondary numbers for parts of the project or job, and dates for revisions of drawings become an important identifying factor. Numbers are obtained from the accession book. The alphabetical card index is an essential key for locating material by name or subject.

Numeric Correspondence Files. Because it is a slow and indirect method, ordinary correspondence today is seldom filed numerically. The need to keep papers confidential is the primary reason for using this system. Numbers are assigned in consecutive order from the accession book, and individual folders are made for each correspondent. All papers for this correspondent are placed in this folder, with the most recent material in the front. An alphabetic index card is made. Neither the accession book nor the card index is available to unauthorized personnel.

Illus. 7-16
Confidential correspondence files which combine numbers and names

Shaw-Walker

Terminal-Digit Filing

Terminal-digit filing is a method of numeric filing based on reading numbers from *right to left*. It is ideal for any large numeric file with five or more digits. In terminal-digit filing, the numbers are assigned in the same manner as for consecutive number filing, but the numbers are read in small groups (00–99) beginning with the terminal (or final) group. It is widely used by banks for depositors' savings accounts, mortgages, and loans; by hospitals for medical case records; and by insurance companies for policyholders' applications.

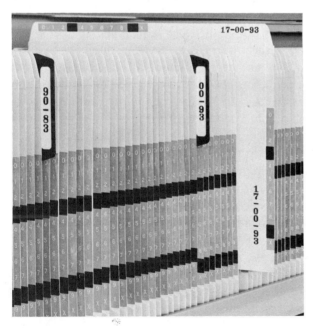

Illus. 7-17
Terminal-digit file
Where individually numbered folders hold records for insurance policies, claims, cases, etc., terminal-digit filing is fast and accurate.

Shaw-Walker

In the terminal-digit system, the primary division of the files is based on the last two digits of a number, the secondary division upon the next two digits, and the final division upon the first digits. For example, if you were to look up life insurance policy number 225101, you would read the numbers from right to left in pairs of digits instead of from left to right as whole numbers.

22	51	01
Final	Secondary	Primary

You would first locate the drawer containing those materials or records whose numbers end with 01. Then you would search down the guides in that drawer for the number 51. Lastly, you would file or find the material in proper order behind the number 22. Numbers of fewer than six digits are brought up to that figure by adding zeros to the left of the number.

When even larger numbers are common, they may be broken down for filing in groups of three digits, 000 to 999.

Alpha-Numeric Filing

Banks now identify the checking accounts of their depositors by numbers. In some banks an individual account number is assigned to each depositor according to an *alpha-numeric plan*. This is a method of assigning numbers to accounts in such a way that, even with additions and deletions, the accounts filed in numeric sequence will also be in alphabetic sequence. Originally the accounts are arranged in exact alphabetic sequence and assigned account numbers with uniform gaps between numbers to allow for additional accounts. This number is printed with a special magnetic ink on a set of blank checks before the checks are given to the depositor. After a check has been drawn, cashed, and returned to the bank, a machine automatically "reads" the number and charges the account of the depositor. The canceled checks are filed daily in front of check size guides, which

accumulated: collected or gathered

usually contain the signature card of the depositor, and are **accumulated** until the time of the month when the statement and canceled checks for the period are returned to the depositor.

There are other alphabetic-numeric filing systems which are highly specialized and are used in large filing departments with special problems that these systems are designed to solve. Your office duties may indirectly bring you into contact with these various filing systems. Filing personnel who work with alphabetic-numeric systems are given on-the-job training before being assigned to the operation of such systems. On-the-job training is normally necessary because of the differences in the systems.

Guides and Folders Used in Numeric Filing

The type and quantity of supplies used in numeric filing will depend on the arrangement that is used. Individual folders can be made for each number, with the number on the tab, or the number and name typed on a label affixed to the tab. Guides are normally inserted for every ten folders.

SUBJECT FILING

Every organization has materials which are important because of their content rather than because of the person to whom or by whom they are written. For these materials a *subject* filing system is necessary. Since subject filing is generally used in the administrative and executive areas of a business, your duties may not bring you into direct contact with this system of filing. However, should you assist with this kind of filing, it is well to have a knowledge of it. Subjects are placed in alphabetical order, and related subjects may be grouped together. A folder labeled "Applications" with the subheading "Salesmen" is an example. The names of all sales applicants are not easily remembered; therefore, the names are of secondary importance in filing, and the letters should be placed in a special subject folder labeled "Applications — Salesmen." As long as there are only a few subject folders they are filed in a regular alphabetic or numeric system along with the other folders.

Illus. 7-18
A subject file

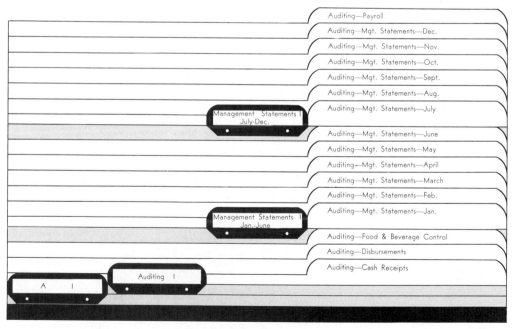

The following list shows some typical subject filing captions:

Advertising	Finance	Payroll
Applications		Personnel
Associations	Government — Federal	Price Lists
Audit Reports	Government — Municipal	Production
	Government — State	Public Relations
Balance Sheets		
Budgets	Insurance	Real Estate
		Reports
Conferences and	Legal Matters	Research
Conventions		
Contracts	Maps	Sales
Credits and Collections	Methods and Procedures	Speaking Invitations
	Minutes	Statistical Data
Directors' Meetings	Mortgages	
		Taxes — Federal
Employee Benefits	Operating Overhead	Taxes — Municipal
Equipment & Supplies	Operating Policies	Taxes — State

Guides and Folders Used in Subject Filing

In a subject file you will make use of several different types of guides and folders. The main subject titles are used as captions for primary guides. These serve the same purpose as primary guides in an alphabetic file. Secondary guides are used for the **subordinate** titles that are related to the main subjects on the primary guides behind which they are placed.

subordinate:
placed in a lower
class or rank

There is a miscellaneous folder for each main subject in which all papers relating to that topic are filed. Individual folders are made for subdivisions of the main subject when sufficient papers (usually six or seven) accumulate for the subtopic. Subdivisions may be made by

Subject: *Name:*

Safety   Associations

    Accident Prevention   American Manufacturers
                                   Association

Date Periods:

Production Reports

    January–June, 197–

    July–December, 197–

When individual folders are used in a subject file, they are placed behind the primary or secondary guides that classify the subject matter of the correspondence in those folders. In this way correspondence is doubly identified — by subject, as shown by the guide captions; and by titles, as shown on the folder captions. Main subject and subdivision captions must be shown on each folder tab.

Cross-Reference to a Subject File

An alphabetic cross-reference is necessary in a subject file for maintaining consistency in assigning subjects. Cross-referencing may be done by using a 5″ x 3″ card index, which is very flexible since additions can be made easily. Photocopies and carbon copies may also be used for cross-reference purposes.

Some companies distribute copies of the main subjects of the filing system (and possibly a definition of each) to each department for its use in dictating letters or when requesting materials from the files.

Subject Filing Procedures

In filing by subject, there are six basic steps which you should follow.

Inspecting. Each letter should be checked to see that it has been released for filing.

Indexing. The letter must be read carefully to determine under which subject it should be filed. Thorough familiarity with the outline of subjects and their subdivisions is necessary.

Coding. When the subject of a letter has been determined, the caption is written on the letter in the upper right corner or it is underlined if it appears in the letter.

Cross-Referencing. If more than one subject is involved in a letter — a very frequent occurrence — a cross-reference caption is underlined and an X is placed at the end of the line in the margin. An extra carbon copy, a photocopy of the letter, a cross-reference sheet, or a 5″ x 3″ index card should also be prepared.

Sorting. Material is sorted first according to the main subjects and second by the main subdivisions.

Placing Material in Folders. Material that is placed in an individual folder is filed with the latest date in front. If there is no individual folder, the material is filed in the miscellaneous folder for the main subject in alphabetic order according to subdivisions or in date order, latest date to front.

GEOGRAPHIC FILING

If you are using a geographic filing system, geographic location is the prime indexing factor. In the United States, for instance, materials would be arranged alphabetically first by states, then by cities or towns within the states, and finally alphabetically by the names of the correspondents in the cities or towns. A geographic file may also be based upon territories of salesmen, upon cities in a single state, or upon districts or streets for local correspondence.

Typical users of geographic filing systems are publishing houses, mail-order houses, radio and television advertisers, real estate firms, and organizations dealing with a large number of small businesses scattered over a wide area. The personnel in many of these small businesses change frequently; therefore, the name of the individual owner or manager is often less important than the location of the business.

Geographic filing is an indirect method of locating folders for individual correspondents. It is slower to operate since papers must be sorted as many as three times, depending on the geographic arrangement that is selected.

Arrangement of a Geographic File

The primary guides in a geographic filing system bear the names of the largest geographic divisions. The specific arrangement will depend on the needs of the company and the volume of records. For example, a geographic filing system based on states would have each guide tab printed with the name of a state; and all correspondence with people in that state would be filed behind that guide. These state guides are usually arranged alphabetically: thus, Alabama is first, followed by Alaska and the other states in alphabetic order. They could also be arranged by a division of the country into areas, such as "West Coast"; and behind these guides the secondary guides or folders for the states of California, Oregon, and Washington would be filed.

The secondary guides bear the names of the geographic subdivisions. For example, behind each primary state guide there are secondary guides with captions that provide for the alphabetic arrangement of cities and towns within that state.

A geographic file may include several different kinds of folders, such as individual folders, city folders, and state folders. Individual folders in a geographic file are used in the same manner as they are in an alphabetic file. They differ, however, in their captions, because in a geographic file, the caption on an individual folder includes the name of the city and state, as well as the name of the correspondent. The geographic identification should appear on the top line, the correspondent on the second. This arrangement of the captions aids in the correct placement of the folders behind the appropriate state and city guides.

Illus. 7-19
Geographic file

Shaw-Walker

If there is no individual folder for a correspondent, his communication is filed in a city folder. If there is not enough correspondence to **warrant** the use of a separate city folder, the communication is placed in a miscellaneous state folder at the back of the appropriate state section of the file.

warrant:
to justify; to be a
reason for

For larger cities, several city folders are sometimes necessary. These are assigned alphabetic captions and placed behind a secondary city guide. For example, five Chicago folders might be used, the first for those Chicago correspondents whose names fall into the alphabetic range of A–C; the second, D–H; the third, I–M; the fourth, N–R; and the fifth, S–Z.

Cross-Reference for Geographic Filing

As in alphabetic filing, there are times when cross-references must be prepared on a letter. The geographic location, the correspondent's name, and other information about the letter are written in the proper spaces on the form.

Card Index

In geographic filing you must know the name of the city and state in which a person or business firm is located to find a letter referring to that correspondent. Because this information is not always known, it is advantageous to keep a card index with a geographic correspondence file. This is usually a 5″ x 3″ card file, which includes a card for each correspondent giving the name and address of the correspondent. The card index is arranged alphabetically by the names of the correspondents.

Illus. 7-20
Card index

Shaw-Walker

Geographic Filing Procedure

The filing procedure for a geographic file is similar to that for alphabetic filing, except that the state and city are of primary importance in coding and filing. In coding it is desirable to mark on each letter the city and state as well as the name of the correspondent. The location may be circled and the name of the correspondent underlined.

Materials are sorted by geographic units, starting with the key unit for the first sorting and continuing until all the units involved in the filing system have been used. For example, the first sorting might be on the basis of states, the second sorting on the basis of cities or towns, and the final sorting on the basis of correspondents.

Letters are arranged in the folders as follows: (1) in an individual folder by date, (2) in a city folder by the names of the correspondents and then by date, (3) in an alphabetic state folder by the names of cities or towns and then by the names of correspondents according to date. In each case, of course, the most recent letter is placed in front.

SUMMARY OF FILING METHODS

Each filing method has its advantages and disadvantages. On page 263 is a summary of the outstanding features of the four methods.

	ADVANTAGES	DISADVANTAGES
Alphabetic	1. Direct filing and reference. 2. No index required. 3. Records may be grouped by individual or by company name. 4. Simple arrangement by guides, folders, and colors. 5. Easy-to-find miscellaneous records.	1. Possibility of error in filing common names. 2. Related records may be filed in more than one place. 3. Too little or too much cross-referencing.
Numeric	1. Most accurate of all methods. 2. Unlimited expansion. 3. Definite numbers to identify name or subject when requesting files. 4. Uniform system of numbers used in departments of company. 5. Cross-referencing permanent and extensive. 6. Complete index of correspondents and subjects.	1. Requires specialized training. 2. High labor cost. 3. Indirect filing and reference. 4. Miscellaneous records require separate files. 5. Cumbersome index.
Subject	1. Records grouped by subject for administrative, executive, technical, or statistical files. 2. Documents from different sources brought together under one heading, an essential tool for management decision-making. 3. Unlimited expansion.	1. Extensive cross-referencing necessary. 2. Difficulty in classifying records for filing. 3. Difficulty in filing miscellaneous folders. 4. Necessary use of index in determining subject heading or subdivision.
Geographic	1. Direct filing and reference for geographic area (indirect for individual correspondence). 2. Provision for miscellaneous records. 3. Records grouped by location.	1. Location as well as name required. 2. Triple sorting necessary — by state, by city, by alphabet. 3. Increased labor cost. 4. Increased possibility of error. 5. Reference to card index necessary. 6. Detailed typed descriptions on folder labels. 7. Confusion in miscellaneous files.

Illus. 7-21

1. Name the three parts of a numeric filing system. What is the purpose of each?
2. How is a number assigned to a correspondent in a numeric file?
3. How is a number assigned to a subject? Give an example.
4. When is a subject filing system used in preference to other methods?
5. What is the major problem in a subject file?
6. How is a letter coded in a subject file?
7. Explain the procedure of cross-referencing in a subject file.
8. What is the basis for geographic filing?
9. What kinds of guides and folders are used with a geographic filing system?
10. What are some of the advantages and disadvantages of the numeric system?

MAKING DECISIONS

1. What are the advantages of using numbers as well as subjects for guide and folder captions?
2. How should an office decide whether it ought to arrange its files by name, number, subject, or geographic location?
3. What is a practical situation where terminal-digit filing may promote office efficiency?

WORKING WITH OTHERS

An office worker filing under a subject system must read letters and papers carefully, since they may contain references to more than one subject. Caryl Carson, with whom you work, fails to read the material to be filed, and, as a result, there is much misfiling and improper cross-referencing.

Whenever the chief file clerk corrects her, Caryl becomes impatient and tells the chief clerk the system is stupid and does not make sense.

How would you help Caryl to improve her work habits and to understand the importance of proper operation of the filing system?

USING LANGUAGE

The relative pronouns *who* and *whom* are quite frequently misused. When a relative pronoun is the subject of a subordinate clause, *who* is used. When a relative pronoun is the object of a verb or preposition, *whom* is used.

Examples: Sam Davis is the man *who* can do the job.

Grace is the girl *whom* we are hiring.

Type each of the following sentences, inserting the correct usage of *who* or *whom*. If you are unsure of your choice, try substituting *he* for *who* and *him* for *whom* before making your final decision.

1. To _____ did you release the Ames folder?
2. _____ signed the substitution card for the letter?
3. _____ does she know in the central filing department _____ can be of assistance?
4. Since if was not signed, we could not tell from _____ the letter was received.
5. _____ said that six or more letters from one firm should be placed in an individual folder?
6. The personnel officer, _____ I saw yesterday, asked me to come back next week.
7. Now you know _____ should get the promotion.
8. Can Agnes, _____ proofreads so accurately, retype the entire report?
9. _____ shall I talk to about this?
10. _____ decided that the lighting was inadequate for our work?

11. Don't you know _____ called me?

12. He told them _____ we had selected as our chairman.

13. For _____ are you waiting?

14. The matter of _____ shall pay for the delay is still to be decided.

15. Do you understand _____ is in charge of the division and _____ will be responsible for the reports?

16. Was it _____ I thought it was?

17. They also serve _____ only stand and wait.

18. _____ wouldn't enjoy a vacation at this time of the year?

19. With _____ shall I go?

20. Have you noticed _____ is always late?

USING ARITHMETIC

1. On a separate sheet of paper reduce the following fractions to their lowest terms.

8/10	9/72
16/24	6/21
5/20	10/12
8/16	15/25
18/20	6/18

2. On a separate sheet of paper state the value of N in the following equations.

Example: $13 + 14 = N$ Answer: 27

$N - 8 = 10$	$N = 14 - 8$
$16 - N = 12$	$6 + 9 = N$
$3 \times N = 9$	$15 \div N = 5$
$4 \times N = 32$	$14 + N = 25$
$N \div 2 = 7$	$N = 9 \times 8$

PERFORMING OFFICE TASKS

Type the following twenty business firm names, addresses, and account numbers on 5″ x 3″ cards. File them three ways: (1) alphabetically, (2) geographically, and (3) numerically.

5001 Cobin & Sons, Washington, D.C. 20013

5004 Connell Manufacturing Co., Seattle, Washington 98111

5009 The Cole Manufacturing Co., San Francisco, California 94101

5006 Crawford, Crawford and Croll, Cincinnati, Ohio 45201

5003 Cone, Lambert and Ulysses, Chicago, Illinois 60690

5002 Corn and Frederick, Dallas, Texas 75221

5005 Max Collier & Sons, Tallahassee, Florida 32302

5007 Conwit Tailors, Gainesville, Florida 32601

5008 Cone, Arnold & Co., New York, New York 10001

5010 Cobbs Corporation, Boston, Massachusetts 01432

5019 Conklin Company, Erie, Pennsylvania 16512

5015 Conner Corporation, Cleveland, Ohio 44101

5016 The Samuel Collins Company, St. Louis, Missouri 63177

5013 Colton Company, Boise, Idaho 83707

5012 Conrad & Matthew, Reno, Nevada 89504

5011 Coyne Corporation, Los Angeles, California 90053

5014 Craig & Stanton Corporation, San Luis Obispo, California 93401

5017 Cole & Monford Co., Nashville, Tennessee 37202

5018 Conners Metal Manufacturing, Inc., Cicero, Illinois 60650

5020 Conover & Sterling, Baton Rouge, Louisiana 70821

PART 4 SPECIAL FILES AND INFORMATION SYSTEMS

Carolyn French has been with the Seattle Chemical Company since it was founded eight years ago. Because of her experience in working with all its projects since the company started in business, Carolyn has an exceptional knowledge of the files. Quite often Mr. Bowman, the President, asks Carolyn to obtain information from the company's electronic data processing center. Usually, however, Carolyn can find, in the files near her desk, all the information Mr. Bowman needs for decision-making. Mr. Bowman has often commented, "I can always count on Carolyn to find the information I need — and find it in a hurry!"

CARD FILES

From small to large, practically all offices make use of card files. You may keep a small card file on your desk that contains the names, addresses, and telephone numbers of people whom you call or write to frequently. Receptionists for doctors and dentists usually have card files containing information about patients; teachers often have a card file for each of their classes; libraries, of course, have card catalogs covering all the books in the library. A card file is needed as a cross-reference in numeric, geographic, and subject filing. Card files are used in almost every department in a business firm; shipping, receiving, purchasing, inventory control, personnel records, payroll, and stock records may be maintained on cards.

Cards used in filing are usually 5″ x 3″, 6″ x 4″, or 8″ x 5″. The size selected usually depends upon the amount of information that is needed on the card. The 5″ x 3″ is the most widely used card size.

When typing information on the cards for the files, follow this simple procedure:

1. Type the name in exact indexing order.
2. If the card is not ruled, begin typing on the third line from the top of the card. If the index card is ruled, begin typing above the printed line.
3. Indent two spaces from the left edge of the card and set a margin.

4. Use upper and lower case letters. They are easier to read.
5. Abbreviations may be used since space is limited.
6. Be consistent in style, spacing, capitalization, and punctuation.

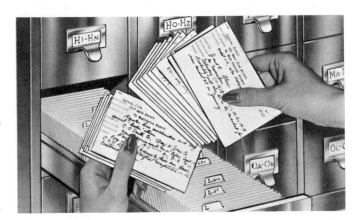

Illus. 7-22
Card files
for drawers

Shaw-Walker

Vertical Card Files

These are the types of files in which the card stands on edge, usually the width of the card. Thus, a 5″ x 3″ card rests on the 5-inch edge; the 6″ x 4″ card rests on the 6-inch edge; the 8″ x 5″ card rests on the 8-inch edge. There are, however, exceptions to this; some cards are filed according to the depth of the card. The cards may or may not be ruled, depending upon whether they will be typed or handwritten.

Illus. 7-23
A card file may be an alphabetic, geographic, numeric, or subject file. Card files may contain current records; while storage card files may contain historical and seldom used records. Cards may be easily replaced as the files are closed and put in storage, and substitute current cards are added or rearranged.

Ohio National Life Insurance Company

Just as guides are needed to divide the file drawer to keep the folders in order, it is also necessary to divide the cards in an alphabetic card file into convenient alphabetic sections with a set of *card guides.* These card guides indicate on **projecting** tabs the various alphabetic sections into which the file drawer is divided. In some cases special primary and secondary guides are used, and color frequently plays an important part.

projecting:
sticking out or up

The notations on the tabs of the guides consist in most cases of letters, such as *Alf, Alli, Alm, Alt, Am, An*; but they may consist of popular surnames such as *Allen, Anderson, Andrews,* as you will notice in the illustration below. They indicate the alphabetic range of the cards filed in each section. The file cards are placed in alphabetic order behind the appropriate guide just as the folders are placed behind the guides in the file drawer.

Illus. 7-24
File cards
with guides

Shaw-Walker

Visible Card Files

These are files in which a portion of the card is visible at all times, that portion generally showing the name, department, or product to which the card record refers. These cards are generally placed in pockets on horizontal trays, or on vertical sheets, or in files that appear in book form. The total card becomes visible as the overlapping cards are raised to provide a view of the whole card.

Illus. 7-25
Visible record
card cabinet

Remington Rand

Signals on Visible Records. In addition to cards that are especially printed for use with visible files, small metal or plastic signals are available. These may be placed in various positions on the cards to indicate something important about the record. For example, if a visible file is used for collection records, the signal may indicate that the account is in good standing or that it is overdue. Some signals may be used to indicate that it is very much overdue or that the firm with the account is no longer to be given credit because of poor standing. These signals are sometimes placed in special positions on the card and frequently are in different colors. For example, blue may indicate a good credit standing, yellow may suggest mildly overdue, orange may mean very much overdue, and red may tell you that no further credit is to be extended.

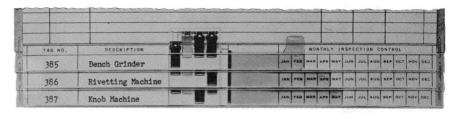

Illus. 7-26
Signals on
visible records

TAG NO.	DESCRIPTION	MONTHLY INSPECTION CONTROL
385	Bench Grinder	JAN FEB MAR APR MAY JUN JUL AUG SEP OCT NOV DEC
386	Rivetting Machine	JAN FEB MAR APR MAY JUN JUL AUG SEP OCT NOV DEC
387	Knob Machine	JAN FEB MAR APR MAY JUN JUL AUG SEP OCT NOV DEC

Acme Visible
Records, Inc.

ITEM	PART NO.	WEEKS SUPPLY ON HAND											
Cam Shaft Gear	398	1	2	3	4	5	6	⑦	8	9	10	11	12
Crank Shaft Gear	225	1	2	3	4	5	⑥	7	8	9	10	11	12
Driving Shaft	187	1	②	3	4	5	6	7	8	9	10	11	12
Feeder Arm Right	339	1	2	3	4	5	6	⑦	8	9	10	11	12
Feeder Cam	358	1	2	③	4	5	6	7	8	9	10	11	12
Feeder Pump Cover	186	1	2	③	4	5	6	7	8	9	10	11	12
Impression Cylinder	116	①	2	3	4	5	6	7	8	9	10	11	12

Reference Visible Systems. These files usually carry only a strip instead of a whole card, the strip containing perhaps a name, address, and telephone number of persons who are called rather often. The strips are usually referred to as visible panels and are generally limited to one or two lines.

Illus. 7-27
Visible panel system
for reference records

E. H. Brown Advertising Agency

Rotary Wheel Files

These are cards to be used where quick reference to a large number of cards is needed. Cards used with this type of equipment are punched or cut at the bottom or at the side, depending upon the style of wheel. There are small wheel files for desk-top use and also large rotary motorized equipment that is used when a great deal of information must be available for fingertip retrieval.

Illus. 7-28
Rotary
wheel
file

Business Efficiency Aids, Inc.

Random Files

In this kind of system, the cards not only have typed or printed information on them, but also are equipped with strips of metal teeth which are attached to the bottom edge of the card. These teeth are cut in relation to magnetic rods that run under the cards. These files are operated by a keyboard, and the depression of certain keys causes one or more cards to be pushed up, thus locating them and making them available

Illus. 7-29
At the touch of the keys this file automatically selects the right card. Valuable time is saved, and delays are avoided.

Acme Visible Records, Inc.

quickly. This system has the advantage of allowing one card to be identified under one of several possible captions. It is often found in banks, savings and loan associations, and finance companies where fast reference to a customer's file assures prompt service and goodwill.

Elevator Files

This type of file is power driven and is in a sense a multiple card file with trays arranged on shelves which may be brought to the level of the operator by the use of an elevator or power-driven system. The shelves in this kind of a file operate on the same principle as a ferris wheel at an amusement park. The shelves may be wide enough to take four, five, or more trays of 5″ x 3″ cards; and any single machine may include a large number of shelves. The operator pushes a button to move any particular shelf into position. At that point she may work directly on some cards, or she may remove a complete tray of cards and turn them over to someone else to work on.

Illus. 7-30
Elevator files

Ohio National
Life Insurance Company

MICROFILMING

Because of increasing information needs, many businesses are using microfilm as a solution to certain of their information problems. Microfilm is a photographic method of copying records in **miniature**. Since microfilm cannot be viewed by the naked eye, a machine called a reader or a reader-printer is used. This machine magnifies the microfilm.

miniature:
in small size

Microfilm makes it possible to store vital records and save storage space at the same time. For example, about 3,000 letter-size documents can be photographed on a 100-foot roll of microfilm. The United States Army Rocket Guided Missile Agency "files" over 100,000 engineering drawings in only four feet of floor space. The microfilming process and equipment, however, are very expensive.

Microfilm is widely used as a method of processing, distributing, and retrieving information. Schools, banks, department stores, libraries, government offices, and research centers are among the many users of microfilm.

Duplication and Copying

With the development and refinement of the reader-printer, *hard copies* of information on microfilm are quickly obtained by pressing a button. The term *hard copies* refers to a photocopy of the material on the microfilm. Duplication by microfilm also eliminates time-consuming manual transcribing and also provides error-free copies.

Retrieval

Motorized electronic equipment is available that is **capable** of retrieving at very high speeds information stored on microfilm and producing hard copies almost immediately. The Social Security Administration, for example, maintains the microfilm records of over 130 million people and can obtain a hard copy of any record in 90 seconds.

capable:
able to do
something

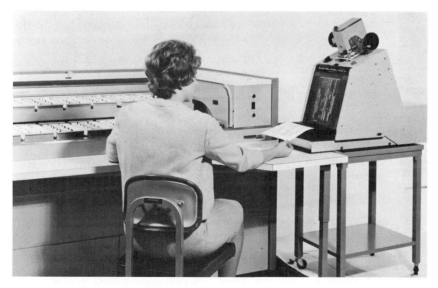

Illus. 7-31
In this typical installation the operator is using a reader-printer to produce a "hard" or paper copy from a microfilmed image. The entire operation from the search to the finished print takes less than a minute.

Remington Rand

What to Microfilm

All documents should not be microfilmed. Although documents reduced to microfilm occupy about two percent of the space required by regular records, microfilm should not be used only as a method of saving space, except in unusual situations. Inactive records should be transferred to low-cost record centers after realistic retention periods have been adopted. The expense of microfilm cannot be justified if infrequent use is made of too many office records. In most cases records must be retained for fifteen years or more before it is economical to microfilm only to save space.

ELECTRONIC DATA PROCESSING

Electronic data processing equipment can store more information and retrieve it faster than any other system. Specially trained people handle the equipment for both input and retrieval of data. If you work in a data processing department, you will be very much concerned with the equipment and how it is used. If you work in any other department, you should be familiar with how the data processing equipment can aid your employer and you. In almost all cases, however, you will need the assistance of the people in the data processing department in order to store or retrieve information.

Tabulating (Punched) Cards

extensive:
large

With the tremendous increase in the use of electronic data processing equipment, most companies have **extensive** tabulating card files. The tabulating or punched cards are often stored in vertical files. In the drawers of the filing cabinets, the cards are stored in removable trays. Alphabetic, numeric, and alpha-numeric indexing systems are used.

Computer Tapes and Disks

Magnetic tapes and disks hold more information in less space than punched cards. The tapes and disks are usually stored in fire-and heat-resistant cabinets or safes.

Some electronic data processing equipment uses punched paper tape to store information. The punched paper tapes themselves are usually placed in specially designed folders that contain pockets for the tape.

Retrieval

Retrieval of information stored in a computer is quite rapid. When you request information from a computer, it may print out the information on a continuous sheet of paper or on specially prepared business forms. It is also possible that you may work in a business that has visual display units for retrieving information. With visual display units, the information you request is shown on a television-like screen.

Illus. 7-32
Visual display unit
for retrieving
information

Ohio National
Life Insurance Company

WHICH FILING SYSTEM?

If a filing system is to operate effectively, considerable time must be given to its development. A good filing system cannot be designed casually. The solution to many records management problems is neither simple nor easy. The development of an effective filing — and finding — system must be based on good planning, careful analysis, clear thinking, and sound experience.

Here are some factors that should be considered when developing a filing system:

1. *The record requirements of the office.* What kinds of records are retained? How are these records created or received? What is the total volume of records retained each week, month, or year? What about future expansion of the system?

2. *Using the system.* How are the records requested and used? How active are the records? How long must the records be retained?

3. *Storing the records.* What type of classification system should be used? Will a centralized or decentralized file plan be most effective? Where will the inactive records be stored?

4. *Equipment and supplies.* What specific types of equipment and supplies — out of the vast array available — would be most appropriate for this system in this office?

Since every office has different records requirements, a system used in one office is not always suitable for another. Remember that you are storing important information that must be retrieved quickly — you are not merely keeping pieces of paper.

Every filing system should be as simple as possible to use. In addition, the system should be efficient and reliable in providing needed information and also should be economical to operate and maintain.

When an office decides to install a new filing system or to change an old one, three methods may be considered. A qualified person in the office may analyze the particular information requirements and develop an "office-made" system, a system may be purchased from a filing equipment and supplies manufacturer, or a records consultant may be engaged to design a tailor-made filing system to meet the company's particular needs.

CARNIVAL   **by Dick Turner**

Illus. 7-33.

© 1971 by NEA, Inc., T.M. Reg. U.S. Pat. Off.

"The reason we have so many drawers marked 'L' Mr. Giltwhistle, is that we get lots and lots of letters!"

Newspaper Enterprise Association

1. What determines the size of the cards used in card filing?
2. What card size is most widely used in business files?
3. Describe the procedure for typing information on a card file.
4. Why are metal or plastic signals used with visible card records?
5. When are cards filed on rotary wheel files?
6. Give one of the advantages of a random file.
7. Give one of the advantages of an elevator file.
8. What is microfilm? Name six users of microfilmed records.
9. What does the term *hard copies* mean in microfilming systems?
10. What are four factors to be considered in developing a filing system?

**MAKING
DECISIONS**

Discuss how each of the following statements will affect your filing duties.

1. The best retention system for *many* records is not to produce the records at all. If a record has a *retention value of only a few days*, it should be *destroyed and not filed*.
2. Considering the marked increase in the cost of labor, equipment, space, and overhead, it has been determined that the cost of retrieving only one misfiled paper may now amount to $92.46.

**WORKING
WITH
OTHERS**

Connie does general office work in a downtown office of a large manufacturing company. Connie always keeps her files up to date and in good order, and she is able to produce a file within seconds after it is requested. On Saturdays, however, her employer, the manager; the assistant manager; and several traveling representatives for the firm come into the office and catch up on reports and other paper work that they do not have time to handle during the week.

Almost weekly Connie finds misplaced files; files are lost; and, on one occasion, she did not locate a file that her employer needed until after he had left town because the assistant manager had used it and placed the folder in the wrong file.

What should Connie do?

**USING
LANGUAGE**

Type each of the following sentences using the correct form of the word in parentheses.

1. We don't have (no, any) more carbon paper.
2. Please (bring, take) that letter here, and I'll photocopy it.
3. Where do the typists place (there, their) initials on the letters?
4. Resort reservations are not (so, as) expensive this summer as they were last summer.
5. Mary (sure, surely) knew her filing rules.
6. (Try to, Try and) picture a more perfect setting.
7. They work (well, good) together.
8. (Leave, Let) me answer the phone, please.
9. (It don't, It doesn't) matter if you are a bit late.
10. Everyone in our class (has, have) seen the filing movie, *It Must Be Somewhere*.
11. You were (very, real) thoughtful to call.
12. They (should of, should have) mailed it sooner.
13. We (differ with, differ from) you on the value of such elaborate planning.
14. Act (as if, like) you were interested in the suggestion.
15. Please (lay, lie) down to rest at the end of the day.

USING ARITHMETIC

On a separate sheet of paper show your answers to the following problems and how you arrived at them.

1. ½% of $855 is what amount?
2. $75 is what percentage of $250?
3. Express 45% as a decimal.
4. Express 27% as a fraction.
5. 25% of $3,200 is what amount?
6. ¾% of $400 is what amount?

PERFORMING OFFICE TASKS

This is the conclusion of the alphabetic indexing exercise begun in Unit 6, Part 3, and continued in Part 1 of this unit.

Prepare your last 25 index cards from the names listed below and incorporate them with the 75 cards you now have from the two previous assignments.

(76) Henry R. Elston, IV, 2728 Germantown Rd., Germantown, PA 19144
(77) Chamber of Commerce, 12th & Olive Sts., Joliet, IL 60433
(78) Chief Engineer, Safety Division, Arkansas State Highway Dept., Ft. Smith, AR 72901
(79) Horace Mann Junior High School, 2500 Euclid Ave., Erie, PA 16511
(80) St. Mark's Episcopal Church, Oakwood, MO 63401
(81) University of New Mexico, Albuquerque, NM 87103
(82) Wm. A. Graves, 1620 N. Vernon Place, Winnetka, IL 60093
(83) Second National Bank, 8th & Race Sts., Spokane, WA 99202
(84) Ye Olde Garden Gate Antiques, 49 W. Elm St., Independence, KS 67301
(85) Security Savings Society, 74 Ohio Ave., Watertown, NY 13601
(86) Vera's Beauty Salon, 29 W. Adams St., Bennington, VT 05201
(87) Jack the Tailor, 536 S. 29th St., Oklahoma City, OK 73129
(88) Downtown Merchants Assn., 1200 Transportation Bldg., Wheeling, WV 26003
(89) Lady Constance Cosmetics, 128 W. 63rd St., New York, NY 10023
(90) Citizens Bank & Trust Co., Manchester, NH 03105
(91) Hartford Water Department, Hartford, CT 06101
(92) U.S. Marshal, Justice Dept., Federal Bldg., Boise, ID 83707
(93) Arnold A. Townley-Jones, 5021 Eastman Blvd., Chicago, IL 60622
(94) Chief Inspector, Food & Drug Administration, Health & Welfare Dept., Post Office Bldg., Butte, MT 59701
(95) United Fine Arts Fund, Terminal Bldg., Dallas, TX 75222
(96) Baldwin-Wallace College, Berea, OH 44017
(97) Harold McArthur & Sons, 4587 Roland Ave., Glendale, CA 91209
(98) MacArthur Sportswear, 688 Jefferson St., Kalamazoo, MI 49007
(99) Bernice L. McAdoo, 3 Alpine Terrace, Trenton, NJ 08610
(100) Perkins-Reynolds Insurance Agency, 200 Nicollet Ave., Minneapolis, MN 55401

UNIT 8

HANDLING RECEPTIONIST DUTIES

RECEPTIONIST
CLERK TYPIST

ccurate typist, good telephor
rsonality, varied duties mu
dependable and efficier
rban location; need ow
rtation.   Reply to B(
quirer.

PART 1 — GREETING AND ASSISTING PEOPLE

Cheryl Burnham is the receptionist for an investment company in the financial district of New York City. Cheryl answered the following advertisement a month before her high school graduation.

> ### RECEPTIONIST
>
> Is greeting people something you do very well? Welcoming our visitors with a warm smile, making them feel comfortable, and announcing them properly are very important to us. To qualify you must be poised, well-spoken, and attractive in appearance. Also, since you will help some of our department heads, typing is necessary. Will consider recent high school graduate. Call Mrs. Boyle, 819-2332.
>
> An Equal Opportunity Employer

Cheryl has been at work for six months, and she believes she has a wonderful job.

PERSON-TO-PERSON MEETINGS

transacted: performed; conducted

You are aware that much business is **transacted** in person. You have undoubtedly seen the receptionist who handles appointments in a dentist's or doctor's office or clinic, or you have been helped by a receptionist-clerk at a local delivery office. Office workers who greet the public are found in all kinds of organizations. They provide valuable assistance and are the link between company and the public.

SPECIAL SKILLS AND ABILITIES OF RECEPTIONISTS

Receptionists must have special skills and abilities to handle their jobs. Their constant communications with the public make their tasks different from many other jobs in the office.

Successful receptionists possess these skills and abilities:

Alertness and Attentiveness.

Receptionists are people who enjoy being with others and being helpful. They, therefore, respond quickly and graciously to others. Callers are greeted immediately on arrival, for the receptionist is always aware of the entrance of another person.

While talking with others, receptionists give their full attention so that they understand the purpose of the visit or inquiry.

Illus. 8-1
Receptionists provide valuable assistance. They are the link between the company and the public.

Knowledge of Company Policies.

Receptionists frequently must answer general questions about their organizations; so they must have a thorough understanding of company policies.

Jennifer works as a receptionist in the office of a large industrial trade association that publishes many bulletins and booklets. Visitors ask her about the availability of these materials. She knows that company policy allows her to give single copies of any of the items to a caller without charge. **Multiple** copies are available by mail only. She gives callers who request multiple copies an order form to assist them in placing an order when they return to their own offices.

Multiple:
more than one;
many

Christopher works in the local REA office. Many people ask him for information about the services provided. He has many **inquiries** about rates, packaging, and crating requirements for express shipments, and also about shipments to rural areas. He knows the policies of the company; so he can give callers the information they need.

inquiries:
requests for information

Illus. 8-2

To assure fast customer service receptionist-clerks provide immediate answers to visitors by getting the information from a computer.

Control Data Corporation

Skill in Using Reference Materials

Many receptionists provide information that they are not expected to know from memory. They are expected, however, to read and understand directories, atlases, maps, timetables, and other references. Receptionists learn how to use such references by carefully reading the introductory material when a new reference is added to their collection.

Donna works in one of the state tourist offices near Omaha, Nebraska. Visitors from all parts of the country, and some from foreign countries, stop by to ask questions about historical sites, distances, and routes. Donna has many reference materials at hand and can quickly locate answers to such questions as:

What is the best route to Fort Kearney State Park?

What kinds of facilities are available in Fort Kearney State Park?

Can we get accommodations near Kingsley Dam without reservations?

Jason works in the maintenance department of a high-rise office building in Chicago. In addition to handling many telephone calls Jason has to receive many callers who are tenants in the various offices of the building. They come to check on cleaning schedules, to discuss redecorating plans, and for other types of information. Jason has on hand some of the information which he is expected to give to callers. He knows how to carefully record what is requested when he doesn't have the information. He then refers such requests to the persons who can handle them quickly and accurately.

TECHNIQUES FOR HANDLING RECEPTIONIST DUTIES

In addition to the special skills and abilities that a good receptionist must have, there are certain techniques that must be developed to become a valuable employee. Mastering these techniques makes a receptionist an asset to the company.

Scheduling Appointments

In most organizations there is a constant need for appointments between business associates and executives. Often a receptionist is responsible for maintaining the calendar of appointments so that arriving visitors are expected, and two appointments are not scheduled for the same time.

Here is a typical procedure that is used in many offices: This office is a law firm with four attorneys. The receptionist maintains a single calendar which shows the schedules for all four attorneys. One page from her calendar is shown in Illus. 8-3. The secretaries to the attorneys keep the receptionist informed of all appointments that have been made. Each morning the secretaries verify the day's calendar. Notice that the names are written clearly so that the receptionist can call the visitors by name easily. Also, telephone numbers for all appointments are recorded so that if adjustments must be made, the receptionist can telephone persons quickly.

JANUARY 14	FOLEY	WALSH	FLYNN	EVANS
9:00	R. Bender 821-4211	L. Timmins 356-8254	C. Basil 789-9339	
9:30				
10:00		V. Stein 215-6129	Mrs. Rodden 981-7991	
10:30	L. Samuels 203 420-1481			Courthouse
11:00			J. Benjamin 201 621-0219	9-5
11:30				
12:00	J. Bunting - Lunch 873-1891	Lunch	Lunch	
12:30			R. Braun 239-7969	
1:00		J. Perez 888-6239	S. Solomon 914-6199	
1:30				
2:00	D. Amos 739-4989	J. Silver 219-4569	Leave for Chicago 3pm flight	
2:30				
3:00		J. Taylor 819-1699		
3:30				
4:00	Out from here	B. Matthews 891-8393		
4:30				
5:00		S. Nelsen 766-7916		
5:30				
6:00				

Illus. 8-3
Appointment
calendar page

Sometimes a client will stop by to reschedule an appointment for a later date. The receptionist then calls the secretary to the attorney with whom the appointment is requested to check on a **convenient** time. The receptionist then gives the client a small card with the rescheduled date and hour of appointment. Illus. 8-4 shows an appointment card.

convenient:
suitable; handy

Illus. 8-4
Reminder of
appointment

FOLEY, WALSH, FLYNN, AND EVANS
ATTORNEYS AT LAW

357 MICHIGAN BOULEVARD
CHICAGO, ILLINOIS 60600

M *r. B. Matthews* _____ has an appointment

with Mr. _____ *Walsh* _____ at _____ *4 p.m.* _____ on

Monday, January 14

W.E.B.

Maintaining a File of Callers

The receptionist in the law firm discussed here also maintains a file of all clients. The names are kept on cards in a rotary file. Illus. 7-28, page 271, shows a rotary file. Notice the ease with which the receptionist is able to find a particular card. Illus. 8-5 shows a card that is in the file.

Illus. 8-5
File
card

```
Matthews, Bernard W.
    1451 East Monroe Street
    Chicago, IL  60603




    Telephone:   392-4320 (Home)
                 891-8393 (Office)
```

The receptionist is responsible for getting full information from callers on their first visit so that a card can be typed and filed in the rotary file.

Illus. 8-6
A receptionist maintains complete and current files so that appointments can be rescheduled if necessary.

Pitney Bowes

Greeting Callers

Executives want their employees to greet callers courteously. If you are a receptionist you will want to show the friendliness of your company. This means that you give immediate attention to the caller as he approaches your desk. Here is the way in which Betsy greets callers:

> As the caller approaches Betsy's desk, she looks up and says: "Good morning. May I help you?"
>
> The caller: "Good morning. Yes, I am Herb Landson, of the Mid-Continent Electronic Company; and I would like very much to talk with Mr. Stanley about some production problems that we think he can solve for us." (Betsy writes his name and company on a pad.)
>
> Betsy: "Will you have a seat while I check with Mr. Stanley's secretary to see if Mr. Stanley can see you now."

Mr. Landson walks over to a chair and sits down. Betsy telephones Mr. Stanley's secretary. Betsy: "Ruth, this is Betsy. Mr. Herb Landson, of Mid-Continent Electronic Company, is here. He would like to talk with Mr. Stanley about some production problems he has in his company. Could Mr. Stanley see him now?" (A pause while Ruth checks and finds that Mr. Stanley can talk with the caller.) "Thank you, Ruth, I'll have Mr. Landson come to your office immediately."

Betsy walks over to Mr. Landson: "Mr. Landson, Mr. Stanley can see you now. His office is on the second floor. If you will take the elevator on the right, to the next floor, you will find his office at the end of the corridor on your left."

Mr. Landson: "Thank you very much."

Betsy used several good techniques that show how efficient and courteous she is.

1. She gave the caller her full attention immediately upon his arrival.
2. She wrote his name and company on a pad as he told her who he was so that there was no need to ask for that information **prior** to making her telephone call.

prior:
before; earlier in
time or place

3. She asked him to be seated so that he would be out of range of the telephone conversation as she attempted to determine Mr. Stanley's availability.
4. She knew whom to call and knew the secretary by name.
5. She walked over to Mr. Landson (she didn't shout from her desk) to give him the message.
6. She gave Mr. Landson the directions for getting to Mr. Stanley's office.

Announcing Callers

You will find that in some offices receptionist duties may involve escorting visitors to executive offices and announcing them. The following are courteous techniques for handling these situations:

An expected caller whom the receptionist knows:	Caller: "Good afternoon."
	Receptionist: "Good afternoon, Mrs. Sayles. Mr. Walsh is expecting you. Let me check to see if he is free. Will you have a seat?"
	The receptionist goes immediately into Mr. Walsh's office and returns quickly.
	Receptionist: "Mrs. Sayles, Mr. Walsh is ready to see you." (The receptionist then returns to her desk.)

An expected caller who has not been in the office before and doesn't know the person with whom he has an appointment:

Caller: "Good afternoon. I am Jack Conley."

Receptionist: "How nice to meet you, Mr. Conley. Mr. Walsh is expecting you. Let me check to see if he is free. Will you have a seat?"

Caller: "Thank you."

The receptionist calls Mr. Walsh's office. She then says, "Mr. Walsh is free and can see you now." The receptionist walks into the office with Mr. Conley and introduces him to Mr. Walsh: "Mr. Walsh, Mr. Conley."

The receptionist then quickly and quietly walks out of the office.

Good techniques in announcing callers include:

1. Being aware of who is expected for appointments
2. Asking the caller to have a seat
3. Checking with the executive to be sure he is free to see the caller
4. Taking the caller into the office when he hasn't been there before
5. Introducing the caller to the executive when necessary

Talking with a Difficult Caller

There are times when you may have to deal with a difficult caller when you are responsible for receptionist tasks. From time to time a caller whom you do not know may refuse to tell you who he is or why he wishes to see someone in the company. Such a caller may speak discourteously and become angry. On such an occasion you must be firm in your responses and try to learn the caller's purpose. If he will not state his purpose, you will have to refuse his request. Here is a technique that is often successful:

Caller approaches the desk with no comment.

Receptionist: "May I help you?"

Caller: "I want to see the president."

Receptionist: "Please, may I have your name and the purpose of your visit?"

Caller: "It is none of your business. What are you, a screening device? I want to see the president."

Receptionist: "I am very sorry, but I am unable to grant your request without this information."

Caller: "Will you tell me where his office is, and I'll go in my-self?"

Receptionist: "I am sorry, but I cannot do this for you. I would suggest that you write the president a letter. If you would like to see him in addition to telling him of your business in the letter, indicate in your letter when you can come in for an appointment."

Caller: "That's not the way I want to handle my business, but I guess I have no choice." (The caller leaves the office.)

The receptionist was successful in handling the difficult caller primarily because she followed these techniques:

1. She remained calm but firm.
2. She did not use the name of the president or say where the president's office was.
3. She suggested that the caller write a letter in which he could state his problem and request an appointment.
4. She promised nothing. While the receptionist told the caller he could ask for an appointment, she did not indicate that he would get one.

Keeping a Record of Callers

Receptionists often receive callers for a number of executives. They must keep track of who is waiting, who is in what office, and other details. Some companies keep a record of callers. Illus. 8-7 shows a form that is sometimes used to register callers. Notice that neat handwriting is important if this register is to be legible.

JANUARY 14, 197-

Time of Arrival	Name and Affiliation	Person Seen	Time of Departure
8:50	R. Bender, Attorney	J. Foley	9:30

Illus. 8-7
Register of callers

Handling Emergencies

As a receptionist, you should maintain in a convenient place the telephone numbers of the organization's doctor, the nearest hospital, the police department, the fire department, the maintenance department, and any other sources that are likely to be of assistance in case of an emergency.

You will find that the receptionist is frequently one of the first persons notified in case of an emergency, and you should remain calm and handle efficiently the tasks that must be done quickly at such a time.

Covering the Receptionist's Desk

Reception desks must never be left unattended. If you are assigned to such a desk, you must be sure that you make arrangements for someone to **relieve** you when you are called away or go to lunch. You must also remember that the responsibility for handling receptionist duties does not allow you to spend your time talking with friends either in person or by telephone. Adequate coverage requires attention to the business matters of your position at all times.

relieve:
take your place

**REVIEWING
WHAT YOU
HAVE READ**

1. What is the primary responsibility of the receptionist?
2. How does the receptionist indicate her interest in the caller?
3. How do reference books help a receptionist who must answer questions from callers who request information?
4. How can a receptionist who makes appointments for several people organize a calendar?
5. What information is ordinarily recorded on an appointment card given to a caller?
6. Why is it a good idea to record the telephone number of each person scheduled for an appointment?
7. Why should a receptionist record the name of an unfamiliar caller when he *first* gives his name?
8. May the receptionist assume that all callers are acquainted with the executives with whom they have appointments? Explain.
9. How should the receptionist respond to the difficult caller who refuses to give his name or purpose of visit?
10. What are some of the telephone numbers a receptionist should have listed for emergency purposes?

**MAKING
DECISIONS**

1. Judy is a receptionist in a large insurance company. One afternoon a woman came to her desk shouting: "That agent from your company is robbing me. I demand that all the premiums I've paid be returned to me. Whom can I see immediately?" What would you suggest that Judy do at this point?
2. A caller comes into the reception area where Marge is serving as receptionist. The caller asks to see Mr. Quinn. She has no appointment. Mr. Quinn had informed Marge about an hour earlier that he did not want to be disturbed for the morning, for he had to finish a draft of a report that he was expected to complete by the end of the week.
   What should be Marge's response to the request?

**WORKING
WITH
OTHERS**

Wanda is the receptionist in a large publishing company. Many callers come to her office daily. Her lunch time is from 12 to 1 and during this hour Vera, who is a typist in one of the offices, relieves Wanda. Vera frequently makes appointments for callers and merely writes on small slips of paper the last name of the caller and the hour of appointment. Sometimes the day of the week is indicated; at other times, it is missing. Wanda finds that she has many problems because Vera doesn't get all the information needed and also she doesn't record it in a form that Wanda can use.

What do you believe Wanda ought to do about this problem?

USING LANGUAGE

Below are responses made by receptionists to callers or to executives. On a separate sheet of paper, indicate for each whether the response is appropriate or inappropriate. Rewrite and improve those that are inappropriate.

1. Linda: "Good morning, Mr. Rowland. Mr. Stern is free, and he is expecting you. You may go right in."
2. Ruth: "Who are you? Do you have an appointment?"
3. Brenda: "Why don't you go in and find out if Mr. Ross is finished with his other appointment. If he isn't maybe he'll hurry it up."
4. Lois: (Angrily) "If you won't tell me your business, you can be sure that I shall not allow you to go one step beyond this desk."
5. Dorothy: "When you get in Mr. Stanley's office, would you just introduce yourself, since he doesn't know your name."
6. Peggy: "I shall call Mr. Burns to see if he is free. Will you have a seat in the meantime?"
7. Vicki: "Goodbye, Mrs. Reins. Have a pleasant day."
8. Winnie: "I am very sorry that Miss Bryant is out of town. Would a time one day next week be convenient for you?"
9. Beverly: "Mr. Collins is in, but he is very busy, and he doesn't want to see anyone this morning. Sorry!"
10. Vivian: "Mr. Bradford, Mr. Thomas Abelson of Electronics Equipment Company; Mr. Abelson, Mr. Theodore Bradford."

USING ARITHMETIC

The receptionist in a small architectural firm in Boston, Massachusetts, was asked to figure out the length of each long-distance call made during the preceding week. These are the figures she recorded on her worksheet. On a separate sheet of paper determine the length of each call as well as the total time spent in long-distance conversations.

	Time Started		Time Ended		Time Started		Time Ended
11/15	10:15	–	10:29	11/17	2:15	–	2:19
	1:15	–	1:21	(Continued)	2:25	–	2:30
	2:10	–	2:30				
	3:15	–	3:19	11/18	10:00	–	10:15
					11:01	–	11:16
11/16	9:15	–	9:20		11:45	–	11:51
	11:45	–	11:50		2:19	–	2:35
	2:10	–	2:20				
				11/19	9:30	–	9:45
11/17	10:05	–	10:25		9:50	–	10:20
	11:10	–	11:45		11:03	–	11:29
	1:45	–	2:09		2:15	–	2:45

1. (a) Assume one of the two roles:

Receptionist in the executive suite of a large city bank. Her name is Marie Van Dyke.

An executive, Mr. Lester Schwartz, from a bank in another city who has an appointment with the vice-president of personnel, Mr. Stewart Whitney, at 2 p.m.

Situation: It is now 9:30 a.m. Mr. Schwartz arrives at the bank hoping that he can see the vice-president during the morning hours, since he must return to his home in the early afternoon.

Act out the conversation between Marie and Mr. Schwartz.

   (b) Assume one of the two roles:

Receptionist in a dress manufacturing company. Her name is Joan Wiggins.

Salesman from a textile firm who wishes to see the production manager. His name is Mr. David Needham.

Situation: Mr. Needham has never sold this company any of his textiles; he now has a new product which he thinks will be very attractive to this company. He wants an opportunity to talk with the production manager. He has no appointment.

Act out the conversation between Joan and Mr. Needham.

2. Assume that you are the receptionist for a textile trade association in Charlotte, North Carolina, which has three executives for whom you schedule appointments. You have made the following appointments for Mr. McNally, Mr. Jones, and Mr. Beech for Thursday, December 7. On a separate sheet of paper draw up an appropriate calendar form and record the appointments.

For Mr. McNally	9:30 appointment with James Hanson from Washington, D.C. (202 567-8900 Ext. 45)
	Noon luncheon engagement with Wesley Horton (354-6789)
	3:00 appointment with John Waterman of Advertising (Ext. 467)
	4:00 appointment with Miss Teresa Sallows (342-2345)
For Mr. Jones	9:00 appointment with Ted Norris (451-4671)
	10:00 appointment with Ralph Manley (567-3791)
	11:30 appointment with William Bates (465-8999)
	2:00 appointment with Walter Colliers from Raleigh (919 567-4689)
For Mr. Beech	9:30 appointment with George Wienberg (532-0975)
	10:30 appointment with Murray Elliott (680-3223)
	Noon meeting at the Towers Inn — Breakmore Room (out until 2:30)
	3:00 appointment with Erick Kamp (567-8643)

PART 2 ORAL COMMUNICATIONS

Kathy Horner is the receptionist in a new medical clinic in Worthington, Minnesota. She is a quiet, gracious young woman and is well liked by others. The doctors for whom she works think her services are invaluable. One of them, Dr. Wolman, when asked why the staff likes Kathy, commented, "Kathy is constantly facing very anxious people. They are ill; they are uncertain about what is wrong. She is reassuring and understanding. She never says anything to discourage our patients. She makes them feel comfortable. We must take care of emergencies, and this means that scheduled appointments are delayed. Kathy remains calm and tries to keep waiting patients contented."

ORAL COMMUNICATION SKILLS

Oral communication is important to the business world today. When you are handling receptionist duties, you will be spending the greater part of your working day in talking with others. The good habits that you have learned in various courses will be valuable to you as you talk with others. Speaking clearly, pronouncing words correctly, using acceptable language and good grammar — all are needed for effective oral communications.

Using Standard Language

Standard language is that vocabulary which is acceptable in personal and business communications, both oral and written.

As you know, the language of a society is constantly changing. In fact, we talk of "living language" because we are always adding new words and dropping words that are no longer used. New developments, such as space exploration, have resulted in adding new words to our vocabulary. Many dictionaries have a special section in which the new words that have been added to the language since the dictionary's last edition are defined. You may want to look through such a section to get an idea of the types of words that are being added to our language.

The language that you learned in your study of English as well as in your other courses is appropriate for the business office. A broad vocabulary will be useful and **beneficial** to you in all **aspects** of your life, including your business career.

beneficial: helpful

aspects: phases

Speaking Clearly

You know how easy it is to listen to someone who speaks clearly. You hear each word that is spoken and can respond to the person accurately. Some of the most common habits that keep people from speaking clearly include:

1. Speaking so rapidly that words run together and the listener is not able to understand what is said
2. Speaking in a very low voice
3. Speaking in a very loud voice
4. Speaking so that the ends of sentences are mumbled
5. Speaking before you know exactly what you want to say so that disconnected phrases and sentences are spoken that have little, if any, meaning to your listener

If you will think of your listener as you talk, you will find that you can improve the **clarity** of your speech. Speak as though you want to be heard. This means that you will speak so that each word is clearly **audible**. You will have in mind what you want to say before you begin to talk.

clarity: clearness

audible: able to be heard

Pronouncing Words Correctly

Most words have standard pronunciations. This means that there is one correct way of saying the word. There are some words, though, that have more than one acceptable pronunciation. For example:

for *progress*, the usual pronunciation is *präg res*; yet *prō gress* is also correct.
for *tomato*, the usual pronunciation is *ta māt o*; yet *ta mät o* is also correct.

You will also find that pronunciation differs from one part of the country to another. What is acceptable in Boston may sound strange in Denver. However, if you work some place other than where you grew up, you will find people **tolerant** of speech differences. In fact, you should refrain from imitating the pronunciation of the new community if it differs from your natural way of speaking. Such imitation is called *affected* speech and may be **offensive** to the listener.

A good habit to follow is to check the preferred pronunciation in a dictionary. Also you should be aware of careless speech habits that cause you to pronounce words improperly. Here are a few speech errors that you should avoid.

tolerant: accepting; forbearing

offensive: unpleasant; painful

Illus. 8-8

Pronunciation varies from
one part of the country
to the other

Avis Rent A Car

	FAULTY	CORRECT
Dropping the ending of words	workin'	working
	talkin'	talking
Substituting one vowel for another	mill	meal
	fill	feel
	winda	window
	fella	fellow
Substituting one syllable for another	libery	library
	granite	granted
	purtty	pretty

Enunciating Words Properly

When you speak each word precisely, you are enunciating
properly. Care in enunciating words is important if you are to be understood by the person listening to you. Among the words that are often
confused because they are not enunciated carefully are the following:

accept	sense
except	since
affect	statue
effect	stature
charted	than
chartered	then
picture	work
pitcher	word
	worth

Avoiding Colloquialisms and Slang

As you learned, our language is constantly changing and the value of certain words and expressions also changes. There are two classes of words that change rather quickly. These are colloquialisms and slang. *Colloquialisms* are words that are satisfactory for informal conversation and are often natural to a person's speech. However, it is wise to avoid such words in written communications and in conversations where standard language is more likely to express your thoughts clearly. Here are three frequently heard colloquialisms that are avoided by careful speakers:

COLLOQUIAL	PREFERRED
around for *about*	He should arrive *about* (not *around*) noon.
contact for *get in touch with* or *call* or *talk with*	Will you *talk with* (not *contact*) Miss Sanders this afternoon?
posted for *informed*	Mr. Keller kept us *informed* (not *posted*) while the negotiations were in progress.

Although colloquialisms are tolerated, slang is seldom acceptable in business offices. *Slang* is the use of nonstandard words with forced meanings. While some slang expressions become standard **ultimately**, most slang words lose their popularity in a short time. While slang phrases such as *on the ball* or *to miss the boat* are less offensive than they were in the past, their use in business offices should be limited.

ultimately:
finally; eventually

A vocabulary made up of slang words such as the following is an indication of a very weak English background:

dig	swell
super	rap
bug	groovy
tough	lousy

Each of these words usually means many, many different things. For example, *tough* is used to mean *pretty, attractive, good, lovely,* etc. The lack of precise meaning for slang expressions makes their usefulness limited.

Using Correct Grammar

Both oral and written communications require that you give attention to correct grammar. It is very easy for grammatical errors to creep into your speech and to become so common that you are not aware that you are speaking incorrectly. Be aware of the errors you tend to make and then try to improve your grammar. Some common errors are listed at the top of page 296.

Using a subject of one number and a verb of another	Incorrect: *He don't* need that many sheets of paper.
	Correct: *He doesn't* need that many sheets of paper.
Using the wrong case for pronouns	Incorrect: Both *him* and *me* will go to the meeting tonight
	Correct: Both *he* and *I* will go to the meeting tonight.
Using adjectives as adverbs	Incorrect: She did *good* in the contest.
	Correct: She did *well* in the contest.
Using the improper past tense for irregular verbs.	Incorrect: He *sat* it on the shelf.
	Correct: He *set* it on the shelf.

Eliminating Offensive Mannerisms

distract:
draw away from

Mannerisms are gestures, facial expressions, or speech habits that **distract** from your ability to communicate clearly with others. It is possible to eliminate unbecoming mannerisms by careful attention to them.

> Jan was a very kind young woman who giggled at the end of every sentence she spoke. This was an annoying habit that often caused people to discount the seriousness of what she was saying. When a friend talked to her quietly about this fault, Jan accepted the criticism well and asked her friend to keep a count of how many times she giggled when they were together. Jan didn't overcome the habit immediately, but she was able to reduce the frequency of the giggling; and, after some months, she was successful in eliminating this shortcoming.
>
> Roger had a habit of talking to people indirectly — that is, he always looked down at the floor or ground and never looked at the person with whom he was talking. This habit caused people to think that Roger was not friendly and lacked interest in others. One of his teachers talked with him about his mannerism. He, like Jan, wasn't aware of how distracting it was; and he began being conscious of his behavior as he talked with others. He eventually overcame the habit.

COURTESY

When someone talks with you, you should give the person your full attention. This is the first rule of courtesy in speaking with others. These were Mr. Darden's comments about Ned:

> Ned is basically a satisfactory worker, but I find it hard to talk with him, for he never seems to be listening to me. He is always looking off to see who is passing by, and he seldom is giving his attention to what I am saying. He often has to ask

questions about instructions I have given him orally. I have talked to him about his lack of attention, and I hope he will improve. We expect our employees to respect what we say to each other, since accurate communication is a very important part of our work.

When you are talking with another person, you should not grow impatient and interrupt before he has completed his thought. At the same time, when you are talking, you should be careful that you give the other person an opportunity to talk. A nonstop talker usually becomes a bore to the listener.

Illus. 8-9

Courtesy should always be observed in talking with others.

IBM Corporation

Courtesy in speaking with others includes careful control of your voice. Many conversations are confidential, and you should not respond in a voice that reveals the content of the conversation. Kristen commented about a young woman who was no longer in the employment of her company:

Rebecca just didn't seem to belong in this office. There are six of us who are typists; and frequently the people for whom we are doing the typing come in to talk about format, placement, and other problems. The work is often confidential, and there is no need for everyone in the room to know what one typist is doing. Rebecca never learned that she didn't have to talk in a loud, distracting voice when she spoke with the supervisors who came to her desk. Not only did she interrupt any other conversations going on at the time, but she was regularly revealing confidential information. Our supervisor talked with her about this, I know, but it didn't seem to do much good.

You will improve your oral communications if you are courteous as you talk with others.

1. What is the meaning of *standard language*?
2. Why are new words constantly being added to our language?
3. What are three habits that cause unclear speech?
4. What is *affected* speech?
5. Give an example of the faulty habit of dropping the endings of words.
6. Why is proper enunciation considered important in speaking?
7. How does a colloquialism differ from a slang expression?
8. Explain why the statement *They will give it to her and I* is incorrect.
9. Mannerisms are considered distractions. Explain what this statement means.
10. How can you show courtesy to another person with whom you are talking?

MAKING DECISIONS

1. Regina was born in Boston and lived there until she was eighteen. Then she moved to Savannah, Georgia, where she got a job as a receptionist. Regina was very self-conscious about her speech, which she felt was totally out of place in the South. She liked the style of speaking in Savannah, and she decided to imitate it. She believed that no one would be able to detect the fact that she was not a native of Georgia. What do you think of Regina's decision?

2. Francis worked as a clerk in the stockroom of a large appliance store that carried all types of recording equipment. One day he and a fellow clerk were asked to check a tape recorder that a customer claimed was defective. Francis and his fellow clerk recorded their conversation so that they could check the machine. Then they listened to the conversation. Francis learned that his friend's speech was clearer than his. In fact, Francis couldn't understand himself. His words ran together, others were mumbled, some were incomplete. What could Francis do about his speech?

WORKING WITH OTHERS

Amelia was recently hired as a clerk in the central filing department of a manufacturing company. Amelia was born in Venezuela and lived there until three years ago when her family moved to New Orleans. She studied English earnestly when she came to the United States, but she continues to have difficulty in speaking English so that the listener will understand her easily. She knows her problem and after she was introduced to Bertha whose desk is next to hers, she said to Bertha, "Will you help me with my English? When you hear me say something wrong, will you please tell me about it? I really want to improve my English."

What do you think Bertha should say and do?

USING LANGUAGE

Some words in the English language are pronounced alike but are different in meaning. Other words have pronunciations which are similar, but not exactly alike. Often people pronounce these words as though they are alike. Below are pairs of words, some of which are pronounced alike but have different meanings and others which are not pronounced the same. Use a dictionary to check the pronunciation of each word, as well as to check the meaning of the word. On a separate sheet of paper write a sentence for each of the words. Underline those words that are pronounced the same.

accept	except	picture	pitcher
affect	effect	then	than
since	sense	sight	site
weather	whether	waist	waste
word	worth	which	witch

Marilyn is a receptionist in a management consulting firm. She has been given a number of duties, including typing reports. But her primary responsibility is to greet callers and handle the telephone calls that come into the company. In an effort to learn how much work there is at her desk, Marilyn has been asked to keep a record of how many callers and how many telephone calls she receives as well as how many she makes each day. Below are the records for five days. Tally each day's record and prepare a report showing how many calls and callers were taken care of for the week of November 5.

Monday, November 5, 19 - -

Outgoing local calls: ~~IIII~~ ~~IIII~~ ~~IIII~~ II

Outgoing long-distance calls: ~~IIII~~ II

Incoming calls: ~~IIII~~ ~~IIII~~ ~~IIII~~ ~~IIII~~ I

Callers: ~~IIII~~ ~~IIII~~ II

Tuesday, November 6, 19 - -

Outgoing local calls: ~~IIII~~ ~~IIII~~ ~~IIII~~ ~~IIII~~

Outgoing long-distance calls: ~~IIII~~ ~~IIII~~ III

Incoming calls: ~~IIII~~ ~~IIII~~ ~~IIII~~ ~~IIII~~ I

Callers: ~~IIII~~ II

Wednesday, November 7, 19 - -

Outgoing local calls: ~~IIII~~ ~~IIII~~ ~~IIII~~ ~~IIII~~ IIII

Outgoing long-distance calls: ~~IIII~~ III

Incoming calls: ~~IIII~~ ~~IIII~~ ~~IIII~~ III

Callers: ~~IIII~~ ~~IIII~~ ~~IIII~~ I

Thursday, November 8, 19 - -

Outgoing local calls: ~~IIII~~ ~~IIII~~ ~~IIII~~ III

Outgoing long-distance calls: ~~IIII~~ IIII

Incoming calls: ~~IIII~~ ~~IIII~~ ~~IIII~~ II

Callers: ~~IIII~~ IIII

Friday, November 9, 19 - -

Outgoing local calls: ~~IIII~~ ~~IIII~~ ~~IIII~~ III

Outgoing long-distance calls: ~~IIII~~ I

Incoming calls: ~~IIII~~ ~~IIII~~ ~~IIII~~ I

Callers: ~~IIII~~ III

Illus. 8-10

1. Make a list of slang words and expressions that you hear daily that you believe would not be appropriate for business communications. For each slang word or expression, write the definition. Opposite the definition, write the word or words of standard English that you believe should be used to express the meaning intended by the slang word or phrase.

2. Write a short paragraph in answer to one of these questions:
   (a) Why is it important for the office worker to enunciate properly?
   (b) Why is courtesy important in the office?
   (c) What are some mannerisms that you believe would be distracting in the office?

3. If a tape recorder is available, make a taping of the following:
   (a) Reading a paragraph from a textbook
   (b) Having a conversation with a fellow classmate about the responsibilities of an office worker who meets the public
   (c) Explaining to a classmate what it means to speak clearly

   Listen to your recording and make notes of speech habits you hear that you would like to change.

UNIT 9

TELEPHONE AND TELEGRAPH SERVICES

CLERICALS

Bright energetic people wante
Good telephone technique
ust. Some positions requ
ing.
ply Personnel 2nd floor
terviews 10-12 & 2-4
W & J STEIN
enue at 40th St.

PART 1   RECEIVING CALLS

Diane Roberts works in the Planning Department of the Northern Construction Company. When Mr. Keller, her boss, is away from his desk or doesn't wish to be disturbed, Diane must answer all his incoming telephone calls. She knows the work of the Planning Department, and she has a very pleasant telephone voice. Through experience, Diane has learned to handle Mr. Keller's incoming calls properly.

Can you imagine working in an office that has no telephone? Of course not! It would be impossible for today's business to run smoothly and efficiently without the rapid communication that is made possible with telephones. In fact, telephones have become so important to business that they are used in about 90 percent of all business transactions.

One of your duties may be to receive and place telephone calls. With each call you will be representing your company. The impression you give over the telephone will reflect — positively or negatively — on the people for whom you work. Therefore, it is important that you understand the proper techniques for using the telephone.

TELEPHONE PERSONALITY

Developing your telephone personality will require careful thought and effort. Since the caller will not be able to see you, you will not be able to rely on good grooming or on an attractive appearance to create a favorable impression. The only image of you that your caller has comes from your voice, your speech, your vocabulary, and your manner. You should try to improve the attractiveness of each. If you speak with a friendly smile in your voice, you will create a favorable impression of your company.

Voice

A voice can convey a spirit of interest, alertness, courtesy, and helpfulness over the telephone; or it can reflect an attitude of indifference, impatience, or inattention. It is often true that it is not what is said but the way it is said that really counts in a telephone conversation. A pleasant voice is much nicer to listen to than one which is loud, harsh, or shrill. You can improve your voice if you think and speak with a smile. Try to think of the caller as a person — not just as an unknown voice — who needs your help. You can have the *voice with a smile* if you talk with callers in a pleasant manner. Here are some suggestions to improve your telephone voice:

Illus. 9-1
The voice with a smile gives the caller a favorable impression.

AT&T

1. *Speak clearly.* A normal tone of voice — neither too loud nor too soft — carries best over the telephone.
2. *Use a low-pitched voice.* A low-pitched voice carries better over the telephone and is kinder to your listener's ear. A high-pitched voice tends to become shrill and **irritating**.

irritating: tending to produce anger or impatience

3. *Use voice inflection.* The rise and fall of your voice not only put your thoughts across but also add personality to your voice. A **monotonous** voice sounds indifferent because it is flat and lacks spirit.

monotonous: uniform, unvarying, same, tiresome

Speech

Your speech habits are just as important as your voice: a pleasant voice makes you easy to listen to; good speech habits make you easy to understand. You should pronounce words clearly and correctly so that callers understand what you are saying. It is important that callers hear your message correctly.

Below are some suggestions for good telephone speech.

Illus. 9-2
Good speech habits convey efficiency to the caller.

General Telephone and
Electronics Corporation

1. *Speak carefully.* Distinct speech is essential, since the listener can neither read your lips nor see your expression. Be careful to pronounce each word clearly; don't mumble or slur syllables.

2. *Talk at a proper pace.* A **moderate** rate of speech is easily understood, but the pace should be related to the ideas you are expressing. You should give some information more slowly: for example, technical information, lists, information the listener is writing down, numbers, names, and foreign or unusual words.

moderate:
reasonable

3. *Use emphasis with words.* The stress or emphasis placed on words, or groups of words, may change the meaning of what you are saying.

Vocabulary

Your ideas should be stated simply with descriptive words when they are needed. Technical, awkward, and unnecessarily lengthy words may confuse the other person and may require an explanation or may even cause a misunderstanding.

Be careful not to use language which will offend the listener or create a bad impression of the company you represent. Avoid trite words, phrases, and slang expressions. *Yes* sounds much better than *Yeah* or *OK*.

Courtesy

Courtesy is just as important in a telephone call as it is in a face-to-face conversation. Callers should not be interrupted or given the "run-around." Listen carefully to what the person is saying. You can develop a good telephone manner that is always courteous, sincere, understanding, and helpful to the caller.

INCOMING CALLS

As part of your office duties, you will probably answer the telephone. You may also be expected to answer your employer's telephone when he is away from his desk. The suggestions given below and on the following pages will aid you in performing this important function.

Answer Promptly

You should answer all incoming calls promptly and pleasantly. No one likes to wait; furthermore, you have no way of knowing who is calling — it may be a very important call. In fact, no matter who is calling, if he thought enough of your business to make a call, you must give him prompt attention. The telephone should be answered on the first ring.

As you reach for the receiver, reach for your notebook. You must be ready to take notes immediately. *You should hold the mouthpiece about an inch from your lips* and speak directly into the telephone in a normal conversational tone of voice.

Identify Yourself

A telephone conversation cannot really begin until the caller knows that he has reached the right number. You should always identify yourself and your firm, office, or department immediately. Never answer by saying "Hello" or "Yes?" — these greetings add nothing to the identification.

If you answer an outside line, give your firm's name, followed by your name, as "Northern Construction Company, Miss Roberts." If your company has a switchboard, your operator has already identified the company; and you may answer your employer's telephone by saying, "Mr. Keller's office, Miss Roberts." When answering an office extension in a department, identify the department and give your name — "Planning Department, Miss Roberts."

Screening Calls

One of your most important duties may be to screen your employer's incoming telephone calls when he is away from his office, has someone with him, or is talking on another line. Explain why your employer cannot talk, and, if possible, suggest another way in which you can help the caller, such as:

> Mr. White, Mr. Keller is attending a committee meeting. Is there anything I can do to help you?
> Mr. White, Mr. Keller is in conference. Would you care to talk to his assistant, Mr. Goetz?

Giving Information

You must be very careful when giving information if your employer is not available for telephone calls. For instance, a reply such as "Mr. Keller left for Minneapolis this morning" may be just enough information to let a competitor know that Mr. Keller is interested enough in a certain construction contract to make a personal trip to the construction site. Unless you are absolutely sure that your employer would want others to have the information, do not give details over the telephone to outside callers.

Say	Rather than
He is out of the city. May I ask him to call you when he returns on Monday?	He was called to New York to help close the Jones contract.
He is not at his desk. May I take a message?	He is discussing the merger with the comptroller.
He will be in tomorrow morning. May I ask him to call you then?	He is at the Bonnie Brook Country Club.

Getting Information

Some telephone callers do not care to give their names; others prefer not to say why they are calling. You will frequently have to find out *who* is calling and, if the name does not help you, *why* he is calling. Try to get the information as tactfully as possible by using an **appropriate** response, such as:

appropriate:
suitable; fitting

Mr. Keller has a visitor at the moment. If you will give me your name and telephone number, I will ask him to call you just as soon as he is free.

Mr. Keller is not at his desk just now. May I give him a message for you?

Mr. Keller is talking on another line. May I help you?

If you must ask a direct question to get the information, state it as a request rather than as a demand: "May I tell Mr. Keller who is calling?"

Taking Messages Accurately

A pad of forms for recording the details of incoming telephone calls should always be kept on your desk next to the telephone to take messages when your employer is out. When your employer returns he can use the messages to return the calls, a practice which promotes better customer relations. It is very important, therefore, that you record all the details of every message accurately.

Illus. 9-3
Always be prepared to make a record of telephone messages.

AT&T

The message, written clearly, should include

1. The exact time of the call and the date

2. The name of the caller and his company (check the spelling of any unusual name)

3. The telephone number, the caller's extension, and area code, if it's a long-distance call (check the number)

4. The details of the message

5. The initials of the person who wrote the message

Illus. 9-4 Memo of call

Transferring Calls

Sometimes you will have to transfer a call to another extension or number. Calls are usually transferred when the caller has reached a wrong extension, when the caller wishes to speak with someone else, or when the caller's request can be handled better by someone else. Tell the caller why the transfer is necessary, and be sure that the call is being transferred to the proper person. In these instances you may say to the caller:

> I am sorry; you have reached the wrong extension. What extension were you calling? . . . I can transfer your call. Just a minute, please.
> I shall be glad to transfer your call to Mr. Williams. His extension is 2368. Just a minute, please.
> Mr. Young has all the information on that matter. May I transfer your call to him?

To transfer a call you should push down and release the receiver button of the telephone *slowly*. This action flashes a signal light on the switchboard which will attract the operator's attention. After the operator answers your signal, you might say, "Please transfer this call to Mr. Williams," or, "Please place this call on Extension 2368."

If you are disconnected during a call made *to* you, hang up, but try to keep your line free to receive the call back. If you placed the call, signal the operator and ask her to place the call again; or, if you dialed the call, dial it again. If you dialed a long-distance call, dial *O* for Operator and explain that you were disconnected.

Automatic Answering and Recording Set

A telephone answering and recording set called *Code-a-phone* will automatically answer the telephone and record a message after business hours or during the regular business hours if there is nobody to answer the telephone. Here is how it works. A message such as the following may be dictated to the set.

> This is John Keller speaking. You are listening to a recording of my voice. If it is important, you may reach me at 701-555-2579. When you hear the tone you can record a message for me if you would like to do so. Thank you.

The recorded messages may be played back later.

Telephone Answering Service

With a telephone answering service you know that all your calls will be answered when you are unable to receive them personally. The telephone answering service operator takes your calls for you and relays the messages to you or your business associates. The names of firms that supply telephone answering service are listed in the Yellow Pages.

TERMINATING CALLS

Try to leave a favorable impression by ending each telephone conversation in a friendly, unhurried manner. It is very bad manners to end a call by hanging up abruptly. As the conversation ends, thank the caller for his call with an appropriate remark such as:

> Thank you very much for calling, Mr. Ames.
> Thank you for your message. I'll ask Mr. Keller to telephone you as soon as he returns.
> Thank you for the information. I'll give it to Mr. Keller.

Be sure to say "Good-bye." After the caller has hung up, replace the receiver *gently*.

PERSONAL TELEPHONE CALLS

The policy of using a business telephone for personal calls varies in different offices. Some firms permit a limited number of personal calls; others permit none at all. However, all firms oppose the overuse of a business telephone for personal calls. Callers who wish to discuss personal matters with you during business hours should be politely discouraged. Personal calls should be made only when they are necessary.

TELEPHONE TIPS

In the business office you will meet many people for the first time over the telephone. Here are some telephone tips to help you make that first impression a favorable one.

1. Answer calls properly by
   (a) Answering at the end of the first ring
   (b) Identifying yourself properly
   (c) Identifying the answered phone properly
   (d) Noting all appropriate information
   (e) Letting the caller end the conversation

2. Always be courteous by
   (a) Greeting all callers pleasantly
   (b) Listening attentively
   (c) Responding appropriately
   (d) Using the caller's name
   (e) Apologizing for any delays or errors

3. Project a pleasing personality by
   (a) Acting naturally
   (b) Being friendly
   (c) Showing interest in the caller
   (d) Speaking expressively
   (e) Displaying alertness

4. Transfer calls with care by
   (a) Being very tactful
   (b) Explaining to the caller why the transfer is necessary
   (c) Signaling the switchboard attendant
   (d) Giving the attendant the proper name and the correct extension number
   (e) Hanging up the receiver *gently*

REVIEWING WHAT YOU HAVE READ

1. On what does telephone personality rely?
2. Give several suggestions for improving telephone speech habits.
3. How should you identify yourself when answering a business call?
4. What information should be recorded when taking a telephone message?
5. How can calls be transferred?
6. What is the best way to terminate telephone calls?
7. Discuss the use and the abuse of the office telephone for personal phone calls.

MAKING DECISIONS

1. Your employer is very busy and wants to be interrupted by as few telephone calls as possible. How would you know which calls to answer yourself and which calls to refer to your employer?
2. The assistant to the purchasing agent of a business buys almost all the office supplies. Therefore, some calls coming to the purchasing department are for the

purchasing agent and some are for the assistant. What should the assistant say when he answers the telephone?

WORKING WITH OTHERS

The Production Department of The Davis Electronics Corporation employs a production typing supervisor, Alice Bennett, and a receptionist, Betty Evans, who works in the reception area. The division has two telephone extensions — 621-2368 and 621-2369. Betty spends about 15 to 30 minutes on the telephone every morning talking about personal matters and office gossip with her co-workers in other offices.

After one prolonged conversation devoted mainly to office gossip, Alice spoke to Betty and told her that she was tying up an office telephone with personal chatter when she should be devoting her time to office business.

Betty responded by pointing out that (a) Shirley Clinton, of the Payroll Department, had called her — she had not called Shirley — and (b) while she has been using Extension 2368 the other extension, 2369, was still available for calls.

Was Alice correct in speaking to Betty about her prolonged telephone conversation with Shirley? Do you approve or disapprove of Betty's responses? Give your reasons for your approval or disapproval.

USING LANGUAGE

Below are three simple rules for helping you correctly add *ing* endings to verbs.

1. An *e* is usually dropped before the *ing*.

   Example: hope   hoping
            prove   proving

2. Before adding *ing*, *ie* is changed to *y*.

   Example: die   dying
            lie   lying

3. When the final syllable contains a long vowel, the *ing* will be preceded by a single consonant.

   Example: conceal   concea*l*ing

   When the final syllable contains a short vowel, the *ing* will be preceded by a double consonant. (However, in recent years usage has been tending toward only a single consonant. It is, therefore, wise to check your dictionary for the preferred usage.)

   Example: program   program*m*ing or program*ing
            cancel   cance*l*ing or cance*ll*ing

On a separate sheet of paper type the following words using the correct *ing* ending. When in doubt check the dictionary for correct usage.

1. advise	11. occupy
2. apply	12. occur
3. argue	13. plan
4. balance	14. put
5. continue	15. study
6. dictate	16. tie
7. dine	17. transcribe
8. drop	18. transfer
9. label	19. type
10. manage	20. verify

USING ARITHMETIC

1. One of your duties is to relieve the switchboard attendant when she is at lunch, absent, or otherwise assigned. A record must be kept and submitted to the office manager of all time you spend at the switchboard. Time less than ¼ hour is not reported. Last week you spent the following time at the switchboard. On a separate sheet of paper list the number of hours for each period and the total hours that you relieved the regular attendant.

Monday — 12:00 to 1:06	Thursday — 12:00 to 1:00
Tuesday — 8:00 to 12:00	Friday — 9:00 to 12:00
— 1:00 to 5:00	— 1:00 to 2:30
Wednesday — 12:00 to 1:13	— 3:00 to 5:00
— 3:20 to 5:00	

2. If in Problem 1 you work 40 hours a week, what percentage of your time did you spend relieving the switchboard attendant? Show the solution to this problem on the same sheet of paper that you use to solve Problem 1.

PERFORMING OFFICE TASKS

1. The following telephone calls were received on March 5, 197–, while the persons called were out of the office. Prepare a report of each call on a form similar to that shown in the illustration on page 308.

   (a) William C. Adams, of Chicago, called Alfred Rogers at 10:30 a.m. regarding Order R-325-C. Mr. Adams' telephone number is 312-891-3456. He will call again at 2:00.

   (b) Mrs. James Arthur called Mr. Arthur (her husband) at 12:30 p.m.

   (c) Mr. James Linden, of Philadelphia, called William Spencer at 11:45. He said that he had received Order 10256 but had not received Order 10245, which had been placed a week before Order 10256. His telephone number is 215-922-8230.

   (d) Earl Kramer called Alfred Rogers at 4:15. He will meet Mr. Rogers at 5:30 at the club.

2. Certain words and expressions used in telephone conversations have little relationship to modern telephone manners. The following trite and outdated telephone usage is still heard too frequently. Reword and type courteous sentences or questions for each.

   (a) Please put Mr. Davis on the phone.

   (b) He's tied up now. Can I have him call you back?

   (c) He's engaged at the moment. Hold the line.

   (d) OK, I'll have him call you back.

   (e) Who do you want to talk to?

   (f) What do you want to talk to him about?

   (g) I'll put Mr. White on the wire.

   (h) I'll have to hang up now.

   (i) Hello, Miss Ames, National Slippers.

   (j) Put the receiver on the hook.[1]

---

[1]There is no hook anymore — it's a cradle.

PART

PART 2 PLACING CALLS

Mr. James Bunker, the Credit Manager of Artcraft Camera Company, places most of his outgoing local calls himself. However, when he wants to make a long-distance call, he has Gayle Kerr, the switchboard attendant, place the call. Gayle understands fully the different kinds of long-distance services that are available, and she knows which service will be best in terms of speed and cost for each call.

OUTGOING CALLS

More and more executives are saving telephone time by answering and placing their own telephone calls. However, you may be expected to make your own telephone calls and to place calls for your employer. In order to make calls courteously and efficiently, you should have a fairly clear idea of the purpose of each call before you make it. You may find it wise to make a list of the points you wish to cover before making an important call. Be sure that your employer is free to talk before you place a call for him, for when you say, "This is Mr. Bunker's office calling. Mr. Bunker would like to speak with Mr. Hardy," you may be speaking with Mr. Hardy.

USING TELEPHONE DIRECTORIES CORRECTLY

Before making calls you should know how to get information from telephone directories quickly and how to operate the telephone properly. Three different telephone directories may be consulted to make outgoing calls: your own personal directory of frequently called persons and firms, the Telephone Directory (the White Pages), and the Yellow Pages.

Be sure you have the correct number before making a call. If you are not sure of the number, refer to a telephone directory to avoid possible delay and **embarrassment.** If you cannot find a number you want to call in the directory, call a Directory Assistance operator. For numbers in your own area, call Directory Assistance by dialing the number listed in the front of the Telephone Directory. To reach an out-of-town Directory Assistance operator, dial the proper area code, then 555-1212. The number 555-1212 is the nationwide Directory Assistance number.

embarrassment:
discomfort;
uneasiness

Personal Telephone Directory

An up-to-date list of frequently called local and out-of-town telephone numbers will save you and your employer a great deal of telephoning time. Booklets to be used as personal telephone directories can be obtained from most telephone companies. For the small firm or office, an "automatic finder" can be used. By moving the indicator to the correct letter of the alphabet, you can reach the desired page immediately. A large personal listing can be kept more easily on cards in a revolving visible file on your desk.

Alphabetical Directory

The names of subscribers are listed alphabetically in this directory. Individual names and firm names are easily located, unless the spelling of a name is unusual, and then it is cross-referenced as:

Gray — See also Grey
Hoffman — See also Hoffmann, Hofmann
Rees — See also Reis, Reiss, Riess

For the convenience of their customers or clients, business and professional people often list their home numbers directly below their business listings: for example,

Banks Jacob groc 4740 ReistwRd..............271-3469
    Res 3516 VaAv.........................271-4092

It is often necessary to call government agencies to request information or to get answers to questions which are constantly arising about government regulations. Government agencies are listed under three **categories:**

Federal agencies under United
States Government..............U.S. Government
                           Agriculture Dept of
                           Labor Dept of

State agencies under state
government...................North Dakota State of
                           Employment Service
                           Highway Dept

County and municipal agencies
under local governments........Minneapolis City of
                           Education Board of
                           Fire Dept
                           Police Dept

categories:
classes; groups

The first few pages of the alphabetical directory contain useful information including instructions for making **emergency** calls, local and long-distance calls, service calls (repair, assistance, etc.) and special calls (overseas, conference, collect, etc.). In addition, area codes for the United States and Canada, sample rates, and telephone company business office addresses and telephone numbers are listed.

emergency:
a pressing need;
something that
calls for immediate
action

Yellow Pages

The Yellow Pages are used when you wish to find out quickly where you may obtain a particular product or service. The names, addresses, and telephone numbers of business subscribers are listed alphabetically under the name of the product or service. Many business organizations use advertising space and artistic displays to tell their customers about the organization's operations, including brands carried, hours, and services. Nationally advertised or trademarked products may be listed with the names, addresses, and telephone numbers of most of the local dealers arranged alphabetically under a word or trademark design.

Illus. 9-5
The Yellow Pages
will provide quick,
accurate information.

AT&T

For instance, your employer may ask you to reorder master sets and copy paper for the A. B. Dick spirit duplicator. Under the heading, "Duplicating Machines & Supplies," the A•B•DICK trademark is displayed. Many local dealers are listed below "WHERE TO BUY THEM."

At another time your employer may ask you to call a certified public accountant named Smith who has an office on North Fifth Street. Since there are so many Smiths listed in the alphabetical section, it will be much easier to refer to the heading in the Yellow Pages "Accountants — Certified Public" to find this particular Mr. Smith.

Smith R R 209 N 5........................721-2626

PLACING LONG-DISTANCE CALLS

At times you may have to place long-distance calls. The two most generally used types of out-of-town calls are *station-to-station* and *person-to-person* calls.

Station-to-Station Calls

A station-to-station call is made to a certain telephone number. Make this type of call if you are willing to talk with anyone who may answer the telephone or if you are fairly certain the person with whom your employer wishes to speak is within easy reach of his telephone.

Person-to-Person Calls

When you wish to speak with a particular person in a large company, place a person-to-person call. A person-to-person call is directed to a specific person, room number, extension number, or department. Make this type of call only if you wish to talk with a particular person or if you are not sure he is within reach of his telephone. You must have assistance from a telephone company operator to place a person-to-person call. This type of call costs more than a station-to-station call.

Direct Distance Dialing (DDD)

Direct distance dialing is a method of placing all station-to-station calls and some person-to-person calls by using the dial on your telephone. No assistance is needed from the operator in order to complete the call. The front pages of the Telephone Directory provide complete directions for direct distance dialing.

Station-to-Station DDD. In order to use direct distance dialing in making a station-to-station call, in many areas you must first dial the number *1*, which is a prefix code that will give you a long-distance line.

Next you dial the three number area code which represents the area of the country you are calling. Area codes are required when calling from one area to another. In those areas of the country where the prefix code is not required, you simply dial the three digit area code to get a long-distance line. Finally, you dial the seven digits of the particular telephone number you wish to reach. For example, suppose you were in Cincinnati and wished to call the Alhambra Book Store in New York City, whose telephone number is 360-8437. You would dial 1-212-360-8437.

> 1 is the prefix code to get a long-distance line.
> 212 is the area code for New York City.
> 360-8437 is the telephone number of the Alhambra Book
> Store.

Person-to-Person with DDD. In more and more cities it is also possible to use direct distance dialing for person-to-person calls. You must first dial a special prefix code. This special prefix code signals the telephone company's computer that you wish to make a person-to-person call with DDD. You then dial the area code and the particular telephone number. The operator will come on the line and ask for the name of the person you are calling. When that person answers, the operator notes the start of the call. This is required for billing purposes.

Person-to-Person without DDD. If you cannot dial the person-to-person call directly, you dial the operator and ask her to place the call for you. Place the call with the operator in this order: area code, telephone number, and the name of the person with whom you wish to speak. For example, you should say, "I'm making a personal call to Area Code 311 and the number is 341-8912. I would like to speak with Mr. James Gordon." Remain at the telephone until your call is completed or until you receive a report from the operator. If your call cannot be completed at the time it is placed, try it later.

Time Factor

It is important that you be aware of the time differences across the country. The United States is divided into four standard time zones: Eastern, Central, Mountain, and Pacific. Each zone is one hour earlier than the zone immediately to the east of it. When it is 3 p.m. Eastern Standard Time, it is 2 p.m. in the Central zone, 1 p.m. in the Mountain zone, and noon in the Pacific zone. Because of time differences, you must remember not to call Los Angeles from New York City before 12 noon because it is only 9 a.m. in California, or New York from California after 2 p.m. because it is then after 5 p.m. in New York and the office you wish to call is likely to be closed.

Illus. 9-7
Map of telephone area codes and time zones

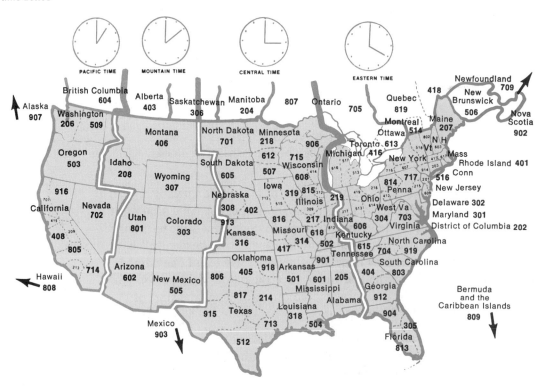

THE COST OF TELEPHONE SERVICE

The cost of telephone service is determined by the kinds of equipment the business has and the ways in which the equipment is used.

Cost for Local Calls

Businesses are charged in many different ways for their telephone service. In most communities the business is charged a basic rate for its telephone service, and it then can make as many local calls as it wishes. In a few large cities a business is allowed a certain number of calls for a base rate and is charged for each extra call.

Costs for Long-Distance Calls

Charges are made for all out-of-town telephone calls or calls made beyond the local service area. The amount of the charge depends upon the distance, the type of call, the time of day or night that the call is made, and the length of the conversation. You should know when it is advisable to make each type of call and the relative costs of the calls.

The cost of a station-to-station call is about 30 percent less than the cost of a person-to-person call because a call can be made to a particular number in much less time than a call to a particular person. The cost of all long-distance calls you dial yourself is lower than calls for which you need assistance from the operator.

The rates for long-distance calls are based on an **initial** charge for three minutes. Lower rates are in effect between 5 p.m. and 8 a.m. on weekdays. These lower rates also apply all day on Saturdays, Sundays, and holidays.

initial:
first; beginning

TELEPHONE TIPS

Whether in your business office or in your own home you can place long-distance telephone calls more effectively by

1. Planning your conversation before placing the call
2. Checking the area code and the number before placing the call
3. Giving the person you are calling time to answer
4. Identifying yourself properly and giving the reason for the call
5. Thanking the person you called for helping you

REVIEWING
WHAT YOU   1. What information would you put in your employer's personal telephone directory?
HAVE READ   2. Under what circumstances would you use the alphabetic telephone directory?

3. When would you most likely use the Yellow Pages?
4. Under what set of circumstances would you recommend the placing of a person-to-person long-distance call?
5. What is direct distance dialing, and how is it used?
6. What information should you furnish the operator when you make a person-to-person long-distance call if direct dialing is not used?
7. What is the quickest and least expensive type of long-distance telephone call?

MAKING DECISIONS

1. Your employer asks you to get a certain customer on the telephone. Should you connect him as soon as someone answers the company's telephone, or should you wait until the particular person your employer wishes to speak with is put on the telephone?
2. You sometimes place calls for your employer. Most of these calls go to the same firms. How should you be prepared so that you can make these calls quickly?
3. Charles Allen, a traveling salesman, makes the long-distance calls described in the following paragraphs. Which type of service should he use in each case?
    (a) Mr. Allen wishes to telephone his home as inexpensively as possible.
    (b) A customer asks for information about a special contract. It is necessary for Mr. Allen to talk personally with the general manager to get this information.
    (c) Mr. Allen receives an order from a customer who asks that the order be telephoned to the company at once.
    (d) Mr. Allen calls the office to get prices on a new item.

WORKING WITH OTHERS

Barbara Washington places most of the calls for her employer, the purchasing agent, Mr. Thomas Downs. Because Mr. Downs spends most of his business day on the telephone with sales representatives, Barbara tries to save his time by not putting Mr. Downs on the telephone until she has the other party on the line.

One Monday morning she is asked to call the executive vice-president, Mr. Bertram Moore. When he is told that Mr. Downs is calling he picks up the receiver and says, "Yes, Tom, what can I do for you." Barbara responds by saying, "I'll put Mr. Downs right on, Mr. Moore." Mr. Moore is visibly annoyed and says, "Tell Mr. Mr. Downs I haven't got time to wait for him," and hangs up.

Barbara thinks that she has caused Mr. Downs unnecessary difficulty with his superior when she was only trying to help him. Discuss ways in which Barbara should place calls to Mr. Downs' superiors in the future.

USING LANGUAGE

The following 20 words are spelled both correctly and incorrectly. On a sheet of paper type the correct spelling of each word.

1. appropriate	appropriete	11. frequently	frequintly
2. assocciates	associates	12. monotoneous	monotonous
3. assurance	assurrance	13. overseas	over seas
4. brusquely	brusquelly	14. preferance	preference
5. convay	convey	14. specific	spicefic
6. courtious	courteous	16. techneques	techniques
7. conversationel	conversational	17. transfering	transferring
8. dailing	dialing	18. terminating	terminateing
9. economical	economical	19. unnecessary	unnecessery
10. efficeint	efficient	20. vocabulery	vocabulary

1. The company for which you work in Charleston, West Virginia, opens its offices at 9 a.m. Your employer asks you to call the Los Angeles office as soon as it opens. At what time in Charleston would you place the call?

2. The company for which you work requires that a record be submitted on the first day of each month for all long-distance calls placed and all long-distance collect calls accepted by the personnel of the district office in which you are employed. Below is the list of calls for the month of May.

	Calls Placed	Collect Calls Received
District Manager	75	3
Assistant Manager	81	2
Office Manager	79	2
Secretary	57	0
Head Order Clerk	25	0

On a separate sheet of paper compute the total of each type of call. Also indicate the grand total.

1. Using your telephone book, look up and list the telephone numbers for
   (a) All emergency call telephone numbers for the fire department, police department, doctor, ambulance, state police, and Federal Bureau of Investigation
   (b) Telephone service calls — business office, repair service
   (c) A large business firm in the community
   (d) One of the banks in the community
   (e) The area codes for New York City, Chicago, Los Angeles, and Philadelphia

2. The questions below require the use of the Yellow Pages.
   (a) If you knew the address of a doctor but not his name, would you look in the Yellow Pages for his name under "Doctors" or under "Physicians & Surgeons (M.D.)"?
   (b) How are lawyers listed in the Yellow Pages — under "Attorneys" or under "Lawyers"?
   (c) If you were to order typewriter ribbons by telephone, under what heading in the Yellow Pages would you look for a firm selling typewriter ribbons?
   (d) Suppose you work in a one-man office and are missing telephone calls (and business) because your telephone is unattended when your employer is traveling and you are out of the office. What service is listed in the Yellow Pages that you could recommend to your employer to remedy the situation?

3. Use the Telephone Directory to type an alphabetical list of names, addresses, and telephone numbers of ten business firms in your area that might employ clerical workers.

PART 3 SPECIAL TELEPHONE EQUIPMENT

During the years that Mary Coleman has worked for The Voight Development Corporation it has grown from a small to a large company. On many occasions Mary has been called upon to assist in handling telephone calls. As a result she has learned how to use the many kinds of telephone equipment that are standard in business offices. Mary's co-workers admire and respect her ability and efficiency in using telephone equipment to its greatest advantage.

oral: spoken

Telephone companies provide special equipment to meet the special needs of every business. All telephone equipment has the same basic purpose: to make rapid **oral** communication possible. When you work in an office, you will be expected to use different kinds of telephone equipment.

SWITCHBOARD

Most businesses have a private business exchange (PBX) or switchboard to aid in handling telephone calls.

A PBX system has three main functions:

1. To receive incoming calls
2. To place outgoing calls
3. To make calls between offices within the business

Usually companies have special switchboard attendants; however, even if you are not a switchboard attendant, you may be asked to relieve at the switchboard at the noon hour or at other times during the day.

Cord Switchboard

Cord switchboards are used in large businesses where many telephone lines are needed. The switchboard operator receives all incoming calls, makes the connection for interoffice calls, and either places outgoing calls or provides the outside line to dial the call.

Cordless Switchboard

There are many kinds of cordless switchboards. Usually companies that do not have a great volume of telephone calls will use a cordless board. A full-time operator is not needed since incoming calls can usually be made to any extension number and employees can place their own outgoing calls. The operator will normally answer only those calls that are of a general nature.

Illus. 9-8
A cordless switchboard has many applications in a modern office. It does not require a full-time attendant.

AT&T

Call Director

The call director permits you to answer many lines from one location. You can also transfer calls and make outside calls. If your employer wishes, he can both make and receive calls without your help.

Illus. 9-9
In a busy office a Call Director is a time-saver.

AT&T

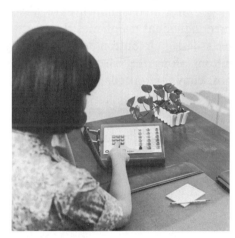

TOUCH-TONE TELEPHONE

rotary:
turning on an axis
like a wheel

Touch-tone telephones have buttons instead of the **rotary** dial. Listen for the dial tone; then depress the numbered buttons for the telephone number. As each button is depressed you will hear a tone.

Touch-tone calling systems are being installed in all major cities and are available to both home and business users. The advantage of this calling system is the increased speed in dialing. In more and more firms touch-tone buttons are also being used to send data to computers.

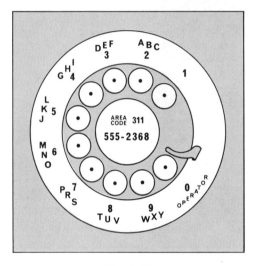

Illus. 9-10
Dial telephone

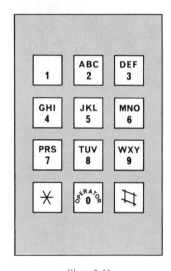

Illus. 9-11
Touch-tone telephone

BUTTON TELEPHONE

Button telephones have almost completely replaced the two or three individual telephones that were formerly found on the busy executive's desk. A button telephone may have anywhere from one to six buttons along the base of the instrument, but the six-button variety is most commonly used.

Arrangement of the Buttons

The buttons on a six-button telephone should be arranged and labeled in this order:

1. The *hold* button is the button on the left side of the telephone. When it is depressed you will be able to hold a call while you make or answer another call. The first caller is then *unable to overhear your second conversation.*

The hold button does not remain depressed but returns to normal when you release it. However, if you do not use it before pressing another button to accept a second call, the first call will be cut off.

2. The pick-up buttons, Buttons 2, 3, 4, 5, and 6, are used to make and receive outside calls. A line will be connected when you depress the correct button.

Illus. 9-12

It is possible to handle several calls on a six-button telephone.

AT&T

Button 1	Button 2	Button 3	Button 4	Button 5	Button 6
Hold	2368	2369	2370	2371	2372

Operating a Button Telephone

A number of calls can be handled on a push-button telephone at the same time. The steps in the receiving and handling of two incoming calls follow:

1. Depress the *pick-up* button connected with the ringing line before lifting the receiver. (Pick-up buttons usually light up when in use.)

2. If a call comes in while you are talking on another line, excuse yourself, depress the *hold* button, then depress the pick-up button connected with the ringing line and answer it.

3. When the second call is completed, return to the first call by depressing the button for that line.

Custom-made arrangements, designed to meet the special needs of a particular office, may be found on the job. For instance, a *signal* button, frequently a buzzer, may be used to signal an assistant in the outer office.

SPEAKERPHONE

You need not pick up the receiver at all when you use the Speakerphone. When a call comes in, you press a button and talk as you would to a visitor in your office. The caller's voice comes from a small loudspeaker on your desk. The volume of the loudspeaker can be adjusted to suit your desires. Your own voice is picked up by a microphone sensitive enough to hear your voice anywhere in your office or all the voices in an office conference. You can talk and listen with both hands free to take notes or to look up records. When you want to make a private call, you can pick up the receiver and your Speakerphone automatically becomes a regular telephone again.

AUTOMATIC DIALING TELEPHONES

There are several automatic dialing telephones commonly used in business offices. Automatic dialing telephones save a great deal of telephoning time, and they eliminate the possibility of dialing a wrong number.

Card Dialer

The Card Dialer uses small plastic cards for numbers you expect to call frequently. They should be coded and placed in the storage area in the unit. To place a call, you insert the proper card in the dial slot, lift the receiver, and when you hear the dial tone, press the start bar.

Illus. 9-13
A Card Dialer is useful for placing volume calls. It is fast, efficient, and reliable.

AT&T

Magicall

The Magicall magnetic tape dialer is also used to save dialing time. The names and telephone numbers of frequently called parties are listed on a magnetic tape. After a name has been brought into position on the "scanner," it can be dialed automatically from the stored telephone number on the magnetic tape by simply pushing the start bar. Up to 1,000 telephone numbers can be stored in the memory of the Magicall.

Call-A-Matic

The Call-A-Matic is a touch-tone automatic dialer. It is a combination of a six-button touch-tone telephone and a magnetic tape dialer with a storage for up to 500 telephone numbers.

Illus. 9-14
The Call-A-Matic tape dialer is another time-saving telephone feature.

AT&T

PICTUREPHONE

The Picturephone is a new kind of telephone equipment — it lets you see the person you are talking to and he sees you. The Picturephone is rather expensive, but it may prove to be a valuable aid to business firms. Conferences and sales demonstrations can be conducted over the Picturephone. This, of course, will save a great deal of time and expense. The Picturephone is being introduced gradually — first in Pittsburgh, then in Chicago, Washington, Detroit, Cleveland, Newark, New York, and Philadelphia. In the beginning it will be available in business areas only, and calls can be made to other firms in the area.

MOBILE TELEPHONE

This radio telephone provides your employer with a listed number for his car that is part of the nationwide dial network. He can make and receive calls from his car just as he would from his office telephone. It helps him avoid the risk of missing important calls while he is on the road and provides him with a way to handle emergencies more efficiently.

More than 33,000 customers now use mobile telephones. They are installed in trucks, buses, planes, trains, and taxicabs, as well as in private automobiles.

REVIEWING WHAT YOU HAVE READ

1. What do the initials *PBX* mean?
2. What are the two advantages of the Speakerphone over the regular telephone?
3. How can the use of the Magicall save telephoning time?
4. Describe a Call-A-Matic tape dialer.
5. Why would an employer install a mobile telephone in his car?

MAKING DECISIONS

1. Discuss the probable business uses of the Picturephone.
2. Discuss the advantages of a touch-tone telephone over the traditional rotary dial telephone.

WORKING WITH OTHERS

Claire Rogers and Ann Brown fill in as relief switchboard attendants during the noon hour. Claire handles a call in this fashion: "Mr. Smith's extension is busy." After about 15 seconds she says, "Still busy." When the extension is free she says, "I'll ring him now."

Ann handles a similar call in this fashion: "Mr. Clark's extension is busy. Will you wait, please?" After about 15 seconds she says, "Mr. Clark is still busy." When the extension is free she says, "You may have Mr. Clark's extension now. Thank you for waiting."

Which of the two approaches to the handling of a delayed call is more likely to make a favorable impression on the caller? Why?

USING LANGUAGE

An adverb is a word that modifies a verb, an adjective, or another adverb. An adverb, like a descriptive adjective, may also be used in comparisons.

Examples: Sheila types *fast*. (Positive adverb *fast* modifies verb *types*.)

Sheila types *faster* than the other girls. (Comparative adverb *faster* modifies verb *types*.)

Of the 25 students Sheila typed *fastest*. (Superlative adverb *fastest* modifies verb *typed*.)

On a sheet of paper list the adverbs in the following sentences and tell the words they modify.

1. Joan merely tried to be kind to the caller, but the visitor misunderstood her.
2. The receptionist was most gracious, but Mr. Smith said that he could wait no longer.
3. Mr. Brown canceled the appointment immediately.
4. Mr. Phillips called and said that he would arrive sooner than he expected.

5. With a little more tact, the switchboard attendant could have soothed the customer's feelings.
6. He operated the machine too efficiently to be in a beginner class.
7. His tire was almost flat by the time he arrived for his appointment.
8. She was less inclined to make the trip after she heard the weather predictions.
9. The farther he traveled the worse conditions became.
10. Her warm smile and sincere interest in people were very valuable assets.

USING ARITHMETIC

On a separate sheet of paper solve the following problems and supply the missing numbers.

(a) $32 minus $\frac{1}{8}$ of itself is _____.

(b) $\frac{1}{8}$ more than $32 is _____.

(c) $28 plus $\frac{1}{4}$ of itself is _____.

(d) _____ is $\frac{1}{6}$ smaller than $36.

(e) _____ is $\frac{1}{4}$ more than $24.

PERFORMING OFFICE TASKS

Prepare an office telephone directory for John Carl Warner and Associates, a firm of architects and planning consultants, from the following list of officers and associates. Arrange the names of the 25 officials in alphabetical order before typing them with their respective titles and home telephone numbers. Type the last name of each official first — in solid capitals.

Name	Title	Home Telephone Number
John Carl Warner	President	566-0101
Carl T. Warner	Executive Vice-President	542-3481
Martin C. Hunter	Vice-President	764-5244
Leonard T. Hart	Vice-President	562-8796
James J. Carroll	Secretary	241-2442
Arthur D. Brown, Jr.	Treasurer	231-2633
Donald R. Stewart	Project Manager	891-7350
Joseph C. Margolo	Systems Manager	764-1121
Emery Hirschman	Personnel Director	732-4575
Eugene C. Davis	Construction Supervisor	231-9367
Jean Wiley	Interior Designer	441-8452
Wallace D. Russell	Comptroller	681-3794
Walter E. Nelson	Office Manager	764-1985
Arthur A. Schiller	Construction Supervisor	562-5521
Josef Ausubel	Chief Draftsman	231-4872
David C. Palmer	Project Manager	764-3363
Walter J. Roberts, Jr.	Transportation Engineer	871-5046
Thomas M. White	Public Relations Director	231-0785
Wayburn Evans	Chief of Shop Drawings	541-6914
Lisa T. Guthrie	Landscape Designer	764-2658
Thomas F. O'Brien	Construction Supervisor	231-1479
Ralph T. Spencer	Project Manager	831-0837
Lawrence A. Adams	Construction Supervisor	321-7525
Joseph A. McMurray	Estimator	922-8240
William C. Peterson	Construction Supervisor	771-3313

PART 4

SPECIAL COMMUNICATIONS SERVICES

"Eve, set up a conference call for 2 p.m. with Howard Walsh in Chicago, Mark Ross in Boston, Earle Carter in Denver, and Arthur Mann in Dallas. Would you also ask Joseph Hummell and Ronald Sigler if they would come to my office for the conference?" These instructions were given to Eve Craft by her employer, Mr. Clifford Pickens. Because of her understanding of special long-distance services available, Eve had no difficulty in setting up the conference.

Conference calls are just one of many special long-distance services provided by the telephone company. These rapid services include both oral and written communications.

SPECIAL LONG-DISTANCE CALLS

Now let us take a look at the special long-distance services with which you should become familiar. These services include collect calls, credit card calls, conference calls, wide area telephone service, and overseas telephone calls. Before placing these calls, check the front pages of the Telephone Directory for instructions. Usually you dial ".0" (Operator).

Collect Calls

If you want the charges reversed — if you want the station or the person you are calling to pay the charges — notify the operator when you place the call. This gives the station or person you are calling an opportunity to accept or refuse the call before the connection is made. The charges may be reversed on both station-to-station and person-to-person calls.

Credit Card Calls

Many business executives have credit cards from the telephone company that allow them to charge long-distance calls. Credit card telephone service provides a convenient way to make long-distance calls when traveling. If your employer should ever ask you to place a credit card call for him, he will give you his card. You should call the long-distance operator and tell her that you wish to place a credit card call. You should then give her the credit card number, the area code, and the telephone number you are calling. The charges for the call will be billed to your employer's account.

Conference Calls

A conference call is a telephone call that enables several persons at different locations to talk to each other at the same time. As many as ten locations can be connected for a conference call. To arrange such a call you should give the operator the names, telephone numbers, and locations of the persons to be connected for the call. Be certain to give the exact time that the call is to be put through. Then be certain that your employer is ready to receive this call!

Wide Area Telephone Service (WATS)

Some of the telephone lines into the company for which you work may be called "WATS" lines, and some phones may be called "WATS" phones. This means that the firm offers its customers, without charge, Wide Area Telephone Service. Firms that use this service believe that, if they offer their customers this free service, they will get more business. Many hotel and motel chains use WATS service in order to make it easier for their customers to make room reservations.

The WATS phones or lines are used only for making and receiving station-to-station long-distance calls. To determine whether the company you wish to call offers this service, dial Area Code 800 and then 555-1212. The 800 is the standard area code for all WATS lines, and the 555-1212 is for operator assistance.

Overseas Telephone Calls

Underseas cables, satellites, and radio now make it possible to telephone 200 countries and areas overseas. Most calls are operator dialed. To place an overseas call or to obtain additional information, see the front pages of the local Telephone Directory. You usually dial "0" (Operator).

Some typical weekday station-to-station rates for the first three minutes from any point in the United States are: to the United Kingdom, $5.40; to Hawaii $5.70; to France and Italy $6.75; to Israel and Vietnam $9.00. The person-to-person weekday rates for the first three minutes to the same areas are considerably higher — to the United Kingdom $9.60; to Hawaii $9.50; to France, Italy, Israel, and Vietnam $12.00.

TELETYPEWRITER SERVICE

"Jean, will you send a message to our New Orleans plant requesting information on the carload shipment of insulation board to Lumbermen's Supply Company in Columbus that was promised for delivery on January 15?" A few minutes later Jean entered Mr. Robertson's office in Dayton, Ohio, with a teletype message reading:

```
AMCO   TWX 410-345-7890   JAN 14   MSG 12
ATTN   JOHN ROBERTSON SALES

LUMBERMEN'S ORDER B-70581 SHPD GULF MOBILE &

OHIO--PENN CENTRAL JAN. 7 CAR SPOTTED PENN

CENTRAL SIDING COL O JAN 14 10:30 AM

JAMES FERGUSON
```

transmitted:
sent or transferred from one person or place to another.

A teletypewriter is a typewriter-like machine which operates on the same principle as a telephone except that the typewritten, rather than the spoken, word is transmitted. Messages typed on the typewriter keyboard of a teletypewriter are **transmitted** and reproduced as they are

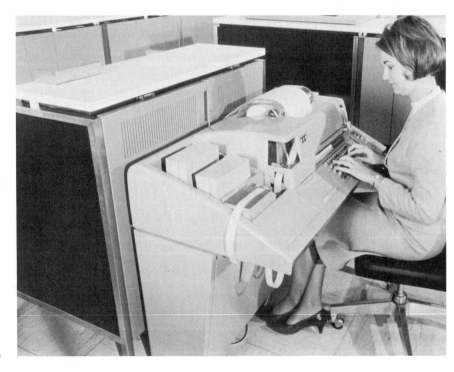

Illus. 9-15
District office teletypewriter attendant transmits message by tape directly to manufacturing plant in distant city.

Teletype Corporation

typed. A message may be reproduced on a single machine or on many machines, depending on the kind of service the business wants. Teletype equipment is often used for communication between offices of the same firm and between offices of different firms when speed is an important factor and when a written record of the message is desired. Usually a special attendant will send and receive the teletyped messages. However, it is sometimes necessary for relief attendants to operate this equipment.

There are two basic types of teletype service — teletypewriter exchange service and teletypewriter private line service.

Teletypewriter Exchange Service (TWX)

Teletypewriter exchange service (TWX) operates through a Western Union service. Each subscriber has a teletypewriter number and is furnished with a directory of all teletypewriter subscribers in the United States.

Before sending a message, the teletype operator signals the TWX equipment she is calling and types the exchange and the number she wishes to reach. After the connection has been made and the called unit is ready to receive, the teletype operator types her message. As the sending operator types the message, the receiving machine instantly copies it. The rates for teletyped messages are much lower than the rates for station-to-station telephone calls.

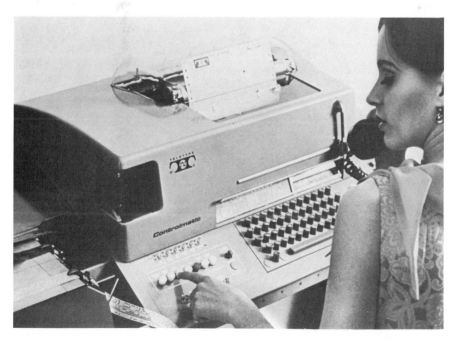

Illus. 9-16
Message received by plant attendant from district office is transferred from tape to hard copy.

Teletype Corporation

Teletypewriter Private Line Service (TWPL)

Teletypewriter private line service (TWPL) or leased wire service messages do not go through a central Western Union office. The machines are connected by direct wires. They are used for interoffice communications by firms with a number of branch offices and plants throughout the country.

Data-Phone Service

Data-Phone service provides the means for sending payrolls, inventories, sales figures, and other business data from one location to another rapidly. Data-Phone data sets can handle data prepared on punched cards, paper tape, or magnetic tape. Machine signals from the punched cards or tape are converted into tones that are sent over regular telephone lines. The Data-Phone data set at the receiving office changes the transmitted tones back into whatever is required — punched cards, paper tape, or magnetic tape.

Data-Phone data sets are capable of transmitting at speeds of up to 4,500 words a minute. The charge for this service is the same as for a regular long-distance call.

Illus. 9-17
District office transmits monthly territory sales figures to home office by Data-Phone data set.

AT&T

REVIEWING
WHAT YOU
HAVE READ

1. What would be an advantage of using a credit card to make a long-distance call?
2. What is a conference call? How would you set up a conference call?
3. Why do businesses provide WATS lines for their customers?
4. What is a teletypewriter? From a business standpoint, what advantage does it have over a telephone?
5. What are three types of business data transmitted frequently by Data-Phone data sets?

MAKING
DECISIONS

1. The number of overseas telephone calls from the United States has increased from 11,750 calls in 1927 to more than 19,500,000 in 1969. Discuss the reasons for this tremendous increase in overseas calls.
2. Consider the types of business firms that might use a teletypewriter installation advantageously.

WORKING
WITH
OTHERS

One day when Louise Hills came back from lunch early, she overheard Rosalind Robinson, a co-worker, placing a long-distance call to her mother. Louise was very startled when she heard Rosalind give her employer's telephone credit card number to the operator. Later when Louise asked Rosalind about the use of her employer's credit card, Rosalind replied, "I had to call my mother right away. I'll tell Mr. Jenkins about it later and pay him for the call."

What do you think of Rosalind's actions? How do you think Mr. Jenkins will react when he is told?

USING
LANGUAGE

Here are seven sets of words that are frequently misused. Type the sentences on a separate sheet of paper using the correct word that applies in each instance.

1. *Don't* and *Doesn't*
   (a) He (don't, doesn't) seem to mind when we use his phone.
   (b) It (don't, doesn't) take long to file a telegram.
2. *Like* and *As*
   (a) It tastes good (like, as) a steak should.
   (b) (Like, As) Maine goes, so goes the nation.
3. *Lie* and *Lay*
   (a) Now I (lay, lie) down my burden.
   (b) The typed letters (lay, lie) on his desk.
4. *Sit* and *Set*
   (a) We (sit, sat) for hours waiting for the test to be given.
   (b) Cares (sit, set) heavily upon the manager.
5. *Can* and *May*
   (a) (May, Can) we tell you about the other types of files in our office?
   (b) (May, Can) you type as well in an emergency?
6. *Affect* and *Effect*.
   (a) What was the (affect, effect) of the announcement?
   (b) The drop in the stock market may have a telling (affect, effect) on employment opportunities.
7. *Raise* and *Rise*.
   (a) Let me (rise, raise) the window for you.
   (b) Price (raises, rises) were announced by the automobile manufacturers.

1. The Better Half has a clearance sale on slacks at $3.45 each or three for $9.45. How much will you save by buying three pairs of slacks at one time rather than three pairs of slacks one at a time?
2. Below is a copy of an actual long-distance telephone bill. In addition to the charges for long-distance calls and the telegram as shown, there are these additional charges: $6.90 for local telephone service and taxes of $4.56. What is the total cost of this telephone bill?

DATE	CODE	LONG DISTANCE CALLS			AMOUNT
5 01		QUEZONPHIL	176	209–1513	18 00
5 12	1	ALBANY NY	518	472–9096	60
5 19	1	SAN FRAN CAL	415	648–4240	2 60
5 19		GUBAO QUEZ		TELEGRAM	3 74
5 22	1	SAN FRAN CAL	415	648–4240	1 10
5 23		QUEZONPHIL	176	209–1513	15 00
5 30	1	SAN FRAN CAL	415	873–0633	1 35

Select a member of the Clerical Office Procedures class to work with you in placing and taking this typical service call. One of you should be prepared to make the call and the other prepared to answer it. Use a Teletrainer or a telephone if either is available. If neither is available, simulate the call.

Information for the Caller

Assume that you are a statistical typist preparing a report in the Advertising Department of an air conditioner manufacturer. The electronic calculator you have been using to verify the figures in the report has broken down, and you are asked to call a serviceman. You will need to know the make and model of the calculator before placing the call. Use the Yellow Pages to find the name and telephone number of manufacturers under the heading: *Adding & Calculating Machines.* If the Yellow Pages in your Telephone Directory do not list office machines service, use the following information:

Adding & Calculating Machines & Supplies
  Monroe — Sales, Service, and Rental 555-2368

Information for the Receiver

Assume that you are taking the service call for the Monroe Calculator Company. When the call comes in, verify the information about the machine, the address of the air conditioner manufacturer, and the room number and floor of the Advertising Department. Tell the caller approximately when to expect the serviceman.

As other members of your class make and answer the service call, evaluate their telephone techniques under the following headings:

1. Placing and Beginning the Call
2. Development of the Call
3. Closing the Call
4. Telephone Personality

PART 5 DOMESTIC AND INTERNATIONAL TELEGRAPH SERVICES

"Joy, Al Stevens and I just reached an agreement on the phone of our purchase of the Little Rock property. Let's send him a written confirmation. Make the telegram read: This will confirm our verbal agreement of July 8, 197–, in which we, Arcade Products, Inc., agree to purchase your property at 1807 Beech Street, Little Rock, Arkansas, for $82,000. Payment to be made as follows: $10,000 by July 15, 197–; remainder by date of occupancy, September 1, 197–. Please confirm if these facts agree with your understanding of our statement." Joy Parsons realizes that great care must be taken to insure the accuracy of this message. Joy also knows that with a message of this importance she will have the telegraph company report back when it has delivered the message.

DOMESTIC TELEGRAPH SERVICE

When you want to send the most rapid *written* communication send a telegram. It can be sent from coast to coast and is usually delivered in a few minutes. You can be sure, too, of getting attention because a telegram carries with it a note of urgency and importance.

Technological progress during the past 30 years has produced a vast chain of high-speed telegraph message centers throughout the United States, Canada, and Mexico. Hundreds of thousands of telegraph messages and money orders are sent over Western Union wires every business day. Most of these messages relate to business transactions: buying and selling merchandise, buying and selling stocks and bonds, making reservations, or sending money.

A telegram can be sent a distance of 1,500 miles and delivered in less than an hour, while the average business letter would spend over a full day en route, even if it were sent by airmail.

After you are employed in an office you will probably be expected to know when to send a telegram and which type of service to use. You may also be expected to know how to compose telegrams and how to get your messages to the telegraph office in the shortest time.

The telegraph company provides two different types of message service. Messages are sent and delivered according to the type of service used. Some are sent and delivered immediately; others are sent during the night and delivered early during the following morning. The two types of service are the

(1) Full-rate telegram
(2) Overnight telegram

Full-Rate Telegram. When there is great urgency about the message or when speed in having the message received is important, you will send the full-rate telegram. A full-rate telegram, usually referred to simply as a telegram, is the faster type of telegraph service. The message is sent immediately at any time during the day or night; and, if it is received during business hours, it is telephoned or delivered to the addressee at once. If it is received after business hours, it is relayed to the addressee as soon as possible. Although it is the more expensive type of service, it is used most frequently by businessmen because of the speed with which it is sent and delivered. The basic charge is made for a message of 15 words or less; a small charge is made for each additional word in the message.

Overnight Telegram. An overnight telegram is more economical than a fast full-rate telegram, but it is a slower type of telegraph service. It will be accepted by the telegraph office any time up to midnight for delivery the following morning. The basic charge is for a minimum of 100 words. Additional words are charged at the rate of 1 to $1\frac{1}{2}$ cents a word. It is used mostly for messages of considerable length such as business proposals, progress reports, and detailed instructions.

Counting the Chargeable Words

Since the cost of a telegram is based on a minimum number of words in the message plus an additional charge for extra words, it is important that you know how to count the chargeable words. The following summarizes the rules for counting words:

1. One address and one signature are free.
2. The punctuation marks below are sent as written but are not counted or charged for.

. (period or decimal point)   - (hyphen)
, (comma)   () (parentheses)
: (colon)   ? (question mark)
; (semicolon)   "" (quotation marks)
— (dash)   ' (apostrophe)

3. Figures are counted as one word for every five characters. With figures the decimal point, the comma, and the dash are considered as punctuation marks and not counted.

 34,785 (five figures with comma as punctuation)................................1 word
 378,534 (six figures with comma as punctuation)...........................2 words
 4.333 (four figures with decimal point as punctuation)........................ 1 word
 10—160 (five figures with dash as punctuation). 1 word

4. The following special characters may be sent and charged for at the rate of one word for each five characters: $, &, # (number or pounds), "(inches or seconds), '(feet or minutes), / (fraction mark).
 The percent sign is transmitted as o/o and counts as three characters.

 83.33% (four figures and % — decimal point as punctuation)...................2 words
 $44.50 (four figures and $ — decimal point as punctuation)...................1 word
 $450.25 (five figures and $ — decimal point as punctuation)....................2 words
 #4,960 (four figures and # — comma as punctuation)....................1 word

5. The special characters ¢ (cents), @ (at), and ° (degree) cannot be transmitted. They are written out and sent as words.

6. Dictionary words from the English, German, French, Italian, Dutch, Portuguese, Spanish, and Latin languages are counted as one word each, regardless of length. Nondictionary words and words from all other languages are counted as one word for every five characters.

7. Geographic names are counted according to the number of individual words contained in them even when they are written without spaces.

 ST. LOUIS ....2 words
 ST.LOUIS ....2 words
 NEW YORK CITY ....3 words
 NORTH DAKOTA ....2 words
 FARGO, N. D. ....3 words

8. Abbreviations of single words are counted as full words.

9. Common abbreviations are counted as one word for every five characters. Spaces between the abbreviations increase the word count. Periods are considered punctuation and are not counted.

NYC ....1 word
N. Y. C. ....3 words
COD ....1 word
FOB ....1 word
a.m. ....1 word

10. Initials in names are counted as separate words. A last name with a prefix, such as "Du" in DuBois, does not count as a separate word if it is not followed by a space. Initials, when separated by spaces, are counted as separate words, but when written together are counted at the rate of one word for each five letters

JOHN F. KELLER......................3 words
JAMES O'DONNELL.....................2 words
CARL VAN TIL.........................3 words
RALPH DUMONT.......................2 words
J. J. WILLIAMS.........................3 words
W.A.R. DAVIS.........................2 words

Preparing a Telegram

You must prepare a telegram carefully if it is to be delivered without delay and if it is to be understood by the one who receives it. The secret of a well-worded telegram is to state your message as clearly and briefly as possible. The suggestions shown on pages 341 and 342 should be kept in mind in preparing a telegram.

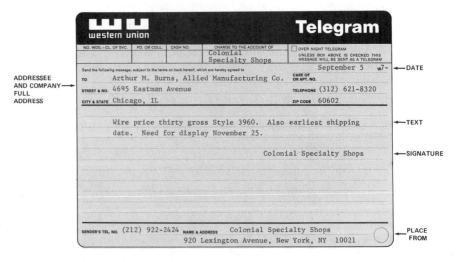

Illus. 9-18
Full-rate telegram
Every telegram should include all the elements shown in the full-rate telegram.

1. *Use Western Union telegram blanks.* You can obtain pads of telegram blanks free of charge at any Western Union office.
2. *Type three copies of the telegram.* Ordinarily the original goes to the telegraph company, the second copy to the correspondence file, and the third to the addressee so that he can check to see that the message was transmitted correctly.
3. *Type the message with capital and lower case letters.* The message should be double spaced. Do not divide a word at the end of a line.
4. *Indicate whether the message is sent paid, collect, or charge.* If it is to be charged, indicate the account below the heading, CHARGE TO THE ACCOUNT OF.
5. *Indicate the type of service desired.* Type an "X" in the box before Over Night Telegram at the upper right of the blank if you want to send an overnight telegram. Unless the box is checked the message will be sent as a full-rate telegram.
6. *Type the date.*
7. *Type the full name of the addressee.*
8. *Type the complete address and telephone number of the addressee.* Whenever possible give the office number. Spell out such words as *North* and *South*. Do not use suffixes with street numbers (34 not 34th Street).

western union **Telegram**

NO. WDS.–CL. OF SVC.	PD. OR COLL.	CASH NO.	CHARGE TO THE ACCOUNT OF	[X] OVER NIGHT TELEGRAM UNLESS BOX ABOVE IS CHECKED THIS MESSAGE WILL BE SENT AS A TELEGRAM
	Pd.			

Send the following message, subject to the terms on back hereof, which are hereby agreed to — October 19 19 7-

TO Bruce J. Harrison — CARE OF OR APT. NO.

STREET & NO. 244 State Street — TELEPHONE (513) 621-4400

CITY & STATE Cincinnati, OH — ZIP CODE 45227

Have no record of order referred to in your telegram. Please send duplicate. No increase in price before beginning of next quarter. No important change expected then.

Gordon A. Eaton
Boston Machine Company

SENDER'S TEL. NO. (617) 781-1620 NAME & ADDRESS Gordon A. Eaton, Boston Machine Co.
2205 Barter Street, Boston, MA 02116

Illus. 9-19
Overnight telegram

9. *Write the message clearly and include punctuation.* The use of punctuation marks makes the message clearer. There is no extra charge for them.

10. *Include your address and telephone number.* After the signature type the sender's telephone number, name, and address. This is important if hotel or travel reservations are requested.

Filing a Telegram

How can you file a telegraphic message? When it is filed, a message is turned over to Western Union for transmission and delivery. A message can be filed in any one of six different ways:

1. *Over the Counter.* A prepared message can be taken to a Western Union office or a message can be written at the counter.

2. *Over the Telephone.* A telegram can be filed over the telephone. When a message is telephoned to a Western Union office care must be taken to be sure that names and unusual words are transmitted accurately. Such words should be spelled out to the operator to avoid confusion.

3. *Tie Line Service.* Tie lines are used when the firm sends and receives a large number of telegrams. A tie line is a system of direct wires between the business and the telegraph company.

4. *Teleprinter Service.* A telegraphic message can be sent on a specially installed printing machine with a keyboard like a teletypewriter. This machine is called a teleprinter. As the message is typed in a business office on the teleprinter, it is being recorded on a tape or message form in the telegraph office. The message is transferred immediately to a telegraph line and transmitted to its destination.

5. *Telex.* The dial-a-wire service, called Telex, permits users to dial other subscribers instantly, regardless of distance. This two-way customer-to-customer teleprinter service links major cities in the United States and also serves many countries in other parts of the world.

6. *Private Wire Systems.* Many telegraph users, with a large volume of communications, require private telegraph systems of their own. Such private networks are built, installed, and maintained for businesses by Western Union. A system may extend hundreds, or even

thousands, of miles and connect a company's offices and plants in as few or as many as a hundred cities.

One of the new and growing developments in the business world is electronic data processing (see Unit 4) — the use of machines to speed the processing of vast amounts of paper work. Since it is necessary to quickly gather sales, payroll, inventory, shipping, and other data from distant cities and branch offices for processing at a central point, many business firms use a private wire system.

Western Union has developed private wire systems, called *data communication*, that, in addition to handling business messages, will also transmit data, either in punched card or tape form ready for instant processing at the destination by business machines and computers.

Cash, Charge, and Collect Service

Telegraph service may be paid for in any one of four ways:

1. With cash at the time the message is sent. Cash may be required of an infrequent telegraph user.
2. Through business charge accounts. Charge accounts are carried by the telegraph company, particularly for large firms that send many telegrams every business day. These accounts are billed on a monthly basis.
3. Through telephone subscribers' accounts. An individual may send a telegram from a telephone or from a Western Union office and have it charged to his telephone bill.
4. By the person receiving the message. A message may be sent collect. This means that the receiver of the telegram pays for it upon delivery. To send a telegram collect, type the word *Collect* beneath the heading PD OR COLL. at the top of the blank.

Delivery of Telegrams

A telegraphic message may be delivered in any one of four ways:

1. *By messenger*. The message may be delivered in a sealed envelope by a Western Union messenger.
2. *By telephone*. The telephone is often used instead of the messenger for speed and convenience, especially when the addressee is located at a distance from the telegraph office. The Western Union operator will mail a copy of

a telephoned message to the addressee upon request at no extra charge.

3. *By teleprinter.* This machine, described under "Filing a Telegram" on page 342, automatically receives and prints messages.

4. *By mailgram.* A new electronic mail service developed by Western Union and the United States Postal Service enables companies to send 100-word messages anywhere in the continental United States for about one third the cost of a 15-word telegram. Mailgrams may be called in, delivered, or sent via Telex to a Western Union office. They are delivered in special envelopes the next business day by a regular letter carrier.

If the telegraph company fails to deliver a message or makes an error in the transmission of the message, it is liable for damages. The limits of liability are stated on the back of each telegraph blank.

Telegraphic Money Orders

One of the quickest and safest ways for you to send money is to send a telegraphic money order. The amount to be sent is turned over to the telegraph office together with the name and address of the recipient and any **accompanying** message. There is a charge for sending the money order and a slight additional charge for any accompanying message. You will be given a receipt for the amount of money sent.

accompanying:
going or being with

The recipient's telegraph office notifies him when the money order arrives; however, he must furnish **evidence** of his identity before the money is given to him.

evidence:
something that
shows proof

PRESS FIRMLY—WRITE CLEARLY

Telegraphic Money Order
western union

Send the following Money Order subject to conditions below and on back hereof, which are hereby agreed to

SENDING DATA	CHECK	OFFICE	DATE AND FILING TIME		
				S	AMT.
					FEE
			ACCTG. INFM.	S	TOLLS
MOD	=			E	TAX
		DO NOT WRITE ABOVE THIS LINE			TOTAL

PAY AMOUNT: One Hundred Sixty-Three--and--75 /100 DOLLARS ($163.75) =
FIGURES   CAU OR VIG

TO: Peter J. Hancock   TEST QUESTION =   =

ADDRESS: 1422 Taylor Avenue   CARE OF OR APT. NO.

CITY - STATE Tampa, FL 33615   SENDER'S NAME: Arthur M. Pennington =

DELIVER THE FOLLOWING MESSAGE WITH THE MONEY: Balance will follow May 31. Regular commission deducted.

=MOD=

SENDER'S FULL NAME Arthur M. Pennington   Louisville, KY   (502) 621 3464
ADDRESS   TELEPHONE NUMBER

● Unless signed below the Telegraph Company is directed to pay this money order at my risk to such person as its paying agent believes to be the above named payee, personal identification being waived. Foreign money orders excepted.

Illus. 9-21
Telegraphic money order

Special Telegram Services

When messages are of a legal nature or of serious concern to both sender and recipient, two additional services are available.

Repeat Back. At the time the message is filed with the telegraph company, you may decide that the message is important enough to need special attention. For example, the message may contain figures, names to be published, or dates. For an additional charge, a message may be repeated back from its destination to the sending office to be checked for possible errors. If errors are discovered, the corrected message is then sent at no additional charge. *Repeat Back* must be typed at the top of the telegraph blank if this additional service is desired.

Report Delivery. Occasionally written evidence of the time of delivery and the address of the person or firm to whom the telegram was delivered is considered necessary. To get this additional information, you must pay the cost of a return telegram and type *Report Delivery* or *Report Delivery and Address* at the top of the telegraph blank. These words of instruction are counted and charged for.

Differences in Time Zones

A branch office in Seattle wishes to contact your office in Miami. It is 5 p.m. in Seattle. It is a long message which will be reported at a branch meeting on the following afternoon. The employee in Seattle wisely sends it as an overnight telegram. You will receive it when you arrive at work the next day. If a telegram is to be sent any great distance east or west, the employee must be aware of the difference in time between the sending office and the receiving office to decide upon the correct service. A home office located on the East Coast is opened and closed three hours earlier than a branch office in San Francisco; a telegram sent anytime after 2 p.m. from a branch office on the West Coast would not arrive in a Boston home office until after closing hours. The message could be sent more economically as an overnight telegram for delivery the following morning. In dealing with telegraphic services, you will be expected to know the different time zones and the present time in each of them.

INTERNATIONAL TELEGRAPH SERVICE

More and more businesses are opening branches in foreign countries. This means that international communications are becoming very important. Cablegrams may be sent to foreign countries by means of cables under the seas and by radio.

Kinds of Service

International telegraph service and domestic telegraph service are similar. There are three types of international telegraph service: *Full-Rate* (FR) messages, *Cable Letters* (LT), and *Ship Radiograms.*

Full-Rate Messages (FR). A full-rate message is the fastest and most expensive type of overseas service. It is transmitted and delivered as quickly as possible. It may be written in any language that can be expressed in letters of ordinary type, or it can be written in code. A minimum charge is made for a message of seven words or less.

Cable Letters (LT). A cable letter, or letter telegram, is transmitted during the night and delivered at its destination the following morning. The message must be written in plain language, not code. A minimum charge is made for a message of 22 words or less. The cost is only one half that charged for full-rate messages.

Ship Radiograms. Plain language or code may be used in sending radiograms to and from ships at sea. A minimum charge is made for a message of seven words or less.

Code Messages

Cablegrams and radiograms are much more expensive than domestic telegrams. Not only are the rates higher but many more words are counted and charged for. In order to reduce the cost of overseas messages, many firms send their messages in code. One five letter code word may be used in place of a common phrase that would normally take four or five words. For example, the code word *ODFUF* may be used in place of the statement, "Please cable at once," and only one word would be charged for instead of four.

You count chargeable words for international messages about the same way that you do for domestic telegrams. Major differences are:

1. Each word in the address is counted and charged for.
2. Code words are counted as five letters to the word.
3. Each punctuation mark is counted as one word.
4. Special symbols, such as ¢, $, and #, must be spelled out because they cannot be transmitted.

Cable Code Addresses

Because each word in the address is counted as a chargeable word, firms that have a great many international messages often use a single code

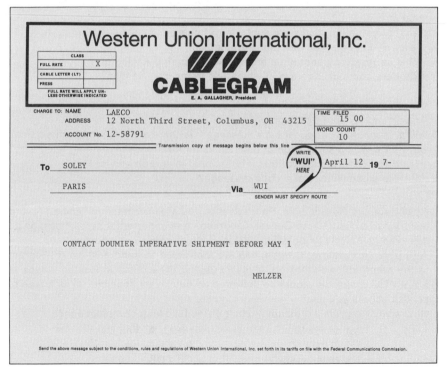

Illus. 9-22
A full-rate cable

word as the business's cable address. The following shows the regular address and the cable code address of Mutual Books, Inc., of the Philippines.

Regular Address	Cable Code Address
Mutual Books, Inc. 465-A A-Mabini Shaw Boulevard Mandaluyong, Rizal Philippines	Mubinc

There is a small annual charge for registering the cable address with the telegraph company.

Differences in Time

Time differences will determine, in part, the service you choose. If you work in an office that has a heavy volume of overseas communications, be sure you have a chart of the time zones around the world.

REVIEWING WHAT YOU HAVE READ

1. What are two types of domestic telegraph service?
2. Give the essential features of each class of domestic service and the relative cost of each.
3. What punctuation marks are sent without charge?
4. How are numbers counted in telegrams?
5. What suggestions should be followed in preparing a telegram?
6. What are some of the ways in which telegrams may be filed?
7. In what four ways may telegraph service be paid for?
8. How may telegrams be delivered?
9. How is money sent by telegraph?
10. What is meant by a repeat back message? Is there a charge for such service?
11. In what way is a knowledge of time zones important when sending telegrams?
12. Name and describe the various international telegraph services.
13. What is an advantage of a code message?

MAKING DECISIONS

1. At 4:30 p.m., in Philadelphia, Pennsylvania, you are instructed to send a 17-word telegram to a customer in Denver, Colorado. It is important that the message be delivered as quickly as possible. Which type of service should you use?
2. At 3 p.m., in Portland, Oregon, you are instructed to send a 30-word telegram to the home office in Boston, Massachusetts. The office in Boston closes at 5 p.m. The message should be delivered as quickly as possible. Which type of service should you use?
3. How many telegram words are in each of the following combinations?

   (a) $1,925.50
   (b) $50.00
   (c) New Jersey
   (d) C. A. Van Dyke
   (e) COD
   (f) FOB

Mr. Edward Collins telephones his New York office from a hotel in Chicago at noon. The call is collect because his wallet with currency, travelers' checks, and credit cards has been either mislaid or stolen. In any event he needs $200, and he needs it immediately. His assistant promises to send the money at once, but later realizes that in the excitement Mr. Collins failed to indicate how the money should be sent.

The assistant sends the money in the form of a cashier's check in a special delivery airmail letter.

Which method of sending the money could the assistant have used?

If you were the assistant, what would you have done?

A conjunction is a word that connects other words, phrases, or clauses. Conjunctions may be *coordinate* or *subordinate*.

A *subordinate* conjunction is dependent in that it connects unequal elements in a sentence.

Example: The receptionist rushed to her desk *when* the telephone rang. . . . *when* is a subordinate conjunction, which connects the subordinate clause, *the telephone rang*.

Type the following sentences and underline the subordinate conjunctions.

1. You will not type attractive letters unless you plan carefully.
2. Although the stenographer was with the company two years, her employer was not pleased with her work.
3. She made a file for the conference so that everything would be in one place.
4. The typist studied shorthand because she wanted to learn to take dictation.
5. Don't leave before you pay your dues.

Below is a reproduction of a Western Union Telegraph Company statement covering a company's charges for the months of March and April. What is this company's current balance?

PAGE 1

AMOUNT ENCLOSED————————

PLEASE DETACH

BATCH	DATE	DESTINATION		TYPE		WD. CNT.	CHARGES	CREDITS	BALANCE
							PREVIOUS BALANCE		47.24
	4/21/7–	PAYMENT						47.24	
35376	3/20/7–	WASHINGTON	DC	PD	D	18	5.61		
35377	3/21/7–	NEWROCHELL	NY	NL			1.70		
35378	3/22/7–	CHICAGO	IL	PD	D	16	5.37		
35378	3/22/7–	BALTIMORE	MD	PD	D	21	5.97		
35378	3/22/7–	BOSTON	MA	PD	D	12	5.25		
35384	3/27/7–	SPARTA	OH	NL			1.30		
35398	4/03/7–	LEONVILLE	LA	NL	D		3.20		
35412	4/13/7–	STPETERSBU	FL	NL	D		3.20		
35416	4/17/7–	CHARLESTON	SC	NL	D		3.20		
35417	4/17/7–	HONOLULU	01	FR		45	9.45		
		FIXED EQUIP					8.00		

In each of the following problems compose the message and select the kind of message to be sent. Type the messages and make two carbons.

1. At 10 a.m., on October 15, 197–, your employer, Thomas A. Evans, Office Manager of the Davis Advertising Agency, San Francisco, California, asks you to send a telegram to the Sheraton Hotel in St. Louis, Missouri, reserving a single room at $18.50 for the night of October 17, 197–. He will arrive at the Sheraton at about 8 p.m. on the 17th. Ask the hotel to wire confirmation immediately. The message is to be charged to the company. It must be delivered as quickly as possible.

2. At 4:30 p.m., on December 10, 197–, you are asked to send a telegram for H. R. Harris, President of the Harris Construction Company, El Paso, Texas, to the Warner Manufacturing Company, Pittsburgh, Pennsylvania, whose office closes at 5 p.m. Ask them to cancel Order 8675 of December 9. Tell them that a letter will follow the telegram.

3. On February 4, 197–, your employer, Mr. E. O. Colby, asks you to prepare a telegraphic money order form for $125 to be sent to the firm's sales representative, Sam D. Browning, at the Hotel Dennis in Atlantic City, New Jersey. You are to include a message informing Mr. Browning that a special sales meeting has been scheduled for February 25 at the Statler Hotel in Boston.

4. Your employer has plane reservations on TWA Flight 204 from O'Hare Airport on Tuesday, March 17. The flight is scheduled to arrive at John F. Kennedy International Airport in New York City at 4 p.m. Eastern Standard Time. He wants the Long Island manager to meet him at the airport.

UNIT 10

COPYING AND DUPLICATING

XEROX OPERATOR
inee for 3600 or 7000 mach
Personnel 753-7770

PART 1 · COPIERS AND REPRODUCING MACHINES

Robin Lynn works as a receptionist for Dr. John Miles, a local dentist. She answers the telephone, schedules appointments, and makes patients comfortable while waiting to see Dr. Miles. At regular intervals throughout the month, she also prepares and mails statements to patients. Robin finds this task easy because she does not type a new statement each month. When a patient first visits the office, Robin types his name and address on a statement. Each time there is a new charge to his account, Robin removes this statement from the files and records the date and the amount of the charge. When it is time to send the patient a bill, she makes a copy of the statement on a photocopier, a machine which makes an identical copy of the statement. She then mails the copy to the patient and files the original. By using the copying machine, Robin reduces the amount of typing she must do and the amount of time she must spend preparing monthly statements.

Robin uses the copying machine in other ways also. Quite often Dr. Miles receives letters from other dentists who are treating former patients of his requesting histories of their dental work. To speed the reply, Robin makes a copy of the dental record and sends it to the dentist making the request. Robin knows that time is important; so she uses modern copying and duplicating machines to save time and increase her efficiency as an office worker.

COPIERS

The demand for a machine that can rapidly copy information on paper has been growing in recent years. Such machines are sometimes called *copiers* and at other times called *photocopiers*. In business the machines are also called by the trade name of the company that manufactures the machine, such as *Xerox* and *Thermo-Fax*. They are now standard equipment in most offices, and you may work in an office that has more than one copier. There may be a floor model which is used when many copies are needed, or there may be a small model on a desk or table near you on which you can make a few copies when necessary.

Advantages of Copiers

Copiers have many advantages, one of which is speed. Copies can be made at the rate of one a second on some machines, and some will enlarge or reduce the material during the copying process. Some other advantages of photocopiers are:

1. Copies of an original can be reproduced. This can be important when the item to be reproduced is a complicated drawing or illustration.
2. They are inexpensive when only a few copies are made from the original. Quite often companies record how much customers owe them on ledger cards. At the end of the month the ledger cards are reproduced on a copier, and the copy is sent to the customer as a monthly statement.
3. Copiers are easy to operate. You simply set the dial for the number of copies desired and insert the original in the copier. The original is scanned by the machine and copied. The copy of the original then comes out of the machine. All colors are reproduced in black.
4. Some models prepare **transparencies** that can be projected on a screen. These may be used by your employer to illustrate an important point in a business meeting.
5. Some models prepare offset masters, fluid masters, and stencils which are placed on duplicating machines. Many copies can then be reproduced rapidly.

transparencies: pictures or designs on films viewed by light shining through them.

Uses of Copiers

Your employer may sometimes use a copier for answering letters, as shown on page 354. Handwritten notations are made on the original letter and it is then copied. The letter is mailed back to the sender, and the copy is placed in the office files. This saves your employer's time; he does not have to dictate an answer to the letter. You will not have to type an answer; so your time is saved also. Both the letter and the reply are on one sheet; so filing space is saved.

Photocopiers may be used to make copies of complicated drawings or illustrations that would be difficult to reproduce on a stencil or master. Special kinds of copiers can send and receive printed information through telephones. A telephone receiver is placed in the copier. The original is placed in the sending copier and a light beam scans the dark printed matter on the white paper. The dark print is converted into sound that is sent through telephone wires. At the receiving end, the procedure is reversed and a copy is reproduced.

Standard
Supply Company   4422 North Seventh Street   Dallas, TX   75208

December 10, 197-

Mr. J. W. Stauffer, Sales Manager
The Arnold Products Company
23 North Redd Street
Roanoke, VA   24014

Your Invoice 31336

Dear Jerry

On November 14 we ordered 12 cases of AA bat- *Sorry, John;*
teries on our Purchase Order 2986. On November 20 *our error;*
we received your invoice showing that the batteries *2 cases placed*
were shipped on November 18. *on back order*

We received 10 cases of the batteries on November 25. As yet we have not received the other two
cases. Will you please let me know immediately if
the additional batteries were placed on back order
or if they were shipped separately?

Also, we need about 250 additional advertising *Shipping today*
sheets on the tape players for distribution to our *by separate*
customers. *package*

Thank you.

Sincerely

John

John Mendes
Manager

st

Illus. 10-1

Copy of letter with notations

Photocopiers may be used to make copies of letters for cross-referencing purposes.

Types of Copiers

There are many types of copying machines, but you will probably use the electrostatic and infrared most frequently in the office.

Electrostatic. The electrostatic copier is probably used more than any other in the office. It produces dark black copy that looks very much like the original. It will copy all colors, but all colors are reproduced in black. Corrections or changes can be made on the original by blocking out the area with correction fluid, a white liquid that is applied with a brush. Corrections, if you make them properly on the original, are not **visible** on the copy.

visible:
seen

The electrostatic copier is simple to operate. After turning on the machine, you place the original in the machine and the copy is automatically **ejected** within a few seconds. Most models have a feature that permits you to set a control for the number of copies needed. On some models the original must be reinserted for each copy.

ejected:
to throw out or
off from within

You can make copies at the rate of one a second on some machines. You can also enlarge or reduce copies on some models during the copying process. For many models you will not need special paper for this process.

This process is frequently called "Xerox," the brand name of one of the companies that makes this type of copier.

Illus. 10-3
Floor model
electrostatic copier

Xerox

Infrared.　Sometimes this process is called "Thermo-Fax," the brand name of a company that makes this type of copier.　To make a copy with this machine you use a special thin paper which is available only in an off-white color.　Colors are reproduced in black; but this machine will not copy all colors, particularly red, blue, and green.

Illus. 10-4
A desk model
infrared copier
reproduces ledger
cards which are
used as monthly
statements.

Thermo-Fax

To operate this copier, start the machine to warm it up. Place a sheet of special copy paper on top of the original and feed both into the machine. The copy is made in a few seconds.

AUTOMATIC TYPEWRITERS

Sometimes your employer may wish to send the same letter to many different people. He may want each letter to look like an original. If the copies are prepared on a copying machine or duplicator, it will be **obvious** that they are not originals. When your employer wants original letters for a large number of people, you can use an automatic typewriter.

obvious:
easy to see

Illus. 10-5
Automatic typewriters produce large quantities of letters that have an individualized appearance.

American Automatic
Typewriter Company

The automatic typewriter produces original typewritten form letters in large quantities. The automatically typed letters are individually typed so that they do not look like form letters. They are used to give the recipient a favorable impression; however, this is an expensive way to reproduce large quantities of an item.

To use the automatic typewriter, you first prepare a master copy of the letter on paper tape, cards, or magnetic tape. (The magnetic tape and card method is described in more detail on page 136.) After the master copy has been prepared, you simply place the tape or card in the console unit, insert paper in the typewriter, and push the button to start the typing.

The machine will automatically type the letter. At specific points in the letter, the machine will stop automatically to allow you to manually type in information that will vary from letter to letter. For example, you might have automatic stops to allow you to insert the date, inside address, salutation, or other special information. Some automatic typewriters also have an attachment for placing the signature on each letter.

COLLATORS

Any time you have a duplication job of two pages or more, you must collate it — that is, the pages must be assembled in proper order and fastened into sets. The simplest method of collating is to place the copies of each page in individual stacks on a table, then lift the top page from each stack until a complete set is assembled. This method, however, is time-consuming if large numbers of sets are needed.

Illus. 10-6
Floor-type copier with automatic sorter-collator

Savin Business Machines Corporation

Mechanical collating machines are often used in offices where there is a great deal of duplicating and collating. Each page of a duplicated job is stacked in a separate compartment of the collator. A rubber-tipped metal rod rests on each stack and pushes a page out of each compartment as the foot control is depressed. The pages are gathered in sets and criss-crossed for stapling or binding after each depression of the foot control. When there is a great deal of collating, an automatic collator may be used. This machine will automatically collate and staple sets of papers.

REVIEWING
WHAT YOU
HAVE READ

1. What are the advantages of a photocopier?
2. When would you use a copier to answer a letter?
3. What two types of copiers are most frequently used in offices?

4. Name an important advantage of an electrostatic copier over infrared.
5. What is one advantage of automatic typewriters?
6. Explain the use of the automatic typewriter.
7. Describe the simplest method of collating.

MAKING DECISIONS

1. What are two office situations in which a copying machine may be used?
2. Your employer is considering the purchase of a copying machine. What facts can you present to help him in making his decision?

WORKING WITH OTHERS

A new copying machine has been installed in the personnel department to reduce copying expense. The director of personnel has decided that it would be more efficient to have just one person in the department operate the machine and control the supplies; and he has asked Mary Sherwood, a new employee, to assume this responsibility.

Immediately after the machine is installed, Mr. Yates, the chief clerk in the payroll department, asks Mary to make a copy of a newspaper clipping covering an account of a naval battle of World War II. Mr. Yates is interested in naval history and considers himself an authority in this field. Mary graciously made the copy of the clipping for Mr. Yates. Since that time he has brought in an ever-increasing number of clippings, photographs, and diagrams of naval battles to be reproduced on the copying device.

The photocopying paper costs more than five cents a sheet. If Mary continues to do all of Mr. Yates's work, she will use up her copy paper stock in half the expected time. Sensing that a difficult or embarrassing time lies ahead, Mary wonders what she should do.

What courses of action could Mary take? Which course of action would you take? Why?

USING LANGUAGE

The word *get* is one of the most overworked terms in the English language. In the sentences below, substitute a word that will improve the sentence by eliminating the *get* construction. (Do not rewrite or rephrase the sentence.)

1. *Get* a reservation for me at the Sheraton Hotel in San Francisco for the night of August 14, late arrival.
2. *Get* me on a flight leaving about 4 or 4:30 Monday afternoon for Kansas City.
3. We ought to *get* a new file cabinet to replace the one in Mr. Smith's office.
4. The office staff was well pleased when everyone *got* a new desk.
5. Her employer *got* upset when she was late for work the third time last week.
6. He *got* control of the company through purchase of the stock.
7. Little time is needed to *get* to the railroad station.
8. He *got* that increase in salary justly.
9. The St. Louis office *got* the award for selling the most subscriptions.
10. He *got* the information, but with great difficulty.

USING ARITHMETIC

Your employer, who is active in a civic organization, has asked you to typewrite a 16-page report and then use the office copier to prepare 8 copies for a meeting. Since this is a meeting for the civic club, he has asked that you figure the cost of the copy paper so that the club can reimburse your company. The copy paper is priced at $4.50 for a hundred sheets. What will be the cost to the civic club for the paper?

1. The following material is to be reproduced on an office copier. Type the copy in an attractive style.

PROGRAM FOR THE SEVENTH ANNUAL BUSINESS EDUCATION CONFERENCE

WEDNESDAY, July 6, 197–. 12:00 noon — Registration. Conference Lounge, Student Union Building, East Wing, 2:00 p.m. — First Session, Baldwin Auditorium: Speaker, Dr. Robert G. Ball, Central Teachers College, Pittsburgh, Pennsylvania, "A Changing, Progressing Business Education." 2:45 p.m. — Intermission. 3:00 p.m. — Speaker, Mr. Henry Reynolds, Philadelphia Public Schools, Philadelphia, Pennsylvania, "Curricular Problems in Business Education As Viewed by a Supervisor of Business Education"; Speaker, Miss Marilyn Donnell, Illinois Junior College, Chicago, Illinois, "Answering the Needs of Today's Business World." 4:15 p.m. — Forum: Moderator, Dr. T. J. Collins, Department of Business Education, Eastern Academy, Newark, New Jersey; Discussants, Dr. Robert G. Ball, Mr. Henry Reynolds, Miss Marilyn Donnell. 6:45 p.m. — Dinner, State Room, Student Union Building, East Wing: Presiding, Mrs. Edith R. Jones, Department of Business Education, Southern University, Atlanta, Georgia; Speaker, Dr. K. T. Lerner, Director of Business Education, Ohio Western College, Toledo, Ohio.

2. Type a guide copy of the following report to the stockholders of the Wakefield Gypsum Company. Use your best judgment in planning the layout of the guide copy. Correct all errors and make the layout as attractive as possible. The report is to be photocopied.

To the stockholders —

Profits for the first nine months and the third quarter of this year, compared with corresponding periods of last year, were as follows —

	this year		last year	
	Amount	Per share	Amount	Per share
9 months				
Consolidated Companies;				
Profit before income taxes	$13,894,371	$4.86	$12,474,298	$4.36
Less United States and Foreign Taxes on Income............	7,030,558	2.46	6,405,100	2.24
Profit after income taxes	6,863,813	$2.40	6,069,198	$2.12
Dividends from *Subsidiaries NOT* CONSOLIDATED...............	$84,725	.03	188,140	.07
3rd Quarter				
Consolidated Companies;				
Profit before Income Taxes........	4,808,157	$1.68	$4,407,167	$1.54
Less United states and foreign Taxes on Income..............	2,469,175	.86	2,253,296	.79
PROFIT AFTER INCOME TAXES.	$2,338,982	$.82	$2,153,871	$.75
Dividends from SUBSIDIARIES NOT CONSOLIDATED.........	22,887.00	.01	71,199.00	.03
NET Income......................	$2,361,869	$.83	$2,225,070	.78

PART **2** STENCIL DUPLICATING

The Standard Manufacturing Company has an information session each year for those employees who are interested in furthering their education in their specific field with company aid. Tanya is a clerk-typist in the company. About a week before the session Mr. Trexler, the Personnel Manager, who arranges the program, said to Tanya, "Will you type this final draft of the program, Tanya, and have it duplicated? We'll need about 100 good copies. Here are the names and titles of the speakers and their topics." Tanya knew that this responsibility involved typing an attractive program and preparing the stencil before it could be duplicated. From experience she knew that to get 100 good copies she would have to prepare a good stencil. She also knew that if her stencil was well prepared she could depend upon the employees in the Duplicating Department to produce good quality copies inexpensively.

FEATURES OF STENCIL DUPLICATING

Many offices today use stencil duplicating, which is also called mimeograph duplicating. There are many advantages to using a mimeograph machine since it is very dependable and **versatile**.

versatile:
having many uses

The stencil duplicator has the following features:

1. It is used when up to 10,000 copies are needed.
2. Copies are inexpensive for long runs and comparatively expensive for short runs.
3. Compared with the fluid duplicator, copies are of better quality; compared with the offset duplicator, copies are of poorer quality.
4. It is not too difficult to cut a stencil or to operate the duplicator.
5. Illustrations can be traced onto the stencil or manufactured insets may be purchased and used.
6. It can be used to reproduce color.
7. Stencils can be stored and used again when more copies of that item are needed. For example, 200 or 300 copies of an inventory form may be run off and the stencil stored until the supply must be **replenished**.

replenished:
filled again;
restocked

8. It prints best on **absorbent**, rough finished paper of any color.

A. B. Dick Company

Illus. 10-7 A stencil duplicator is used
when many copies are needed.

PREPARING A STENCIL

stylus:
a sharply pointed
instrument used to
write or draw on a
stencil

A stencil is prepared by pushing aside the wax coating on the stencil sheet with a typewriter key or **stylus**. (Preparing a stencil with a machine stencil maker is discussed in Part 4, page 384.) This is called *cutting a stencil.* When the stencil is placed on the mimeograph machine, ink flows through the openings made by the typewriter keys and forms an impression on the copy paper. To get good copies on a stencil duplicator requires careful planning. The steps for preparing a stencil correctly are discussed on the following pages.

Collect Supplies Needed

The supplies you will need to prepare a stencil are the stencil itself, a burnisher, and a stencil correction fluid.

The Stencil. Most stencils have guidelines to aid you in properly placing the material to be duplicated on the page. If you carefully follow the guidelines and numerals on a stencil as illustrated on page 363, you will be assured of attractively positioned copies.

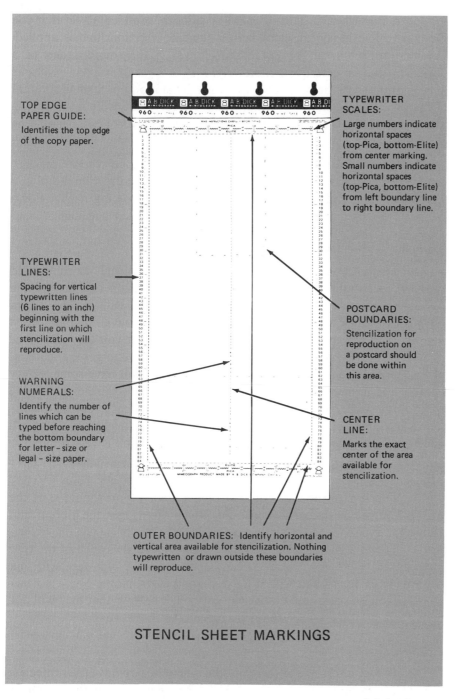

TOP EDGE PAPER GUIDE:
Identifies the top edge of the copy paper.

TYPEWRITER LINES:
Spacing for vertical typewritten lines (6 lines to an inch) beginning with the first line on which stencilization will reproduce.

WARNING NUMERALS:
Identify the number of lines which can be typed before reaching the bottom boundary for letter – size or legal – size paper.

TYPEWRITER SCALES:
Large numbers indicate horizontal spaces (top-Pica, bottom-Elite) from center marking. Small numbers indicate horizontal spaces (top-Pica, bottom-Elite) from left boundary line to right boundary line.

POSTCARD BOUNDARIES:
Stencilization for reproduction on a postcard should be done within this area.

CENTER LINE:
Marks the exact center of the area available for stencilization.

OUTER BOUNDARIES: Identify horizontal and vertical area available for stencilization. Nothing typewritten or drawn outside these boundaries will reproduce.

STENCIL SHEET MARKINGS

A. B. Dick Company

Illus. 10-8 Stencil sheet markings

A Burnisher. A burnisher is any smooth, rounded object that you can use to lightly rub an error before stencil correction fluid is applied. Special burnishers can be purchased; however, the rounded end of a paper clip can be used quite effectively.

Burnishing helps correct the error by smoothing a small amount of the surrounding stencil coating over the error. To insure an unnoticeable correction, you must very carefully burnish each error before applying correction fluid.

Stencil Correction Fluid. To complete the correction process, stencil correction fluid must be applied. Stencil correction fluid is a chemical compound much the same as the stencil coating itself. For a complete discussion on correcting errors on stencils, see page 365.

Plan the Guide Copy

To assure proper positioning on the stencil and on duplicated copies, you should type the material for the stencil on ordinary typing paper first. (Be sure to use the same size paper that will be used to run off the duplicated copies.) Since you will be using the guide copy when you begin typing the stencil, it is very important that you carefully place each item on the page. Stencils are expensive; be sure to get the material placed correctly on the stencil the first time. You will have some leeway because the mimeograph machine can be adjusted to raise or lower the copy on the page, but it will save time if the placement is correct on the stencil itself. As you gain experience in preparing a stencil, usually it will not be necessary to prepare a guide copy unless the job is very difficult.

Prepare the Typewriter

To prepare the typewriter to type a stencil, you should shift the ribbon control to the *stencil* position. This disengages the ribbon and allows the type face to strike the stencil directly.

To get a good *cut* on the stencil, you should always clean the type faces on the typewriter before beginning to type. A type face with ink deposits from the ribbon will not give a good clear image.

Finally, you should move the paper bail rolls so that they will not roll over any of the markings on the stencil.

Prepare the Stencil

Before inserting the stencil in the typewriter, remove the protective sheet that is usually over the stencil and place the guide copy that you have prepared directly beneath the stencil sheet. Be sure that the top edge of the guide copy is aligned with the paper guide markings on the stencil.

On the stencil mark the position of important parts (such as paragraphs and illustrations) of the guide copy with dots of correction fluid so that you will have no trouble in positioning the material when you begin typing. After you have marked the stencil, remove the guide copy and type from it as you prepare the stencil.

If the stencil assembly you are using has a protective sheet, discard it. This sheet protects the stencil sheet only until it is ready for use.

Insert a cushion sheet between the backing sheet and the stencil sheet. If you are using a waxed cushion sheet, insert the cushion sheet with the waxed side up. A tissue cushion sheet may be inserted with either side up since it is the same on both sides. A tissue cushion sheet helps to produce fine-line copy. A waxed cushion sheet helps to produce medium- to bold-line copy.

If the stencil set has a cellophane film, place it on top of the stencil sheet, aligning the bottom edges. Smooth the cellophane film over the stencil sheet. You are now ready to insert the stencil set in the typewriter.

Type the Stencil

With the backing sheet next to the platen, carefully roll the stencil set into the typewriter, taking care to avoid wrinkling the stencil. To straighten the stencil, disengage the paper release, match top and bottom right corners and top and bottom left corners of the stencil set, and engage the paper release.

An electric typewriter automatically gives the even pressure needed for typing a stencil. If you use a manual typewriter, however, you will probably obtain better results if you type a little slower than your usual rate. Strike with greater force those letters and special characters that have a large printing surface, such as *M*, *W*, *E*, *A*, *$*, *#*, *&*, and *@*, so that the entire typeface area will cut through the stencil. Strike with less force letters and punctuation marks having small sharp printing surfaces, such as *c* and *o*, the comma, and the period. Notice the difference between a poorly cut stencil and a correctly cut stencil illustrated on page 366.

Correct Errors

Errors should be corrected as you are typing to prevent your overlooking them later. To correct an error you should

1. Lift the paper bail and turn the stencil up several lines so that you may work at the point where the typing error occurred.
2. If you have a cellophane film over the stencil, pull it loose from the top of the stencil set and lay it over the

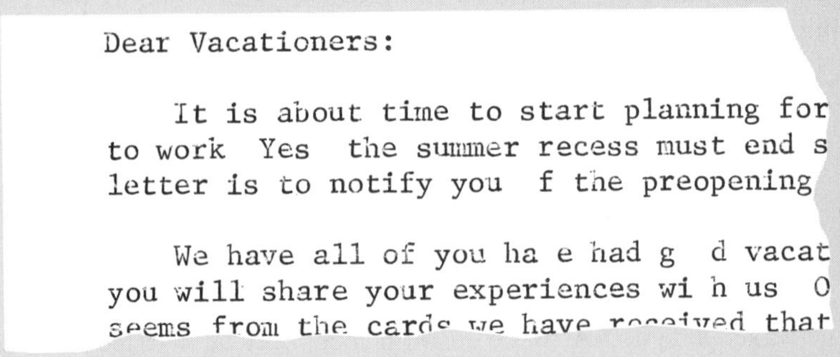

Dear Vacationers:

It is about time to start planning for
to work Yes the summer recess must end s
letter is to notify you f the preopening

We have all of you ha e had g d vacat
you will share your experiences wi h us O
seems from the cards we have received that

Illus. 10-9
A poorly cut
stencil

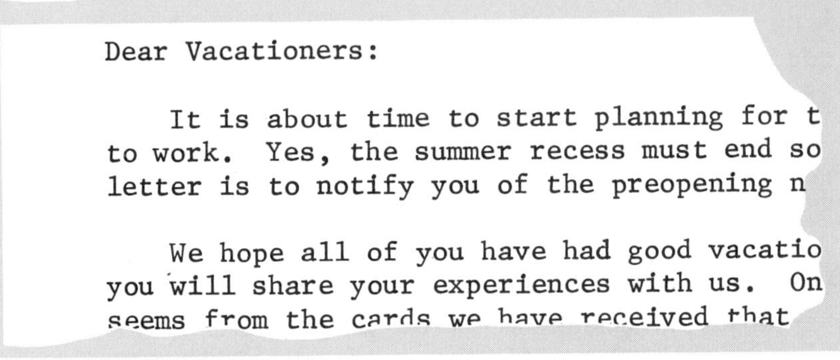

Dear Vacationers:

It is about time to start planning for t
to work. Yes, the summer recess must end so
letter is to notify you of the preopening n

We hope all of you have had good vacatio
you will share your experiences with us. On
seems from the cards we have received that

Illus. 10-10
A correctly cut
stencil

A. B. Dick Company

front of the typewriter. The correction must be made
on the stencil sheet itself.

Illus. 10-11
Burnishing to
correct an error

A. B. Dick Company

3. Lightly rub a rounded object such as a paper clip or a special glass rod burnisher in a circular motion over the error. Burnishing smoothes a small amount of the surrounding stencil coating over the error.

4. Apply a thin coat of stencil correction fluid with a single upward stroke for each incorrect character.

Stencil correction fluid, after drying, is similar to the stencil coating itself. You are actually covering up the error so that you can recut the correct letter or letters. Replace the brush in the bottle and cap the bottle as quickly as possible to prevent the fluid from becoming dry and thick. Allow 30 to 60 seconds for the fluid to dry.

5. Roll the stencil back to the typing position and type the correction.

Proofread

Although you have been proofreading as you have been typing, you still must reread the entire page and make any additional corrections before removing the stencil from the typewriter. It is much more difficult to correct an error after the stencil has been removed from the typewriter because you must **realign** the stencil in the typewriter in the same position as it was originally.

realign:
to bring into line
again

Illus. 10-12
Replace stencil
coating with
correction fluid

A. B. Dick Company

Before removing the stencil from the typewriter, check to make sure that you have not left out a paragraph. Also be sure you have enough space remaining for any illustrations.

Prepare Illustrations

Drawings and illustrations can be placed on a stencil by using a lighted drawing board and one of several styluses. You can purchase a stylus to draw straight or curved lines, dotted lines, shaded lines, or shaded areas. Several stencil manufacturers also provide booklets or leaflets with cartoons and drawings which you can trace onto a stencil. These drawings are easy to use and make very attractive copies. A machine stencil maker, described on page 385, is sometimes used to prepare stencils, especially when detailed drawings must be copied.

OPERATING A STENCIL DUPLICATOR

Detailed instructions of operation may be obtained from the manufacturer of your machine. Some machines have step-by-step directions mounted on the duplicator. Since these instructions are designed for a particular machine, it is wise to study them carefully before attempting to duplicate copies.

The following is an outline of the general steps involved in duplicating on a stencil machine, regardless of the brand of machine that may be used.

1. *Prepare the stencil.* After the stencil has been cut and proofread, remove the cushion sheet and the cellophane film — if one was used.

2. *Attach the stencil.* With the backing sheet up, attach the stencil face down. Tear the backing sheet from the stencil sheet along the perforation. Stretch the stencil sheet carefully around the cylinder.

3. *Load the copy paper.* Place a supply of copy paper on the feed table. Adjust the left and right paper guides so that the paper fits snugly into the area appropriate to the size paper you are using.

4. *Preparing the receiving tray.* The completed copies drop neatly into the receiving tray. This is particularly important when duplication is necessary on both sides of the paper. As is true of the feed table, the receiving tray can be adjusted to accommodate various lengths and widths of paper.

5. *Review and follow carefully the instructions given for inking and counting copies.* Duplicate a trial copy;

inspect it to see if the margins are correct. Copy may be raised or lowered by adjusting controls on the machine. Side margins can easily be adjusted by moving the left and right paper guides on the feed tray.

If the copies are too light the duplicator may not be receiving enough ink. If necessary, add ink according to instructions on the machine. Run off a few more copies. If copies are dark enough and evenly inked, run off the desired number.

All machines have some mechanism by which copies may be automatically counted as they are run through the machine. Some machines register one on the counting device each time a sheet of paper is fed through. When the machine begins to produce the quality desired, the operator sets the counter register at zero and operates the machine until the counter shows that the desired number has been reproduced.

On other models, it is possible to preset the counting device to the number of copies desired. When that number has been fed through the machine, a bell will sound and the feeding mechanism will automatically stop the flow of paper into the machine.

6. *Remove the stencil.* If the stencil is not to be reused, discard it by placing it inside an old newspaper and depositing it in the wastebasket.

STORING THE STENCIL

Since up to 10,000 copies can be made from a single stencil and since it is difficult to store large amounts of duplicated copies, a small number of a particular item may be duplicated and the stencil can be saved for reuse when the supply must be replenished.

To prepare a stencil for filing, clean the stencil by placing it between two sheets of newspaper and gently rubbing the entire surface to remove as much ink as possible from the stencil. You may have to repeat this process several times with clean newspaper until all ink is removed.

Stencils can be stored in special stencil wrappers or in legal size file folders. They can be filed in a legal size file cabinet, or they can be placed in a stencil box where they are kept dry and clean until they need to be used again.

To identify which stencil is in a particular folder, attach a copy of the duplicated material to the file folder or write a description of the item on the file folder.

REVIEWING WHAT YOU HAVE READ

1. What is another term for a stencil duplicating machine?
2. What are some of the features of stencil duplication?
3. Which instruments are used to cut a stencil?
4. What is a burnisher?
5. Describe the guide markings shown on a stencil sheet.
6. Why is it advisable to prepare a guide copy?
7. How do you prepare the typewriter to cut a stencil?
8. Describe how to make a correction on a stencil.
9. Why should you proofread a stencil before removing it from the typewriter?
10. Describe the method for storing a stencil.

MAKING DECISIONS

1. In your office considerable time is spent in preparing carbon copies of certain reports for as many as twenty people. What better method could be used for making this number of copies plus additional copies for incidental use and for the files?

2. Which typewriter do you think will prepare better stencils — one with pica type or one with elite type? If you think there is a difference, how do you account for it?

WORKING WITH OTHERS

The stencils typed by Mary Brady, an employee in the publicity department, failed to produce the sharp, clear, and clean copies so necessary for publicity purposes. At first she attributed the difficulty to the rubber surface on the type-writer platen, which was slightly pitted; so she had the platen replaced. Later she increased the pressure on the type bars; but both changes, though they brought about improvements, failed to produce the desired quality.

Finally she noticed that duplicated copy bearing the initials of the director's secretary was invariably sharp and clean. She asked the secretary for suggestions for improving her copy and received two:

1. Always clean the type before typing a stencil.

2. Brush the type faces occasionally as you type the stencil to prevent paper lint from collecting on them.

Mary had never cleaned the type faces before or during the typing of a stencil; so she frankly told the director's secretary that her suggestions were worthless.

If you were Mary, how would you handle the suggestions that were made? What is your evaluation of the manner in which Mary dealt with the director's secretary?

USING LANGUAGE

Semicolons are used to punctuate complex elements in a sentence. Below are two uses of the semicolon:

1. Between independent clauses not joined by a conjunction
   Example: She prepared the stencil; it was then run off on the mimeograph.

2. Before a conjunction joining two independent clauses when one clause (or both) has internal punctuation
   Example: She had three stencils to type, four letters to file, and a report to complete; but she completed the work, with time to spare, before her employer left on his trip.

On a separate sheet of paper type the sentences below punctuating them based on the two rules you have reviewed above.

1. Tom was preparing a large stencil job Bill was running off each job on the mimeograph as Tom gave it to him.

2. The office manager told the new employee that the company used several kinds of duplicating machines depending on the size of the job but he should consult Bill Smith the supervisor or Joe Camp the assistant supervisor if he was not sure which method to use.

3. There were four stencils that had to be prepared three of which had to be run off that day however Susan had to delay the work because the data processing department did not have the information completed.

4. Paul Ken and Fred worked in the duplicating department Walt Dick and Al worked in the mail department.

5. Because of the flood water in the duplicating room it was impossible to do any work there so the company had to send the work out and the employees in the duplicating department helped out in the mail room and shipping department temporarily.

USING
ARITHMETIC Figure the total cost for the following supplies you are ordering for your office from the Gibson Office Supply Company.

1 dozen ballpoint pens at 25 cents each
2 reams of bond paper at $3.75 a ream
6 stenographer's notebooks at $3.90 a dozen
1 stapler at $3.25
1 dozen rolls of cellophane tape at 35 cents a roll

PERFORMING
OFFICE
TASKS The material shown below is to be reproduced on a stencil duplicator. Type the material in tabular form on a stencil. Rule the form. If stencils are not available, use plain paper.

Comparison of Estimated and Actual Expenses.

Last year:

Sales Salaries: Estimated, $7,000.00; Actual, $7,118.00
Office Salaries: Estimated, $7,500.00; Actual, $7,556.00
Delivery Expense: Estimated, $1,600.00; Actual, $1,591.05
Advertising: Estimated, $300.00; Actual, $312.95
Rent: Estimated, $1,500.00; Actual, $1,500.00
Supplies: Estimated, $300.00; Actual, $287.60
Insurance: Estimated, $2,100.00; Actual, $2,100.00
Depreciation: Estimated, $500.00; Actual, $521.16
Miscellaneous: Estimated, $350.00; Actual, $357.35

This year:

Sales Salaries: Estimated, $7,500.00; Actual, $7,439.00
Office Salaries: Estimated, $7,800.00; Actual $7,780.00
Delivery Expense: Estimated, $1,650.00; Actual, $1,612.45
Advertising: Estimated, $350.00; Actual, $365.75
Rent: Estimated, $1,500.00; Actual, $1,500.00
Supplies: Estimated, $350.00; Actual, $342.75
Insurance: Estimated, $2,250.00; Actual, $2,250.00
Depreciation: Estimated, $550.00; Actual, $565.32
Miscellaneous: Estimated, $400.00; Actual, $392.40

PART 3 FLUID DUPLICATING

Miriam Kathman works in a suburban office of the Missouri National Life Insurance Company. She is an assistant to Mr. Orth's secretary, Louella Bethel. Seven salesmen work out of the office under Mr. Orth's supervision. Miss Bethel mentioned to Miriam yesterday that Mr. Orth is planning a meeting of the salesmen for Friday. She said, "Miriam, here is a report that Mr. Orth wants to present at the meeting. Will you type it for me on a fluid master and make twenty copies on the fluid duplicator?" As Miriam gathered the supplies she needed to type the report, she recalled the things she has learned in her office procedures class in high school about typing on fluid masters. She knew that it was important to have a good master in order to get clear copies on the fluid duplicator.

FEATURES OF FLUID DUPLICATING

You will probably find that the fluid duplicating process is the easiest to learn. When many copies are needed but the quality of the copies is not of great importance, you should probably use a fluid duplicator. Fluid duplicators have the following features:

1. They are used when up to 200 copies are needed; although, with a well-typed master and careful operation of the duplicator, as many as 300 copies can be made from one master.
2. This is probably the least expensive duplicating process for about 10 to 30 copies.
3. It is easy to prepare a master and easy to operate the duplicator.
4. Copies are not as attractive as most other duplicating methods.
5. Several colors can be duplicated.
6. They print best on smooth-finished, glossy paper of any color.
7. The masters can be saved to be used again.
8. The purple dye from the master soils your hands very easily.

PREPARING A FLUID MASTER

achieve:
attain; earn;
receive

You will find fluid masters easy to prepare, and you will **achieve** the best results by following these steps:

Collect the Supplies Needed

The materials you will need to prepare a fluid master are the master itself and a razor blade or knife.

The Master Set. The master set is composed of a sheet of master paper and a sheet of carbon which are fastened together at one end. The master set has a tissue sheet between the master and carbon sheet, which you should remove before you insert the set in your typewriter. Save the tissue sheet to use to protect the master sheet after it has been typed.

Razor Blade. You need a razor blade or knife when correcting errors. When you are typing a fluid master, your typing puts carbon deposits on the back of the master sheet. When you make an error, you have carbon where you do not want it. Use the razor blade to carefully scrape off the unwanted carbon.

Plan the Placement of the Materials on the Master

Unlike the stencil process, you will seldom find it necessary to type a guide copy; however, you will have to plan the placement of the material on the master before you begin typing. When planning the placement, you must remember to leave at least one-half inch blank space at the top or bottom of the fluid master. This allows space for the master to be clamped onto the fluid duplicator (either end of the master can be attached to the fluid duplicator).

Prepare the Typewriter

To insure good copies when using the fluid duplication process, you must carefully clean the type faces on the typewriter. Give extra attention to type faces where ink is likely to accumulate, such as *e, a, w, g,* and *o.*

Type the Fluid Master

Remove the tissue sheet from between the master sheet and the carbon sheet before inserting the fluid master in the typewriter. As mentioned before, the carbon sheet and master are fastened together on one end. To aid in correcting any errors you may make, insert the open end of the master set in the typewriter first, with the carbon sheet next to the platen. In this way you can make corrections on the back of the master sheet without first separating the master sheet from the carbon sheet.

IBM Corporation

If your typewriter does not have a smooth, medium hard platen, place a sheet of heavy paper or thin, flexible plastic behind the carbon sheet to serve as a backing sheet.

An electric typewriter automatically gives the even pressure needed for typing a master. If you are using a manual typewriter, you will probably obtain better results if you type a little slower than your usual rate. Type with firm, even strokes.

Correct Errors

To correct an error on a fluid master, follow these steps:

1. Separate the master sheet from the carbon sheet. It was suggested that you insert the open end of the master set in the typewriter first. Corrections are made on the reverse side of the master sheet. By inserting the open end of the set into the typewriter first, you can simply pull the master sheet toward you; and the reverse side of the master sheet, on which you will make your corrections, is exposed.

The section of the master sheet where you will be making the correction should rest on the flat part of the typewriter or on a flat surface, such as a typewriter shield, that you have placed on top of the typewriter.

2. Lightly scrape off the unwanted carbon with a razor blade or knife, being careful not to make a hole in the master sheet.

3. Fluid carbon paper can be used only once; and, at that point where you typed an error, you have already used the carbon. Therefore, you must provide some new carbon before you can type in the correction. You can cut fresh carbon from the unused portion of that carbon sheet, or you can cut a small piece from another carbon sheet that you are using for that purpose. Insert this fresh carbon behind the error with the carbon side facing the master sheet. Type the correction. Remove the extra carbon slip before **resuming** your typing.

resuming:
beginning again

Although the above described method is used most often, there are several other ways to correct errors on a fluid master. If you have several lines to **delete**, you can simply cut them out with a razor blade; or you can cover them with cellophane tape. You can also buy a special adhesive correction tape which has the same surface as the master sheet. To correct an error, you place this special tape over it and type the correction. This eliminates the need to scrape off the unwanted carbon.

delete:
eliminate; do away
with; take out

Proofread

Always proofread and make corrections before removing the fluid master from the typewriter. Even though you have been proofreading as you are typing, reread the entire page.

Remove the Fluid Master from the Typewriter

Disengage the paper release and remove the master, being careful not to wrinkle the master sheet. Cover the carbon side of the master sheet with the tissue sheet to protect it until it is attached to the machine for duplicating.

Prepare Illustrations

You may use a pencil, a ball point pen, or a stylus for drawing illustrations on a fluid master. You will usually save time and get a better copy if you first draw the illustration on bond paper because you can make corrections easily and quickly. Place the drawing on top of the fluid master set and trace the outlines, using an even pressure. A machine master maker (see page 384) is sometimes used to produce the masters, especially when detailed drawings must be copied.

OPERATING A FLUID DUPLICATOR

In a large office with a separate duplicating department, you would be expected to run off copies only in an emergency. In a small office, however, preparing masters and turning out copies on a fluid duplicator may be one of your duties. Instructions for operating the various makes of fluid duplicators vary slightly, but the following general instructions apply to all makes.

1. *Attach the master.* Clamp the master copy to the cylinder, carbon side up. To avoid wrinkling the master copy, take care to insert the master copy across the width of the drum in the slot *evenly*. Then hold lightly to the unattached end while you turn the drum one complete revolution.

Illus. 10-16
Turn the drum one complete revolution to test for fluid control, pressure, and margin alignment.

A. B. Dick Company

2. *Adjust the fluid control.* This mechanism determines how much the paper being fed into the machine is moistened. The wetter the paper when it comes into contact with the master copy the more carbon is transferred from the master copy to the paper. Therefore, when this mechanism is set on *high*, each individual copy produced will be very dark; but, you will get fewer copies than with a low setting.

3. *Position the copy paper in the feed tray.* Align the sides of the copy paper on the feed tray with the sides of the master copy on the drum. This permits the duplicated copies to have the same margins as the master copy.

4. *Set the pressure control.* This mechanism controls the force with which the moistened paper is pressed against the carbon side of the master copy. When a low setting is used, each moistened sheet will be pressed only *slightly* against the master, resulting in relatively light copies. More copies, even though light in color, can be produced in this manner.

Illus. 10-17
Inspect first copy and make any adjustments before proceeding to run remaining sheets.

A. B. Dick Company

5. *Run the copies.* Both electrically operated and manually operated machines are available. The speed of manual machines may be varied. The greater the speed the weaker the color strength of the copies produced and the greater the number of copies possible. Slower speeds give shorter runs with greater color strength.

STORING THE FLUID MASTER

Although the total number of copies a fluid master can produce is limited, fluid masters can be stored and used again. Copies will not be as good, however, if the fluid master is very old and dried out. You should protect the carbon side of the fluid master sheet with the tissue paper that comes with the fluid master set before you store it.

Fluid masters can be placed in a regular file folder and stored in a file cabinet, or they can be laid flat and stored in the fluid master box. They should be protected from the sun and extreme heat to prevent them from drying out.

REVIEWING WHAT YOU HAVE READ

1. When would you probably use a fluid duplicator?
2. What are the three parts of a master set?
3. Explain the statement: One-half inch should be left blank on the master copy at the top or at the bottom.
4. How do you prepare the typewriter for typing a fluid master?
5. Describe how the master set should be inserted in the typewriter.
6. Describe the method of correction most often used on a fluid master.
7. Name two other correction methods for fluid masters.
8. What two machine controls can be adjusted to determine color strength of copies and length of run? Explain.
9. What is the relationship of the speed of operation to color strength and length of run?
10. Explain how you would store a fluid master.

MAKING DECISIONS

1. In your office there is frequently a need for multiple copies. What factors should be considered in deciding which method of duplication would best fit your needs?
2. Many operators of duplicating machines learn the methods of operation on the job. What then are the advantages, if any, of becoming familiar with these machines while in school?

WORKING WITH OTHERS

You work in the office of an insurance company that has a fluid duplicator used by nine of the employees. It seems that the machine is frequently out of order when you want to use it. On several occasions you notice that the pressure has been left on and the fluid has not been turned off when you must use the machine. Also, there always seems to be a great deal of wasted copy paper around the machine because users are not getting good copy all of the time. This seems to be a case of "everyone's responsibility is no one's responsibility." What should you do?

USING LANGUAGE

1. Quotation marks are used to enclose the beginning and end of a *direct* quotation.
   Example: The supervisor said, "Be sure to clean the typewriter before preparing a master."
2. Quotation marks are used to set off quotations that are *built into* a sentence.
   Example: His letter said that there are "several kinds of duplicating machines" and that he "intends to learn how to operate all of them."

3. Quotation marks are used to set off a specific part of a complete work. (The title of the complete work is put in italics or underlined if you are typing.)

Example: She studied the section entitled "Tracing and Handwriting" in her *Duplicating Machine Processes* textbook.

Type the sentences below on a separate sheet of paper and correctly insert the quotation marks.

1. On page 376 the author states you may use a pencil, a ball point pen, or a stylus for drawing illustrations on a fluid master.
2. Stencil Duplicating and Fluid Duplicating are two parts of Unit 10 of Clerical Office Procedures.
3. Mr. Orth's instructions stated clearly that he will need 40 copies of the report completed and ready for use by Friday morning.
4. On page 377 the textbook clearly says, Clamp the master copy to the cylinder, carbon side up.
5. What is another name for a stencil duplicating machine? her teacher asked.

USING ARITHMETIC

On a separate sheet of paper show your computations and answers for the following problems:

1. 170 is what _____% of 3400?
2. 39 is 10% of _____?
3. 81% of $279 = _____?
4. .23 = _____%.
5. .023 = _____%.

PERFORMING OFFICE TASKS

The schedule below is to be prepared on a fluid duplicator for distribution to all company salesmen. Use the calendar for next month. Set the schedule up on a fluid master and insert the following information in the correct dates. (If fluid masters are not available, use plain paper.)

First Saturday, 7:30 p.m.: Company awards banquet
First and third Monday, 9:30 a.m.: Sales meeting
Second weekend, Friday through Sunday: Chicago sales convention
Each Tuesday: Weekly sales reports are due by 5:00 p.m.
Third Thursday, 10:30 a.m.: Meeting for all salesmen with the company president
Fourth Wednesday: Deadline for submitting material for monthly newsletter
Last day of the month: Monthly report due by 5:00 p.m.

PART 4 OFFSET DUPLICATING

The American Survey Company specializes in conducting nationwide surveys for businesses, nonprofit organizations, and political groups. This company prepares questionnaires for gathering needed information. After the people to be surveyed are selected, the company conducts the survey and presents its findings to its clients. Donald Mahaney works in the American Survey Company's office as a clerk-typist gathering results of surveys. He does a great deal of typing as well as answering telephone inquiries and operating stencil and fluid duplicators. As Donald was leaving for lunch, his supervisor, Mr. Robert Kippenberg, said, "Would you take this questionnaire to the Central Duplicating Department on your way to lunch? We want it duplicated on the offset and need 5,000 copies. Be sure to find out when it will be finished." Donald often delivered materials to be duplicated on the offset. His office has both a mimeograph and a fluid duplicator; but, when a great many high quality copies are needed, an offset master is prepared and the copies are made on offset equipment.

FEATURES OF OFFSET DUPLICATING

Copies made on an offset duplicator are of a much finer quality than those made on a stencil or fluid duplicator. The offset duplicator has the following features:

1. Copies of excellent quality are produced. The copy looks like the type on the page of this book.
2. Thousands of copies can be produced from a master.
3. Cost is moderate for short runs and inexpensive for long runs.
4. Masters are easily prepared, but machine operation is difficult.
5. Copies can be produced in many colors.
6. Many copies can be produced quickly.
7. Copies can be printed on a variety of weights, sizes, colors, and quality of paper.

PREPARING AN OFFSET MASTER

Preparing a master is a simple process if you follow the steps outlined below.

Collect the Supplies

The only supplies needed for typing an offset master are the duplicating master and a soft, nongreasy eraser.

The Offset Master. There are two types of offset duplicating masters — paper masters and metal masters (sometimes referred to as aluminum plates). Short-run, medium-run, and long-run masters may be purchased. Up to 5,000 copies can be obtained from a single long-run paper master, but 25,000 or more copies can be run from an aluminum plate. The short-run paper masters are the least expensive; the aluminum plates are the most expensive.

Special techniques and supplies are necessary to prepare an aluminum plate. Since you will seldom be required to do this, the paper master will be described here. The paper master is made of a specially treated paper. It contains guide marks similar to those on the stencil on page 363.

Eraser. You will need a very soft, nongreasy eraser to get best results when making corrections on the offset master. You can purchase special offset erasers or use a soft typing eraser.

Plan the Placement of Materials on the Master

Typing a paper master is very similar to typing on regular paper because you don't have to work with carbon (as you do in the fluid process), nor do you have additional sheets that require special care (as you do in the stencil process). Nevertheless, planning how you are going to put the material on the page is very important because you do not want to waste masters. You should try to get the placement right the first time you type it. A special pencil can be purchased that will enable you to write directly on the master as you are planning the layout of the material. The pencil marks will not reproduce when the master is run.

Prepare the Typewriter

When typing an offset master, the typefaces should be clean and the paper bail rollers and platen free of ink smudges. You must use typewriter ribbons of carbon plastic, carbon paper, or special grease fabric because they are **receptive** to the special offset ink.

receptive:
ready to receive

Move the paper bail rollers outside the left and right boundary markings on the master to prevent the rollers from smearing the type.

Type the Offset Master

Insert the offset master in the typewriter so that the markings on it face you. Use the markings on the master to guide you as you type with an even, firm touch. You should type so that you get an evenly dark image; a touch that is too heavy results in **embossing** on the reverse side of the master and appears as hollow-looking letters on the duplicated copy. Set the pressure control on an electric typewriter to the lowest position where all characters will print.

embossing: standing out from a surface.

Correct Errors

Use a soft, nongreasy eraser or a special offset eraser to make corrections on a paper master. Erase the image very lightly with a *lifting* motion, being careful not to damage the slick finish on the master. It is necessary only to remove the greasy deposit. It is not necessary to remove the ghost image left as this image will not reproduce. Keep the eraser clean by frequently rubbing it on a piece of clean paper.

Proofread

Offset masters are easy to proofread since the copy is clear. Carefully proofread to catch every error before removing the master from the typewriter.

OPERATING AN OFFSET DUPLICATOR

As mentioned earlier, it is relatively easy to type a master to be run on the offset duplicator, but it is difficult to actually run the duplicator. In fact, a skilled operator is needed to run these machines. Your job will probably be to prepare the offset master, and a central duplicating department will do the actual duplicating. However, should your duties involve operating an offset duplicator, you will receive special training on the particular machine you are to run.

STORING THE OFFSET MASTER

Storing an offset master is very important because the master can be used many times. Storing it correctly will insure good copies no matter how many times you run it.

Before storing the master, carefully wipe the surface with a ball of cotton containing a special fluid which will remove any ink or grease

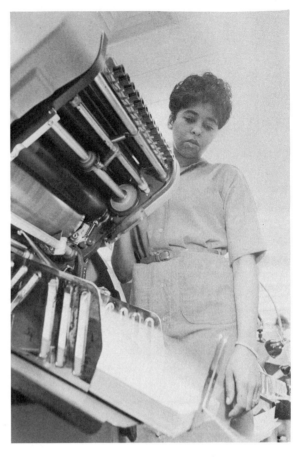

Illus. 10-18
Offset duplicating
requires the skill
of a well-trained
operator.

Addressograph-
Multigraph Corporation

smudges. Cover the master with a thin coat of gum solution to preserve the typed images. Allow it to dry. Place the master in a file folder and store it in a file cabinet. If several paper masters are stored in one file folder, slip a piece of clean paper between them to prevent small amounts of oil and ink from being transferred from one master to another. If this is not done, when the master is rerun, smudges will appear where the ink and oil were deposited.

MACHINE PREPARATION OF MASTERS AND STENCILS

Placing information on an offset master, fluid master, or stencil is called *imaging*. When you typewrite, write, draw, or rule information on the master or stencil as explained in this unit it is called *direct imaging*.

There are many ways of preparing masters and stencils. As mentioned on page 353, you can insert special masters and stencils instead of copy paper into regular copiers and complete the imaging process.

Illus. 10-19
A master maker will
serve a variety of
needs in a busy
office.

A. B. Dick Company

Image makers, also called *master makers*, that are similar to copiers will prepare masters, stencils, and transparencies. Some machines will make all these items; others will prepare only one or two of them.

An electronic scanner will prepare stencils. The original is wrapped around one half of the cylinder, and the stencil is wrapped around the other half of the cylinder. When the machine is started the original is exactly reproduced on the stencil.

Machine preparation of masters and stencils is faster than direct processing. Also, it completely eliminates the need for proofreading the master or stencil because an exact copy is produced, whether it is an engineer's drawing, a complicated tabulation, a detailed business form, or an interoffice communication.

For fast production of much duplicated work, the image maker can be connected in **tandem** to an offset duplicator as shown in Illus. 10-20. The originals are fed into the image maker at the right and an offset master

tandem:
one behind another

is prepared. The master moves on a belt to a machine at the right of the offset duplicator that processes the master without being touched by the operator. The master is then automatically attached to the cylinder of the offset machine where many copies are duplicated very rapidly. The process is sometimes called a continuous total copy system.

Addressograph-Multigraph Corporation

REVIEWING WHAT YOU HAVE READ

1. What are the features of offset duplication?
2. Describe the two types of offset masters.
3. What type ribbon is used for typewriting offset masters?
4. What causes embossing? How does it appear on the duplicated copy?
5. Describe the eraser used on offset masters.
6. Why should an offset master be properly stored?
7. How do you store an offset master?
8. Define the term *imaging*.
9. What are two advantages of a machine stencil maker?
10. What is the purpose of a continuous total copy system?

MAKING DECISIONS

1. How would you help your employer decide which type of copying machine or duplicator should be purchased for your office?
2. Under what circumstances would you use each of the following methods of preparing several copies of material in preference to the other methods?

    (a) Typewriter
    (b) Stencil duplicator
    (c) Fluid duplicator
    (d) Offset duplicator
    (e) Copier

WORKING WITH OTHERS

Howard Lansing, the assistant office manager, is also secretary of a local service organization. Almost every week he brings in a job to be done on one of the duplicating machines. With equal frequency he also brings in several papers to be reproduced on one or more of the copying devices. He never offers to pay for any of this service, nor for any of the supplies.

Some companies permit this practice as a goodwill gesture to the local service clubs when one of their own men is an officer. Others charge for the service. Still others have a rigid rule against such practices.

Assume that you are in charge of the duplicating service for the firm. If you were asked to do this work, what steps would you take?

USING LANGUAGE

On a sheet of paper, write the plural form for each of these words.

1. city
2. report
3. businessman
4. class
5. address
6. opportunity
7. job
8. company
9. activity
10. procedure

USING ARITHMETIC

On a sheet of paper, complete the following problems.

1. 429×220

2. $5,280 - 4,633$

3. 398
   28
   142
   42
   41
   667
   80

4. $39/15,288$

5. $8\ 3/4 \times 9\ 2/7 =$

PERFORMING OFFICE TASKS

1. Prepare a guide copy of the following letter and certificate. The material will be duplicated on an offset duplicator. The material should be arranged in such a way that the customer can tear the certificate from the letter to mail in with his order.

Best Products Co., Inc.
4722 South Wayland Road
Indianapolis, Indiana 46227

Dear Customer:

This may be the last catalog we can send you. We have been happy to send you catalogs since you requested your first one. But, in order to keep our prices low, we must keep our costs down. And to do this we have to send catalogs only to those people who buy from us.

We know that you have enjoyed our catalogs and have been amazed at our money-saving prices. Just one order from you will make it possible to keep you on our mailing list. And as an added incentive to order, the attached certificate entitles you to a five percent discount on anything you order.

Your first order will show you how easy and economical it is to order from us. Just attach the certificate to your order and claim your discount. It's that simple.

Sincerely yours,

Sales Manager

Special Discount Certificate

This certificate is worth five percent discount on anything in our catalog. Attach this certificate to your order to claim your discount. Please use this certificate within 30 days of its date.

Date:

2. Set up the following in tabulated form on a guide copy. The material is to be duplicated on an offset duplicator.

Perry Altmann Company

Sales Comparisons

1973–1974

January: 1973 sales 392 units, 1974 398 units, up 1.53%

February: 1973 sales 403 units, 1974 427 units, up 5.96%

March: 1973 sales 401 units, 1974 399 units, down .50%

April: 1973 sales 401 units, 1974 408 units, up 1.75%

May: 1973 sales 411 units, 1974 420 units, up 2.19%

June: 1973 sales 427 units, 1974 427 units, no change

July: 1973 sales 399 units, 1974 410 units, up 2.76%

August: 1973 sales 397 units, 1974 401 units, up 1.01%

September: 1973 sales 368 units, 1974 392 units, up 6.52%

October: 1973 sales 390 units, 1974 388 units, down .51%

November: 1973 sales 387 units, 1974 400 units, up 3.36%

December: 1973 sales 399 units, 1974 402 units, up .75%

Year: 1973 sales 4,775 units, 1974 4,872 units, up 2.03%

UNIT 11

OFFICE TYPEWRITING

STATISTICAL TYPIST

Position in headquarter offic
r large national corporatio
nveniently located dow
n. Accurate typing, fam
y with preparation of repor
ning statistical table
e benefits program i
beral employee d
nient parking a
urgical insu
ointme

PART 1 PREPARING BUSINESS REPORTS

Trice Electric Company is a manufacturer of electronic parts and equipment. Paula Sadler, one of three technical typists, has worked for three years in the Research Department. Mr. Marvin Taylor, the Research Director, is in charge of all research on the various electronic equipment which the company manufactures. He must prepare many reports on the results of the department's research findings. Paula was typing a research report when Mr. Taylor brought several pages of material to her desk and said, "Paula, will you include these pages in the Appendix of that report? And will you also add these books to the Bibliography?" Paula has typed many reports for Mr. Taylor; so she knows exactly where the pages should be placed and how to add the books to the Bibliography.

IMPORTANCE OF BUSINESS REPORTS

A business report may be only one or two pages and be in the form of a memo or letter; or it may be a long, formal report of several hundred pages. As businesses continue to grow and as the amount of information needed to operate a business increases, it is more and more *vast:*
great in size, amount, or degree
difficult to communicate this **vast** amount of knowledge in person. There is a great need for written communications in the form of business reports, because they make it possible for a busy executive to present information to others without talking to each person individually. Some reports are sent to personnel within the company while others are sent to interested people outside the company. Since so many people will be reading the report, it is extremely important that the information it contains be accurate.

When you work in an office, you will no doubt have an opportunity to type reports. As you gain experience and show the ability to assume responsibility, you may be asked to help gather the information that is used in the reports.

Illus. 11-1
Gathering and checking information for a report is an exacting task that requires care and responsibility.

Ken Lauben

PARTS OF A REPORT

A long and detailed business report may contain a dozen, more or less, specific parts which are classified under three main headings: the introductory parts, the body of the report, and the supplementary parts. Before binding, they are arranged in this order:

A. Introductory Parts
   1. Cover
   2. Title page
   3. Preface or letter of transmittal
   4. Table of contents
   5. List of tables, charts, and illustrations
   6. Summary

B. Body of the Report
   1. Introduction
   2. Main body or text
   3. Conclusions and recommendations

C. Supplementary Parts
   1. Appendix
   2. Bibliography

The body of the report must be developed first; so it is usually typed first. Then the supplementary parts and the introductory parts of the report are typed.

Cover

The cover should contain this information: the title of the report, the name of the person submitting it, and the date it was submitted.

Title Page

The items of information that usually appear on the title page are the title of the report, the name of the author, the date, and the place of preparation. Sometimes reports include the name of the person (with his title) for whom the report was prepared.

Preface or Letter of Transmittal

The purpose of the preface or letter of transmittal, illustrated on page 406, is to interest the reader and encourage him to read the entire report. The preface or letter of transmittal is written in a less formal and more personal style than the body of the report.

The preface or letter of transmittal usually will contain the following information:

1. The name of the person or organization that asked that the report be prepared
2. The main purpose of the report
3. The scope, or extent of coverage, of the report
4. Acknowledgments of assistance in the preparation of the report

If a separate summary is not included in the report, usually it is included in the letter.

Table of Contents

The table of contents, shown on page 406, gives an overview of the material covered in the report by listing the main topics or chapter titles with their page numbers.

Before you type the final copy of the Table of Contents, check the titles and page numbers to make sure they are correct, particularly if any last minute changes were made.

List of Tables

A list of tables is actually a separate table of contents used in reports which contain several tables, charts, figures, or other illustrations. The List of Tables contains the title of each illustration and indicates the page on which it can be found. Usually the List of Tables is typed as a separate page, but it can be a part of the Table of Contents.

Summary

The summary of the report is written after the entire report is completed. It gives the reader a quick overview that saves his time and makes it easier for him to understand the detailed statements contained in the body of the report.

Introduction

The purpose of the introduction is to tell the reader exactly what problem is going to be studied in the report. The reader is told how the problem developed and how the report will analyze and deal with the problem.

Main Body

The main body of the report presents the information which was collected and applies this information to the problem with the idea of presenting a **solution** to the problem. The main body, of course, is the bulk of the report. It is where the information is analyzed and compared and where relationships and trends are identified, considered, and evaluated.

solution: answer to a problem

Conclusions and Recommendations

The conclusions are the results of what has been presented in the report. The recommendations contain the writer's suggestions about action that should be taken as a result of the conclusions.

Appendix

The text of a long report or a manuscript may be followed by an appendix; it is omitted in a short report. It usually contains extra reference material not easily included in the text. The appendix may also include tables containing complete original data, general reference tables, and other materials which will help to interpret and to add interest in the report.

Bibliography

All documentary sources (written material) referred to in a business report — books, articles, and periodicals — should be included in the bibliography. It should also include all the references consulted which had worthwhile information related to the report. The references listed in the bibliography should be arranged in alphabetical order by authors, by editors, or by titles if the authors' names are not available. Examples of references in a bibliography are illustrated on page 411.

STEPS IN REPORT WRITING

There is no *one* best way to write a report; there are many ways. However, in drafting and revising a business report you and your employer will usually take these steps:

1. He develops a broad idea of the problem to be covered in the report.
2. He prepares either a sketchy or a detailed outline of the contents.
3. He composes the first draft. He may write the entire draft in longhand, or he may record it on a dictating machine.
4. You type the first draft in rough draft form.
5. He reorganizes and edits the first draft for content, wording, and sentence structure (usually with your help).
6. You type a second draft of the report.
7. He edits the second draft to insure the best presentation of the contents.
8. You type the report in its final form.
9. You double-check each page for accuracy, particularly accuracy of figures.
10. You **collate** pages of the report.

collate:
arrange in order

Illus. 11-2

An employer may record the first draft or the revision of a report on a dictating machine.

Philips Business Systems, Inc.

GATHERING INFORMATION

Your employer may not have all the information that is needed to complete the report. He may have only a little information to give you such as, "I think the title of the book is *Business Organization and Management,* and the author is Tyler, but I'm not sure." He may not even remember how to spell the author's name. In these instances, he may call on you to find the information and insert it in the correct place.

Sometimes your employer may want to quote a particular person, but he doesn't remember the exact wording; or he has an approximate date, but he needs an exact date. After checking the original sources, you must insert the changes in the manuscript in the correct places, always double-checking dates, amounts, and page numbers.

You may have to check reference books such as the *Readers' Guide to Periodical Literature,* the *New York Times Index,* and the *World Almanac and Book of Facts.* You may use the public library or a company library to find original sources. Thus, you will find that, in **compiling** reports or writing manuscripts, you will need to know what to look for, where to look, and how to get the information rapidly and correctly.

compiling: collecting into a volume

Illus. 11-3
To compile a report it may be necessary to gather information from many sources.

Remington Rand

TYPING THE OUTLINE

Before writing the report itself, your employer will prepare an outline for you to type. An outline is necessary because it gives your employer a chance to organize his thoughts and rearrange the contents of the report before it is actually written. It also permits him to see if everything is included in the report.

Parallel:
corresponding to;
similar in form or
style

An outline may be written in complete sentence form or in topical form. *Topical form* means that the topics or headings of the parts of the report are listed. **Parallel** construction should be used; that is, if one part of the outline is in sentence form, all parts should be in sentence form. Words, phrases, and sentences should not be mixed throughout the outline. No main heading or subheading should stand alone. For every Roman numeral "I," there should be a Roman numeral "II"; for every letter "A," a letter "B"; for every Arabic "1," an Arabic "2."

In the outline illustrated, each identifying number or letter is followed by a period and two spaces and begins just below the first word of the previous line.

```
                    An Outline of a Report on

            PUNCHED CARD DATA PROCESSING OPERATIONS


      I.  Introduction

          A.  Purpose
              1.  To review present operations
              2.  To develop an improved system
          B.  Approach
              1.  To make detailed studies of present equipment
              2.  To prepare flow charts of present operations
                  a.  Accounting department
                  b.  Payroll department
                  c.  Purchasing department

     II.  Proposed system

          A.  Staff requirements
              1.  To retrain present personnel
              2.  To employ systems manager
          B.  Equipment requirements
              1.  To study rental costs of additional machines
              2.  To study other costs
                  a.  Auxiliary equipment
                  b.  Additional cards and tapes
              3.  To study additional wiring costs
```

Illus. 11-4 A topical outline of a report

REVIEWING WHAT YOU HAVE READ

1. Why are business reports important?
2. What are the three main parts of a business report?
3. List the items of information usually given on the title page of a report.
4. What is the purpose of a letter of transmittal?
5. Why is a table of contents used in a business report?
6. What is the purpose of the introduction?
7. Describe how the main body of a report treats information.
8. What are conclusions and recommendations?
9. What is the purpose of the outline for a report?
10. What is the difference between preparing an outline in sentence form and preparing one in topical form?

1. What advantage does a written report have over direct oral communication?
2. Why would a bibliography be included in a report?

Laura Bates has been assisting her employer, Mr. Engels, in the preparation of a very important report for the president of the company. Twice Laura had completely typed the final draft when Mr. Engels decided to make further revisions which required starting over. Yesterday Laura completed the final version of the report and prepared it for mailing.

While reading the newspaper at home last night, Laura read an article that contained new information on the subject of Mr. Engels' report. In fact, the newspaper article indicated that some of the key information in the report was no longer true. What should Laura do?

The question mark has three usages:
1. After a direct question: "What are you doing?"
2. In a series, if special emphasis is desired: "Where is my book? my pen? my eraser?"
3. To indicate uncertainty: "He was born in 1955(?)."

(It is not necessary to use a question mark after a polite request: "Will you let us have the information quickly.")

On a separate sheet of paper type the following sentences and insert question marks and other punctuation where needed.
1. Where are the figures for May he asked.
2. What happened to the title page the table of contents the list of tables.
3. He asked her to retype the letter of transmittal.
4. The figures for 1970, 1971, 1972, and 1937 were given to the sales manager.
5. Can't this report be reduced to something less than 45 pages the president asked.
6. Please include these pages in the Appendix.
7. What happened to my first draft my carbon paper my notes.
8. When do you expect to have the final draft completed.
9. The amounts for the five-year period 1968–1973 were included.
10. He asked her if the information was current.

Gwen Newcomb works from 9 a.m. until 5 p.m. five days a week. She gets an hour for lunch. Today (Tuesday), as soon as she arrived at work, her employer handed her the final draft of a 52-page report to be typed and ready for him to take on a business trip. He must leave the office at 4 p.m. Wednesday to get the plane. What is the least number of pages Gwen can type an hour to meet her boss's deadline?

1. You have just completed typing a report except for the table of contents. You have not numbered the pages as yet but have clipped all pages of sections together. Someone brushed the entire report off your desk. Show the proper order for collating the papers by listing on a separate sheet the specific report parts shown at the top of page 398.

Bibliography	Introduction
Title Page	Letter of Transmittal
List of Illustrations	Conclusions and Recommendations
Cover	Main Text
Appendix	Summary
Table of Contents	

2. Type the following in correct, topical outline form, making all necessary corrections in numbering, capitalization, or punctuation:

An Outline of a report on
COST OF ELECTRONIC CALCULATORS FOR HOME OFFICE

1. introduction:

   A. Purpose
      1. To recommend Improvements
      2. to increase profitability

   B. Need for Study
      1. To Examine effectiveness of present calculators:
      2. To determine Future calculating machine requirements.
      3. to Investigate costs of Various Models.

   B. Procedure —
      1. To secure Information from company files
      2. To Observe hours spent Using calculators
      3. To gather information from Salesmen.

2. Analysis of Information:

   A. Strong Points

   B. Weak Points

III. Proposed Solution:

IV. Conclusions and recommendations.

PART 2 TYPING BUSINESS REPORTS

Annette Perkins has typed many reports since she graduated from high school and is quite familiar with the procedures for setting margins, typing headings, numbering pages, and typing quoted material and footnotes. However, every report presents new problems in typing that must be solved either by checking a reference book or by deciding which way of presenting an idea, a picture, a graph, or a chart will be easiest for the reader to understand. Annette's employer, Mr. Raymond Marshall, allows Annette to make most of the decisions about such matters because she has displayed an unusual ability to apply rules to different situations and to present information in a logical way. Since Annette always considers the reader's reaction to Mr. Marshall's reports, her finished copies reflect her care in making them attractive.

One of the major responsibilities in preparing a report is typing the copy. By having a good understanding of procedures, methods, and shortcuts in typing a report, you can type the copy with great confidence of success. Carefully read the following material keeping in mind that you no doubt will type reports both in school and in the office.

SETTING THE MARGINS

The margins for typed reports are determined by the binding. If the following table of margins for unbound, side-bound, and top-bound reports is carefully followed, the report will be attractive.

MARGINS FOR TYPING BUSINESS REPORTS

Margins	Unbound	Side Bound	Top Bound
Top margin			
First page	2 inches	2 inches	2½ inches
All other pages	1 inch	1 inch	1½ inches
Side margins			
Left	1 inch	1½ inches	1 inch
Right	1 inch	1 inch	1 inch
Bottom margin	1 inch	1 inch	1 inch

Illus. 11-5

A light pencil mark about 1½" from the bottom edge of the page will alert you that you have but one line left to type at the bottom of the page. Be sure to erase this pencil mark when you are proofreading your final copy.

It may be helpful to use a guide sheet such as the illustration below. On a plain sheet of paper, make rulings with very dark ink to show the left and right margins. Numbering the horizontal lines on the right edge of the page is useful in allowing space for footnotes. The guide sheet is placed behind the original in the typewriter and followed for proper placement.

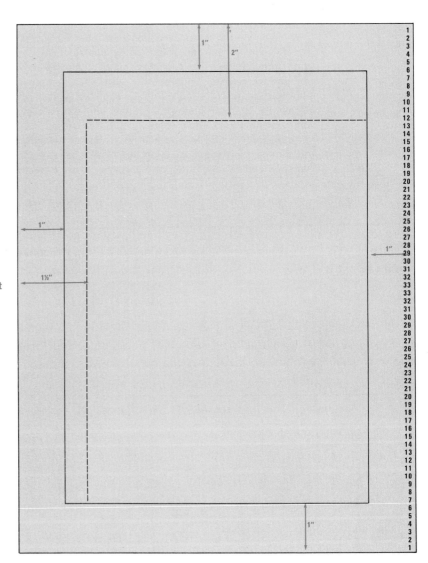

Illus. 11-6
Guide sheet
for reports

TYPING THE ROUGH DRAFT

A rough draft is your employer's first attempt to get his thoughts down on paper where they can be edited and improved. The draft may be revised and retyped many times; therefore, you will find the following ten suggestions helpful:

1. Use typing paper strong enough to withstand erasing easily. Do not use onionskin paper or expensive letterhead paper.
2. Type with double or triple spacing so that changes can be clearly marked and easily seen and followed.
3. Allow ample margins (1½ to 2 inches) at the top, bottom, and on both sides of each page to provide enough room for corrections.

Illus. 11-7
Preliminary work often precedes preparation of a report.

National Cash Register Company

4. *X* out typing errors and deletions in the first draft instead of taking time to erase them.
5. A carbon copy should be made in case the original is misplaced. You may also wish to have an extra copy to cut up when reorganizing the material.
6. Number each page in the draft in its proper sequence. Also assign a number to each successive revision of a draft and type the date on it.

7. Type a long insertion on a separate sheet of paper and give it a corresponding page number and letter. For example, the first insertion to be included on page 8 should be numbered "8A" and clearly marked "Insert 8A" at the point where it is to be inserted.

8. Type quoted matter of four lines or more single spaced and indent it in the same form as it will appear in the final draft.

9. Type footnotes single spaced at the bottom of the page, on a separate sheet, or, preferably, insert them in this manner immediately after the reference in the text but separated from the text by solid lines:

---

[1]James R. Meehan, William R. Pasewark, and Mary Ellen Oliverio, Clerical Office Procedures (5th ed.; Cincinnati: South-Western Publishing Co., 1973), p. 410.

---

10. Keep all rough drafts in a file folder until the final draft has been approved. Your employer may decide to include words, phrases, and sentences deleted from previous drafts in the final draft of his report.

Need for Proofreading

statistics:
a collection of
numerical data

All typewritten reports and manuscripts should be proofread carefully. The text can be checked most effectively, particularly if it contains **statistics**, by having one of your co-workers read the original copy aloud to you while you check the reading against the final copy.

You must also be absolutely sure that all figures in the report are accurate. An incorrect letter in a word is undesirable, but seldom does this kind of error cause the reader to misunderstand the entire report. An incorrect figure, on the other hand, may mean the difference between a profit and a loss on a business transaction. You will find the following suggestions for reading and checking figures helpful:

1. Read 2948 as *two nine four eight*.
2. Read 0 (the number) as *oh*.
3. Read decimal point as *point*.
4. Read .00032 as *point oh oh oh three two*.
5. Read down columns, not up or across.
6. Verify totals by addition. This is a double check on the original and on the copy.

The names of persons, places, and other proper nouns should be spelled by the reader, at least the first time that they appear in the copy, in order to avoid errors.

Use of Proofreaders' Marks

Proofreaders' marks are used to indicate corrections and revisions in rough drafts of business reports because they are clearly understood and easily followed. Their use greatly reduces the chance of error in the retyping of a draft. Standard proofreaders' marks, as they are indicated in a rough draft and corrected in the text, are shown below. You will need to know their meanings to type rough drafts of business documents efficiently.

PROOFREADERS' MARKS

Mark in Margin	Meaning of Mark	Correction or Change Marked in Text	Corrected or Changed Copy
⋀	caret; indicates insertion is to be made	If you are interested⋀we	If you are interested, we
⌒	close up	on the pay⌒roll	on the payroll
≡ or caps	capitalize	Mutual life of New York	Mutual Life of New York
¶	new paragraph	two or more lines. ¶One caution	two or more lines. One caution
⌐	move to right	centered over the ⌐columns and then typed	centered over the columns and then typed
⌐	move to left	cc: Joseph H. Morrow ⌐Gerald A. Porter Allen A. Smith	cc: Joseph H. Morrow Gerald A. Porter Allen A. Smith
tr or ∼	transpose	monthly be⌒fits	monthly benefits
ℒ	take out; delete	We wished you	We wish you
stet	leave it as it was originally	commencing starting next month	starting next month

Illus. 11-8 Proofreaders' marks

TYPING THE FINAL DRAFT

The final draft of a business report should be typed on white bond paper (8½″ x 11″ in size) of good quality, preferably of 20-pound substance. The body of the report, except for footnotes and long quotations,

CHAPTER ~~11~~ III

PROPOSED SYSTEM IN PRINCIPLE

stet The system ~~discussed~~ *outlined* below would eliminate the need for all punched card installations in any of the branch offices. This would virtually eliminate the need for over time during the peak season. It would also provide weekly reports of the expenses and remaining balances in all branches. An improved method for planning and controlling the work is outlined to *caps* enable the computer center to handle this system. ¶Savings under the proposed system are estimated at about $26,000 annually. The system anticipates continued growth in the size of Palmer Products and contemplates that in the future other processing functions will be added to those now processed by the Computer Center.

The following procedures are recommended for developing *stet* branch office budgets, for ~~ordering~~ *obtaining* all goods and services, for processing payments, and for preparing budgetary reports. The Budget Office would consolidate all funds for each branch office, regardless of the source, into single line amounts for each of the various items in order to facilitate control over expenditures. The line items would differ among branches, depending on what the largest items were. Many branches, however, would require ~~most of~~ the following line items: personal services, supplies,

Illus. 11-9
Rough draft report with proofreaders' marks

should be double spaced. The report should be typed so that it is attractive and easy to read. The typing line should be 6 to 6½ inches long: 60–65 pica spaces or 72–78 elite type spaces.

Title Page

The title page must be attractively typed with the information carefully spaced to give the page a balanced look. The information presented on the title page should be centered horizontally on the line of typing.

Letter of Transmittal

The letter of transmittal may be typed in any acceptable letter style. An illustration of an acceptable letter of transmittal appears on page 406.

```
                DATA PROCESSING OPERATIONS
                  PALMER PRODUCTS, INC.




                          For
               William L. Henderson, Vice-President
```

Illus. 11-10
Title page of a report

```
                          By
                Michaels, Singer & Smith
                 Management Consultants
                   708 Market Street
                San Francisco, CA  94102
                    415-621-6693


                  November 14, 197-
```

Table of Contents

The heading, *Table of Contents*, should be centered two inches from the top of the page and typed entirely in capital letters. Double spacing is used before the titles of chapters or main topics, and single spacing in all other instances. All important words in the chapter or main topic title should be capitalized. Important words include the first word and all others except articles (a, an, the), conjunctions (and, but, for, neither, nor, or), and prepositions (to, in, of, on, with). Each chapter title should be preceded by its number which is typed in capital Roman numerals and followed by a period and two spaces. The Roman numerals should be lined up with the periods directly beneath each other. Leaders (periods and spaces alternated) should extend across the page from each title to guide the reader in finding the page number at the right.

MICHAELS, SINGER & SMITH

708 Market Street   Management Consultants

San Francisco, CA 94102   415-621-6693

November 14, 197-

Mr. William L. Henderson
Vice-President
Palmer Products, Inc.
555 Madison Avenue
New York, NY 10022

Dear Mr. Henderson

Accompanying this letter is the report covering our study of data processing operations at Palmer Products, Inc. The report proposes a new data processing system for your firm--first in principle and then in detail-- and suggests a plan of action.

The system proposed would eliminate the need for a punched card installation in any of your branch offices and would provide you with weekly reports of the expenditures and remaining funds in all your branches.

We estimate that annual savings of $26,000 would result from installing a new system. An initial outlay, however, of about $6,500 would be required for the new equipment which we are recommending.

We were materially assisted in our study by the cooperation of your staff and the others we interviewed. We would be pleased to discuss the contents of this report with you after you have had an opportunity to review it.

Sincerely yours

David R. Singer

David R. Singer

rkm

ii

Illus. 11-11
Letter of transmittal

TABLE OF CONTENTS

iii

Illus. 11-12
Table of contents

The periods in the leaders should be in vertical **alignment** also. This can be done easily by typing all periods at even numbers on the typewriter line scale. Before it is finally typed, the table of contents should be checked for correctness of titles and accuracy of page numbers.

alignment:
in line; lined up

List of Tables

The heading *List of Tables*, like all other main headings, is centered two inches from the top of the page and typed entirely in capital letters. The table numbers are typed in Arabic numerals followed by a period and two spaces. The first letter of every important word in the title of a table is typed with a capital letter. Leaders extend from the title to the Arabic page numbers at the right. Lists of charts and other illustrations are typed in the same form as the *List of Tables*.

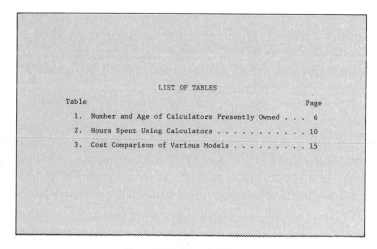

Illus. 11-13 List of tables

Body of the Report

The division headings in the body of the report should be the same as the titles that appear in the table of contents. Each division should begin on a new page with the word *Chapter* or *Section* centered two inches from the top of the page. It should be typed entirely in capital letters and followed by a chapter or section number typed in large Roman numerals. The title of the chapter or section is centered two line spaces below and also typed in capital letters. A very long title should be broken into two or more lines and divided at the point where the thought in the title changes. With a long title the **inverted** pyramid style may be used — the top line longer than the second, and the second line longer than the third. Three line spaces should be left between the title and the first paragraph of the report.

inverted:
turned upside
down

Page Numbers

Small Roman numerals (ii, iii, iv, etc.) are used to number the pages of the introductory parts of the report. The title page is considered as page "i" but no number is typed on it. The numbers are centered and typed one-half inch from the bottom of the page, and they are not followed by periods or any other punctuation.

consecutively:
following one after
the other;
continuously

Arabic numerals, without punctuation, are used to number the pages in the rest of the report. They begin with "1" and run **consecutively** throughout the report. The number on the first page of each section is centered and typed one-half inch from the bottom of the page. The pages that follow are numbered one-half inch from the top and even with the right margin. If the report is to be top bound, all page numbers are placed at the bottom of the page.

It is wise to number all pages at the same time after the entire report has been typed. If you type the numbers on the pages as you type the report and a rather long change has to be made, you will then have to renumber all pages following the change. Before page numbers are typed, they can be written in pencil on the first carbon copy, which will assist in keeping the pages in numerical order.

Headings

You will choose from several types of headings to improve the appearance of the typed matter and to indicate the relationship of its parts. Headings make a report easier to read and understand. If the material is well organized, the headings and subheadings will serve as a basic outline for the report.

Main Headings. Main headings are usually centered on the page and typed in all capital letters. A main heading is normally followed by a triple space.

Subheadings. There are basically two kinds of subheadings — side headings and paragraph headings.

Side Headings. Side headings are used to indicate major divisions of the main topic. They are typed even with the left margin with the main words starting with a capital letter. Side headings are followed by a double space. They may also be underlined.

Paragraph Headings. If the copy needs to be divided further, paragraph headings may be used. Paragraph headings are indented and underlined. Usually the main words of the heading are capitalized, and the heading is followed by a period.

CHAPTER VIII

FINANCIAL IMPLICATIONS

The proposed changes in the data processing system would result in substantial financial savings. An initial outlay of $6,500 would be required to get the proper equipment needed to perform all the functions of the consolidated operation. In spite of the initial outlay, however, it is estimated that the proposed system will save about $26,000 annually.

Projected Savings

By consolidating the data processing operations in the home office and eliminating the punched card installations in the branch offices, cost savings will accrue in many areas. The major areas where cost savings can be expected are equipment rentals, personnel, mailing, floor space, and storage.

Equipment Rentals. At the present time, each of the five branch offices is equipped with four punched card machines. The annual cost of renting each of these machines is $960. Since these machines would not be utilized in the proposed system, the gross annual savings in rental cost would be $19,200.

Illus. 11-14
A portion of a typed page of a report with headings and subheadings

Quoted Material

Material from other sources is frequently quoted in a business report to increase the effectiveness of the writer's point of view. All direct quotations should be typed exactly as they are written in the quoted source — in wording, spelling, punctuation, and paragraphing.

1. A brief quotation of fewer than four lines is typed in the text and enclosed with quotation marks.
2. A quotation of four lines or more is started on a new line and typed on shorter, single-spaced lines — indented from both the left and right margins. No quotation marks are used.
3. A quotation of several paragraphs need not be indented, but a quotation mark should precede each paragraph and should follow the final word of the last quoted paragraph.
4. A quotation within a quotation (an inside quotation) is enclosed with single quotation marks. The apostrophe is usually used to indicate a single quotation in typed material.

5. Omissions in a quotation are shown by typing an ellipsis — three spaced periods for an omission within a sentence. Four periods are used for an omission at the end of a sentence.

Permission should be obtained to quote copyrighted material if it is to be widely distributed in duplicated reports or printed manuscripts. Material may be quoted from government publications without permission.

Footnotes

Footnotes refer the reader to information outside the text of a report. They are inserted to acknowledge and identify the source of the quoted information, to support points made by the author, to provide additional material for the reader, or to elaborate on the meaning within the text. The Arabic number of a footnote is typed in the text just after the statement to be documented but slightly above the line of writing. For raised numbers, the platen is turned toward the typist a half space before the number is typed. The footnote itself, if it is the first reference to a particular work, should identify the author and the title of the work referred to, give facts about the publication of the work and the copyright date, and cite a specific page reference.

Later references to the same source need not repeat all these details; only *ibid.*, the abbreviation for *ibidem* (meaning in the same place), and the page number are used when references to the same work follow each other. The author's name, *op. cit.*, the abbreviation for *opere citato* (meaning in the work cited), and the page number are used when a previous reference has been made to the same source but other references are between. The author's name and *loc. cit.*, the abbreviation for *loco citato* (meaning in the same place), are used to refer to the same passage in a reference previously cited.

The footnotes below show the use of *ibid.*, *op. cit.*, and *loc. cit.*

----

[1]H. Webster Johnson, How to Use the Business Library (4th ed.; Cincinnati: South-Western Publishing Co., 1972), p. 148.

[2]Robert R. Aurner and Paul S. Burtness, Effective English for Business Communications (6th ed.; Cincinnati: South-Western Publishing Co., 1970), pp. 537-592.

[3]Ibid., p. 646.

[4]Johnson, op. cit., pp. 142-146.

[5]Aurner and Burtness, loc. cit.

Footnotes should be typed according to the following guides:

1. They are separated from the text by a short, solid horizontal line of 15 pica or 18 elite spaces.
2. The first line of the first footnote is typed two lines below the short horizontal line and is indented. The succeeding lines of the footnote begin at the left margin.
3. The reference number is typed slightly above the line of writing. It is typed without punctuation or a space between it and the first word of the footnote.
4. All footnotes are typed single space. A double space is used between footnotes.

Appendix

The word *Appendix* can be centered horizontally and vertically on a separate sheet of paper and used as the first page of the Appendix; or you can treat the first page of the Appendix as a special page and center the word *Appendix* two inches from the top of the page, and then continue with the material you want to include in the Appendix.

Bibliography

The Bibliography is a list of publications which are referred to in the report. They are listed in alphabetical order by author.

BIBLIOGRAPHY

One Author → Laurie, Edward J. Computers and Computer Languages. Cincinnati: South-Western Publishing Co., 1968.

Three Authors → Arnold, Robert R., Harold C. Hill, and Aylmer V. Nichols. Introduction to Data Processing. New York City: John Wiley & Sons, Inc., 1966.

Four or More Authors → Boynton, Lewis D., et al. Century 21 Accounting. Cincinnati: South-Western Publishing Co., 1972.

Magazine Article → Ockene, Arnold. "Computer Simulation--Can It Work for You?" Computer Decisions (January, 1970), pp. 32-37.

Yearbook → Arnstein, George E. "The Impact of Automation on Occupational Patterns," Recent and Projected Developments Affecting Business Education, National Business Education Yearbook, edited by Theodore Woodward. Washington: National Business Education Association, 1970, p. 39.

Unpublished Material → Wall, Lewis E. "Data Processing Institute Evaluation." Doctoral dissertation, Colorado State University, 1968

Newspaper → "President Declares War on Government Red Tape." Tulsa Herald. January 27, 1971, Sec. C, p. 2.

Government Document → U. S. Congress, Senate, Committee on the Judiciary. Implications of Computers in the Judiciary Process. 91st Congress, 2d Session. Washington: U. S. Government Printing Office, 1970.

Illus. 11-15
Examples of bibliographical forms

1. What determines the margins of typed reports?
2. How can a guide sheet help you in typing a report?
3. What is a rough draft?
4. What is the purpose of proofreading?
5. What are the advantages of using proofreaders' marks to show corrections in reports and manuscripts?
6. Why are leaders used in tables of contents and lists of tables?
7. Give the two kinds of numerals used to number the pages of a report or a manuscript, and indicate where each kind is used.
8. Describe two kinds of subheadings.
9. Why are materials from other sources quoted in business reports and manuscripts?
10. What information is contained in a footnote?

MAKING DECISIONS

1. Why is a typist permitted to *X* out typing errors and deletions in a rough draft of a report?
2. Give three suggestions for proofreading figures.

WORKING WITH OTHERS

After she graduated from high school, Roberta Butler was employed by an export-import firm as a stenographer. She was responsible for typing reports. When she was interviewed for the position, she was specifically told that her immediate superior would be Miss Hayes, the transcription supervisor.

Roberta became quite disturbed when Tina Davis, the stenographer at the next desk, gave her instructions about the typing of the reports, because Tina's instructions conflicted with those given by Miss Hayes.

Every afternoon Tina gave Roberta some of her own work. Tina said that she had too much work, but she was often away from her desk talking with the other girls.

Should Roberta have told Miss Hayes that Tina gave her conflicting instructions? Suppose Roberta did not tell Miss Hayes. How could she have handled the situation by herself?

USING LANGUAGE

On a separate sheet of paper type the following sentences and insert punctuation marks where needed. Change the dollar and decimal fractions to numbers.

1. We are studying the use of the period
2. The F B I is investigating Dr Green
3. The report was written in our office at St Louis, Mo on Jan 11, 197–
4. His grade average was eighty-seven point five
5. James H Smith recently won an award
6. It was two pm when he finished reading the report which left him little time to drive to the airport for his 345 pm flight
7. He bought 2 lbs of nails and 6 oz of tacks
8. The total account was eleven dollars and twelve cents
9. He read pp 120–25 before writing his summary
10. J N Jones left town today

USING ARITHMETIC

You have a pica typewriter (10 spaces to an inch). There are 6 vertical typewriter spaces to an inch. On a separate sheet of paper answer the questions at the top of page 413.

1. Where would you set your left and right margins for an unbound report?
2. Where would you set your left and right margins for a side-bound report?
3. How many lines from the top would you go down to type the page number?
4. What is the center point for a report that will be bound at the side?
5. If a report is to be bound at the side, at what point would you start typing each of the following lines on the title page:

COST OF ELECTRONIC CALCULATORS FOR HOME OFFICE
By
John A. Murray
January 11, 197–
El Paso, Texas

PERFORMING OFFICE TASKS

1. Prepare a guide sheet like the one shown on page 400.
2. Type the following five items of information in the form of a title page for a report:
   (a) Title: RESEARCH REPORT ON NEW PRODUCTS AND DEVELOPMENTS.
   (b) For: Thomas B. Carleton, President of the Smith Paper Company
   (c) By: Walter A. Starr, Director of Research and Development
   (d) At: Chester, Pennsylvania
   (e) On: November 30, 197–
3. Type the following TABLE OF CONTENTS with appropriate margins on a single page:

	Page
Letter of Transmittal	ii
Table of Contents	iii
List of Tables	iv
List of Charts	v
Summary	vi
Chapter	
I. Introduction	1
Prices	2
Outlook	3
Earnings and Dividends	4
Employment	5
II. Directors and Officers	6
III. Statement of Earnings	7
IV. Balance Sheet	8
V. Comparative Balance Sheets	9
VI. Accountants' Certificate	10
VII. Property, Plant, and Equipment	11
VIII. Inventories and Investments	13
IX. Disposition of Income	15
X. Research and Development	16

4. Type the following paragraphs in manuscript form with indented paragraph headings.

Incorporating an Established Business. Owners of sole proprietorships or persons doing business as a partnership may wish to incorporate the business and continue its operations as a corporation. In such a case, the same type of information is provided in the application for a charter as that provided when a corporation is formed to promote a new business. Each subscriber to the capital stock of the corporation indicates on the subscription list the number of shares of stock subscribed to and the method of paying the subscription when the charter has been granted. The owner or owners of the established business usually take stock in payment for their interest in the business.

Goodwill. Frequently the incorporators of a corporation being formed to continue the operations of an established business will agree to pay the owner of the established business more than the value of his proprietary interest in the assets of the business as shown by the balance sheet. This excess value is known as goodwill. The incorporators agree to pay more for the assets of the business than the owner's proprietary interest because the owner has an established trade, and the customers he has served will continue as customers of the corporation.

5. Type the following page from an annual report to the stockholders. The page is to be typed double space with margins set for binding at the side. The heading is *Research and Development.*

The Corporation's long-standing emphasis on research and development continues to be directed to new products, to improved products, and to more economical processes and equipment. These activities, located at Yorktown Heights, New York, are conducted to assure the future success of the Corporation. The organization is composed of separate groups with personnel well trained in scientific fields related to the Corporation's business, that is, in chemistry, in physics, in engineering, and in textile technology. Each group has adequate up-to-date facilities and equipment to do modern research in fields of expanding technology. (¶) The combination of the various technical talents at one location enables groups to conduct coordinated research on new fibers and packaging films — and basic or exploratory research directed toward the discovery of new products. Through research the competitive position of fiberglass tires has been improved by developing a method of processing fiberglass so that it is flexible and strong. As a result of this development, passenger car tires have been made even more durable under difficult road conditions.

PART 3

TYPING FINANCIAL STATEMENTS

Raymond Osby, while in high school, had taken a bookkeeping course in which he learned about financial statements that businesses use to let their owners and prospective investors know how the business is progressing. Not until he began to work for DuBois Chemical Company was he asked to actually process these statements. The manager of DuBois Chemical Company, Mr. Dennis Tolleson, placed some rough draft accounting reports on his desk and said, "Ray, these financial statements must be typed before Friday. Since you have had some training in bookkeeping, I am going to ask you to do this. If you have any problems, ask Mrs. Estes for help. You may get copies of previous statements from the files." Raymond realized that there is a big difference between studying financial statements and typing them. He realized that he would need considerable skill in setting the tabs and centering the material both vertically and horizontally on the page.

UNDERSTANDING FINANCIAL STATEMENTS

A business, like an individual, at times, needs a checkup. An individual reports to his family doctor to get a check on his physical condition. After examining the patient thoroughly, the doctor analyzes his findings and locates the cause of any physical problem the patient may have. The doctor is then able to prescribe medication for the problem.

Those who manage a business can discover the financial health of a business by studying reports called *financial statements*. The two reports common to all types of businesses which furnish the information necessary for management to determine the financial health of a business are the *balance sheet* and the *income statement*.

Balance Sheet

A balance sheet, like a physical examination, **reveals** whether a business is healthy on a particular date. Analysis of the three main parts shown in the balance sheet on page 420 enables management to tell whether, on a specific date, the business is well or sick. These three parts

reveals: shows; makes known

are (1) *assets* (what the business owns), (2) *liabilities* (what the business owes), and (3) *proprietorship* (the owner's share of the business). The proprietorship part tells what the business is worth, or assets minus liabilities.

On every balance sheet, the total assets always equal the total liabilities plus the proprietorship ($A = L + P$). The form of the balance sheet should make this basic bookkeeping equation obvious to the reader. Double lines typed beneath the figure representing *Total Assets* and beneath the figure representing *Total Liabilities and Proprietorship* attract the reader's attention so that he can see at a glance that the figures are equal.

Income Statement

The income statement shows the financial progress of the business. It shows how successful, or unsuccessful, a business has been during the period stated in the heading of the report: for example, "For the Year Ended December 31, 197–." Success is measured in terms of net income, or net profit. A *net profit* results when the income is greater than the expenses. A *net loss* occurs when the opposite happens.

Below the heading, the income statement shows in convenient form the income of the business, the cost of merchandise sold, the expenses, and the net income, or net loss, that resulted from the operation of the business during the fiscal period. The *fiscal period* is the time covered by the financial statement.

Some employers require that income statements include a column to show the percentage that each item listed is of net sales. For example, the income statement on page 421 shows that Merchandise Inventory, January 1, is 10 percent of sales; that Gross Profit is 13.9 percent; and that Net Income after Deducting Federal Income Taxes is 1.4 percent.

The double lines beneath the last dollar amount listed on page 421 make the Net Income after Deducting Federal Income Taxes of $28,594 immediately noticeable to the reader. Since this is the most important figure on the income statement, the emphasis is justified. By studying the remaining figures in the same column, the reader can understand why and how the profit or loss occurred. For more detailed information, the reader may study the remaining columns on the report.

PRODUCING TYPEWRITTEN FINANCIAL STATEMENTS

You will have several major responsibilities in producing final copies of the financial statements. If the statements are to be correct and pleasing in appearance, careful study and planning are necessary before you begin to type.

Study Previous Reports

Before you type any financial statements for your employer, it is a good idea to examine earlier copies of income statements and balance sheets in the company files. Because businessmen compare new financial statements with previous ones, they usually prefer that the same general form be followed year after year.

Check Accuracy of Calculations

With a calculating machine, check to make sure that the addition and subtraction shown on the rough draft submitted for typing are correct. It is also wise to verify, by machine, the accuracy of the addition and subtraction of the figures typed on the final typewritten product. This checks the typing accuracy of numbers.

Illus. 11-16
It is wise to use a calculating machine to verify the accuracy of the addition and subtraction of the figures on the final typewritten product.

Eastman-Kodak Company

Type the Financial Statements

A look at the financial reports of several companies would show many similarities, but no doubt would reveal some minor differences in style. Points of similarity might include the following:

1. *Use of descriptive titles to introduce groups of similar accounts.* For example, in the balance sheet on page 420, assets which, during the normal course of business operations, will be converted to cash are listed under the title Current Assets. Notice that the first letter of the first word and important words in these introductory titles is capitalized.

2. *Indentations from the left to indicate subdivisions of larger units of information.* In the income statement on

page 421, the depth of the horizontal indentations before Selling Expenses and Administrative Expenses indicates that both types of expenses are of equal importance; also that both are subdivisions of a larger grouping labeled Operating Expenses. The additional depth of indentation before Delivery Expense shows that it is a subdivision of Selling Expenses.

3. *Listing of important figures in the last column to the right on the financial statement.* A busy executive can get a good overview of the important parts of the balance sheet on page 420 by reading only the figures listed in the last column at the right.

4. *Use of commas in the amount columns to separate each three digits, beginning to the left of the decimal point.* For example, in the income statement on page 421, the Sales figure is $2,111,755.

5. *Vertical alignment of the decimal point in a column of figures.* Also, when one or more of the items in the amount columns indicate cents, every entry in any column should contain a decimal. For example:

$2,550.42
350.00
1,670.90
80.00

6. *A single line extending the width of the longest item in the column, typed beneath the last figure, to indicate addition or subtraction.*

7. *Double lines typed beneath a figure to identify the final figure in a column.*

8. *Use of leaders (a line of either spaced or unspaced periods) to guide the reader's eye from the explanation column to the first column of amounts.* Leaders are especially necessary when the items in the explanation column vary widely in the amount of horizontal space used or when, on single-spaced copy, there is so much space between the explanation column and the first amount column that the reader may lose his place as he reads across. Leaders should be aligned vertically on either even or odd spaces on the typewriter scale and should end at the same horizontal point.

9. *Information given in the heading of the financial statement.* Answers to each of the questions, Who?, What?, When?, should be given on separate lines in

that order. The balance sheet should answer the question, When?, with a specific date; the income statement will answer it with a phrase which identifies the fiscal period covered.

10. *Use of the dollar sign with the first figure listed vertically in each amount column.* In the balance sheet on page 420, notice that in the first column the Accounts Receivable figure ($96,500) includes a dollar sign. The same is true of the Cash figure ($31,534) in the second column and the Total Current Assets figure ($390,034) in the third column. Use a dollar sign with every figure which has double lines typed directly beneath it.

The important guideline to apply for minor points of style is to *be consistent.* Apply the test of consistency when making decisions related to the following points:

1. *Vertical spacing.*

    In deciding whether to single-space or double-space within a financial statement, consider:

    (a) Length of statement relative to the amount of vertical space available. The common practice is to avoid, if possible, two-page financial statements.

    (b) Ease of reading. Those who analyze financial statements are normally top-management people who have many demands on their time, attention, and efforts. Blank vertical lines scattered among single-spaced copy attract attention; therefore, use them for emphasizing especially important figures.

2. *Capitalization*

    (a) In the heading. Some businessmen prefer that the entire heading of financial statements be typed in all capitals; others require all capitals for only the name of the business. The current **trend** seems to be away from the practice of using all capitals for every word in the heading of a financial statement.

    trend:
    general direction

    (b) In the explanation column. Common practice is to capitalize the first letter of the first word and each important word included in the explanation column. (This practice is followed in both the income statement on page 421 and the balance sheet on page 420.) However, some businessmen prefer that only the first character of an account title be capitalized: for example, Accounts payable.

STANDARD PRODUCTS
Balance Sheet
December 31, 197-

Assets

Current Assets:
```
  Cash....................................   $ 31,534
  Notes Receivable......................     26,120
  Accounts Receivable...................   $96,500
    Less Allowance for Bad Debts.......    1,900      94,600
  Merchandise Inventory.................              232,600
  Store Supplies........................                4,817
  Office Supplies.......................                  154
  Prepaid Insurance.....................                  209
  Total Current Assets..................                          $390,034
Fixed Assets:
  Store Equipment.......................   $27,000
    Less Allow. for Depr.--Store Equip.    8,860    $ 18,140
  Delivery Equipment....................   $20,000
    Less Allow. for Depr.--Del. Equip..    5,940      14,060
  Office Equipment......................   $ 8,000
    Less Allow. for Depr.--Off. Equip..    4,200       3,800
  Buildings.............................   $75,000
    Less Allow. for Depr.--Buildings...   21,600      53,400
  Land..................................              20,000
  Total Fixed Assets....................                          109,400
Total Assets............................                         $499,434
```

Liabilities

Current Liabilities:
```
  Notes Payable.........................   $ 40,900
  Accounts Payable......................     71,614
  Employees Income Taxes Payable........      1,490
  FICA Taxes Payable....................        435
  State Unemployment Taxes Payable......        147
  Federal Unemployment Taxes Payable....        930
  Federal Income Taxes Payable..........     19,518
  Total Current Liabilities.............                        $135,034
Long-Term Liabilities:
  Mortgage Payable (20-year, 5%)........                          65,000
Total Liabilities.......................                        $200,034
```

Proprietorship

```
Capital Stock...........................   $250,000
Retained Earnings.......................     49,400
Total Proprietorship....................                         299,400
Total Liabilities and Proprietorship....                        $499,434
```

Illus. 11-17 A balance sheet

STANDARD PRODUCTS
Income Statement
For Year Ended December 31, 197-

				% of Net Sales
Income from Sales:				
Sales...............................		$2,111,755		100.6
Less: Sales Returns and Allowances...... $	5,642			
Discount on Sales.................	6,113	11,755		.6
Net Sales............................			$2,100,000	100.0
Cost of Merchandise Sold:				
Merchandise Inventory, January 1, 197-..		$ 209,800		10.0
Purchases............................ $2,288,650				
Less: Purchases Ret. & Allow....$152,900				
Discount on Purchases..... 304,850	457,750			
Net Purchases........................		1,830,900		87.2
Cost of Merchandise Available for Sale..		$2,040,700		97.2
Less Merchandise Inventory, Dec. 31,197-		232,600		11.1
Cost of Merchandise Sold...............			1,808,100	86.1
Gross Profit on Sales....................			$ 291,900	13.9
Operating Expenses:				
Selling Expenses:				
Delivery Expense...................... $	20,573			1.0
Depreciation of Delivery Equipment....	4,813			.2
Depreciation of Store Equipment.......	2,420			.1
Miscellaneous Selling Expense.........	6,294			.3
Sales Salary Expense.................	112,894			5.4
Store Supplies Expense................	15,117			.7
Total Selling Expenses...............		$ 162,111		7.7
Administrative Expenses:				
Bad Debts Expense..................... $	1,100			.1
Depreciation of Buildings.............	3,000			.1
Depreciation of Office Equipment......	932			*
FICA Taxes............................	5,800			.3
Federal Unemployment Taxes............	930			*
Insurance Expense.....................	2,037			.1
Miscellaneous Administrative Expense..	3,195			.2
Office Salary Expense.................	58,403			2.8
Office Supplies Expense...............	1,951			.1
State Unemployment Taxes..............	3,139			.1
Total Administrative Expenses........		80,487		3.8
Total Operating Expenses.................			242,598	11.6
Net Income from Operations...............			$ 49,302	2.3
Other Income:				
Interest Income......................		$ 940		*
Other Expense:				
Interest Expense.....................		2,130		.1
Net Subtraction.......................			1,190	.1
Net Income before Deducting Federal Income Taxes			$ 48,112	2.3
Less Federal Income Taxes...............			19,518	.9
Net Income after Deducting Federal Income Taxes			$ 28,594	1.4

*Percent is less than .1

Illus. 11-18 An income statement

3. *Colon*

A colon following a title is used to introduce like accounts (for example, on the income statement a colon following Income from Sales:). The colon indicates that a listing follows.

4. *Indentations*

The depth of the indentations depends on the amount of horizontal space available in relation to the number of horizontal spaces needed to type the necessary columns across the page. The important thing to remember is that units of equal importance (such as Selling Expenses and Administrative Expenses on the income statement on page 421) should be indented the same number of spaces.

5. *Abbreviations*

Since two-line entries in the explanation column are commonly avoided (because they interfere with readability), abbreviations within financial statements are acceptable. However, an abbreviation assigned to any one word (such as "Allow." for "Allowance") should be consistently used in the same financial statement. (See the balance sheet on page 420.)

Proofread the Final Product

Proofreading is easier, faster, and more accurate if the person reading the final typewritten product does not have to glance back and forth from the original to the copy being proofread. Either (1) ask another worker in the office to help — choose one who is particularly good at noticing details, or (2) dictate from the original copy onto a dictating machine and then check the final draft as you listen carefully to the recording.

The oral reader should be careful to indicate all capitalization, punctuation, use of dollar signs in figure columns, underscores, blank vertical spacing, and depth of indentations. Unless emphasized orally, these are details which are likely to be overlooked by the proofreader.

A common technique for proofreading columns of dollar amounts is to read down the columns, rather than across the columns.

File Carbon Copy of Final Draft

Before filing the carbon copy, write on it the name of the person responsible for the original preparation of the financial statement. Some businessmen require that the rough draft original submitted to the typist be filed along with the carbon copy of the final typewritten product.

1. Name three kinds of information contained in a balance sheet.
2. What basic bookkeeping equation should be obvious to one looking at a typed balance sheet?
3. What is the purpose of the income statement?
4. What is *net profit*?
5. Why do businessmen ordinarily prefer that financial statements follow the same basic form, or design, year after year?
6. Of what use is a calculating machine when processing a financial statement?
7. What is the purpose of leaders extending from the explanation column to the first column of figures?
8. What questions are answered by the heading of a balance sheet and income statement?
9. What is the most important guideline to remember when making a decision on typing style?
10. Of what significance are depths of indentation from the left margin on financial statements?

1. Some believe that the person who typed the final copy of the financial statement should proofread while a second person reads orally from the original. Others believe that the person who typed the final copy should be the oral reader and a second person, one unfamiliar with the task, should do the proofreading on the final copy. Which is your choice and why?
2. Should a typist redesign the form and style of financial statements?

Barbara is a part-time employee working at Mr. Jones's office during the summer. It is time for the Monthly Production Report to be typed, and Mr. Jones has given Barbara the necessary information to complete the final copy. Barbara is uncertain about the style she is to use.

What action should Barbara take before attempting to type the final report?

Three important uses of the colon are:

1. To introduce a long or formal *direct* quotation

   Example: The President began his talk with these words: "It is on an occasion such as this that we must all remember that we are bound by ties of brotherhood, tradition, and learning."

2. To introduce a number of examples or a formal list of any sort which contains a *summarizing* word

   Example: The company introduced the following five products in one year: Filcron, Vinylplas, Polycrest, Nycrin, and Depron.

3. To introduce an independent sentence or clause when the second gives an illustration of a general statement in the first

   Example: The purpose of a newspaper should be twofold: It should be the friend of all that is good and the foe of all that is evil.

Type the following sentences on a separate sheet of paper and apply the above colon uses correctly.

1. The Chairman of the Board began his address by saying it is with deep emotion that I must submit my resignation effective June 30, since the United States

Government has requested that I assume the presidency of an organization in South America dedicated to relieve the poverty and suffering of our neighbors in Peru and bordering countries.

2. Bring with you the income statement, the balance sheet, the December monthly report, and the sales and production figures for January to date.

3. Every detail indicated that Jim was interrupted at his work and intended to return to it the uncovered calculator, the unfinished income statement in his typewriter, the totaled columns of figures on his desk, the uncapped fountain pen.

4. Her original contention was justified that in time those who study, prepare their assignments, and apply themselves to their classes will receive good grades and be ready to accept positions in business offices.

5. We learned that the following six terms are found on the balance sheet current assets, fixed assets, current liabilities, long-term liabilities, capital stock, and retained earnings.

USING ARITHMETIC

On a separate sheet of paper work the following problems and then verify your answers with a calculator, if available.

1.	$	799.85		4.	$	869.97
		432.02				745.32
		108.70				587.03
		569.65				730.25
		634.98				696.50
		853.04				507.61
		227.13				122.03
	$				$	

2. $997,982.74
  − 865,897.99
   $

5. $21,080.04
  − 9,549.77
   $

3. $2,546.74 ÷ $7,097.45 =

PERFORMING OFFICE TASKS

1. Prepare a balance sheet dated December 31 of this year for the Watson-Vaughn Company using the following information:

Current Assets: Cash $29,290; Notes Receivable $10,340; Accounts Receivable $92,300; Less Allowance for Bad Debts $1,500; Merchandise Inventory $194,320; Store Supplies $6,127; Office Supplies $538; Prepaid Insurance $369; Total Current Assets $331,784.

Fixed Assets: Store Equipment $21,400, Less Allowance for Depreciation of Store Equipment $4,310; Delivery Equipment $25,000, Less Allowance for Depreciation of Delivery Equipment $4,100; Office Equipment $7,300, Less Allowance for Depreciation of Office Equipment $2,500; Total Fixed Assets $42,790.

Total Assets: $374,574.

Current Liabilities: Notes Payable $8,000; Accounts Payable $24,000; Employees Income Taxes Payable $1,200; FICA Taxes Payable $539; State Unemployment Taxes Payable $152; Federal Unemployment Taxes Payable $1,300; Federal Income Taxes Payable $20,412; Total Current Liabilities $55,603.

Long-Term Liabilities: Mortgage Payable (20-year, 5%) $55,000.

Total Liabilities: $110,603.

Capital Stock $238,000; Retained Earnings $25,971; Total Proprietorship $263,971.

Total Liabilities and Proprietorship: $374,574.

Be certain to check the calculations with a calculating machine.

2. Prepare an income statement for the Allison Cosmetics Company for the year ended December 31 of this year with the following information:

Income from Sales: Sales $3,250,850; Less Sales Returns and Allowances $6,420; Less Discount on Sales $8,750; Net Sales $3,235,680.

Cost of Merchandise Sold: Merchandise Inventory (January 1) $350,000; Purchases $3,540,600; Less Purchases Returns and Allowances $190,200; Less Discount on Purchases $540,700; Net Purchases $2,809,700; Cost of Merchandise Available for Sale $3,159,700; Less Merchandise Inventory (December 31) $420,000; Cost of Merchandise Sold $2,739,700. Gross Profit on Sales $495,980. Operating Expenses: Selling Expenses: Delivery Expense $28,500; Depreciation of Delivery Equipment $6,200; Depreciation of Store Equipment $3,600; Miscellaneous Selling Expense $8,300; Sales Salary Expense $132,500; Store Supplies Expense $20,400; Total Selling Expenses $199,500. Administrative Expenses: Bad Debts Expense $2,100; Depreciation of Buildings $4,500; Depreciation of Office Equipment $1,500; FICA Taxes $6,600; Federal Unemployment Taxes $1,300; Insurance Expense $3,900; Miscellaneous Administrative Expense $4,800; Office Salary Expense $72,700; Office Supplies Expense $2,400; State Unemployment Taxes $4,300; Total Administrative Expenses $104,100; Total Operating Expenses $303,600.

Net Income from Operations $192,380.

Other Income: Interest Income $1,400.

Other Expense: Interest Expense $3,300; Net Subtraction $1,900.

Net Income before Deducting Federal Income Taxes $190,480.

Less Federal Income Taxes $91,430.

Net Income after Deducting Federal Income Taxes $99,050.

PART 4 TYPING LEGAL PAPERS

Joyce Keith has been employed by Mr. Herman Packard and Mrs. Jane Porterfield, attorneys-at-law, since she graduated from high school two years ago. Joyce has always had an interest in legal work; so she welcomed the chance to learn more about the field of law by working in an attorney's office. Joyce types a wide variety of legal documents, including contracts, wills, deeds, and leases that have been recorded on a dictating machine. Joyce has accumulated a file of the most commonly used kinds of legal documents and uses these to guide her when typing the documents which Mr. Packard and Mrs. Porterfield give her each day.

legal:
lawful; valid

witnesses:
those who observe the signing of an instrument and later can swear that a signature is genuine

There are various kinds of **legal** papers, or documents — contracts, wills, deeds, leases, affidavits, powers of attorney. Some may be typewritten; others are printed and merely require filling in various blanks to complete them. Some require the services of a notary public; others require **witnesses** only. You will at one time or other be called upon to type or complete a legal document.

TYPEWRITTEN LEGAL PAPERS

Legal documents may be typed on standard 8½″ x 11″ paper; however, most are typed on legal size paper which is 8½ inches wide and varies from 13 to 15 inches in length. This paper may have printed left and right margin lines. The left margin rule is usually a double line; the right margin, a single line. In typing material on legal paper with printed margin rules, you should set the margin stops on your typewriter so that the margins of the typewritten material will be at least two spaces within the printed margin lines. If paper without printed margin rules is used for typing a legal paper, you should allow a 1½-inch left margin and a ½-inch right margin. Minimum margins of 2 inches at the top and 1 inch at the bottom are usually allowed. You should prepare enough carbon copies of all legal papers so that each person affected by the paper will have a copy, including at least one copy for the lawyer and one for the court record. Or your office may use a photocopying machine which will eliminate carbons by allowing you to type the original and photocopy the other needed copies. An example of a typewritten legal document is shown on page 432. Note particularly the space between the printed margin lines and the left and right margins of the typewritten material, the spacing (triple spacing between the title and the first line, double spacing thereafter), the use of all capitals for certain words in the contract, the punctuation, and the arrangement of the closing lines.

Spacing

Typewritten legal documents are usually double spaced, but you may single-space some of them, including wills and affidavits (a sworn statement in writing made under oath).

Legal paper may be purchased with consecutive numbers printed down the page at the left of the printed left margin line. The number "1" is approximately two inches from the top edge and indicates the position of the typewritten title. The other numbers indicate the positions of the typewritten lines of material and make possible easy reference to any particular part of the legal paper when its contents are under discussion. If the legal paper used does not contain these printed numbers, and if your employer wants to have them on the completed document, it will be a simple matter for you to type them as you type the document.

Erasures

Because a legal paper states the rights or privileges and duties or obligations of the parties who sign it, and later may be submitted in a court of law as evidence, you should prepare each paper accurately and proofread it carefully. You may erase and correct some errors in typing legal papers; others may not be corrected. If the error and erasure affect only one or two letters in a relatively unimportant word, you may erase and make the correction. If, on the other hand, the error you make involves a word which might be important to the meaning of that part of the contract — substituting the word *may* for *must*, for example — or, if an error involves an amount of money, name, or date, the erasure should not be made but the complete paper should be retyped. In some cases, however, such corrections may be made if the corrected paper is initialed by all parties. If you are in doubt, you should ask your employer if it is necessary to retype the legal paper or if it is permissible to erase and correct the error.

Numbers, Dates, and Titles

Quantities in legal documents are usually written in both words and figures, as shown on the next page.

Illus. 11-19
Some corrections
will require retyping
a legal document.

IBM Corporation

A scholarship of one thousand dollars ($1,000)
Under the terms of the will he will receive five thousand
(5,000) dollars
A twenty- (20) year mortgage
Fifty (50) shares of Woolworth common stock
Five (5) percent interest

Dates are written in several forms. No one form, however, is more legal than another; therefore, there is no reason why you should not type a date in a legal form as you would type it in a letter. Variations are:

On this, the sixteenth day of June, 19—
This 16th day of June in the year 19—
This sixteenth day of June, in the year of our Lord, nineteen hundred and seventy-three

Personal titles — Mr., Mrs., Miss — are not used with names in legal documents. Professional titles — Dr., Prof. — are not ordinarily used either.

PRINTED LEGAL FORMS

Legal documents may be prepared by typing the necessary information on a printed legal form. Standard forms for bills of sale, deeds, leases, mortgages, and wills may be purchased in stationery stores. However, important legal documents, even though they are on a printed form, should be checked by a lawyer.

When typing on printed legal forms, if the item of information that is filled in is important, such as a sum of money, the space that remains on either side of the item after it is typed should be filled in with hyphens. This eliminates the possibility of figures, letters, or words being added later to change the meaning of the typewritten insertion.

The same margins used for the printed matter should be used for the typewritten matter. When carbon copies are prepared, the position of the printed matter on each copy must be checked carefully so that the typewritten additions will appear in the proper places on all copies. Unless this check is made, the typewritten matter on a carbon copy may be written over some of the printed matter, and the copy may be illegible.

NOTARIZED LEGAL PAPERS

Many legal documents are *notarized*. This means a signed statement is added by a notary public (a public official authorized by the state) to show that the paper has been signed in the notary's presence and that the signers have sworn that they are the same persons referred to in the document. The statement by the notary public usually is typed at the bottom of the same paper on which the legal document is typed. It may be typed on a separate page, however, if there is no room for it on the page that contains the legal material.

Illus. 11-20
Statement of a
notary public

State of   FLORIDA, DADE   **County. ss.**

Be It Remembered, *That on the*   first   *day of*   May

in the year of our Lord nineteen hundred and   --   *, before*

me a   notary public   *in and for said county, personally came*

John E. Hansen, Evelyn M. Hansen, and Charles L. Burroughs

the parties named in the foregoing Lease, and acknowledged the signing thereof to

be   their   *voluntary act and deed.*

In Testimony Whereof, *I have hereunto subscribed my name, and affixed my*

official seal on the day and year aforesaid.

(SEAL)   _Judith F. Mahle_
                                        Notary Public
                                        My commission expires May 31, 197-

Do not be surprised if your employer wishes you to become a notary public. In large offices one of the employees usually acts in this **capacity**. In an office building containing a number of small offices, an employee in one of them may act as a notary public for all the offices.

The laws for becoming a notary public differ in the various states. In many states an application accompanied by statements that show that the applicant is a citizen and a resident of the state, of the required age, and of good character is submitted to the governor's office. If the application is granted, the notary public obtains a notary's seal, which is a metal, hand-operated instrument that embosses on a legal paper the design of a seal containing the name of the notary. A notary's commission is for a limited period of time, usually for two years, but it may be renewed.

TYPICAL LEGAL DOCUMENTS

A discussion of a simple contract, a will, a deed, a lease, an affidavit, and a power of attorney — legal papers that are frequently prepared in a business office — will explain the typing problems involved.

Simple Contract

A *contract* is an agreement that can be enforced at law. It creates legal rights and responsibilities. It may be either oral or written; however, some contracts, such as those for the purchase of real estate, must be in writing. Before you type a contract, you should check to see that it includes the essential information listed on page 431.

Illus. 11-21
Accuracy is necessary for the legal typist.

Allied Chemical
Corporation

1. The date and the place of the agreement
2. The names of the parties entering into the agreement
3. The purpose of the contract
4. The duties of each party
5. The money, services, or goods given in consideration of the contract
6. The time period
7. The signatures of all the parties

The illustration on page 434 shows parts of a simple contract prepared on legal paper with printed margin lines.

Will

A *will* is a legal document in which a person provides for the distribution of his property after his death. The person who makes the will is the *testator* (man) or *testatrix* (woman). He may designate an *executor* (man) or *executrix* (woman) to probate his will, that is, prove its **validity** to the court for the purpose of carrying out its provisions. Making a will is a technical matter and should be entrusted only to a qualified attorney. Illustration 11-22 on page 432 shows a properly prepared and correctly typed will.

validity:
having objective truth or generally accepted authority; soundness

Deed

A *deed* is a formal written instrument by which title to real property is transferred from one person to another. All the details of the transaction should be approved by a lawyer before it is registered with the proper government agency.

Lease

A *lease* is a contract by which one party gives to another the use of real or personal property for a fixed price. This relationship exists when one person, the *lessee*, under an express or implied agreement, is given possession and control of the property of another, the *lessor*. The amount given by the lessee is called *rent* (for real property) or *consideration* (for personal property).

The lease shown on page 433 illustrates the typing problems involved in completing a printed form for a legal document. Observe where typewritten material has been inserted, the method of indicating the amount in words and figures, and the completion of certain words by adding letters that keep the sentences containing those words consistently in plural form.

LAST WILL AND TESTAMENT OF WILLIAM H. STEWART

I, WILLIAM H STEWART, a resident of the City of Trenton,
State of New Jersey, declare this to be my Last Will and Testament, and revoke all former Wills and Codicils.

FIRST: I declare that I am married, and wife's name is
MARJORIE DAVIS STEWART; I have two children now living, DAVID
H. STEWART and STEPHEN C. STEWART.

SECOND: I direct that my just debts and funeral expenses
be paid.

THIRD: I give, devise, and bequeath to my wife, MARJORIE
DAVIS STEWART, all the rest of my estate both real and personal
and wheresoever situated, which I may own or have the right to
dispose of at the time of my decease.

FOURTH: I appoint as Executrix of my Will my wife,
MARJORIE DAVIS STEWART, to serve without bond. In the event
she is unable or unwilling to serve, or to complete such service as Executrix, then it is my wish that HOWARD PATTON, a
long-time friend of mine, shall be appointed as Executor.

This Will and Testament is subscribed by me on the eighth
day of December, 1972, at Trenton, New Jersey.

William H. Stewart

The foregoing instrument, consisting of one page, was subscribed on the date which it bears, by the testator, WILLIAM H.
STEWART, and at the time of subscribing was declared by him to
be his Last Will and Testament; and we, at the testator's request and in his presence and in the presence of each other,
have signed such instrument as witnesses.

Ida M. Turner residing at 703 Bunker Hill Avenue
Trenton, New Jersey

Anne Hemmerle residing at 513 New York Avenue
Elizabeth, New Jersey

Illus. 11-22 The format of a will

This Lease Witnesseth:

THAT   John E. Hansen and Evelyn M. Hansen, husband and wife,

HEREBY LEASE TO   Charles L. Burroughs

the premises situate in the   City   of   Miami   in   the   County   of

Dade   and State of   Florida   described as follows:

     Building to be used as a restaurant located at 232 Collins Avenue, Miami, Florida

with the appurtenances thereto, for the term of   ten (10) years   commencing

June 1,   19 72 at a rental of Two hundred fifty (250)

dollars per month   , payable monthly.

     SAID LESSEE AGREE S to pay said rent, unless said premises shall be destroyed or rendered untenantable by fire or other unavoidable accident; to not commit or suffer waste; to not use said premises for any unlawful purpose; to not assign this lease, or underlet said premises, or any part thereof, or permit the sale of his interest herein by legal process, without the written consent of said lessor S; to not use said premises or any part thereof in violation of any law relating to intoxicating liquors; and at the expiration of this lease, to surrender said premises in as good condition as they now are, or may be put by said lessor S, reasonable wear and unavoidable casualties, condemnation or appropriation excepted.   Upon nonpayment of any of said rent for thirty days, after it shall become due, and without demand made therefor; or if said lessee or any assignee of this lease shall make an assignment for the benefit of his creditors; or if proceedings in bankruptcy shall be instituted by or against lessee or any assignee; or if a receiver or trustee be appointed for the property of the lessee or any assignee; or if this lease by operation of law pass to any person or persons; or if said lessee or any assignee shall fail to keep any of the other covenants of this lease, it shall be lawful for said lessor s, their   heirs or assigns, into said premises to reenter, and the same to have again, repossess and enjoy, as in their first and former estate; and thereupon this lease and everything herein contained on the said lessor s ' behalf to be done and performed, shall cease, determine, and be utterly void

     SAID LESSOR S AGREE   (said lessee having performed   his   obligations under this lease) that said lessee shall quietly hold and occupy said premises during said term without any hindrance or molestation by said lessor s, their   heir or any person lawfully claiming under them.

     Signed this   first   day of   May   A. D. 19 72

IN THE PRESENCE OF:

Louis K. Whitfield   John E. Hansen

Robert R. Crowell   Evelyn M. Hansen

                         Charles L Burroughs

Illus. 11-23 Lease

Affidavit

An *affidavit* is a written statement made under oath that the facts set forth are sworn to be true and correct. It must be sworn to before a proper official, such as a judge, justice of the peace, or a notary.

Illus. 11-24
Parts of a legal
document typed on
legal paper

AGENCY CONTRACT

This agreement, made and entered into on this, the fifth day of June, 19--, by and between THE JOSLYN MANUFACTUR-ING COMPANY, a corporation of Muncie, Indiana, the party of the first part, and ROBERT M. BERGOLD, of Dallas, Texas, the party of the second part,

WITNESSETH: That, whereas, the party of the first part is about to open a branch office to be located in Dallas, Texas, for the sale of its products, the said party of the first part hereby engages the services of Robert M. Bergold, the party of the second part, as manager of that office.

The party of the first part hereby agrees to pay the

first part from time to time.

IN WITNESS WHEREOF, The parties have hereunto affixed their hands and seals on the day and in the year first above written.

THE JOSLYN MANUFACTURING COMPANY

Witnesses:

G. M. Van Pelter   *Francis P. Burnett* (Seal)
                              President
                       Party of the First Part

Ken A. Maclin

                       Robert M. Bergold (Seal)
                       Party of the Second Part

Power of Attorney

A *power of attorney* is a legal instrument authorizing one person to act as the attorney or agent of the grantor. An employer may give a trusted employee his power of attorney — the power to act for him. It may authorize the employee to sign checks and other legal documents for him. The power of attorney specifies the acts which the agent (the employee) is authorized to perform for the principal (the employer). It may be granted for an indefinite period, for a specific period, or for a specific purpose only. It must be signed by the principal and should be notarized.

REVIEWING WHAT YOU HAVE READ

1. In what ways does legal paper differ from other paper used in business?
2. What are the minimum margins usually allowed on typewritten legal paper?
3. What is the advantage of using legal paper on which the lines are numbered?
4. What type of error may be erased and corrected in a legal paper?
5. How are quantities usually written in legal papers?
6. How should words be filled in on a printed legal form?
7. What is meant by the term *notarized*?
8. What is a contract?
9. Describe the difference between *rent* and *consideration* as used in lease agreements.
10. What is an affidavit?

MAKING DECISIONS

1. Is a typing error in a legal paper more serious than a similar error in an important business letter?
2. Why is it an advantage for an office worker to be a notary public?

WORKING WITH OTHERS

Rosa was busy with her usual work when her employer, Mr. Adams, asked her to type a contract at once so that it could be signed by Mr. Lara and Mr. Cook who were waiting in his office. When proofreading the contract later Rosa found an error in the amount of money. What should she do?

USING LANGUAGE

There are four important usages for parentheses ():

1. To enclose figures or letters that mark a series of enumerated elements.

    Example: Mr. Keith asked for three things: (1) the contract, (2) his reference book on business law, and (3) the addresses of the persons who signed the contract.

2. To enclose figures verifying a number which is written in words.

    Example: The agreement specified that two thousand dollars ($2,000) would be paid monthly for the use of the equipment.

3. To enclose matter that is only indirectly related to the main thought of the sentence.

    Example: At 3:30 p.m. (the time agreed upon at the conference the evening before) the meeting began.

4. To enclose matter introduced as an explanation.

    Example: He told her to check the *Federal Reserve Bulletin* (March, 1971) page 103 for a review of the case.

Type the following sentences and insert parentheses where necessary.

1. Some typical legal documents are a a will, b a deed, c a lease, and d a power of attorney.
2. The lease specified that for a term of ten 10 years rent was to be two hundred fifty 250 dollars a month payable monthly.
3. He left at 4:30 he had told them he would leave at 3:30, but he arrived at the airport in time to get on the plane.
4. You may name an executor man or an executrix woman to probate your will.
5. The amount given by the lessee is called *rent* for real property or *consideration* for personal property.

USING
ARITHMETIC

Jan Collins has worked in a law office a number of years. Her employer has asked her to prepare a schedule of payments for a lease agreement. The lessee agrees to pay rent monthly for a leased building at the rate of $10 a day for one year, beginning January 1 of next year. Rent is due in advance on the first day of each month. On a separate sheet of paper prepare a schedule showing each month's payment.

PERFORMING
OFFICE
TASKS

1. Type the following power of attorney, making one carbon copy. Use the current date. If printed forms are available, complete the form by adding the information printed in italics. You may also use ruled legal paper (or you may rule in ink the necessary vertical lines on regular 8½" x 11" paper) and type all parts.
   NOTE: *A power of attorney is a formal written document used for the appointment of an agent.*
   KNOW ALL MEN BY THESE PRESENTS, That *I, Ernest W. Dunn, of the City of Beverly, County of Essex, State of Massachusetts*, have made, constituted, and appointed, and by these presents do make, constitute, and appoint, *Merrill J. Martin, of the City of Salem, County of Essex, State of Massachusetts, my* true and lawful attorney, for *me* and in *my* name, place, and stead, *to sign my name to any and all checks drawn on the First National Bank against my deposits in the same, for the purchase of the property situated at the corner of State Avenue and Congress Street, known as the Randolph property; and I hereby ratify and confirm all that my said agent or attorney will lawfully do, or cause to be done, in connection with this purchase.* (¶) IN WITNESS WHEREOF, *I* have hereunto set *my* hand and seal this _____ day of _____ in the year of our Lord nineteen hundred and _____.

   _____

   Witnesses:

   _____

   _____

   State of Massachusetts ⎫ ss.
   County of Essex ⎭

   The above signed authority, *Ernest W. Dunn*, personally appeared before me on the _____ day of _____ in the year of our Lord nineteen hundred and _____, and in due form acknowledged the attached instrument to be his act and deed and declared that it may be recorded as such.
   (SEAL)

   _____
   Notary Public

2. If printed forms for a warranty deed are available, complete an original copy and one carbon copy of that form by adding those parts of the following information that are printed in italics. Use the current date.

   If printed forms are not available, type an original copy and one carbon copy of all parts of the following warranty deed.

KNOW ALL MEN BY THESE PRESENTS:

THAT I, William W. Fredericks, of Rochester, in the County of Strafford and State of New Hampshire for and in consideration of the sum of *One Dollar and other valuable consideration* to *me* in hand before the delivery hereof, well and truly paid by *James McGuire, of said Rochester*, the receipt whereof I do hereby acknowledge have granted, bargained and sold, and by these presents do give, grant, sell, alien, enfeoff, convey and confirm unto the said *James McGuire, his* heirs and assigns, forever, *a certain tract of land situated in Wakefield, in the County of Carroll and State of New Hampshire, on the easterly side of Route 16, so-called, the same being the highway from Wakefield to North Wakefield, bounded as follows:*

Beginning on the easterly sideline of said highway at a stone wall at land formerly of B. Hull, thence by said wall easterly and thence northerly by wall and by stakes and stones and by trees marked "line" to land formerly of M. C. Denicore at Blake field, so-called; thence easterly by said field to land formerly of John C. Peak and the Peter Carroll lot, so-called, formerly owned by John W. Matthews; thence southerly by said Carroll lot to the Peter Carroll place, as it was once called; thence westerly by said Carroll lot and George L. Williams lot, as it was once called, to the aforesaid highway; thence northerly by said highway to the bounds begun at, the same containing forty (40) acres, more or less.

For title reference see deed of Edward Daniels to Albert Swain dated July 30, 1914, recorded Carroll County Records, Book 160, Page 306, the grantor hereof having obtained his title by devise under the will of the late Albert Swain, see Carroll County Probate Records.

TO HAVE AND TO HOLD the said premises, with all the privileges and appurtenances to the same belonging, to *him* the said *James McGuire* and *his* heirs and assigns, to *their* and *their* only proper use and benefit forever, and *I* the said *William W. Fredericks* and *my* heirs, executors and administrators do hereby covenant, grant and agree, to and with the said *James McGuire* and *his* heirs and assigns, that until the delivery hereof *I am* the lawful owner of the said premises, and *am* seized and possessed thereof in *my* own right in fee simple; and have full power and lawful authority to grant and convey the same in manner aforesaid; that the premises are free and clear from all and every incumbrance whatsoever, except _____ and that *I* and *my* heirs, executors and administrators, shall and will WARRANT and DEFEND the same to the said *James McGuire* and *his* heirs and assigns, against the lawful claims and demands of any person or persons whomsoever.

And, I, *Josephine Fredericks*, wife of the said *William W. Fredericks*, in consideration aforesaid, do hereby relinquish my right of dower in the before mentioned premises.

And we, and each of us, do hereby release, discharge and waive all such rights of exemption from attachment and levy or sale on execution, and such other rights whatsoever in said premises, and in each and every part thereof, as our Family Homestead, as are reserved, or secured to us, or either of us, by Chapter

260, Revised Laws of the State of New Hampshire, or by any other statute or statutes of said State.

IN WITNESS WHEREOF, *we* have hereunto set *our* hands and seals this *23rd* day of *January* A. D. 197–.

_____

_____

STATE OF NEW HAMPSHIRE
County of *Strafford*

On this *23rd* day of *January* 197–, before me, the undersigned officer, personally appeared *William W. Fredericks and Josephine Fredericks* known to me (or satisfactorily proven) to be the persons whose names *are* subscribed to the within instrument and acknowledged that *they* executed the same for the purposes therein contained.

IN WITNESS WHEREOF, I hereunto set my hand and official seal.

(SEAL)

_____

_____

Title of Officer

UNIT 12

PURCHASING AND RECEIVING

CLERK

Good at figures. Assist M
handise Manager & Buyers
ving office of major d
e.
MR. BELL   274-9

Part 1 The Purchasing Function
Part 2 Clerical Purchasing and Receiving Procedures

PART 1   THE PURCHASING FUNCTION

Over two hundred years ago Benjamin Franklin warned about the dire consequences of not having enough supplies on hand when he wrote in *Poor Richard's Almanac*, "A little neglect may breed great mischief . . . for want of a nail the shoe was lost; for want of a shoe the horse was lost; and for want of a horse the rider was lost."

When Ralph Lyons graduated from high school, he accepted a position as a general clerk in the Purchasing Department of Allied Industries. Ralph's starting assignment was to work with purchase requests for office supplies and equipment that amounted to less than $500. First, he had to be sure that each requisition had been signed by the person who was actually responsible for ordering. He then had to decide where to get the requested items, usually beginning with the suppliers' (sellers') office products catalogs.

Ralph soon found out that his work covered only the first step, but a very important one, in the ordering process. The purchasing process required the cooperative efforts of many people — some in Allied Industries and others in outside firms. He discovered that, after the purchase requisitions left his desk, the items were listed with their stock numbers on purchase orders, receiving orders, inventory records, and accounts payable records. Finally, after the sellers' invoices had been verified and approved, Allied Industries issued checks to pay for the requisitioned items.

After he had been on the job for about a month, Ralph realized that he had a great deal to learn about purchasing and that it would require at least a year of training and on-the-job experience before he could be considered for promotion. He hoped, however, that within a few years, with the necessary experience and proper supervision, he would become an assistant buyer, the first position in the Purchasing Department requiring highly specialized knowledge of buying products and services.

Let's review the procedures of the important function of purchasing. Understanding them will help you to succeed in a position like Ralph's and make it easier for you to be promoted to a better position.

THE IMPORTANCE OF PURCHASING

Have you ever gone to a store to get a special brand of jeans or slacks or a particular record or album or perhaps a special food product, only to be told that the item was not in stock or had not been unpacked or was not carried by that store? Annoying, isn't it? Not only has the store lost your confidence in its ability to serve you, it has also lost a sale — if you don't settle for a substitute. So, purchasing goods and receiving them are important functions of that store and, in fact, are important in all businesses.

Let's take a look at why purchasing is important in a large company. In companies that manufacture goods, the amount of money used to purchase materials that go into the final product is one of the largest single costs in the entire operation. Did you know that more than half of every dollar that the typical manufacturer receives for selling his product goes toward paying for the material he purchased to make that product? Moreover, inability to obtain materials causes slowdowns in delivering goods to the market. You can readily see that purchasing is a vital function of the typical manufacturing firm. This is true of all types of businesses.

In your home there are probably many "purchasing agents" for the many articles your family uses. In large firms the job of obtaining materials, supplies, and services is handled by a separate purchasing department headed by a purchasing agent. The purchasing agent may have people working for him, called *buyers*, who buy special products for the firm because they know those products or materials very well and know which companies provide the best quality at the lowest price. The purchasing agent and his buyers in a large firm are assisted by a staff of office workers who know how to handle all the steps in the purchasing process. In small companies the purchasing agent or a department head, assisted by one or more purchasing and receiving clerks, may make up the entire purchasing section.

GUIDELINES FOR PURCHASING GOODS

Whether the buying is done by a purchasing agent, a department head, a purchasing clerk, or a general clerk, the aims are the same — to obtain the needed materials, supplies, and services of the desired quality for the firm at the most reasonable price. The responsibility for purchasing is often described as "*buying materials from the right source, of the right quality, in the right quantity, at the right time, and at the right price.*"[1]

---

[1]S. F. Heinritz and P. V. Farrell, *Purchasing: Principles and Applications* (4th ed.; Englewood Cliffs, New Jersey: Prentice-Hall, Inc., 1965), p. 7.

The Right Source

Choosing the right source from which to purchase goods and services is very important. In fact, many purchasing agents believe that if you choose the right source you will automatically get the right quality, the right price, and delivery will be on time.[2]

In order to buy properly, you must find the right source — a reliable supplier. You can then enter into an agreement with the supplier not only upon the price, but also upon the quality of the product and a suitable schedule of delivery as well. A supplier, or seller, who can be depended upon to meet delivery deadlines and standards of quality can very often ask and get a higher price for his products. The buyer, in looking for a dependable supplier, is often willing to pay more for this "right source."

Salesmen. When you shop, do you ever ask the salesman, "Which is better? Which gives the best wear? Which is the more popular? Which would *you* buy?" Do you depend on his advice, or at least take it into consideration when deciding on what to buy?

Salesmen are perhaps the most important source of information for all types of purchases. An effective salesman can give you the uses, advantages, and limitations of every product in his line of **merchandise**. He can suggest new uses for some of his products and can give advice on ways to cut costs and increase productivity by using his company's

merchandise:
things bought and
sold; goods; wares

---

[2]*Ibid.*, p. 157

products. When new products or ideas are introduced, he may be the first to tell you about them. Very few products or services are sold without the efforts and assistance of salesmen.

In all businesses, salesmen call regularly to acquaint buyers with their products. They may call to introduce a new or less expensive item, to discuss a proposed change in price, to help solve problems created by the use of their products or services, to obtain a larger share of the business, to talk about a new contract for supplies or services, or to answer a call for information or assistance.

One of the most important duties of the employees in the purchasing department is **conferring** with salesmen. If you are employed in a department that receives salesmen, you should treat them in a courteous, businesslike manner and see to it that their appointments are properly scheduled and promptly kept. Professional and courteous treatment of salesmen will establish the best kind of business relationship between the buyer and the seller.

conferring:
talking;
exchanging ideas

Catalogs. If you are asked to buy a product, the best place for you to find it may be in the catalogs of the leading suppliers. Trade catalogs with price lists are available to all business firms interested in purchasing a particular line of products. In addition to stock numbers and descriptions of the products, catalogs usually provide the **list prices** for single and quantity purchases of the specific items.

list price:
basic price of an item as published in a catalog, but subject to trade, quantity, and other discounts

Trade Directories. You will find that nationally and internationally known products and services are listed in publications known as *trade directories.* These directories list the names, addresses, and telephone numbers of most of the manufacturers and wholesalers of a particular product or service. One widely used type of trade directory is the Yellow Pages of the telephone directory. It lists the dealers and distributors in your town in alphabetic order under subject headings. For example, under "Air Conditioning Equipment & Supplies" the first three listings might be A & A Air Conditioning and Heating, ABM Air Conditioning and Refrigeration, and AC Air Conditioning and Heating.

Wholesalers. When a company buys in small quantities, it will probably buy from a local wholesaler. A *wholesaler* is a middleman who buys in large quantities from the manufacturer and sells in small quantities to small firms and to individual buyers. After the wholesaler buys the merchandise from the manufacturer he usually stores it in a warehouse and sells it mainly through salesmen. Ordinarily he grants credit to his customers and makes deliveries to their places of business. The wholesaler is the retailer's usual source of supply for goods in steady demand.

Central Markets. There will be times when a purchasing agent or buyer won't be able to get all the purchasing information he needs from salesmen, catalogs, or trade directories. He may then visit the central market for the goods he needs. Central markets are large cities where many suppliers of a particular line of goods are located. For example, New York City, Dallas, San Francisco, and Los Angeles are central markets for wearing apparel. Central markets for furniture are located in Chicago; Grand Rapids, Michigan; Jamestown, New York; and High Point, North Carolina. Central markets for shoes are found in Boston, Chicago, and St. Louis. Chicago leads in the producing and marketing of radio and television sets.

There are several advantages to making a trip to a central market. Often, looking at an illustration in a catalog or even seeing a salesman's samples will not tell a buyer what he needs to know. By going directly to the central market, he can look at the actual goods. In addition, many different suppliers are usually located close to each other in the central market so that he can see and compare all their merchandise in a relatively short time. This also permits him to make a better selection from the goods offered by the various suppliers.

The Right Quality

How do buyers get the right quality of merchandise for their firms? If you are a buyer, you would probably buy the highest grade of bond paper for typing contracts and other important legal documents that will be kept for years. On the other hand, you would probably buy an inexpensive grade of paper for telephone message forms which will be destroyed just as soon as the call is returned.

Once the decision about the right quality is made, the buyer attempts to obtain goods of that quality. The practices of buyers differ widely in their efforts to obtain merchandise of the right quality. To be **assured** of the right quality, one buyer may choose only brands produced by well-known manufacturers. Another may prefer products sold by established suppliers with reputations for making good if the buyer is not completely satisfied with the purchase item. The right quality may have to be obtained by matching a sample, and the buyer will purchase only from the seller who can come closest to the sample.

There may be times when products will have to be made especially for your firm. In those cases the purchasing department will give several suppliers all the details, or **specifications**, about the product. The buyer then orders the product from the supplier that can produce goods closest to the specifications and at the best price.

assured:
sure; certain

specifications:
detailed descriptions of requirements, dimensions, materials, etc.

The Right Quantity

The right quantity means the right amount to buy at a given time—a quantity that will permit the operation to continue on schedule without any interruption. Some items must be purchased to fill an immediate shortage or to fill specific departmental **requisitions**. So that better prices can be obtained, whenever possible the needs of all departments are combined into a single large order and are usually limited to one quality or grade, such as one grade and size of business envelopes, letterheads, carbon paper, and office pencils. Complete and accurate records on the buying and distribution of stocked items can serve as a very reliable guide in deciding whether a stocked item should be bought in small, medium, or large quantities.

The Right Time

An efficient buyer always tries to buy at the right time. Items should not be purchased in such small quantities that frequent purchases create a great deal of unnecessary paper work, nor should purchases be in such large quantities that they create large inventories and cause storage problems. Nor should the buying of an item be delayed until a rush order has to be placed, because the delivery charges for rush orders greatly increase the cost per unit. If you work in a purchasing department, one of your duties may be to keep an exact count of stock items on file cards; and, when the supply drops to a certain level, you will have to reorder the item immediately. Reordering in large manufacturing companies that have hundreds of thousands of stock items, such as aircraft companies, is often done almost automatically because the stock inventories are kept by computers.

The Right Price

Price is also a very important factor which must be considered when buying a product. However, price should not be the only factor to be considered. Other important factors to be taken into account are the quality of the product, the delivery charges, the credit terms, and whether or not the supplier is dependable. The price of a product is determined by several factors including (1) the cost of producing it, (2) the supply available and the number of customers who want it, (3) the delivery charges, and (4) the price of a competing product.

PAYING FOR GOODS

Before a transaction is completed, both the buyer and the seller should have a clear understanding of the terms of purchase — the time that the buyer is given to pay his bill and any discounts that will be offered. Sometimes goods are sold on a COD (cash on delivery) basis, and the customer has to pay for the goods when he receives them. In most instances, however, the buyer is allowed to pay for the goods sometime after the shipment is made, usually thirty days later.

Three general types of discounts are available to the buyer — a quantity discount, a trade discount, and a cash discount.

Quantity Discount

gross:
12 dozen or
144 items

A quantity discount is offered to the buyer as a reward for ordering in large quantities. For example, pencils may be listed in a wholesale stationer's catalog at 90 cents a dozen or $7.20 a **gross**. If bought by the dozen, the pencils cost 7½ cents each ($.90 \div 12 = .075$); if bought by the gross, the same pencils cost 5 cents each ($\$7.20 \div 144 = .05$). The quantity discount for buying by the gross in this transaction amounts to 2½ cents a pencil or 33⅓ percent.

Trade Discount

A trade discount is a special discount offered by manufacturers to wholesalers and retailers to encourage them to stock that particular manufacturer's line of goods. Trade discounts are based on the suggested list price, the price printed in the manufacturer's catalog. For example, the catalog of an office equipment manufacturer may show the suggested list price of a five-drawer, letter-size file cabinet with a lock as $100. To retailers this file may be subject to a 40 percent trade discount. In that case the retailer would pay only $60 for the filing cabinet.

$100.00 — Suggested list price
—40.00 — Trade discount ($100 \times 40\% = \$40$)
$ 60.00 — Retailer's cost price

The retailer would then sell the file cabinet at the list price of $100 and would make a *gross profit* of $40 on the transaction. Expenses for rent, taxes, store utilities, salaries, employee fringe benefits, and so on must then be deducted from the gross profit of $40 to arrive at a *net profit* of approximately $4 on each $100 sale for the retailer.

Instead of offering just one trade discount, many manufacturers offer a series of two or more discounts. One of the advantages of offering a series of discounts is that it permits the manufacturer to raise or lower prices without going to the expense of printing and distributing new catalogs. If the prices must be changed, all the manufacturer has to do is send a notice to all potential buyers that the discount rates have been changed. For example, suppose the manufacturer of file cabinets found that his costs had increased. He might send a notice to his customers saying that instead of a single trade discount of 40 percent they would now receive a discount series of 20 percent, 20 percent, and 2 percent. The file cabinet with the suggested list price of $100 would then cost the retailer slightly more than $60. This is true because the three discounts are applied to the ever-decreasing amounts and would actually be less than 40 percent. The series discounts of 20 percent, 20 percent, and 2 percent on $100 would be figured as follows:

$100.00 — Suggested list price
−20.00 — *First* discount of 20 percent ($100 × 20% = $20)
$ 80.00 — Amount remaining after taking the first discount
−16.00 — *Second* discount of 20 percent ($80 × 20% = $16)
$ 64.00 — Amount remaining after taking the second discount
− 1.28 — *Third* discount of 2 percent ($64 × 2% = $1.28)
$ 62.72 — Retailer's cost price — the amount remaining after taking the third discount

The retailer would then sell the file cabinet at the list price of $100 and make a gross profit of $37.28.

Cash Discount

A cash discount is offered to customers to encourage prompt payment within a specified period, usually ten days after the date of the sales invoice. It differs from a quantity discount or a trade discount because it is a reward for prompt payment.

Illus. 12-2
Document conveyor routes checks to clerks to be checked against bills

To be granted a cash discount it is seldom necessary for the buyer to pay as soon as the goods are shipped or even as soon as they are received. The usual practice is to allow the buyer ten days from the date of the sales invoice, which is usually the date the goods are shipped. The ten-day period generally provides enough time for the goods to arrive, for the buyer to unpack and inspect them, and to process the sales invoices for payment. Thus, if you, the buyer or customer, receive goods costing $700 shipped on September 15 with terms of 2/10, net 30 days, what can you do? You can decide to take advantage of the 2 percent discount of $700 by paying in ten days; or you can wait 30 days and pay the full amount of the bill. If you decide to pay by September 25 to take advantage of the discount, you save $14 and pay $686.

$700.00 — Full amount of invoice shipped on September 15
—14.00 — Less cash discount of 2 percent ($700 × 2% = $14)
$686.00 — Net amount payable by September 25

If you decide not to take advantage of the cash discount, the full amount of the invoice, $700, is due and payable exactly 30 days from September 15 — on October 15.

REVIEWING WHAT YOU HAVE READ

1. What are the typical duties of a buyer in a purchasing department?
2. What factors would you take into consideration in trying to find the right source for the buying of goods or services?
3. What is perhaps the most important single source of information about all types of purchases?
4. What is a *list price* and how does it differ from other prices?
5. What services, other than permitting them to buy in small quantities, does a wholesaler ordinarily grant to retailers?
6. What are the advantages of buying at a central market?
7. What are the major disadvantages of buying small quantities in rush orders?
8. What are four factors that determine the price of a product?
9. Why is a cash discount granted to a buyer?
10. If the terms of an invoice dated April 19 are 2/10, net 30 days, what is the last date on which you may take advantage of the cash discount? On what date will the full amount of the invoice become due and payable?

MAKING DECISIONS

Assume that you are employed as an assistant buyer in the purchasing department in the home office of a large oil company. One day just after closing, a stationery salesman phones from a firm you have never heard of, the Comet Office Products Company, and offers to sell you cotton fiber paper at $2 a ream less than the normal market price. You know that cotton fiber paper, originally called rag content paper, is one of the finest grades of paper and is ideally suited for the stationery needed in the executive offices.

However, the salesman says that he cannot give you a written report on the quality of the paper, the price, and the quantity to be shipped, which you ask for, because the paper is selling out so fast. Furthermore, he claims that, because of the very low price, all shipments must be made on a COD basis.

Should you (1) accept the salesman's offer for the low-priced cotton fiber paper?, (2) reject the offer?, (3) tell the salesman that you will have to talk to the purchasing agent who has left for the day before making a decision? The salesman points out that the paper may be completely sold out by the time he hears from you.

WORKING WITH OTHERS
Early one very rainy morning, as Carol Martin was going into the lobby of her office, she noticed a peddler on the sidewalk doing a brisk business in telescopic umbrellas. Suddenly, on an impulse, she bought one from the street merchant for $3.

During her lunch hour Carol priced umbrellas in a nearby department store. To her great satisfaction, she found that a telescopic umbrella with a lifetime guarantee that looked almost exactly like hers sold for $12. During the afternoon coffee break Carol, with a little encouragement from her co-workers, opened and displayed her new umbrella. Everything went well until she wanted to close it. Although almost everyone tried, no one could close it until a maintenance man succeeded with a pair of pliers. He then explained loudly that it was probably a second because the frame was bent but that "it would work all right if Carol used a pair of pliers every time she closed it."

Word of Carol's purchase spread through the office. When the messenger arrived for the last mail, he was humming "Raindrops Keep Falling on My Head." A few minutes later one of the buyer trainees approached Carol's desk and said, "Tomorrow is my wife's birthday. She wants a telescopic umbrella. I understand that you are an authority on buying these. Could you tell me where I could get the best buy?"

Leaving the office Carol confided to you that she had to control herself to keep from hitting the young buyer over the head with the umbrella.

What would you say to soothe Carol's ruffled feelings? Do you think Carol is justified in becoming angry because of her co-workers' teasing?

USING LANGUAGE
Three frequent uses of the dash are:

1. When a sentence is broken off and something entirely different added.
   Example: The company picnic will be — by the way, are you going to the picnic?
2. Before a statement, or even a single word, which summarizes a series.
   Example: Freight, salaries, raw material costs, use of equipment — these are some of the factors that affect the price of products.
3. In place of a comma to show emphasis.
   Example: If — and only if — great care is taken, the records will be accurate.

On a separate sheet of paper type the following sentences and insert dashes where required.

1. The purchasing agent, the assistant purchasing agent, one of the buyers these three were out of the office when the call came in.
2. When will the report be finished if it ever is?

3. When if ever will he complete the purchasing department's list of supplies needed?

4. When he learned how to figure the various kinds of discounts then and only then was he promoted to his present position.

5. Salesmen, catalogs, trade directories, wholesalers, central markets these are sources that purchasing departments use for buying goods.

USING ARITHMETIC

On a separate sheet of paper show your solutions to the problems below.

1. Figure the trade discount and the retailer's cost price of an executive's desk with a list price of $320 in the wholesaler's catalog less a trade discount of 40%.

2. Find the trade discount and the net amount of a sales invoice amounting to $1,500 if the trade discounts are 20% and 10%.

3. Which is greater — and by how much — a single trade discount of 25% on a sales invoice amounting to $360 or a series of trade discounts of 10%, 10%, and 6% on the same invoice?

PERFORMING OFFICE TASKS

Below are three typical office problems. Show your solutions to each on a separate sheet of paper.

1. If a wholesaler offers a retailer a series of trade discounts of 20%, 10%, and 10% on an onyx clock and pen desk set that lists for $125 in his catalog, what is the total amount of the discounts and what is the retailer's cost price?

2. If a filing cabinet with a suggested list price of $80 is sold by the wholesaler with a series of trade discounts of 20%, 20%, and 5%, what is the wholesale price of the filing cabinet?

3. If the terms of a sales invoice amounting to $645 shipped on October 19 are 2/10, net 30 days, what is the amount of the cash discount, the last date on which the cash discount can be taken, and the net amount payable on that date? If the cash discount is not taken when is the full amount of the invoice due and payable?

2 CLERICAL PURCHASING AND RECEIVING PROCEDURES

Fred Collins, president of the Camera Club during his senior year, answered the following Help Wanted advertisement when he graduated from high school:

Receiving-Stock Clerk

Responsible for receiving and storage. Able to handle paper work. Knowledge of cameras helpful. Call John Beck, Odell Camera Company, 4840 Robinson Road, 681-7388.

An Equal Opportunity Employer

Fred was interviewed and hired by this company which was a nationwide mail order business for cameras and film.

As a receiving clerk, he was expected to examine and count each shipment before signing the deliveryman's receipt book. He then checked the shipment with his copy of the purchase order before filling out the receiving record. He assigned a receiving number to each shipment before storing it.

Fred soon learned that the shipments received did not always agree with their purchase orders — some were incomplete, others arrived in unsatisfactory condition — thereby creating additional work for him and his co-workers. He found that shipments had to be handled carefully and the paper work completed accurately. The work proved to be most interesting because he was learning a great deal about cameras and the camera business.

PURCHASING PROCEDURES

Whether you are working in the purchasing or receiving department or in one of the other departments of a business, you will have to know and use correct purchasing procedures. Business firms have well-planned purchasing procedures. Each step is based upon the step before it. All purchasing usually follows this order: requesting the goods, supplies, or services needed; getting price quotations on what is needed; preparing the purchase order; checking the incoming shipment when it arrives; submitting any claims for overages, shortages, and damages (OS&D claims); and, finally, paying for the goods.

Stockroom Requisition

If you work as a file clerk in a large business and find that you need some file folders and guides, you request them from the stockroom. The request form that you give to the stockroom is called a *stockroom requisition*. On the stockroom requisition you give your name and department, the date, and a list of the supplies or materials which you need. Usually there is a space for your supervisor to sign the form indicating his approval.

Most businesses require several copies of the requisition in order to provide

1. An original and a carbon copy for the stockroom. The original will remain in the stockroom records. The

Illus. 12-3
Stockroom
requisition

STOCKROOM REQUISITION

Deliver to: SDR No. E-72-123

Name *Helen Mathis*   Department *Engineering* Authorized by *KEB*

Date *July 26, 7—* Unit *Filing* Tel. Ext. *356* Charge to Account No. *76-8557*

Quantity	Code No.	Description--Use Separate Line for Each Item	Accounting Use (Do not write in this space.)
50	56 WL-503	Blank metal tab pressboard guides	
100	56 WL-325	Manila folders	
150	56 WL-350-3	Heavyweight 3-tab manila folders	

carbon copy will be returned to you when you receive the materials or supplies that you ordered. If any of the items which you ordered are not in stock, this will be noted on the carbon copy that is returned to you.

2. A carbon copy for your supervisor, since he approved the requisition and may need a copy for accounting purposes.

3. A carbon copy for your files. When the requested materials or supplies are delivered, you may destroy this copy and keep only the copy that is returned by the stockroom.

Purchase Requisition

Sometimes you will order items that the stockroom does not normally have. You must then fill in a *purchase requisition* to let the purchasing agent or buyer know which specific items you need.

The purchase requisition must contain detailed information about the requested items. Unlike the stockroom requisition which remains within your firm, the purchase requisition must be sent to an outside firm in the form of a purchase order. In most cases you will find the detailed information you need in suppliers' catalogs. Information you need will include the name of the item, its catalog number, size, color, and price. The purchase requisition may also indicate the name and address of a firm from whom the goods may be obtained.

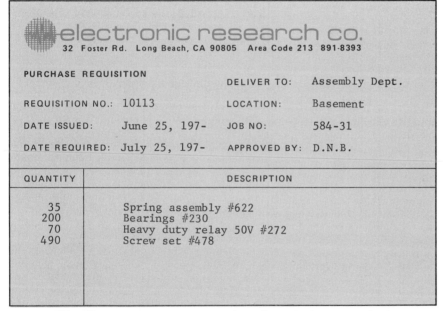

Illus. 12-4
Purchase
requisition

Usually you prepare two copies of a purchase requisition. You send the original to the purchasing agent and keep the duplicate in your files. Before forwarding the purchase requisition to the purchasing agent, you will need the approval of the person for whom you work. If you are employed by a large organization, you will probably be required to prepare an additional copy of each purchase requisition so that it will be available for the accounting department.

Request for Quotation

When your purchase requisition reaches the purchasing department, the quotation file is checked for prices. Purchasing departments keep a quotation file of the latest prices for the products that they buy, together with the names and addresses of the suppliers that furnish them. The quotation file is usually made up of 6″ x 4″ cards on which the necessary information about the products and their prices is recorded. The product will probably be ordered immediately if the latest prices are on file. If the latest prices are not available in the quotation file, it is customary to send a *request for quotation* to the business firms that sell the product. The purchasing agent decides which companies are most likely to furnish the product by referring to his own catalog file, to the *Thomas Register of American Manufacturers*, or to a similar general purchasing directory.

The request for quotation contains the name of the firm making the request, the current date, a description of the product, the quantity needed, and desired delivery date. To avoid any confusion on the part of the seller, the form is sometimes marked THIS IS NOT AN ORDER! in all capital letters.

Purchase Order

The products that you requisition may be ordered in any one of a number of ways — by giving an order to a salesman, by writing an order letter, by making a telephone call, by sending a telegram, by filling out and mailing an order blank that is included as part of a catalog, or by filling in a *purchase order* that has been especially designed for the purpose.

Illus. 12-5
Purchase order

electronic research co.
32 Foster Rd. Long Beach, CA 90805 Area Code 213 891-8393

PURCHASE ORDER

TO:	DATE	TERMS
BYRON JACKSON COMPANY 4998 Michigan Avenue Chicago, IL 60614	June 27, 197-	2/10 net 30

	ORDER NO.	SHIP VIA
	05202	REA

QUANTITY	CAT. NO.	DESCRIPTION	PRICE	TOTAL
35	622	Spring assembly	14.35 ea.	502.25
200	230	Bearings	3.35 ea.	670.00
70	272	Heavy duty relay 50V	7.50 ea.	525.00
490	478	Screw set	.03 ea.	14.70
				1,711.95

Illus. 12-6
The accuracy of all figures should be checked before mailing the purchase order.

Victor Business Machines

As a general rule, business firms prefer to use purchase orders which they mail to the **vendors**. If the products are needed immediately, they often are ordered by telephone or telegraph; but then a purchase order covering the transaction is prepared and mailed to the vendor or seller to serve as written confirmation of the order.

vendors: sellers

The purchase order bears the name, address, and telephone number of the firm issuing the order, the date the product is needed or the delivery schedule, the name and address of the vendor, the purchase order number, the quantity, the description of the items with their catalog numbers, the size of the items, the color, the price, the total amount of the purchase order, and the shipping instructions. Normally several copies of every purchase order are needed. Purchase order forms are made with carbon sheets between them so that all copies are made with one typing. After the copies have been signed by the purchasing agent, they are usually distributed in this manner:

Original.................To the vendor
First carbon copy........To the purchasing department to serve as a follow-up on the purchase order
Second carbon copy......To the department from which the requisition came
Third carbon copy........To the accounting department
Fourth carbon copy......To the receiving clerk

RECEIVING PROCEDURES

All purchases should be handled in a series of orderly steps when they arrive. These steps include the receiving, checking, recording, identifying, and storing of goods.

Receiving

A complete and accurate record should be made of all incoming shipments as soon as they are received. When goods arrive at the receiving point, the receiving clerk should examine the unopened cartons, packages, boxes, or barrels very carefully. The receiving clerk should count the packages, inspect the condition of each, and see that the number and condition of the packages are recorded in the deliveryman's receipt book. After the delivery receipt has been signed, a copy should be kept in case a claim for loss or damage should arise.

Checking

The receiving clerk next checks the goods received against a copy of the purchase order. If the check of the goods actually received does not agree with the quantities listed on the purchase order, the differences are brought to the attention of the purchasing agent. The receiving clerk also notes any items received in damaged condition. The purchasing agent will then inform the supplier of any differences in quantity or of any damaged goods.

Illus. 12-7
Receiving
record

RECEIVING RECORD

Date July 23 197- _____ No. 05202

From Byron Jackson & Co., Chicago, Illinois 60614

VIA REA _____ Express Charges $24.93

Memo _____

Quantity	Description of Articles
35	622 spring assembly
200	230 bearings
70	272 heavy duty relay 50 V
490	478 screw sets

Received by John Melvin

Recording

As the goods are checked, the receiving clerk fills in a *receiving record.* This is a record of the number of items received, the date, the vendor's name, the method of shipment, the transportation charges, and other facts about the receipt of the goods. The receiving record is very important because it is the first record of an incoming shipment. It is useful in determining whether goods have been received and whether they were in perfect condition.

The receiving record is completed accurately and carefully and often is distributed in this way:

Original................To the purchasing department
First carbon copy........To the accounting department
Second carbon copy......To be filed in the receiving department
Third carbon copy.......To the stockroom

Identifying

As soon as the shipment has been completely entered in the receiving record, it must be identified. This means that the receiving clerk must assign a receiving number to the entire shipment and must then mark each package in the shipment with that number. The clerk writes on each carton with a crayon or marking pencil the receiving number assigned to the shipment, the department for which the goods are intended, and the number of packages in the entire shipment. For example, the first carton in an eight-carton shipment for the Filing Department, with the assigned receiving number 33, would be marked *#33, Filing Dept., 1 of 8.*

Storing

Often goods received will not be used or needed immediately; so they must be stored properly. Items should be stored as close as possible to the location where they will be used and in such a way that the identifying marks can be read easily.

PURCHASING AND RECEIVING FORMS

There are many forms related to the purchasing and receiving functions which you will have to complete. Although some of the forms are handwritten, most are typed. All forms must be completed thoroughly and accurately.

Purchase Invoice

When the vendor ships the merchandise you ordered, he usually mails an invoice to your purchasing department on the same day. The invoice is known to the vendor as a *sales invoice* and to the purchaser as a *purchase invoice*. An invoice usually includes the current date, the name

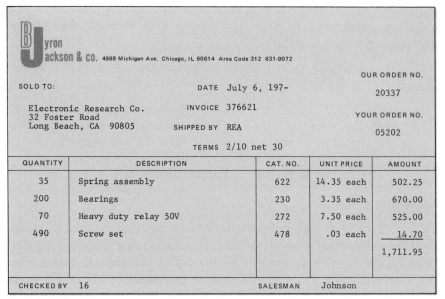

and address of the vendor, the name and address of the purchaser, the invoice number, the buyer's purchase order number, the terms of payment, and the method of shipment. In addition, for each item it lists the quantity shipped and a brief description of the item with its price and amount. The total amount of the invoice, with the shipping charges included, is usually shown at the bottom of the last column. The invoice may also show trade discounts and other deductions.

If you become a clerk in a purchasing department, it may be your responsibility to check the purchase invoice against the terms and conditions of the purchase order to be sure that they agree in quantity and price. If they agree, the date, amount, and invoice number are entered on the reverse side of the purchasing department's copy of the purchase order. When the invoice is approved by the purchasing department, it is stamped *APPROVED*, initialed by the proper authority, and then sent to the accounting department for payment.

Credit Memorandum

Sometimes goods will have to be returned to a supplier for one reason or another. The merchandise may have been delivered too late to be of value; it may be the wrong kind, style, or color; or it may arrived in a damaged condition. In cases such as these, the goods will be returned to the supplier with a letter requesting credit. The supplier will then issue a *credit memorandum* to your firm. The credit memorandum lists the items that were returned and the amount by which your firm's account has been reduced.

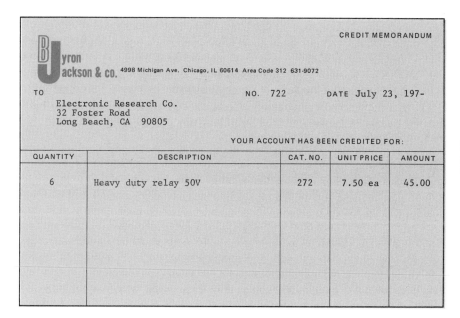

Illus. 12-9
Credit
memorandum

Follow-Up of an Order

You may find it necessary to write or call a supplier about the shipment of an order that you have placed with him, especially if the delivery date has been postponed; but there are times when suppliers are unable to meet their delivery schedules because of strikes, shortages, and other circumstances beyond their control.

A follow-up may be a personally dictated letter or a form letter, depending upon how much the shipment is needed. Sometimes telegrams are sent to indicate the very urgent need for a particular shipment. However, in some instances you will place a telephone call or send a teletypewriter message to the supplier to find out immediately why the shipment has not been made and when you may expect it.

A follow-up file should be kept in which copies of purchase orders are filed according to the date of their expected delivery. Late delivery may hold up production and prove to be very costly. A prolonged delay in a shipment of an order for seasonable or fashionable items may make the shipment worthless and cause cancellation.

PURCHASING ETHICS

Since the buyer and the seller need each other for the success of their businesses, they should both work to bring about a business relationship that is based on honesty and fair play. Experienced buyers and sellers know that it is to their mutual advantage to work together. When a seller makes an honest mistake and tries to correct it, the buyer, knowing that he is not always right, should allow the seller to do so. To be **inflexible** is not good business practice; keep in mind that if you, as the buyer, make a mistake, you will not want the same harsh treatment. As a buyer, you must consider the interests of your company first and try to carry out its established purchasing policies. You should try to buy wisely and with no favoritism to any organization. You should try to get the very best value for every dollar of the firm's money that you **expend**.

inflexible:
unyielding; rigid;
unable to bend

expend:
pay out; use

REVIEWING WHAT YOU HAVE READ

1. What is the purpose of a *stockroom requisition*?
2. What is the purpose of a *purchase requisition* and how does it differ from a *stockroom requisition*?
3. How does a *request for quotation* differ from a *purchase order*?
4. When placing orders, why do business firms prefer to use purchase order forms?
5. What information is contained in a *receiving record*?
6. If goods are not to be used as soon as they are received, where and how should they be stored?
7. What information is contained in a *purchase invoice*?
8. When is a *credit memorandum* issued?
9. Why would a business firm keep a *follow-up file* of purchase orders?
10. What would you do if one of your regular suppliers made an honest mistake in the price of an item sold to you?

MAKING DECISIONS

A large business organization placed notices in trade publications and sent letters to vendors saying: "Please do not give Christmas gifts to our purchasing agents or buyers. It is against our company's policy."

Despite these announcements, a vendor sent a portable color television set to a purchasing agent's home during the Christmas season.

What should the purchasing agent do about this gift? Would the fact that it was sent to his home rather than to his business office make any difference?

WORKING WITH OTHERS

Mary Young, the receptionist for Dr. Allan Brooks, a very prominent dentist, types and mails out the monthly bills.

Unfortunately, the bills rarely are mailed before the tenth of each month. If the statements were mailed earlier, payments would be received sooner.

Mary is confident that she could get out the statements earlier if she were permitted to use a new form. The present form contains horizontal lines for the name and address of each patient, but the lines do not agree with the vertical spacing on the typewriter, and the variable line spacer must be used to move from one line to another.

If you were Mary, what recommendation would you make for redesigning the statement? How would you convince the dentist of the value of a change in statement form?

USING LANGUAGE Several words listed below are misspelled. Type the entire list giving the correct spelling for each word.

1. appreciation
2. inclueded
3. industral
4. guarantee
5. government

6. jugment
7. neccessary
8. percentage
9. specefications
10. services

USING ARITHMETIC On a separate sheet of paper show your solutions to the problems below.

1. You recently purchased a used automobile for $750 plus 4% sales tax. The dealer offered you a discount of 2% if you paid cash for the car, which you accepted. How much did you pay for the car?

2. An office chair is listed at $50 with trade discounts of 30% and 10%. If the terms of sale are 2/10, net 30 days, and the invoice is paid within the cash discount period, what is the net cost of the office chair?

PERFORMING OFFICE TASKS If blank business forms are not available for the following office assignments, use plain paper and type forms that are similar to the illustrations in this part.

1. Type the following stockroom requisition in duplicate. (If you do not have a blank stockroom requisition, type one that is similar to the illustration on page 452.)

The following six requested items should be listed in the body of the stockroom requisition:

2 dozen	lead pencils No. 2
6 rolls	adding machine tapes, 2¼" wide
1 dozen	Erase-Rite typewriter eraser pencils
3 boxes	Swingline heavy duty standard staples
1 package	second sheets, color canary, size 8½" x 11"
2 boxes	carbon paper, plastic base, size 8½" x 11½"

2. Type the following purchase requisition in duplicate. (If you do not have a blank purchase requisition, type one that is similar to the illustration on page 453.)

The heading should contain the following information:

REQUISITION NO.: 1914; DATE ISSUED: May 18, 197–; DATE REQUIRED: June 18, 197–; DELIVER TO: Advertising Dept.; LOCATION: Second Floor; APPROVED BY: J. J. T.

The body of the purchase requisition should contain the following four items:

2 double pedestal general office desks, top size 60" x 30", No. 7401
2 swivel chairs, No. A4229
4 side chairs with arms, No. A4259
3 open front bookcases (3 shelves)
  42" high, 34½" wide, 11¼" deep, No. S42A

3. Type the following purchase order in duplicate. (If you do not have a blank purchase order, type one that is similar to the illustration on page 454.) The quantities and unit prices are given; you are to make all extensions and calculate the total.

PURCHASE ORDER NO. 1715 from:

MELROSE CORPORATION
7600 Tallman Avenue
Melrose Park, IL 60161

TO:

Vacarro Brothers
65 East South Water Street
Chicago, IL 60601

DATE: May 31, 197–; TERMS 2/10, net 30 days; SHIP VIA: ICRR

2 double pedestal general office desks, top size 60″ x 30″, No. 7401, List price $185.50 each

2 swivel chairs, No. A4229, List price $100.50 each

4 side chairs with arms, No. A4259, List price $74.25 each

3 bookcases (3 shelves), open front,
42″ high, 34½″ wide, 11¼″ deep,
No. S42A, List price $52.75 each

4. Type the following purchase invoice in duplicate. (If you do not have a blank purchase invoice, type one that is similar to the illustration on page 458.) The quantities and unit prices are given; you are to make all extensions and calculate the total.

MELROSE CORPORATION
7600 Tallman Avenue
Melrose Park, IL 60161

TO:

Sterling-Franklin Company
1000 South Elmora Avenue
Elizabeth, NJ 07207

DATE: June 16, 197–; INVOICE NO. 5251; SHIPPED BY: Penn-Central; TERMS 2/10, net 30 days; OUR ORDER NO. 3037; YOUR ORDER NO. 5104

9 Five-Drawer File Cabinets, Standard Finish, No. 1805, Price: $95.35 each

15 Counter-Height (3-drawer) File Cabinets, Standard Finish, No. 1865, Price: $72.25 each

6 Lateral Files (2-drawer with lock), Standard Finish, No. 1845, Price: $111.50 each

87 Frames for Suspension File Folders, No. 8221, Price: $1.45 each

CHECKED BY 19   SALESMAN Johnson   DEPARTMENT 6A

UNIT 13

SELLING

CLERK-TYPIST

Order Dept. Type sales orders
redit memos & entering or
ers. Some filing. Would b
pected to type invoices oc
ionally. Typing accurac
important than speed. Ex
t fringe benefits.
al opportunity Employe
ply in person at
R MFG. CORF
r Ave.,

Part 1   The Selling Function
Part 2   Clerical Selling Procedures

THE SELLING FUNCTION

During her senior year in high school, Joan enrolled in the clerical cooperative program. Students enrolled in the program attended classes one week and worked full time at starting office salaries the next. Joan worked in the Sales Department of the New Operations Company as a clerk-typist. The New Operations Company is a large nationwide mail-order clothing company that sells men's and women's clothing. At first her tasks were routine: typing address labels from a state mailing list and inserting four items in each labeled envelope — a form letter, a business reply order card, a two-page advertising folder, and a set of eight cloth samples. A few months later, after window envelopes replaced the standard envelopes with the labeled addresses, she was assigned to operate an automatic typewriter. Here she typed the inside address and salutation at the top of each form letter and then typed each customer's name and hometown in the spaces provided in the body of each form letter.

Because Joan was very efficient and also got along very well with her co-workers, she was offered full-time employment when she graduated. She was asked to take a four weeks' training program to prepare her to work with records in the Billing Department. She was told that she would receive an increase of $10 a week when she successfully completed the training program, with another increase after she had been on the job for six months, as well as a bonus at Christmas. After talking it over with her family, Joan decided to accept the offer.

IMPORTANCE OF SELLING

Selling means assisting and persuading customers to obtain goods and services so that both the buyer and the seller are satisfied. Probably no business activity is more important. If a business has no sales, it has no income. Without income, there will be no profits. If there are no profits, the firm cannot continue to operate. When a business can no longer operate there are no jobs. Every job in every business in one way or another is **dependent** upon successful selling.

dependent: relies upon; subject to

What Businesses Sell

All businesses sell something. They may sell *goods*, such as clothing, portable radios, soft drinks, or cameras. They may sell *services*, such as movie theaters, dry cleaners, and amusement parks. Many businesses sell both goods and services. For instance, a store may service as well as sell television sets; an automobile agency will usually provide repair service for the cars it sells.

No matter what a business sells, customers must be satisfied if the company is to be successful. Its purpose is to provide those goods and services that the customers want. In addition, the firm must sell its goods and services in such a way that customers will come back.

All Employees Are Salesmen

Every employee of a business can be considered a salesman of the firm. Each employee a customer meets helps to form the customer's opinion of the firm. If the customer's opinion is favorable, there is a good chance that he will continue to **patronize** the store. It is, therefore, very important that all customers be treated fairly and courteously.

patronize:
buy from

Sales Personnel. Those who have the most frequent and direct contacts with customers are the sales personnel. These are the employees who directly assist the customer in buying those goods and services which will provide the most satisfaction. Like all other employees in a business, sales personnel are specially trained in assisting customers.

Nonselling Personnel. Although clerical workers are occasionally asked to perform direct selling functions, usually this is not the case. Rather, as a clerical worker, you may assist the salesman and the customer

Illus. 13-1
No matter what your job, you always represent the company — its products, its image, its goodwill.

Wilbe Incorporated

in other ways. For example, you may answer telephone inquiries or complaints from customers, you may type invoices for sales, or you may handle routine correspondence related to sales.

Even though it is unlikely that you will be involved in direct selling, you will affect the way in which customers view your business. If you treat customers in the office with courtesy and respect, a good impression of your company will be formed. On the other hand, if you are indifferent — or what is worse, rude — to customers or if you make an error in typing their monthly statements, a poor impression will be formed.

Every employee of the firm makes an impression on the customer. If that impression is not good, the customer and his future purchases may be lost.

METHODS OF SELLING

How your business goes about selling its goods or services is very important to you because the income from sales pays your salary. There are two general methods of selling — personal selling and nonpersonal selling.

Personal Selling

potential:
possible; can
develop into

In personal selling a sales person speaks directly with a **potential** customer. This meeting may take place on the sales floor, in the customer's home, or over the telephone. Although as a clerical worker you probably won't be dealing with the customers on the sales floor or in their homes, it is possible that you may do some telephone selling. In that case you will have to study the product, and learn how to deal with customer questions. You may also have to prepare reports on your telephone contacts.

Nonpersonal Selling

influence:
to persuade;
to alter; to affect

Nonpersonal selling takes place when an attempt is made to **influence** customers to buy without meeting them or talking with them. Three common methods of nonpersonal selling are advertising, sales letters, and catalog selling.

Advertising. Everyone is exposed to hundreds of advertisements daily in newspapers and magazines, on billboards, on buses, and on radio and television. Advertisements try to inform potential customers about goods and services for sale by various businesses. Preparing advertising copy requires special training. A knowledge of advertising methods and techniques is very helpful to a clerical worker in an advertising agency or in a store that prepares most of its own advertisements.

Sales Letters. Most businesses use sale letters to inform customers of special goods and services that they have to offer. Sales letters are often used to announce preseason sales, anniversary sales, and clearance sales

Harry and David
at Bear Creek Orchards, Medford, Oregon 97501

THESE FARM FRESH GIFTS ARE SO GOOD WE
GUARANTEE THEM 100 % . . . OR YOUR MONEY BACK !

You'll never hear the end of it when you give <u>these</u> Christmas gifts to your family, friends and important customers. Here's <u>something</u> <u>different</u> they won't get from anyone but you . . . guaranteed to delight everyone you send them to . . . or your money back!

Down-to-earth Christmas **VALUES** ! Harry and I have the old-fashioned notion that a dollar ought to buy you 100 cents worth of value. So we grow our fruit, handweave our own baskets, bake our own cakes, put up our own preserves, pack, gift-wrap and deliver straight from orchards to your friends. The savings are yours.

OUR PRICES INCLUDE EVERYTHING ! . . . all the extras you usually pay for at stores, like packing, fancy wrapping AND delivery charges. No crowds to fight and no waiting around. Just easy, guaranteed shopping from the pages of these Christmas Books for gifts that stand out above all others . . . perfect for anyone whether they live in a castle or a cottage.

IT'S AWFULLY IMPORTANT TO ORDER EARLY.   Right now is a wonderful time!

Happy shopping, **David**

P.S. Why not have your secretary tell us of your probable requirements? We'll gladly confirm a RESERVATION for the gifts you want (subject to change or cancellation as you may wish) and thus protect you until your list is received.

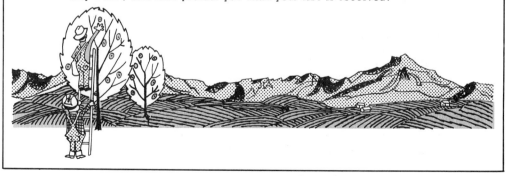

Illus. 13-2
Sales
letter

to regular customers. These letters must be so carefully written that some firms employ specialists to write them. Even though you probably won't be writing sales letters, you may be responsible for typing them. If a large volume of sales letters is being sent to prospective buyers, you may have to use an automatic typewriter to prepare them.

Catalog Selling. Many clerical workers are employed in mail-order or catalog selling. You may work in the department that takes telephone orders from customers. In that case you prepare an invoice for the order and send it to other departments for processing. In other firms using catalog selling, you may receive written orders from customers. You will have to check the accuracy of the customer's order, make sure that the arithmetic is correct, and send the order to the billing and shipping departments.

REVIEWING WHAT YOU HAVE READ

1. How would you define *selling*?
2. Why does a businessman believe that selling is very important?
3. Some firms sell goods, others sell services, and still others sell both goods and services. Give two examples of all three.
4. Why are satisfied customers so necessary for business firms?
5. What is the difference between sales personnel and nonselling personnel?
6. Give three examples of nonpersonnel selling.
7. Why should *every* employee of a firm try to make a favorable impression on customers and prospective customers?
8. A tire manufacturer has been known to spend over $100,000 to advertise snow tires on a 30-second commercial on a nationwide televised sports program. Why do you think the manufacturer is willing to spend so much on a single commercial?
9. About 50 million newspapers are sold every day and it is said that their advertisements are read by everyone — the rich and the poor; the young and the old; men, women, and children. If this is so, do you think that newspapers are well suited for advertising products which are in general use?
10. Why do business firms use sales letters?

MAKING DECISIONS

Ruth Green's first job was in a one-girl office. She was employed by Automated Lawn Care Service, a service company that guaranteed to take complete care of homeowners' lawns, except for cutting and watering, with automated equipment, for 3 cents a square foot.

By the middle of May the demand for the service had increased so rapidly that Automated Lawn Care Service could no longer accept any new lawn care service contracts. About a week after this became known, the manager of a competing service that provided about the same lawn care service for 3½ cents a square foot called Ruth at home. He offered to send her a gift certificate for $100 if she would give him a list of the homeowners whose lawns Automated Lawn Care Service was unable to care for.

Should Ruth accept or reject this offer? Give reasons for your answer.

WORKING WITH OTHERS

Clark Miller is employed in the Sales Division of J. P. Lippincott and Company. One of his duties is to prepare monthly sales summaries based upon the sales reports received from all the salesmen in the northwest area of the United States. Mr. Harry Kendrick, a salesman in the state of Washington, is consistently late in submitting his reports. For this reason, Clark must work many hours of overtime. He knows that the sales summaries for all areas are usually distributed at the regular monthly meetings of the Board of Directors on the second Wednesday of each month. However, Clark cannot begin his work until he has received all the sales reports from the northwest area. Mr. J. P. Lippincott, President of the company, has recently announced that extra pay will no longer be given for any office overtime.

What should Clark do about this situation?

USING LANGUAGE

The apostrophe has three principal uses:

1. To form the possessive of nouns and indefinite pronouns
   Example: Mary's (possessive) typewriter should be repaired.

2. To denote the omission of letters or figures
   Example: He hasn't been here today.

3. To form the plural of figures, letters, signs, and words (In some cases of current usage, it is not incorrect to omit the apostrophe — the 1960s.)
   Example: When *and's* and *the's* are used in titles, they should not be capitalized, unless they are the first word.

On a separate sheet of paper type the following sentences, inserting apostrophes where necessary.

1. He wasnt clear about how he wanted the sales figures handled.
2. Why did she type the *2s* and *8s* so lightly?
3. The report of the womens division will be ready tomorrow morning.
4. Her *Ts* and *Fs* were too much alike and also her *vs* and *us*.
5. The purchasing and sales departments reports were parallel in construction.
6. Mens shoes, childrens shoes, and ladies shoes were on sale all week.
7. He used $+s$ and $-s$ to indicate if sales for the month were ahead or behind.
8. The class of 70 had its reunion here.
9. Hers was the last test to be turned in.
10. "Its very warm in here," he said.

USING ARITHMETIC

1. Marian Davies, a high school student, sells greeting cards in her spare time. She is paid a straight commission of 25 cents on each box of cards that she sells. During the month of May she sold 90 boxes of cards. What was the amount of her commission?

2. Bill Porter, a salesman, is paid a straight commission of 7 percent on the amount of his sales. During September his sales amounted to $8,500. What was the amount of his commission?

3. The cashier at a local amusement park had $45 in change in the cash box of the ticket-selling window at the start of the day last Saturday. During the day she sold 213 90-cent tickets and 92 45-cent tickets. How much money should have been in the cash box when she proved the cash at the close of the day?

Prepare a Quarterly Sales Summary for Baldwin Laboratories, Inc.

1. Type a rough draft of the quarterly sales summary.
2. Complete the figure work on the rough draft:

   (a) Subtract the listed amount of the Sales Returns and Allowances for each salesman from his Gross Sales to find his Net Sales for the first quarter of the year.

   For example, the Net Quarterly Sales for the first salesman, Harry S. Abrams, are $62,036 ($65,555 − $3,519 = $62,036)

   (b) Compare the amount of each salesman's net first quarterly sales with his net quarterly sales for the first quarter of last year. Record the amount of the increase or decrease in the proper column.

   For example, Harry S. Abrams' net quarterly sales have increased by $2,248 ($62,036 − $59,788 = $2,248)

   (c) Add the columns and record their totals at the bottom of the Quarterly Sales Summary.

3. Type the final draft of the Quarterly Sales Summary on plain paper with two carbon copies.

BALDWIN LABORATORIES, INC.
Quarterly Sales Summary
PERIOD ENDING March 31, 197–

Salesman	Gross Sales for the First Quarter	Sales Returns and Allowances First Quarter	Net Sales for the First Quarter	Net Sales First Quarter (Last Year)	Comparison Amount of Increase	Amount of Decrease
Abrams, Harry S.	$65,555	$3,519	$	$59,788	$	$
Becker, Norman T.	68,706	4,221		64,823		
Carr, Frank J.	97,376	5,720		90,231		
Davis, Robert R.	72,064	4,472		70,947		
Ehrlich, Walter C.	57,649	2,170		54,923		
Fulton, Ross N.	62,630	3,702		57,005		
Goldberg, Seymour	70,480	6,042		66,122		
Hansen, John C.	88,290	5,170		79,162		
Iorizzo, Salvatore	90,592	5,517		80,216		
Johnston, David G.	72,575	3,433		67,980		
Kraft, George A.	62,195	2,155		59,944		
Lang, Oscar P.	66,444	3,414		65,082		
Mazer, Harold H.	70,188	4,560		61,201		
Neale, Henry J.	50,780	2,158		57,160		
O'Brien, Thomas E.	98,490	7,269		85,396		
Parker, Herbert A.	56,333	3,908		55,013		
Quinn, Peter D.	72,403	5,501		65,161		
Roberts, Jack	61,512	4,094		50,057		
Tsuyuki, John Y.	73,488	3,408		66,567		
Van Tassel, Charles	55,304	2,129		59,041		
TOTALS.............	$	$	$	$	$	$

PART 2 CLERICAL SELLING PROCEDURES

Rosalind Bennett and two other girls work in the Order Department of Byron Jackson & Co., an electronic supplies manufacturer. In addition to being an accurate and rapid typist, Rosalind also must be skilled in using the electronic calculator to check the arithmetic on the invoices. Rosalind knows that to be efficient she must be very careful about checking each order received. The price indicated by the customer must be the same as the price shown in the catalog. Extensions and totals must be checked for accuracy. She must check to see if the product ordered is still manufactured by the company or if it has been replaced by a new, improved product. If the product ordered by the customer is no longer in stock, she must either send the correct form letter or write a routine letter to the customer requesting the action to be taken. Rosalind is a good order clerk. She takes her job seriously, and her supervisor knows that she can depend on Rosalind.

SALES OFFICE RESPONSIBILITIES

As was mentioned in Part 1, as a clerical worker you probably will not be responsible for selling directly to customers. However, it is quite likely that you will perform clerical functions that will aid your sales personnel and customers in successfully completing sales. You may be responsible for handling telephone or mail orders from customers. A large amount of your time may be taken up in typing and filing the business papers related to selling. No matter what your responsibilities are, you must remember that every action you take may affect the customers' **attitude** toward your money.

attitude:
mental position;
feeling; emotion

Routine Correspondence

Much of the correspondence that comes into a business contains routine requests for catalogs, information about products or services, and information about company policies. Clerical workers are often responsible for answering these requests. Since many customers ask similar questions, *form letters* are often used to answer their requests. All you have to do is find the form letter that will answer the customer's question. You may have to type in special information on points not covered in the basic form letter. Space is provided on the form letters for this information.

Illus. 13-3
Filled-in form letter

Byron Jackson & CO. 4996 Michigan Ave. Chicago, IL 60614 Area Code 312 631-9072

March 12, 197-

Mr. James R. Dewey
Purchasing Agent
R & D Electronic Supplies
1414 Third Avenue
San Diego, CA 92101

Dear Mr. Dewey

Thank you for your order P-5131 dated March 10, 197-,
which has just been received.

Your order specified   20   S44 switches. We are no
longer producing the S44 switch. Because of improvements
in materials and production methods, we are now producing
a new switch--the S52--which has greater durability and
flexibility. Even though the S52 switch is superior to
the S44 switch, it costs only 50 cents more. This change
will be shown in our November 1 catalog.

We are taking the liberty of substituting   20   new S52
switches at a total cost of $220 (20   at $11 each).
If this substitution does not meet with your approval, please
notify us at once so that we can delete this item from your
order.

The remainder of the items you have ordered will be shipped
as specified.

Sincerely yours

(Miss) Rosalind Bennett

Rosalind Bennett
Order Department

Salesmen's Records

If you work for a firm that has salesmen who call on customers at their places of business, you may have the responsibility of assisting the

Illus. 13-4
Order department clerk receives copy of order and telephone call from salesman in one minute.

Xerox

salesmen in serving their customers. The salesmen may either work out of your office, or they may work in another city or state. If the salesmen work out of your office, they will talk with you several times each week concerning the needs of their customers. Should the salesmen work in another territory, you will be receiving mailed reports and telephone calls from them.

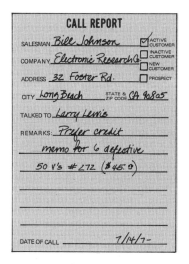

Illus. 13-5
Daily call report

Each time a salesman calls on a customer he makes a record of their conversation on a *call report*. On the call report the salesman records who he called upon, the subjects discussed, and what action needs to be taken. The call reports are then taken or mailed to the sales office.

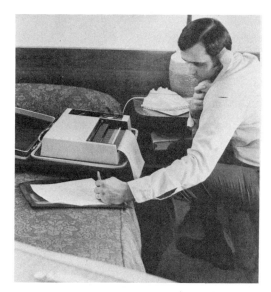

Illus. 13-6
Traveling salesman transmits rush order to office by telephone and portable telecopier.

Xerox

When call reports come in, you must read and **interpret** each one carefully. If the customer requested a price list or catalog, you will send a notice to the mailing room to that effect. If the customer requests information that you can provide, you will write to him. If the call report contains an order for goods, you will type the invoice and send it to the appropriate departments.

After the proper action has been taken, the call report should be filed in the customer's file folder. Any letters or invoices related to the customer should also be placed in his file. In this way the customer's file becomes a complete history of his dealings with your company.

Mail Requests

Mail-order houses are not the only businesses that receive mail orders. Most businesses get letters every day ordering goods. Some businesses include mail-in coupons in their advertisements to make it easier for customers to place orders.

Special procedures are usually necessary for handling mail orders.

1. If you are responsible for opening the envelopes, take care that you don't damage the contents.
2. Don't throw the envelope away until you are sure that the customer's name and address are included in the contents of the letter or order.
3. Handle with extreme care any checks or money orders received. Usually you will note on the letter or order that a check was received and indicate its amount.

Illus. 13-7

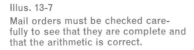
Mail orders must be checked carefully to see that they are complete and that the arithmetic is correct.

H. Armstrong Roberts

Checks are then normally sent to the cashier or the accounting department.

4. Check the order to be sure that it is complete and the arithmetic is correct. Consult your supervisor if any important details are missing or incorrect. If the customer lives in your town, you may be told to call and get the information needed. If the customer lives in another town, you may have to send a written request for missing information (often form letters are available for this purpose).

5. Usually you will type an invoice for the order received. A copy of the invoice will go to the credit department for approval before charge sales are shipped.

Telephone Requests

Every day business firms receive thousands of telephone requests for information about products and services. By using the telephone, the customer is indicating that he wants action in a hurry. You must perform your duties in such a way that the customer is not disappointed.

Many businesses include their telephone numbers in their advertisements so that customers can call to order goods and services. If your duties include taking telephone orders, you should have copies of the latest advertisements handy for reference. This will aid you in answering questions and in knowing which goods the customer is ordering.

When a customer calls, you should have *sales order forms* and pencils and pens ready. You must listen very carefully to be sure that you

Illus. 13-8
When a customer calls, order form and pencil should be at hand. Listen carefully to what the customer says.

Bearings, Inc.

know exactly what the customer wants. If the customer says anything you do not completely understand, politely ask him to repeat the information. When writing the information on the order form, make sure that you write legibly. Be certain to get the customer's name (spelled correctly), address, telephone number, and charge account number, if it is a charge sale. Carefully record the items desired, the prices, and how the goods are to be shipped. To be sure that you have recorded the information correctly, read the order back to the customer.

concluded: ended

After you have **concluded** your conversation with the customer, you should recheck the order for completeness and accuracy. Then you or a co-worker will usually type an invoice from the order form. Copies of the invoice are sent to the proper departments, including shipping and accounting.

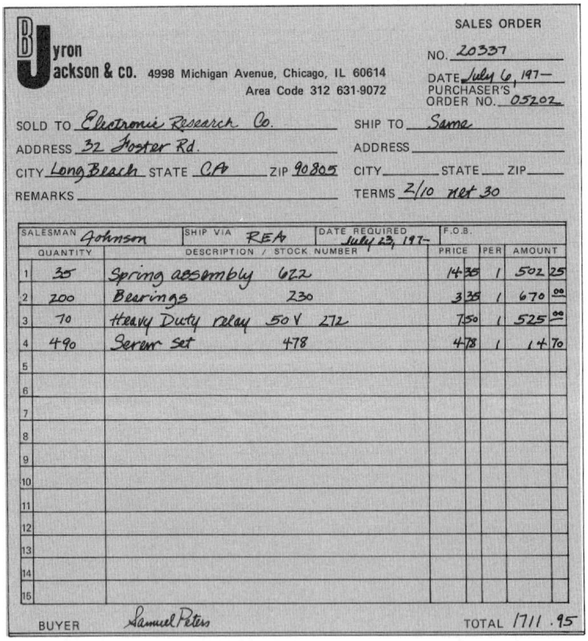

Byron Jackson & co. 4998 Michigan Avenue, Chicago, IL 60614
Area Code 312 631-9072

SALES ORDER
NO. 20337
DATE July 6, 197–
PURCHASER'S ORDER NO. 05202

SOLD TO Electronic Research Co.
ADDRESS 32 Foster Rd.
CITY Long Beach STATE CA ZIP 90805
REMARKS

SHIP TO Same
ADDRESS
CITY STATE ZIP
TERMS 2/10 net 30

SALESMAN Johnson | SHIP VIA REA | DATE REQUIRED July 23, 197– | F.O.B.

	QUANTITY	DESCRIPTION / STOCK NUMBER	PRICE	PER	AMOUNT
1	35	Spring assembly 622	14 35	1	502 25
2	200	Bearings 230	3 35	1	670 00
3	70	Heavy Duty relay 50 V 272	7 50	1	525 00
4	490	Screw set 478	4 78	1	14 70
5					
6					
7					
8					
9					
10					
11					
12					
13					
14					
15					

BUYER Samuel Peters TOTAL 1711 .95

Illus. 13-9
Hand filled-in sales order

PROCESSING ORDERS

As you know, an order for goods or services may come to your business in many ways. It could come as a purchase order; it could come as a letter or telephone call; it could come from a customer visit; or it could come as a result of a salesman's call. No matter how the order is received, you must process it accurately and rapidly. Remember that the customer's purchase is providing the income that pays your salary. Every action you take must be directed toward providing customer satisfaction.

Checking the Order

When an order is received, you must check it to be certain that all needed information is available and that what is provided is correct. You should also check to see that the goods ordered are in stock. If the ordered goods are not in stock, your supervisor will decide whether to contact the customer or to send goods that are very similar to those ordered.

You must also check the accuracy of the prices shown on the order. Use a calculator to check all the arithmetic.

Approving Credit

When an order is received without an accompanying payment, it usually must be approved by the credit department before the merchandise is shipped. Most orders are from established customers who have proved their reliability. Those orders are given rapid credit approval.

Illus. 13-10
A customer's credit rating is checked before an order is shipped.

Wilson Jones Company
Division of Swingline, Inc.

If the order is from a new customer without an established credit rating or from a firm with an unsatisfactory record of past payments, the credit department may recommend that the goods be shipped *COD*, which means *cash on delivery*. The goods must be paid for as soon as they are delivered to the buyer. When a COD shipment is necessary, the seller often writes to the buyer to ask him **tactfully** if he wants the goods shipped under these terms.

tactfully:
with consideration

Preparing the Sales Invoice

The sales invoice (illustrated on page 458) gives all the details of the sale. You must take great care in typing invoices to be sure that all the information is correct. The sales invoice shows a complete listing of the goods shipped, including the following information about each item: the quantity, description, catalog number, unit price, and the extension (the multiplication of the unit price by the quantity of an item shipped). For example, a line on an invoice for office products might include

```
8 DZ  MEDIUM BALL-POINT PENS  873   2.70 DZ  21.60
```

The sales invoice also carries the firm's name, the customer's name and address, the method of shipping, the customer's order number, the sales invoice number, the terms of payment, and the total amount of the invoice.

The copies of the sales invoices are usually distributed as follows:

Original...............To the customer
First carbon copy.......To the Accounting Department for accounts receivable
Second carbon copy.....To the Filing Department for placement in the customer's file
Third carbon copy......To the Shipping Department
Fourth carbon copy.....To the Sales Department or salesman

Every well-organized business firm has an established procedure for preparing sales invoices. This procedure will differ with the number and the difficulty of the invoices prepared by each firm. If they require very little mathematical work, a small number of invoices can be prepared on a typewriter. Invoices with more complicated arithmetic will require the use of a desk calculator as well as a typewriter. If a large number of invoices is prepared every day, it may be more economical and efficient to use either special billing machines or data processing equipment. Most sales invoices prepared on billing machines or data processing equipment are written on continuous invoice forms with carbon paper between the copies.

Billing the Customer

When the order is shipped by your firm, the bill or invoice is mailed to the customer. This important office operation is known as *billing*.

Statements. In addition to the invoices that are sent to customers when an order is shipped, most businesses send out monthly statements for each customer's account. The statement shows the amount the cus-

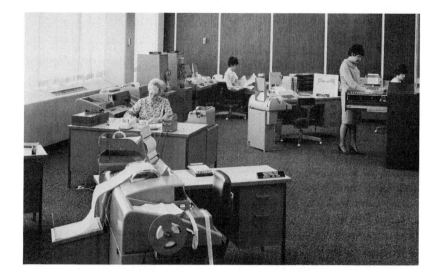

tomer owed at the beginning of the month, the charges and payments made during the month, and the balance the customer owes at the end of the month.

Statements are usually prepared on bookkeeping machines, punched card tabulating machines, and other electronic data processing equipment, depending upon the number of statements sent out each month. Although the preparation of the statements is the responsibility of the accounting department in all but very small business firms, it is sometimes necessary for the office workers in other departments to help in preparing statements, especially during rush periods.

Cycle Billing. The firm you work for may not send out all its statements at the end of the month. Some companies mail some of their statements on the first of the month; others on the fifth; still others on the ninth; and so on. This procedure is called *cycle billing.* Most department stores, telephone companies, and gas and electric companies have divided their lists of customers and mail out statements on different dates in the month, rather than mail out all statements at the end of the month. This makes it possible for the billing department to work steadily throughout the month, to avoid peak loads and overtime at the end of every month, and to send out statements as they are completed. Some companies divide their customer lists alphabetically; for example, statements may be mailed to customers whose last names are in the middle of the alphabet, beginning with either *M* or *N,* on the fifteenth of the month. Other companies divide their customer lists by districts, geographic locations, or sales territories.

DEALING WITH CUSTOMER COMPLAINTS

Even though you and your co-workers take great care in processing sales, there will always be some customers who will return merchandise for one reason or another. The merchandise may have been delivered too late to be of value; the merchandise may have been the wrong kind, style, or color; or the merchandise may have been received in a damaged condition. Then, of course, there are also instances when a customer returns goods because what he ordered simply will not fit his needs. Usually after the customer tells the seller that he is not satisfied with the shipment, he will be asked to return the shipment. In some cases, however, it may be more advantageous to the seller to grant a special allowance to the customer to cover his loss if he keeps the merchandise.

Every time a customer has a complaint there is an opportunity to build goodwill for your firm. The degree of attention and courtesy the customer receives will help to form his opinion of your business.

Credit Memorandums

When merchandise is returned to the seller or when an allowance is granted to the customer, a credit memorandum (illustrated on page 459) is issued. This credit memorandum is very much like a sales invoice and carries about the same information that appears on an invoice. At least three copies are made — the original for the customer, the second copy for the accounting department to be used in crediting the customer's account, and the third copy for the customer's file. Frequently additional copies are prepared — one copy for the receiving department to indicate the goods to be returned, and one for the sales department as a record of sales returns and allowances. All businesses try to keep sales returns and allowances at the lowest possible level.

Adjustment Letters

Some customer complaints involve problems that cannot be solved by simply sending a credit memorandum. An adjustment letter may be necessary to more fully explain what caused the problem and what action will be taken. Beginning office workers are seldom asked to write adjustment letters; however, as you gain experience this may become one of your responsibilities. Adjustment letters usually contain the following elements:

1. A cordial acknowledgment of the complaint
2. An explanation and an expression of regret
3. A suggestion for the adjustment of the complaint

You should present the facts in a forthright manner, without anger or trying to fix the blame. Suggest the adjustment in a tone and manner that will reassure the customer. An example of an adjustment letter is shown in Illus. 13-12.

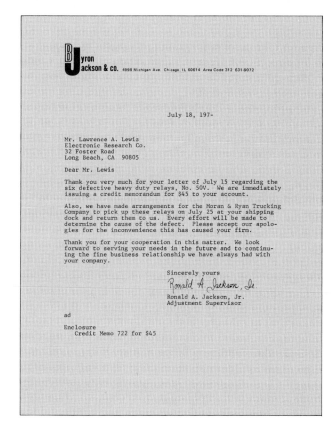

Illus. 13-12
Adjustment letter

REVIEWING
WHAT YOU
HAVE READ

1. What is the purpose of a form letter?
2. What is a call report and why should it be carefully read and interpreted?
3. Where is a call report filed?
4. How should you handle checks and money orders enclosed in letters ordering goods?
5. What is the purpose of a sales order form?
6. Under what circumstances would a credit department recommend that goods be shipped COD?
7. What is the meaning of the term *extension* in a sales invoice?
8. What information is shown on a customer's statement?
9. What is the main advantage of using a cycle billing system?
10. When is a credit memorandum issued to a customer?

MAKING
DECISIONS

1. Do you think that the purchasing department or the sales department is more important in a small furniture manufacturing company? Give reasons for your answer.
2. Give the reasons why you agree or disagree with the statement: Every time a customer has a complaint there is an opportunity to build goodwill for your firm.
3. Why do all business firms try to keep sales returns and allowances at the lowest possible level?

WORKING
WITH
OTHERS

A new salesman bursts into the sales department and happily displays his first large order — an order for over $1,000 from Wells Associates. You suddenly remember that the credit department has been trying to collect $1,200 from Wells Associates for over a year for a previous order.

Should you (a) type the sales invoice for Wells Associates and let the salesman get the bad news from the credit department in a few days or (b) tell the salesman that you do not think the order will be approved because Wells Associates still owes the company $1,200 for a previous order? Do you think he will hold it against you if you tell him now?

USING
LANGUAGE

The hyphen is used for dividing words at the end of a line when you don't have sufficient space to complete the full word. Rules to follow in dividing words are:

1. Words should be divided between syllables only.
   Right: regret-able   Wrong: regr-etable

2. Single syllable words are not to be divided.
   Right: paint   Wrong: pa-int

3. Hyphenated words should be divided at the hyphen only.
   Right: self-reliance   Wrong: self-rel-iance

4. A one-letter syllable should not be typed at the end of a line or at the beginning of the next line.
   Right: award   Wrong: a-ward
          area   are-a

5. A two-letter syllable should not be carried to the next line.
   Right: bodily   Wrong: bodi-ly

6. A single-letter syllable should be typed with the beginning portion of a divided word rather than with the end of the word.
   Right: dedi-cation   Wrong: ded-ication

On a separate sheet of paper type each of the following words indicating all the places where the word could be hyphenated if it appeared near the end of a line of typewriting.

1. automation	6. feeling	11. impatience	16. seldom
2. brilliant	7. forgotten	12. moment	17. selfsatisfaction
3. contrast	8. found	13. oblige	18. thorough
4. declaration	9. formality	14. permissible	19. timeless
5. encouragement	10. gainful	15. seemingly	20. unadvised

On a separate sheet of paper show the calculations and the answers to the problems below.

1. How much does the customer pay for a travel clock marked $9.75 if a retail discount of 16% is allowed?
2. Wool sweaters formerly priced at $16.50 were marked down 22%. What was the markdown price?
3. During a special sale, the price of a dinette set is marked down 20% from $69.50. What is the special sale price?
4. The price of a desk lamp is reduced 40% from the original price of $15.95. How much will the desk lamp cost the purchaser at the reduced price?
5. For a special sale $27.50 tires were marked down 12%. What was the sale price of the tires?

1. If blank business forms are not available for this and the following problems, use plain paper. Type the information that is ordinarily printed on such forms as shown in the illustrations in this part.

Type sales invoices in duplicate for the following sales made by the National Furniture Company, 1440 Jefferson Avenue, Forest Hills, NY 12068, on December 3, 197–, terms 2/10, net 30 days. The quantities and unit prices are given; you are to make all extensions and calculate the totals.

(a) The Kramer Publishing Company, 784 Catherine Street, Unionville, CT 06085. Ship by EAK Trucking Company. Our Invoice NF 325 C. Customer Order K 725. Salesman Canter. Department 16

   8 Open Storage Bookcases (2 shelves), 48"H x 36"W x 12"D, Walnut veneer finish, No. SW47-1130. Price $86.50 each.
   2 Single Pedestal Desks, 60" x 30", Walnut veneer finish, No. SW48-976. Price $127 each.
   36 Desk Trays, Letter size, Walnut veneer finish, No. SW45-1360. Price $66 a dozen.
   4 Side Chairs with Walnut Arm Rests, Seat 18½" x 18"W x 3"D, No. SW44-204. Price $62.75 each.

(b) The Dutchess Distributing Company, 66 Canterbury Drive, Poughkeepsie, NY 12603.
   Ship by Robinson Transfer Company. Our Invoice NF 329 C. Customer Order DD 3184. Salesman Smythe, Department 16.

   6 Fluorescent Desk Lamps, 18" high, Translucent shade and wood grain walnut base, No. SD77-108. Price $32.95 each.
   24 Desk Pads with Walnut Panels, 20" x 34", No. SD78-3960. Price $92.25 a dozen.
   8 Reception Room Chairs, Seat 18½" x 20"W x 3"D, color: spice brown, No. SW43-241. Price $41.50 each.
   4 Walnut Oblong Waste Baskets, 16" x 9", 14" high, No. SD75-356. Price $12.75 each.

2. Type credit memorandums in duplicate for the following credits allowed customers on January 14 by the Modern Furniture Company, Coral Gables, FL 33926.

(a) Mr. J. B. Young, 1462 Alhambra Circle, Coral Gables, FL 33926:
   1 Captain's Chair.................$55.00
   1 Night Table....................$39.50

(b) Mrs. Ellen Baker, 3714 Ponce de Leon Boulevard, Coral Gables, FL 33926.

    2 Arm Chairs....................$99.50 each

    1 End Table....................$35.00

3. Type monthly statements of account in duplicate to be sent to the following customers of Haines and Williams, wholesale grocers, Knoxville, TN 37903, May 1, 197–.

(a) Robert L. Wilkins, 2580 Moorman Avenue, Knoxville, TN 37905.

Date	Code	Division	Charges	Credits
April 1	C-111	83	142.80	
6	C-113	83	129.65	
10	R-201	90		142.80
15	R-212	90		4.95
21	C-119	83	18.50	

(b) Anthony M. Upshaw, 501 Klotter Street, Athens, TN 37303.

Date	Code	Division	Charges	Credits
April 15	C-151	83	39.20	
26	R-171	90		39.20
28	C-155	83	14.95	

UNIT 14

INVENTORIES
AND THEIR
CONTROL

INVENTORY
CLERK

Responsible young person,
curate and neat with simp
athematics, to maintain p
tion and inventory recor
ur week, in medium-siz
rk office. Apply in p
J. Manning, Textil
uthland Rd., C

PART 1   THE INVENTORY FUNCTION

Bob Langley is a stock clerk in the printing and supply department of a large securities brokerage firm in New York City. He spends each day filling requisitions, ordering, and receiving supplies of forms, such as certificates, letterheads, envelopes, stationery, punch cards, and other items needed to handle the work of the firm. Bob also takes inventories, makes counts of stock, adjusts stock for better use of space, and arranges for disposal of old stock. He works with three other stock clerks, with whom he is constantly cooperating since they often make group decisions about what should be done about problems that develop. This staff of four makes it possible for all the offices in this large firm to have supplies on hand to carry on their work.

THE NATURE OF INVENTORIES

An *inventory* is a collection of materials and products kept on hand by a business so that it can operate effectively. An inventory generally includes many items. The quantity of each item on hand is referred to as a *stock*. For example, a clerk will say, "We must reorder letterheads because our *stock* is low."

Steel manufacturing plants carry inventories of raw materials needed for the production of steel. Bookstores carry inventories of books. Rug and carpet departments of large stores carry inventories of **various** types of rugs and carpeting. Each of these businesses is aware of the importance of its inventories. The steel plant will have to stop operations if it runs out of raw materials for its ovens; the bookstore will lose customers if a popular book is out of stock; the rug and carpeting department will have dissatisfied customers if they select gold from the floor samples and then learn from the salesman, who checked with the stockroom, that there is only one five-foot piece of gold left, and it will take about six weeks to get a new shipment from the manufacturer.

various:
many kinds

Systems for Keeping Inventories

Companies have developed systems for keeping records of their inventories so that they know exactly how much of each item will be required. Companies want to have on hand as much of each item as they will need, but they do not want to build up large inventories of items for which there is very little demand.

The profits that companies earn depend, to some extent, on how well they purchase the materials and products needed to carry on their businesses. If they have too little stock, the work of the firm is interrupted. If they have too much stock, they are spending funds needlessly. Therefore, ways of knowing what is the best size for inventories are important to a firm.

Workers Needed

Many clerical workers are needed in all types of businesses to properly maintain inventories. Clerical tasks related to inventories and their control are interesting and highly important. These tasks require alertness, accuracy, neatness, and orderliness. You will find it helpful to understand this important aspect of modern business management.

INVENTORY CONTROL

Having the right materials and supplies at the time they are needed means there must be control of inventories. Many office workers are needed to maintain inventories properly. Generally there is a manager who is responsible for the procedures to be followed for keeping the records. Working with the manager are assistants and inventory clerks who also bear considerable responsibility for inventory control. Aspects of inventory control that are the tasks of clerical workers include keeping track of stock on hand, reordering items, receiving items, keeping an orderly arrangement in the stockroom, filling requisitions, and checking the **adequacy** of inventories.

adequacy:
enough to meet
the needs

Keeping Records of Inventories

The manager of a stockroom decides the right amount of each item to be kept on hand. He knows that he is tying up too much of his firm's money if he keeps in inventory more of an item than is needed for normal operations. He, therefore, carefully reviews the past demand for each item and makes judgments about future needs. Clerical assistants then see that the stocks are maintained at the levels established. There are two basic ways of keeping inventory records.

One method is a *perpetual* (continuous) inventory system, which means that a record is made each time an item leaves the stockroom. This system is often used with major items. For example, a large department store keeps a perpetual inventory of all major appliances, such as washing machines, dishwashers, and refrigerators. At any time, the card for a particular item indicates exactly how many of the items are still available with no need to actually count the stock.

intervals:
a space of time
between events or
units

The other method that is used for maintaining the inventory is to actually count each item in stock at regularly scheduled **intervals**. For example, a manager of a large stockroom of small items commented, "In our stockroom, we use UBC, that is, Unit Buying Count. Every two weeks our clerks make an actual count of all the stock on hand and make a record of this count."

Reordering Goods

minimum:
the least;
the smallest;
the lowest

Well-organized stockrooms have a reordering procedure when an item reaches the **minimum** level. The minimum level is that point below which there is just enough stock to take care of normal requests until the new stock is delivered. Stockroom managers are responsible for establishing what the minimum levels are. Generally, there is some mechanical procedure for noting that the level has been reached. For example, in one

large stockroom of office supplies, the clerk described their procedure in this way:

> Each of us in this Department is constantly filling orders for supplies that come in from all the offices in this building. Inserted in each stack of a particular item is a bright red reorder card. As soon as we take an item from a stack and find that red card below the last item we took, we are to pull the card, which is already marked with the item name, code number, and other specifications and fill in a reorder form as soon as possible. Generally, we hold these cards on our desk until near the end of the day after all requisitions for supplies have been filled. Then we fill in the forms.

Keeping an Orderly Stockroom

You will find that good housekeeping habits are important in your work in a stockroom. Goods must be located quickly if they are to be available to the people who need them. Therefore, finding the goods must not be an exercise in guessing. Goods not readily **accessible** are practically useless, for requests cannot be filled, and needed goods are denied the various departments of the company. One manager of a large stockroom in a dress manufacturing company commented:

accessible:
easy to find;
obtainable

We operate this stockroom very much like a systematic library. Every clerk here is automatically following the same procedure each time he handles an item. When he works with incoming goods, he knows that the goods are to be placed in their regular locations immediately. When a new item is ordered, arrangements are made for its placement on the shelves or in the bins immediately so that when the goods arrive, there is already on the master location layout an indication of the location. We have buttons, hooks, belts, buckles, trimming, thread — in all kinds and styles — plus fabrics for dresses, for linings, and for interfacings. You can walk through our stockroom at any time and find it a clean, organized place. We don't like to work in chaos.

Requisitioning Goods

There must be an accounting for the total quantity of each item that is placed in stock. Therefore, you will find that every stockroom has a procedure for taking items out of stock. Persons from many departments in the company are likely to need goods from the stockroom. They must be informed of the procedures which are usually in written form. You as an employee of the stockroom may have to explain the procedures to callers who fail to read them or who expect exceptional treatment. One clerk in a supplies stockroom commented:

dispense:
to distribute

We supply all the materials that secretaries and other office workers need to do their work. We receive requisitions by interoffice mail and in person. In case of emergencies, we do accept requests by telephone. All the office workers have the requisition forms in their offices, but we also carry a supply for those who arrive at the window without one filled in. We are instructed not to **dispense** any item without a requisition form that clearly identifies the budget to which the item is to be charged. Furthermore, every requisition must be signed by the person who is to get the goods.

VARIATIONS IN INVENTORIES

Different kinds of businesses have different kinds of inventories. Inventories in distributive firms, such as stores, are organized differently from inventories of manufacturers which, in turn, are different from inventories of service organizations, such as hotels, beauty salons, and plumbing companies.

Inventories in Distributive Firms

Firms that buy goods for the purpose of resale are called *distributive firms*. Department stores, drugstores, bookstores, supermarkets, wholesale fruit companies, and shoe stores are examples of the millions of distributive firms in the United States and Canada. You are aware of how important inventories are to such businesses. A customer who finds a shirt that he likes and then learns from the salesclerk that it is out of stock in his size is not likely to enjoy shopping in that store. This is an instance of an inadequate inventory.

Illus. 14-3
Retail stores must maintain large inventories of stock.

Paul L. and Sally L. Gordon

Inventories in distributive firms are organized by types of goods. You are likely to find many different stockrooms in a large firm. While some stockrooms may carry only one type of goods, such as a shoe stockroom for a large department store, there will be some stockrooms that carry several types of goods. In a store with a small linens department, you may find that linens are in the same stockroom with towels, fabrics, bedspreads, and draperies. Each distributive firm determines an appropriate division of its total merchandise lines for inventory maintenance purposes.

Inventories in Manufacturing Firms

A *manufacturing firm* is a firm that combines raw materials in order to make a product. Steel companies, dress companies, shoe companies are examples of manufacturing firms. Each uses raw materials and changes their nature.

Important inventories for a manufacturing firm are these:

1. *Raw materials inventory*. Materials needed in the production process, such as coal, iron ore, leather, cotton goods, buttons, thread.

Components:
parts; members;
contents

2. **Components** *inventory*. Items that are semiproduced and are used in a particular step of the production process, such as belts which a dress company purchases from another manufacturer and does not produce itself or tires and batteries which an automobile manufacturing company purchases from other manufacturers.

3. *Goods in process inventory*. Products which represent the output of a manufacturing firm at each step prior to the *final* step in the manufacturing process. For example, shoes are not made in one step. There are several steps, and at each one there is a partial shoe. The goods in process inventory is a means of keeping account of how many items are at each stage of production. This inventory provides a means of determining if there are sufficient items at the beginning of the next step to maintain production at the scheduled rate.

4. *Finished goods inventory*. Final output of a manufacturing company, such as dresses from a dress manufacturing company or automobiles from an automobile manufacturing company.

Illus. 14-4
Finished goods
inventory of a food
processing company

Towmotor

Inventories in Service Businesses

As you know, service businesses provide some useful work rather than products to their customers. Plumbers, appliance repairmen, beauty salons, laundries, hotels, and motels are service businesses. Lawyers, doctors, accountants render professional services. In all instances, these businessmen need equipment and supplies to do their work.

Service firms have the following inventories:

1. Supplies and equipment needed to operate the business. For example, a motel or hotel needs a wide variety of items to keep its facilities clean. Mops, dust cloths, brooms, paper towels, and many other items must be kept in stock.
2. Supplies and equipment for direct customer services. For example, a motel or hotel needs stationery, soap, furniture, water glasses, linens, and many other items in the rooms for guests to use.

MAINTAINING SECURITY

The goods kept in stockrooms are valuable. Easy access to them may lead to many losses. Persons who deal with inventories must be honest. Sometimes stockroom personnel who handle valuable goods are bonded, which provides insurance for the company if goods are stolen.

AUTOMATION IN INVENTORY CONTROL

Many companies are replacing manual methods of keeping control of inventories with systems that are linked to computers. It is possible for a retail store, for example, to keep a record of its inventory through connecting all sales registers with a computer that updates quantities on hand every time a sale is made.

The computer introduced new procedures for handling inventories. However, the basic purposes of inventory control remain the same. If you understand these purposes, a computer system will not be a mystery to you.

REVIEWING WHAT YOU HAVE READ

1. How would you describe an *inventory*?
2. How would an inventory in a manufacturing firm differ from an inventory in a small jewelry store?
3. Why is it important that firms develop systems for keeping inventories?
4. What are important traits of clerical workers in stockrooms?
5. How would you describe an inventory that is well controlled?
6. Describe how a perpetual inventory system works.

7. Is it a good idea to wait until an item is out of stock before reordering it? Explain.

8. Why is it necessary to keep a stockroom orderly?

9. If a person needs an item quickly from the stockroom, should he have to fill in a requisition form? Explain.

10. Explain the types of inventories manufacturing firms must carry.

MAKING DECISIONS

1. Sid is a clerk in a large stockroom of a china and glassware store in a shopping center. One afternoon a salesclerk came in to get some goblets that were in the receiving area. There were none on the stockroom shelves. Sid knew the salesclerk needed them; so he removed the carton from the stack, opened it, and gave the salesclerk the six goblets he wanted. Sid knew he would remember what he did and would make the adjustment when the stock was checked the next morning.

What do you think of Sid's decision?

2. Flora is a clerk in the supply stockroom of a large law firm. One morning she was opening new stock and found an item that had not previously been in the stockroom. She looked around the shelves and found a place to put the new form. She decided that she would remember where she put the stock, and if anyone needed it she could tell the person where it was.

What do you think of Flora's decision?

WORKING WITH OTHERS

Chuck and Craig became friends soon after they began to work together in the stockroom of a large office supplies company. They worked in a well-organized department, and they enjoyed their work. One day Craig realized that Chuck was taking small items such as pens, scotch tape, and writing pads from stock for his personal use. While there were strict rules about stockkeeping, Chuck had obviously figured out a way of taking these small items without the manager seeing him. Craig was sure that Chuck would lose his job if the manager found out what was going on.

What do you think Craig should do?

USING LANGUAGE

Below is a list of frequently misused words and expressions. On a separate sheet of paper list each word and beside it substitute a word or expression that is better English usage.

no place	lots of
anywheres	might of
in back of	off of
brainy	outside of
could of	seldom ever
different than	show up
enthuse	superior than
every so often	these kind
hisself	no good

USING ARITHMETIC

On page 495 is the inventory data for one display case in Location 1. Compute the Total Cost for each item and the Page Total Cost.

Magini Inventory Service, Inc.	HOME OFFICE: 325 Olive Street St. Louis, MO. 63102 TEL: 314-351-4040							

Magini Inventory Service, Inc.

HOME OFFICE:
325 Olive Street
St. Louis, MO. 63102
TEL: 314-351-4040

Date _____ Page **2601**

Customer **E CC**

Address _____

Location **1**

Caller _____
Writer **CW**
Mag. No. _____
Side No. _____
Team Page No. _____

Description	Brand or Mfr.	Size or No.	Code	Qty.	Unit	Unit Price	Total Cost
pen points	Speedball			214		29	
ruler, 6" pocket				9		10	
ECC pens				19		29	
pens pinky				58		29	
pen Flair exec.				7		98	
refill, Flair				7		59	
marker	el Marko			60		59	
"	" "			6		19	
pen	Paper Mate			18		98	
refill for	Bic Clic			28		25	
pen, Bic Clic				26		49	
pen, cartridge	Shaeffer			9		1 00	
pencil	Scripto			1		49	
pencil, charcoal	Blaisdell			11		29	
" colored	Venus Paradise			297		25	
marker, major	Accent			90		41	
marker	Sanford	Big Sig		59		29	
"	"	Mr. Sketch		46		49	
"	"	Marker King		6		89	
magic marker				4		59	
marker	Sanford	Marker		66		69	
"	Esterbrook	water color		33		49	
"	"	" "		18		49	
"	Sanford	Transport		7		59	
"	"	Sharpie		19		49	
"	"	King		24		89	
						Page Total Cost	

Illus. 14-5

PERFORMING OFFICE TASKS

1. Assume that you are a clerk in a stockroom where two new clerks have been hired. Your supervisor has asked you to explain to the new clerks why it is important to follow the procedures for maintaining and dispensing stock. Write an outline of the points you would plan to cover in your discussion with the new clerks.

2. Write a letter of two to three paragraphs to your teacher on one of the following topics: The Importance of Maintaining Adequate Inventories in a Retail Establishment. The Value of Neatness in the Stockroom of an Insurance Company. The Kinds of Inventories Maintained by Manufacturing Companies and the Value of Each Kind. The letter should be block style with mixed punctuation.

PART 2 CLERICAL INVENTORY PROCEDURES

Jack Walls is a stock clerk in the central stockroom of Buffalo's largest television dealer. Not only does the company sell television sets, radios, and stereo equipment, but it also repairs equipment for customers. The stockroom has several thousand different parts that must be kept in stock if repairs are to be made quickly and satisfactorily. Jack finds his work varied, which he likes. Jack not only checks new stock, but he also answers the telephone. At times servicemen call in for parts. Jack gets the needed parts from the stockroom and then drives the company truck to the customer's home, so that the serviceman can finish the repair job.

STOCKROOM RECORD KEEPING

In order to maintain inventories in every kind of business, accurate record keeping is necessary. From the time a copy of a purchase order reaches the stockroom until the time goods are reordered, there is a series of steps that must be followed to keep supplies of stock on hand ready for use when needed.

Receiving Goods

The stockroom keeps on file a copy of the purchase order (see Illus. 12-5, page 454) for goods to be received. When goods arrive, you will have to check what is received against what was ordered. The usual procedure for handling this task is:

1. Note the invoice that accompanies the goods received that will indicate your company's order number.
2. Take from your files the copy of the original purchase order and check it against the invoice to be sure you have the right order.
3. Compare the items listed on the invoice accompanying the goods against the listing on the copy of the purchase order. If there are any differences between these two, you should note the difference on the invoice received as well as on the copy of the purchase order.

4. Open the goods and count them against the file copy of the purchase order. Every company has an established procedure for doing this. You will generally have assistance in opening cartons and placing the contents on a table or stand so that counting can be done easily. Counting should be done carefully, so it is important that you check the total contents of each carton.

5. Check the quality of the goods received. For example, if you are checking letterheads, one ream should be opened to determine if the printing is clear and in the style and color requested.

Recording the Receipt of New Stock

For each item received in the shipment, you will find a control sheet or card. You will have to note the receipt of the order on this sheet or card. Illus. 14-6 shows you the supply control card for personnel time sheets. Notice that there is a record of the date the time sheets were ordered, plus the quantity ordered. If the quantity received is the same as the quantity ordered, then a check is all that is needed. If there is a difference, then the actual quantity received is recorded.

Illus. 14-6
Supply control card

Min. Quantity *120 pads*			**SUPPLY CONTROL**							Location Dept. ____92____
			Store Room No. ____129____							Cabinet ____14____
Max. Quantity *720 pads*			Form Title: *Personnel*							Shelf ____5____
			____*Time Sheets*____							Position ____C____

Date Order	Quantity Ordered	Rec'd	Date Order	Quantity Ordered	Rec'd	Date Order	Quantity Ordered	Rec'd	Date Order	Quantity Ordered	Rec'd	Reminders for Peak-Orders
4/11	500	✓										
6/9	600	550										
7/30	600	✓										

Arranging Stock

Because many businesses must carry a wide variety of items in their stockrooms, stockrooms must be orderly places if you and your fellow workers are to work easily. After goods have been checked, they should immediately be placed in their correct locations. You will find that the stockroom is organized much the same way that a library is organized. Note the specification of location shown in Illus. 14-7.

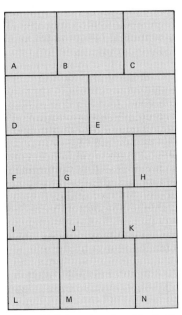

Illus. 14-7 Inventory location form

Location of Forms		Shelf Location
A3216	Premium—first notice	D
B4391	Change of premium rate	L
C8381	Policy—straight life	A
C9132	Policy—endowment	C
D4211	Policy—annuity	B
D9311	Policy—term	G
F3311	Policy—varied	F
G3576	Policy—rider	H
H8210	Policy—change of	E
H9325	Policy—termination of	J
J4101	Policy—application	L
K4210	Policy—health examination	I
L3210	Premium—change of payment	M
M2100	Policy—change of beneficiary	N

The stock should be arranged neatly at its correct location. It is standard practice to place old stock in the front so that it will be used first. This means that you will move the old stock to the side, while you stack the new stock to the rear of the location.

Counting Stock

As you learned in Part 1, companies find it important to know how much stock is on hand. The two most common systems for keeping a count of the inventory are the perpetual inventory system and the direct counting system.

The Perpetual Inventory Card. The card used in a perpetual inventory system includes a great deal of information. The following items usually are included on the perpetual inventory control card.

1. The stock number of the item—which is the key identification for the item. Notice on Illus. 14-8 that the bottom line contains the same information as the top line. This is done so that the card can be arranged in a visible file for easy access.
2. The description of the item, including its size, finish, color. This card is used for appliances in a major retailing establishment with stores in many parts of the world.

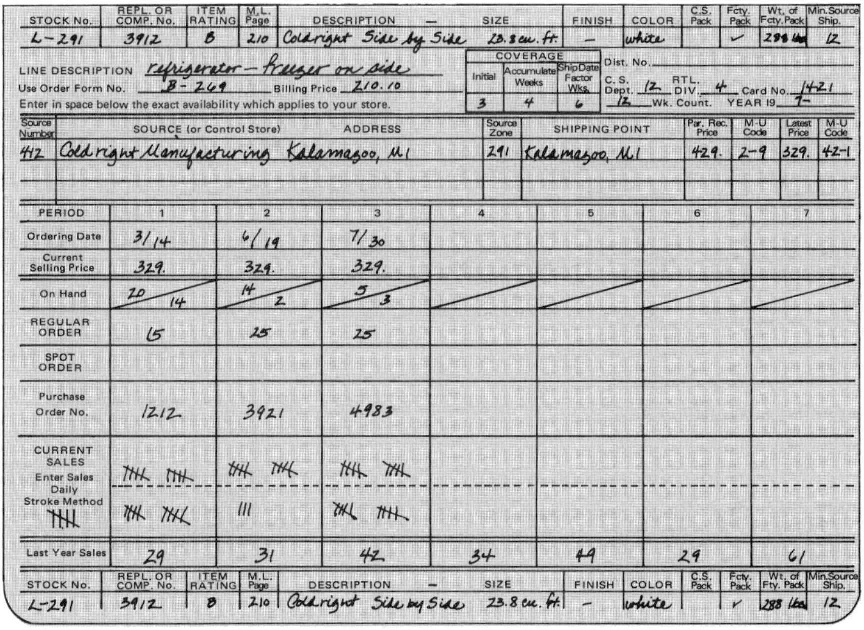

STOCK No.	REPL. OR COMP. No.	ITEM RATING	M.L. Page	DESCRIPTION — SIZE		FINISH	COLOR	C.S. Pack	Fcty. Pack	Wt. of Fcty. Pack	Min. Source Ship.
L-291	3912	B	210	Coldright Side by Side	23.8 cu. ft.	—	white		✓	288 lbs	12

LINE DESCRIPTION refrigerator—freezer on side
Use Order Form No. B-269 Billing Price 210.10
Enter in space below the exact availability which applies to your store.

COVERAGE		
Initial	Accumulate Weeks	Ship Date Factor Wks.
3	4	6

Dist. No.
C. S. Dept. 12 RTL. DIV. 4 Card No. 1421
12 Wk. Count. YEAR 19 7-

Source Number	SOURCE (or Control Store)	ADDRESS	Source Zone	SHIPPING POINT	Par. Rec. Price	M-U Code	Latest Price	M-U Code
412	Coldright Manufacturing	Kalamazoo, MI	291	Kalamazoo, MI	429.	2-9	329.	42-1

PERIOD	1	2	3	4	5	6	7
Ordering Date	3/14	6/19	7/30				
Current Selling Price	329.	329.	329.				
On Hand	20 / 14	14 / 2	5 / 3				
REGULAR ORDER	15	25	25				
SPOT ORDER							
Purchase Order No.	1212	3921	4983				
CURRENT SALES Enter Sales Daily Stroke Method							
Last Year Sales	29	31	42	34	49	29	61

STOCK No.	REPL. OR COMP. No.	ITEM RATING	M.L. Page	DESCRIPTION — SIZE		FINISH	COLOR	C.S. Pack	Fcty. Pack	Wt. of Fty. Pack	Min. Source Ship.
L-291	3912	B	210	Coldright Side by Side	23.8 cu. ft.	—	white		✓	288 lbs	12

Illus. 14-8
Perpetual inventory control card

3. Source of the item as well as shipping point. In this instance, the source may be either a store within the company or an outside vendor.
4. The ordering date for additional stock, that is, the length of time that it takes from the time goods are re-ordered until they arrive.
5. The current price at which the item is sold at retail.
6. Current sales which, you will notice, are recorded daily.

The Record for Periodic Counting. A form that is used for maintaining the periodic count of small items is shown in Illus. 14-9. This form is used in a stockroom that makes a quick physical count once every two weeks. The count usually is taken at the beginning of the first working day of the week. This count has two purposes:

1. To have an updated record of the actual amount of stock on hand
2. To reorder items that have reached minimum levels

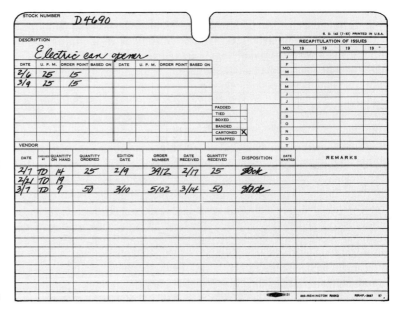

Illus. 14-9
Periodic count record

Remington Rand

In addition to recording the count, you will be expected to note the items that have reached their minimum levels (those which must be reordered if an adequate stockroom supply is to be maintained). Supply room bin tickets (descriptive labels which identify an item in a bin) indicate the code number for the item as well as the minimum level. When you notice that an item has reached its minimum level, make a record of this on a supply room order memo form, such as that shown in Illus. 14-10.

SUPPLY ROOM ORDER MEMO

Supply Room: List below the Supply Record Card Number for each item having reached its Minimum Low Stock. This information is obtained from the Supply Room Bin Tickets. Refer this Order Memo to the Control Office for ordering.

Control Office: Remove cards with corresponding numbers from the Supply Record Card File Box. Enter the quantity to be ordered. Write order. Replace cards.

CARD NO.	CARD NO.	CARD NO.	CARD NO.	CARD NO.
B-491				
F-398				
G-491				
G-891				
H-411				
I-519				
L-919				
M-219				
N-488				
P-462				
R-121				
R-532				

Illus. 14-10
Supply room order form

The Annual Count. Most businesses find it necessary to take a thorough count of all items in inventory at least once a year. This inventory-taking activity often requires closing the stockroom for a day or longer. This process is often necessary to get an accurate financial picture of the year's activities.

Preliminary to the actual counting, you will have to do some housekeeping chores in the stockroom. Even the best managed stockroom is likely to have a few items out of order. Therefore, you and your fellow workers will be involved in straightening all the shelves, rearranging any items that are out of place, and putting on the shelves any unpacked items.

Preliminary: before; preceding

Generally you will work in teams of two for this job. There are procedures that must be followed for doing the job so that it is done completely. Also, the counting is generally checked by others; so it is important that the same procedures are used by everyone.

REQUISITION OF STOCK

Items may be requested from the stockroom over the telephone or in person, but normally the request must be written. Once items have been properly requisitioned, the person making the request may either take the items with him or have the stockroom personnel deliver them.

Requesting Stock

Each company has organized procedures that are used by all persons who need items from the stockroom. In most instances, a written request is required. However, many stockrooms do accept requests, especially emergency ones, by telephone. A written form is then prepared by the stockroom and the form is signed by the receiving office at the time of delivery.

Illus. 14-11
Signed requisition form

Illus. 14-11 is a requisition form which is filled in by a clerk in the stockroom. It is signed by the person who gets the stock. Notice that the quantity, code number, and a brief description of each item are listed.

183700031	0547-2		10843								CHECK DATA PRINTED WITH DELIVERED ITEMS
BUDGET NO.	DATE	CODES	QTY. 1	CODE	QTY. 2	CODE	QTY. 3	CODE	QTY. 4	CODE	QTY. 5 CODE

BUDGET NO.- SUPPLIES EXPENSE	DATE	DEPARTMENT - PROJECT - OFFICE	FOR STORES USE ONLY
18 -3700 -031	5 24 7-	*Advertising*	0 05361

REQUESTED BY	DELIVER TO		RECEIVED BY
Toni Blair	RM 351	*Macy Bldg.*	*Toni Blair*

QUANTITY	CODE	DESCRIPTION	B.O.*
1 *1*	0843	*Cassette Tape C 120*	
2			
3			
4			
5			

B.O.* QUANTITY IN THIS COLUMN INDICATES ITEMS OUT OF STOCK OR PARTIALLY DELIVERED. PLEASE REORDER UNDELIVERED ITEMS.

DELIVERY COPY

Delivering Stock

Persons who go to the stockroom for items will frequently carry them back to their desks with them if they are manageable. However, many times stockroom supplies are ordered. On such occasions, one of the employees of the stockroom may be responsible for putting all the items requested by one person, or one office, together and later delivering them by cart to the proper location. If you are given the responsibility for delivering goods, you will find it useful to always check on the following:

1. The items listed on the requisition should match the items you have packed.
2. You should have accurate information about the location to which the items are to be delivered.
3. Someone at the receiving office should sign a copy of the requisition so that you have evidence that you have delivered the supplies.

1. For what reason does a stockroom keep a copy of a purchase order?
2. Why is it necessary to count the merchandise received in the stockroom?
3. Why is stock placed on shelves rather than kept in the cartons in which it is received?
4. Why is stock placed on shelves according to a predetermined order?
5. Why is new stock placed behind old stock?
6. Name three types of information you would be *likely* to find on a perpetual inventory card.
7. Which kinds of items are frequently maintained according to a perpetual inventory plan?
8. What is the meaning of *reaching a minimum level*?
9. What should a stockroom clerk do when an item reaches a minimum level?
10. For what purpose is an annual count made?

**MAKING
DECISIONS**

Some new books arrived in a large bookstore in St. Louis, where Cynthia is employed as a stockroom assistant. She opened the books and recalled that they had been ordered. She saw no need to check them against the purchase order, since book publishers seldom made mistakes when shipping orders. She put the books, which were all reorders, on their proper shelves and threw away the carton.

What do you think of Cynthia's decision to trust her memory of the original order?

**WORKING
WITH
OTHERS**

Bert is a clerk in a large stockroom of an insurance company. Requisitions are received through local mail, in person, and by telephone. Bert is a hardworking young man and is very courteous to all the persons who request supplies. There is a new assistant to one of the vice presidents who always seems to need supplies. She, however, never anticipates her needs and regularly makes emergency calls to the stockroom requesting that small items be delivered immediately. She generally says, "As soon as I hang up, please deliver the supplies I need *right* now." Bert doesn't want to be discourteous toward her, but he feels that she is unreasonable in her constant requests. What would you suggest that Bert do?

**USING
LANGUAGE**

Write or type each of the following sentences on a separate sheet of paper, correcting the misspelled words.

1. It is not ture that we will recieve all the questionaires by the end of the week.
2. We can get acommodations for you very quickily.
3. He is very conscientous about his work, don't you think?
4. There are three seperate packages that must be delivered latter.
5. Tommorrow is going to be a busey day for everone.
6. On what ocassion do you think that would be appropriate?
7. Will they aprecaite the work you are doing now?
8. Betsy isnt going to be able to mannage all those tasks at the same time.
9. The referrence to the report was uncorrect.
10. He will precede to do the hole job by the time we are able to help him.

Assume that you have been assigned the task of determining which items are to be reordered, that is, which have reached their minimum level. In the left column is a list of the minimum levels for five items in your stockroom. In the right column are the actual amounts on hand when you are checking. On a separate sheet of paper list items that must be reordered.

Minimum Quantities	*Quantity on Hand*
1. 12 dozen	154 items
2. 10 gross	15 packages (Each contains a dozen items.)
3. 2 gross	23 packages (Each contains a dozen items.)
4. 100 yards	305 feet
5. 20 reams	250 sheets

**PERFORMING
OFFICE
TASKS**

Assume that you have taken the following information from three reorder inventory cards that were pulled from the shelves. Draw up an order form like that illustrated and use it for reordering the following from A. G. C. Supply House, 39 Atlantic Avenue, Albany, NY 12204.

12 gross Pencils No. 456 @ 37 cents a dozen
15 doz. 3M Scotch Tape $\frac{1}{2}$ x 1296 in. @ 49 cents a roll
12 doz. Yellow Pads $8\frac{1}{2}$ by 11 No. 134 @ $1.80 a dozen

Illus. 14-12

TRAVELERS' INN
1224 AMSTERDAM AVE., NEWARK, NEW JERSEY 07105
TELEPHONE: (201) 870-4307

PURCHASE ORDER

2900

THIS NUMBER MUST APPEAR ON ALL
SHIPPING LABELS AND INVOICES.

DATE:

**INSIDE DELIVERY TO
SOUTH SIDEWALK CHUTE ONLY**

TO:

PLEASE INVOICE IN TRIPLICATE

QUANTITY	ITEM NUMBER	D E S C R I P T I O N

Authorized _____

UNIT 15

FINANCIAL DUTIES

ACCOUNTING CLERK

Career opportunity for hig
school grad who enjoys worl
ng with figures. Some a
unts receivable or cost wo
ful but we will train. Ge
accounting and cleric
Legible handwriting
bus line, 10 minute
Free parking. Ca
961-03

Part 1 Using a Checkbook

Part 2 Banking Activities

Part 3 Using the Petty Cash Fund

Part 4 Computing Wages

Part 5 Recording and Paying Earnings

PART 1

USING A CHECKBOOK

Karen Haines works in the office of the Lakeview Bank. Quite often in her work she finds checks with amounts of money that she can't read. Occasionally she finds a check that isn't signed or one on which the amount written in figures does not agree with the amount written in words. Karen knows that checks with errors like these cannot be cashed; so she returns them to the person to whom the check was written. She has learned how important it is to write a check correctly.

As with most of your other duties, the size and type of firm for which you work will determine the extent of your contact with banks. For example, if you are employed by a large firm with a separate accounting department, your contacts with banks may be limited. On the other hand, if you are employed by a small firm or by one engaged mainly in financial transactions (for example, a loan company), dealing with banks may be one of your most important daily tasks.

The information presented in this part will not only help you in your office work it will also be helpful for your personal use.

ADVANTAGES OF CHECKING ACCOUNTS

There are several advantages to keeping money in a checking account which apply to individuals as well as to businesses. Business firms prefer to keep money in the bank because it is safer than keeping it at the place of business. Paying bills by check is usually preferred because the **canceled check** is returned to the one who wrote it and is a receipt for payment. It is safer to send checks through the mail than to send cash. Also, check stubs provide a record of what has been paid out by the company.

canceled check:
a check paid by
the bank

OPENING A CHECKING ACCOUNT

When you open a personal checking account, the bank may want to have you identified and/or introduced by one of its **depositors**. If you

depositors:
persons who put
money in the bank

are not known by a depositor, the bank may ask for one or more **references** — usually a reference from another bank where you may have had an account or a reference from your present employer. This request is made so that the bank may check the references to be fairly sure that it is dealing with a responsible person who will use the account properly.

Before your account is opened you will be asked to fill out a *signature card*, which will be kept on file at the bank. The signature which you use to sign your checks should always agree with your signature on the card. If you have used a given name and a middle name on the signature card, *Mary Alice Downs*, for example, you should not use initials, such as *M. A. Downs*, when you sign your checks.

When more than one person is to sign checks for a firm — the president, vice-president, and the treasurer, for example — all must fill out signature cards. If you are asked to handle the checking account for a business, a letter must be sent to the bank authorizing your signature; and you will have to fill out a signature card before you will be permitted to sign checks.

Authorized Signatures of Blanch, Robert L.	ACCOUNT NUMBER
FOR THE PLAINS NATIONAL BANK, LUBBOCK, TEXAS	326 004 31

Below are duly authorized signatures, which you will recognize in the payment of funds or in the transaction of other business on my account. In making this deposit and at all times in doing business with this bank, I specifically agree to all of the terms and conditions printed on the reverse side hereof.

Date *April 4, 19--*

Signature *Robert L. Blanch*

Signature   Telephone No. *799-0624*

Signature *Robert L. Blanch*   Account

Signature *by Mary Alice Downs*   Accepted by *M T.*

Address   257 Mt. Vernon Avenue

Business   Mt. Vernon Insurance Agency

Introduced by   Philip E. Owens

Please honor the above signature on checks against my account or as endorsement on checks or drafts in my favor.

Illus. 15-1 Signature card This card shows the employee's authorization to sign checks.

WRITING CHECKS

A *check* is a written order directing a bank to pay out the money of a depositor; therefore, it should be written very carefully. An incorrectly written check can cause a great deal of inconvenience — not to mention the risks involved if the check should fall into the hands of a dishonest person.

The Check Stub

The first step in writing a check is to fill out the check stub. You must do this *before* you write the check, or you may forget to fill it out and to subtract the amount from your account balance. If this happens, your check stub balance will be greater than the amount you actually have in the bank; and you will not have a record of the check until the bank returns your canceled checks or notifies you that your account has been **overdrawn.**

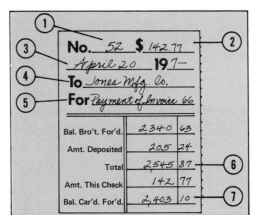

Illus. 15-2
Check stub

Usually the check stubs are bound into the checkbook to the left of the blank checks. The stubs provide space for this information (see Illus. 15-2): (1) check number, (2) amount, (3) date, (4) name of the **payee**, and (5) purpose. The amount of the check should be subtracted from the (6) previously recorded balance and the (7) new balance entered on the stub. This amount will also be written on the next stub (No. 53) as the "Bal. Bro't. For'd."

Writing Checks

Checks must be written properly because, if an amount of money or a name on a check is illegible or incorrect, many problems are created for you, your employer, the person to whom the check is written, and the bank. It is up to you to make sure that you don't make out a check for $556.28 when the bill was for $56.28 or that you don't write a check to Elton G. Tipton when the check was to be written to Elton H. Tipton. Here are some suggestions for writing checks:

1. *Type checks or write them in ink — never in pencil.*
2. *Number* each check, if numbers are not printed on them. Be sure that the number of the check is the same as the number on the check stub.

3. *Date* the check on the exact date that it is written. Do not *postdate* a check, that is, date it ahead with the hope that there will be enough money in the account by that time to cover the check.

Illus. 15-3
Check with stub

4. Write the name of the payee in full. If you are not sure of the correct spelling, check it in the telephone directory or from previous correspondence. Omit titles such as Mr., Mrs., Miss, Dr., or Prof.

5. *Write the amount* of the check in large, bold figures close enough to the printed dollar sign to prevent anyone from adding any other figures. In spelling out the amount, start at the extreme left, capitalize the first letter only, and express cents as fractions of one hundred:
   Three hundred thirty-four no/100- - - - - - - - - -*Dollars*
   One thousand five hundred fifty 75/100- - - - - -*Dollars*
   If you should write a check for less than a dollar, precede the spelled-out amount with the word *Only* and cross out the printed word *Dollars* as:
   Only eighty-nine cents- - - - - - - - - - - - - - - - - -~~Dollars~~

6. *Fill in all blank spaces* after the written amount with hyphens, periods, or a line to prevent anyone from changing the amount.

7. *Write the purpose of the check*, such as *In Payment of Invoice 3960*, at the bottom of the check. Some checks have a special blank line for this purpose.

8. *Do not erase* on a check. If you should make an error in writing a check, write the word **Void** across the face of both the check and the check stub. Save the voided check and file it in numerical order with the canceled checks when they are returned by the bank.

Void:
of no legal effect

9. *Do not sign blank checks* — that is, checks which do not have the name of the payee and the amount filled in — because anyone can fill them in and cash them.

10. *Do not make a check payable to "Cash"* unless you plan to cash it at once, because if it is misplaced, anyone who finds it can cash it.

11. *Write legibly.* An illegible signature can cause problems at the bank and is no protection against forgery.

A firm issuing a large number of checks usually will print the amount of each check with a checkwriter, a machine that prints the amount into the check paper to prevent any alteration.

Duplicate Checks

Your firm may prefer to prepare checks in duplicate with a ball-point pen or a typewriter instead of taking the time to fill in regular check stubs. The original of each check is sent out, but the duplicate copy is kept for reference purposes and for entering the transaction in the company records.

Writing Checks for Bills

Paying bills by check is a great responsibility. If writing checks for paying bills is one of your duties in the office, you should know the proper procedure for writing checks and the **precautions** you should take to prevent errors.

precautions: care taken in advance

The usual procedure for paying bills is:

1. Make sure all bills are approved for payment by your immediate supervisor or whoever is responsible for releasing bills for payment. Some bills may be sent to the company that include items which were not received, and the bill should not be paid until the matter is cleared up. In a large company, the shipping clerk is responsible for checking each invoice against the shipment of goods to make sure all items are there. In a small company, you may be responsible for performing this task.

2. Verify all computations on the bill. This may involve multiplying the number of items received times the cost of each, adding items to arrive at totals, figuring discounts, and subtracting the discount from the total amount due.

3. Fill in the check stub first. Be sure to give enough information so that the stub can be used in preparing the financial records such as the Cash Payments Journal.

4. Fill in the check. Make sure that the number on the check stub and the number on the check are the same.

5. Write on the bill or invoice the date and the check number used to pay the bill.

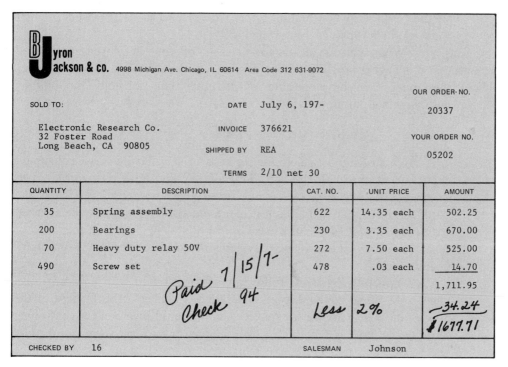

Illus. 15-4
Invoice
showing
discount

Filing Paid Bills

A procedure must be established and followed for filing paid bills. You may file them alphabetically according to the name of the firm. In a small business, you may file them all together under "Bills Paid," although the file may become quite bulky. Another method is to file them according to subject. You should keep all utility bills in one folder, all bills for supplies in another folder, and so on.

Whatever method is used, you should be consistent and file all bills the same way each month. In this way, you will be able to find a paid bill if there is a question about it.

Writing Checks for Cash

Occasionally you may be asked to get cash for your employer from his checking account. To do this you should write a check to *Cash*, that is, the word *Cash* should be written in the blank where the payee's name would usually go. Your employer must sign the check, and you can then take it to the bank and receive the cash. Usually the bank will require the person who receives the cash to *endorse* the check, that is, to sign it on the back.

negotiable:
easily transferred
to another person
or cashed

Since a check made out to *Cash* is highly **negotiable**, extreme care should be taken when handling this type of check. If the check is lost, whoever finds it can cash it immediately.

When you are asked to get cash for your employer, make sure that it is kept completely separate from your own money. It is best to put the money in an envelope and seal it rather than put it in your billfold with your own money.

STOPPING PAYMENT ON CHECKS

One of the firm's employees calls to say that he has lost his paycheck. You must call the bank immediately and have payment stopped on the check. If the check has not already been cashed or deposited, the bank will refuse payment when it is presented. Payment may be stopped for a number of reasons: if a check is lost or stolen, if it has been made out incorrectly, or if it represents payment for goods or services which have been canceled.

drawer:
the person who
signed the check

confirming letter:
letter sent to
verify something

You must give the following information to stop payment on a check: the name of the **drawer**, the date of the check, the amount of the check, and the name of the payee. You should also send a **confirming letter** to the bank immediately or fill out a stop payment form supplied by the bank. This form gives the bank written instructions not to cash the check described.

OVERDRAFT

An overdraft occurs when a depositor writes a check on an account in which he does not have enough money to cover the full payment. This happens when checks that have not been entered and deducted on the check stubs are cashed or when an error is made in computing or recording the checkbook balance on the stubs.

When a personal checking account is overdrawn, a bank may return the check marked *Insufficient Funds*. A charge is made by the bank for handling the overdraft. Thus, an overdraft is expensive as well as embarrassing to the individual.

**REVIEWING
WHAT YOU
HAVE READ**

1. Name four advantages of keeping money in a checking account.
2. How is a checking account opened?
3. What is the purpose of a signature card?

4. When should the check stub be filled in, and what information should be on it?
5. Give ten suggestions that will enable you to write checks correctly.
6. What is a checkwriter?
7. For what purposes are duplicate checks used?
8. What procedure should you follow when paying bills by check?
9. Why should you be very careful with a check made out to Cash?
10. Under what conditions should payment be stopped on a check, and what procedure should be followed?

MAKING DECISIONS

What can you do to make it less likely that your check could be altered?

WORKING WITH OTHERS

You work for Mrs. Phillips who owns a small dress shop. Today Mrs. Phillips hands you an invoice and says, "Please make out a check for this invoice and get it in the mail today. The terms are 2/10, n/30; so be sure to take the discount." While looking over the invoice, you see that it is dated June 7. This is the 18th of June — one day past the time allowed for the discount.

Mrs. Phillips made a specific point of telling you to take the discount. How should you handle this situation?

USING LANGUAGE

In addition to the uses mentioned in Unit 10, Part 2, semicolons are used

1. Before such words and abbreviations as *e.g., i.e., viz., for example, namely*, and *to wit* when they introduce a long list of items. A comma precedes the list.
   Example: Some words cause students difficulty; for example, farther and further, affect and effect, fewer and less, good and well.

2. Between elements in a listing when there are commas within the elements.
   Example: Dr. John R. Jones, of St. Mary's Hospital; Dr. William Blase, of Taft Memorial Clinic; and Dr. Joseph Craig, of Cranley, Meese, Hafner and Craig, won awards for surgical exhibits.

3. Before connectives when such words introduce sentences, principal clauses, or an abrupt change in thought. Some of these connectives are *accordingly consequently, hence, however, in fact, moreover, nevertheless, therefore, thus, whereas, yet.* (A comma usually follows the connective.)
   Example: We warned him that the bridge was out and the road dangerous; nevertheless, he went ahead.

   On a separate sheet of paper type the sentences below punctuating them based on the five semicolon rules you have learned (see page 371).

   1. Before they left for camp they bought bread coffee and eggs at the grocery store bacon sausage and hamburger at the meat market soap and toothpaste at the drug store and some waxed paper at the dime store
   2. They used a new method of pitching their tent therefore it was put up faster
   3. He did not join the Air Force he joined the Navy
   4. They took their checkbook cash and travel checks with them but Tom used up his checking account balance Bill ran out of cash and Sam's travel checks were not sufficient
   5. On their trip they went to the Grand Canyon by Route 66 which skirts the Ozarks and from the Grand Canyon they turned south going to Phoenix and Tucson Arizona but from there they turned back towards home

6. The portrait was removed from the school lobby in its place was hung a modern painting

7. The membership of the finance committee was as follows Blake School 4 representatives Anderson High School 5 representatives Mt. Hope Commercial School 2 representatives Taho Business School 1 representative

8. He said he wanted to take a long trip this summer yet he appeared to be making no plans

9. He used a new method of cultivation therefore his yield was greater.

10. The third game of the World Series was rained out moreover several players could not play because of injuries

USING ARITHMETIC

On the morning of March 18, you had a checkbook balance of $2,785.65. During the day you wrote checks for $175.83, $187.25, $32.31, and $17.18. What was your checkbook balance on the morning of March 19?

PERFORMING OFFICE TASKS

You are employed by Johnson & Sears and have been authorized to write and sign checks. If forms are available, complete the check stubs and write the checks for these checks issued on the 10th of November. If forms are not available, find the checkbook balance after each transaction.

The balance according to the last check stub is $2,735.17.

Check 515, Linton Service Company, $189.53, for invoice of November 2.

Check 516, Copeland Exterminators, $759.15, for services performed on November 9.

Check 517, Howard A. Johnson, $85, for personal use.

Check 518, Hilton Office Supply, $35.17, for typing paper and paper clips.

PART 2   BANKING ACTIVITIES

Jim Green is an accounting clerk for the Rice Supply Company. One of his duties is to prepare money for deposit and take it to the bank. The daily deposit consists of checks, money orders, and cash. Jim knows that he must be very careful in making up the deposit slip since the Accounting Department depends on the accuracy of the information on the slip, and the Rice Supply Company accounting records must balance with the bank records. Mr. Harry Krenek, the Manager, trusts Jim's ability to take care of the daily deposits because he knows that Jim is capable, honest, and exact in preparing the company's bank deposit.

MAKING A DEPOSIT

A deposit is made in a checking account by presenting to the bank teller a deposit slip and the cash, checks, and money orders to be deposited. Usually a deposit slip is made in duplicate, and the duplicate copy is given back to the depositor as a receipt after it has been stamped by the teller.

Illus. 15-5
Care must be given to preparing and making bank deposits.

First National City Bank

Preparing Cash for Deposit

The money to be deposited in the bank will usually consist of coins, bills, checks, and money orders. For ease in handling, coins and bills should be put in money wrappers furnished by the bank. Coins are placed in paper rolls, and bills are wrapped in paper bill wrappers. Coin and bill wrappers should have the amount and the depositor's name on them so that if a mistake is made in counting the money, the correct amount can be credited to the right account. Pack coins in paper rolls in the following quantities:

Denomination	Number of Coins to a Roll	Total Value of Coins in Roll
Pennies	50	$ .50
Nickels	40	2.00
Dimes	50	5.00
Quarters	40	10.00
Halves	20	10.00

If you have many bills of different denominations, you should package each denomination in amounts of $50, $100, and so on. Be sure that all bills face the same way.

Preparing Checks and Money Orders for Deposit

All checks or money orders which are to be deposited must be endorsed. The endorsement may be handwritten in ink or stamped with a rubber stamp across the back of the check at the top of the left end.

Before preparing the deposit slip, make sure that all checks are properly endorsed. The most common types of endorsements are restrictive, blank, and full endorsements.

A *restrictive endorsement* enables you to send an endorsed check safely through the mail. *For Deposit Only* is written above the signature of the endorser. If you endorse a check in this way, it can only be deposited in your account. Since the check cannot be cashed by anyone else, there is little danger if the check is misplaced, lost, or stolen. This is why the restrictive endorsement is used by most business firms.

A *blank endorsement* consists only of a signature across the back of the check. It makes the check payable to anyone who may possess it. You should use this type of endorsement only when you plan to cash or deposit a check immediately. It is not the correct endorsement for a check that is sent through the mail or for a check that could be lost or misplaced, because the check can be cashed by anyone who holds it — even if he has no right to it.

An *endorsement in full* or *special endorsement*, as it is sometimes called, shows the name of the person to whom the check is being trans-

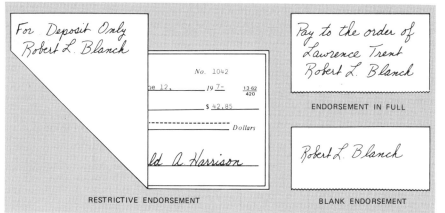

For Deposit Only
Robert L. Blanch

No. 1042
ne 12,   19 7-   13 62 / 420
$ 42.85
-------------------- Dollars
ld A. Harrison

RESTRICTIVE ENDORSEMENT

Pay to the order of
Lawrence Trent
Robert L. Blanch

ENDORSEMENT IN FULL

Robert L. Blanch

BLANK ENDORSEMENT

Illus. 15-6

ferred. For example, the words, *Pay to the order of Lawrence Trent*, may be written before the endorser's signature. A check endorsed in this way cannot be cashed by anyone without Lawrence Trent's signature. Therefore, you may send a check endorsed in this manner through the mail without danger in case of loss.

Preparing a Deposit Slip

A deposit slip is a form supplied by the bank on which the money to be deposited is listed. Deposit slips are usually prepared in duplicate. The information to be filled in on a deposit slip includes the account number, the name of the depositor, the date, the items to be deposited, and the total. The items to be deposited may be currency (paper money), silver (coins), endorsed checks, and /or money orders.

Illus. 15-7
Deposit slips

You may list the checks on the deposit slip by the ABA (American Bankers Association) number, which is in fraction form in the upper right corner of the check; by name (if it is a local bank); or by the city and state of out-of-town banks. You should add the checks, currency, and silver together and put the total at the bottom of the deposit slip.

When you go to the bank and present the deposit slip and items to be deposited to the teller, he will check the items with the deposit slip. The deposit slip is then stamped either by the teller or by a machine, and you are given one of the copies of the deposit slip as a receipt.

RECONCILING A BANK STATEMENT

Statement of Account: a list of additions to and subtractions from a checking account

Sometime during each month your employer will receive a **Statement of Account** and the canceled checks that the bank paid out of your firm's account during the previous month. Some banks send the statement early in the month to all their customers; other banks mail customers' statements at different times of the month.

As shown on page 519, the Statement of Account lists the Statement period—A; the Beginning Balance—B; Total Deposits—C; Total Checks—D; the Service Charge—E—deducted by the bank for handling the account; and the Ending Balance—F—of the period.

When you receive the canceled checks and the bank statement, you should compare the final balance on the bank statement with the checkbook balance. If the two figures are not the same, you must find out why there is a difference. This process of accounting for the difference is called *reconciling the bank statement*. For the convenience of their depositors, many banks print a reconciliation form on the back of the monthly statements. The following steps should be taken to reconcile an account:

numerical: by number

1. Arrange the canceled checks in **numerical** order.

2. Compare the returned checks with the stubs in the checkbook. Place a check mark on the stub of each check that has been returned.

outstanding checks: those checks that have not been paid and returned by the bank

3. Make a list of the **outstanding checks**. Include on the list the number of each outstanding check and the amount.

4. Add the amount of outstanding checks and deduct the total from the balance shown on the bank statement.

service charge: amount charged by the bank for keeping an account

5. Subtract the amount of the **service charge** listed on the bank statement from the checkbook balance.

6. After the service charge has been deducted from the checkbook balance, the remaining amount should agree

| THE PLAINS NATIONAL BANK LUBBOCK, TX 79408 | STATEMENT OF ACCOUNT | | |

Jeanne Morris
3105 Auburn Avenue
Lubbock, TX 79409

ACCOUNT NO.	PAGE NO.
63 072 8	1

5-17-7-	6-18-7
A FROM	TO

STATEMENT PERIOD

B	C		D		E	F
BEGINNING BALANCE	TOTAL DEPOSITS		TOTAL CHECKS		SERVICE CHARGE	ENDING BALANCE
	NO.	AMOUNT	NO.	AMOUNT		
499.02	2	929.49	12	847.01	1.50	530.00

AMOUNT	CODE	AMOUNT	CODE	AMOUNT	CODE	DATE	BALANCE	CODE
16.81						05/18	432.21	
9.80		25.20				05/21	397.21	
5.77		680.19	DP			05/22	1,071.63	
6.00						05/23	1,065.63	
15.30		146.01				05/26	904.32	
350.00		249.30	DP			05/30	803.62	
165.00						06/05	638.62	
44.72		19.50				06/15	574.40	
26.09		1.50	SC	16.81		06/17	530.00	

CODE EXPLANATION

SC – SERVICE CHARGE	OD – OVERDRAFT	DM – DEBIT MEMO	EC – ERROR CORRECT
RT – RETURNED CHECK	OC – OVERDRAFT CHARGES	CM – CREDIT MEMO	RC – RETURN CHARGE

Illus. 15-8
Statement
of account

with the balance shown on the bank statement after the total of the outstanding checks has been deducted.

Here is an example of a reconciliation:

RECONCILIATION OF BANK ACCOUNT
June 18, 197–

Balance as shown on bank statement...	$530.00	Balance as shown on checkbook.......	$375.50
Less checks out-standing:		Less June service charge..........	1.50
No. 143... $50.00			
No. 144... 16.00			
No. 147... 90.00	156.00		
Adjusted bank balance.........	$374.00	Adjusted checkbook balance..........	$374.00

CHECKS OUTSTANDING NOT CHARGED TO ACCOUNT		THIS FORM IS PROVIDED TO HELP YOU BALANCE YOUR BANK STATEMENT	
NO.	$		
143	50 00		
144	16 00		
147	90 00	1. Check Book Balance	$ 375.50
		2. Less Service Charges (if any) shown on this statement (This amount) should be deducted from your book balance.)	$ 1.50
		ADJUSTED CHECK BOOK BALANCE (Item 1 Less Item 2)	$ 374.00
		Bank Balance Shown on This Statement	$ 530.00
		ADD +	
		Deposits not shown in this statement (if any) $ _____ $ _____	
		TOTAL	$
		Subtract- Checks Outstanding	$ 156.00
		BALANCE (should agree with adjusted check book balance above)	$ 374.00
TOTAL	156 00		

Illus. 15-9
Bank reconciliation prepared on printed form on reverse side of bank statement.

These are some of the financial duties you may perform. They are not difficult, but they require accuracy, neatness, responsibility, and efficiency on your part.

Illus. 15-10
Accuracy, neatness, dependability, and efficiency are necessary for the employee who handles banking transactions.

Vincent Nanfra

THE PATH OF A CHECK

A check is passed from person to person and finally returns to the person who wrote it. When a check is written on a bank and deposited in another bank, the check follows the path illustrated on page 521.

The Path of a Check

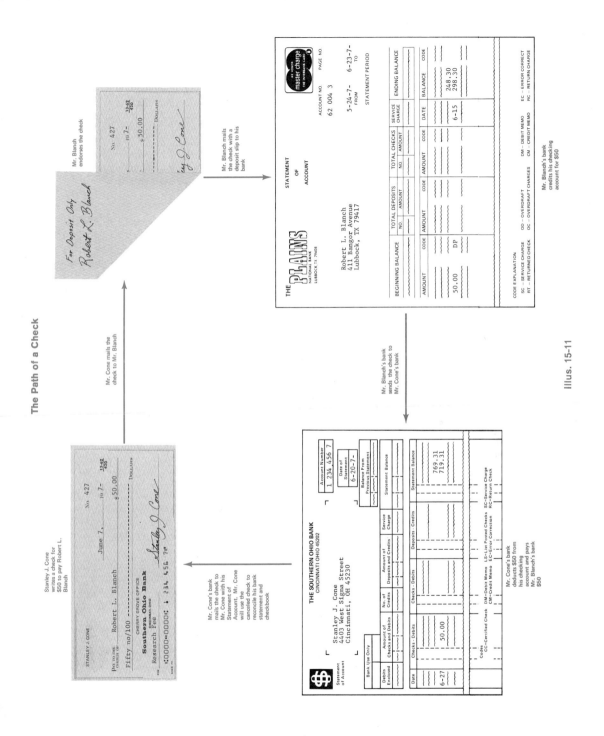

Stanley J. Cone writes a check for $50 to pay Robert L. Blanch

Mr. Cone mails the check to Mr. Blanch

Mr. Blanch endorses the check

Mr. Blanch mails the check with a deposit slip to his bank

Mr. Blanch's bank sends the check to Mr. Cone's bank

Mr. Blanch's bank credits his checking account for $50

Mr. Cone's bank mails the check to Mr. Cone with his Statement of Account. Mr. Cone will use the cancelled check to reconcile his bank statement and checkbook.

Mr. Cone's bank deducts $50 from his checking account and pays Mr. Blanch's bank $50

Illus. 15-11

1. How is a deposit made?
2. Name three types of endorsements.
3. Which endorsement is used by most businesses? Why?
4. When should you use a blank endorsement?
5. What must be done to a check that has a full endorsement before it can be cashed?
6. A deposit slip contains what information?
7. How may checks on a deposit slip be listed?
8. What information is included on a bank statement?
9. How is a reconciliation of the bank statement made?
10. What is the last step in the path that a check follows?

MAKING DECISIONS

Some persons believe that making a bank reconciliation is too much trouble. What is your reaction to this opinion?

WORKING WITH OTHERS

You are a bank teller in the State Security Bank. Mr. Templeton, who recently opened a laundromat, comes to your window with a bagful of coins to make a deposit.

If you stopped to count all the coins, the customers behind Mr. Templeton would have to wait a long time. What should you do?

USING LANGUAGE

Type the following paragraph and insert the necessary capitalization.

on wednesday i met with a committee that was planning a picnic. it will be held on july fourth at the glenwood city park located on the banks of the ohio river. mr. james j. kay will act as chairman of the committee. he is vice-president of the peoples savings bank of watertown. he is a westerner by birth but has made his home in the state of kentucky for many years. mr. kay has invited charles de forest, of brookfield township, to take charge of the sports events of the day. de forest is a vice-president of the howard hardware company and is treasurer-elect of the watertown rotary club. a group of policemen from division g will control traffic at the picnic grounds, and a reporter from the watertown herald will be on hand to give the affair good news coverage.

USING ARITHMETIC

The checking account balance of the Art Craft Company on the first of March was $932.15. During the month the Art Craft Company deposited $2,530.15 and issued checks totaling $2,777.81. Checks amounting to $298.60 have not been cashed.

What is the checkbook balance at the end of the month? What is the bank balance?

PERFORMING OFFICE TASKS

1. You are employed by Johnson & Sears and have been authorized to make deposits for the company. If forms are available, prepare the deposits for November 13 and November 16. If forms are not available, find the total of each deposit slip. The account number of Johnson & Sears is 531-15397.

    November 13 Deposit: currency, $14; silver, $2.25; checks — First National Bank, $59.70; Syracuse, New York, $212.75; Cincinnati, Ohio ,$193.80.

    16 Deposit: currency, $15; checks — Central Trust Company, $221.40; First National Bank, $129.62; Rochester, New York, $279.33.

2. During the month of June the following checks were issued by the Fuel Oil Products Company:

No. 146	$ 16.10	No. 166	$ 65.00
" 147	4.31	" 167	191.84
" 148	4.24	" 168	84.56
" 149	10.23	" 169	2.04
" 150	166.81	" 170	254.68
" 151	204.68	" 171	27.13
" 152	15.31	" 172	19.00
" 153	4.06	" 173	118.34
" 154	.52	" 174	125.00
" 155	18.93	" 175	50.00
" 156	16.77	" 176	6.60
" 157	22.54	" 177	8.14
" 158	18.30	" 178	14.67
" 159	281.69	" 179	178.34
" 160	346.06	" 180	101.47
" 161	2.85	" 181	11.12
" 162	46.81	" 182	219.00
" 163	5.00	" 183	1.92
" 164	8.50	" 184	10.13
" 165	105.25		

The check stub balance on June 1 was $932.15. The deposits for the month were as follows: $401.68, $664.00, $593.45, $432.18, $187.67, $251.17.

The bank statement for the month of June showed a balance of $981.59. A service charge of $1.50 had been deducted. All checks written were returned with the bank statement except Checks 173, 179, 183, and 184.

Prepare the reconciliation of the bank statement.

If you have a workbook, use the reconciliation form similar to those provided by banks in preparing this problem. If you do not have a workbook, prepare your answer following the form shown on page 520.

PART 3 · USING THE PETTY CASH FUND

Alice Ryan, who does general office work at the Hamilton Printing Company, completed a business course in which she learned that, when a package is sent COD, it means that the person who receives the package must pay cash for it when it is delivered. She remembered also that the initials COD mean Collect on Delivery. She knew what to do, therefore, when the deliveryman brought a package to her desk and said, "Here is a COD, Miss Ryan." Since this was a small expense, Alice knew that she must pay cash for the package out of the petty cash fund. As one of her regular office duties, she makes small cash payments for her firm. Alice must know about all of the records necessary to operate the petty cash fund.

THE PETTY CASH FUND

The petty cash fund is used for paying small expenses, such as buying stamps, paying COD charges, and paying for inexpensive office supplies. The petty cash fund should be handled by only one person. Since most of the records on petty cash are handwritten, it is important that they be written so that you and your supervisor can read them easily.

About $25 is usually placed in the petty cash fund; however, the amount may range from $10 to $100, depending upon how much money is needed for small expenses. The money in the fund is usually kept locked in a metal cashbox in the desk of the person handling it, and is placed in the office safe at night.

STARTING THE FUND

To start a petty cash fund

1. Write a check payable to *Petty Cash* for the amount to be placed in the fund, $25 for example. The check may be written by your supervisor or boss if you are not responsible for writing checks.

authorized:
the right or
permission to do
something

2. Have the check signed by an **authorized** person and cashed at the firm's bank.

3. Place the money in the petty cash box.

MAKING PAYMENTS FROM THE FUND

Each time that you make a payment from the petty cash fund you should make out a receipt for the amount and have it signed by the person receiving the money. The receipts should be numbered consecutively. Each should show the date, to whom the payment is to be made, and the purpose of the payment. The signed receipts should be kept in the petty cash box. At all times the cash on hand plus the total amount of the receipts should equal the original amount placed in the fund. Be sure to get a receipt each time you make a payment because *you* are responsible for the money, and the receipts are proof of your proper use of the fund.

```
                        CARSON & BLACK
                     PETTY CASH RECEIPT

No. 311                    Date  July 20            197__
Received of Carson & Black                  $ 1 25
One 25/100 _____ Dollars
For  Miscellaneous store supplies
_____
Account Charged: Store supplies    Signed  J. D. Dean
```

Illus. 15-12
Petty cash receipt

REPLENISHING THE FUND

Additional cash should be placed in the fund whenever the amount of cash gets low. To replenish the fund, follow these steps:

1. Add all receipts and count the cash in the petty cash box.
2. *Prove* the petty cash fund by adding the amount of cash on hand to the total of all petty cash receipts. The sum should equal the amount originally set aside for the fund. An illustration of a proof follows:

Total of petty cash receipts.........	$22.04
Petty cash on hand................	2.96
Total...........................	$25.00

3. Prepare a summary report of petty cash **expenditures** and attach the receipts for them.
4. Write a check payable to *Petty Cash* for the total amount of the receipts shown in the summary report ($22.04 in the illustration on page 526).

expenditures: payments for goods or services

SUMMARY REPORT OF PETTY CASH
July 1 to 31, 197–

Balance on hand, July 1............. $25.00

Expenditures:

Office Supplies............. $4.19
COD Payments............... 3.35
Advertising................ 4.75
Stamps..................... 1.35
Miscellaneous.............. 8.40

Total expenditures................. 22.04

Balance on hand, July 31........... $ 2.96

5. Submit the summary and the attached receipts to your employer with the check payable to the petty cash fund.
6. After your employer has signed the check, cash it and place the money in the petty cash box, thus replenishing the fund.

Sometimes a more permanent record is made of the petty cash fund by using a Petty Cash Book as illustrated below. The amount on the first line shows the balance in the petty cash fund on July 1. As expenditures are made from the fund, the amount is recorded in the Payments column. Several additional columns are provided in a Petty Cash Book to show the distribution of the payments — that is, how much is spent for office supplies, how much for store supplies, and so forth. When writing in an expenditure, place the amount of the expenditure in one of the special columns. Place all items that don't fit the special columns in the miscellaneous column.

PETTY CASH BOOK

Illus. 15-13
Columnar petty
cash book

Date	Explanation	Receipts	Payments	Office Supplies	Store Supplies	Advertising	Messenger	Miscellaneous
July 1	Balance	25 00						
2	Ad in school program		4 75			4 75		
10	Registered letter		90					90
15	Cleaning office		7 50					2 50
19	Delivery of a contract		1 00				1 00	
20	Twine for store		1 25		1 25			
22	Ink		75	75				
25	Immediate delivery of a sale		35				35	
27	Postage stamps		4 85	4 85				
29	Miscellaneous office supplies		69	69				
31	Totals	25 00	22 04	6 29	1 25	4 75	1 35	8 40
31	Balance		2 96					
		25 00	25 00					
31	Balance	2 96						
31	Check No. 475	22 04						

1. What is the purpose of a petty cash fund?
2. How many people should handle the petty cash fund?
3. How much money should be kept in the petty cash fund?
4. How is a petty cash fund established?
5. What information should appear on the petty cash receipt?
6. Why should a receipt for each payment from the petty cash fund be kept?
7. What steps are necessary to replenish the petty cash fund?
8. What information should be included on the summary report of petty cash?
9. What should appear on the first line of the petty cash book?
10. Where are expenditures recorded in the petty cash book?

**MAKING
DECISIONS**

1. Why should you exercise care in maintaining a petty cash fund?
2. Why should only one person handle the petty cash fund?

**WORKING
WITH
OTHERS**

You handle the petty cash fund for the Jackson Realty Company. While proving the petty cash fund this morning, you discover that it is $5 short. After a thorough search, you report the shortage to your employer, Mr. Jackson. He replies, "Oh that. I borrowed $5 from the petty cash fund the other day. I just forgot to tell you." How would you react to Mr. Jackson's news?

**USING
LANGUAGE**

On a separate sheet of paper write the plurals of the following words.

analysis	genius
good-for-nothing	teaspoonful
tomato	shelf
hoax	dwarf
parenthesis	two-year-old
sister-in-law	child
attitude	ox
library	life
passer-by	half
belief	appendix
self	leaf
gentleman	crisis
cargo	lawyer
photocopy	memorandum
money	proof

**USING
ARITHMETIC**

You handle the petty cash fund for the Taylor Implement Company. The fund had $50 in it originally, but now it has only $2.65. There are receipts in the petty cash box of $15.19, $10.16, $7.00, and $15.

1. What is the total of the receipts?
2. Prove the petty cash fund (see page 525).

**PERFORMING
OFFICE
TASKS**

The following transactions pertain to the petty cash fund kept by the Jones Drug Company during the months of September and October.

Sept. 1 Check No. 175 for $25 was cashed to establish a petty cash fund.
    3 Paid Bill Smith $6 for cleaning the store and office.
  13 Paid the Lake Supply Company 95 cents for store supplies.

17 Paid Johnny Stone 75 cents for delivering merchandise.
24 Paid $3 for postage stamps.
29 Paid the Stevens Hardware Company 50 cents for a duplicate key for the office.
30 Check No. 221 for $11.20 was cashed to replenish the petty cash fund.

Oct. 4 Paid the Howsam Stationery Company $1.15 for office supplies.
10 Paid Bill Smith $6 for cleaning the store and office.
17 Paid Central High School $5 for advertisement in school paper.
22 Paid the Jackson Paper Company 85 cents for store supplies.
29 Paid REA $6.75 for COD charges on merchandise purchased.
31 Check No. 256 for $19.75 was cashed to replenish the petty cash fund.

Prepare a summary report of petty cash expenditures similar to the one illustrated on page 526. If receipt forms are available, write a receipt for each of the payments made during the month of September. If receipt forms are not available, list the information that should appear on each receipt. Use the illustration on page 525 as a guide.

PART 4

COMPUTING WAGES

Judy works as a payroll clerk for United Wholesale Supply Company. Some of the employees at United Wholesale Supply Company are paid a salary; some are paid by the hour; and some are paid on a commission basis. It is Judy's responsibility to figure the gross pay, deductions, and net pay for each employee. Judy has a printing calculator to help her in the computations. During the past six months, United Wholesale Supply Company has become very busy, and almost all the employees have had to work overtime. Therefore, Judy's supervisor, Mrs. Carolyn Lawson, has taught her how to compute overtime pay. Now Judy can easily compute the overtime pay, gross pay, deductions, and net pay for each employee.

GROSS EARNINGS

One of the duties you may be required to perform in an office is computing wages for employees. Some of these employees may be paid by the hour; while some may be paid a weekly, semimonthly, or monthly salary. For example, Larry Stevens, a messenger, is paid by the number of hours he works. Thomas Anderson, a manager, is paid a monthly salary. A salesman may be paid by commission; that is, his earnings are a percentage of the amount of goods he sells during the month. A factory worker may be paid a certain amount for each item he produces. This is called the *piece-rate* method. You will need to know how to compute the wages of all employees, no matter how they are paid.

The first item that must be computed when figuring wages is the gross earnings of each worker. The *gross earnings* of an employee are the amount earned before any items are deducted. From the gross earnings, the *payroll deductions* (amounts subtracted from gross earnings for items such as taxes and social security) are subtracted to arrive at the net pay for an employee. The *net pay* is the amount actually received by the employee. For example, Linda earns $134 a week. Her *take-home* salary or net pay is computed as follows:

$$\text{Gross Pay} - \text{Deductions} = \text{Net Pay}$$
$$\$134.00 - \$27.54 = \$106.46$$

SALARY METHOD

If an employee is paid a salary, he receives a stated amount of money for each pay period. It is easy to compute the gross pay for salaried people because their stated salary is the gross pay. For example, if Anita Douglas is hired at a salary of $135 a week, her gross pay is $135 a week. This is illustrated as follows:

Salary = Gross Pay
$135 = $135

If an employee's salary is stated on a weekly basis, to figure the monthly rate you multiply the weekly salary by 52 (the number of weeks in a year) and divide that figure by 12. For example, a weekly salary of $100 is a monthly salary of $433.33. One hundred dollars a week multiplied by 52 is $5,200 a year; $5,200 a year divided by 12 is $433.33 a month.

HOURLY RATE METHOD

If an employee is paid a stated amount of money for each hour worked, the gross pay is computed by multiplying the number of hours worked times the rate of pay an hour. If Andy Jamison is paid $2.50 an hour, you figure his gross pay like this:

Hourly Wage × Hours Worked = Gross Pay
$2.50 × 40 = $100

The workweek is usually 40 hours. If Andy works only 30 hours a week, you multiply his hourly wage by 30 to arrive at his gross pay.

Some companies use a time clock to record the number of hours an employee works. A time clock is illustrated below.

Illus. 15-14
Some businesses use a time clock to record the hours each employee works.

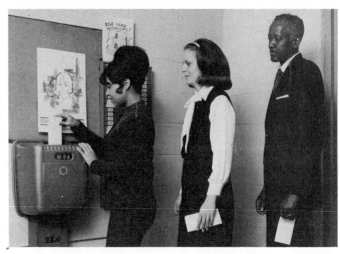

When an employee arrives at work, he puts his time card into the time clock, and it automatically records the exact time he arrived. Each employee has his own time card which is used throughout the week.

When an employee leaves for the day, he again inserts the time card in the time clock, and the exact time of departure is recorded. Some firms require employees to check in and out at the lunch hour also. If a time clock is used where you work, when preparing the payrolls you will record the daily totals in the column on the time card. Then you will fill in the information at the bottom of the time card to arrive at the gross pay. The time card in Illus. 15-17, page 538, shows how it will look after this information has been filled in.

PIECE-RATE METHOD

When an employee is paid by the *piece-rate* method, he is paid a certain amount for each item he produces. Quite often this method is used in factories as an **incentive** plan. If an employee produces more units, he will increase his pay.

incentive: a promise of reward for producing more units

To determine the gross pay of an employee using the piece-rate method, you multiply the number of units produced by the rate paid for each unit. For example, if Robert Calhoun produces 860 units a week and is paid 20 cents a unit, his gross pay is computed as follows:

$$\text{Units Produced} \times \text{Rate per Unit} = \text{Gross Pay}$$
$$860 \qquad \times \qquad \$\,.20 \qquad = \qquad \$172.00$$

COMMISSION METHOD

Some businesses use the *commission* method of determining payment for services. This means that an employee is paid a certain percentage of the dollar value of what he sells. The commission method can be an incentive for an employee to work harder. The more he sells the higher his income. If Victor Adams sells $10,465 worth of insurance in a month, and his commission is 5 percent of what he sells, his gross income is computed as follows:

$$\text{Amount Sold} \times \text{Percentage} = \text{Commission}$$
$$\$10,465 \quad \times \quad .05 \quad = \quad \$523.25$$

FIGURING OVERTIME PAY

Whenever an employee works longer than his regular hours, he receives *overtime* pay. Usually overtime pay is figured on a weekly basis. If an employee normally works a 40-hour week but works 45 hours this week, he is paid overtime for 5 hours.

Overtime pay is generally computed at one and one-half times the regular rate of pay. If a clerk earns $3 an hour, his overtime pay is $4.50 an hour — regular time ($3) + one half of regular time ($1.50) = overtime ($4.50). Let's assume that David Colgate usually works 40 hours a week for Artcraft Industries. David receives $3 an hour. Last week David worked 48 hours. His gross pay is computed like this:

$$40 \text{ hours} \times \$3.00 = \$120.00 \text{ (Regular pay)}$$
$$8 \text{ hours} \times \$4.50 = \underline{\quad 36.00} \text{ (Overtime pay)}$$
$$\$156.00 \text{ (Gross pay)}$$

Salaried employees usually are not paid for overtime. They are expected to complete the work required of them no matter how much time it takes. Of course, the work expected of them can usually be completed in the normal workweek.

PAYROLL DEDUCTIONS

Gross pay is the total amount an employee earns. To determine the amount an employee will take home with him, you must subtract several payroll deductions. There are two kinds of payroll deductions — those required by law and those not required by law, called **voluntary** deductions.

voluntary:
freedom of choice or action

Required Deductions

The payroll deductions required by law are federal income tax, social security tax, state income tax (depending on the state), and city tax.

The money which is withheld for federal income tax is applied toward your taxes for the year. Your employer pays this amount **periodically** each year to the federal government. The amount of income tax withheld by your employer depends on the number of *exemptions* you claim and your income. (Your exemptions are the dependents you can lawfully claim to cover that portion of your income which will not be taxed.) You will fill out an Employee's Withholding Exemption Certificate (called a Form W-4) when you begin working which indicates the number of exemptions you claim. This information is used to figure the amount of money withheld for federal income tax using a table similar to the one shown on page 533.

periodically:
at regular times

If you claim yourself as an exemption and earn at least $110 a week but less than $115 a week, you pay $15.50 a week for federal income tax. Notice that as the number of exemptions increase, the amount of the deduction decreases. In other words, the more dependents you have, the less tax you have to pay.

Form **W-4**
(Rev. Dec. 1971)

Department of the Treasury—Internal Revenue Service
Employee's Withholding Exemption Certificate

Type or print full name

Bruce Robert Benner

Social security number
201-26-8341

Home address (Number and street or rural route)

74 Main Avenue

City or town, State and ZIP code

Johnstown, Pennsylvania 15909

Marital status—check one (if married but legally separated, or spouse is a nonresident alien, check "Single"): ☒ Single
☐ Married

If you expect to owe more tax than will be withheld, you may either claim fewer or zero exemptions or ask for additional withholding on line 8.

1 Personal exemption for yourself. Write "1" if claimed **1**

2 If married, personal exemption for your wife (or husband) if not separately claimed by her (or him). Write "1" if claimed . . . .

3 Special withholding allowance.¹ (See instruction 2.) Write "1" if claimed . . . .

4 Exemptions for age and blindness (applicable only to you and your wife but not to dependents):
   (a) If you or your wife will be 65 years of age or older at the end of the year, and you claim this exemption, write "1"; if both will be 65 or older, and you claim both of these exemptions, write "2" . . . . .
   (b) If you or your wife are blind and you claim this exemption, write "1"; if both are blind, and you claim both exemptions, write "2" . . . .

5 Exemptions for dependents. (Do not claim an exemption for a dependent unless you are qualified under instruction 5.) . . . .

6 Additional withholding allowances for itemized deductions. . . . .

7 Add the exemptions and allowances (if any) which you have claimed above and enter total **1**

8 Additional withholding per pay period under agreement with employer . . . . $

Under the penalties of perjury, I certify that the number of withholding exemptions and allowances claimed on this certificate does not exceed the number to which I am entitled.

(Date) January 1, 19 7- (Signed) *Bruce Robert Benner*

Illus. 15-15
Employee's Withholding Exemption Certificate (Form W-4)

Businesses also withhold social security tax. This tax is deducted under the Federal Insurance Contributions Act and is also called FICA tax. The social security tax is used to pay for old-age, survivors', and disability benefits. It also provides an insurance program for elderly people called Medicare.

SINGLE Persons — WEEKLY Payroll Period

At least	But less than	0	1	2	3	4	5	6	7	8	9	10 or more
$70	$72	$9.90	$7.30	$4.70	$2.40	$.40	$0	$0	$0	$0	$0	$0
72	74	10.30	7.70	5.10	2.70	.70	0	0	0	0	0	0
74	76	10.70	8.00	5.40	3.00	.90	0	0	0	0	0	0
76	78	11.10	8.40	5.80	3.20	1.20	0	0	0	0	0	0
78	80	11.50	8.80	6.20	3.60	1.50	0	0	0	0	0	0
80	82	12.00	9.10	6.50	3.90	1.80	0	0	0	0	0	0
82	84	12.40	9.50	6.90	4.30	2.10	0	0	0	0	0	0
84	86	12.80	9.80	7.20	4.60	2.30	.30	0	0	0	0	0
86	88	13.20	10.20	7.60	5.00	2.60	.60	0	0	0	0	0
88	90	13.60	10.60	8.00	5.40	2.90	.90	0	0	0	0	0
90	92	14.10	11.00	8.30	5.70	3.20	1.20	0	0	0	0	0
92	94	14.50	11.40	8.70	6.10	3.50	1.40	0	0	0	0	0
94	96	14.90	11.90	9.00	6.40	3.90	1.70	0	0	0	0	0
96	98	15.30	12.30	9.40	6.80	4.20	2.00	0	0	0	0	0
98	100	15.70	12.70	9.80	7.20	4.60	2.30	.30	0	0	0	0
100	105	16.50	13.40	10.40	7.80	5.20	2.80	.80	0	0	0	0
105	110	17.50	14.50	11.50	8.70	6.10	3.50	1.50	0	0	0	0
110	115	18.60	15.50	12.50	9.60	7.00	4.40	2.20	10	0	0	0
115	120	19.60	16.60	13.60	10.50	7.90	5.30	2.90	.80	0	0	0
120	125	20.70	17.60	14.60	11.60	8.80	6.20	3.60	1.50	0	0	0
125	130	21.70	18.70	15.70	12.60	9.70	7.10	4.50	2.20	.20	0	0
130	135	22.80	19.70	16.70	13.70	10.70	8.00	5.40	2.90	.90	0	0
135	140	23.80	20.80	17.80	14.70	11.70	8.90	6.30	3.70	1.60	0	0
140	145	24.90	21.80	18.80	15.80	12.80	9.80	7.20	4.60	2.30	.30	0
145	150	25.90	22.90	19.90	16.80	13.80	10.80	8.10	5.50	3.00	1.00	0
150	160	27.50	24.50	21.40	18.40	15.40	12.30	9.50	6.90	4.30	2.00	0
160	170	29.60	26.60	23.50	20.50	17.50	14.40	11.40	8.70	6.10	3.50	1.40
170	180	31.70	28.70	25.60	22.60	19.60	16.50	13.50	10.50	7.90	5.30	2.80
180	190	33.80	30.80	27.70	24.70	21.70	18.60	15.60	12.60	9.70	7.10	4.50
190	200	35.90	32.90	29.80	26.80	23.80	20.70	17.70	14.70	11.70	8.90	6.30
200	210	38.10	35.00	31.90	28.90	25.90	22.80	19.80	16.80	13.80	10.70	8.10
210	220	40.40	37.10	34.00	31.00	28.00	24.90	21.90	18.90	15.90	12.80	9.90
220	230	42.70	39.30	36.10	33.10	30.10	27.00	24.00	21.00	18.00	14.90	11.90
230	240	45.10	41.60	38.30	35.20	32.20	29.10	26.10	23.10	20.10	17.00	14.00
240	250	47.80	43.90	40.60	37.30	34.30	31.20	28.20	25.20	22.20	19.10	16.10

Illus. 15-16
Sample federal income tax table

The amount of social security tax that you will pay will be matched by your employer. For example, if your social security tax is $4 a week, your employer will also pay $4 a week.

You are required to pay social security tax only up to a certain amount earned during a year. The maximum amount now is $10,800, although this figure may be changed as the law changes. If you earn any amount over $10,800, you do not have to pay social security tax on that amount. For example, if you earn $11,000 a year, you do not pay social security tax on $200 ($11,000 − $10,800).

Another deduction required by law is a state income tax. Not all states, however, have a state income tax. The amount withheld for state income tax is also figured on gross earnings and the number of exemptions.

Voluntary Deductions

Most businesses also have other deductions which may be deducted from an employee's earnings if the employee wishes. These may include voluntary deductions for group insurance programs, United States Savings Bonds programs, and retirement programs.

A group insurance program is usually less expensive than buying insurance individually. A deduction for insurance is treated the same way as the required deductions; the deduction is made each pay period before you receive your earnings.

The savings bonds program permits you to save money by having a certain amount of money deducted from your earnings for the purchase of United States Saving Bonds. If not enough is taken out each pay period to buy a bond, the payroll department accumulates the deductions until there is enough money to purchase a savings bond, which is given to you.

A retirement program is also provided by most businesses. In some companies, the retirement program is required for all employees; in others, it is on a voluntary basis.

The total of your payroll deductions is subtracted from your gross pay to arrive at your net, or take-home, pay.

REVIEWING WHAT YOU HAVE READ

1. What is the first item that must be computed when figuring wages?
2. How do you compute net pay?
3. What is the gross pay for a salaried person?
4. If an employee's salary is stated on a weekly basis, how do you figure his monthly rate of pay?
5. How is gross pay computed for an employee who receives an hourly rate of pay?
6. How do you determine the gross pay of an employee who is paid by the piece-rate method?
7. Explain the commission method of determining payment for services.
8. How is overtime pay usually computed?

9. Name two types of payroll deductions and briefly explain them.
10. What is the amount of earnings on which you must pay social security taxes?

What are the advantages of the various types of wage returns for services rendered: weekly or monthly salary; piece-rate method; hourly rate; commission?

You work in the Payroll Department of the Collins-Reed Motor Company. Cindy, a new employee, confronts you with the following statement, "Here is my paycheck. It is not correct. Mr. Collins told me that I would be paid $134 a week. This check is made out for only $106.46. This attached voucher says something about deductions, but I don't understand. What have you done with the rest of my paycheck?"
How would you answer Cindy's question?

The following sentences contain frequently misused terms. On a separate sheet of paper type each sentence using the correct form of each word.

1. The assistant (accepted, excepted) the invitation to the dinner meeting in his employer's name, since the employer was out of the city.
2. Her employer told her before he left to attend the meeting that it would be (all right, alright) for her to leave the office early.
3. Mr. Jones was (all ready, already) committed to give the breakfast address at the meeting when the program director asked him to be the (principle, principal) speaker at the final dinner meeting.
4. Although the president of the company was (reared, raised) in France, his travels in America made him a (real, very) enthusiastic baseball fan.
5. When Mr. Lower did not (appear, show up) in time to address the convention, the chairman became alarmed and telephoned the former's office.
6. (All together, Altogether) ninety persons were on the airplane when it left the Kansas City airport.
7. Although the weather (affected, effected) his past football injury, it did not prevent the executive from making many business trips.
8. The (farther, further) he was away from the office the more (likely, liable) he was to call his secretary at any time.
9. The motel was (luxurious, luxuriant), but the noise from the swimming pool (in back of, behind) his room (irritated, aggravated) him.
10. There was agreement (between, among) the four officers of the company that traveling was necessary if the company was not to (lose, loose) money.

Tom Jones earns $2 an hour working for Medlock Industries. He usually works a 40-hour week. This week, he worked 52 hours — 12 hours overtime. Compute his gross pay.

1. You are employed as a payroll clerk for Madison Equipment Company. Compute the gross pay for the week for each of the following employees.
   (a) Anita Johnson receives a salary of $115 a week.
   (b) Andy Jackson works for $2.75 an hour. This week he worked 40 hours.
   (c) Tom Hancock receives 25 cents for every unit he produces. Tom produced 823 units this week.

(d) Larry Owen works for a 5 percent commission. His sales for the week amounted to $3,100.

2. Complete the information needed on the time cards for these employees of Stark Manufacturers. Determine the total hours worked, overtime rate, regular and overtime earnings, if any, and total earnings. If a workbook is used, complete the information on the forms provided. Use the illustration of a time card on page 538 as a guide. If a workbook is not available, present the information in the form of a table. For column headings use Name, Total Hours Worked, Overtime Rate, Regular Earnings, Overtime Earnings, and Total Earnings.

Payroll Number	Name	Hours Worked Regular	Hours Worked Overtime	Regular Rate
20	Bates, Barbara	40	5	$2.40
37	Davis, Joe	30		$2.80
12	Fairbanks, John	40	2	$3.50
19	Parkins, Linda	37		$2.35
24	Scott, Richard	40		$2.50
27	Tennell, Marlene	40	8	$2.90

PART 5 RECORDING AND PAYING EARNINGS

Esther Payne has worked for some time in the general office of the Harrison Paint Company, which employs about 100 full-time employees. Mr. Tublian, the office manager, said to Esther, "Joan is sick today. Can you take over the payroll for us?" Esther had worked occasionally in the Payroll Department and had also taken a business course at school where she learned about the different payroll forms and records. She answered, "I'll be glad to, Mr. Tublian. My regular work can wait till tomorrow. I know the payroll work is important around the first of the month." And with that comment Esther took over in Joan's absence and helped complete the payroll for her employer.

PAYROLL RECORDS

After you have computed the employee's gross pay and deductions, you are ready to record the earnings of each employee. This information must be recorded so that it can be sent to state and federal agencies which require it. Payroll information is usually recorded on two records — the payroll register and the employee's earnings record.

Payroll Register

Companies may use time cards to record each employee's working hours. The information concerning total or gross earnings recorded on the *payroll register* is taken from time cards.

If the Wakefield Publishing Company uses a time clock, the record of employees' working hours is shown on time cards. You will collect the time card of each employee at the end of the week. You then fill in the total hours worked, overtime (if any), rate of pay, and gross pay on each time card. The information on each time card is transferred to the payroll register.

The time card for Joseph A. Butler is illustrated on page 538. Notice that the gross earnings have been computed.

Joseph Butler's number, name, and gross earnings are taken from the time card and recorded on the payroll register (as shown on the first

Illus. 15-17
Punched time card containing hand-written totals, hourly rate, and gross earnings.

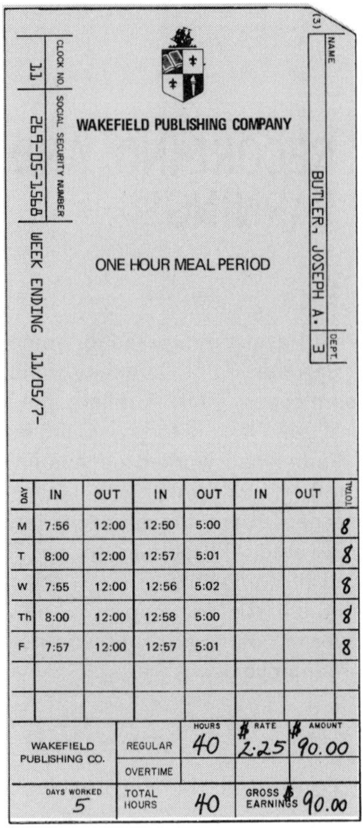
WAKEFIELD PUBLISHING COMPANY

(3) NAME: BUTLER, JOSEPH A. DEPT. 3

CLOCK NO. 11 SOCIAL SECURITY NUMBER 269-05-1568 WEEK ENDING 11/05/7-

ONE HOUR MEAL PERIOD

DAY	IN	OUT	IN	OUT	IN	OUT	TOTAL
M	7:56	12:00	12:50	5:00			8
T	8:00	12:00	12:57	5:01			8
W	7:55	12:00	12:56	5:02			8
Th	8:00	12:00	12:58	5:00			8
F	7:57	12:00	12:57	5:01			8

WAKEFIELD PUBLISHING CO.		HOURS	RATE	AMOUNT
	REGULAR	40	$2.25	$90.00
	OVERTIME			
DAYS WORKED 5	TOTAL HOURS	40	GROSS EARNINGS	$90.00

line below). The deductions are then figured using the number of exemptions and the gross earnings of Mr. Butler. All deductions are totaled in the Total Deductions column. Finally, the Total Deductions are subtracted from the Gross Earnings to arrive at the Net Earnings, or take-home pay, for Mr. Butler.

Illus. 15-18
Payroll register

THE WAKEFIELD PUBLISHING COMPANY

PAYROLL REGISTER — DATE November 5, 197-

EMPLOYEE NUMBER	EMPLOYEE NAME	EXEMPTIONS	GROSS EARNINGS	DEDUCTIONS: FEDERAL WITH. TAX	F.I.C.A.	GROUP INSURANCE	HOSP.	BONDS	TOTAL DEDUCTIONS	NET EARNINGS
11	BUTLER, JOSEPH A.	1	90 00	11 00	5 27	1 60	1 75		19 62	70 38
32	CAVALLO, ROSE M.	2	150 39	17 90	8 80	2 85	2 25		31 80	118 59
13	DYER, LENA B.	1	90 00	11 00	5 27	1 60	1 75		19 62	70 38
24	FAIRBANKS, JOHN	2	101 00	9 50	5 91	2 85	1 75		20 01	80 99
35	GROSSMAN ISIDORE	4	162 92	14 90	9 53	4 10	2 25	5 50	36 28	126 64
26	JUNG, FOO Y.	3	104 00	7 20	6 08	2 85	2 25	3 00	21 38	82 62
9	KIRKLAND, MURRAY	1	78 00	8 80	4 56	1 60	1 75		16 71	61 29
			776 31	80 30	45 42	17 45	13 75	8 50	165 42	610 89

Employee's Earnings Record

An individual record is kept for each employee on an *employee's earnings record*. The earnings record for each employee is usually kept in alphabetic order on cards in a file or on loose-leaf sheets in a binder.

Joseph Butler's employee's earnings record is illustrated below.

The employee's earnings record provides space for information for 13 weeks or a quarter of a year. The information to record on the employee's earnings record is taken from the payroll register. The date for the pay period is entered in the first column. Gross earnings are recorded under the Earnings column and the individual deductions for each pay period are recorded under Deductions. The amount actually paid each employee is recorded in the Net Pay column. Another column is added to the employee's earnings record. This is the Taxable Earnings Accumulated. This tells at a glance the total gross earnings of the employee. When an employee's earnings reach a certain amount, some taxes, such as social security, no longer apply. By using this column, you can make sure all deductions are accurately figured.

Illus. 15-19
Employee's
earnings record

EMPLOYEE'S EARNINGS RECORD

| Butler | | Joseph | | | A. | | | | | 269-05-1568 | | |
| LAST NAME | | FIRST | | | MIDDLE | | | | | SOC. SEC. NO. | | |

			DEDUCTIONS							NET PAY		TAXABLE
WEEK	PERIOD ENDING	EARNINGS	FED. WITH. TAX	F.I.C.A.	GROUP INS.	HOSP.	OTHER	TOTAL		AMOUNT		EARNINGS ACCUMULATED
	TOTAL FIRST THREE QUARTERS	3531 60	434 80	206 95	62 40	68 25		772 40		2765 20		3531 60
1	10/8	90 00	11 00	5 27	1 60	1 75		19 62		70 38		3627 60
2	10/15	90 00	11 00	5 27	1 60	1 75		19 62		70 38		3717 60
3	10/22	83 50	9 50	4 88	1 60	1 75		17 73		65 77		3801 10
4	10/29	90 00	11 00	5 27	1 60	1 75		19 62		70 38		3891 10
5	11/5	90 00	11 00	5 27	1 60	1 75		19 62		70 38		3981 10
6												

PAYING EMPLOYEES

After the payroll has been prepared, the next step is to pay each employee the amount due him. In many firms payment is by check; in other firms, in cash; in still others, certain employees are paid in cash, and the remainder are paid by check.

Paying by Check

Payroll checks, after being prepared by a clerk, must be signed by the person designated by the firm to do this. As a rule, however, if there are many checks, a check-signing machine is used.

Deductions are often shown on payroll checks in such a way that the employee will know the amount of each deduction. This information is usually printed on an attached check stub, or voucher, that the employee removes before cashing the check.

Checks for office employees are usually enclosed in envelopes for privacy and presented in packets to department heads, who **distribute** them to the individuals in their departments. In some organizations, checks are mailed to the employee's home or bank. Checks for salaried factory workers are sometimes enclosed in envelopes so that they will not become soiled from handling. They are distributed to the department heads or foremen, who pass them on to the employees. Checks for salaried store employees are usually given to department heads for distribution. While methods of payment vary with different businesses, the information provided on the check will always be the same as that developed in the payroll register; therefore, the check should be prepared using the payroll register as a source of information.

distribute:
to pass or give out

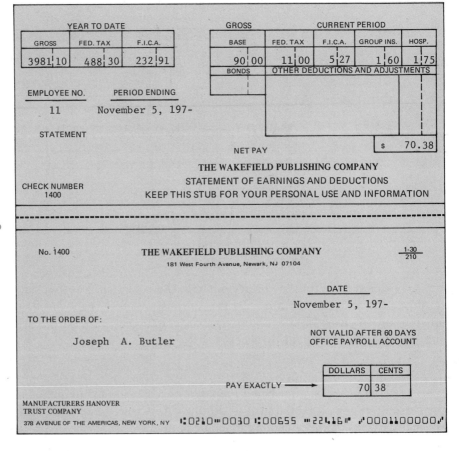

Illus. 15-20
Paycheck and stub

Paying in Cash

As a general rule, employees need their money immediately on payday. Therefore, some firms, as a service to their employees, pay by cash rather than by check.

When it is the policy to pay all or some of the employees in cash, a check is drawn for the net amount of the payroll, that is, the amount of the payroll less all deductions. The check is cashed and the money, along with a slip of paper showing gross pay, deductions, and net earnings, is placed in pay envelopes, which are distributed. Before someone is sent to the bank for the payroll money, it is customary to prepare two forms — a payroll change sheet and a payroll cash slip.

Payroll Change Sheet

A payroll change sheet or money tally shows the name of each employee and the amount of money he has earned. In the columns to the right of each employee's name are indicated how many bills and coins of each denomination will be needed to pay the worker. For example, if Joseph A. Butler makes a net amount of $70.70, he will be given three $20 bills, one $10 bill, a half dollar, and two dimes. After the salary amounts

PAYROLL CHANGE SHEET

DATE November 5, 197-

EMPLOYEE	AMOUNT PAID	$20	$10	$5	$1	50¢	25¢	10¢	5¢	1¢
Butler, Joseph A.	$ 70.38	3	1				1	1		3
Cavallo, Rose M.	118.59	5	1	1	3	1			1	4
Dyer, Lena B.	70.38	3	1				1	1		3
Fairbanks, John	80.99	4				1	1	2		4
Grossman, Isidore	126.64	6		1	1	1		1		4
Jung, Foo Y.	82.62	4			2	1		1		2
Kirkland, Murray	61.29	3			1		1			4
TOTAL	$ 610.89	28	3	2	7	4	4	6	1	24

Illus. 15-21
Payroll change sheet

have been broken down into the various denominations and all columns have been totaled, the totals are transferred to a payroll cash slip so that the bank will know how many of each of the denominations are needed.

You will also notice that the payroll clerk handles the least number of pieces of currency and coins in the lists shown on the payroll change sheet. For Joseph A. Butler she handles *seven* pieces of currency and coins for a total of $70.70. However, if she totals Butler's wages by using three $10 bills, eight $5 bills, two quarters, and four nickels, she will handle *seventeen* pieces of currency and coins for a total of $70.70. The fewer pieces of money handled, the fewer the mistakes that will occur.

Payroll Cash Slip

Using the payroll change sheet as a source of information, the clerk prepares a payroll cash slip (illustrated below). This form shows the number of $100, $50, $20, $10, $5, and $1 bills and the number of half-dollars, quarters, dimes, nickels, and pennies that are needed. Because people find it difficult to change large bills, most firms use nothing larger than $20 bills.

MANUFACTURERS HANOVER TRUST COMPANY
REQUISITION FOR PAYROLL

Wakefield Publishing Co.
NAME OF DEPOSITOR

DATE *November 5, 197—*

THIS COLUMN FOR USE BY BANK ONLY	DENOMINATIONS	DOLLAR AMOUNT ONLY	CENTS ONLY
	$100 BILLS		
	$ 50 "		
	$ 20 "	560	00
	$ 10 "	30	00
	$ 5 "	10	00
	$ 1 "	7	00
	HALVES	2	00
	QUARTERS	1	00
	DIMES		60
	NICKELS		05
	PENNIES		24
	TOTAL ⟶	610	89

238
1250M   1-66

Illus. 15-22 Payroll cash slip

Distribution of Payroll Money

After the money has been received from the bank, it is usually counted and separated into various denominations and inserted in pay envelopes which have been prepared in advance. After the money and the slip **itemizing** the deductions have been inserted, the pay envelopes are ready for distribution. If there are only a few employees in an organization, the pay envelopes are usually distributed to them by an executive, the cashier, or the bookkeeper. In a large organization, where it might be unsafe and inconvenient to carry all the pay envelopes around to them, the employees are asked to call at a certain place for their pay. The employees are often asked to sign a receipt when they receive their pay.

itemizing: listing

PAYROLL ACCOUNTING MACHINES

Many large offices use accounting machines, as illustrated on page 127, in the preparation of their payroll records. The use of such machines saves time and helps reduce errors. Time is saved because one payroll accounting machine can prepare several payroll records in one operation. Errors are reduced because there is no need to transfer information from one record to another.

Earnings and deductions are usually computed by a payroll clerk and are recorded by hand on the time cards. From these time cards, the payroll accounting machine operator quickly and efficiently prepares the remaining payroll records. The machine prints the information for each employee on the payroll register and on the employee's earnings record at the same time that it completes the payroll check and the employee's statement of earnings and deductions.

ELECTRONICALLY COMPUTED PAYROLLS

Increasingly you will find payrolls in large companies computed by electronic data processing equipment. Once the basic information regarding salary and hours or days worked is entered in the machine, the

Illus. 15-23
Producing paychecks and other payroll information has become a specialized clerical function for young people trained in data processing.

IBM Corporation

properly programmed equipment will automatically complete all computations including deductions. As part of its work, it will produce the paycheck, the stub, and all other records needed. Some large firms now have their payrolls prepared at data processing centers or at their bank. This type of service is becoming very popular, and is providing employment of a specialized nature for clerical office workers trained in data processing.

REVIEWING
WHAT YOU
HAVE READ

1. Name two records on which payroll information is usually recorded.
2. What information will be found on a typical payroll register?
3. The employee's earnings record provides space for information for what length of time?
4. What information appears on the employee's earnings record?
5. What is the source of information for the preparation of paychecks?
6. Name two forms that are prepared before someone is sent to the bank to get the payroll money.
7. What is the purpose of a payroll change sheet?
8. What information appears on the payroll cash slip?
9. How does the use of payroll accounting machines save time and reduce errors?
10. How is electronic data processing equipment used in payroll work?

MAKING DECISIONS

Do you consider it a sign of poor planning by certain employees when they prefer to be paid in cash because it would be inconvenient for them to wait until the following day to have a check cashed?

WORKING WITH OTHERS

Judy Ames, a payroll clerk for the Downing Aircraft Corporation, has recently had several of her office friends ask her about the earnings of fellow employees. Since Judy prepares the employee's earnings records for the company, she has the information that her friends are requesting.

What should Judy say to her friends when they question her about the pay of co-workers?

USING LANGUAGE

The following ten terms are among the 1,500 most frequently used words in the business world. You will use each word often when you begin your working career. On a separate sheet of paper write a sentence relating to something that you have learned in this course and use the word correctly. If you do not recall the meaning, you may check it in the dictionary before composing the sentence.

1. analysis   (noun)
2. capacity   (noun)
3. conference   (noun)
4. initial   (verb)
5. maintain   (verb)
6. maximum   (adjective)
7. participate   (verb)
8. procedure(s)   (noun)
9. range   (noun or verb)
10. specific   (adjective)

USING ARITHMETIC   Assume that you are preparing a payroll change sheet like that illustrated on page 541. Allen James is to receive $92.13. What denominations of money will you use to pay Allen James so that you will handle the least number of pieces of currency?

PERFORMING OFFICE TASKS

1. On a separate sheet of paper prepare forms to complete the three parts of this problem.

   (a) Prepare a payroll register similar to the one illustrated on page 538. Use the following information to complete the payroll register.

	Employee			Deductions			
No.	Name	Exemp-tions	Gross Earnings	Fed. With. Tax	Grp. Ins.	Hosp.	Bonds
11	Butler, Joseph A.	1	68.00	7.00	1.00	1.25	
32	Cavallo, Rose M.	2	121.88	12.70	1.25	1.50	2.00
13	Dyer, Lena B.	1	66.75	6.60	1.00	1.25	
24	Fairbanks, John	2	80.00	6.10	1.00	1.25	
35	Grossman, Isidore	4	155.75	13.30	1.50	1.50	2.00
26	Jung, Foo Y.	3	80.00	3.80	1.25	1.25	1.00
17	Kyoto, Fusai	2	100.00	9.50	1.25	1.50	1.00
28	Maloney, Michael J.	1	75.00	8.00	1.00	1.25	
19	Nielsen, Ingar	1	89.05	10.60	1.00	1.50	
10	Presley, Thelma M.	2	63.75	3.30	1.00	1.25	
21	Reid, Ruth P.	2	88.43	7.40	1.25	1.25	
12	Sanchez, Julio P.	1	60.00	5.50	1.00	1.25	
23	Tenney, Mabel A.	3	111.25	8.80	1.25	1.50	1.00
34	Upton, Charlotte	1	80.62	9.10	1.00	1.25	
25	Walker, Arlene N.	2	64.75	3.60	1.00	1.25	

Compute the FICA (Federal Insurance Contribution Act) tax at the rate of 5.85 percent of the total earnings of each employee.

After the various deductions have been filled in, add them across to get the total deductions. Deduct the total deductions from gross earnings in order to determine the net earnings — the amount that should appear in the final column. Prove your work by adding all columns vertically. Add the totals of all deductions horizontally. This should equal the grand total of deductions. This amount, subtracted from the total gross earnings, should equal the total net earnings.

   (b) Complete the payroll change sheet.

   (c) Complete the payroll cash slip.

2. You are to complete the employee's earnings record of Thomas P. Randall, Social Security Number 463-86-0526, for the last quarter of the year.

   (a) Prepare an employee's earnings record by entering the information on page 546 on it.

Deductions

Week	Period Ending	Earnings	Federal With. Tax	FICA*	Group Ins.	Hosp.	Other
Total First Three Quarters		4,200.50	565.50	245.73	78.00	87.75	45.00
1	10/8	125.00	18.70	7.31	2.00	2.25	5.00
2	10/15	125.00	18.70	7.31	2.00	2.25	
3	10/22	142.85	21.80	8.36	2.00	2.25	
4	10/29	100.00	13.40	5.85	2.00	2.25	
5	11/5	135.71	20.80	7.94	2.00	2.25	5.00
6	11/12	75.00	8.00	4.39	2.00	2.25	
7	11/19	149.99	22.90	8.77	2.00	2.25	
8	11/26	125.00	18.70	7.31	2.00	2.25	
9	12/3	125.00	18.70	7.31	2.00	2.25	5.00
10	12/10	159.68	24.50	9.34	2.00	2.25	
11	12/17	130.00	19.70	7.61	2.00	2.25	
12	12/24	130.00	19.70	7.61	2.00	2.25	
13	12/31	152.26	24.50	8.91	2.00	2.25	

*FICA Tax computed at 5.85%

(b) Complete the employee's earnings record by (1) adding each line horizontally to find the total deductions, (2) subtracting the total deductions from the total earnings to find the net pay, (3) extending the total earnings for the first three quarters to the Taxable Earnings Accumulated column and adding the successive total earnings for each week to the accumulated total to find the taxable earnings accumulated, and (4) adding vertically all columns except the Taxable Earnings Accumulated column to find the totals for the quarter and for the year. After the totals have been recorded, check the accuracy of your work by subtracting the deductions total from the earnings total; the remainder should equal the total of the Net Pay column. The last entry in the Taxable Earnings Accumulated column should be equal to the earnings total. *Note:* The items in the Other column represent payments made by Mr. Randall for goods purchased from the company store.

UNIT 16

YOUR BUSINESS CAREER

CLERK

Permanent position for amb
tious high school graduate wh
desires business experienc
ith expanding chemical com
ny. Duties include light typin
filing.
cants should have goc
chool record in busines
m.
nce required. We o
salary, fully pai
ition refun
to M

PART 1 — JOB OPPORTUNITIES

Maria Lopez, a senior in a large high school in New York City, is planning to work in a business office when she graduates in June. She is very much interested in finding the kind of job for which she has the right qualifications. The local newspapers list job openings, but she wonders about other ways of learning of job opportunities.

THE JOB MARKET

What jobs are available in the business community? Is there a need for office workers? While automation has transferred many tasks from the desk to the machine, there continues to be a great demand for office workers of all kinds. Beginners with limited or no experience find many jobs available to them. Often high school graduates who do outstanding work in beginning jobs quickly move into positions of greater responsibility. Businessmen are eager to use every talent and skill available, and their efforts to reward new employees who show special interest in their work result in promotional opportunities for good workers.

Beginners generally are typists, accounting clerks, clerk-typists, transcribing machine operators, receptionists, office machine operators, and file clerks.

TYPES OF ORGANIZATIONS

Organizations are classified in a number of ways. A classification based on the nature of activity carried on in the organization is given on page 549. You will want to consider the kind of organization which you find especially interesting.

Doris always enjoyed the work she did on the high school newspaper. Doris organized the jobs and saw that they got done. She kept the small office in order and set up a filing system. She liked the excitement of getting out a newspaper — the rush, the unexpected events, the editorial problems. When she graduated from high school, she applied for a position at the local newspaper office. The manager was impressed with

ORGANIZATIONS CLASSIFIED BY ACTIVITIES

Organization	Activity
Manufacturing	Producers of household appliances, glass products, pianos, carpeting, textiles, and the whole range of manufactured products
Mining	Coal, copper, silver
Construction	Housing construction, mobile home construction, office construction, hospital and other institutional construction
Transportation and Public Utilities	Trucking, airlines, railroads, bus lines, electricity, gas, telephone
Trade	Wholesale, central retailing chain, department store, grocery store, specialty store
Finance, Insurance, and Real Estate	Commercial banks, savings banks, security dealers and brokers, insurance companies, real estate brokers
Health Services	Hospitals, clinics, doctor's office, dentist's office
Community Agencies	YMCA, YWCA, Red Cross, 4-H, Boy Scouts, Girl Scouts
Religious	Church, synagogue, mission services of coordinated religious groups
Communications	Periodicals, newspaper, book publishing, radio, television
Government	City government, state government, federal government
Education	Preschool centers, elementary school, secondary school, community college, college, university, research center
Professional	Law office, counseling service, consultant services, architect's office

Illus. 16-1

her volunteer experience in high school. She was hired to be a clerk-typist and was assured she would have a good opportunity to learn all about publishing a daily newspaper in a city of 35,000 people.

Fred liked construction — and the materials used for building houses, furniture, and cabinets appealed to him. His hobby of building things required his visiting lumberyards and hardware stores. While in high school, he worked part-time as a delivery assistant for a large building materials center. After completing his course in clerical procedures, he applied for a job in the stockroom of the center. The manager knew his dependability as a part-time worker; the center needed stockroom clerks so Fred was hired.

Office workers are needed everywhere. It is important that you give thought to the **environment** in which your interests will have an opportunity to develop.

environment: surroundings

SIZES OF ORGANIZATIONS

Organizations range from small firms where an individual works alone with an office assistant to giant companies where there are thousands of employees located in a large office complex. Which size do you prefer? You will want to give attention to this question. Some office workers like large companies that have specific rules and policies about job tasks, promotional possibilities, and salary scales. Others, however, choose to work in very small, informal surroundings where everyone is acquainted with everyone else in the organization.

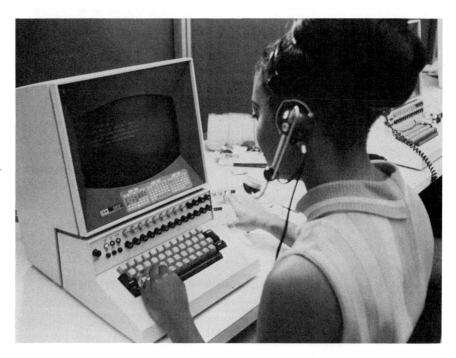

Illus. 16-2
Clerical workers are found everywhere — from large airline reservations offices to small one-girl offices.

AT&T

When Evelyn was a senior in high school her class visited a large insurance company in Hartford, which was about 20 miles from her hometown. She liked the large company; it seemed orderly and calm. She felt she would enjoy working in such a company, for there would certainly be more opportunities for a young person in such a place than there would be in a small office in her local community. She thought she would enjoy meeting many new people and working with them.

Arlene was not like Evelyn. Arlene had gone on the field trip with Evelyn, but her impression was unfavorable. She thought that a large company was impersonal and that the chances that she would ever get to know anyone were slight. She knew that she wanted to work in a small office. She firmly believed that if she did a good job, it would be recognized. She didn't think that it was important to be concerned with opportunities for promotions before she began her first job.

LOCATION

Where do you want to work? Your choice is wide! There are jobs in downtown centers of large metropolitan areas, in suburban communities, in small villages. Jobs are available in places as different as Portland, Maine, and Miami Beach, Florida, or London, England, and Lima, Peru. Some beginning office workers expect to **commute** from their homes when they are working; others plan to relocate so that they may live near the place of their work.

commute: travel back and forth regularly

Paul loved his hometown, which he realized was smaller than many places in the region, and had no desire to find a job elsewhere when he graduated from high school. He liked to be with people whom he knew; and strange, large cities were no lure for him. He, therefore, applied at the public utilities office in his hometown when his high school graduation approached. He was hired as a mailroom clerk and messenger. His knowledge of the town made him a valuable employee immediately.

Maryann had always dreamed of the time when she would have the skills to earn her own living and would be able to go to Washington, D.C., to work. She knew that Washington would be very different from the small town of 11,000 in Indiana where she had lived all her life. She took the Civil Service Examination for typist, which she passed. Soon after her high school graduation she left for Washington, where she began working for the Department of Commerce.

LEARNING OF JOB OPPORTUNITIES

There are many ways you can learn about the job opportunities in the community where you want to work. Use as many as necessary to aid you in finding a job that is best for you.

Placement Office in Your School

Many high schools have placement offices that receive notices of local job openings and also of federal and state government openings. These placement offices help students find jobs. If your school has a placement office, you may want to file an application so that you will be told about jobs for which you are qualified. Generally a placement counselor will talk with you to learn of your interests and abilities. Sometimes job openings are posted on a bulletin board which you should check regularly to see if there is a job listed for which you want to apply.

If you promise a placement counselor that you will go on an interview, it is important that you follow through. Also, you should let the placement counselor know the results of the interview. The placement

Illus. 16-3
A placement counselor will talk with you to
learn first-hand your interests and abilities.

office is a service that is provided to help you find employment; so it is important that you follow the established procedures.

recruit:
enlist; engage

Many companies **recruit** employees through school placement offices, and you may find that this is the only source you need to find a job when you graduate.

Employment Agencies

In many communities there are both private and public employment agencies that will provide aid to you in your efforts to find a position. Private employment agencies are sometimes specialized; so you will want to be sure that you are inquiring at one that does place office personnel. Private employment agencies earn their income from fees which are paid either by the individual who secures a position through services provided by the agency or by the company that hires the new employee. The fee is a percentage of salary, generally based on a week's or a month's salary.

Public employment agencies provide a service without fee. Such agencies are supported through public funds. You may register at a public employment agency for aid in seeking a position. In large cities public agencies are specialized; so you will want to be sure that you visit the department that handles office vacancies.

Classified Advertisements

Many companies as well as employment agencies use the classified section of newspapers to announce vacancies. While many of the advertisements identify the company or agency seeking personnel for positions, some are listed as blind advertisements. A *blind advertisement* is one that lists only a box number so that the identity of the company seeking an employee is not revealed. Blind advertisements are used so that some

TYPIST

Exciting Int'l Hotel Corp.
Wholly Owned Subsidiary of

PAN-AM

is seeking a bright, RECENT GRADU-
ATE who has excellent typing skills,
pleasant telephone voice, and a desire to
meet a job challenge requiring adapta-
ability and a sense of humor. This Gal
Friday opportunity will afford exposure
to an exciting department of the international hotel field.

EXCELLENT COMPANY BENEFITS

Apply in person or call 973-2164

Inter-Continental Hotel Corp.
Pan-Am Bldg., 200 Park Ave.

An Equal Opportunity Employer

CLERK-TYPIST—Good job for average
typist who wants to learn. Starting
salary $90-$100 a week. Fine company
with handsome offices and friendly
people to work with. For an immediate
appointment see Robert Pack at Employers Service Agency, 18 East 48th St.,
or call 383-6665. FEE PAID.

Illus. 16-4
Identified
advertisement

Illus. 16-5
Employment
agency advertise-
ment

RECEPTIONIST-TYPIST. Some
clerical work. Bright, alert, pleasant
person with good telephone voice. Con-
genial law office. Will consider beginner. Send resume and salary requirements. Box Y2868. Post-Times.

Illus. 16-6
Blind advertisement

preliminary screening can be done on the basis of written letters and data
sheets that are submitted by interested applicants.

Direct Inquiry to Organization

Some people learn about office positions through relatives and
friends who are employed in companies that are seeking new employees.
If you are informed of an opening through such a source, your relative or
friend may make the initial inquiry to the personnel department and
arrange an interview for you. You will be expected to visit the company
and indicate to the personnel officer who made the suggestion to you.

Illus. 16-7
A company will form
its first impression
of you in the personnel
office.

Modern Partitions, Inc.

Part 1 / Job Opportunities

553

If there is a company in which you have special interest, it is proper to write a letter of inquiry and to indicate your skills and the type of position you are seeking. If you are writing to a company that often hires beginning workers, your chances of being granted an interview are very good.

Civil Service Announcements

Many positions in government require that candidates take examinations and, therefore, there are general public announcements about the dates of such examinations. If you are interested in employment in government, you will want to note the announcements that are posted in public buildings and that appear in newspapers. Announcements for federal positions are often displayed in post offices and in regional civil service offices throughout the country. You can also write directly to the United States Civil Service Commission, Washington, DC 20415, asking for information on forthcoming examinations. Announcements of city civil service examinations are usually posted in the City Hall; announcements of county and state examinations, in the County Courthouse or principal county building. Also, you can check your local telephone directory to find the Civil Service Commission office in your city and request information directly from that office.

REVIEWING WHAT YOU HAVE READ

1. What kinds of jobs are generally available to beginning office workers?
2. If you are interested in communications, in what kinds of organizations will you look for employment?
3. In what ways does working for a large company differ from working for a small company?
4. What considerations will influence you in selecting the location for your first job?
5. What kinds of services are provided by school placement offices?
6. Why do private employment agencies charge a fee?
7. How do public employment agencies differ from private employment agencies?
8. In what section of the newspaper can you find notices of job openings?
9. What information is missing in a blind advertisement?
10. How can you learn about examinations for civil service positions in the federal government?

MAKING DECISIONS

1. A friend of yours has always been interested in travel. She thinks all aspects of travel are exciting. She is now considering the types of positions for which she should apply since she will be graduating from high school and has taken typing and clerical procedures. She asks you, "Where should I look for a job?"

   What would you say to your friend?

2. You are interviewed for a position in a small law office in your own hometown. There are two office workers in the office now, and you will be the only new person to be employed. There are two lawyers who share the practice. As you walk home following the interview, which ended with the lawyers offering you a position at an acceptable salary, what kinds of questions will you ask yourself to determine if this is the job you wish to accept?

WORKING WITH OTHERS

A friend is interested in moving to a large city and working in an office in the center of the city. She talks to you about going to the city with her. She says, "I know we can get jobs. We can wait until we get there to find work. Why worry ahead of time? We can find a place to live, and then we can begin to look for jobs."

What is your reaction to your friend's suggestion?

USING LANGUAGE

Some of the words below are hyphenated; some are two words; some are one word. On a separate sheet of paper retype the list according to current correct usage.

recurrent	selfreproach
selfsufficient	semifinal
sellout	bimonthly
multistory	trademark
aboutface	tradename
devolve	cooperate
deplane	postpaid
NeoLatin	postoffice
neocolonial	antiknock
neoclassic	nonrenewable

USING ARITHMETIC

Below are listed weekly salaries for several office employees. The table on page 556 shows the withholding tax deducted from a single person's salary. Also the employer deducts 5.85 percent of the gross salary for social security benefits levied under the Federal Insurance Contributions Act. On a separate sheet of paper indicate in the form of a table the net salary for each of these single employees, assuming that each claims one exemption.

Beverly Sharpe, a beginning worker, earns $89 a week.
Tom Walsh, who has a year's experience, earns $115 a week.
Raymond Mosely, who has three years' experience, earns $143 a week.
Peggy Ellman, who has been working for about two years, earns $121 a week.

Name	Gross Salary	Federal With. Tax	FICA Tax	Net Salary
Beverly Sharpe				
Tom Walsh				
Raymond Mosely				
Peggy Ellman				

SINGLE Persons — WEEKLY Payroll Period

And the wages are —		And the number of withholding exemptions claimed is —		
		0	1	2
At least	But less than	The amount of Income tax to be withheld shall be —		
$80	$82	$12.00	$ 9.10	$ 6.50
82	84	12.40	9.50	6.90
84	86	12.80	9.80	7.20
86	88	13.20	10.20	7.60
88	90	13.60	10.60	8.00
90	92	14.10	11.00	8.30
92	94	14.50	11.40	8.70
94	96	14.90	11.90	9.00
96	98	15.30	12.30	9.40
98	100	15.70	12.70	9.80
100	105	16.50	13.40	10.40
105	110	17.50	14.50	11.50
110	115	18.60	15.50	12.50
115	120	19.60	16.60	13.60
120	125	20.70	17.60	14.60
125	130	21.70	18.70	15.70
130	135	22.80	19.70	16.70
135	140	23.80	20.80	17.80
140	145	24.90	21.80	18.80
145	150	25.90	22.90	19.90

PERFORMING OFFICE TASKS

1. Make a list of the sources of placement information that are available to you and your classmates who are seeking employment as office workers.

2. From your local newspapers, clip the advertisements for office positions that have appeared in the past week which you are qualified to fill. Be ready to discuss these job opportunities in class indicating why you believe you are able to meet the job requirements.

PART 2 APPLYING FOR A JOB IN PERSON

Peggy Colmer began to think about the kind of work she would prefer several months before graduating from high school. As she considered all the tasks — typing, filing, proof-reading, record keeping, filling in forms, receiving callers, handling telephone calls — she put them in order of preference. Peggy soon realized that she enjoyed typing very much, but she also liked working with people. As she studied newspaper advertisements she decided that she was qualified for a clerk-typist or a receptionist-clerk position. Either of these positions seemed to provide a variety of tasks, which she would enjoy.

Ken Williams also thought about his interests. The experiences dealing with purchasing, selling, and inventory control of goods were among his favorites. He believed that he would like maintaining merchandise and supplies, moving them in and out of a warehouse or storeroom, and keeping records of the merchandise. He decided that he would look for a job in the stockroom of a large department store or in a large manufacturing firm in a purchasing, shipping, or inventory control department.

Both Peggy and Ken are young people who want to make the most of their education and interests as they start to look for rewarding job opportunities. You, like Peggy and Ken, may apply for a job in person. You should prepare yourself carefully, for you will probably have to complete an application form, take one or more tests, and be interviewed.

PERSONNEL DEPARTMENT HOURS

Many companies have personnel departments that interview applicants during certain hours, such as 9 to 3, Monday through Friday. The information you receive about job openings will generally indicate when you should apply. For example, many newspaper advertisements state *Apply in person between 10 and 2, Monday through Friday*. Announcements that your school placement office receives will often specify *Apply in person*. In some cases, you are asked to call for an appointment. When an appointment is scheduled, you should be sure to arrive promptly at the hour stated.

When you know where and when you are to apply for a job, you should give attention to what you will wear, what information you should have with you, and how to prepare yourself for a favorable interview.

YOUR APPEARANCE

Business offices vary in what they consider appropriate dress for work. Clothing that is acceptable in your community and does not call attention to yourself is preferred in business offices. Fads in fashions that may be acceptable for parties or informal occasions generally are not appropriate for the business office. The office is not the place to be a fashion pacesetter. Therefore, you should plan carefully just what you will wear for your interview. Plan to wear clothing that is basically standard for meeting people in your community. Your clothing should not be the casual, comfortable kind that you wear for leisure hours; neither should it be the formal clothing that you wear for special parties. Your appearance should give the impression that you are a well-groomed, neat, confident person. Your choice of clothes should show that you are aware of what is appropriate and what is becoming to you.

ARRIVAL AT THE OFFICE

In most firms you will find a receptionist who will direct you to the right office. She may also explain to you the procedure that you will follow in being interviewed.

When you arrive at the right office, walk quietly and directly to the receptionist, if she is free. If she is talking on the telephone or is busy at her desk with someone, remain standing far enough away from her desk so that you cannot possibly overhear her conversation. When she is free tell her your reason for being in the office and listen carefully to the directions that she gives you. Here is a portion of a typical conversation between a receptionist and an applicant:

Receptionist: "Good morning. May I help you."
Applicant: "Good morning. I am Valerie Ferguson. Miss Montague, the placement counselor at Edgewood High School, suggested that I come to apply for the clerk-typist position."
Receptionist: "I am very happy to meet you, Miss Ferguson. Will you please come with me. (The receptionist and the applicant walk to an office down the

corridor.) Won't you please sit down here and fill in this application form. Be sure to fill it in completely. When you have filled in the form, please come back to my desk and I'll give you our clerical aptitude test. While you are taking the test, I'll arrange for your typing test. Would you prefer an electric or a manual machine for the test?"

THE APPLICATION FORM

Most companies require that the job applicants complete an application form. Although application forms vary from company to company, most of them request the same basic information.

To help you in filling in all the spaces on the application blanks accurately and completely, you may want to take with you the information that you may not quickly recall when you are writing details on a form. Among the facts that you may want to have on a small card or slip of paper are the following:

1. Your Social Security Number.
2. Your weight and height.
3. A list of your activities while in high school.
4. The names and addresses of any summer or part-time employers.
5. The periods of time during which you held jobs, the kind of work you did, and the weekly salary received.
6. The full names, addresses, and telephone numbers of at least three persons who would be willing to give references for you. Ask these persons for their permission to list their names. Former employers, your teachers, and your minister are references for your abilities, interests, and character. You should tell these persons that you are applying for a job and that they may be hearing from prospective employers.

Application forms should be filled in carefully and legibly. Since office workers must be careful in their work, interviewers look at the application form as an example of the kind of attention you will give to your work. Print the information where printing is requested. Print all the information if your printing is more legible than your writing.

If the question does not apply to you, write the notation NA (not applicable) or a dash (—) so that the interviewer will know that you did not overlook the item.

APPLICATION FOR EMPLOYMENT

WITH

UNIVERSAL MANUFACTURING COMPANY

GENERAL INFORMATION

Name Lynn R. Huntley		Date May 12, 197-	
Street Address 425 Glenview Avenue		Phone Number 761-2759	
City Boise State ID Zip Code 83704		Social Security Number 222-43-1896	

Date of Birth	Month June	Day 7,	Year 1951	Height 5'7"	Weight 125

Type of work desired Clerk-typist

Any defects in sight, hearing, or speech ? Yes. Wear glasses.

How much time have you lost through illness in the past two years ? Four days	Nature of illness Colds

Marital status Single	Number of children None	Ages of children NA

If married, is your spouse working? NA	If so, where ? NA

Have you ever served in the United States Armed Forces ? No	Rank and branch of service NA	Date of induction NA

Date of discharge NA	Type of discharge NA	Primary service duties NA

Give names of any members of our organization with whom you are acquainted. None

Are you related to any of these people? NA	If so, to whom ? NA

Who referred you to us for employment ? Eagle Employment Agency

Are you now employed ? Yes	If so, where ? Gilford Insurance Agency

EDUCATION

High School attended Boise Central High School	City & State Boise, ID	Year graduated 1970

Business School attended Norbert Business School	City & State Boise, ID	Number of months attended Nine

College or University attended None	City & State NA	Year graduated NA	Degree NA

Business subjects studied while in school	HIGH SCHOOL Gen. Business, Acct., Typing, Office Procedures
	BUSINESS COLLEGE Typing,Bus.Law,Communications,Office Procedures
	COLLEGE

Are you studying now ? Yes	If so, what ? Economics	Where ? Boise State Col.

Other special training None	System of shorthand studied None

In the space to the right indicate your present speed in shorthand and typing if you have these skills. Place an (X) after the office machines you can operate.

Shorthand		Typing 55 words a min.	Keypunch	
Adding Machine	X	Transcribing Machine	X	Verifier
Calculator		Mimeograph	X	Tabulator
Accounting Machine	X	Offset		Collator
Bookkeeping Machine	X	PBX Board	X	Other

Illus. 16-8

Page 1 — Application form

EXPERIENCE AND REFERENCES

Business Experience and References (Show last position first)

	From	To	Period Yrs.	Period Mos.	Name of Company	City & State	Person to whom you reported
1	7/71	Now	1	10	Gilford Insurance Agency	Boise, ID	Mrs. Ruth Kramer
2							
3							
4							

Business Experience and References (Continued)

	Give title and nature of your work	Why did you leave ?
1	General clerk	Am seeking work with more responsibility
2		and higher potential earnings.
3		
4		

Character References: Do not refer to previous employers or relatives.

Name	Address	Occupation
Mrs. Barbara Powell	294 Elmwood St., Boise	Personnel Manager
Mr. Frank Kreger	1250 Delta Ave., Boise	Teacher, business subjects
Miss Vivian Graham	5568 Sycamore Rd., Boise	Owner of florist shop

By signing this application I affirm that all statements made herein are true to the best of my knowledge.

Lynn R. Huntley
Signature of Applicant

APPLICANTS SHOULD NOT WRITE BELOW THIS LINE

Interviewed by:	Date of interview	Date applicant available for work	E G F P

Remarks:

Date Employed	Clock Number	Department	Classification
Enrolled in Group Insurance		Enrolled in Pension Plan	Blue Cross-Blue Shield Coverage ☐ Ind. ☐ Fam. ☐ Surg.
Date Employment Terminated	Reason		Consider for Reemployment

Illus. 16-9

Part 2 — Application form

TAKING TESTS

Many companies will ask you to take typewriting and clerical tests. You will find that these tests are **similar** to those you took in high school. The same general rules for taking tests apply in both situations. You should be relaxed and calm about the tests. Personnel interviewers try to make the situation as easy as possible and you should not be overly anxious about your performance.

similar:
almost the same;
alike; not different

Clerical Tests

Clerical tests which some companies require determine the applicant's general knowledge of clerical procedures. Listen carefully to all instructions as they are given to you. If permitted, take notes of the instructions. Read written instructions carefully so that you know what you should do. Be sure to find out whether you are to be timed or are to proceed at your own pace and, if you are, let the person **administering** the test know when you have finished it. Note the following instructions:

administering:
giving

> INSTRUCTIONS: Read the following sentences carefully. Determine whether the practice is one that you would follow as an office worker. If it is a practice that you would follow, place a check mark in the "Yes" column. If it is a practice that you would not follow, mark the "No" column. Answer all the questions. You will have ten minutes to complete this part.

> Example: An office worker arrives at her desk no later than 30 minutes after the beginning of the work day

Yes	No
	✓

From these instructions, you learned that one of two responses is possible and how you are to mark each response. You also learned how much time you will have for this section of the test and that you should attempt to answer all of the items.

If you finish a timed test before time is called, use the extra time to reread the items and to check your answers. Careful attention to **comprehending** each item can help you avoid errors due to misunderstanding.

comprehending:
understanding

Performance Tests

The most common performance test given to applicants for office jobs is a typewriting test. It may be a timed typing test from straight copy, or it may be an office style job, such as typing a letter from a rough draft.

Listen carefully to the instructions so that you will know what you are to do and how long you will have for the completion of each test.

Generally you will have a chance to get used to the typewriter you are to use. Even though you find that you will be working on a machine that you have never used, you will quickly adjust to it during the practice period. Remember that typewriters are alike as far as basic structure is concerned. In just a few minutes you can learn how margins and tabulator stops are cleared and set. Then you can do a little straight typing to get the feel of the stroking mechanism of the machine.

The interviewer is interested in learning about your general typewriting skill. You will have had sufficient practice in school so that the performance test should be relatively easy for you.

THE INTERVIEW

In some companies, you will fill in an application form, take tests, and see an interviewer during the same visit. In other companies, the interview may come after you have filled in the application form, and you will be asked to return for the tests if the interview was considered satisfactory. In still other companies, you are asked to fill in an application form and take tests, which are evaluated before you are asked to come in for an interview. In some firms, you will be hired on the basis of your application form and the interview. Some companies use the information about your skill development in school as the basis for evaluating your abilities and, therefore, give no tests.

Whether the interview takes place early or late in the hiring process, there is some general information that you should keep in mind.

Purpose of Interview

You should remember that the interviewer has before him your application form and the results of your tests. He is talking with you in order to tell you about the company and the job and to get additional information that may be helpful in deciding whether you are the best person for the job. He will try to put you at ease so that you will be relaxed in answering questions and in talking with him. The interviewer will tell you about the following:

1. The nature of the company's business and what its general policies are.
2. What the specific job for which you are being interviewed requires and in what department it is located.
3. What the hours of work are, the salary, the benefits, including coffee breaks, health insurance, pension

plan, vacation, holidays, and tuition reimbursement arrangements, if provided.

You should feel free to ask questions about the topics which the interviewer mentions. The interview has a threefold purpose: It permits the interviewer to become acquainted with you; it permits you to become acquainted with the company; and it provides information about the nature of the work you will be doing if you are offered the job.

Answering Questions

In addition to giving you information, the interviewer will ask you questions to get an idea of your interests and attitudes, as well as to learn how well you respond to questions. Listen carefully to the questions asked; respond directly to them. Make your answers brief, but not so brief that you give an incomplete answer. Here is a portion of an interview between an applicant and an interviewer:

Interviewer: "What activities did you enjoy in your course in office procedures?"

Applicant: "Oh, we did so *many* things in that class! The teacher introduced us to just about every job that she believed we would need to know in the office. I really learned a great deal from all the things we did."

This applicant obviously did not listen to the question. The interviewer wanted her to tell him about those activities that she enjoyed and not how extensive the activities were in the class. Answering a question inadequately causes an interviewer to wonder if this is the way the applicant will respond on the job when she is asked a question about her work or her plans.

A more appropriate response to the interviewer's question would have been

> Applicant: "I enjoyed the typewriting jobs best, I believe. I liked typewriting form letters, manuscripts, rough drafts, final copy, and tables and forms. However, I also enjoyed the assignments where we learned how to make telephone calls and where we learned how to deal with callers to an office.

Forming an Impression

The interviewer, as he talks with you, develops an impression of you as a worker in his company. He will note particularly the following:

1. Your alertness in answering the questions he raises
2. Your use of the English language
3. Your voice
4. Your appearance and your poise
5. Your interest in the job to be filled

If the interviewer gets a favorable overall impression on these qualities, he will decide that you are a good candidate for the position.

Conclusion of Interview

When the interview is over, the interviewer will tell you what the next step will be. In some companies the interviewer may offer you a position immediately, if he is favorably impressed and your skills are satisfactory. In other companies, the interviewer may tell you that you will hear from him within a few days.

If a position is offered to you, you will be given some time to consider the offer. You should not respond at the time of the interview unless you are sure that this is the job you want.

Regardless of what the interviewer says in ending the interview, you should thank him for talking with you and indicate that you will either call or write within the time given for a reply or you will await his call. You should then leave quickly.

Follow-up of Interview

If you are offered a job at the end of the interview, you should call or write your decision within the time allowed you. Illustration 16-11 is a sample response.

Illus. 16-11
Letter of
acceptance

```
                              5624 Sunnybrook Drive
                              Fort Worth, TX  76108
                              June 8, 197-

Mr. Joseph Zinn
Personnel Department
Northern Hills Glass Company
11 Greenfield Road
Fort Worth, TX  76101

Dear Mr. Zinn

The position you offered me last Wednesday
sounds very interesting, and I am happy to
accept it.

As you requested, I shall report for work
on Monday, June 15, at 9:00 a.m.

                      Sincerely yours

                      (Miss) Carol Kemper

                      Carol Kemper
```

If the interviewer promised to call or write to you, as soon as you hear from the company you should respond. If the interviewer calls you, it is appropriate to respond by telephone. However, a letter in response to an offer is considered a satisfactory procedure.

REVIEWING WHAT YOU HAVE READ

1. During what hours are many personnel departments open for applicants?
2. What kind of clothing is considered appropriate for office wear?
3. At what point in the hiring procedure is an application form filled in?
4. What information should an applicant list on a sheet of paper ahead of time so that filling in an application form will be easier?
5. How does an applicant indicate that a particular question on the application form doesn't apply to him?
6. What kinds of tests may an applicant for a clerical job be expected to take?
7. Why should an applicant listen to and read instruction for tests carefully?
8. What is the purpose of the interview between a company interviewer and an applicant?
9. How should an applicant respond to questions asked?
10. What does an interviewer observe about applicants in order to decide who will be satisfactory for the company?

MAKING DECISIONS

1. One day about a month before the end of the school year and his graduation, Tom learned about an interesting job in the accounting department of a local real estate company. He was dressed in his casual school clothes, but he decided that he would not take time to go home and change his clothes; so he went to the personnel office to inquire about the job.

   What do you think of Tom's decision?

2. When Gail Leitman was asked to take a typewriting test, the personnel clerk took her to the work station where she would be typewriting. Gail looked at the typewriter and immediately said, "Oh! I have never used a typewriter like that. I won't know how to use it. Will you show me? Will you give me some time to practice."

   What do you think of Gail's decision to ask for help?

WORKING WITH OTHERS

Regina Adams and Alice Curry were good friends, and they wanted to work in the same company; so they decided to go together to inquire about jobs. They visited a large publishing company where they were asked to fill in application forms and to wait to talk with an interviewer. When the interviewer was free, the receptionist asked Regina to go into the interviewer's office. Alice rose to go with her. The receptionist said, "Miss Trumper would like to see each of you separately." Then Regina said, "Well, if we can't do this together, we don't want jobs in this company."

What do you think of Regina's comment?

USING LANGUAGE

The exclamation point (!) is used to represent a full stop after an enthusiastic or strong comment.
   Examples: We won the game!
             The job was completed by noon!
The exclamation point is typed inside the quotation marks if the exclamation applies only to the quoted matter. It is placed outside the quotation mark if it applies to the entire sentence.
   Examples: We heard the crowd shout "bravo!" as we entered the concert hall.
             Ruth exclaimed, "Come with us *now*"!

On separate sheet of paper write or type each of the following sentences with correct punctuation.

1. The young boy called to his friend Look do you see that strange bird
2. How many of you would like to attend the workshop next Friday
3. Hurrah I wasn't sure you would be able to get that job done so quickly
4. What a wonderful surprise this party is for me
5. Business as usual is the slogan of our office isn't it

USING ARITHMETIC

Clerks in many offices must compare numbers to see if they agree. Clerical tests administered to job applicants often include checking numbers for agreement. On page 568 are two columns of numbers. On a separate sheet write these lists of numbers. Then place a check beside those that agree.

Example: 4,567   4,568
             34,223   34,223 √

1.	467,987	467,987
2.	321,302	321,203
3.	56,789	56,798
4.	41,321	42,231
5.	56,675	65,675
6.	35,432	35,332
7.	781,098	718,098
8.	964,323	945,323
9.	13,134	13,143
10.	14,541	14,541

PERFORMING OFFICE TASKS

1. Assume that you are preparing for an interview in a local company and you want to take with you information that would help you in filling in the standard application form. Make a list of the items you would include in this information and then type in the facts related to each item of information.

2. Assume that you have been asked to complete an application form for a clerical position. If an application form is available, complete it carefully in ink. If a form is not available, type a copy of the illustration on pages 560 and 561 and fill in the information with pen and ink.

PART 3 — APPLYING FOR A JOB BY LETTER

> Joan Brewster wanted to work in Denver, which is over 100 miles from her hometown; so she applied for a job with a large company there by letter. She knew that personnel interviewers not only read personal data sheets thoroughly but they are also impressed with the attractiveness of the format used. She planned a brief letter to accompany her personal data sheet, and she hoped that the two would impress the interviewer to write and ask her to visit them for an interview.

You may apply for a job by letter. In that case your letter and personal data sheet should represent you in the best possible way.

THE PERSONAL DATA SHEET

When you apply for a job by mail, you should include a personal data sheet. The personal data sheet tells potential employers who you are and what you are trained to do by both education and actual employment experience.

Its Purpose

A prospective employer needs to become acquainted with you in very little time. A personal data sheet is helpful in achieving this purpose. A personal data sheet outlines in clear form the important facts about your background that will be of value in determining whether you are a good candidate for a position.

Its Content

Generally personal data sheets are organized into the following parts:

Personal information	Experience
Education	References
Extracurricular activities	

Personal Information. The personal information includes your name, home address, telephone number, your age (date of birth), your height, your weight, your marital status, and your physical condition (a general statement is sufficient).

Education. Under education you will give the complete name of your high school, plus the curriculum that you studied or the major courses taken, and the clerical skills that you have developed. You should add any scholastic awards that you received while in high school.

Extracurricular Activities. Extracurricular activities are of interest to prospective employers; so you will want to list all your organizational activities while you were a student and those activities in the community in which you continue to be active. Any offices that you held in a class or club should also be listed. This section of your personal data sheet reflects your special interests, your ability to work with others, and your leadership qualities.

Experience. Experience at work, even though limited, should be listed. Begin with your most recent experience and list all jobs you have held. Give the job title first, then the name of the firm or organization, and the dates of your employment. If you have had little or no work experience for which you were paid, list all volunteer jobs that you have held in the community.

Illus. 16-12
List on your personal data sheet any previous working experience that you have had.

traits:
qualities of
personal character

References. In evaluating candidates, prospective employers review references carefully. You will want to list as references persons who know you sufficiently to judge you on the **traits** and attitudes that

will be given the name of the firm and perhaps the name of the person in charge of employment. If a person's name and title are given, address your letter in this manner:

```
Mr. T. G. Gaines, Personnel Manager
The Abraham Jones Corporation
3689 Jefferson Street
Denver, CO 80200
```

The salutation should be *Dear Mr. Gaines:*

3. State your interest in the first paragraph:

```
May I present my qualifications for the
clerk-typist position which you advertised
in The Denver News on Monday, June 3?
```

or

```
Miss _____ _____, the Placement Counselor
at Central High School, has suggested that I
apply for the clerk-typist position which
is available in your firm.  May I present
my qualifications for this position?
```

4. In the second paragraph, refer to your personal data sheet which is enclosed. This paragraph should highlight the main points of your education and experience. You might write

```
As you will note from the enclosed data
sheet, I will graduate from Central High
School in June.  While in high school
I successfully completed several business
courses, including typewriting, office
machines, and clerical office procedures.
I have also held two summer jobs where I
have had opportunities to use my business
skills and abilities.
```

5. In the final paragraph of your application letter, you should indicate your interest in a personal interview as well as the times when you are available:

```
May I have an interview for the clerk-
typist position which you have available?
I could arrange to be in Denver during
our spring recess, which is the week of
April 21.
```

6. The complimentary close may be a simple *Sincerely yours* or *Yours very truly*, depending upon your salutation (see page 70). Be sure to sign your name and indicate the enclosure.

FOLLOW-UP OF A LETTER OF APPLICATION

Most companies that ask persons interested in a position to write to them will respond quickly to all applicants. However, there are times when the number responding is greater than anticipated and the task of answering letters of application may take several weeks. If you have not heard from a company to which you wrote in response to an advertisement, it is appropriate to write a brief letter after two weeks, in which you state that you wrote earlier and that you hope to hear from the company.

If you write to a company seeking a job when you had no information about the need of the company for employees, you can expect to hear from the company. However, you should allow at least three weeks for a response. If you don't receive a letter or telephone call, it is generally an indication that workers with your skills are not needed. It is usually not fruitful to follow up with another inquiry. However, if you are especially interested in the company, you could write a second brief letter and enclose another copy of your resume. Your chances of getting a response are slight, but there is always the possibility that your first letter was misplaced or misdirected and the second one will arrive at a time when the company needs persons with your skills and interests.

REVIEWING WHAT YOU HAVE READ

1. What is the purpose of a personal data sheet?
2. How should a personal data sheet be organized?
3. What is the value of the information about education on a personal data sheet?
4. What is the value of listing extracurricular activities on a personal data sheet?
5. What work experience would an applicant for a clerical position want to list on a personal data sheet?
6. What is the purpose of references on a personal data sheet?
7. What should the references listed by an applicant be able to judge?
8. Why should people listed as references be called prior to their being listed by a job applicant?
9. How should a personal data sheet be prepared?
10. What should a letter accompanying a personal data sheet state in general?

MAKING DECISIONS

1. Larry Bainford was organizing information for his personal data sheet, and he knew he had to list some references. He decided that it would be easiest to list two of his uncles who lived in the same town as he did and an aunt, who worked in the town, also.

   What do you think of Larry's decision?

2. Judy Holbrook was applying for a position that was advertised in the local paper. She didn't think it was necessary to tell her whole story in a letter; the company could learn about her during an interview. So, Judy wrote a short letter in which she said, "I saw in last night's paper that you need a clerk-typist. I feel qualified for that position. Could I come in for an interview?"

What do you think of Judy's decision to write a brief letter and wait for an interview to explain her background?

WORKING WITH OTHERS

Lynn Yarwood answered an advertisement of a local company that was hiring office workers. In its advertisement the company stated that only applicants who had the required qualifications would receive a reply. Lynn mailed her letter on Monday afternoon and did not receive a response by the end of the week. On Friday afternoon she called the personnel office and said, "I wrote your company a letter on Monday. I know that I have the qualifications needed for the positions you have open. I haven't heard from you. May I come in for an interview on Monday?"

What do you think of Lynn's manner of handling this situation?

USING LANGUAGE

Suffixes are word endings that change the spelling of base words. Common suffixes include -ing, -ly, -ily, -ally, -ness, -able, -ible.

On a separate sheet of paper correctly spell each of the following words, using the suffix indicated.

Add -ing to each of the following:
hit
plan
change
charge
accept

Add -ly, -ily, or -ally to each of the following:
merry
usual
frequent
realistic
heart

Add -ness to each of the following:
neat
happy
ready
clean
fit

Add -able or -ible to each of the following:
change
depend
prevent
manage
defense

USING ARITHMETIC

Many clerical tests that companies give to applicants require basic arithmetic computations. On a separate sheet of paper record each of these problems and perform the operation indicated.

Add:

1. .69	2. 1.98	3. 567.31
.54	4.67	156.71
.45	8.02	290.53
.30	9.35	658.95
.15	10.24	135.24
	15.29	350.80

Subtract:

4.	18.45	5.	700.00	6.	4513	7.	5790.19	8.	76.50
	− 1.99		− 14.50		− 985		− 190.89		− 1.97

Multiply:

9.   56 × 12 =   12. 146 × 122 =

10. 146.10 × 24 =   13. 158.98 × 17 =

11. 198.96 × 38 =

Divide:

14. $15\overline{)5970}$ 15. $132\overline{)6892}$ 16. $3.75\overline{)5381.25}$ 17. $1.2\overline{)766}$

Add: Subtract:

18. 1/4 + 1/3 =   20. 7/8 − 1/4 =

19. 2/3 + 1/3 =   21. 4 1/2 − 1 1/4 =

Multiply: Divide:

22. 2 1/2 × 2 1/2 =   24. 3/4 ÷ 3/4 =

23. 4 1/3 × 12 1/2 =   25. 5/6 ÷ 1/3 =

PERFORMING OFFICE TASKS

1. Prepare a personal data sheet, using Illus. 16-13, page 571, as a model. Type an original and a carbon of your personal data sheet.

2. Type a letter of application in response to an advertisement in a local paper. Indicate in your letter that you are enclosing a personal data sheet.

PART **4** YOUR BEGINNING JOB
AND BEYOND

Yvonne Long was hired by a large bank in Atlanta, Georgia. She liked the modern building and the attractive offices. It was an impressive place; and, as she began her first day on the job, she wondered if she would meet the standards set by the bank. Yvonne knew her supervisor would expect her to produce a full day's work to earn her salary, but she also realized that there would be a period of adjustment to her new job.

YOUR ADJUSTMENT TO WORK

You have received a general introduction to the work of the office and to procedures that are typical in many organizations. However, as you know, organizations differ in the kinds of work they perform and in the manner in which employees carry through the **directives** of their executives. Therefore, the procedures you may use for a particular task will differ from the general ones you know. Do not let this disturb you. The general procedures you have learned will be related to those that you will use in the office. Organizations have reasons for their particular procedures and, as you learn these reasons, you will understand what is to be accomplished.

directives:
guides;
instructions
issued by officials

Because organizations differ from each other, they do not expect beginners to know exactly how to perform their job on their first day of work. Many organizations provide job **orientation** sessions for new employees. Some organizations have formal orientation sessions; others assume that the person under whom you will work will provide informal orientation to the company and your job.

orientation:
acquainting with
surroundings and
position; learning

Formal Orientation

While there are various methods of formal orientation of new employees, a popular method is to plan for new employees to meet together for the first day at work. During this day new employees are introduced to the company and to the department in which each will work. Here is a schedule for a group of new high school graduates who began clerical positions in a large company on July 1.

9:00 to 10:30	Meeting in Conference Room — 13th floor
	1. Greetings from the Vice-President of the company, Mr. Stuart Strasman
	2. Discussion of the objectives of the company — Personnel Director, Mr. Walter Crowley
	3. Film — showing the range of activities of the company
10:30 to 10:45	Coffee break
10:45 to 12:00	Discussion of company organization and how the work flows through the organization — Mr. Stanley Fenwick and Mrs. Delores Phillips, of the Personnel Department
12:00 to 1:30	Lunch in company cafeteria with each new employee seated with an experienced co-worker; tour of headquarters; discussion of neighborhood resources
1:30 to 5:00	Opportunity to learn about specific job location and to do several tasks with assistance

On the second day the new employees report to their job locations at 9:00 a.m. After two weeks all new employees are called together for a one-hour session. At this session they are encouraged to ask questions about the company's policies and operations.

Illus. 16-14
In a large company you may learn several tasks on your first day.

Wang Laboratories Inc.

Informal Orientation

Most small companies and some medium and large companies make no formal arrangements for a program of orientation. Usually a supervisor introduces and guides the new employee so that company policies and job procedures are learned in a reasonable time. The new employee usually reports to the supervisor at the regular hour for beginning work each day and is given details about the work that is to be done. Here is a portion of a supervisor's comments to a new clerk in a central records department:

> "Jane, we are happy to welcome you. I hope you are going to like working here. First, I want you to meet the other five clerks in this department. (At this point, Jane walks with the supervisor to the work stations of the five and is introduced to each.) . . .
> "I think the easiest way to understand the work you are to do is for me to give you some specific jobs, explain them, and then let you do them. As soon as you have a question, just let me know. We don't expect you to understand all parts of the job immediately. I am here to help you; so please don't hesitate to ask questions."

In this company the new employees are scheduled for a brief meeting with someone in the personnel office who discusses the company's policies and benefits. Also, the supervisor is responsible for explaining the coffee break and lunch arrangements for the departmental staff.

EXPECTATIONS OF SUPERVISORS

The cost of doing the paperwork of an organization is watched closely by company executives. Executives try to keep these costs to a minimum the same as *all* costs are kept to a minimum. Executives want their employees to enjoy their work, but they also want them to earn the salaries they receive. Supervisors are the persons responsible for maintaining an environment that encourages each worker to do his work responsibly and pleasurably.

There are many ways that supervisors will observe you to learn what help you need and to enable them to make recommendations for salary increases and promotions. Among the considerations of supervisors are these:

1. Your **punctuality** in the morning and in returning from coffee breaks and lunch periods
2. Your attention and accuracy in doing your work

*punctuality:
promptness;
on time*

3. Your accomplishments each day (Do you hold up others because you fail to finish your part of the task?)
4. Your response to extra demands during emergencies
5. Your general attitude toward your work

Supervisors realize that people should work comfortably and at a reasonable pace. There may be times, however, when you will be expected to increase your **pace**; but, as a general rule, the number of employees assigned to a task can do the job efficiently on a normal workday. Companies try to minimize periods of pressure as well as periods of insufficient work to keep employees busy.

pace:
rate of movement
or progress

YOUR REVIEW OF YOUR OWN PERFORMANCE

As a beginning office worker, you will find that giving attention to how well you do your own work will help you improve your performance. Some of the questions you can raise about your own performance are these:

1. Am I always on time—in the morning, after coffee breaks, after lunch?
2. Am I keeping up with the quantity of work I am expected to do?
3. Am I doing all tasks right the first time and checking my work?
4. Am I working at a reasonably fast pace?

You will find that as you learn your job your performance will improve and you will work faster. Your attention to doing a good job will result in your doing the kind of work supervisors appreciate.

EDUCATIONAL OPPORTUNITIES

With your high school education completed, you will have basic preparation for many office positions. You will learn much as you work and think about your job. Developments in every job give you a chance to learn something new.

In addition to the knowledge that you acquire through your job, you may have chances to take courses or attend workshops that are sponsored by your company, professional organizations in the community, adult education centers, or colleges. You should carefully consider any announcements that you see and enroll in those courses that you think will be valuable to you in your work or personally.

Many communities have evening programs in adult education centers and in community colleges that may be of value to you. Many office workers, for example, enroll in community college programs on a part-time basis. A student who completes the full-two-year program in a community college earns an associate degree, which may be an A. A. (Associate in Arts), A. S. (Associate in Science), or A. A. S. (Associate in Applied Science). The degree earned depends on the program studied. Many four-year colleges accept the credits earned in the community college, so that a person may transfer to a four-year college after two years of work at the community college level. He can then earn a bachelor's degree. Many business people have earned bachelor's degrees at night while working during the day. Both community colleges and four-year colleges offer evening courses in all business areas, including accounting, office skills, data processing, and management.

Many companies encourage employees to gain further education through providing tuition fees. These plans vary, with some providing full tuition for all courses taken and passed; in other cases, the company refunds only a portion of the tuition charges for the courses passed. While some companies make refunds only for courses related to the work the employee is doing, other companies make refunds for all college-level studies completed satisfactorily by employees.

Consider furthering your education. In our rapidly changing society, you may find that going to college may be a rewarding way of keeping yourself aware of the world in which you live and work.

PROMOTIONAL OPPORTUNITIES

During this course you have learned about many jobs that are available to beginning workers with little or no experience. You have realized that these jobs are foundations for better positions. Every organization needs people who can and will assume more responsibility. There are many levels of responsibility in every organization. People do not move up from the low levels to the high levels automatically. Personnel staff members are constantly **assessing** the talents and potential abilities of employees to discover who are most likely to meet the demands of higher level jobs.

assessing: determining the value of

Promotions in the Same Type of Work

In the first Unit of this book, you learned about job classifications (page 9). You saw there two grades for several typical clerical positions in the offices of one state government. You noticed there that the Grade II job required greater skill than the first grade. There are also additional grades for these positions. For example, Illus. 16-15 describes skills required for a Grade III clerk-typist.

```
Clerk-Typist III    Same requirements as for Clerk I and Clerk II, plus
                     Considerable knowledge of modern office practices, proce-
                        dures, and equipment
                     Considerable knowledge of English, spelling, and arithmetic
                     Working knowledge of the principles of office management
                        and supervision and of standard record maintenance
                        procedures
                     Ability to maintain complex clerical records and to prepare
                        reports from various statistical or accounting infor-
                        mation
                     Ability to carry out routine administrative and supervisory
                        detail independently and conduct correspondence
                        without review
                     Ability to understand and follow moderately complex oral
                        and written directions
                     Ability to plan, assign, and coordinate the work of a
                        moderate-size clerical staff
                     Ability to instruct and train clerical subordinates effectively
                     Ability to develop, lay out, and install clerical procedures
                        from general instructions
                     A high degree of clerical aptitude and general intelligence
                        as evidenced by a passing grade in a practical written
                        test
                     Ability to type accurately from plain copy at the rate of
                        40 words a minute as evidenced by a passing grade
                        in a typing performance test

                Source:  Missouri Personnel Division
                         117 East Dunklin Street
                         Jefferson City, MO 65101
```

Illus. 16-15

competent:
able; fitted; skillful

Persons who become **competent** in beginning positions and show evidence of the abilities needed in higher level jobs will earn promotions.

Promotions in Other Areas of Work

Transfers are often made from one type of work to another when there are common aspects of the work in the two departments. The abilities that supervisors value highly for promotions are the following:

initiative:
first step;
preliminary action

1. Ability to be responsible for the accuracy of your own work
2. Ability to take **initiative** and make decisions
3. Ability to work with others and supervise their work
4. Ability to learn new procedures, new techniques, new information
5. Ability to improve the procedures that you have used

Many employees have earned promotions because of their success in doing their jobs. Here are two instances.

Marianne Roth's first job was as a typist in the home office of a large paper manufacturing company. The supervisor

Illus. 16-16
Efficiency in improving
procedures often leads
to new areas of
responsibility.

observed that Marianne was one of the best proofreaders she had ever had in the department. Seldom did Marianne's work have an uncorrected error. After Marianne had been with the company for about a year, there was an opening for an assistant to one of the public information executives. He needed someone who was extremely accurate. All press releases and bulletins that went out had to be perfect. There were other qualifications, including good typewriting skills and general ability to work on one's own; but the skill in proofreading was of primary importance. Marianne met all the requirements and was offered the position. She accepted it, for she believed that she would find the more responsible position interesting and challenging.

Stephen Lockwood is now a supervisor in the accounting department. However, his first job, when he graduated from high school five years ago, was as a clerk in the same accounting office. He liked this large insurance company and found the company offered him many opportunities. He enrolled in an evening college program in accounting. He continues to go to college and hopes to complete the requirements for a bachelor's degree. After he had been with the company about a year he was promoted to a junior accounting clerk, and later he became an accountant. He has been a supervisor for almost a year. The personnel director believes there will be more promotions ahead for this fine employee.

OUTLOOK FOR CLERICAL EMPLOYMENT

As you complete this course, clerical and related occupations represent millions of employment opportunities. A recent study[1] indicates the following openings in the next ten years.

Occupation	Presently Employed	Annual Openings Forecast
Bank clerks	510,000	29,600
Bank tellers	153,000	14,700
Bookkeepers	1,340,000	74,000
Cashiers	847,000	64,000
Computer operators	200,000	34,200
File clerks	169,000	15,300
Hotel clerks	61,000	4,500
Office machine operators	365,000	20,800
Shipping clerks	379,000	12,000
Stenographers	2,833,000	247,000
Stock clerks	500,000	23,000
Telephone operators	420,000	28,000
Typists	671,000	61,000

Illus. 16-17   Ten-year clerical employment forecast

YOUR FUTURE IN THE OFFICE

Today's business office is undergoing many changes. Some projections include far more use of computers as well as marked basic changes in handling paperwork. Microfilm, automatic retrieval, and picture telephones have been introduced into offices. These **innovations** are likely to become commonplace in the future.

innovations: new ideas, methods, or devices

You are prepared not only for your first job but for learning new tasks. You have been introduced to basic skills and problem-solving methods that will be useful in different kinds of offices. If you do your job with an understanding and an awareness of how it relates to what is going on in the office around you, you will develop the new skills and abilities to cope with the innovations that are introduced into your own work.

REVIEWING WHAT YOU HAVE READ

1. Why do companies not expect beginning workers to know how to do all the tasks they will have to do on their jobs?
2. What are the purposes of formal orientation sessions?
3. How does informal orientation differ from a formal orientation period?
4. What do supervisors observe about the work of beginners in a company?

[1]Ernie Hood, Newspaper Enterprise Association, July, 1972.

5. What are two questions a beginning worker can ask about his own performance?

6. What kinds of educational benefits do some companies provide?

7. Do office workers combine their full-time jobs with part-time study? Explain your answer.

8. What kinds of promotional opportunities are open to clerical workers?

9. Name four abilities that are considered important for promotion.

10. How does the office worker remain "in step" with changes in the way jobs are done?

MAKING DECISIONS

Jeanne was a new receptionist in the headquarters of a large chemical company. Miss Erickson, whom she was replacing, had been promoted. On the first day, Miss Erickson worked at the receptionist desk so that Jeanne could observe how the job was to be done and could learn about the company. At midafternoon, Miss Erickson told Jeanne that she would go back to her own office and if any questions arose, she should feel free to call her. Shortly after Miss Erickson left, a visitor arrived and inquired about a conference that was being held in the headquarters office. Jeanne didn't know about a conference; so she decided to tell the visitor: "I am sorry, but you have the wrong company. There is no conference here." Did Jeanne make a good decision? Explain.

WORKING WITH OTHERS

Brad Collins was a new bookkeeping clerk in a large accounting office. One day, shortly after he began working, a fellow clerk told him, "I've been noticing you. You work too hard. Why are you killing yourself on this job? The work will be here long after you're gone. You ought to slow down. Why are you such an eager beaver?"

What do you think Brad should say to his fellow worker?

USING LANGUAGE

Knowing the meaning of prefixes can aid you in adding words to your vocabulary. The definitions of some common prefixes are:

ab — away; from; off; under
con, com, col — together; with; jointly
contra — counter to; against
dis — opposite to; absence of
fore — beforehand; ahead of; previous to
mis — opposite of; lack of; wrong
pre — in front of; before
trans — across; beyond

Below is a list of words that use the prefixes above. On a separate sheet of paper write or type a sentence using each of these words correctly.

abnormal	miscount
compressed	misfile
contradiction	predispose
disadvantage	prerecord
forecast	transatlantic
foresee	transcontinental

Clerical tests that applicants for jobs take often include arithmetic reasoning problems. Here are some typical questions you may have to answer. On a separate sheet of paper record the figures needed to compute an answer to the question asked.

1. What is the total cost of the following items: a red pen at 69 cents, two lead pencils at 39 cents each, and a green felt-tipped pen at 98 cents?

2. If a sales tax of 6 percent is added to an item costing $16.95, what is the total cost?

3. What is the interest earned in a year on a savings account of $550 if the rate of interest is 5 percent?

4. A receptionist earns $90 a week and saves $13.50 a week. What percent of her weekly earnings is she saving?

5. If each typist uses two dozen envelopes a day, how many envelopes are needed for 12 typists in a week (5 days)?

1. Assume that you are inquiring about evening courses on a part-time basis in local adult education centers or colleges. What are the courses that you believe you would find helpful? Make a list of these courses and briefly outline what you would like to learn in each of them. You may list courses that you would enjoy personally as well as those that you believe you would use in a business career.

2. Write a short essay, of approximately two to three paragraphs, in which you describe your career goals for the next three years. Be sure to include a description of the kind of work that you would like to be doing about three years from now.

APPENDIX A

GRAMMAR

Grammar is important in speaking and writing. Knowing the rules of grammar is necessary if you are to carry out your responsibilities confidently.

Grammar is a study of the words of a language, but particularly a study of the relationship of those words to one another. Words are divided into nine classifications that are known as parts of speech.

I. Nouns	V. Verbs
II. Pronouns	VI. Adverbs
III. Adjectives	VII. Prepositions
IV. Articles	VIII. Conjunctions
	IX. Interjections

I. Nouns

A noun is a word that is used as

A. A name of a person (Thomas Jefferson)
B. A place (Washington, D.C.)
C. A thing (desk)
D. A quality (goodness)
E. An action (fishing)
F. An idea (immortality)

Proper Noun. A proper noun names a particular being or thing. It is always capitalized.

Alexander Graham Bell, New York, Empire State Building

Common Noun. A common noun names any of a class of beings or things.

man (men), tree (trees), table (tables)

Collective Noun. A collective noun is a common noun that names a group.

company, committee, crowd, jury, group

II. Pronouns

A pronoun is a word that is used instead of a noun. Most of the problems with pronouns involve personal and relative pronouns. Use of the correct pronoun after the verb *be* may also present a problem.

Personal Pronouns and Their Antecedents. A personal pronoun is a pronoun that shows by its form whether it represents the

    A. Speaker (first person)
    B. Person spoken to (second person)
    C. Person spoken of (third person)

The antecedent of a pronoun is the noun for which it stands. The pronoun must be in agreement with its antecedent in person, number, and gender. There are several uses of antecedents that require particular attention.

1. When two or more singular antecedents of a pronoun are connected by *and*, the pronoun must be plural.

   The clerk and the mail boy received *their* checks.

   If, however, the antecedents are merely different names for the same person or thing, the pronoun must be singular.

   The well-known businessman and public servant has received *his* award.

2. When two or more singular antecedents of a pronoun are connected by *or* or *nor*, the pronoun must be singular.

   Either Joyce or Linda must bring *her* notebook.

   If one of the antecedents is plural, it should be placed last, and the pronoun should be plural.

   Neither the general manager nor his assistants realized that *they* had so little time.

3. If the antecedent of a pronoun is a collective noun that expresses unity, the pronoun must be singular.

   The committee quickly reached *its* decision.

   If the collective noun refers to the individuals or parts that make up a group, however, the pronoun of which it is the antecedent must be plural.

   The class brought *their* own lunches.

4. The number of an antecedent is not changed when it is followed by such connectives as *in addition to* and *as well as*.

   The boy, as well as his brothers, did *his* duty.

5. Since there is no third person, singular number, common gender pronoun, the masculine *he*, *his*, or *him* is generally used when the antecedent requires such a pronoun.

   Each office worker must do *his* best.

   When it is especially important to be accurate, both masculine and feminine pronouns may be used.

   Every employee should be careful about *his* or *her* personal appearance.

Relative Pronouns. A relative pronoun is one that joins a subordinate clause to its antecedent. *Who, which, what,* and *that* are the relative pronouns.

Office workers *who* know grammar are valuable.

Some compound relative pronouns are *whoever, whosoever, whichever, whichsoever, whatever,* and *whatsoever.* Relative pronouns present two problems:

1. Using the correct relative with reference to persons and things.

2. Using the correct case form — for example, *who* refers to persons and, sometimes, to highly trained animals; *which* refers to animals or things; *that* refers to persons, animals, or things.

Who, whoever, and *whosoever* are in the nominative case and are the correct forms when a relative pronoun is the subject of a subordinate clause.

Mr. Johnson is a man *who* can do the job.

Whose is in the possessive case and is used as is any possessive.

Whose hat is this?

Whom, whomever, and *whomsoever* are in the objective case and must be used when a relative pronoun is the object of a verb or preposition.

Grace is the girl *whom* we are addressing.

The Pronoun after *Be*. The same case must be used after the verb *be* in any of its forms (*am, are, is, was, were, be, being, have been*) as appears before it. This is usually the nominative case. When the object of a transitive verb, however, precedes the infinitive *to be*, the objective case must follow it.

It was *she* (not *her*).
If I were *he* (not *him*).
Did you expect those children to be *them* (not *they*)?

III. Adjectives

An adjective is a word that is used to modify a noun or a pronoun. There are two types of adjectives:

A. A *descriptive* adjective names some quality of or describes the person or object expressed by the noun or pronoun that it modifies.

pretty girl, *handsome* child, *white* frock

B. A *definitive* adjective points out or expresses the number or quantity of the object named by the noun or referred to by the pronoun.

eight people, *this* book, *that* desk, *ten* pages

Proper Adjectives. Proper adjectives are those derived from proper nouns, and they are always capitalized.

French language or *American* interests

Comparison of Adjectives. Comparison is the expression of an adjective to indicate an increasing or decreasing degree of quality, quantity, or manner. There are three degrees of comparison:

1. The *positive degree* is expressed by the simple form of the adjective.

   light, pretty

2. The *comparative degree* is used to compare two objects. The comparative degree of almost all adjectives of *one* syllable, and of a few of two syllables, is formed by the addition of *r* or *er* to the simple form.

   lighter, prettier

   The comparative degree of most adjectives of *two* or more syllables is formed by the placing of *more* or *less* before the simple form of the adjective.

   more beautiful or *less* useful

3. The *superlative degree* is used to compare *three* or more objects. The superlative degree of most adjectives of one syllable, and some of two syllables, is formed by the addition of *est* to the simple form.

   lightest, darkest

   The superlative degree of most adjectives of two or more syllables is formed by the placing of *most* or *least* before the simple form of the adjective.

   most satisfactory or *least* attractive

Some adjectives are compared irregularly. The following are a few:

Positive	*Comparative*	*Superlative*
good	better	best
much	more	most
little	less	least
far	farther	farthest

IV. Articles

A, *an*, and *the* are articles.

A. *A* and *an* are *indefinite* articles since they merely limit a noun to any one in a class.

   a person, *an* application

B. *The* is a *definite* article because it singles out a particular person or thing in a class.

   The manager read *the* application.

V. Verbs

A verb is a word that shows action or state of being of the subject. There are two classifications of verbs:

A. A *transitive verb* is one that requires an object to complete its meaning. The object may be a noun or a pronoun and it *must be* in the objective case. The object is used to complete the meaning of the verb.

To determine the object of a transitive verb, ask *What?* or *Whom?*

He *reported* the accident.

B. An *intransitive verb* does *not* require an object to complete its meaning.

The light *shines.* The boy *ran.*

Many verbs may be used both as transitive and intransitive verbs. For example, in the sentence, *The boy* ran, *ran* is an intransitive verb requiring no object.

The verb *ran* may, however, be used as a transitive verb: for example, *The boy* ran *a* race. Here *race* is the object of the verb *ran,* and the verb becomes transitive.

Some verbs, however, may be used correctly only as intransitive verbs. *Sit, lie,* and *rise* are examples of verbs that are always intransitive verbs since they permit no object; while *set, lay,* and *raise* are examples of verbs that are always transitive because they require an object to complete their meaning.

Voice of Verbs. Voice indicates whether the subject of the verb is (1) the doer of the action or (2) the receiver of the action that is expressed by the verb.

A verb in the *active voice* identifies the subject as the doer of the action.

The new stenographer *typed* the letter.

A verb in the *passive voice* identifies the subject as the receiver of the action.

The letter *was typed* by the new stenographer.

Any transitive verb may be used in either the active or the passive voice.

In the independent clauses of a compound sentence or in a series of related statements, verbs of the same voice should be used. This is known as *parallel construction.*

(Wrong) The letter *was dictated* by the executive, and the stenographer *transcribed* it.

(Right) The executive *dictated* the letter, and the stenographer *transcribed* it.

Tense. Tense expresses the time of the action. There are three primary tenses:

1. The *present tense* of a verb is used to denote the present time. It is used in expressing a general truth or that which is generally customary. The present tense is also used to describe more vividly what took place in past time. This is known as *historical present.*

Washington *crosses* the Delaware and immediately *attacks* Trenton.

2. The *past tense* indicates past time.

   We *shipped* your order yesterday.

3. The *future tense* indicates that which will take place in the future. The future tense is expressed by the use of *shall* or *will* with the present form of the verb.

   I *shall go* early. You *will arrive* on time.
   She *will come* in at eight o'clock.

Frequent errors are made in the use of *will* and *shall*. The future tense may be used to express simple futurity or to express determination or promise. Simple futurity is denoted by the use of *shall* with the first person, and *will* with the second and the third persons.

   I *shall be* happy to see you when you arrive.
   He *will be* home early.

If determination or promise is to be expressed, the rule for futurity is reversed. Use *will* with a first person subject, *shall* with a second or third person subject.

   I *will be* there without fail.
   You *shall* certainly *go*.
   They *shall return* tomorrow.

In asking questions, use *shall* when the subject is in the first person (I, we).

   Shall we go?

When the subject is in the second or third person, either *shall or will* may be used, depending upon which form is expected in the answer.

   Will you write the letter? (Answer expected: I *will* write the letter.)
   Shall you miss your friends when you move? (Answer expected: I *shall* miss my friends.)

In addition to the primary tenses, there are three verb phrases, known as the perfect tenses, that represent completed action or being.

1. The *present perfect* tense denotes an action or an event completed at the present time. It is formed by the placing of *have* or *has* before the perfect participle.

   I *have read* several chapters.
   He *has studied* his French.

2. The *past perfect* tense indicates an action or an event completed at or before a stated past time. It is formed by the placing of *had* before the perfect participle.

   They *had completed* the picture by the time dinner was served.
   I *had assumed* you would come by plane before we received your letter.

3. The *future perfect* tense indicates that an action or an event will be completed at or before a stated future time. It is formed by the placing of *shall have* or *will have* before the perfect participle.

I *shall have gone* before you arrive.
He *will have arrived* home before you can get there.

Whether *shall have* or *will have* is used depends upon the basic rule for the use of *shall* or *will*.

Mood. Mood is that property of a verb that indicates the manner in which the action or state of being is expressed.

1. The *indicative mood* is used in asserting something as a fact or in asking a question.

2. The *imperative mood* is used in expressing a command, a request, or an entreaty.

3. The *subjunctive mood* is used in expressing a doubt, a wish, or a condition contrary to reality.

   (a) A condition contrary to *present* reality is expressed with *were*, not *was*.

      (Wrong) If I *was* tall, I could reach the book.
               If Ann *was* going, you could go along.

      (Right) If I *were* tall, I could reach the book.
               If Ann *were* going, you could go along.

   (b) A condition contrary to *past* reality is expressed by *had been*.

      If the plane *had been* on time, this might not have happened.

Agreement of Verb and Subject. The agreement of verb and subject sometimes causes trouble. A verb must agree with its subject in person and number. The verb *to be* has person and number forms: *I am, you are, he is, we are, you are,* and *they are*; *I was, you were, he was, we were, you were,* and *they were*. Other verbs have only one expression for number and person. When the subject is in the third person, singular number, a verb or an auxiliary in the present or the present perfect tense must end in *s*.

   Mr. White *dictates* very slowly.
   Miss Stewart *has* been his assistant for a long time.

A very common error is the use of a singular verb with a plural subject.

1. When the verb and the subject are separate in the sentence, the verb must agree with its subject. A common error is to make the verb agree with the word near it rather than with the real subject.

      (Wrong) The *activity* of the board at its meetings *are* always interesting.

      (Right) The *activity* of the board at its meetings *is* always interesting.

2. If the subject is plural in form but singular in meaning, a singular verb is required.

   The news *has* been good.

3. Two or more singular subjects connected by *or* or *nor* require a singular verb.

   Neither Kurt nor Bill *is* at the office.

4. When two or more subjects connected by *or* or *nor* differ in number, the plural subject is placed nearest the verb and the verb made plural.

   Neither the office staff nor the executives *are* to have that bulletin.

   When two or more subjects connected by *or* or *nor* differ in person, the verb must agree with the subject that is nearest to it.

   Either you or I *am* at fault.

   It is frequently better to rephrase the sentence so as to use a verb with each subject.

   Either you *are* at fault or I *am*.

5. Two or more singular subjects connected by *and* require a plural verb.

   The typewriter and the adding machine *are* both in need of repair.

6. When the subjects connected by *and* refer to the same person, a singular verb must be used.

   The great novelist and playwright *is* on his way home.

7. When the subjects connected by *and* represent one idea or are closely connected in thought, a singular verb should be used.

   Ice cream and cake *is* a popular dessert.

8. When either or both subjects connected by *and* are preceded by *each*, *every*, *many a*, etc., a singular verb is required.

   Each stock boy and foreman *is* expected to work late on inventory.

9. When one of two subjects is in the positive and the other in the negative, the verb agrees with the one in the positive.

   The teacher, and not the students, *is* planning to attend.

10. The number of a subject is not affected by words connected to it by *as well as*, *and also*, *in addition to*, etc.

    Mother, as well as the rest of the family, *is* expecting to go.

11. When a collective noun expresses unity, a singular verb is used.

    The jury *is* asking that a point be clarified.

Contractions. Contractions may be used in informal communications.

In writing contractions, remember that *don't*, the contraction of *do not*, is plural and is used with plural nouns and the pronouns *I*, *we*, *you*, and *they*. *Doesn't*, the contraction of *does not*, is singular and is used with singular nouns and the pronouns *he*, *she*, and *it*.

It *doesn't* bother me much, but I *don't* like it.

Infinitives. An infinitive is a form of the verb that asserts nothing, but merely names in a general way the action or the state of being. It is expressed by the word *to* placed before the verb: *to be, to walk, to talk, to cry*. The infinitive may be used as a noun, the subject of a sentence, a predicate noun, or the object of a verb. It may also be used as an adjective or an adverb.

The sign of the infinitive is omitted after such verbs as *bid, dare, feel, see, need, help, hear, let,* and *make*.

She saw him *open* the door.

Participles. A participle is a verb form used as an adjective having the double function of verb and adjective. There are three forms of the participle:

1. The *present participle* is formed by the addition of *ing* to the simple form of the verb. It expresses action as being in progress, usually at the same time as some other action. It is used as an adjective and at the same time retains some of the properties of a verb.

   The clerk *counting* the money is new here.

   In this sentence *counting* is an adjective modifying the noun *clerk*; it also has the property of a verb in that it takes the object *money*.

2. The *past participle* expresses action prior to that of the governing verb. It is used as an adjective and is usually formed by the addition of *d* or *ed* to the present tense of the verb.

   The machine *used* by the bookkeeper was defective.

   The teacher, *interrupted* by the students, did not complete her grading.

3. The *perfect participle* is formed by the combination of *being, having,* or *having been* with some other participle.

   Having written the letters, she was free to go.

   In the preceding sentence the perfect participle *having written* modifies the subject of the sentence *she*.

   A common error is that of putting at the beginning of a sentence a participial phrase that does not modify the subject. This is referred to as a *dangling* participle.

   (Wrong) Having completed the statement, it was time to file the letters.

   (Right) Having completed the statement, she found it was time to file the letters.

VI. Adverbs

An adverb is a word used to modify a verb, an adjective, or another adverb.

A. An adverb modifies a verb by answering the questions *how? when? where?*

She walked *lightly.*
He arrived *early.*
The report is *here.*

B. An adverb modifies adjectives and other adverbs by expressing degree (*how much? how little?*) and by answering the questions *in what manner?* and *to what degree?*

The clerk will file *more.*
She spoke *less.*
He worked *very* hard.
Julia writes *rather* well.

Comparison of Adverbs. Like adjectives, adverbs are compared to show degree.

1. A few adverbs are compared by the addition of *er* or *est* to the positive form of the adverb.

soon, sooner; often, oftener, oftenest

2. Some adverbs are compared irregularly:

well, better, best; far, farther, farthest

3. Most adverbs, however, are compared by the use of *more* or *most* or *less* or *least* with the simple (positive) form of the adverb.

more brightly, *most* often, *less* lightly, *least* likely

Placing the Adverb. Ordinarily an adverb follows the verb it modifies, but it may precede it. It should be placed where its meaning is most clearly shown. *Only, merely,* and *also,* which are sometimes adverbs and sometimes adjectives, give the most trouble in placing, since they may convey very different meanings in different positions in a sentence.

Only I saw him.   I saw *only* him.
I *only* saw him.   I saw him *only.*

Other Problems with Adverbs. There are a few errors in the use of adverbs that frequently are made.

1. *Very* or *too* should not be used to modify participles.
   (Wrong) She was *very* pleased.
   (Right)   She was *very* much pleased.

2. *Too,* which is an adverb that means *also* or *more than enough,* should be spelled correctly and not confused with *to* or *two.*
   By *two* o'clock she had *too* much work *to* do.

3. *Well* is usually an adverb. In speaking of health, however, *well* is used as an adjective. Be careful not to use *good* as an adverb in place of *well*.

(Wrong) He does his work *good.*
I don't feel very *good.*

(Right) He does his work *well.*
I don't feel very *well.*

4. *Very* is an adverb of degree, while *real* is an adjective of quality. Do not use *real* in place of *very.*

(Wrong) He had a *real* beautiful office.

(Right) He had a *very* beautiful office.

5. Adverbs of manner, those ending in *ly*, are frequently confused with adjectives derived from the same root. Adverbs of manner modify verbs that express action.

She sings *sweetly.* (Adverb)
Her singing is *sweet.* (Adjective)

6. Two negatives should not be used to express negation.

(Wrong) The clerk will *not* wait for *nobody.*

(Right) The clerk will *not* wait for *anybody.*

(Right) The clerk will wait for *nobody.*

VII. Prepositions

A preposition connects a noun or a pronoun with some other element of the sentence and shows the relationship between them. The noun or pronoun that follows the preposition is its object.

There are two kinds of prepositions:

A. Simple — *to, for, at, through, of*

B. Compound — *into, in spite of, instead of, in regard to, on account of, because of, according to, out of, as to.*

Prepositional Phrases. A group of words made up of a preposition and its object, together with any words used to modify the object, is called a *prepositional phrase.* The object of a preposition may be determined by asking *whom* or *what* after the preposition; what the phrase modifies may be determined by asking *what* or *who* before the preposition.

Prepositional phrases, like adjectives and adverbs, should be placed as close as possible to the words they modify to make the sentence as clear as possible.

Choice of Prepositions. Many errors are made in the use of prepositions because some words demand certain prepositions: *angry with* is used in reference to persons, and *angry at* is used in reference to things, animals, or situations. There are many situations in which prepositions are misused. Some of the most common follow.

1. *Into* should be used after a verb that indicates the motion of a person or a thing from one place to another. *In* is used after a verb expressing the idea of rest or, in some cases, motion within a certain place

   The girl went *into* the classroom.
   The clerk is *in* the filing department.

2. *Between* should be used only in reference to two persons or objects. *Among* should be used when referring to three or more persons or objects.

   The two boys divided the work *between* them.
   Gifts were distributed *among* the natives.

3. Prepositions that are not needed should not be used.

   (Wrong) The wastebasket is *in under* the desk. Where is it *at*?

   (Right) The wastebasket is *under* the desk. Where is it?

4. Do not omit prepositions that are needed to make sentences grammatically correct. Avoid telegraphic style in letters.

   (Wrong) Mr. Finley will arrive North Station 11:00 Sunday.

   (Right) Mr. Finley will arrive at the North Station at 11:00 a.m. Sunday.

VIII. Conjunctions

A conjunction is a word used to connect words, phrases, or clauses. There are three kinds of conjunctions:

A. A *coordinate conjunction* connects words or clauses of the same grammatical relation or construction, neither dependent upon the other for its meaning.

   You *and* I are elected.
   Their father is out of town, *and* their sister is on a vacation.

B. A *subordinate conjunction* connects a subordinate clause with some word in the principal clause upon which it is dependent for its meaning.

   The man left hurriedly *lest* he be seen.

C. *Correlative conjunctions* are conjunctions that are used in pairs; the first introducing, the second connecting the elements. They must be placed just before the elements that they introduce or connect.

   (Wrong) I will *either* meet you in Boston *or* Washington.
   I will meet you *either* in Boston *or* Washington.

   (Right) I will meet you in *either* Boston *or* Washington.
   I will meet you *either* in Boston *or* in Washington.

Or should always be used with *either; nor* with *neither*. They are used in reference to two things only.

(Wrong) *Either* Bob, Jack, *or* Don will pitch today's game.
Neither the superintendent, the principal, *nor* the teachers agreed with him.
Neither Jack *or* Don will pitch today's game.

(Right) Bob, Jack, *or* Don will pitch today's game.
The superintendent, the principal, *and* the teachers disagreed with him.
None of them — the superintendent, the principal, the teachers — agreed with him.
Neither Jack *nor* Don will pitch today's game.

As . . . as is used when equality is expressed, while *so . . . as* is used for a negative comparison.

I earn *as* much *as* you do but not *so* much *as* your brother does.

Some things to watch in the use of conjunctions follow.

1. Conjunctions should not be used in place of some other part of speech.

   (Wrong) Seldom *or* ever should such an example be used.
   You should try *and* improve your speech.

   (Right) Seldom *if* ever should such an example be used.
   You should try *to* improve your speech.

2. A clause, which is a part of a sentence containing a subject and a predicate, having meaning in itself, is connected to the other parts of the sentence by either a conjunction or a relative pronoun. A phrase, which contains no verb and has no meaning in itself, is introduced by a preposition, participle, or infinitive, but not by a conjunction.

   The project cannot be completed *without* your help.
   (*Without* is a preposition.)
   The project cannot be completed *unless* you help us.
   (*Unless* is a conjunction.)

3. *Except* and *without* are prepositions and should not be used in place of *unless*, which is a conjunction.

   (Wrong) You will not master shorthand *except* you concentrate.

   (Right) You will not master shorthand *unless* you concentrate.

4. *Like* is not a conjunction and should never be used in place of the conjunction *as*.

   (Wrong) She walks *like* you do.

   (Right) She walks *as* you do.

IX. Interjections

Interjections are exclamatory words or phrases used in a sentence for emphasis or to indicate feeling. They have no grammatical connection with the rest of the sentence. Interjections are set off by commas or by exclamation marks.

Oh, so you saw it?
Ouch! that hurt.

Grammar Reference Books

Although many questions concerning grammar can be answered by using a good dictionary, you should have available a standard reference book on English grammar.

In Appendix H you will find a list of recommended books. A ready reference on grammar will help you produce better letters and reports for your employer.

APPENDIX B

PUNCTUATION

Punctuation is used to make more forceful and to indicate more clearly the relationships of written thoughts. Punctuation is the written substitute for the change in voice, the pause, and the gestures that are used in oral expression.

The excessive use of punctuation marks is not considered good form. However, the importance of an accurate usage of punctuation marks is illustrated daily by the serious errors that may be found in office correspondence.

You will be responsible for the correct punctuation of business letters and reports. Although you are not expected to be an authority on punctuation, you should be familiar with the most important rules. The following rules are accepted and generally used wherever English is written.

Period (.)

The period is used

1. After complete declarative or imperative sentences.
   Today we shall study the use of the period.

2. After initials in a name.
   H. L. Andrews

3. After most abbreviations. The following are some exceptions approved by several authorities.
   (a) Mme (Madame), Mlle (Mademoiselle)
   (b) IOU, c/o, OK, SOS, A1
   (c) Chemical symbols: H_2O, Zn, Pb
   (d) Offices and agencies of the federal government: SEC, FBI, FCC

4. Before decimal fractions, and between dollars and cents when expressed in figures, and after the abbreviations *s.* and *d.* for shilling and pence.
   3.45, $16.13, 13s., 7d.

5. For ellipses. Usually three periods or dots are used to indicate the omission from quoted matter of one or more words when the omitted portion does *not* end with a period. Four periods are used when the omitted portion does end with a period.
   The path was long and narrow . . . the weary boys walked slowly . . . .

Comma (,)

The comma is the most frequently used form of punctuation; therefore, errors in its use are frequent. The comma is used

1. To set off a subordinate clause preceding a main clause.
   When the bell rings, you may leave.

2. To set off a nonrestrictive phrase or subordinate clause. (A phrase or a clause is nonrestrictive if the main clause in the sentence expresses a complete thought when the nonrestrictive phrase or clause is omitted.)
   My doctor, who is now on his vacation, will prepare the report next week.

3. To separate long coordinate clauses that are joined by the conjunctions *and*, *but*, *for*, *neither*, *nor*, and *or*. The comma precedes the conjunction.
   He worked far into the night, for the deadline was noon the next day.

4. To set off phrases or expressions at the beginning of a sentence when they are loosely connected with the rest of the sentence.
   Nevertheless, we feel the way you do about it.

5. To separate words, phrases, or clauses in a series. Note that a comma precedes the last item in the series.
   The group now has no meeting place, no supplies, and no money.
   They told us when they heard it, where they heard it, and from whom they heard it.

6. To separate two or more adjectives if they both precede or follow the noun they modify, provided each adjective modifies the noun alone. If an adjective modifies a combination of a noun and another adjective, however, no comma is used between the two adjectives.
   An old, shaggy, forlorn-looking dog came limping out to greet us.
   Happy young people come here frequently.

7. To set off words and phrases used in apposition.
   My cousin, whose name is Jean, will arrive soon.

8. To set off parenthetical words, clauses, or phrases.
   Tomorrow, on the other hand, business will be much better.

9. To set off words in direct address.
   Finally, children, we must all be ready when the time comes.

10. To set off *yes* or *no* when used in sentences.
    Yes, you may go now.
    Frankly, no, I don't care.

11. To set off the name of a state when it is used with a city.
   They lived in Denver, Colorado, for many years.

12. To separate the day of the month from the year and to set off the year when used with the month.
   The project must be completed by August 20, 1973, at the latest.

13. To set off a mild interjection.
   Ah, he surely enjoyed that story.

14. To set off a participial expression used as an adjective.
   Smiling pleasantly, she entered the office.

15. To separate unrelated numbers.
   In 1960, 25 new students enrolled.

16. To divide a number of four or more digits into groups of three, counting from right to left.
   1,567,039

17. To set off phrases that denote residence or position.
   Professor William Smith, of Harvard, will speak.

18. To indicate the omission of a word or words readily understood from the context.
   In June the book sales amounted to $523; in July, to $781.

19. Before a short, informal, direct quotation.
   The employer asked, "Have you transcribed those letters?"

Semicolon (;)

The semicolon is used

1. In a compound sentence between clauses that are not joined by a conjunction.
   That is good taste; it suggests discretion.

2. In a compound sentence if either clause contains one or more commas. The semicolon is placed before the conjunction.
   The rainy, windy weather made her cold; but she continued on her journey.

3. Before such words and abbreviations as *e.g., i.e., viz., for example, namely*, and *to wit* when they introduce a long list of items. A comma precedes the list.
   Some pairs of words are bothersome to students; for example, affect and effect, loose and lose, sit and set.

4. Between elements in a listing when there are commas within the elements.
   James Craig, Newport High; William Parker, Forest Hills High; and Ken Caldwell, Jefferson High were the winners.

5. Before connectives when such words introduce sentences, principal clauses, or an abrupt change in thought. (The comma follows the connective when used in this manner only if the connective is to be emphasized.) Some of these connectives are *accordingly, consequently, hence, however, in fact, moreover, nevertheless, therefore, thus, whereas, yet.*

It is February; therefore, we have many holidays.

Colon (:)

The colon is used

1. To introduce formally a word, a list, a statement, or a question; a series of statements or questions; or a long quotation:

The book had many good points: it contained an interesting story; it contained humor; it was well illustrated.

2. Between hours and minutes:

8:30 a.m.   1:45 p.m.

3. After salutations in some styles of business letters:

Dear Sir: Gentlemen:

Question Mark (?)

1. The question mark is used after a direct question, but not after an indirect question.

Are you ready?
He asked what caused the fire.

It is not necessary to use a question mark after a polite request.

Will you please let us know your decision at once.

2. The question mark is used inside parentheses to indicate uncertainty.

The applicant was born in 1952(?).

3. In a series, a question mark may follow each question if special emphasis is desired. When it is used in this way, it takes the place of the comma; and each element begins with a small letter.

Where is my pen? my notebook? my file?

Exclamation Point (!)

Like the period, the exclamation point represents a full stop. It is used at the end of a thought expressing strong emotion or command. The thought may be represented by a complete sentence, a phrase, or a word.

Ha! We caught you this time!

Apostrophe (')

1. **To form possessives.** There are several rules that govern the formation of the possessive case of words, depending on the final letter or syllable of the word and whether the word is singular or plural. A few important rules follow:

   (a) The possessive of singular and plural common and proper nouns not ending with the *s* or *z* sound (excepting *ce*) is usually formed by the addition of an apostrophe and *s* to the singular form.

   assistant's letter   women's hats
   Shaw's plays   Lawrence's mail

   (b) The possessive of singular and plural common nouns ending in *s* is formed by the addition of only the apostrophe.

   boys' hats   ladies' manners
   committees' reports

   (c) The possessive of a monosyllabic proper noun ending in an *s* or *z* sound is generally formed by the addition of an apostrophe and *s*, although in newspapers addition of only the apostrophe is frequently seen.

   Burns's poems   Marx's ideas
   Liz's book

   (d) The possessive of proper nouns of more than one syllable ending in an *s* or *z* sound (excepting *ce*) is formed by the addition of an apostrophe only.

   Essex' papers   Adams' chronicle
   Burroughs' house

   (e) The possessive of a compound word is formed by the addition of the apostrophe or the apostrophe and *s* [according to Rules (a), (b), and (c)] to its final syllable.

   mother-in-law's visit
   City of Detroit's council
   letter carrier's route
   passers-by's expressions

   (f) The possessive of a series of names connected by a conjunction showing joint ownership is indicated by the apostrophe or apostrophe and *s* to the last name.

   Simon and Walter's garage
   Adams and Anderson's firm

   (g) If joint ownership does not exist in a series of names, the possessive case is formed by the addition of an apostrophe or apostrophe and *s* to each proper name in the series.

   Macy's and Haynes's stores
   Jack's, Joe's, and Bill's gloves

(h) The possessive of abbreviated words is formed by the addition of an apostrophe and *s* to the last letter of the abbreviation.

YMCA's membership
the X's function
the Mr.'s position in the heading
the OK's presence

(i) The apostrophe is *not* used to form the possessive of pronouns.

2. To show contraction or the omission of figures.

don't (for *do not*)   Class of '67 (for *1967*)
it's (for *it is*)

3. To form the plurals of figures, letters, signs, and words.

If you have no *6's*, use *9's* turned upside down.
Her *v's* and *u's* and *T's* and *F's* are too much alike.
The +*'s* and −*'s* denoted whether the sentences were correct or not.
There were too many *and's* and *the's* in the essay.

4. Followed by a *d* to form the past tense of arbitrarily coined verbs.

She OK'd the copy.
He X'd out three lines.

Dash (—)

The dash is formed in typewriting by the striking of two hyphens without a space preceding or following them. The dash is used

1. To indicate a change in the sense or the construction of a sentence.
Hemingway, Wolfe, Greene — these are my favorites.

2. Instead of a comma to emphasize or to guard against confusing the reader.
The laborer is worthy of his hire — if his labor is.
If — and only if — we go, the day will be complete.

3. To indicate an omission of letters.
Mr. K—, of P—Street

4. To precede a reference.
No, the heart that has truly loved never forgets.—Moore.

Parentheses ( )

Parentheses are used

1. To enclose figures or letters that mark a series of enumerated elements.

She wanted three things: (1) a promotion, (2) a salary increase, and (3) more responsibility.

2. To enclose figures verifying a number which is written in words.

   twenty (20) dollars
   twenty dollars ($20)

3. To enclose material that is indirectly related to the main thought of a sentence.

   We shall postpone (at least for the present) a decision.

4. To enclose matter introduced as an explanation.

   The answer (see page 200) is puzzling.

The rules covering the use of other marks of punctuation with parentheses are:

1. If needed in the sentence, a comma or dash that normally precedes a parenthetic element is transferred to follow the closing parenthesis.

   He sent a belated, though clever (and somewhat personal), greeting.

2. Punctuation at the end of a parenthetic expression *precedes* the parenthesis if it applies to the parenthetic material only; it *follows* the parenthesis if it applies to the sentence as a whole.

   When I heard him (he shouted, "Who goes there?"), I was surprised.
   (See the discussion on page 78.)
   This experiment had interesting results (see Table I).

Brackets [ ]

Brackets are used

1. To enclose a correction, an addition, or a comment which a writer inserts in matter he is quoting.

   "In 1942 [a typographical error for 1492] Columbus discovered America."

2. To enclose the term *sic*, Latin for *thus*, to show that a misspelling or some other error appeared in the original and is not an error by the one quoting.

   In applying for the job he wrote, "I am very good in athleletics [*sic*], and I can teach mathmatics [*sic*]."

3. When it is necessary to place a parenthesis within a parenthesis; but, in general, such complicated usages should be avoided.

   At 3:30 p.m. (the time agreed upon at the conference [see John Coleman's letter of April 9]) the announcement of the new salary agreement was made to the news media.

Quotation marks are used

1. To enclose direct quotations. Single quotation marks are used to enclose a quotation within a quotation.

   The director said, "I hope you are familiar with this play." She said, "Unkind as it may be, I can't help saying 'I told you so' to her."

2. To enclose the titles of articles, lectures, reports, etc., and the titles of subdivisions of publications (that is, the titles of parts, chapters, etc.). The titles of books and magazines are not enclosed in quotation marks, but underscored or typed in all capital letters.

   She thought the chapter "Producing Mailable Transcripts" was helpful.

3. To enclose unusual or slang terms.

   Her "five o'clocks" were famous.
   When they saw us, they "flipped."

4. To enclose words used in some special sense, or words to which attention is directed in order to make a meaning clear.

   He said "yes," not "guess."
   The term "title by possession" is often used.

5. To enclose the titles of short poems, songs, and televison and radio shows.

   "Trees" (poem)
   "Fire and Rain" (song)
   "Gunsmoke" (TV show)
   "Arthur Godfrey Time" (radio show)
   "Lowell Thomas and the News" (radio show)

6. When consecutive paragraphs of the same work are quoted, at the beginning of each paragraph but at the end of only the last paragraph.

Quoted Matter. When quoted matter appears within a letter, an article, or a report, it is advisable that it be indicated as a quotation. This may be done in three ways:

1. The material may be indented from the regular margins on the left and right.

2. It may be underscored throughout.

3. It may be enclosed in quotation marks.

Sometimes the quoted matter is both indented and enclosed in quotation marks. The practice of using quotation marks is the most widely used.

A long quotation is single spaced, even though the rest of the copy is double spaced.

Quotation Marks with Other Marks of Punctuation. At the end of quoted material, a quotation mark and another mark of punctuation are often used together. The rules governing the order of these marks are not entirely logical; but since they are well established and generally accepted, you should follow them.

1. A period or a comma should precede the quotation mark even though it may not be a part of the quotation.
   "I saw you," he said, "when you left."

2. A semicolon or colon should follow the closing quotation mark, even though it may be a part of the quotation.
   Mary, Ruth, and John visited that "house of antiques"; and the "antiques" were really unusual.
   There is this to say about his "mission": it is fictitious.

3. Other marks of punctuation should precede the closing quotation mark if they apply to the quotation only, and should follow the mark if they apply to the sentence as a whole and not just to the quotation.
   She asked, "Will you go?"
   Did you read the article "Better Sales Letters"?

Spacing after Punctuation Marks

One space is left after punctuation marks within a sentence, with the exception of the colon. *Two* spaces are left after colons and all punctuation marks at the ends of sentences.

Exceptions to the basic rules above are that you do *not* space after:

1. A period used within an abbreviation written in small letters.
   a.m., etc., e.g., i.e.

2. A period used as a decimal point within a series of figures.
   3.111, 10.5

3. A comma used to separate a number into groups of three.
   1,268,749

4. An apostrophe written within a word.
   don't

5. The first punctuation mark when two marks are used together.
   "Why not?"

Italics (The Underscore)

A typist can emphasize an important word, phrase, or sentence in typewritten material in several ways. The kind of copy and the purpose for which it is being typed determine to some extent the relative emphasis that should be indicated.

In typewriting, underscoring takes the place of printed italics and is the method most often used to give prominence to a word or group of words. Punctuation marks (except the hyphen in compound words) and the spaces between words are not underscored. Emphasis is also achieved by typing in red in the midst of copy typed in black or blue, and by making characters darker by typing over them several times.

In addition to emphasizing a word or words, italics (underscore) should be used

1. To refer to a word or letter taken out of its context.
   Always dot your i's, and cross your t's.

   Do not write and and the slantwise across the line.

2. To designate a foreign word not yet anglicized.
   Her faux pas was noticeable.

3. To indicate titles of plays, motion pictures, musical compositions, paintings, art objects, books, pamphlets, newspapers, and magazines. (Parts of these, such as chapters in a book or articles in a magazine or newspaper, are designated by quotation marks.)
   Have you seen My Fair Lady?
   El Greco's View of Toledo was on display at the museum.
   We also saw Rodin's The Thinker.
   She found Unit 4, "Processing Data" in Clerical Office Procedures very helpful.
   The Wall Street Journal contains a regular feature entitled "Washington Wire."

4. To designate the names of ships, airplanes, and spacecraft.
   U.S.N.S. Nautilus
   Lindbergh's Spirit of St. Louis
   Apollo 15

APPENDIX C

WORD CHOICE

Always use correct words. Know their spelling, their meaning, their appropriateness. You should maintain a continuous vigilance over the words you use. Never become indifferent to words. For, if you do, you will soon be letting misspelled words slip by as you proofread copy; you will allow words that are not precise for the meaning intended to remain in the copy; and you will soon be guilty of inadequate communication skills.

A dictionary is a regularly used reference in every office. Become acquainted with your dictionary. Learn to understand all abbreviations that are used. Your dictionary will dispel uncertainties about proper spelling and meanings of words.

Good Usage

To convey messages precisely, it is important that you use words that conform to current good usage. *Colloquialisms*, which are words and phrases that are acceptable in informal conversations and sometimes in letters, are not considered good usage in formal business correspondence. *Provincialisms*, which are terms that are used informally in particular areas of the country, are also to be avoided in formal communications. *Archaic* and *obsolete* words, which are words that were once standard, are no longer in fashion and should be avoided.

Below is a list of *colloquialisms* that should be avoided in business communications.

Incorrect in Formal Writing	*Correct in Formal Writing*
all-round (adj.)	generally serviceable
around	about, nearly
back of, in back of	behind, at the back of
bit	a short time, a little while
calculate	think, plan, expect
cute	clever, amusing
enthuse	enthusiastic
get hold of	to learn, to master
have got to	must, have to
lots of	many, much
most	almost, nearly
not a one	not one

Incorrect in Formal Writing	Correct in Formal Writing
off of	off
over with	finished, done
quite some time	a long time
show up	arrive

Some *provincialisms* which may fail to convey meaning when used outside a local area, and which should be avoided, are shown below.

Use	Rather than
declare, maintain	allow
raise	rear
short distance	piece
think, suppose, guess	reckon
want to come in	want in
you	you all

Words That Are Pronounced Alike.

Words that are pronounced alike but differ in meaning are called *homonyms*. These words are often confusing and require close attention to the meaning of the sentence so that the correct word is used.

Some typical homonyms are:

aid, aide	hoard, horde
aisle, isle	incite, insight
allowed, aloud	knew, new
altar, alter	lead, led
bare, bear	lean, lien
bases, basis	loose, lose
berth, birth	right, rite, wright, write
brake, break	role, roll
creak, creek	through, threw
elusive, illusive	ware, wear, where

Words That Are Not Pronounced Alike

There are many words that should not be pronounced alike but often sound alike. Frequently used words of this type include those listed below. Are you able to distinguish the meaning of each?

accept, except	assent, ascent
adapt, adept, adopt	formerly, formally
allusion, illusion	council, counsel
addition, edition	instance, instants
affect, effect	local, locale
carton, cartoon	patience, patients
contend, contest	test, text
costume, custom	personal, personnel
all ways, always	stationery, stationary

Compound Words

In the regular routine of daily business, one class of words that gives considerable trouble is made up of compound words. Compound words fall into three groups: hyphenated compounds, single-word compounds, and two-word compounds.

There are a few rules that will assist you in becoming familiar with certain groups of compound words that use the hyphen.

1. A hyphen is always used in a compound number.
   twenty-one, fifty-eight

2. A hyphen is used between the numerator and the denominator of a fraction written in words, except (a) when one of of the elements contains a hyphen and (b) when the fraction is used as a noun.

   four-fifths share   forty-one hundredths
   two-thirds interest   forty one-hundredths
            one half of the total
            two fifths of the class

3. A hyphen is used between two or more words when the words serve as a single adjective *before* a noun. In applying this rule you must be careful that the words are not a series of independent adjectives. The exception to the rule is that proper nouns made up of two or more words are not hyphenated when used as adjectives.

   a well-liked boy, *but* a boy well liked
   a fresh-water fish, *but* a fish from fresh water
   a New England dinner, a New Jersey product
   a large black horse; a deep, clear pool

4. Groups of three or more words used as a single word are usually hyphenated.
   four-in-hand, well-to-do, sister-in-law, up-to-date

5. A hyphen is used after a prefix
   (a) when the prefix is joined to a proper noun
   (b) to prevent confusion between some verbs and a few compounds
   (c) to prevent an awkward piling up of consonants
   Ordinarily, however, a prefix is written as a part of the main word.
   pro-English, re-form (meaning to form again), re-sign (meaning to sign again), bell-like

   When *any*, *every*, *no*, and *some* are combined with other words, the compound is a single word: *anything, everyone, nowhere, somehow.* Sometimes, however, the parts of the compound expression are written as separate words: *no one, every one.*

Compound words are always changing. Some become single-word compounds through constant usage. At some time in the past most were hyphenated compounds.

When in doubt, consult a good dictionary. The following compounds are used frequently and therefore deserve attention:

Hyphenated Compounds

by-line	man-hours
by-product	self-confidence
cross-reference	vice-president

Single-Word Compounds

billboard	network
bondholder	nevertheless
bookkeeper	northeast
bylaws	notwithstanding
checkbook	outgoing
guesswork	overdue
handwriting	overhead
headline	payday
headquarters	payroll
henceforth	policyholder
hereafter	postcard
laborsaving	postmarked
letterhead	takeoff
meantime	trademark
middlemen	viewpoint

Two-Word Compounds

account book	income tax
bank note	parcel post
card index	price list
cash account	trade union
civil service	vice versa

The Plural Forms of Words

Some words exist in only the plural form (*annals, news, thanks*), and other words are the same in both the singular and the plural forms (*deer, corps, chassis*). Still other words are irregular in form (*man, men; child, children; foot, feet*). Generally speaking, however, the plural of a word is formed by adding *s* if the plural has the same number of syllables as the singular; or *es* if the plural has an extra syllable. An exception to this rule is found in some words ending in *o* (*motto, mottoes; potato, potatoes*), although other words ending in *o* follow the rule (*piano, pianos; folio, folios; cameo, cameos*).

You will find the following rules for the forming of plural words helpful.

1. Form the plurals of nouns ending with *y* preceded by a consonant by dropping the *y* and adding *ies*. When the *y* is preceded by a vowel, add *s* only.

lady, ladies	alley, alleys
salary, salaries	lawyer, lawyers
story, stories	turkey, turkeys

2. Form the plural of a hyphenated compound noun by changing the principal word of the compound from singular to plural. The principal word of a compound is not always the last word.

   sisters-in-law, cross-purposes, passers-by

3. Form the plural of a single-word compound by adding *s* to the end of the word.

   cupfuls, viewpoints, headquarters

4. The plurals of some words of foreign origin are formed in accordance with the rules of the language from which they are derived.

axis, axes	datum, data
alumnus, alumni	alumna, alumnae

5. A few words of foreign origin have both foreign and English plural forms. In some cases, one form is preferred over the other (*strata* instead of *stratums*); while in other cases both forms are considered equally acceptable (*indexes* and *indices*, *memorandums* and *memoranda*). Consult a dictionary for the preferred usage of plural words of foreign origin.

6. Two persons bearing the same name and title may be referred to in the following manner: *The Messrs. Haviland, The Misses McKenzie, The Doctors Butler*, or *The Mr. Havilands, The Miss McKenzies, The Doctor Butlers*. In formal and business language, the plural form of the title is preferred.

7. The plurals of letters, noun-coinages, proper nouns of more than one syllable ending in a sibilant, and words used as words only are formed by the addition of an apostrophe and *s*.

p's and *q*'s	Her *I-don't-care*'s were . . .
the *and*'s	The Curtises' house . . .
Ulysses' voyage	others' ills

Word Division

Frequently a word must be divided at the end of a line in order to keep the right margin even. Words should be divided only between syllables. In case of doubt, consult a dictionary. The rules on page 616 apply to typewritten copy.

1. When a final consonant preceded by a single vowel is doubled before addition of a suffix, divide the word between the two consonants (prefer-*r*ing, program-*m*ing).

2. A single-letter syllable at the beginning or the end of a word should not be separated from the remainder of the word (*above* not *a-bove*).

3. A two-letter syllable at the end of a word should not be separated from the rest of the word (*calmly* not *calm-ly*).

4. A syllable that does not contain a vowel should not be separated from the rest of the word (*couldn't* not *could-n't*).

5. Hyphenated words should be divided only at the hyphens (*follow-up* not *fol-low-up*).

6. A four-letter word should not be divided; it is seldom permissible to divide five- or six-letter words (*into* not *in-to*), (*camel* not *cam-el*), (*never* not *nev-er*).

7. When a word containing three or more syllables is to be divided at a one-letter syllable, the one-letter syllable should be written on the first line rather than on the second line (*maga-zine* not *mag-azine*).

8. When a word is to be divided at a point where two vowels that are pronounced separately come together, these vowels should be divided into separate syllables (*continu-ation* not *continua-tion*).

9. Compound words are preferably divided between the elements of the compound (*turn-over* not *turno-ver*).

10. Proper names should not be divided; and titles, initials, or degrees should not be separated from names (*President* not *Pres-ident*).

11. Avoid dividing words at the end of more than two successive lines, at the end of a page, or at the end of the last complete line of a paragraph.

12. Avoid awkward or misleading divisions that may cause difficulty in reading (*carry-ing* not *car-rying*).

13. When the single-letter syllable *a, i,* or *u* is followed by *ble, bly, cle,* or *cal,* do not separate the single-letter syllable and the suffix.

14. Avoid the division of figures and abbreviations, the parts of an address or date. If it is necessary to separate an address, keep together the number and street name, the city and ZIP Code.

| 2143 Market | *not* | 2143 |
| Street | | Market Street |

In separating a date, leave the day with the month.

| March 3, | *not* | March |
| 197– | | 3, 197– |

APPENDIX D

ABBREVIATIONS

Abbreviations are abridged contractions. They provide a means of conserving the space required for words and phrases. With the extensive use of computers and related equipment, there has developed the need for the use of more abbreviations than was true at an earlier time. The use of abbreviations is guided by custom and equipment restrictions. A general rule that continues to be followed is that abbreviations are used sparingly in correspondence. Abbreviations, on the other hand, are common in the typing of forms, such as invoices and statements, where there are space limitations.

Abbreviations of Proper Names

For proper names there are generally accepted rules to be followed.

1. A person's family name should never be abbreviated. Given names may be represented by initials, but it is desirable for others to conform to a person's own style or signature. For example, if a person signs his name *Henry R. Grimm*, it is good form for others to write his name that way, rather than *H. R. Grimm*. As a general rule, given names such as *Charles* or *William* should not be abbreviated to *Chas.* or *Wm.*, unless the person himself uses the abbreviation so consistently that it is obvious that it is the spelling he prefers.

2. Names of cities, with the exception of those containing the word *Saint* (*St.*), should not be abbreviated.

3. Names of states and territories should be spelled out, except in lists, tabular matter, footnotes, bibliographies, and indexes. In such cases the standard abbreviations listed below should be used. The United States Postal Service has authorized the two-letter all-capital abbreviations listed below for use *only* with ZIP CODES.

State	Standard Abbreviation	ZIP Code Abbreviation
Alabama	Ala.	AL
Alaska	*	AK
Arizona	Ariz.	AZ

*No standard abbreviation

State	Standard Abbreviation	ZIP Code Abbreviation
Arkansas	Ark.	AR
California	Calif.	CA
Canal Zone	C.Z.	CZ
Colorado	Colo.	CO
Connecticut	Conn.	CT
Delaware	Del.	DE
District of Columbia	D.C.	DC
Florida	Fla.	FL
Georgia	Ga.	GA
Guam	*	GU
Hawaii	*	HI
Idaho	*	ID
Illinois	Ill.	IL
Indiana	Ind.	IN
Iowa	*	IA
Kansas	Kans.	KS
Kentucky	Ky.	KY
Louisiana	La.	LA
Maine	*	ME
Maryland	Md.	MD
Massachusetts	Mass.	MA
Michigan	Mich.	MI
Minnesota	Minn.	MN
Mississippi	Miss.	MS
Missouri	Mo.	MO
Montana	Mont.	MT
Nebraska	Nebr.	NE
Nevada	Nev.	NV
New Hampshire	N.H.	NH
New Jersey	N.J.	NJ
New Mexico	N. Mex.	NM
New York	N. Y.	NY
North Carolina	N. C.	NC
North Dakota	N. Dak.	ND
Ohio	*	OH
Oklahoma	Okla.	OK
Oregon	Oreg.	OR
Pennsylvania	Pa.	PA
Puerto Rico	P. R.	PR
Rhode Island	R. I.	RI
South Carolina	S. C.	SC
South Dakota	S. Dak.	SD
Tennessee	Tenn.	TN
Texas	Tex.	TX
Utah	*	UT
Vermont	Vt.	VT

State	Standard Abbreviation	ZIP Code Abbreviation
Virginia	Va.	VA
Virgin Islands	V. I.	VI
Washington	Wash.	WA
West Virginia	W. Va.	WV
Wisconsin	Wis.	WI
Wyoming	Wyo.	WY

Abbreviations in the Body of a Letter

The shortening of words in the body of a letter can convey a lack of care and time in presenting an attractive, thoughtful message. One should not write: The advt. can be supplied for your dept. @ 50¢ per p. The sentence should be written: The advertisement can be supplied for your department at the rate of 50 cents a page.

Abbreviations that are commonly recognized symbols, such as SEC, FTC, CIO, and YMCA, may be used in the body of a letter. A letter should be understood rather than made to follow a single practice. If, therefore, a letter is written to someone who may not understand an abbreviation it is better to spell it out in the first sentence of its use so that the reader understands the term when it later appears in abbreviated form. For example, the complete term *Securities and Exchange Commission* may be used first; then, in subsequent references, SEC may be used if the document is not a formal one.

Frequently used abbreviations are listed in the dictionary. Each field of work has developed specialized abbreviations, and office employees learn these when they begin work in a new office.

Periods in Abbreviations

The tendency seems to be to drop the periods from an abbreviation when it is commonly recognized and does not require the periods for clarity. For example, NBC, SEC, and FTC are written without periods and without spaces between the letters. The omission of a period in some abbreviations, however, might be confusing. For example, without the periods, *in.* for *inch* might be mistaken for the preposition; *a.m.* for *morning* might be confused with the verb form. If, in order to avoid confusion, periods are used with an abbreviation, such as *a.m.*, they should also be used in *p.m.* in order to maintain a consistent style.

Abbreviations with Numbers

The abbreviations *st, d*, and *th* should not follow the day of the month when it is preceded by the name of the month. Correct usage is

He was planning to leave on the 21st of August.
He leaves for London on August 21.
Mr. Smith went to Los Angeles on the 3d of July.

In enumerations, it is better to write first, second, third rather than 1st, 2d, 3d. The abbreviations *st*, *d*, and *th* do not require the use of a period.

Diagonal Lines in Abbreviations

The use of the diagonal signifies the omission of such words as *per*, *of*, *to*, *upon*. In abbreviated forms, including the diagonal, the period is not usually used, as in *B/L* (bill of lading). The period is sometimes retained, however, in three- or four-word combinations, as *lb./sq. ft.*

Plurals of Abbreviations

Most plural forms of abbreviations are formed by adding *s* to the singular form. The singular and the plural forms of some abbreviations, however, are the same.

(plural) chgs., lbs.
(singular and plural) cwt., deg., ft., in., oz.

Several plural forms of abbreviations are double single letters.

pp. for pages, ll. for lines.

Plurals of capitalized abbreviations may be formed simply by adding a small *s*. Apostrophe *s* may be added to form the plurals of abbreviations composed of letters (capital and small), signs, and symbols. There is no definite rule, however, that completely governs all cases that may arise.

YMCAs, a.m.s, IOU's, P's, Q's, 6's, FOB's, OK's, #'s.

Coined Verbs

Often an abbreviation is used as a verb in informal correspondence. To make the necessary change, an apostrophe may be added with *s*, *d*, or *ing* to the abbreviation.

OK'd

Possessives of Abbreviations

Generally the singular possessive is formed by adding the apostrophe and *s*, as *Jr.'s, RR's, Sr.'s, SOS's.*

The plural possessive is formed by adding an apostrophe to abbreviations whose plural forms end in *s*, as *Jrs.', Drs.'.*

APPENDIX E

TITLES,
CAPITALIZATION,
AND NUMBERS

Titles

The use of titles is governed by customs that are accepted by the people of a given society. Office workers should learn the correct titles of the persons with whom they associate. There is one principle for the use of titles in oral communication that should always be remembered: *Never use a title alone.* For example, a person who holds a Ph.D. should never be addressed as *Doctor*. The proper address is *Doctor Jones*. Current practice governing the use of titles in writing follows.

Birthright Titles. The title of *Mr.*, *Miss*, or *Mrs.* is customary for adults who have no other title.

Mr. is used before the name of a man who has no other title. *Messrs.*, the abbreviation of *Messieurs* (French for *gentlemen*), is the plural of *Mr.*

Mrs. is the title given to married women and usually to widows. A married woman is usually addressed by her husband's name, as *Mrs. John Brown*. A widowed woman may be addressed by her Christian name, such as *Mrs. Helen Brown*, or by her deceased husband's name, such as *Mrs. John Brown*, whichever she prefers. With the names of two or more married women, the title *Mesdames*, or its abbreviation, *Mmes*, is used, as *Mmes Clark, Wright, and Grant*.

Miss is the correct title for an unmarried girl or woman. If there is doubt as to whether the person is married, it is a good policy to use *Miss* or the abbreviation *Ms.*, until her marital status is ascertained. *Misses* is the plural of *Miss*, as the *Misses Alice Henderson* and *Dorothy Jones*.

Doctor. *Dr.* is the title of one who holds any one of the various doctors' degrees. It is usually abbreviated. When two doctors are being addressed, the word *Doctors* or the abbreviation *Drs.* may be used. Since there are so many different types of doctors, doctors of medicine and dentistry frequently use the degree letters after their names and no title preceding, as *Frank B. Dana, M.D.* This practice, of course, could be used by anyone possessing a doctor's degree.

Reverend. This title is properly carried by a minister, priest, or rector. The abbreviation *Rev.* is commonly used, although it is considered better usage to write the word in full. Ordinarily when a person with this title is *spoken* of, the word *the* precedes his title and given name or initials. More than one *Reverend* may be addressed as *Reverend Messrs.* or the repetition of the word *Reverend* before each name.

Abbreviated Titles Following Personal Names. *Senior* and *Junior*, the distinction between a father and son of exactly the same name, are written after the name as the abbreviations *Sr.* and *Jr.* The abbreviation is capitalized, followed by a period, and usually separated from the name by a comma. *Second* and *Third*, the distinction between members of the same family or close relatives whose names are the same, are indicated by the abbreviations *2d* and *3d*, or by the Roman numerals, *II* or *III*. The former style is now more common. Note that these abbreviations are not followed by a period, but they may be separated from the name by a comma.

The abbreviation *Esq.* is used after a gentleman's name in England. In this country it is rarely used. When it is used, the title *Mr.* is omitted.

Double Titles. A title may be used both before and after a person's name if the two titles have different meanings, but two titles that indicate the same honor or degree should not be used. For example, it is correct to say *Dr. H. C. Samuel, Moderator*, but not *Dr. H. C. Samuel, M.D.*

Titles in Addresses and Salutations. Except for *Mr.*, *Mrs.*, and *Dr.*, all titles used in the addresses and salutations of letters are better written in full. Abbreviations, however, are not uncommon. Whenever you are in doubt, type the title in full. No one will be offended by seeing his title in full.

The correct titles and salutations to be used for federal and state officials, and educators, are given in Appendix G. Whenever you are unsure of a title or salutation, refer to an authoritative source.

Capitalization

A good dictionary is an excellent source for determining practices in capitalization that are most acceptable. A person who must refer to the dictionary for the most elementary information of this type, however, consumes much time. An understanding of the purpose for and a knowledge of the principles of capitalization should be a part of the training of an office employee.

One of the purposes of capitalization is to designate the names or titles of specific things, positions, or persons. Overuse of capitalization, however, tends to detract from the effectiveness of the written matter.

The following are the most common rules of capitalization:

1. Every sentence begins with a capital letter.
2. The pronoun *I* and the interjection *O* are always capitalized.
3. The salutation and the complimentary close of a letter begin with capitals.
4. The days of the week, holidays, and the months of the year are capitalized.
5. All important words in the titles of the main agencies of a government begin with capital letters.
6. Direct quotations begin with a capital letter.

Business Titles and Positions. Titles are capitalized when they immediately precede or follow individual names and are directly related to them, or when they refer to specific persons.

> President W. L. Matthews will speak.
> Mr. R. Hubert McGraw, Jr., Vice-President, Investors Corporation
> Mr. Samuel Jones is Executive Secretary and Treasurer of Hammett Co.

Business titles are not capitalized when they do not refer to specific persons.

> Three men have been president of this company.
> A treasurer will be elected at the meeting tomorrow.

Geographic Names. Names of countries, cities, rivers, bays, mountains, islands, commonly recognized names given to regions of countries, and sections of cities are capitalized.

> Ohio River, Pacific Ocean, Union County, Harlem, the Great Plains, the Mississippi Valley

A geographic term such as *river*, *ocean*, *county*, *city*, and *street* that is not a part of the name but is used before the name, or a geographic term that is used in the plural, should not be capitalized.

> the river Danube
> county of Hamilton
> the city of San Diego
> the Atlantic and Pacific Oceans
> at the corner of Grant and Lee streets

Points of the compass designating specific geographic sections of the country are capitalized.

> the South, the Midwest, the Northwest

The points of the compass that merely indicate direction are not capitalized.

> South Dakota is south of North Dakota.
> The wind is coming from the west.

A noun that refers to the inhabitants of a particular part of the country is capitalized.

> Westerners, a Southerner, a New Englander

Proper names denoting political divisions are always capitalized.

> British Empire, Ward 13, Platt Township, the Papal States

Words before Figures. With the exception of *page*, *line*, and *verse*, words used in connection with figures in typewritten references are usually capitalized. It is important that one rule be followed consistently. If the word *figure* is capitalized when followed by a number in one place, it should be capitalized in all other places in the text.

Individual Names. Capitalize all names of individuals, except some surname prefixes. *Von, du, van,* or *de,* as a part of a surname, might not be capitalized, depending upon how the person uses it himself, unless it begins a sentence or stands alone within a sentence (that is, is not preceded by a given name or title).

> Charles de Gaulle *but* De Gaulle
> George Louis du Maurier *but* Du Maurier

Hyphenated Words. In general, there are three rules that govern the capitalization of the parts of a hyphenated word.

1. If both parts of a hyphenated word would ordinarily be capitalized when written alone, then both parts should be capitalized in the hyphenated word.

   Senate-House debate
   Spanish-American War

2. In a heading or title, it is permissible to capitalize the parts of a compound word to conform to a general style.

   Forty-Second Street   Mid-January Sales

3. In straight text material, the manner in which a word is used determines the part of a compound word that should be capitalized.

Thirty-first Street	anti-Nazi
mid-January	pro-British
Treasurer-elect	French-speaking
ex-President	pre-Pueblo

Headings and Titles of Articles and Reports. Only the first word and important words in headings or titles — nouns, pronouns, verbs, adverbs, and adjectives — are capitalized. Short, unimportant words are not capitalized. Examples of such words are the conjunctions *and, but,* and *or*; the articles *a, an,* and *the*; and the prepositions *of, in, to,* and *but*. If the word needs to be stressed, however, it may be capitalized. Frequently long prepositions such as *between, after, before,* and *among* are capitalized.

Numbers

Numbers can be written as figures or as words. Although figures are used almost exclusively in business forms, both figures and words are used in letters and other types of transcripts that are written in sentence and paragraph form. If there are two or more ways in which an amount can be expressed, it is usually written in the way that requires the fewest words. A number such as 1,300 is written as *thirteen hundred* rather than *one thousand three hundred*. The following rules specify the proper usage in writing numbers.

Numbers at the Beginning of a Sentence. A number that begins a sentence should be spelled out, even though other numbers are expressed in figures in the same sentence. It is wise, therefore, to avoid beginning a sentence with a large number that is cumbersome in words.

Amounts of Money. Amounts of money, except in legal documents, should be written in figures. Amounts less than one dollar are written in figures with the word *cents* following. In writing even sums of money, the decimal and ciphers are omitted.

> We enclose our check for $21.75.
> He paid 22 cents for the paper.
> He will pay $125 for the painting.

Round Numbers. Round numbers are spelled out, unless such numbers are used with others that cannot be expressed conveniently in words.

> We have fifty employees.
> We have 50 salesmen in our group of 295 employees.

Dates. Except in formal or legal writing, the day of the month and the year are usually written in figures. When a date appears in the body of a letter, the year is customarily omitted if it is the same as that which appears in the date line. It is unnecessary to use *st*, *d*, or *th* in dates, unless the day is written before or is separated from the month.

> the 3d of June
> in July, either the 3d or 4th

Streets. It is considered good form to use words for the names of streets that are numbers that are ten or less; figures should be used for numbers above ten. When the name of the street is a number that is written in figures, it is separated from the number of the building by a dash. If the street name is preceded by one of the words *South, North, East,* or *West,* that word should not be abbreviated.

Tenth Street	Fifth Avenue
72 — 125th Street	72 Fifth Avenue
19 West 115th Street	173rd Street
22 West 110th Street	1 West 12th Street

Time of Day. The abbreviations *p.m.* and *a.m.* may be written in capital or small letters but should be used only with figures. The hour is spelled in full when *o'clock* is used.

> School starts at 8:30 a.m.
> He will leave the office at four o'clock.
> 12 midnight is written 12 p.m. or 12 P.M.
> 12 noon is written 12N. (12M, while correct for 12 noon,
>   can be mistaken for 12 midnight.)

Measurements. Practically all measurements are written in figures.

> Size 7½ AA shoe   12-gal. bottle

Fractions and Decimals. Common fractions appearing alone are spelled out in ordinary reading matter. Mixed numbers are written as figures. Decimals are always expressed in figures.

Miscellaneous Usage. Sessions of Congress and the identifying numbers of various military bodies, political divisions, and dynasties are always written in words.

> the Thirty-sixth Congress   Sixteenth Infantry
> Thirteenth Ward

The result of a ballot is written in figures.

> The count was 34 in favor of the motion, 36 against it.

Page, chapter, section, and footnote numbers are always written in figures.

> pp. 45–67   Section 7
> [2]Hawley, J.   Chapter 9

When two numbers immediately follow each other, it is better that the smaller one be spelled out and the larger one be expressed in figures.

> 125 two-cent stamps   Five 100-dollar bills

Unrelated groups of figures that come together should be separated by commas. Hundreds should be divided from thousands by a comma except in dates, policy numbers, street numbers, and telephone numbers.

> In 1970, 417,296 gallons were sold.
> The policy number is 73288.

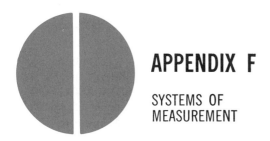

APPENDIX F

SYSTEMS OF
MEASUREMENT

There are two commonly used methods of measurement. One, the *English*, or *imperial*, system, is used in the United States; the other is the *metric* system which is used in most parts of the world. In the English system, for example, units used for measuring lengths are inches, feet, yards, and miles. The basic unit in the metric system for these measurements is the meter. The metric system is a decimal system, which means that you change from one measurement to another by merely moving a decimal point. For example: 10 decimeters = 1 meter. By moving the decimal point one place to the left, you have converted decimeters into meters.

Lengths

English System	Metric System	Equivalencies
12 inches = 1 foot	10 millimeters = 1 centimeter	1 inch = 2.540 centimeters
3 foot = 1 yard	10 centimeters = 1 decimeter	1 foot = 30.48 centimeters
5,280 feet = 1 mile	10 decimeters = 1 meter	39.37 inches = 1 meter
	10 meters = 1 decameter	1 mile = 1.609 kilometers
	10 decameters = 1 hectometer	
	10 hectometers = 1 kilometer	

Weights

English System	Metric System	Equivalencies
16 ounces = 1 pound	10 milligrams = 1 centigram	1 ounce = 28.35 grams
100 pounds = 1 hundredweight	10 centigrams = 1 decigram	1 pound = 453.6 grams
2,000 pounds = 1 ton	10 decigrams = 1 gram	1 ton = 907.2 kilograms
	10 grams = 1 decagram	
	10 decagrams = 1 hectogram	
	10 hectograms = 1 kilogram	

Dry and Liquid Measures

English System

Dry Measure:
  2 pints = 1 quart
  8 quarts = 1 peck
  4 pecks = 1 bushel

Liquid Measure:
  2 pints = 1 quart
  4 quarts = 1 gallon

Metric System

Dry and Liquid Measure:
  10 milliliters = 1 centiliter
  10 centiliters = 1 deciliter
  10 deciliters = 1 liter
  10 liters = 1 decaliter
  10 decaliters = 1 hectoliter
  10 hectoliters = 1 kiloliter

Equivalencies

Dry Measure:
  1 pint = 0.550 liters
  1 quart = 1.101 liters
  1 peck = 8.809 liters
  1 bushel = 35.238 liters
Liquid Measure:
  1 pint = 0.473 liters
  1 quart = 0.946 liters
  1 gallon = 3.785 liters

APPENDIX G

SPECIAL FORMS OF ADDRESS, SALUTATIONS, AND COMPLIMENTARY CLOSINGS

Appendix G lists the correct forms of address with appropriate salutations and complimentary closings for the following special groups:

United States Government officials
State and local government officials
School officials

The correct forms of address for envelopes and letters are shown at the left. Open punctuation is used in addresses. The appropriate salutations and complimentary closings are given in the order of decreasing formality.

United States Government Officials

Address	Salutation	Complimentary Closing
The President of the United States		
The President The Executive Mansion Washington, DC 20500	Sir Mr. President Dear Mr. President	Respectfully yours Very truly yours
The Vice-President of the United States		
The Vice-President United States Senate Washington, DC 20510	Sir Dear Sir Mr. Vice-President Dear Mr. Vice-President	Respectfully yours Very truly yours Sincerely yours
The Chief Justice of the United States		
The Chief Justice The Supreme Court of the United States Washington, DC 20543	Sir Mr. Chief Justice Dear Mr. Chief Justice	Respectfully yours Very truly yours Sincerely yours
Associate Justice of the Supreme Court		
Mr. Justice (Name) The Supreme Court of the United States Washington, DC 20543	Sir Mr. Justice Dear Mr. Justice	Very truly yours Sincerely yours

The Speaker of the House

The Honorable (Name)
Speaker of the House of Representatives
Washington, DC 20515

Sir
Dear Sir
Dear Mr. Speaker

Very truly yours
Sincerely yours

Member of the Cabinet

The Honorable (Name)
Secretary of (Office)
Washington, DC 20520

Sir
Dear Sir
Dear Mr. Secretary

Very truly yours
Sincerely yours

Senator

The Honorable (Name)
The United States Senate
Washington, DC 20510

Sir (Madam)
Dear Sir (Madam)
Dear Senator
Dear Senator (Name)

Very truly yours
Sincerely yours

Representative

The Honorable (Name)
The House of Representatives
Washington, DC 20515

Sir (Madam)
Dear Sir (Madam)
Dear Representative (Name)
Dear Congressman (Name)

Very truly yours
Sincerely yours

Head of a Government Bureau

The Honorable (Name), Chairman
Commission of Fine Arts
Interior Building
18th and C Streets, N. W.
Washington, DC 20240

Sir
Dear Sir
Dear Commissioner
Dear Mr. Chairman
Dear Mr. (Name)

Very truly yours
Sincerely yours

State and Local Government Officials

Governor

His Excellency, the Governor of New York
The Executive Chamber, Capitol
Albany, NY 12224

Sir
Dear Governor
Dear Governor (Name)

Respectfully yours
Very truly yours
Sincerely yours

State Senator

The Honorable (Name)
State Capitol Building
Trenton, NJ 08625

Sir (Madam)
Dear Sir (Madam)
Dear Senator (Name)

Very truly yours
Sincerely yours

State Representative

The Honorable (Name)
The State Assembly
Albany, NY 12224

Sir (Madam)
Dear Sir (Madam)
Dear Representative (Name)

Very truly yours
Sincerely yours

Mayor

The Honorable (Name)
Mayor of the City of Chicago
City Hall
Chicago, IL 60602

Sir (Madam)
Dear Sir (Madam)
Dear Mr. Mayor
Dear Mayor (Name)

Very truly yours
Sincerely yours

School Officials

President of a University or College

(Name), President
Teachers College
Columbia University
525 West 120th Street
New York, NY 10027

Dear Sir (Madam)
Dear President (Name)
Dear Dr. (Name)

Very truly yours
Sincerely yours

Dean of a College

(Name), Dean
School of Education
New York University
Washington Square East
New York, NY 10003

Dear Sir (Madam)
Dear Dean
Dear Dr. (Name)

Very truly yours
Sincerely yours

Professor of a College or University

(Name)
Professor of Business Administration
Indiana University
Bloomington, IN 47401

Dear Sir (Madam)
Dear Professor (Name)
Dear Dr. (Name)

Very truly yours
Sincerely yours

Superintendent of Schools

Superintendent (Name)
Tupper Lake Central Schools
Tupper Lake, NY 12986

Dear Sir (Madam)
Dear Superintendent (Name)
Dear Mr. (Name)

Very truly yours
Sincerely yours

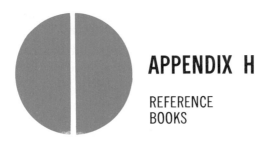

APPENDIX H

REFERENCE
BOOKS

For its clerical and secretarial employees, an office should have at least three reference books available for immediate use — a desk-size dictionary, a secretarial or clerical handbook, and a telephone directory.

Dictionaries

You will find the dictionary indispensable in verifying the spelling, syllabification, and proper usage of words as you prepare and type business papers. It contains not only the realistic pronunciation and derivation of words but also the meanings of foreign expressions and standard abbreviations, the names of places and notable people, and other essential information.

Four of the acceptable desk dictionaries with recent additions to the vocabulary of the language are:

> *The American College Dictionary.* New York City: Random House, Inc., 1968.
>
> *Funk & Wagnall's Standard College Dictionary*, 3d ed. New York City: Harcourt Brace Jovanovich, Inc., 1965.
>
> *Webster's New World Dictionary of the American Language*, 2d college ed. Cleveland, Ohio: World Publishing Company, 1965
>
> *Webster's Seventh New Collegiate Dictionary.* Springfield, Mass.: G. &. C. Merriam Company, 1971.

If a desk-size dictionary is not readily available, you should invest in a paperback pocket-size one. The *Merriam-Webster Pocket Dictionary* is recommended as a transcription tool because it contains definitions for 25,000 words. In addition, it includes guides to correct spelling and pronunciation; lists of synonyms and antonyms; commonly used abbreviations, foreign words and phrases; and population figures for the United States and Canada.

Secretarial Handbooks

The secretary's handbook is a compact, thoroughly indexed reference book encompassing a wide range of secretarial practices and procedures. It is an authoritative souce of information on such topics as proper grammatical construction, plural and possessive forms, pronunciation and punctuation, and the correct writing of numbers in letters and reports. It can be of great help in deciding, for example, where to place the *subject line* in a business letter, whether to place the apostrophe before or after the letter *s* in *women's salaries*, and when to capitalize direction in geographic areas such as on the *East Coast* or in *western Montana*.

Some of the outstanding secretarial handbooks are:

Doris, Lillian, and Bessie May Miller. *Complete Secretary's Handbook*, 3d ed. Englewood Cliffs, N.J.: Prentice-Hall, Inc., 1970.

Hanna, J Marshall, Estelle L. Popham, and Rita Sloan Tilton. *Secretarial Procedures and Administration*, 6th ed. Cincinnati: South-Western Publishing Co., 1973.

House, Clifford R., and Apollonia M. Koebele. *Reference Manual for Office Personnel*, 5th ed. Cincinnati: South-Western Publishing Co., 1970.

Hutchinson, Lois Irene. *Standard Handbook for Secretaries*, 8th ed. New York City: McGraw-Hill, Inc., 1969.

Telephone Directories

The most frequently consulted reference book in any office is the telephone directory. It is used not only to find the telephone number of listed subscribers but also to verify the spelling of their names and the correctness of their addresses. The Yellow Pages, or classified section of a telephone directory, may also serve as a buyer's guide because the names, addresses, and telephone numbers of business subscribers are listed under their product or service.

A small booklet supplied by the telephone company, designed for use as a personal telephone directory, can save considerable telephoning time. On alphabetically arranged pages it provides spaces for writing the names, addresses, area codes, and telephone numbers of frequently called local and out-of-town telephones.

Writing References

The content and format of all types of business communications can be improved if appropriate reference books are consulted.

Business Communications. A recommended reference book for the writing of business letters and other communications of a business nature is

Aurner, Robert R., and Morris P. Wolf. *Effective Communication in Business*. Cincinnati: South-Western Publishing Co., 1967.

Business Reports. Manuals and style books are available to serve as references on how to present papers and reports. Two widely used manuals and two style books are listed at the top of page 634.

A Manual of Style. The University of Chicago. 12th ed., rev. Chicago: University of Chicago Press, 1969.

United States Government Printing Office Style Manual, rev. ed. Washington: U. S. Government Printing Office, 1967.

Perrin, Porter G. *Writer's Guide and Index to English*, 4th ed., Glenview, Illinois: Scott, Foresman and Company, 1968.

Strunk, William, Jr., and E. B. White. *The Elements of Style*, 2d ed., New York City: The Macmillan Company, 1972.

Business Speeches. A wide variety of reference books may be consulted to provide the prospective speaker or master of ceremonies at a business function with words, phrases, ideas, and quotations that will enhance and enliven his presentation. Some of these are:

Bartlett, John. *Familiar Quotations*, 14th ed. Boston: Little, Brown and Company, 1968.

Evans, Bergen. *Dictionary of Quotations*, New York City: Delacorte Press, 1968.

Fernald, James C. *Funk & Wagnalls Standard Handbook of Synonyms, Antonyms, and Prepositions*, rev. ed. New York City: Wilfred Funk, Inc., 1947.

Stevenson, Burton E. *Home Book of Quotations*, rev. ed. New York City: Dodd, Mead & Company, 1967.

The Original Roget's Thesaurus of English Words and Phrases. New York City: St. Martins Press, Inc., 1969.

Webster's New Dictionary of Synonyms. Springfield, Mass.: G. & C. Merriam Company, 1968.

Specific References

Reference books in all fields from many different sources, ranging from the *American Library Association Catalog* to the *Zweng Aviation Dictionary*, are listed and annotated in a single volume, the *Guide to Reference Books*. To determine what, if any, reference books are available on a specific subject, the office worker should first consult this guide:

Winchell, Constance M. *Guide to Reference Books*, 8th ed. Chicago: American Library Association, 1967.

Specific information on business and related subjects may be obtained from many reference books. The information includes statistics on all major industries, directories of all large corporations, biographies of notable people, and factual information on a wide variety of business topics. The examples that follow are arranged alphabetically by subjects.

Accounting. The standard handbook in which leading authorities cover the major divisions of accounting is

Wixon, Rufus, *et al. Accountants' Handbook*, 5th ed. New York City: The Ronald Press Company, 1970.

Almanacs. Published annually, there are four widely used and comprehensive American almanacs of miscellaneous information.

Information Please Almanac. New York City: Simon & Schuster, Inc.

New York Times Encyclopedic Almanac. New York City: Book and Educational Division, The New York Times Company.

Reader's Digest Almanac and Yearbook. Pleasantville, New York: The Reader's Digest Association, Inc.

World Almanac and Book of Facts. New York City: Doubleday & Company, Inc.

Banks. The Bankers Blue Book, one of the leading bank directories published semiannually with monthly supplements, is

Rand-McNally Bankers Directory. Chicago: Rand-McNally & Company.

Biographical Information. Revised and reissued every two years, the best known and generally the most useful biographical dictionary, with full biographical sketches of more than 80,000 notable living American men and women, is

Who's Who in America. Chicago: Marquis-Who's Who, Inc.

Books. An extensive list of available books, new and old, including hardcovers, paperbacks, trade books, textbooks, and juvenile books is published annually with full ordering information in the following volumes:

Books in Print. Authors, Vol. I, New York City: R. R. Bowker Company.

Books in Print. Titles and Publishers, Vol. II, New York City: R. R. Bowker Company.

Subject Guide to Books in Print. A to J, Vol. I, New York City: R. R. Bowker Company.

Subject Guide to Books in Print. K to Z, Vol. II, New York City: R. R. Bowker Company.

A world list of books in the English language is published annually with monthly supplements in the following:

Cumulative Book Index. New York City: The H. W. Wilson Company.

Business Libraries. A reference book that should be consulted to be sure that the business library is used efficiently and that no available source of business information has been overlooked is:

Johnson, H. Webster. *How to Use the Business Library with Sources of Business Information*, 4th ed. Cincinnati: South-Western Publishing Co., 1972.

City Directories. City directories are compiled, published, and sold commercially for most of the cities of the United States and Canada. Each directory contains the names, the addresses, and the occupations of all individuals residing in a community. It usually contains a street directory and a map of the city.

City Officials. A directory of city officials is usually published annually for each large city. *The City of New York Official Directory*, for example, lists all branches of the city government, the courts, and the state and federal government agencies with offices in New York City. It contains an index of the names of all executives listed in the directory.

> *The City of New York Official Directory.* Room 2213 Municipal Building, New York City 10007.

Colleges. A widely used college guide gives the entrance requirements, accreditation, and other factual information about more than 2,800 American colleges and universities. It also contains related information about junior colleges, community colleges, and technical institutes.

> Lovejoy, Clarence I. *Lovejoy's College Guide*, 11th rev. and enl. ed. New York City: Simon and Schuster, Inc., 1970.

A comparative guide to American colleges analyzes every accredited four-year college in the United States. It provides a sound basis for college selection with data on admission requirements, academic opportunities offered, special programs, faculty qualifications, and enrollment figures.

> Cass, James, and Max Birnbaum. *Comparative Guide to American Colleges*, rev. ed. New York City: Harper and Row, Publishers, 1970–1971.

A book of information published annually with facts about 1,350 colleges and universities recognized by the regional accrediting associations. It includes their admissions standards and policies for freshmen and transfer students, programs of study, student life programs, as well as facts about their costs and financial aid.

> Fine, Benjamin. *Barron's Profiles of American Colleges.* Woodbury, New York: Barron's Educational Series, Inc.

A directory of 829 colleges that provide special help for students from minorities and low-income families. It includes a table that indicates for each college the closing date for admission, the closing date for financial aid, and whether or not it will accept nonacademic diplomas and equivalency diplomas.

> College Entrance Examination Board. *A Chance to Go to College.* Princeton, New Jersey: College Entrance Examination Board, 1971.

Junior Colleges. Information about the 751 recognized, nonprofit junior colleges in the United States, the Canal Zone, and Puerto Rico is published by the American Council on Education. Each exhibit for each college includes full information on admission and graduate requirements, enrollment, curricula offered, calendar, staff, student aid, graduates, foreign students, library, publications, finances, buildings and grounds, history, control, and administrative officers.

> Gleazer, Edmund J. Jr. (ed.). *American Junior Colleges,* 8th ed. Washington: American Council on Education, 1971.

Congress. A directory containing the names, addresses, and brief biographies of all congressmen and chief executives of the federal government is issued annually. In it are also listed the members of all congressional committees, the executives of all departments and agencies of the federal government, and all diplomatic representatives. It may be obtained by writing to the United States Government Printing Office.

> *Congressional Directory.* Superintendent of Documents, U.S. Government Printing Office. Washington 20402.

Corporations. A complete national directory of executive personnel in approximately 28,000 companies engaged in all branches of business and industry is published in *Poor's Register of Corporations, Directors, and Executives.* Each company listing includes the names and addresses of all officers, directors, and other executive personnel; the number of employees and the approximate annual sales; and all products and services of the company in the order of their importance.

The register is sold commercially and is available in many public libraries. It may be obtained from Standard & Poor's Corporation.

> *Poor's Register of Corporations, Directors, and Executives.* Standard & Poor's Corporation. New York City 10014.

Credit Ratings. Credit ratings and credit reports are distributed for retail, wholesale, and manufacturing companies. The reports are not available to the general public, but may be obtained by annual subscription.

> *Dun & Bradstreet Ratings and Reports.* Dun & Bradstreet, Inc. New York City 10007.

Encyclopedias. The value of an encyclopedia is that it provides authoritative information on a great number of subjects in concise and convenient form. Because no other single reference book can offer so extensive a survey of universal knowledge, it is often wise to start an inquiry with an encyclopedia. Two outstanding encyclopedias are:

> *Encyclopaedia Britannica* (24 volumes). Chicago: Encyclopaedia Britannica, Inc., 1971.
> *Encyclopedia Americana* (30 volumes). New York City: Grolier Incorporated, 1971.

A compact single-volume general encyclopedia available for instant reference with concise articles on places, persons, and subjects is published in hardcover and paper editions.

Columbia Viking Desk Encyclopedia, 3d ed. New York City:
    The Viking Press, Inc., 1968.

Etiquette. Business and social etiquette is covered in a number of
books on etiquette, but the two prominent authors are:
    Post, Elizabeth L. *Emily Post's Etiquette*, 12th ed. New York
        City: Funk & Wagnalls, Inc., 1969.
    Vanderbilt, Amy. *Amy Vanderbilt's Etiquette*, rev. ed. Garden
        City, New York: Doubleday & Company, Inc., 1972.

Geographic Information. Atlases and gazetteers are reference sources
for all kinds of geographical information. An atlas is a book of maps with sup-
porting geographical statistics and population figures for each area. Such a
book may be an atlas of the world, of a country, of a state, of a county, or of
a city. Three of the atlases frequently used in business offices are:
    Commercial Atlas and Marketing Guide, published annually,
        Chicago: Rand McNally & Company.
    Hammond's Contemporary World Atlas. Garden City, New
        York: Doubleday & Company, Inc., 1967.
    Rand McNally New Cosmopolitan World Atlas, rev. ed.
        Chicago: Rand McNally & Company, 1968.

A gazetteer, on the other hand, is a geographical dictionary giving, in
alphabetic order, the names and descriptions of towns, villages, cities, rivers,
mountains, and countries with pronunciations and related historical and
geographical information. One of the most comprehensive gazetteers with
information about all important places in the world and all incorporated
cities, towns, and villages in the United States and Canada with populations of
1,500 or more is
    Webster's Geographical Dictionary, rev. ed. Springfield, Mass.:
        G. & C. Merriam Company, 1967.

Law. A five-volume law directory, published annually, with a complete
list of the lawyers in the United States and Canada given in Volumes I through
IV and digests of the laws of the states in the United States and the provinces of
Canada in Volume V is available.
    Martindale-Hubbell Law Directory.   Summit, New Jersey:
        Martindale-Hubbell, Inc.

Magazine Articles. Articles in a selected number of periodicals are indexed according to author, title, and subject and listed in an annual publication with monthly supplements which is available in all public libraries.
    Readers' Guide to Periodical Literature. New York City: The
        H. W. Wilson Company.

Manufacturers. A list of almost all American manufacturers with a
classification of their products, trade names, and brands is published annually
by the Thomas Publishing Company.

Thomas Register. New York City: Thomas Publishing
   Company.

Medicine. A register of legally qualified physicians of the United States
and Canada with related medical biographies and a list of approved medical
schools and hospitals is published every two years.

American Medical Directory. Chicago: American Medical
   Association.

Newspaper Articles. All items and reports printed in the *New York
Times* are briefly summarized, indexed, and cross-referenced by subject and
name. They are listed alphabetically with the date, page, and column of publication.

New York Times Index. New York City: The New York
   Times Company. (Published every two weeks and annually).

Postal Information. A complete listing of the postal services in the
United States with detailed regulations and procedures covering these services,
together with up-to-date postal rates, is given in the following publication:

Postal Service Manual. Superintendent of Documents, U.S.
   Government Printing Office. Washington 20402.

A list of all the five-digit ZIP Code numbers in the United States, indexed alphabetically according to the states with appendixes for the large cities,
is published annually in the

National Zip Code Directory. Superintendent of Documents
   U.S. Government Printing Office. Washington 20402.

Shipping Information. Shipments are frequently made by means other
than parcel post — by rail, truck, bus, ship, and, more frequently, by air express. A complete shipper's guide containing rates and routings for parcel post,
express, and freight shipments is published in separate editions for different
parts of the country. This guide also includes information concerning Cana-
dian and foreign parcel post.

Leonard's Guide. New York City: G. R. Leonard & Company, Inc.

A complete list of all post offices, railroad stations, shipping lines, and
freight receiving stations is published.

*Bullinger's Postal Shipper's Guide for the United States, Canada,
   and Newfoundland*. Bullinger's Guides, Inc., Westwood,
   New Jersey.

Information about air express, the newest and swiftest method of door-
to-door transportation service, may be obtained by referring to the following
publication:

Official Air Express Guide. Air Express Division of REA
   Express, New York City.

Travel Information. Travel information is available in many forms of guide books, bulletins, and directories.

Guides. Ratings for approximately 20,000 accommodations and restaurants in the United States are published in the paperback editions of the *Mobil Travel Guides* by Simon & Schuster, Inc., New York City. The guides also list the outstanding historical, educational, and scenic points of interest throughout the country. Regional guide books are revised and reprinted annually for California and the West, the Great Lakes Area, the Middle Atlantic States, the Northwest and Great Plains States, the Northeastern States, the Southeastern States, and the Southwest and South Central Area.

Bulletins. Travel bulletins may be obtained from all travel agencies. Two of the better known agencies with offices in all the principal cities of the world are *Thomas Cook & Son* and the *American Express Company*.

Directories. Travelers are almost as interested in their accommodations as they are in their means of transportation. The most frequently consulted directory which annually lists hotels and motels approved by the American Hotel Association with their respective rates, accommodations, and plans of operation is the following:

> *Hotel & Motel Red Book.* New York City: American Hotel
> Association Directory Corporation.

Overseas Guides. A recent innovation is *The Businessman's Guide to Europe*, available at most overseas airlines offices.

A world guide, containing travel facts about 138 countries, has become a worldwide best seller. It is published by Pan American Airways.

> Whitted, Gerald W. (ed.). *New Horizons World Guide.* Distrib-
> utors, New York City: Simon & Schuster, Inc.

Eugene Fodor edits a complete guide to Europe which is revised annually.

> *Fodor's Guide to Europe.* New York City: David McKay
> Co., Inc.

Separate editions of Fodor's guides are published for all the major countries of Europe. Separate editions are also published for Hawaii, India, Israel, Japan and East Asia, South America, the Caribbean. the Bahamas and Bermuda, and many other areas of the world.

The Reference Section of The Public Library

If a particular reference book is not readily available, look for it in the reference section of your local public library. As a rule, public libraries have many more reference books than either business libraries or high school libraries. Furthermore, the librarians in the reference section have been professionally trained to assist you in obtaining information.

INDEX

tors, 125; ten-key listing machine, 124
Calculators, mechanical printing, 124
Call-A-Matic, 327
Call Director, 323
Call report, daily, illustrated,, 473
Callers, greeting, by receptionist, 285; keeping a record of, 288; register of, 288; talking with difficult, 287; techniques for announcing, 286–287
Canceled check, defined, 506
Capitalization, 196; Appendix E, 622; business titles and positions, 623; geographic names, 623; headings and titles of articles and reports, 624; hyphenated words, 624; individual names, 624; words before figures, 623
Captions, file, 221; consistency in typing, 225
Carbon copies, hints for handling, 85; making, 82
Carbon copy notations on a letter, 72
Carbon packs, assembling, 82; defined, 82; desk drawer assembly, illustrated, 83; inserting in typewriter, 83; preassembled, using, 84
Card deck in data processing cycle, 117
Card Dialer, 326
Card files, 266–272; elevator, 272; random, 271; rotary wheel, 271; vertical, 267; visible, 268
Card index, illustrated, 262
Card punch, 109
Card punch machine, 128
Cards, business reply, 89; stamped, used in outgoing mail, 153
Carrier folders, 244
Cash, paying employees in, 541; writing checks for, 511
Cash discount, 447
Cash registers, 126
Catalog selling, 468
Catalogs, used in purchasing, 443
Central markets, used in purchasing, 444
Central processing unit (CPU), 127
Certified mail, 161
Chain feeding of envelopes, 166
Charge-Out, 243–246; length of time for, 245
Charge-Out forms, 244; carrier folder, 244; out folders, 244; out guides, 244; substitution cards, 245
Check, ABA number on, 518;

blank endorsement on, 516; defined, 507; full endorsement on, 516; overdrawn, defined, 508; path of a, illustrated, 521; paying employees by, 539; restrictive endorsement on, 516; special endorsement on, 516
Check endorsements, illustrated, 517
Check stub, 508
Check with stub, illustrated, 509
Checking account, advantages of, 506; opening a, 506
Checkbook, using a, 506–512
Checking receipt of goods, 456
Checks, duplicate, 510; overdraft, 512; paying bills by, 510; preparing for bank deposit, 516; stopping payment on, 512; suggestions for writing, 508–510; writing 507, 508; writing for cash, 511
Checkwriter, defined, 510
Chronological files, 186
City directories, Appendix H, 636
City, state, and ZIP Code line in a letter, 68
Civil Service announcements, as job source, 554
Clerical positions, Missouri, requirements, 9, 582
Clerical positions, rewards of, 10; fringe benefits, 11; opportunities for employment, 11; salaries, 10; working conditions, 10
COD, defined, 477; service, 161
Code-a-phone, 309
Code telegraph messages, 347
Coded letter, illustrated, 211
Coding, in filing, 231
Coined verbs, 620
Collator, 109; illustrated, 130
Collators, 358
Collect calls, 330
Collective noun, 587
College reference books, 636
Colloquialisms, 611
Colon, 423, 604
Comma, 163, 249, 602
Commission method of determining pay, 531
Common machine language used in data processing, 118
Common noun, 587
Communications services, 330–334; long-distance calls, special, 330; teletypewriter service, 332
Comparison of adjectives, 389; of adverbs, 596
Complaints, dealing with customer, 480; by adjustment letters, 480; by credit, 480

Complimentary close in a letter, 70
Complimentary closings, Appendix G, 629
Components inventory, 492
Compound words, 613
Computer addressing of mail, 168
Computer, electronic system of processing data, 111; how it works, 134; input, 135; magnetic disks, 136; magnetic plastic tape, 136; output, 138; processing, unit of, 137; punched paper cards, 136; punched paper tape, 135
Computer tapes and disks, 274
Computers, features of electronic, see Electronic computers
Conference calls, 331
Confirming letter, defined, 512
Conjunctions, 112, 249, 349, 598, 599
Consecutive number filing, 253
Consideration, defined, 431
Continuous total copy system, illustrated, 386
Contract, agency, illustrated, 434; simple, defined, 430
Contractions, 595
Control section of a computer, 137
Control tape in data processing cycle, 117
Coordinate conjunctions, 112, 598
Coordination of efforts, 15
Copiers, 352–356; advantages of, 353; copy of letter with notations, illustrated, 354; electrostatic, 355; infrared, 356; types of, 355, uses of, 353
Copying, see also Copiers, Fluid duplicating, Offset duplicating, Stencil duplicating
Cord switchboard, 322
Cordless switchboard, 323
Correlative conjunctions, 598
Corrections, making, on letters, 85–87
Correspondence, routine, used in selling, 471
Courtesy, on telephone, 305
Credit, approving, 477
Credit card calls, 330
Credit memorandums, 458, 480; illustrated, 459
Credit rating and reports, 637
Cross-reference, for geographic filing, 261; for letter, illustrated, 233; for subject filing, 259
Cross-reference record, 233
Cross-reference sheet, illustrated, 211

transferring, 247; twenty hints for, 237

Filing, alphabetic name, 185; alphabetic subject, 185; alphanumeric, 256; defined, 184; electronic data processing used in, 274; folders, used in, 257; geographic, 260; guides used in, 257; key words, 240; microfilming used in, 272; numeric, 251; photocopies used in, 245; routine for, 236; subject, 257–259; systems of, 185–186; terminal-digit, 255; twenty hints for 237; *see also* Charge-Out, Follow-Up, Retention, Transfer

Filing accessories, 227

Filing equipment, 217–220; lateral files, 219; shelf files, 219; vertical files, 218

Filing methods, summary of, illustrated, 262

Filing procedures, basic, illustrated, 235

Filing rules, 190–196

Filing supplies, 220–226; folders, 223; guides, 221; labels, 224

Filing systems, factors to be considered in developing, 275

Final draft, typing the, 403

Financial duties, clerical, 515–544; performing, 7

Financial statements, balance sheet, 415; calculations, checking accuracy of, 417; consistency of, 419; final draft, filing carbon copy of, 422; illustrated, 420, 421; income statement, 416; proofreading, 422; similarities in, 417; previous, study of, 417; producing typewritten, 416; typing the, 417; understanding, 415

Finished goods inventory, 492

First-class mail, 157

Fiscal period, defined, 416

Flow chart symbols used in data processing cycle, 116; illustrated, 116

Fluid duplicating, 373–379; features of, 373; operating a fluid duplicator, 377; preparing a fluid master, 374; storing the fluid master, 379

Fluid duplicator, instructions for operating, 379

Fluid masters, correcting errors, 375; machine preparation for use of, 384; master set, 374; placement of materials on master, 374; preparing the, 374; preparing illustrations, 376; preparing typewriter, 374;

proofreading, 376; razor blade, 374; removing from typewriter, 376; storing, 379; supplies needed, 374; typing the, 374

Folders, 223; arranging materials in, 237; capacity of, 224; carrier, 244; dated follow-up, 246; illustrated, 223; individual, 224, 237; miscellaneous, 223, 237; numeric filing, 257; out, 244; placing materials in subject, 259; positions of, 226; special, 224, 237; subject file, 258; transferring file, 248

Folding and inserting letters, 151–152

Follow-Up, 246; card tickler files, 246; dated folders for, 246

Follow-up of order, 459

Footnotes, guides for typing, 411; illustrated, 402, 410

Form letters, 98; prospective customer, 98; requesting reference, 99; used in selling, 471

Fourth-class mail, 157

Fractions and decimals, 52

Frequently misused terms, 535

Fringe benefits for clerical workers, 11

Full endorsement on check, 516

Full-keyboard listing machine, 125

Full-rate telegraph message (FR), 346

G

Geographic files, 186

Geographic filing, 260–262; arrangement of, 260; card index for, 262; cross-reference for, 261; procedure for, 262

Geographic information reference books, 638

Good language usage, 611

Goods, receiving for inventory, 496; reordering for inventories, 488; requisitioning, 490; selling of, defined, 465

Goods in process inventory, 492

Grammar, Appendix A, 587–600; see individual parts of speech

Grammar reference books, 600

Greeting people, 5

Grooming, personal, 22

Gross earnings, defined, 529

Guides for files, 221; card, 268; illustrated, 222; kinds of, 221; number of, 222; numeric filing, 257; out, with pocket, 244; positions of, 226; primary, 221; ruled out guide, 244; secondary, 221; subject filing, 258

Guide sheet for reports, illustrated, 400

H

Handbooks, secretarial, 632, 633

Handwriting, acceptable styles of, 38; improving your, 39; reading, 42

Hard copy, 97, 273

Headings in a report, 408; main, 408; paragraph, 408; side, 408; sub, 408

Health, 20; exercise, 21; food, 21; rest, 20

Homonyms, 103, 612; used in dictation, 101, 102

Hourly rate method of computing pay, 530

Hyphen, 482, 555; used in compound words, 613

Hyphenated compounds, 614

Hyphenated words, capitalization of, 624

I

Ibid., use of, 410

Identifying receipt of goods, 457

IDP (integrated data processing), 118

Image makers, 385

Imaging, defined, 384

Imperial system of measurement, 627

Important records, defined, 187

Income statement, 416; illustrated, 421

Incoming calls, 305–309; answering promptly, 305; answering service, 309; automatic answering and recording set, 309; getting information, 306; giving information, 306; identifying yourself, 305; messages, taking accurately, 307; screening calls, 306; telephone tips, 310; terminating calls, 309; transferring calls, 308

Incoming mail, dating the, 144; distributing the, 147; handling the, 142–147; opening the, 142; photocopying the, 146; routing the, 144; sorting the, 144; time stamping the, 144

Index control cards, 253

Indexing, 231; abbreviated first or middle names, 193; abbreviations, 202; articles, 201; business firms, 199–209; capitalization in, 196; churches, 206; compound geographic names, 204; compound last names, 192;

Purchasing, 7
Purchasing ethics, 460
Purchasing forms, 457; credit memorandum, 458; follow-up of an order, 459; purchase invoice, 458
Purchasing function, the, 440–448; importance of the, 441; paying for goods, 445–448; *see* Purchasing goods, guidelines for
Purchasing goods, guidelines for, 441; catalogs, 443; central markets, 444; right price, 445; right quality, 444; right quantity, 445; right source, 442; right time, 445; salesmen, 442; trade directories, 443; wholesalers, 443
Purchasing procedures, 451–455; purchase order, 454; purchase requisition, 453; request for quotation, 453; stockroom requisition, 452

Q

Quantity discount, 446
Questions marks, 397, 604
Quotation, request for, 453
Quotation marks, 379, 608; with other marks of punctuation, 609
Quoted material, 409, 608

R

Railway freight service, 176
Random access in data processing, 136
Random files, 271
Raw material inventory, 492
REA Express, 174
Readers' Guide to Periodical Literature, 395
Reading, 28; a dictionary, 30; instructions, 30; for specific information, 30, 31; for understanding, 28
Receiving forms, 457
Receiving procedure, 456–457; checking, 456; identifying, 457; recording, 457; storing, 457
Receiving record, illustrated, 456
Receptionist, covering desk of, 289; handling emergencies, 288; language of, 292–296; oral communication skills of, 292–296; skills and abilities of, 280–282; *see* Callers
Receptionist duties, techniques for handling, 283–289
Reconciling a bank account, 518; a bank statement, 518
Record, employee's earnings, 539

Record retention schedules, 248
Record of a sale in data processing cycle, illustrated, 117
Record keeping, *see* Stockroom record keeping
Recording receipt of goods, 457
Records, care of, 186; important, 187; keeping inventory, 488; maintaining, 4; nonessential, 187; useful, 187; vital, 186
Records center, 248
Records control, 183–187; information retrieval, 183; files management, 183; records protection, 183; records retention and disposition, 184
Reference books, Appendix H, 632–640; accounting, 634; almanacs, 635; banks, 635; biographical information, 635; books available, 635; business communications, 633; business libraries, 635; business reports, 633; business speeches, 634; city directories, 636; city officials, 636; colleges, 636; Congress, 637; corporations, 637; credit ratings, 637; dictionaries, 623; encyclopedias, 637; etiquette, 638; geographic information, 638; junior colleges, 636; law, 638; magazine articles, 638; manufacturers, 638; medicine, 639; newspaper articles, 639; postal information, 639; secretarial handbooks, 632; shipping information, 639; telephone directories, 633; travel information, 640; writing references, 633
Reference initials on a letter, 72
Reference visible systems, 270
Register, or accession book, 253
Register, of callers, 288; of expected mail, illustrated, 146; of insured, special delivery, registered mail, 146
Registered mail, 160
Relative pronouns, 588
Release mark on files, 230; illustrated, 235
Remote control dictating systems, 95
Rent, defined, 431
Repeat back telegraph service, 345
Report delivery telegraph service, 345
Reports, preparing business, 6; *see also* Business reports
Reproducing machines, *see* Copiers, Fluid duplicating, Offset duplicating, Stencil duplicating

Request for quotations, 453
Requisition, defined, 445; for payroll, illustrated, 542; purchase, 453; stockroom, 452
Requisition card, 243
Rest, 20
Restrictive endorsement on a check, 516
Retention of files, 248
Retrieval, from a computer, 274; in microfilming, 273
Rotary calculators, 125
Rotary dial telephone, 324
Rotary wheel files, 271
Rough draft of a report, illustrated, 404; typing the, 401
Rounding numbers in multiplication, 49
Routing mail, 144
Routing slip, illustrated, 145

S

Salaries, clerical, 10
Salary method of computing pay, 530
Sales invoice, preparing the, 478
Sales letters, 467
Sales office responsibilities, 471–476; routine correspondence, 471; salesmen's records, 472
Sales order form, illustrated, 476
Sales personnel, described, 465
Salesmen, used in purchasing, 442
Salesmen's records, 472; daily call report, submitted by salesmen, 473; mail requests, 474; telephone requests, 475
Salutation in a letter, 68
Salutations, Appendix G, 629
School placement office as a job source, 551
Sealing envelopes, 152
Second-class mail, 157
Selling, 7, 464–468; advertising used in, 466; by catalog, 468; defined, 464; importance of, 464; methods of, 466; nonpersonal, 466; nonselling personnel, 465; personal, 466; by sales letters, 467; sales personnel, 465
Selling procedures, clerical, 471–481; complaints, dealing with customer, 480; order processing, 476; sales office responsibilities, 471
Semicolon, 371, 603
Sender's Application for Withdrawal of Mail, Form 1509, 162
Separate cover notation on a letter, 76
Service businesses, inventories in, 493